Services Marketing

Text and Cases

SECOND EDITION

Vinnie Jauhari

Director
Education Advocacy
Microsoft Corporation India Pvt. Ltd
Gurugram

Kirti Dutta

Dean and Professor (Marketing)
G.L. Bajaj Institute of Management and Research
Greater Noida

OXFORD

UNIVERSITY PRESS

OXFORD
UNIVERSITY PRESS

Oxford University Press is a department of the University of Oxford.
It furthers the University's objective of excellence in research, scholarship,
and education by publishing worldwide. Oxford is a registered trade mark of
Oxford University Press in the UK and in certain other countries.

Published in India by
Oxford University Press
22 Workspace, 2nd Floor, 1/22 Asaf Ali Road, New Delhi 110 002

First Edition published in 2009
Second Edition published in 2017
Fifth impression 2023

ISBN-13: 978-0-19-945616-1
ISBN-10: 0-19-945616-X

Typeset in Baskerville
by Welkyn Software Solutions Pvt Ltd, Coimbatore
Printed in India by Rakmo Press, New Delhi 110 020

For product information and current price, please visit www.india.oup.com

To
my family and friends

Special thanks to Sunil and Shaurya who have been my greatest strength

Vinnie Jauhari

To
the two pillars of guidance and support who gave meaning to my existence—my parents
—Mrs and Mr K.K.M. Mehta and the one who guides and motivates me through the ebb and
flow of life—my husband—Anil and my two angels—Yoshita and Ridhima

Kirti Dutta

Learning Objectives

Focus on the learning and knowledge you should acquire by the end of the chapter.

OBJECTIVES

After reading this chapter you will be able to understand the

- concept of service processes
- relationship between profitability and service process
- essentials of a service blueprint
- importance of a customer's role in service delivery
- characteristics of a service guarantee
- dimensions of service process matrix

Opening Cases

Help the students connect with the theory explained in the chapter.

30 Minutes or Free

With the addition of 110 outlets in FY13, Domino's, with over 550 outlets, is the fastest growing pizza outlet in the country today. As of now, Domino's accounts for over 70% of the pizza home delivery market.

Ajay Kaul, CEO, Jubilant Foodworks, the master franchisee for Domino's Pizza and Dunkin' Donuts in India, credits this expansion to the customer insight developed by the company since its advent in 1990. Domino's is credited of converting the parantha eating Indian people into pizza aficionados.

The proposition of delivery in 30 minutes was one such action taken to cash in on paucity of time with the working couples. Another way to cash in on this was to offer the pizza free if the delivery was late. This was a risky undertaking given that traffic in India and maze-like residential areas could derail the profitability of the venture. However, it

was achieved by scouting for most efficient delivery routes months before an outlet opened in any area. Equipped with clipboards, paper, and pencil, employees painstakingly sketched maps of every lane, and landmarks such as fire stations and temples, and marked the address of every building, to prepare for deliveries in the area. Armed with hand-drawn maps, these delivery men test-drove through lanes to familiarize themselves with the topography of the area and also chart out the shortest possible routes to the nearest landmarks.

Once on the job to deliver pizzas, the delivery men are also not allowed to race to their destinations either—their motorbikes are modified to restrict their maximum speed to 45kph. That means riders must know every street, pothole, traffic light, choke point, construction site, and police roadblock in their sectors of fast-changing, densely populated

Exhibit 6.2 Car Dealers in China

China has a number of first time car buyers who have a limited knowledge of cars and these customers visit the showroom a multiple times to look at the cars. On these multiple visits they also bring along family and friends for their opinion and also to negotiate the price. Therefore, the car dealers in China are more patient with these customers and are also working out strategies for these multiple visits from customers to make them feel special and welcomed. There are more than 100 car brands available in China and dealers have to ensure creative ways for return visits. In Shanghai's Pudong district, Ford Motor Showroom provides in-house manicurist and shoe-shiner. Singers perform at barbeques for customers and periodically the dealers hold drawings for gifts such as iPads and TVs. In Foshan, a city in southern Guangdong provinces, a Honda Motor outlet holds talks on feng shui, shows recent hit films from Hollywood and Chinese studios, and offers massage chairs for relaxation. The three-story Mercedes Benz dealership in Shanghai's Putuo district has a 12 seat theatre (often showing movies that feature Mercedes vehicles), a cigar room for repeat customers, a library, a fitness centre, and a game room that includes pool tables and driving games. At lunch there is a buffet with five different meat and vegetable dishes, and a full-time tea artist brews various types of Chinese tea.

Exhibits

Help in understanding the application of the theory discussed in the chapter.

Table 14.1 Direct recipients of service

Nature of service act	People	Possession
Tangible action	Service directed at people's bodies (health-care services)	Service directed at people's possessions (car repair)
Intangible action	Service directed at people's minds (art performance and religion)	Service directed at intangible assets (religion and counselling)

Tables and Figures

Illustrate the topics discussed in the chapter.

Fig. 14.2 The service blueprint

the Book

SUMMARY

Managing services is a complex task, which requires a lot of planning for front as well as back office operations. Various categories of services are offered, which can be classified in numerous ways. Marketers have to plan their strategies appropriately so that they address issues of demand management. Service experience is a critical element and the service encounters have to be managed well. The role of the customer in a service process has to be assessed carefully. Also, service guarantees have to be looked into. The chapter has discussed the roles that service providers will have to manage. It has also examined the case of a leading

KEY TERMS

Foreign investment Investment in the domestic economy by foreign individuals or companies. It takes the form of either direct investment in productive enterprises or investment in financial instruments, such as a portfolio of shares.

Liberalization To remove or loosen restrictions on an economic or political system.

Marketing mix The factors controlled by a company that can influence consumers' buying of its products. Product, pricing, promotion, and place are the four components of a marketing mix. The potential profitability of a particular Marketing mix and its acceptability to its market are assessed by marketing research.

Promotion An activity designed to boost the sales of a product or service. It may include an advertising campaign, increased PR activity, a free-sample campaign, offering free gifts or trading stamps, arranging demonstrations or exhibitions, setting up competitions with attractive prizes, temporary price reductions, door-to-door selling, telemarketing, mailers, etc.

Place Activities such as sales and distribution of the product, transportation services, and desirable stock levels.

Service Any activity or benefit that one party can offer to another that is intangible and does not result in the transfer of ownership of any physical object.

EXERCISES

Concept Review Questions

1. Critically discuss the importance of services in the economic growth of a developing country.
2. Which extended elements of the marketing mix are absent in the marketing of traditional products? Critically discuss their importance in the marketing of services.
3. What are the different ways by which services can be classified? Discuss any two.
4. Should services be classified? Discuss.

Critical Thinking Questions

1. Discuss how services are increasingly forming an important component in the marketing of traditional products.

Project Assignments

1. Visit any pure services outlet, such as a hotel or a bank, and examine the marketing strategies employed to overcome the different characteristics of services.
2. Visit the government website of any developing Asian country and try to identify the importance of the service sector in the development of their economy. (*Hint*: you can consider services as a percentage of GDP, employment generated, exports and imports of services, etc.)

Internet Exercises

Identify two organizations whose services are possible only because of the Internet.

Summary

Draws together the main concepts discussed within the chapter. This will help you reflect and evaluate important concepts.

Key Terms

Help you retain all the new technical terms that you have learnt in the chapter.

Chapter-end Exercises

Contain concept review and critical thinking questions as well as project assignments that highlight the major topics covered in the chapter. The questions enhance learning and can be used for review and classroom discussion.

Chapter-end Cases

Consolidate your understanding of the chapter subject and broaden your financial decision-making skills.

CASE STUDY The Online Advertising Food Chain*

Online advertising is growing by leaps and bounds, but are there opportunities for smaller players?

It is said that during any economic downturn, the first sector to get impacted is advertising as it is the first place where companies like to cut back. However, thanks in part to a small base, the Indian online advertising and marketing sector is growing at a fast pace offering many opportunities for different classes of people.

From around ₹150–200 crore in the financial year 2007, online ad spends targeting Indians are expected to have jumped to around ₹500 crore in FY 2008, according to industry estimates. 'In 2008–09, we expect it to hit ₹900 crore', says Mahesh Murthy, whose firm Pinstorm alone would have bought ₹115 crore worth of ads by the end of this year (Fig. 17.1).

In other words, Pinstorm, which claims a market share of around 15 per cent in India, will alone oversee ad sales almost 50% higher than the total industry turnover of ₹80 crore during 2006.

While still accounting for just around 5% of the estimated ₹15,000 crore spent on advertising in India, online promotions account for between 15 to 20% in places like the US and parts of Europe (Fig. 17.2). Recently, a new media specialist research firm eMarketer, revised down its estimate for online promotion expenditure by US companies due to the economic recession. Yet, the new estimate for 2008 for US companies alone stood at

* Eluvangal, S. (2008), 'The online advertising food chain', *The Online Advertising Food Chain*, DARE, 31 August 2008. Reprinted with the permission of Mr Krishna Kumar, Group Editor, DARE, www.dare.co.in.

Companion Online Resources

Visit india.oup.com/orcs/9780199456161 to access both teaching and learning solutions online.

Online Resources

The following resources are available to support the faculty and students using this text:

For Faculty
• Instructor's Manual
• PowerPoint Slides
• Multiple Choice Questions

For Students
• Flashcard Glossary

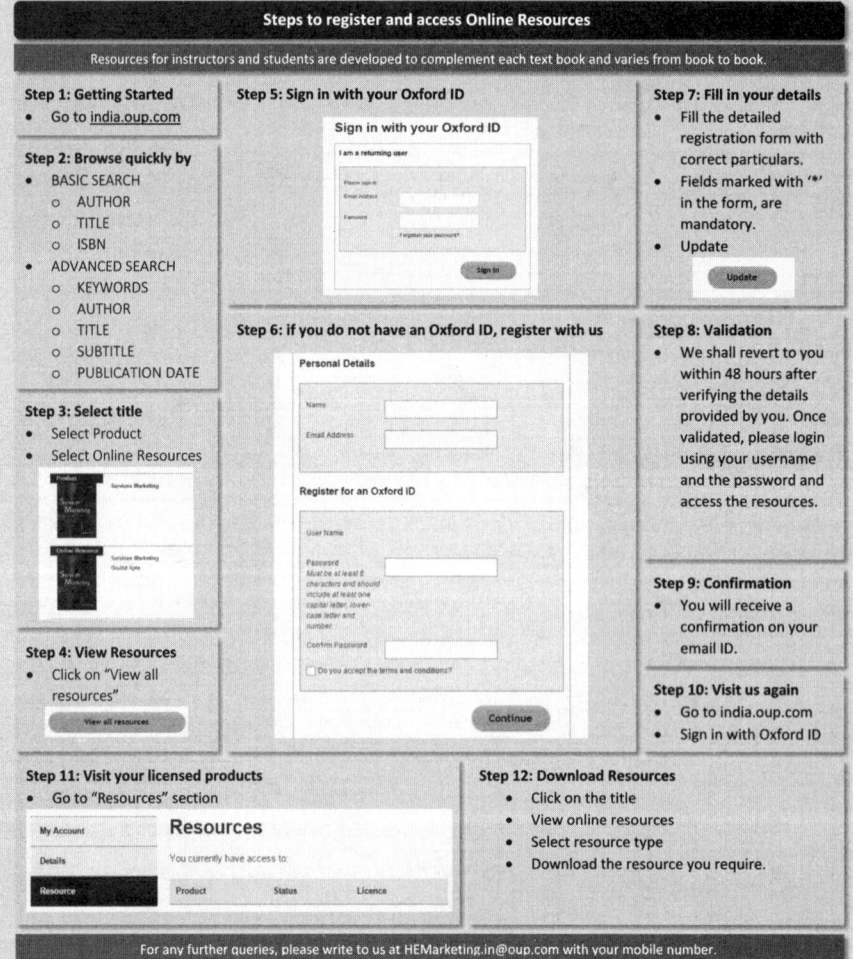

Steps to register and access Online Resources

Resources for instructors and students are developed to complement each text book and varies from book to book.

Step 1: Getting Started
• Go to india.oup.com

Step 2: Browse quickly by
• BASIC SEARCH
  o AUTHOR
  o TITLE
  o ISBN
• ADVANCED SEARCH
  o KEYWORDS
  o AUTHOR
  o TITLE
  o SUBTITLE
  o PUBLICATION DATE

Step 3: Select title
• Select Product
• Select Online Resources

Step 4: View Resources
• Click on "View all resources"

Step 5: Sign in with your Oxford ID

Sign in with your Oxford ID

I am a returning user

Please sign in
Email Address
Password
I register your password?

Sign In

Step 6: if you do not have an Oxford ID, register with us

Personal Details

Name
Email Address

Register for an Oxford ID

User Name
Password
Must be at least 8 characters and should include at least one capital letter, lower-case letter and number
Confirm Password

Do you accept the terms and conditions?

Continue

Step 7: Fill in your details
• Fill the detailed registration form with correct particulars.
• Fields marked with '*' in the form, are mandatory.
• Update

Update

Step 8: Validation
• We shall revert to you within 48 hours after verifying the details provided by you. Once validated, please login using your username and the password and access the resources.

Step 9: Confirmation
• You will receive a confirmation on your email ID.

Step 10: Visit us again
• Go to india.oup.com
• Sign in with Oxford ID

Step 11: Visit your licensed products
• Go to "Resources" section

My Account
Details
Resource

Resources
You currently have access to:
Product   Status   Licence

Step 12: Download Resources
• Click on the title
• View online resources
• Select resource type
• Download the resource you require.

For any further queries, please write to us at HEMarketing.in@oup.com with your mobile number.

Preface to the Second Edition

The contribution of the services sector towards the growth of the global economy is significant. It plays a crucial role in a country's development—helps in poverty alleviation along with better access to amenities such as health and education. Services results in inclusive growth due to the manufacturing and employment linkages. As per the World Bank Group's Global Economic Prospects report, 2015, the growth in South Asia (5.5% in 2014) is promising after a 10-year low (at 4.9% in 2013) and is expected to rise to 6.8% by 2017. As per the report, the country driving this growth in South Asia is India. India's services sector (at 57% in 2014) is leading all other sectors and has contributed considerably towards the nation's income, employment, investment, and trade*.

Since the publication of the last edition, we have received valuable feedback from faculty members regarding the inclusion of certain topics and have included their suggestions while revising the text.

The second edition of this textbook continues to provide an exhaustive yet lucid coverage of the various aspects of the services industry. We sincerely hope that this edition of the book will further aid students in understanding the basic concepts and applications of this subject.

About the Book

Services Marketing is designed to meet the needs of the students of undergraduate, postgraduate, and diploma courses in management. The comprehensive nature of the text along with case studies, review questions, and practical exercises makes it useful for faculty. It provides information for industry practitioners who are involved in marketing services in their current organization. The book is relevant for individuals who wish to gain a sound knowledge of services so as to apply these skills in the future roles they hope to play in the organization, non-marketing professionals who wish to get leadership positions in their organizations, and business leaders of various functional areas in the services industry. Individuals who want to start a business in the services sector will also find this book beneficial as it provides a comprehensive discussion of services management and marketing.

Key Features

- Integrates theory with corporate examples and provides rich insights into the dynamics of the services sector
- Discusses the practices of Indian and global companies
- Explains concepts through examples, exhibits, tables, and case studies
- Includes Internet-based exercises which will help students apply the concepts learnt to different business situations

---

*http://commerce.nic.in/

New to This Edition

- **New chapters** on Managing the Services Brand and Managing Demand and Supply
- **New sections** on Managing E-service and E-service Quality, Employee Engagement in Service Industry, Creating an Empowered Employee, and Customer Feedback and Service Management Orientation
- **Updated and revised content**
- **New case studies** on Café Coffee Day Lounge, Music World, Bluestone, Zomato, Visa, Online Shopping, Online Grocery Retailing, and Yatra

Online Resource Centre

The following resources are available to support the faculty and students using this text:

For Faculty

- Instructor's Manual
- PowerPoint Slides
- Multiple Choice Questions

For Students

- Flashcard Glossary

Coverage and Structure

The book is divided into 21 chapters. It discusses various aspects of the services industry. Each chapter starts with an opening exhibit to introduce the topic and concludes with one or more case studies so that readers can practically apply the learnings from the chapter. The case studies are contemporary and will help in the development of analytical skills. The book has critical review questions, caselets, and Internet-based exercises, which help the readers apply the theory to real-life situations.

Chapter 1, *Introduction to Services*, gives an introduction to the services sector in the global and Indian context. The chapter delineates the characteristics of services and compares them with the characteristics of products. It also brings out the importance of services in case of manufactured products. The challenges for the services industry have been discussed and the critical success factors have also been elaborated upon. The services marketing environment and the service mix elements—product, price, place, promotion, people, physical evidence, and process—have been explained.

Chapter 2, *The Service Product*, gives an understanding of the product in the context of services. It discusses the levels of service offering and the steps involved in new product development. The concept of the product life cycle as well as the strategies involved in managing the product during the different stages of the life cycle have also been discussed.

Chapter 3, *Managing the Services Brand*, highlights the relevance of branding a services product. Concepts such as brand equity, brand knowledge, and brand associations have been discussed. Creating a brand and building brand loyalty are explained along with managing the service brand portfolio over a period of time.

Chapter 4, *Marketing Research*, emphasizes the importance of market research in understanding and delivering services to markets. The chapter gives an overview of the marketing research process. The methodology for conducting research and the tools and techniques of research have been elaborated upon. The chapter also gives an insight into the marketing research strategies followed by firms in the Indian market and the challenges faced by the marketing research firms.

Chapter 5, *Understanding Consumer Behaviour*, gives insights into understanding consumer behaviour before, during, and after consuming the service. It analyses the values and perceptions of customers and their disposition towards the purchase process. The chapter discusses the dynamics of Indian consumers and examines the factors leading to increased consumption of new services. It also gives an overview of the factors influencing consumer behaviour. It further discusses the concepts of relationship marketing, consumer loyalty, customer delight, and consumerism in the context of the services sector.

Chapter 6, *Segmentation, Targeting, and Positioning for a Services Firm*, gives an overview of the strategies involved in helping the service marketer to arrive at the basis of segmentation in the marketplace. The chapter delineates the criteria that help service organizations to choose the segment in which they are going to focus on for marketing the service product. Keeping the target segment in mind, the chapter highlights the different strategies for positioning the service in the mind of the consumers.

Chapter 7, *Customer Perceptions of Service*, highlights the service quality dimensions affecting the customers' perception of services. It further discusses the gaps in service delivery and their effect on consumer perceptions. Managing e-service and e-service quality are also explained keeping in mind the growing online market. It also delineates the concept of service encounter and touches upon the Gap model of service quality. It discusses the concept of service quality and also the SERVQUAL model.

Chapter 8, *Customer Expectations*, examines customers' anticipation about a service based on their perceptions. The chapter also gives a perspective on managing customer expectations, thus leading to customer satisfaction and even 'delight' with the services provided.

Chapter 9, *Pricing Strategies for Services*, explains the various pricing strategies which could be adopted by service firms. These could be cost-based or market-based strategies. There are a range of options that service firms could initiate in each category. The chapter helps to bring in a perspective on implications of pricing strategies for the service provider.

It gives insights into the pricing strategies adopted by the current service providers in India keeping in mind the value to the customer.

Chapter 10, *Strategies for Promotion for Service Sector*, discusses the management of the marketing communications for a service organization. It covers advertising, sales promotion, personal selling, direct marketing, and public relations, and focuses on the management of these different channels of marketing communications to position the product in the minds of the customers and create realistic expectations. It also explains the concept of e-marketing.

Chapter 11, *Managing Distribution Channels in Service Industry*, discusses the distribution channels available for the services sector. It discusses the management of these channels so that there is optimization of service availability for the customer. It also studies the impact of the Internet on distribution.

Chapter 12, *Physical Evidence*, delineates the different factors that have a bearing on the customer's perception about the service provider. It further elaborates on the management of different dimensions of physical evidence to create a perception, which is in line with the services being provided.

Chapter 13, *Managing People in Service Industry*, provides an understanding of the importance of managing people in the process of service delivery. Individuals employed in the services industry have to be involved and highly motivated as well as committed to the job to deliver to the best of their abilities. This has numerous implications for the service managers to manage their teams well. The kind of people recruited by the service organization depends on the availability of people in the labour market in a country or region. The demand and supply dynamics in labour markets also influences the availability of skills and competencies for a particular industry. The chapter also gives an understanding of the role of culture, which influences individuals' behaviour in the organizational setting. The chapter further discusses service culture and the aspects that influence it. The issues of recruitment, retention, teamwork, training and development, rewards, and job security have been explained.

Chapter 14, *Managing Service Processes*, analyses the management of service processes by service firms. The chapter establishes the relationship between profitability and service process. It details the blueprinting process, which maps all the activities right from the time that the customer begins the contact with the marketer to the time that he departs from the service provider's premises. The chapter also gives insight into managing the demand and supply dynamics.

Chapter 15, *Managing Demand and Supply*, is an important aspect of services as it greatly impacts the profitability of the firm and has a strong bearing on the customer satisfaction level. The waiting line strategies have also been discussed in the chapter. The chapter discusses the importance of managing demand and supply, demand issues, capacity constraints and more. It also discusses the solutions to overcome demand–supply issues.

Chapter 16, *Customer Feedback and Service Recovery*, examines the issues that need to be managed when the service delivered falls short of customer expectations. It discusses the strategies to retain customers after a service delivery failure. Customer feedback is an extremely important way to improvise the service processes. The recovery mechanisms enable a firm to reduce the attrition level and could have an immense bearing on consumer loyalty. It discusses various ways of managing the service recovery and also examines the issue of service warranties.

Chapter 17, *Impact of Technology on Marketing of Services*, gives an overview of the technology issues that are faced by the service firms. Technology influences the strategies adopted by the service firms. They impact the way the service is provided. The chapter delineates the impact of technology on different aspects of the business such as productivity, new services, control mechanisms, distribution networks, new relationships, and customer relationships. The chapter also traces the impact of online technologies on service businesses. It also discusses the concepts of service innovation and key influencers. The concepts of data mining and data warehousing have also been discussed.

Chapter 18, *Managing Quality and Excellence*, gives a perspective on the management of services in totality. It discusses different service excellence models such as the Malcolm Baldrige Quality Award, ISO, European Quality Award, and CII awards in India. It develops a critique on these models and discusses a blueprint for service excellence in the form of the balanced scorecard model.

Chapter 19, *Ethics in Service Firms*, introduces the concepts of ethics and values. The global businesses will have to imbibe the models of sustainable development in order to perform well. The chapter argues the need for pursuing ethical business practices.

Chapter 20, *Strategies for Business Growth,* gives insight into the strategies adopted by service firms for growth. The chapter discusses the various options such as green field ventures, joint ventures, mergers and acquisitions, strategic alliances, franchising, and management contracts. The advantages and disadvantages of the same have also been elaborated upon.

Chapter 21, *Emerging Service Sectors in India,* discusses four important service sectors in India—healthcare, biotechnology, retailing, and banking. Each sector is discussed in detail, along with the industry structure, critical success factors, and major challenges faced by it.

Acknowledgements

We would like to express our heartfelt gratitude to a number of institutions, publications, and individuals without whose support and encouragement we would have not been able to complete this work. First of all we would like to thank our host institutions which have always been supportive of our efforts.

We would like to express deep thanks to the following publications and institutions, which have been very supportive of sharing the resources for publication: *Emerald Group of Journals, The Business Standard, Hindustan Times, The Times of India, Business World, Journal of Services Research, International Journal of Contemporary Hospitality Management, Indian Management, The Economic Times,* World Bank, Institute for International Management and Technology (IIMT), and Institute of Chartered Financial Analysts of India (ICFAI).

I would like to thank my husband Sunil and son Shaurya for their love and support. I would like to acknowledge the role of my parents and parents-in-law and the entire family for the encouragement that I have always received. It has been a blessing to have such a loving family. The role of Prof. Chihiro Watanabe for all his motivation and support for my research endeavours is something I really cherish. His constant encouragement has had a big influence on my research agenda and work. I would also like to thank all my friends and professional mentors for their inspiration and guidance. We would like to thank the entire team of Oxford University Press for the standards laid by them and in motivating us for improving our earlier drafts. The painstaking efforts of the team are indeed commendable.

Vinnie Jauhari

The constant encouragement provided by my husband Mr Anil Dutta and daughters Yoshita and Ridhima has been a big influence in my research agenda. This work would not have been possible without their inspiration and dedicated support. The interest shown by Yoshita and Ridhima in the field of management and their participation and assistance have provided an impetus in developing and redefining this work. The motivation by my parents (Mrs Sudesh and Mr K.K.M. Mehta), brother Vijay Bali and Yash Mehta and sister Jaya Rishi Kinger, and their families—Neelam, Tarun, Ankita; Archana, Kshamta; Rishi, Mahima, Devya, and Abhijat has helped me in hours of strife. The guidance provided by Dr Parsa, Kirti and Pankaj Madan, and Dr Urvashi and Haren Makkar has helped me in my research endeavours.

Kirti Dutta

Preface to the First Edition

The contribution of the services sector in the growth of the global economy is significant. Business operations are getting more complex on account of liberalization of economies and rapid changes in technology. In light of the changing market structures, aspirations of the consumers, and internationalization of firms, it is important to understand the changing business dynamics in India and other emerging economies. India is one of the faster growing economies in the world. The estimates of the Organisation for Economic Co-operation and Development (OECD) indicate that India would emerge to be the third largest economy by 2026. The service industry in India contributes to more than 53 per cent of the GDP (World Development Indicators 2007). This book is an attempt to understand the dynamics of the services industry, especially in the Indian and South Asian context.

About the Book

This book is targeted to meet the requirements of management students, faculty, and practitioners by presenting a comprehensive overview of services management. To understand services management, it is important to have an understanding of the specific characteristics of the services industry. There is a need to understand the broad economic environment as well as elements of the service mix, such as the service product, price, place, promotion, people, physical evidence, and process. A business manager should also have an understanding of consumer behaviour, segmentation, targeting, positioning, perceptions, and customer expectations to deliver a commercially viable service product. The understanding of services management also requires an insight into technological issues, ethical issues, and future options available for growth of the business. There is a need to appreciate alternatives to implement excellence in service businesses, as short-term approach may not be conducive for long-term survival.

Pedagogical Features

The book explores the emerging issues in the services sector from an Indian perspective. It touches upon various key concepts by bringing in examples from the business world. The practices at Indian and global companies, such as HDFC, Hewlett–Packard ITC, HUL, KFC, and McDonald's, have been discussed.

Every chapter begins with outlining the scope of the chapter. The key definitions and summary at the end of each chapter help the reader in better assimilation of the content. The text in each chapter is interspersed with the suitable corporate examples in the form of boxed exhibits to facilitate the understanding of various concepts relating to services.

The book captures the changing business dynamics of the services sector. It discusses emerging issues in the services sector, which business managers would need to address—excellence, innovation, technology, and strategy. The Internet-based exercises will provide the reader with a wider exposure to the key areas in services management.

The following are the key highlights of the book:
- Integrates theory with corporate examples
- Provides rich insights into the dynamics of the service sector

- Includes aspects such as technology management, ethics, strategies for growth, business excellence, and balanced scorecard approach
- Gives a perspective on emerging service sectors such as software and ITES, healthcare, banking, and retailing
- Discusses the practices of Indian and global companies such as HDFC, Hewlett–Packard, LIC, Ferns 'n' Petals, KFC, and McDonald's
- Contains exhibits which give insights into the Indian service industry
- Explains concepts through examples, exhibits, tables, caselets, and case studies
- Includes Internet-based exercises which will help the students to apply the theory to business situations

Acknowledgements

We would like to express our heartfelt gratitude to a number of institutions, publications, and individuals without whose support and encouragement we would have not been able to complete this work.

First of all, we would like to thank our host institutions which have been supportive of our efforts. The leadership at IIMT, Dr R. Kapur, Mr K.B. Kachru, and the entire team, including Dr Kamlesh Misra, Dr Umashankar Venkatesh, Kamal Manaktola, have all been wonderful colleagues and have always stood by us. Ashok Sahu has always been a source of great strength and his contribution is beyond description. Amit Sexena and Manjit have always worked very hard in our endeavours and have rendered outstanding support.

The team at Hewlett–Packard, especially Michel Benard and Rob Bouzon, have been a source of inspiration.

A very warm word of thanks to dear Shivangi Gupta and Himani Kaul whose support has been immeasurable during very tough periods. They played a very important role in evolving the final draft version of this book. We would remember their contribution forever.

We would like to express deep thanks to the following publications and institutions, which have been very supportive of sharing the resources for publication:

Emerald group of journals, *The Business Standard*, *Hindustan Times*, *The Times of India*, *Business World*, *Journal of Services Research*, *International Journal of Contemporary Hospitality Management*, *Indian Management*, *Economic Times*, World Bank, Institute for International Management and Technology (IIMT), and Institute of Chartered Financial Analysts of India (ICFAI).

The role of Prof. Chihiro Watanabe for all his motivation and support for my research endeavours is something I really cherish. His constant encouragement has had a big influence on my research agenda and work. The presence of friends, such as Amee Yajnik, Charla-Griffy Brown, Meenakshi, Jagdeep, Ajay Jugran, Vinayshil Gautam, Vipin Gogia, Pankaj, and Kirti Madan, have helped me cope with very challenging periods in my life.

We would like to express our heartfelt thanks to our families. Our respective spouses Sunil and Anil as well as children Shaurya and Yoshita, and Ridhima, brothers Shallen and Yash, sister Jaya, parents, and in-laws, who have always been on our side to help us progress in our professional careers. Without them it would never have been possible to accomplish all this.

We would like to thank the entire team of Oxford University Press for the standards laid by them and in motivating us for improving our earlier drafts. The painstaking efforts of the team are indeed commendable.

Vinnie Jauhari
Kirti Dutta

Brief Contents

Detailed Contents

1   Introduction to Services

OBJECTIVES

After reading this chapter you will be able to understand the

- essentials of a service economy
- concept of a service and its characteristics
- classification of services, and the importance of classification
- difference between goods and services
- factors responsible for the growth of the services sector and the challenges thereof
- critical factors for success of the services sector
- concepts of service management
- ingredients of the traditional marketing mix

Indian Online Retail

The Indian online retail space seems to have come of age. The industry is said to be worth around $12.6 billion (₹76,700 crore) and is said to grow further. Flipkart, Jabong, and SnapDeal are some of the home-grown e-commerce majors that enjoy top-of-the mind customer recall. The presence of Amazon, the global online retail giant, indicates the interest of global palyers in the Indian e-commerce space.

Indian online retail has some unique characteristics. The majority of transactions are carried out using the cash-on-delivery system. This adds to the cost to the e-retailers as courier companies charge extra to handle such transactions. There is also a high rate of return, which translates into longer credit cycles. High growth rates and fierce competition has fuelled high customer expectations.

Although the country's e-commerce companies are finding it difficult to become profitable in a capital-intensive business, long-term growth potential is luring global investors into investing in online retail ventures. Recently, Russian billionaire Yuri Milner's fund DST Global invested $210 million in Flipkart, the country's largest online retailer. Bangalore-based Flipkart recently acquired a majority stake in e-fashion vertical Myntra, in a deal that is reportedly worth $300 million (₹1770 crore).

After going through the chapter, you will be able to answer the following questions:
1. What could be the reasons for online retailing to take off in India?

2. How important is customer involvement in a service-oriented business?

Sources: *Business Standard* (2014); IAMAI (2013), Ghosh (2014).

INTRODUCTION

As the economy grows, the demand for services increases. The services sector, which has registered a five per cent annual growth in 2012–13, it is expected to grow at the rate of 6.1 to 6.7% in 2013–14, accounts for 60% of India's GDP and is currently the fastest growing sector of the economy (Indian Budget 2013–14). The services sector, which witnessed a double-digit annual growth, includes transportation (air, rail, or road), telecom, health care, financial services such as banking and insurance, business services such as advertising, legal services, etc. The growth of the service industry has been uniform, with sectors such as accountancy, facility management, hospitality, entertainment, and personal services also showing impressive growth. Table 1.1 depicts the growth of commercial services exports by category and region between 1990–2012.

Table 1.1 The growth of commercial services exports by category and region for 1990–2012 (Annual percentage change)

(Annual percentage change)	World	North America	South and Central America	Europe	CIS	Africa	Middle East	Asia
Commercial services								
1990–95	8	8	9	–	–	7	–	14
1995–00	5	7	6	4	–	4	–	4
2000–05	11	5	8	13	18	–	–	–
2005–10	9	8	10	7	14	9	–	12
2011	11	9	19	12	20	0	11	12
2012	2	5	4	–2	9	6	13	6
Transportation services								
1990–95	6	4	7	–	–	6	–	11
1995–00	3	1	1	3	–	–1	–	3
2000–05	10	3	11	11	15	14	–	11
2005–10	7	6	9	6	13	9	9	9
2011	9	11	17	10	16	6	22	4
2012	1	3	–1	–2	5	9	13	4

(Contd)

Table 1.1   *(Contd)*

(Annual percentage change)	World	North America	South and Central America	Europe	CIS	Africa	Middle East	Asia
Travel								
1990–95	9	7	10	–	–	8	–	14
1995–00	4	6	7	2	–	6	–	3
2000–05	8	2	6	9	18	15	12	11
2005–10	6	4	7	3	9	8	15	13
2011	12	10	8	13	28	–4	2	18
2012	4	8	5	–2	12	6	6	10
Other commercial services								
1990–95	9	11	10	–	–	5	–	16
1995–00	7	10	9	6	–	6	–	5
2000–05	13	8	11	15	25	–	13	–
2005–10	11	10	16	10	19	11	–	13
2011	12	8	30	12	20	3	14	14
2012	2	4	6	–2	11	4	20	6

Source: Based on the WTO data on 'Trade in Commercial Services by Category 1990–12'.

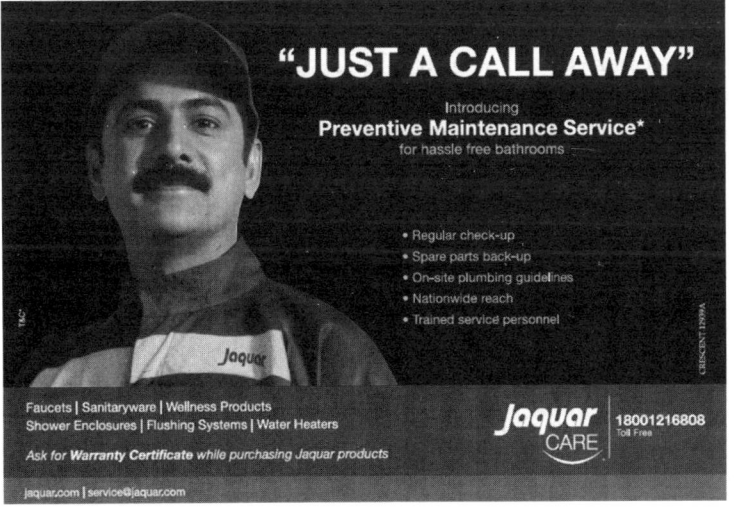

Jaquar understands the important of service in retaining their customers

Courtesy: Jaquar & Co.

Owing to the economic down turn, the growth rate of services sector declined to 6.6% in 2012–13, which is also lower than that achieved in 2011–12. The slowdown in the growth of the economy in 2012–13 is attributable to the slowdown in the industrial sector, which is estimated to grow at 3.1% in 2012–13 as against 3.5% in 2011–12. This is

Table 1.2 Services: The new profit imperative in manufacturing

Category	Total expenditure
Personal computers	5 times the product cost
Locomotives	21 times the product cost
Automobiles	5 times the product cost

Credit: Adapted from Howells (2004). Used with permission.

significantly lower to the growth of 1.8% in the agriculture sector as against a growth rate of 3.6% achieved in 2011–12 (*India Economic Survey* 2012–13).

The distinction between goods and services is slowly getting blurred. Given the demands of global competition, and thanks to the increasingly sophisticated production, it makes more economic sense for companies to combine services with the product they offer. Manufacturers are now moving downstream (towards the customer) as they are appreciating the fact that, it is in services that the profit lies (Wise and Baumgartner 1999).

They now understand that the sale of products forms just a small portion of the overall revenue and it is services, which generate the big money. It is the experience dimension of the product consumption which is becoming important.

Table 1.2 shows the product cost in terms of total expenditure for a manufacturer. As manufacturers have an intimate knowledge of their products and the market, they are in a better position to provide the service activities related to their products. Today, they consider product sales as an entry point for foraying into services.

For instance, Ford had long been engaged in finance (Ford Credit), and in maintenance and car components (Visteon). Eventually, the company moved into car insurance and general after-sales care and web retailing (fordjourney.com). To add to its list of customer services, it formed a joint venture, Wingcast, with Qualcomm, a wireless electronics company, and Cartell, a telematics equipment supplier, to provide 'in-vehicle' navigational assistance, and Internet and entertainment services. Similarly, Fiat took over full control of Toro Assicurazioni some years ago to provide insurance and other financial services to its customers. Primarily, all these activities are closely associated with selling the manufactured product, the car. IBM and Siemens derive more than half of their turnover from services activities (Howells 2004).

This trend is also evident in the aerospace industry wherein aircraft builders are offering finance and leasing options along with providing repair and overhaul facilities. For example, GE has a major finance and leasing company (GE Capital Services), and also provides a range of purchasing, leasing, and rental options. Thus, engines can be rented from GE Engine Services (GEES) for a period ranging from 24 hours to more than a year. It also offers 'GE On Wing Support', which provides wide ranging maintenance service package including engine inventory, long-term preservation, and facilities support. Similarly, Rolls Royce has acquired aero-engine repair and maintenance companies worldwide. This aspect of marketing or 'servicization' phenomenon is termed as 'service encapsulation' of goods and materials. Table 1.3 highlights the service encapsulation phenomenon, wherein goods are not offered to the consumers in their own right, but in terms of their wider service attributes.

More and more countries are finding that the majority of their gross national product (GNP) is being generated by the services sector. An examination of the World Bank development indicators for 2011–13 indicates that the services sector is the major source of economic activity across the world (Table 1.4) and the Americas, the average growth

Table 1.3   Service dimensions through life cycle of a product

Pre-purchase activities	During purchase activities	Post-purchase activities
Seeking advice	Financing	Disposal
Consultation services	Leasing	Recycling
Purchase facilitation	Information sharing	Repair and maintenance
		Delivery

Credit: Adapted from Howells (2004). Used with permission.

Table 1.4   World Bank Development Indicators 2013

Region	GNI Atlas methodb $ billions	GNI per capita		GDP per capita average annual real growth %	Services % of GDP	Gross capital formation % of GDP	Exports of goods and services % of GDP	Total debt service % of exports of goods, services and primary income
		Atlasb $	PPPc $					
	2012	2012	2012	2012	2012	2012	2012	2011*
East Asia and Pacific	9,650,422	4,846	7,788	6.7	44	44	37	4.7
Europe and Central Asia	1,805,390	6,636	11,856	1.2	59	21	43	24.5
Latin America & Caribbean	2,661	8,999	12,008	1.8	62	22	24	13.3
Middle East and North Africa	–	–	–	–	–	–	–	5.0
South Asia	2,345,191	1,422	3,534	2.3	56	32	23	6.7
Sub-Saharan Africa	1,224,537	1,345	2,247	1.5	59	22	34	3.4

Source: Based on the data from Facts and Figures: The World Bank Development Indicators (2013).

*Figures available till 2011 in the World Bank report (2013)

figure for per capita GDP is 7%. The overall trend in the world's economic activities shows that barring the services sector, all other major activities such as agriculture and industry have showed a downward curve. An insight into the kind of profits generated by the services industry can be seen in Table 1.5. According to a sector-wise analysis of India by CapitalinePlus, some 7830 services listed in the country, netted a profit of ₹163,875.91 crore during the financial year 2012–13 compared to the manufacturing sector that earned a profit of ₹146,106.77 crore from 9425 listed companies. The total number of service firms in the country might be larger, but they do not feature here as many of them are unlisted firms.

Table 1.5 Sector-wise comparison statistics from India

Name	Number of companies	Year 2012–13	
		Sales (₹ in crore)	Net profit (₹ in crore)
All companies	23583	8,058,905.07	403,677.92
Commodities	1114	481,024.19	88,154.99
Diversified	25	32,256.58	645.73
Manufacturing	9425	4,620,874.79	146,106.77
Miscellaneous	4052	167,679.43	6,992.83
Services	7830	2,245,632.68	163,875.91
Trading	1102	449,820.88	1,236.21

Source: Based on the data from CapitalinePlus: Fact Sheet Industry (2013).

Exhibit 1.1 **Growth of the Indian Hospitality Industry**

The Indian hospitality sector is poised for a huge inflow of world's leading hotel brands. With ever increasing business activity, flourishing leisure travel, and booming middle class, India is poised to be the third largest market in hospitality and tourism by 2015.

In 2012, in terms of travel and tourism, India was ranked 12th among 184 countries for total contribution to GDP. This contribution is expected to grow at the rate of 7.8% per annum during 2013–23 against the world average of 4.2%.

It is estimated that the sector will create 78 jobs for every investment of USD 18,366, as compared to 45 in the manufacturing sector. The contribution of travel and tourism to capital investment is expected to grow at the rate of 6.5% per annum during the year 2013–23. This is above the global average of 5.0%. Additionally, it is also estimated that against the world average of 4.0% in visitor exports to total exports, India's share will increase by 5.7% per annum during the 2013–2023 period.

The boom in tourism industry evidently has had a cascading effect on the hospitality sector, which has seen an increase in the occupancy ratios and average room rates. As new sectors—rural tourism, luxury tourism, medical tourism, heritage tourism and eco-tourisms are creating new venues of growth and expansion, Indian hotels are expected to flourish as there is a severe shortage of quality rooms. With the demand continuing to surge, many a global hospitality major has shown a keen interest in the Indian hospitality sector. For example, US-based brand Starwood is all set to enter India with its tie-up with ITC group. Unitech has joined hands with Marriott to operate three new hotels in Kolkata, Gurgaon, and Noida. DLF has already developed plans to set up over 100 business and 4-star hotels in 50 cities over the next 10 years.

With prospects being so bright, Indians can look forward to exciting management career opportunities in the field of international hospitality. Due to the severe shortage of skilled workforce in this industry, well-educated hospitality managers with an international perspective and professional experience will be in high demand.

Source: Based on articles from *The Economic Times* (2006, 2008) and India Brand Equity Foundation (August 2013).

India's hospitality industry is another service segment that is poised for growth and has very bright prospects in terms of generating revenue as well as jobs. Increasing business activity, flourishing leisure travel, and a booming middle class are encouraging global brands to line up for a slice of the Indian hospitality pie (Exhibit 1.1).

SERVICES: CONCEPT AND CHARACTERISTICS

What exactly are services? There are several definitions of services in services market-ing literature. Grönroos (1990) defines services as 'An activity or series of activities of more or less intangible nature that normally, but not necessarily, take place in interac-tions between the customer and service employees and/or physical resources or goods and/or systems of the service provider, which are provided as a solutions to customer problems.' Kotler (1991) defines services as 'Any act or performance that one party can offer to another that is essentially intangible and does not result in the ownership of anything. Its production may not be tied to a physical product.'

Zeithaml et al. (2006) have reflected upon services as, 'An act or performance offered by one party to other. Although the process may be tied to a physical product, the performance is transitory, often intangible in nature and does not normally result in ownership of any of the factors of production.' Kasper et al. (1999) define services as, 'Services are originally intangible and relatively quickly perishable activities whose buying takes place in an interaction process aimed at creating customer satisfaction but during this interactive consumption this does not always lead to material possession.' The various definitions of services include several features such as element of tangibil-ity, which could vary on a spectrum of being very high to low. This would mean that services such as consultancy could be highly intangible while certain others, such as education may be more tangible. Thus we can define services as 'A set of activities or benefits which produce a product, which is normally intangible in nature, per-ishable, involving temporary transfer of ownership or as long as the service is being used and which gratify the customers needs or problems. Services can also be provided in connection with sale of tangible goods for creating value perceptions among customers.' Table 1.6 highlights the elements of tangibility in vari-ous service areas.

Table 1.6 Tangibility element in various service sectors

Higher intangible content	Higher tangible content
• Teaching	• Cosmetics
• Consulting	• Detergents
• Financial investment	• Furniture
	• IT equipment
• Hospitality	• Sugar

Characteristics of Services

A review on the subject by Lovelock and Gummesson (2004) and Parker (1960), identified intangibility and perishability as the two most important characteristics of services. Regan (1963) identified intangibility, inseparability, perishability, and ubiq-uity as the four characteristic features of a service. However, he neither defined nor explained them. Rathmell (1966) identified as many as thirteen characteristic differ-ences between goods and services. The first authors, according to the review, to cite all four characteristics were Sasser et al. (1978), who presented them in a pioneering services operations textbook. However, they used the term 'simultaneity' instead of 'inseparability'. Zeithaml et al. (1985) identified four characteristics of services that all service marketers must bear in mind—intangibility, inseparability, variability, and perishability.

Intangibility

Services are 'experiences' created for customers. They comprise actions rather than objects. Bateson (1977) first described services as intangibles because 'Services are performances rather than objects, they cannot be seen, felt, tasted, or touched in same manner in which goods can be touched.' He identified intangibility as the critical difference between goods and services from which all the other differences emerge. Bateson further categorized intangibility into physical intangibility, which is 'not palpable or cannot be touched' and mental intangibility, which is difficult for the consumer to grasp or measure even mentally. For example, it is not easy to judge how thoroughly a car has been serviced immediately after the service. He thus concluded that services are doubly intangible.

The intangibility of services results in the following implications for marketers:

- Services cannot be stored.
- Services cannot be patented legally, hence they can be easily copied by competitors.
- Services cannot be readily displayed or easily communicated leading to difficulty in assessing its quality.
- Decisions regarding advertising and promotions are difficult.
- Pricing services is difficult as it is hard to determine the actual cost of a 'unit of service' and price/quality relationship is complex.
- It is less efficient than goods production.
- Design of total service package is not possible.

Some of the possible solutions for service marketers to overcome intangibility issues can be:

- use tangible cues
- stimulate, manage, and promote word-of-mouth communication
- use personal sources of information more than non-personal sources
- use post-purchase communication
- strengthen internal and external marketing
- use relationship marketing
- create strong organizational image
- use cost accounting to help set prices.

Inseparability

This stands for inseparability of production and consumption. Services are created (by the provider) and consumed (by the client/user) simultaneously and cannot be stored like goods. Hence a mobile phone (product), which is manufactured in Korea and shipped to Sweden, is sold four months later, and is used for years. On the other hand, the transportation services of an airplane are first sold, and then produced and experienced or consumed simultaneously (Zeithaml et al. 1985). This also implies that the customers have to be present during service production. Consumers frequently interact with each other and may influence each other's experience. Thus a service must be provided at the right time, in the right place, and in the right way. Service producers themselves play an important role as part of the product itself, as well as an essential ingredient in the service experience for consumers.

We can thus summarize that 'Inseparability involves the presence of the customer, customer's role as co-producer, customer to employee and customer to customer interaction' (Lovelock and Gummesson 2004). A case in point has been the emergence of health care tourism in India. Efficient and skilled health care at affordable costs has made India a favourite global health destination. As services are 'inseparable' and aimed at giving the customer an 'experience of a lifetime', several leading medical care chains are tying up with hospitality chains to provide a unique combination of health and tourism.

Exhibit 1.2 highlights this facet of the services sector.

The inseparability of services results in the following challenges for those marketing services:

- Centralized mass production becomes difficult if not impossible.
- Customer experience depends upon the action of employees and interaction between employees (service providers) and customers.
- Operations need to be decentralized so that the service can be delivered directly to consumers at convenient locations.

Exhibit 1.2   **Booming Health Care Tourism in India**

Inspite of the global downturn, India has emerged as the most promising medical tourist destination in the world. The Indian health care sector is emerging as the preferred choice for 'medical' tourists from Middle East, Africa, Britain, US, and Canada. The government support combined with, improved health care infrastructure, low cost, and its rich cultural heritage, has helped Indian medical tourism to attain a position among the global leaders in health care. India has become one of the world's most cost-efficient medical tourism destinations.

It is expected that the Indian medical tourism industry will register a CAGR of more than 20% during 2013–2015. It is estimated that by the end of 2013, the global share of India's health care tourism would be around 3%, and in all likelihood generate a revenue of around 3 billion USD. Additionally, by the end of 2015, it is expected that the medical tourism market of India will grow by 30% annually.

Tourism is an important industry in India, contributing around 6.8% to the national GDP, and providing employment to over 41 million people. Medical tourism is playing a significant role in this upsurge. This is mainly due to the fact that private hospitals in India are world class and have the latest medical technologies in place. The doctors and nurses in the country have a very high degree of proficiency and have the capability to outshine any hospital in the West. India's knowledge of Ayurveda, Unani, Reiki, and other alternate forms of medicine is also highly valued across the world. Additionally, many tourists come to India to look for and discover the peace and curative powers of these alternative medical therapies. There are over 3,000 hospitals and around 726,000 registered practitioners catering to the needs of traditional Indian health care.

According to a Planning Commission report, India is a cheaper option for health care as compared to countries such as Thailand, UK, or US. A cosmetic surgery would cost $3500 in Thailand, $20,000 in US, and about $10,000 in UK. The same in India would cost just about $2000.

Besides being home to some of the best privately-owned hospitals, tourists from the West face relatively lesser communication problems as English is a widely spoken language here. Moreover, the waiting list for these foreign patients is low. All these advantages point towards one main point—medical tourism is riding a growth curve and is all set to drive India's economy in the years to come.

Source: Based on the articles from *The Times of India* (2008), Booming Medical Tourism in India, 2013 and Healthcare.in (2013)

- Due to simultaneous production and consumption, the customer involvement is high and this influences the outcome of the service transaction.
- Involvement of other customers in the production process becomes an imperative.

Some of the probable solutions to overcome inseparability problems of services can be:
- having strong selection and training programmes for personnel who would be dealing with public/clients
- announcing strong incentives and motivations to attract and satisfy the customer
- marketing at multi-site locations
- innovating techniques of indirect interaction
- achieving standardization to the maximum extent possible
- resorting to consumer management
- focusing on personal attention
- developing a distribution network with quality control mechanism.

Variability

Services face the difficulty of achieving uniform output, especially labour-intensive services. Sasser et al. (1978) described the challenge of setting up standards when the behaviour and performance vary not only among service workers, but even between the same employee's dealings with different customers, and on different days. Variability or heterogeneity also results because no two customers are alike in their demands.

Thus, quality and essence of service vary from producer to producer, customer to customer, and from day to day (Zeithaml et al. 1985), and is largely the result of human interaction and all the vagaries that accompany it. The implications for marketing due to variability in services are:
- difficulty in achieving standardization
- difficulty in setting quality controls
- determination of quality possible only after performance of service
- difficulty in communicating to the clients what exactly they would get.

The strategies that can help in overcoming this aspect of services are:
- stress upon standardization and performance
- focus on employee training programme, performance evaluation, and internal marketing.
- consider licensing and other forms of credential requirements
- position variation as a strength of innovation
- promote research and innovation
- industrialize service: Levitt (1972) suggested 'Specific techniques to substitute organized pre-planned systems for individual service operations (for example, travel agents could offer pre-packaged vacation tours to obviate the need for the selling, tailoring, and haggling involved in customization). This strategy is the opposite of customization.
- customize services

Perishability

This implies that 'services cannot be saved' (Zeithaml et al. 1985). Goods once produced can be stored and then sold at a later date but services peter out. They cannot

Table 1.7   Applicability of unique characteristics of services to different types of services

Physical action to a person	Physical action to the object of a customer	Non-physical action at the mind	Non-physical action directed at data
Hair cut	Repair and maintenance of equipment	Advertising	Information processing
Beauty treatment	Interior designing	Theatre	Consulting
Medical surgeries	Transportation of goods	Lectures/talks	
Restaurant food service			

Credit: Adapted from Lovelock & Gummesson (2004). Used with permission.

be stored. An unutilized service capacity cannot be utilized further. For example, an unoccupied hotel room, airline seats, etc. cannot be saved, stored for reuse later, resold, or even returned if the customer is unhappy (Lovelock and Gummesson 2004). The marketing implications as a result of perishability of services are:

- short-lived value of services
- services cannot be inventoried
- there is a lot of time pressure in sales
- capacity of services is finite.

Marketing strategies that can be adopted to overcome the marketing implications are:

- demand forecasting and creative planning for capacity utilization to close gaps between demand and supply
- formulate strategies to cope with fluctuating demand
- devise strong recovery strategies when things go wrong
- focus on competence and expertise
- continuous study of demand patterns and competitive parameters
- develop creative pricing options such as early bird or frequent flier specials.

Lovelock and Gummesson (2004) have applied the four characteristics of services to categorize services into four types based on whether the service offering is physical or non-physical in nature and whether people themselves, owned objects, or information, represent the central element that is processed to create the service. These four categories are—(1) physical actions to the person of the customer (people processing); (2) physical actions to an object belonging to the customer (possession processing); (3) non-physical actions directed at the customer's mind (mental stimulus processing); and (4) non-physical actions directed at data or intangible assets (information processing). Representative examples of services in each category are highlighted in the Table 1.7.

CLASSIFICATION OF SERVICES

Services can be classified in several ways. Various authors have tried to classify services on the basis of different features/aspects such as the market segment, tangibility factor, skill type, etc. Figure 1.1 shows the numerous factors along which services can be classified. They are enlisted as follows:

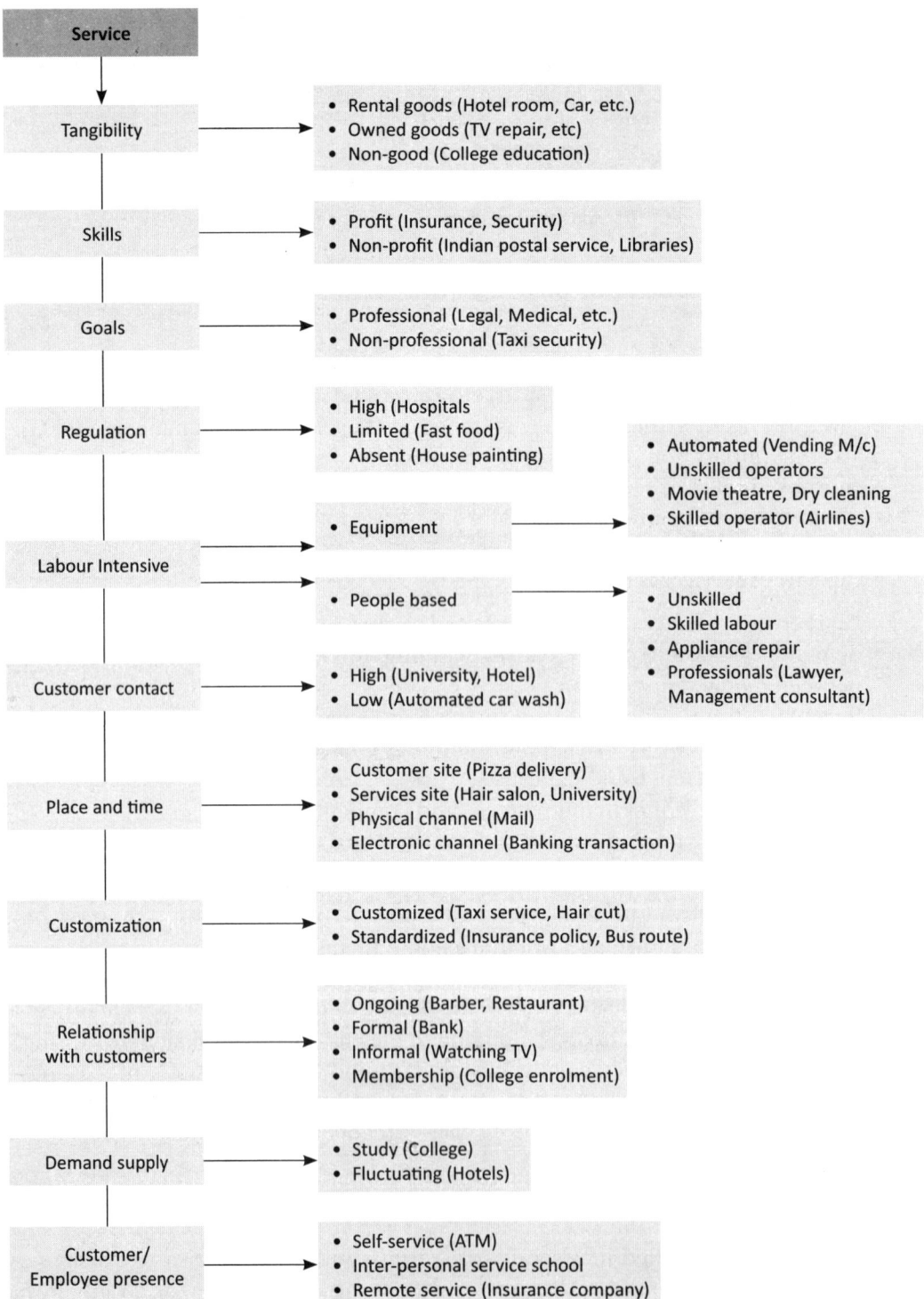

Fig. 1.1 Classification of service

- tangibility component
- skill-type involved
- goals of the business
- regulatory dimension
- intensity of labour used

- consumer contact
- place and timing
- customization
- relationship with customers
- demand and supply

Categorizing Service Processes

Various authors have classified services on the basis of the processes, which in turn are differentiated on numerous factors. The various service classifications are discussed in detail in this section.

Market segment Services can be classified on the basis of the market segment they are catering to. Thus, we can have services catering to end-consumers, such as the hair salon and beauty services, coaching classes, and car wash services or services catering to organizational consumers such as management consulting, repair and maintenance services for machines, and legal services (Lovelock 1983, and Rampal and Gupta 2002).

Degree of tangibility According to Lovelock and Wright (1999), services can be classified into tangible offerings, such as food services or dry cleaning, and intangible services, such as teaching and medical services. Judd (1964) classified services as rental goods services, such as hotel and lodging services, and car rental; owned-goods services such as laundry, cleaning, repair of gadgets, etc. which involves repair or improvement of goods owned by the customer; and non-goods services that cover personal experiences such as legal services, educational services, and social services (family and counselling services, job training, etc.).

Skills of the service provider Services can be provided by highly skilled labour or unskilled labour (Rampal and Gupta 2002). Thus, services can be classified as professional, such as health/medical services, engineering, accounting, research, management, etc., and non-professional services such as shoe shining, laundry, cleaning services, etc.

Goals of the service provider At times, services are differentiated on the basis of the goals they pursue—whether they are profit making or non-profit making. For example, an organization can be a profit-oriented entity, such as airlines, hotels, or restaurants. Non-profit organizations or services include state-owned post and telegraph services, public libraries, etc. (Kotler 1980). For example, the government-owned India Post has over 1,55,015 Post Offices (as on 31 March 2009) of which 1,39,144 (89.76%) are in the rural areas (India Post, 2014).

Degree of regulation Services are also classified according to the extent of government regulation on them (Rathmell 1974). Services, such as mass transportation systems, which include airlines, railways, and roadways are highly-regulated, while some face limited regulations. The hospitality sector faces limited government regulation. There are some services; for example, barber and beauty services, domestic help services, etc that are very difficult to regulate in developing countries such as India.

India Post: The world's largest postal network

Degree of labour intensiveness Service employees play a vital role in the delivery of services and sometimes are also a part of the service delivery (Varoglu and Eser 2006). However, services may vary according to the extent of the labour involved. Thus, there can be equipment-based services on the one hand and people-based services on the other (Thomas 1978). Equipment-based services, as the name suggests, could include completed automated services such as ATMs and vending machines, or an offering through a machine with little or unskilled human intervention, as in movie theaters, dry cleaners, etc. They also include services that are operated by skilled professionals, such as airlines, BPOs, etc. People-based services can again be classified into unskilled (guards and cleaning services); skilled (appliance repair, printing, catering, etc.); and professionals like engineering, management consulting, data processing, medical services, etc.

Degree of customer contact Chase (1978) classified organizations on the basis of the contact time between the customers and the service staff. Thus, organizations could be high-contact or low-contact ones depending upon the time a customer spent with the service provider. High contact services are those, where the customer spends hours, days or weeks in the service system, such as in education and hospitality industry; while low contact service is one in which the contact with service system ranges from a few minutes to some hours. For example, appliance repair services, postal services, etc.

Place and time According to Lovelock (1983), services can be classified on the basis of the place and time of service delivery. Thus, there can be service-site, customer-site, and service-delivery services. In case of a service-site service, the customer needs to visit the service location to avail the service; for example, watching a movie in a theatre. In customer-site service, the service is delivered to the customer, like home delivery of food items. Service delivery involves the interaction between the customer and the service provider through a physical channel such as e-mail, as in case of online reservations of airline, railway tickets, etc.

Customization   According to Silvestro et al. (1992), 'a high degree of customization is when the service process can be adapted to suit the needs of individual customers'. Lovelock (1983) has also classified services as customized and standardized. A standardized service is where the service to be provided is predetermined and pre-designed. A customer may be offered several options, all of which are predetermined and the customer can make a choice.

Relationship with customers   Lovelock (1983) classified services according to the nature of relationship with customers. According to him, the relationship can be formal, informal, ongoing, or a membership-based one. A formal relationship is exemplified in banks, where each transaction is noted; while an informal relationship is one in which customers are anonymous and the transactions are short-lived, as in case of watching television. An ongoing relationship is epitomized by services of a barber or in a restaurant, where proactive measures need to be taken to enjoy continued patronage of clients. A membership relationship is one in which patrons (clients) must apply to become members and their performance is reviewed over time. Sometimes service providers create special memberships or frequent user programmes to reward loyal users. For example, airline companies offer frequent flyer programmes for regular customers.

Demand and supply   Some service organizations can be classified according to the demand for the service and the ability of the service organizations to match the demand (Lovelock 1983). Thus the grouping can be categorized as steady, like colleges where there is a 'steady' demand for the services; or 'fluctuating' as in the hospitality industry where the demand is not constant over a period of time.

Facilities, equipment, and people   Equipment, facilities, and people form the tangible elements of service delivery. It is important because customers use tangible clues to assess the quality of a service provided. The more intangible a service is, the greater is the need to make it tangible (Rafiq and Pervaiz 1995). For example, in a college the classrooms, tables and chairs, the overhead projector, and the faculty form a part of the tangible elements (Lovelock and Wright 1999).

Degree of discretion   Silvestro et al. (1992) classified services according to the degree of discretion. A high degree of discretion is exercised when front office personnel can use judgment in altering the service package or process without referring to superiors, as in the case of management consultancy. A low degree of discretion is where changes to service provision can be made only with authorization from superiors, like in services by news agents and confectioners.

Value addition   Silvestro et al. (1992) grouped services on the basis of value addition done by the front-office or the back-office staff. According to this parameter, services can be classified into back-office and front-office services. 'A back-office-oriented service is (one) where proportion of front-office (customer contact) staff to total staff is small, and a front-office-oriented service is (one) where proportion of front-office staff to total staff is large.' For example, in management consultancy and in hospitality sector the focus is on front-office orientation, whereas in transport service, back-office orientation is predominant.

Product and process   Silvestro et al. (1992) also classified services as product-oriented, where emphasis is on what the customer buys, and process-oriented, where the focus is on how the service is delivered to the customer. Thus, restaurants and transport services are product-focused, whereas hotels are process focused.

Utility creation perspective   Hsieh and Chu (1992) classified the services business from the utility creation perspective. According to them, the value of a service business depends on its ability to create a utility. They identified time utility and space utility as dimensions of the service product, and people or things as the service recipients. For example, they classified hair styling and beauty salon as time utilities where recipients could obtain better appearance in a short while. Similarly, a space utility for people is created by a hotel to widen the area of lodgers' activities.

Service as a Process

A process involves the conversion of an input into an output. In services, two broad categories—people and objects—are processed. The nature of service act can be tangible or intangible. From an operational perspective, Lovelock and Wright (1999) categorized service process into four broad groups—people processing, possession processing, mental stimulus processing, and information processing. All categories have different forms of process with vital implications for marketing, operations, and human resource managers.

People processing   This involves noteworthy actions directed towards people, in particular, the bodies of persons, such as haircut, surgery, etc. Here customers must enter

People processing is an important aspect of managing medical services

the service factory/location where service providers (people/machines or both) deliver the service benefits to them. Sometimes service providers, come to the customers along with their tools to provide the desired benefits at locations of customers' choice.

Management implications   If managers think about the process and output in terms of people/or objects being processed, it helps them to identify the benefits being created and the non-financial costs—time, fear, pain, and mental and physical effort—that customers incur.

Possession processing   This includes concrete actions to physical goods belonging to customers. In this case, customers need not be present, but objects requiring processing must be present. For example, lawn mowing, warehousing, laundry, etc. Many such activities are quasi-manufacturing operations, and do not always involve simultaneous production and consumption.

Management implications   The managers should note that the output in each instance should be a satisfactory solution to the customer's problem/need or there must be some tangible enhancement/improvement of the item in question.

The nature of services needs to be understood. Depending on the target segment, the offering needs to be packaged appropriately.

Mental stimulus processing   This kind of service focuses on intangible actions directed at the minds of people. It includes education, news, entertainment, sport, theatre, etc. In such instances customers must be present mentally, but could be physically located either in a specific service facility, or in a remote place connected by broadcast signals or telecommunication linkages. This is in sharp contrast to people processing where people must be present physically, e.g. hair cut, or air travel. As these kind of services, that is, advertising, consulting, etc. pertain to people's minds and have the power to influence attitudes, there is lot of scope for manipulation; hence, strong moral standards and cautious oversight is required on the part of the service providers.

Management implication   As core content of all services in this category is information-based, which can easily be recorded and transformed to manufactured product, this service can thus be 'inventoried'.

Information processing   This describes indistinguishable actions directed at the customer's belongings or assets. In services sectors such as insurance and banking, little direct contact is needed with the customer, once the request for service has been set in motion. The extent of customer involvement is determined more by convention, and a personal desire to meet the supplier face to face than by operational need.

Management implication   Information is the most intangible form of service output but can be transformed into more enduring tangible forms such as reports, books, tapes, diskettes, etc. Although professionals and clients prefer one-to-one meetings to know more about each other's needs and disposition, management should try to build successful personal relationships based on trust. This relationship can also be created and maintained through telephone or e-mail, thus saving the firm from all the complexities of managing people-processing service.

Importance of Classification System

The purpose of the development of classification system for services can be multi-dimensional. Hafer (1987) compiled the following reasons to classify products/services and the advantages thereof:

- Classification helps to understand the needs of consumers and their motivation for making purchases. This helps a marketer to stay abreast of changes in the needs of the consumers.
- It helps a marketer to understand the pre-purchase and post-purchase buyer behaviour. This provides insights into the consumers approach at evaluating services, their sources of information, and judgment of a product's absolute and relative performance.
- Classification can help service providers formulate strategies for groups of products/services. Such strategies save time and effort and can become the foundation for the marketing mix of the firm.
- Classification helps to identify whether products/services have complements in other industries or businesses and identify strategies for possible adoption. It is a benchmark to list the service types or organizations, which are felt to fit into the groupings.
- Classifying services acts as a checklist of service dimensions possessed by service providers and helps to determine their strategic positioning. This further helps to determine the strengths and weaknesses of a particular service, that is, determine areas of excellence as well as areas that need to be worked upon, abolished, or reduced.

It also helps to determine the competitor set. This also leads to the determination of the competitor's strengths and weaknesses, which could enable a marketer to identify strategic gaps that represent growth potential or high risk.

DIFFERENTIATION BETWEEN GOODS AND SERVICES

A product is the core output of a firm. It can either be a service or a manufactured good produced by the firm. Goods are described as physical objects or devices that provide benefits to the customer through ownership or use. In contrast, services are actions, deeds, or performances. The basic differences between goods and services are:

Ownership On purchasing goods customers obtain tangible ownership of a product. But while purchasing services, customers do not obtain permanent ownership of tangible elements. They can only derive values or some mental satisfaction either by renting, or hiring or availing the benefits of using certain products. Here they purchase the experience of using the service product, instead of the service itself.

Performance The performance of goods is tangible, and the products can be used to perform their functions time and again. Services on the other hand are intangibility predominant performances. The benefits of owning and using manufactured products emanate from their physical characteristics, whereas in services benefits arise from the nature of performance.

Another interesting way to distinguish between goods and services is to place them on a scale from tangible dominant to intangible dominant. This section describes some of the parameters of this scale.

Customer involvement Performance of a service involves the participation of the customer, either actively (e.g., ATM) or by their cooperation with service personnel (e.g., hotels, schools, etc.), in the production process. In contrast during the production of goods, customers do not have to play an active role—they just purchase the standard finished goods.

People as part of the product In high-contact services, such as the hospitality sector, customers not only come in contact with service personnel but with other customers as well. Thus the distinction between service businesses often lies in the quality of employees who are serving the customers and type of customers patronizing the service business. People constitute an important part of the product in many services. It is the task of the management (service providers) to manage the service encounters in such a manner as to create favourable experiences for the customers in order to generate customer loyalty.

Variability Products can be standardized but there is a great degree of variability in services. Since service personnel, influenced by other customers in the system, perform operational inputs and outputs, this makes it difficult to standardize and control variability in services. However, service providers are trying hard to customize services to the maximum extent possible.

Evaluation Since goods are made up of tangible attributes, it is easier to search for a product suiting the customer's requirements. In services, on the other hand, the entire emphasis is on experience attributes, which makes it harder for even customers to evaluate it after consumption. For example, the service aspects related to a surgery are difficult to evaluate.

Inventory Goods can be inventoried till they are sold or consumed. In contrast, services are perishable and cannot be stored.

Distribution channel Goods are distributed through proper distribution channels which are industry specific. Services, however, either use electronic channels or combine the service factory, retail outlet, and point of consumption at a single location. Also, service firms have to manage the behaviour of their personnel as well as customers to ensure smooth running of operations.

FACTORS RESPONSIBLE FOR GROWTH OF SERVICES SECTOR

There are both global factors as well country-specific factors, which have led to the growth of the services sector across the world over the last two decades. This section discusses the factors that led to the growth of the services sector in India.

Liberalization of services sector Certain services sectors in India have been liberalized and thrown open to the private sector. This has led to enhanced competition leading to higher degree of entrepreneurship in these areas. In India, for example the insurance and banking sectors have been opened to foreign direct investment (FDI). Similarly, the software and telecommunication sectors have been liberalized. Figure 1.2 indicates the growth of the liberalized sectors in India. Service sectors, such as information technology (IT) and telecommunications, have attracted significant FDI, created more

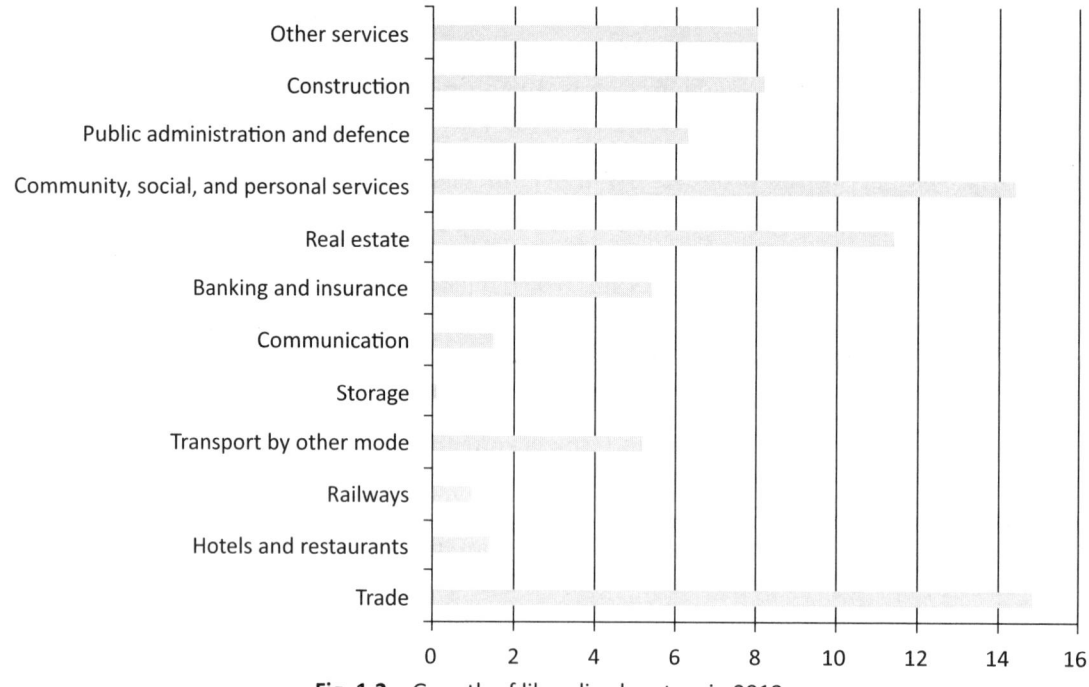

Fig. 1.2   Growth of liberalized sectors in 2013

Source: Based on the data from Services:business-india.in

employment opportunities, and galvanized other sectors of the economy as well. Over the years the growth rate of the Indian services sector has outpaced that of the agricultural and manufacturing sectors. The services sector contributes to nearly 60% of the GDP of India. It has a growth rate of about over 10% and generates almost 25% of the total job opportunities in the country. Additionally, opportunities in business process outsourcing and allied commercial activities, created by overseas companies have contributed significantly to the exports and foreign currency inflow. However, sectors such as retail and other professional services, that have not been exposed to sufficient domestic and foreign competition, and where the regulatory framework is weak, have failed to create income or employment opportunities for the economy.

Foreign direct investment   Liberalization has led to increased foreign direct investment (FDI) in the services sector. This has led to increased investment by multinationals in India and hence stiffer competition. Domestic firms have also tried to meet the growing customer aspirations resulting in commitment to offering superior services. The flow of FDI in India in the first quarter of 2013 (January–June), amounted to US$13.6 billion and is expected to increase significantly in the years to come, according to the UNCTAD 2013 report.

Higher flows of FDI have also been associated with more exports in the services sector.

India's IT and BPO sector exports are expected to grow by 12–14% in FY14 to touch US$84 billion–US$87 billion, according to Nasscom (2013).

The IT/ITeS sector has created 2.8 million direct and 8.9 million indirect employment opportunities. Both these opportunities are expected to grow to about 14 million by 2015 and to around 30 million by 2030, according to an industry estimate. Table 1.8 highlights the contribution of IT/ITeS services to foreign exchange earnings in YR12–13 (₹billion).

Figure 1.3 highlights the positive correlation between FDI and growth in various services sectors.

Among the individual segments of the services sector, there appears to be a strong association between FDI growth and exports. The IT sector is a case in point. Figure 1.4 illustrates the relationship between FDI and IT exports in select states in India.

Better living standards The standards of living are getting better thanks to increased employment opportunities for people. This has been led by high disposable income, double household income, and convenience factors.

Table 1.8 Software services export from India: 2011–12

Activity	2010–11	2011–12	Growth (%)
	(1)	(2)	(3)
A) Computer services	1598.4	1867.1	16.8
Of which: i) IT services	1492.2	1661.8	11.4
ii) Software product development	106.2	205.3	93.3
B) ITeS/BPO services	571.7	617.2	8.0
Of which: i) BPO services	468.7	523.0	11.6
ii) Engineering services	103.0	94.2	–8.5
Total export of software service (A + B)	2170.1	2484.3	14.5

Source: Reserve Bank of India (2013).

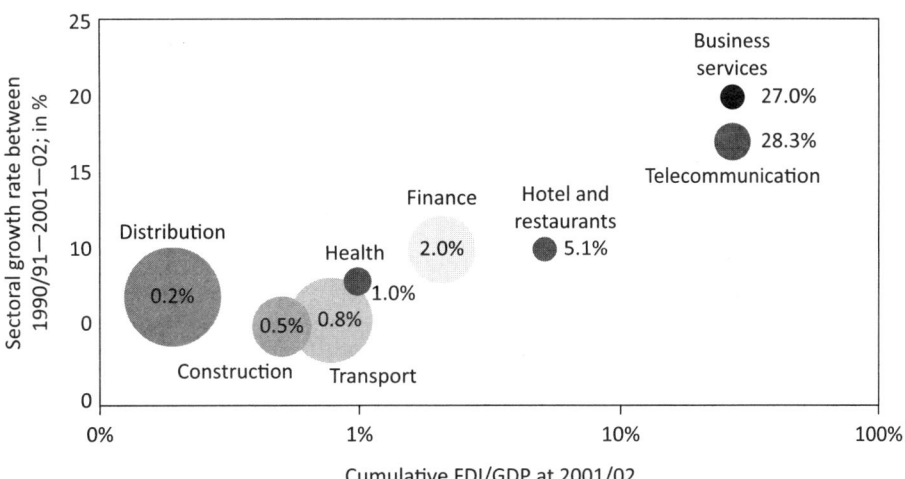

Fig. 1.3 Positive association between FDI and growth

Source: The World Bank.

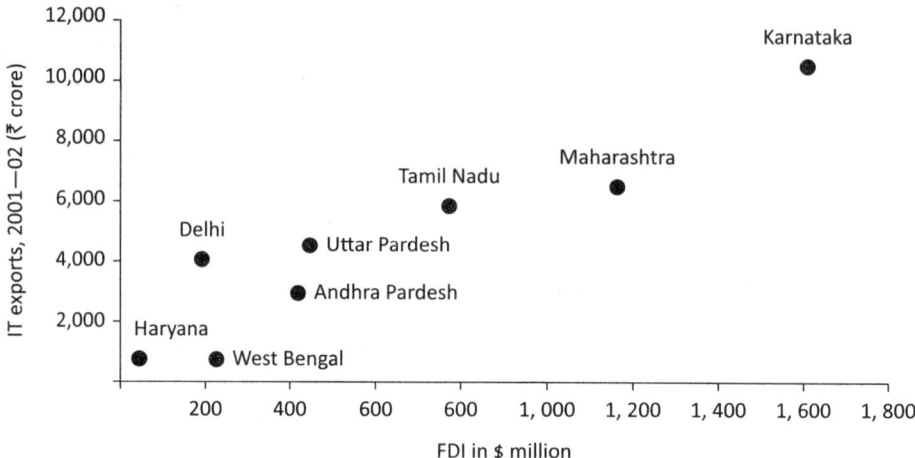

Fig. 1.4 FDI and IT exports in some Indian states

Source: NASSCOM (2008).

High disposable incomes   The incomes of consumers have increased manifold in the years of liberalization. People now have bigger amounts of money to spend. With more disposable incomes consumers tend to spend on services that make their life convenient. A case in point is the proliferation of mobile phone services in the country. The percolation of the mobile phones to literally every segment of the society has made life convenient and improved lifestyles as also the way of doing business. Thus, several cellular phone service providers keep devising new attractive schemes for consumers to make it easier for them to acquire mobile phones as well as services.

Convenience factors   As incomes of people rise, there is a proclivity towards convenience-related services. For example, laundry services, house-keeping, and repairing are some of the services which are increasingly being outsourced. There is also a rush for baby-sitting services, home delivery grocery outlets, and transport providers. The idea is to utilize money in improving one's lifestyle and making it comfortable.

Dual income households   With both spouses working, the spending power increases and so does the paucity of time. Thus, home-care services, salon services, and service apartments are some of areas that have seen a lot of growth in recent years. This has also led to emergence of convenience retailing formats. The success of superstores such as Big Bazaar is an evidence of this change.

New technological devices   New advancements in technology and their commercial applications have led to the emergence of new services such as gaming, entertainment, and satellite and cable networks. Also, convergence of technological applications have led to the emergence of products, such as tablets and smart phones, which could be used to download text, video, and audio signals. This creates a new room for service providers for such products. Thus, the creation of new platforms of technology has led to the demand for a new stream of content developers for the new services.

Concern for productivity Technology has helped change the dynamics of business transactions. For instance, banking has become so convenient with new standards being set in customer delivery. The options of ATMs, online banking, payments through the Internet, and credit cards have all contributed to convenience, and at the same time resulted in more business and cost savings by the provider. Many product and service firms have set up call centres that take care of customer queries and after-sales servicing. These factors have contributed to higher revenues and business growth in the services segment.

CHALLENGES CONFRONTED BY SERVICES SECTOR

The services sector faces a lot of challenges. If we take into account the various stakeholders into account, then there are numerous challenges that need to be addressed. These stakeholders are the government, consumers, society, financial investors, suppliers, and the firms or service providers themselves.

Infrastructure

The growth of any segment depends upon the presence of adequate and good infrastructure. Despite India's average performance in the manufacturing segment as compared to China, it fares better in terms of service industry, especially the software industry. The support by the government in terms of providing and developing software technology parks has been largely instrumental in the emergence of world-class Indian software firms such as Infosys and Tata Consultancy Services. Technology facilitates a lot of value drivers in the service industry. For instance, call centres help in putting together a customer response system. But these can function well and are meaningful only if the roads are proper, the transport sector is well developed, and the power, water, and bandwidth availability is adequate. Thus, the biggest challenge in India is the creation of world-class infrastructure to match the demands of the growing economy. The airports and local transport system needs to be revamped, and investments in civic amenities need to be hiked.

Technology

Technology has dramatically changed the nature of business. E-commerce, for instance, has opened up an additional channel for sales for many organizations. This has implications on nature of transactions, procurement, and delivery processes for firms that have integrated IT in their business. Distribution channels stand greatly enhanced due to instance availability of e-tickets for airline and train travel, direct room reservations, etc. Also, shopping on the Internet opens up new options for consumers. While IT enables convenient purchase for consumers, it throws up several issues of secure transactions and security of consumer databases for the service firms. Also, firms will have to look for larger volumes of business to make their online businesses commercially viable. Technology sophistication and availability also implies that the same service can be copied as anyone can buy the technology off the shelf. It is a challenge to remain competitive in the long run. It implies that firms need to invest in enduring relationships with consumers to survive.

Employees

It is a big challenge to find the right kind of people who can create a distinct experience for consumers. Sectors such as retail and IT enabled services (ITeS) operating in India face the challenge of high attrition. This implies that new people have to be hired continuously and trained. In fact, many BPOs frequently place large recruitment ads for walk-in interviews. There are also high attrition rates in the Indian hospitality sector, and firms face a big challenge in retaining talented workers. The employee attitude is a key factor that influences the service experience of a customer. It is, therefore, important that an employee has the right attitude, and is well trained so that services could be standardized, and deviations on account of human errors be avoided. Service firms will have the following challenges relating to the workforce:

- How to recruit the right talent and nurture it as well?
- How to retain the people?
- How to imbibe the right competencies in the manpower?
- What interventions are required at the education level to have both the right output for the industry, and the right trainers?
- How could best practices be instituted and benchmarked?

Consumers

Rising education levels have resulted in higher levels of consumer awareness. Higher incomes have also resulted in higher expectations on delivery. With competition having increased, consumers are willing to experiment to get maximum value for their money. Thus, for a service firm, sustaining growth is a big challenge. Today, the consumers benchmark internationally and their expectations are also higher, thanks to the Internet and global satellite channels. Also, the level of domestic and international travel has gone up dramatically, which has contributed to higher aspirations and expectations. Many desperate service firms, in the name of relationship marketing, make innumerable unsolicited calls for selling credit cards or offering loans in order to achieve higher sales. These are not viable solutions for the businesses. Better ways of engaging customers would have to be thought of rather than hitting the same database with the same enquiries about potential association. The consumer courts have also become stronger in India. They provide relief to hassled consumers, thus making the business of providing services more challenging than before.

Competition

Competition also becomes an important challenge for service firms. With similar technologies available, the search for different value drivers becomes difficult. The firms face a tough time constantly striving to achieve a higher market share. The long-term solution should be not to compete against each other, but go in for cooperative arrangements to prevent wastage of resources. For example, global majors in the business of sustainable energy sources have fostered alliances for commercializing alternate fuel technologies. Similarly, in the field of information technology (IT), Intel, Hewlett-Packard (HP), and

Princeton University have fostered an alliance, 'Planetlab' which works on Linux technologies on Itanium platform.

Suppliers

Suppliers are becoming more and more dynamic, and this has given rise to new kind of industry relationships in the services sector. In certain high-technology industries these relationships have a profound impact on the business and the shape of the industry itself. For instance, the relationship of Intel with various personal computer (PC) manufacturers has set new technology standards. Similarly, the alliance of Microsoft with various PC vendors has led to several tie ups for the operating systems. These alliances have long-term impacts on the nature of industry relationships. In the travel industry, the global reservation systems, which most firms adopt, have become the default standards, and, hence have a unique place for suppliers of such software. In the years to come, service providers will have to ponder over the following questions:

- How will the supplier impact my future growth?
- Should I go with a few exclusive suppliers, or should I deal with multiple vendors?
- How would future change in technology influence the relationship with current vendors?

Service firms will have to assess the above-mentioned challenges and devise a strategy to cope with them.

CRITICAL FACTORS FOR SUCCESS

Every service segment has some distinct aspects that contribute towards its success. However, there are some generic aspects which can be addressed keeping in mind the general characteristics of the service industry.

Focus on Customers

It is always important for a service firm to remember that the consumer is the most important entity and all its processes and activities need to be aligned to ensure a better service delivery. Many a time, in the process of adopting a particular technology system or quality initiatives, firms alter the processes of service delivery, which may or may not be convenient for the customer. For example, the automatic response system set up by many service providers, such as banks or airlines, sometimes takes a lot of time for resolving a query. The technology, people, systems, and policies are all facilitators, and are not an end by themselves. So a service firm always needs to address issues such as:

- Who are my customers?
- What do they want?
- How much are they willing to pay?
- What could be the quickest way of delivery without compromising quality?

Caring for Employees

People management is one of the most critical factors in services management. Employee satisfaction leads to better performance at work resulting in customer satisfaction and hence increased market share. This has been discussed extensively in Chapter 17. It is, therefore, important for companies to take care of their employees. Satisfied and loyal employees could facilitate a happy experience for a customer, which is translated into increased business. Thus, managing attrition, training people, and helping chart a bright career path for them, are key challenges in managing human resources.

Identification of Value Drivers

Every business has its own value chain as has been pointed out by Porter (1985) in his theory of value chain analysis. In some businesses, it is the experience such as multiples as in adventure; tourism, or in some services sectors it may be technological superiority, which are the essential or key value drivers that can be identified and worked upon. A firm, if it does not have a unique or a distinct advantage, will not last long in business. Hence, identification of unique elements, which would extend longevity, is one of the critical challenges for these companies.

Deploying Technology to a Firm's Advantage

Technology opens new vistas of business for a service firm. It is, therefore, important to identify the technology which could add value to the service being provided and the firm. The Internet offers an immense challenge. The dynamics of online purchase are also very different as compared to traditional channels of marketing. Also, it offers new ways of reaching out to consumers through various portals. One critical success factor is to evolve the right communication strategy to drive the business.

Demand Management

Since services cannot be stored, it is a big challenge to manage the demand. The pricing strategy has to be such that it generates volumes to keep the business going. Necessity-based entrepreneurship always leads to a lot of challenges for service firms. In India, the small-scale sector faces a huge challenge of demand management. Technology can be utilized to leap frog to higher growth, provided customer focus is in place.

Adequate Systems

It is essential to invest in adequate systems and procedures. Lack of proper service delivery systems can ruin the brand. Work flow systems have to be in place with clear reporting relationships. The implementation of services need to be closely monitored.

SERVICE MANAGEMENT

This section discusses the traditional marketing mix, the expanded marketing mix, and the variables and elements of the marketing mix.

Traditional Marketing Mix

Culliton (1948) developed the idea of a marketing mix from the notion of a marketer as a 'mixer of ingredients' where a marketer plans various means of competition and blends them together so that a profit function is optimized. The term and concept of 'marketing mix' was introduced by Neil Borden in the 1950s. According to Baron et al. (1991), the marketing mix is defined as 'those activities that show similarities to the overall process of marketing, requiring the combination of individual elements'. After the Second World War, Cullotin coined the 'P' philosophy of marketing, proposing a long list of Ps which typified profit, planning, production, etc. and represented the key activities of running a business. According to Czinkota, one could differentiate between a 'sales orientated' and a 'manufacture oriented' company by examining the amount of emphasis given to the various 'Ps'. Thus, the idea, and eventually, the practice of a marketing-orientated company emerged. McCarthy (1960) further developed this idea and refined the principle to what is today generally known as the four 'Ps'—product, place (distribution), promotion, and price.

Product

The definition of the first 'P', that is, product, according to Kotler et al. (2006) is, 'anything that can be offered to a market for attention, acquisition, use or consumption; it includes physical objects, services, personalities, places, organization services and ideas'.

The service industry has to develop the right service package. A service package includes the service delivery process also, because, in services, the delivery process is part of the product. Since the product is the main offering which the clients covet, any failure in it will ring a death knell for the service.

Place

'Place' in marketing stands for distribution of services. A client can engage a service if he/she has possession of it, at the right time and location convenient to him/her. Thus, place is concerned with the 'possession of service that is accessible to the client at the right place and at the right time'. It includes distribution channels, levels of distribution, logistics, etc. However, for service industries, strategic location is of prime importance, and by occupying strategic locations, the advantages and resources can be optimized (Low and Tan 1995).

Promotion

Once the organization has decided to market their services, they need to inform the customers or the public in general about their existence, what services they can provide, and how they are different from the other providers of the same service so that they can influence the purchasing decisions of the customers. Promotion, or the third 'P' in marketing, is all about this. In order to effectively strengthen the customer's view of the organization, the promotion mix must be integrated with the marketing mix to deliver a consistent message and strategically position the company and the product. The four main promotion tools are advertising, sales promotion, public relations, and personal selling.

Price

This is the only marketing mix element which generates revenue and is set in relation to the other three 'Ps' as all the others represent cost. According to Kotler et al. (2006), 'Price is the amount of money charged for a good or service'. It is 'The sum of the values consumers exchange for the benefits of having or using the product or service'. Pricing is a difficult area of marketing due to the number of variables such as capacity, efficiency of the firm, competitors' prices, relationships with suppliers, economic conditions, and company's policy on the mark-up.

Expanded Marketing Mix for Services

Services are produced and consumed simultaneously (Bitner 1990). Thus the customers are present 'in the firm's factory' and 'interact directly with the firm's personnel'. The contact employees are then playing a dual role—that of marketing and operations.

According to Shostack (1977), customers are frequently searching for 'surrogates' or 'cues' to help determine a firm's capabilities to overcome 'intangibility'. And often the only cues available are the physical facility and the employees. On the basis of this reasoning Booms and Bitner (1981) broadened the traditional four 'Ps' into seven 'Ps' of services by adding 'physical evidence (the physical surroundings and all tangible cues), participants (all human actors in the service encounter including firm personnel and other customers), and process (procedures, mechanisms and flow of activities)' thus including all elements, which an organization can control in order to satisfy its target market. Although these new elements could be covered within the traditional mix, separating them draws attention to the factors that are significant to service firm managers.

People

Booms and Bitner (1981) included all the 'human actors in the service encounter including firm's personnel and other customers' in the people concept. Organizational personnel are very important in a services firm as they are the only component that can deliver the services. In many services, customers influence the service delivery and thus affect the service quality not only of their own services, but of services of other customers as well. Bitner (1992) identified three types of service organizations based on who performs actions within the 'servicescape' (i.e., physical facility where the service is offered). These are as follows:

Self-service   Organizations in which few employees are present, and level of customer activity is high. For example, ATMs, vending machines, etc.

Inter-personal service   These are organizations where both employees and customers are present, and perform actions within the servicescape. For example, restaurants and hospitals.

Remote service   This is the other extreme of the spectrum. Organizations of such kind have little or no customer involvement, and sometimes even little employee involvement in the servicescape. For example, voice messaging services.

Physical Evidence

According to Zeithaml and Bitner (2003), physical evidence is 'The environment in which the service is delivered and where the firm and customer interact and any tangible components that facilitate performance or communication of the service'. It is important because customers use tangible clues to assess the quality of service provided. Hence, if a service is highly intangible, the marketing need is to make it more tangible so that customers can evaluate it easily. The physical evidence thus includes all the tangible representations of the service such as layout/decor, ambience, cleanliness, equipment, employee dress, quantity, guarantees, etc. Bitner (1992) emphasized the importance of managing the physical aspects of the servicescape as a sensory package designed to elicit emotional responses facilitate to shape customer behaviour and enable efficient flow of activities differentiators to distinguish a service provider from its competitors.

These signal the intended market segments at which the service is targeted, and differentiate higher priced offerings from the less expensive ones. Customers may be specifically attracted to an expensive service by the availability of superior tangible elements, such as a more elegant and better equipped hotel room.

According to Bitner (1992) the servicescape can be of any of the following kinds:

Lean These environments are very simple with few elements, few spaces, and few forms. For example, Federal Express drops off kiosks where the service is provided from one simple structure. For lean servicescapes, design decisions are relatively straightforward, especially in self-service or remote service situations in which there are no interactions between customers and employees.

Elaborate Servicescapes which are very complicated with many elements and many forms are termed elaborate environments. For example, a hospital with many floors, rooms, sophisticated equipment, and complex variability in functions performed within the physical facility. Firms positioned in the elaborate interpersonal service cell face the most complex servicescape decisions.

Process

Process is the actual manner in which the services are delivered. Since the customers are present at the time of service delivery, the service process is a prime consideration in customer satisfaction. Services, by concentrating on this aspect, can turn customer satisfaction into customer delight and thus gain a customer for a lifetime.

The importance of physical setting depends on the nature of the job and the nature of the consumption experience.

In Exhibit 1.3, the 7Ps have been applied to the McDonald's fast food chain to give a fair understanding of the marketing mix elements and variables.

Expanded Mix for Services

Within the marketing mix elements we can have a number of variables. Variables can be defined as 'A set of controllable factors that a firm can use to influence the buyer's

Exhibit 1.3 **McDonald's Marketing Mix Elements and Variables**

The concept of marketing mix can be further illustrated by examining the practices followed by McDonald's, the world's largest fast food chain. It has 25,000 restaurants in over 100 countries and continues to expand its presence globally.

Product

Although McDonald's aims to create standardized items, adaptation to local cultures, tastes, laws, and customs has become a key feature of its marketing strategy. While India was the first outlet where the beef burger was not sold, in Malaysia and Singapore, the chain underwent rigorous inspections to ensure the absence of pork products. Quality assurance remains its main focus and is the global practice that distinguishes the chain from others in the market.

McDonald's is a very good example of prudent and strategic expansion. About 4403 restaurants in 1825 days were added during 1999–2004, i.e., more than 2 restaurants each day for 5 years. This reflects globalization with a glocal focus.

Price

Even the pricing strategy of McDonald's is one of localization than globalization. In order to select the right price for the right market, a price objective is selected, demand is determined, cost is estimated, competitor's cost is analysed, a pricing method is selected, and a final price is determined.

Promotion

Although the company's overall objective is to promote a global image, the entire marketing communications strategy is localized to adapt to the cultural differences that are faced in each country. Footballers Alan Shearer and Fabien Barthez adve r tise for the company in UK and France respectively. In India, McDonald's is promoted as a family restaurant. The company sponsors a vast array of sports and seeks to enhance a brand name during the Olympic Games and the World Cup. It paid an estimated 20 million pounds for the right to use its logo in an international football event.

McDonald's concentrates on helping children and families facing problems. The company is strongly committed to staffing locally and promoting from within its ranks. Its policy of satisfying all its customers all the time is one of the main reasons for its sustained success.

Process

Stringent criteria are followed for each food item and these procedures are identical globally.

Physical Evidence

'To focus on consistent delivery of quality, service and cleanliness through excellence in our restaurants.' This message is visible in every McDonald's franchise around the world. Thus all around the world, every McDonald's restaurant offers a family environment to its customers.

response' (Vignali and Davies 1994). The variables and elements of the extended marketing mix are illustrated in Table 1.9.

An Integrated Approach

From the earlier discussion it is clear that an intelligent marketer should balance all parts of the marketing mix to convey a harmonious message.

Table 1.9 The extended marketing mix—variables and elements for services

Elements	Product	Place	Promotion	Price
Variables	Brand	Outlet type	Personal selling	Price level
	Features	Outlet nos	• Selection	Strategy
	Quality	Accessibility	• Training	Determinants
	Quantity	Location	• Incentives	Discount
	Style	Stocks	Advertising	Trade-ins
	Accessories	Intermediaries	• Targets	Credit
	Packaging	Transportation	• Media types	Terms
	Warranties	Managing	Sales promotion	
	Product lines	channels	Public relations	
Elements	**People**	**Physical evidence**	**Process**	
Variables	Customers	Layout/Decor	Blueprinting	
	Age	Ambience	Automation	
	Social group	Cleanliness	Control	
	Employees	Equipment	procedures	
	Quantity	Employee		
	Quality	dress		
	Training	Quantity		
	Motivation	Guarantees		
	Promotion			
	Rewards			
	Teamwork			

RESEARCH INSIGHT

International Market Selection: Measuring Actions Instead of Intentions

Nicholas Alexander, Mark Rhodes, Hayley Myers, (2007), 'International market selection: measuring actions instead of intentions', *Journal of Services Marketing*, vol. 21, issue 6, pp. 424–434.

This paper aims to consider factors that determine the direction of international market selection. It does this with specific reference to service companies operating in the retail sector.

The paper shows that language and hence, by implication, culture plays a fundamental role in determining direction of expansion. This has important implications for the way psychic distance is understood and service company responses to psychic distance.

SUMMARY

Services constitute a major portion of the world trade and are growing at an increasing rate. However, they are different from the traditional product marketing in a number of ways. These differences make the marketing of services challenging for the management.

This chapter highlights some of the strategies the marketers can adopt to overcome these concerns. The chapter also gives an understanding of the factors responsible for the growth of the services sector and the critical factors for its success. This is important to understand the services sector and form a background for a detailed study in services management. This section highlights the initiatives taken to promote trade in the services sector. The next section discusses the various aspects of marketing mix applicable to services. A rationale has been developed for the extended marketing mix and an integrated approach to services management is discussed.

--- **KEY TERMS** ---

Foreign investment Investment in the domestic economy by foreign individuals or companies. It takes the form of either direct investment in productive enterprises or investment in financial instruments, such as a portfolio of shares.

Liberalization To remove or loosen restrictions on an economic or political system.

Marketing mix The factors controlled by a company that can influence consumers' buying of its products. Product, pricing, promotion, and place are the four components of a marketing mix. The potential profitability of a particular Marketing mix and its acceptability to its market are assessed by marketing research.

Product Anything that can be offered to a market for attention, acquisition, use, or consumption that might satisfy a need. It includes physical objects and services.

Pricing The setting of selling prices for the products and services supplied by an organization. Prices can be based either on market prices or costs.

Promotion An activity designed to boost the sales of a product or service. It may include an advertising campaign, increased PR activity, a free-sample campaign, offering free gifts or trading stamps, arranging demonstrations or exhibitions, setting up competitions with attractive prizes, temporary price reductions, door-to-door selling, telemarketing, mailers, etc.

Place Activities such as sales and distribution of the product, transportation services, and desirable stock levels.

Service Any activity or benefit that one party can offer to another that is intangible and does not result in the transfer of ownership of any physical object.

Service economy With the decline of heavy engineering and rise of the knowledge-based economy, the service industry constitutes an ever-increasing proportion of the national income in nearly all the developed countries.

--- **EXERCISES** ---

Concept Review Questions

1. Critically discuss the importance of services in the economic growth of a developing country.
2. Which extended elements of the marketing mix are absent in the marketing of traditional products? Critically discuss their importance in the marketing of services.
3. What are the different ways by which services can be classified? Discuss any two.
4. Should services be classified? Discuss.
5. What are the different challenges being confronted by the services industry. Which according to you is most important and why?

Critical Thinking Questions

1. Discuss how services are increasingly forming an important component in the marketing of traditional products.

2. Identify any three services you are using the most in your daily life. Discuss the levels of their intangibility.

Project Assignments

1. Visit any pure services outlet, such as a hotel or a bank, and examine the marketing strategies employed to overcome the different characteristics of services.
2. Visit the government website of any developing Asian country and try to identify the importance of the service sector in the development of their economy. (*Hint*: you can consider services as a percentage of GDP, employment generated, exports and imports of services, etc.)
3. Visit the website of the WTO and find out the latest developments pertaining to the GATS.

Internet Exercises

Identify two organizations whose services are possible only because of the Internet.

CASE STUDY   The Housing Finance Sector in India: A Focus on HDFC

The mortgage financing industry, which is primarily known as the housing finance industry in India, has grown by leaps and bounds in the past few years. The sector has emerged as one of the outstanding successes over the last decade, second, perhaps, only to the country's software industry. According to ICRA (2013) estimates, the total housing credit outstanding in India as on June 30, 2013 was over ₹7,991 billion as against ₹7,592 billion as on March 31, 2013, indicating a growth of 21% (annualized) (as against 18% in 2012–13). However, the mortgage to GDP ratio (ratio of outstanding home loans to GDP), which is used to determine the extent of penetration of housing finance in the country, is one of the lowest for India as compared to developed countries where it ranges from 25% to 80%. The mortgage to GDP ratio stood at an abysmal 9% in India when compared to 17–41% in Southeast Asia, 88% in UK, 81% in USA, 20% in China, and 17% in Thailand. Hence, there is a great deal of promise for this industry in India, as the penetration of housing is very low and there are immense growth opportunities in the long run (CapitalinePlus, 2013). The housing finance industry has grown at a compounded annual growth rate (CAGR) of 18 to 20% over the last decade. It is expected to grow at the rate of 25% approximately over the next few years.

Factors Driving the Mortgage Market

According to the National Housing Board, the age-old concept of a house as a 'shelter' has transformed with time to mean a popular 'investment' for a significant segment of the population who consider this as a good source of returns on capital. This has further been facilitated by low and stable interest rates. Some of the main fiscal, social, and regulatory drivers that have fuelled the growth are:
- Changes in demographic profile, including increase in the rate of household formation, due to a structural shift from joint family system to nuclear family.
- Ever increasing middle class, migration of population, and increasing urbanization resulting in acute shortage of housing units.
- Increase in disposable income levels due to decrease in marginal tax rates and increase in total income levels.
- Tax benefits and other fiscal incentives announced in the Union budget.
- Increasing affordability of housing property purchase due to declining interest rates and stable property prices.
- Increased demand from software and other services sectors.
- Decline in the average house cost to annual income ratio to around 4–5 from 11–14 during the last decade, resulting in an affordable equated monthly instalments (EMI) as a percentage of monthly income.
- Apart from this, India, with vast untapped opportunities, is already on its way to becoming the desired location for real estate investors.
- The Indian real estate market is growing at an annual rate of 30% with steady growth in residential properties, shopping malls, multiplexes, food outlets, office spaces, and convention and business centres across India.
- 80% of the demand for commercial space is being fuelled by the IT and ITeS sector with the emergence of India as the knowledge capital of the world.
- Foreign developers, architects, and planners are playing a crucial role in the development of integrated/luxury townships.

Structure of Housing Finance System in India

The housing finance industry can be broadly classified into the formal and informal sector. In the formal sector there are housing finance companies, HUDCO, commercial banks, etc., accounting for around 30% of the total housing finance needs. The remaining 70% is met by the informal sector sources such as household savings, disposal of existing property, borrowings from friends, relatives, and local moneylenders, etc.

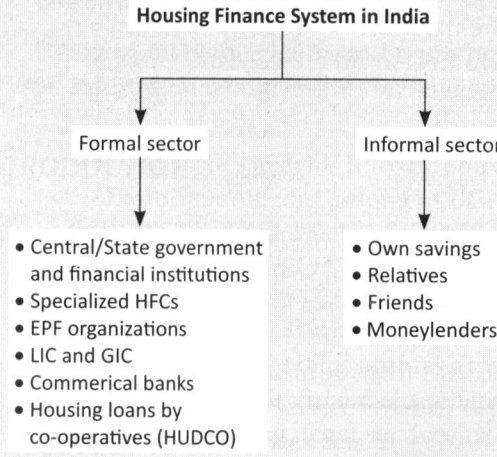

have outpaced its counterpart and and today the ratio stands in favour of SCBs. SCBs have also grown at a rate much higher than the industry growth rate. The growth rate for HFCs in first nine months of 2012–13 was 25% which was much lower to SCBs, which stood at over 70,000 crore in FY 2012.

Performance of Major HFCs

Among the insurance housing subsidiaries, GIC Housing Finance Ltd (GICHFL) has approved home loans to the tune of 1424 crore in FY13. Disbursements on the other hand showed a growth rate of 17% in FY13. LIC Housing Finance Ltd (LICHFL), on the other hand, has shown an 11% growth in its home loan approval figures, while disbursements showed a growth rate of 13%.

Among the private players, HDFC has shown a 29% growth in its home loan approval figures, in FY12–13. Disbursements have shown a growth rate of 33%. DHFL, on the other hand, has shown a 41% growth in its home loan approval figures while disbursements have had a growth rate of 35%.

HDFC, the market leader with over 50% market share in housing loans, has consistently clocked a 40–50% growth rate during the last six years as against the industry growth rate of 33% (Business India 2002). However, a look at consensus Bloomberg estimates suggests this (at ₹8,424 crore) in 2013–14 will be only 25.2% more than last year (*Business Standard* 2013)

Even in the slowdown period of 2008–09, it delivered 41% growth in net profit to ₹2,249 crore. This is higher to other HFCs and GICHFL during the same period

Among SCBs, ICICI Bank is the leader in the retail finance arena. Its loan book grew by 17.2% in 2012. Mortgage disbursements (excluding developer financing) grew by 26.80% in FY12, though this growth was partly offset by repayments and prepayments out of the existing portfolio resulting in a portfolio growth of 7.50%.

Retail loans have exhibited 14.95% YOY growth in 2013 while housing loans have exhibited a 16.28% YOY growth in 2013 and stand at 1,19,467 crore as on March 2013.

Increasing Share of Banks

The Housing Development Finance Corporation Limited (HDFC) pioneered individual lending based on market principles for homeownership in India. The success of HDFC over the years indicates that financing houses can be a profitable business. This has motivated many new housing finance companies to venture into the housing finance business. An important event of the 1980s was the formation of the National Housing Bank (NHB) in 1987. The objective of NHB is to channel formal sector resources to housing finance (urban and rural) through the promotion of a sound, healthy, and cost-effective housing finance system.

Despite being a late entrant, banks have overtaken the HFCs in the home loan market. The share of banks in total home loan disbursements has risen to 2795.9 in the year 2013–14P (KPMG 2013). Banks have increased their focus on the retail finance market, particularly in housing finance due to lower non-performing assets (NPA) levels.

During 1999–2000, the share of home loan (HL) disbursements among HFCs and scheduled commercial banks (SCB), (which include public sector banks, private sector banks, and foreign banks in India) stood equal. However, with gradual progress, SCBs

HDFC Bank

HDFC was amongst the first to receive an 'in principle' approval from the Reserve Bank of India (RBI) to set up a bank in the private sector, as part of the RBI's liberalization of the Indian banking industry in 1994. The bank was incorporated in August 1994 in the name of 'HDFC Bank Limited', with its registered office in Mumbai, India. HDFC Bank commenced operations as a scheduled commercial bank in January 1995.

HDFC is India's premier housing finance company and enjoys an impeccable track record in India as well as in international markets. Since its inception in 1977, the company has maintained a consistent and healthy growth in its operations to remain the market leader in mortgages. Its outstanding loan portfolio covers well over a million dwelling units. HDFC has developed significant expertise in retail mortgage loans to different market segments and also has a large corporate client base for its housing-related credit facilities.

Business Focus

HDFC Bank's mission is to be a world-class Indian bank. The objective is to build sound customer franchises across distinct businesses so as to be the preferred provider of banking services for target retail and wholesale customer segments, and to achieve healthy growth in profitability, consistent with the bank's risk appetite. The bank is committed to maintain the highest level of ethical standards, professional integrity, corporate governance, and regulatory compliance. HDFC Bank's business philosophy is based on four core values—operational excellence, customer focus, product leadership, and people. In a study conducted by Apnaloan.com to discover how the different institutions score, HDFC has emerged as the top scorer in two categories and one of the top scorers in two other categories, and clearly leads the other institutions.

Distribution Network

HDFC Bank is headquartered in Mumbai. The bank, at present has an enviable network of over 3,251 branches spread over 2,022 cities across India. All branches are linked on an online real-time basis. Customers in over 1,397 locations are also serviced through telephone banking. The bank's expansion plans take into account the need to have a presence in all major industrial and commercial centres where its corporate customers are located as well as the need to build a strong retail customer base for both deposits and loan products. Being a clearing/settlement bank to various leading stock exchanges, the bank has branches in the centres where the NSE/ BSE have a strong and active member base. The bank also has a network of about over 11,177 networked ATMs across these cities. Moreover, all domestic and international Visa/ MasterCard, Visa Electron/Maestro, Plus/Cirrus, and American Express credit cardholders can access HDFC Bank's ATM network.

In a milestone transaction in the Indian banking industry, Times Bank Limited (another new private sector bank promoted by Bennett Coleman & Co/Times Group) was merged with HDFC Bank Ltd, effective 26 February 2000. The acquisition added significant value to HDFC Bank in terms of increased branch network, expanded geographic reach, enhanced customer base, skilled manpower, and the opportunity to cross-sell and leverage alternative delivery channels.

Apart from giving housing loans, HDFC also provides services such as HDFC realty in which they provide assistance required at various stages of property dealings for financial, legal, taxation and valuation, and for sale, purchase, and lease of commercial and residential property. As a goodwill gesture, HDFC has come up with a grievance cell where, if you are at your wits end regarding a newly purchased property, all you have to do is provide details like name and address of your building, name of the developer, date of purchase, etc., mention your problem as briefly as possible, and HDFC takes it up with the developers.

Outlook for the Housing Finance Industry

The Indian housing finance industry is on solid ground and has interesting prospects ahead. Given the size of the market, and the huge shortage of housing and low penetration levels, housing loans will continue to grow rapidly and show strong growth for the next few years. Realistic property prices, low interest rates, tax incentives, and innovative products offered by housing finance companies augurs very well for the growth of the housing sector. Further, the Indian housing finance industry mainly caters to the organized or the employed sector, and is traditionally confined to metros and other big cities. The housing finance industry has to go a long way to cover the vast populace of semi-urban and rural towns that live outside the formal sector. However, the HFCs will face stiff challenges from banks, which will definitely put pressure on their margins. Hence, profitability growth will come mainly from loan growth. According to CRISIL (2013), HFCs are expected to maintain a net profit margin of 1.6–1.7% of loan book as against banks at 1.5–1.6% of loan book based on incremental disbursements.

Questions

1. What are the different factors driving the growth of the home loan industry in India. Can you draw similes with the growth of the services sector in India?
2. Critically evaluate the growth of the home loan sector vis-à-vis the different institutions providing the loans.
3. Evaluate HDFC's strategy to capture the home loan market. What critical factors is it focusing on for its success?
4. Comment on the distribution of services employed by HDFC.

REFERENCES

Baron, J. (1991), 'Beliefs about thinking', in Voss, J.F., D.N. Perkins, and J.W. Segal (eds), *Informal Reasoning and Education*, pp. 169–186. Hillsdale, Erlbaum, NJ.

Bateson, John E.G. (1977), 'Do we need service marketing?', *Marketing Consumer Services: New Insights*, Report #77115, Marketing Science Institute, Cambridge, MA.

Bitner, M.J. (1990), 'Evaluating the service encounters: The effects of physical surroundings and employee responses', *Journal of Marketing*, April, vol. 54, no. 2, pp. 69–82.

Bitner, M.J. (1992), 'Servicescapes: The impact of physical surroundings on customers and employees', *Journal of Marketing*, vol. 56, no. 2, pp. 57–71.

Booms, B.H. and M.J. Bitner (1981), 'Marketing strategies and organization structures for service firms', in Donnelly, J.H. and W.R. George (eds), *Marketing of Services*, American Marketing Association, Chicago.

CapitalinePlus (2006), 'Services: Banks and housing finance', Capitaline Plus, Mumbai.

Chase, R.B. (1978), 'Where does the customer fit in a service operation?', *Harvard Business Review*, vol. 56, no. 6, November–December, pp. 137–142.

Culliton, James W. (1948), *The Management of Marketing Costs*, Division of Research, Graduate School of Business Administration, Harvard University, Boston.

Freeman, N.L. (2005), 'Extended marketing mix drives service delivery', *Opthalmology Times*, vol. 30, no. 20, p. 106.

Grönroos, C. (1994), 'From marketing mix to relationship marketing: Towards a paradigm shift in marketing', *Management Decision*, vol. 32, no. 2, pp. 4–22.

Hafer, J.C. (1987), 'Developing and operationalizing a product/service classification system for health care providers', *Journal of Health Care Marketing*, vol. 7, no. 3, pp. 25–36.

Hibbert, E. (2003), 'The new framework for global trade in services—All about GATS', *The Service Industries Journal*, vol. 23, no. 2, pp. 67–78.

Hoffman, K.D. and J.E.G. Bateson (2002), *Essentials of Services Marketing: Concepts, Strategies and Cases*, 2nd edn, Orlando, Harcourt College.

Howells, J. (2004), 'Innovation, consumption and services: Encapsulation and the combinatorial role of services', *The Services Industries Journal*, vol. 24, no. 1, pp. 19–36.

Hsieh, Charng-Horng and Tzong-Yau Chu (1992), 'Classification of service businesses from a utility creation rerspective', *The Service Industries Journal*, vol. 12, no. 4, pp. 545–557.

Judd, Robert C. (1964), 'The case for redefining services', *Journal of Marketing*, vol. 28, no.1, January, pp. 58–59.

Kasper, H., P.V. Helsdingen, and W.D. Vries (1999), *Services Marketing Management: An International Perspective*, John Wiley & Sons, Chichester, UK.

Kasper, H., P.V. Helsdingen, and Wouter de Vries Jr (1999), *Services Marketing Management: An International Perspective*, John Wiley and Sons, New York.

Kotler, P., J.T. Bowen, and J.C. Makens (2006), *Marketing for Hospitality and Tourism*, Pearson Education Inc., New Jersey.

Kotler, Philip (1980), *Marketing Management*, Prentice Hall, London.

Kotler, Philip (1991), *Marketing Management*, Prentice Hall, London.

Levitt, Theodore (1972), 'Production line approach', *Harvard Business Review*, September–October, pp. 41–52.

Lovelock, C. (1983), 'Classifying services to gain strategic marketing insights', *Journal of Marketing*, vol. 47, pp. 9–20.

Lovelock, C. and E. Gummesson (2004), 'Whither services marketing? In search of a new paradigm and fresh perspectives', *Journal of Services Research*, vol. 7, no. 1, pp. 20–41.

Lovelock, C. and J. Wirtz (2006), *Services Marketing*, 5th edn, Pearson Education, New Delhi.

Lovelock, C. and L. Wright (1999), *Principles of Services Marketing and Management*, Prentice Hall, New Jersey, p. 14.

Low, Sui Pheng and C.S. Martin Tan (1995), 'A convergence of western marketing mix concepts and oriental strategic thinking', *Marketing Intelligence and Planning*, vol. 13, no. 2, pp. 36–46.

McCarthy, E.J. (1960), *Basic Marketing: A Managerial Approach*, Richard D. Irwin, IL.

National Housing Board (2004), Report on trend and progress of housing in India, June.

Parker, Donald D. (1960), *The Marketing of Consumer Services*, University of Washington, Seattle.

Porter, M. (1985), *The Competitive Advantage*, Free Press, New York.

Rafiq, Mohammed and Pervaiz K. Ahmed (1995), 'Using the 7Ps as a generic marketing mix: An exploratory survey of UK and European marketing academics', *Marketing Intelligence and Planning*, vol. 13, no. 9, pp. 4–16.

Rampal, M.K. and S.L. Gupta (2002), *Service Marketing: Concepts, Applications and Cases*, Galgotia Publishing Company, New Delhi.

Rao, R.M. (2005), *Services Marketing*, Pearson Education, New Delhi.

Rathmell, John M. (1966), 'What is meant by services?', *Journal of Marketing*, vol. 30, October, pp. 32–26.

Rathmell, John M. (1974), *Marketing in the Service Sector*, Winthrop Publishers, Cambridge, MA.

Regan, W.J. (1963), 'The service revolution', *Journal of Marketing*, vol. 47, pp. 57 – 62.

Sasser, E.W., P.R. Olsen, and D.D. Wyckoff (1978), *Management of Service Operations: Text, Cases, and Readings*, Allyn & Bacon, Boston, MA.

Shostack, G. Lynn (1977), 'Breaking free from product marketing', *Journal of Marketing*, vol. 41, no. 2, pp. 73–80.

Silvestro, R., L. Fitzgerald, and R. Johnston (1992), 'Towards a classification of service processes', *International Journal of Service Industry Management*, vol. 3, no. 3, pp. 62–75.

Sinha, Kounteya (2008), 'Medical tourism booming in India', *The Times of India*, 4 April, p. 19.

Thomas, Dan R.E. (1978), 'Strategy is different in services businesses', *Harvard Business Review*, July.

'The art of leveraged living' (2002), Business India, April 15–28, pp. 47–53.

Unnikrishnan, Rajesh and Prince Matthew Thomas (2006), 'Global brands line up for a slice of the Indian hospitality pie', *The Economic Times*, 24 July.

Vargo, S.L. and R.F. Lusch (2004), 'The four service marketing myths: Remnants of a goods-based manufacturing model', *Journal of Service Research*, vol. 6, no. 4, pp. 324–335.

Varoglu, D. and Z. Eser (2006), 'How service employees can be treated as internal customers in hospitality industry', *The Business Review*, Cambridge, vol. 5, no. 2, pp. 30–36.

Vignali, C. (2001), 'McDonald's: Think global, act local– the marketing mix', *British Food Journal*, vol. 103, no. 2, pp. 97–108.

Vignali, C. and B.J. Davies (1994), 'The marketing mix redefined and mapped: Introducing the MIX', *Management Decision*, vol. 32, no. 8, London, pp. 6, 11.

Wise, R. and P. Baumgartner (1999), 'Go downstream the new profit imperative in manufacturing', *Harvard Business Review*, Sep–Oct 1999.

World Trade Organization (2001), *Trading into the Future: WTO, The World Trade Organization*, 2nd edn.

Zeithaml, V.A. and M.J. Bitner (2003), *Services Marketing*, Tata McGraw-Hill Publishing Company Limited, New Delhi.

Zeithaml, V.A., A. Parasuraman, and L.L. Berry (1985), 'Problems and strategies in services marketing', *Journal of Marketing*, vol. 49, no. 2, pp. 33–46.

Zeithaml, V.A., M.J. Bitner, and D.D. Gremler (2006), *Services Marketing: Integrating Customer Focus across the Firm*, 4th edn, McGraw-Hill, Singapore, p. 117.

Booming Medical Tourism in India, http://www.rncos.com/Report/IM123.htm, accessed on 8 December 2013.

Debojyoti Ghosh, DST Global pumps $210 million into Flipkart, 28 May 2014, http://forbesindia.com/article/special/dst-global-pumps-$210-million-into-flipkart/37870/1, accessed on 28 May 2014.

e-Commerce Rhetoric, Reality and Opportunity (Report), 04 Sep 2013, Internet Mobile Association of India, http://www.iamai.in/rsh_pay.aspx?rid=XvXKtpsoDMg=, accessed on 28 May 2014.

http://icra.in/Files/ticker/SH-2013-Q2-1-ICRA-Housing%20Finance.pdf, accessed on 8 December 2013.

http://indiabudget.nic.in/es2012–13/estat1.pdf, accessed on 28 May 2014.

http://rbi.org.in/scripts/BS_PressReleaseDisplay.aspx?prid=29029, accessed on 8 December 2013.

http://www.capitaline.com/user/FramePage.asp?id=1, accessed on 8 December 2013).

http://www.hdfcbank.com/aboutus/News_Room/hdfc_profile.htm, accessed on 8 December 2013.

http://www.ibef.org, accessed on 8 December 2013.

http://www.indiahospitalityreview.com/article/using-technology-better-guest-experience, accessed on 8 December 2013.

http://www.indiapost.gov.in/Our_Network.aspx, accessed on 27 May 2014.

http://www.kpmg.com/IN/en/IssuesAndInsights/ArticlesPublications/Documents/KPMG_ICC_Indian_Banking_The_engine_for_sustaining_Indias_growth_agenda.pdf, accessed on 8 December 2013.

http://www.wto.org/english/res_e/statis_e/its2013_e/its13_trade_category_e.htm, accessed on 8 December 2013.

http://www.wttc.org/site_media/uploads/downloads/India_sector_release_study.pdf, World Travel and Tourism Council, accessed on 21 January 2014.

https://www.kpmg.de/docs/Performance-benchmarking-report-FY-2012.pdf, accessed on 8 December 2013.

'India seems to be the most promising medical tourism destination', Posted by Vinay Grover on 22 October 2013, See more at: http://healthandcare.in/india-seems-to-be-the-most-promising-medical-tourism-destination/#sthash.ogXc4404.dpuf, accessed on 8 December 2013.

'ITC upgrades hotel brand', *Business Standard*, 7 August 2006, http://www.itcportal.com/newsroom/press_dec16_04.htm.

'Strangling e-commerce; Policy hurdles continue to slow growth of online retail', *Business Standard* Editorial Comment, 27 May 2014, http://www.business-standard.com/article/opinion/strangling-e-commerce-114052701713_1.html, accessed on 28 May 2014.

www.apuhf.info/Country%20Highlights%20India%20-%20V%20S%20, accessed on 8 December 2013.

2 The Service Product

OBJECTIVES

After reading this chapter you will be able to understand the

- concept that in services, the product is 'missing'
- features of a services product
- process of new product development
- concept of product life cycle and the strategies adopted for the different stages of a service product

F1 and More

The year 2011 saw 'Jaypee Sports International Ltd, a subsidiary of Jaiprakash Associates Limited (JAL), develop India's premier motorsports destination—Buddh International Circuit (BIC)—at Greater Noida, near India's capital city New Delhi. BIC hosted India's first ever F1TM Grand Prix in 2011 to a full house' (Jaypee Sports 2013). This business proposition was being questioned as Jaypee had invested $400 million in the F1 race. But it was going to lose $35 million every time it organized the F1 race and this loss was going to happen when it was assumed that it would draw a full house.

F1 is controlled by Formula One Management (FOM), which does not pay the circuit to host a race. It is the circuit that has to pay FOM an annual fee. 'Circuits reportedly pay FOM $35–45 million a year as licence fee; the initial contract is for five years. Jaypee will also spend $15–20 million in operational

costs-track and event management, logistics, and transport. That's a total operating cost of $50–65 million. On the revenue side, the 125,000-seater circuit has basically one contributor: ticket sales. Tickets are priced in six slabs, from ₹2,500 to ₹40,000. Then, there are 55 corporate boxes, which reportedly went for ₹30 lakh each initially. Gaur expects ₹80–150 crore ($15–30 million) from ticket sales. Revenues from everything else that matters-title rights (sold to Airtel for $6–8 million a year), track advertising, the privileged $5,000 per person 'paddock club' goes to FOM. In other words, Jaypee Sports will lose $35 million from the race. And it also has to recover the track's $200 million capital cost'.

F1 built BIC's brand image as a quality place for a racing venue in India. This would open many more doors and this was what S. Sameer, Gaur Managing Director and CEO, Jaypee Sports International, was hoping. The business that the circuit would be able to manage in the other 51 weeks would be the tie-breaker and the tipping point towards profit.

'Besides F1, there's only one motor-racing series that requires a circuit to pay its race organisers: MotoGP, the F1 equivalent of motorcycle racing. The amount, though, is much lower—reportedly $3–4 million per year. All other lower series—Formula 3, Formula Asia and GT3, among others—pay the circuit.' 'Lower series are packaged for TV,' said Sanjay Sharma, head of JK Motorsports. For example, Formula 3 logs about 12,500 hours of TV time in 100 countries. Series like this share TV and ad revenues with circuits. Sharma felt lower series would come to India because of the economic shift towards Asia that was taking place. He said, 'Anyone with any interest in Asia will look at India.' According to Gaur, once the F1 race was over, Jaypee Sports circuit should finalize terms with MotoGP and Superbike Series. Besides holding races, the circuit was planning to rent it out to teams for testing, and similarly to automobile and tyre manufacturers too, either for testing or for experiential marketing. 'This can fetch ₹10–20 lakh a day,' said Sharma (Pande and Sharma 2011). The main grand stand and 10 other stands with massive seating capacity could also be used for other events apart from racing such as gala events, award ceremonies, concerts, etc.

BIC includes 41 pit garages, 18 team buildings, a paddock club, and a media centre. These have been showcased as a 'one-stop destination for all corporate requirements and a whole host of other events like a car launch, conferences, seminars, company off-sites, rock concert, award function,' etc.

The pit lane and pit garages (where each garage can accommodate 50 people) 'is ideal for showcasing the product, touch and feel experience for customers, witnessing live action on the track, customer briefing sessions etc. The twelve halls with capacity up to 6,500 can be used to host theme events, conferences, exhibitions, fashion shows, cocktail evenings, etc. The media centre with a capacity of 600 and the press conference room with a capacity of 150 are ideal for press conferences, product launches, training sessions, etc. The 1,30,000 square metre of grand plaza area and 4,00,000 square metre of total area makes it an ideal location for trade shows, exhibitions,' etc. BIC also has 6 helipads and provides chopper services too (JPSiBrochure 2013).

It was reported that 'For around 200 days a year, Gaur's Buddh International Circuit—India's only Formula 1 track—is kept alive by adrenaline junkies like Singhania and Oberoi as they take a break from their corporate schedules and unwind under the Greater Noida sky vrooming their Ferraris, Maseratis and assorted superbikes. And for Gaur's Jaypee Sport's International that owns and operates the track, such private events—test drives, live shows et al.—translate to almost half of the track's annual revenues' (Rathore 2013).

After going through the chapter, you will be able to answer the following questions:
1. What is the service product that Jaypee offers?
2. Discuss the various sources of revenue open for the 'product' Buddh International Circuit.

Source: Based on Jaypee Sports (2013); Pande and Sharma (2011); JPSiBrochure (2013); and Rathore (2013a).

INTRODUCTION

A product/service forms the core focus around which the firm's activities revolve. All the grand plans of marketing activities can fail if the product/service is flawed or does not meet the customer expectations. The marketing environment is dynamic and to be successful, the product/service offering should be reconsidered from time to time so that it can cater to the changing demands. Competitive pressures compel an organization to reconsider its service offering.

In traditional product marketing, a product is a physical commodity, which is an outcome of a production process. The marketing activities revolve around this pre-produced product. However, services are different as there is no readymade, pre-produced article of marketing and utilization. There is only a process; some part of which may be prepared before the customer enters, but the crucial part of the service cannot start until the consumer or user enters the process and interacts with the service providers. The service is ultimately performed and delivered in the presence of the customer. Thus, Grönroos (1998) came up with the idea of the 'missing product' and stated that, 'Services are processes, and hence service firms do not offer products that are comparable to pre-produced bundles of physical resources and features that are provided by manufacturing companies. Instead, the outcome of the process is an integral part of the service process, which is consumed by customers as a solution to perceived problems. Thus, the use of a service can be characterized as process consumption as opposed to outcome consumption, where only the outcome of a process is consumed or used'. Thus, in services marketing, a product can be a vacation package, a meal at a restaurant, a financial service, a health service, educational service, or service for hosting events and conferences.

THE SERVICE PRODUCT

There are numerous perspectives on a service product. Kotler et al. (2006) defines a product as, 'Anything that can be offered to a market for attention, acquisition, use, or consumption that might satisfy a need or want. It includes physical objects, services, place, organizations, and ideas'. This definition includes both tangible and intangible offerings. It also places emphasis on meeting the customer expectations.

The American Marketing Association defines a product as, 'Anything that can be offered to a market for attention, acquisition or consumption including physical objects, services, personalities, organizations and desires'. In this definition, the focus has been on the offering to the consumer. The emphasis is not on satisfaction.

Adcock and Halborg (2001) define services as 'Everything that the customer receives that is of value in terms of perceived want, need or problem'. This definition attaches importance to the value that is offered to the consumer.

Thus, it can be seen that a product can be a tangible object, or an intangible service or idea, which a marketer has to offer to satisfy the needs and wants of the customers. A service is an offering, including both tangible and intangible offerings, which satisfies customer needs through an integrated approach and at the same time contributes to the societal welfare. BIC, as discussed in the chapter-opening case, provides a quality place for racing where the race track, halls, press conference room, etc. are the tangible part and the maintenance, kind of chopper service etc. it is providing over there constitute the intangible part.

Nature of a Service Offering

Customers adopt a product based on the perception that the benefits derived are worth more than the cost of the product. Thus, service organizations must develop and offer

> **Exhibit 2.1** **Service Offering at Flipkart.com**
>
> Flipkart started its journey in the year 2007 as an online book retailer. The initial assumption that 'every book available in India would be available in Bengaluru' proved to be wrong and so within a year they shifted base to Delhi to capture the huge market and also re-looked at their business model. To overcome their mistakes they set up their own logistics, their own warehouses, and a very large network support team in place. They developed their own 'dedicated Flipkart delivery partners who work round the clock to personally make sure the packages reach the customers on time'.
>
> Today, apart from books, they offer a host of other products such as movies, games, mobiles, computers, cameras, toys, apparel, etc. The year 2012 saw them acquire Letsbuy—a specialized e-commerce site selling digital gadgets by raising $150 million from IndoUS, Tiger global, Accel, and IDG. The services provided are 'cash-on-delivery, a 30-day replacement policy, EMI options, free shipping', and bargain prices. To deliver a better customer experience, use of technology such as mobile apps and simple texting services emails, etc. are encouraged. To ensure that the customer is present at the time of delivery of the product, SMSes and emails are sent stating the estimated time of delivery. In case the customer is not available, the same delivery person is sent so that customer relationship is built over time.
>
> As per Alexa (a global company studying online traffic ratings) rankings, Flipkart is among the top twenty Indian websites and is the largest online bookseller with over 11 million titles on offer. This is further reinforced by the fact that the ₹3 crore sales by the company in the year 2010 rose to ₹100 crore by the year 2012.
>
> *Source*: Based on Ojha 2013 and Flipkart.com 2013.

a service product that meets or exceeds customer expectation (Gordon et al. 1993). According to Gibney and Luscombe (2000), 'When industries are competing at equal price and functionality, design is the only differential that matters'. When designing the service product, marketers need to strategize, keeping in mind the customers wants and expectations regarding the service product. The element of experience in the service product is of prime importance. The design of the service product must thus address three key components—core product, augmented service offering, and delivery process (Lovelock and Wirtz 2006).

Core product

According to Lovelock and Wirtz (2006), the core product is a vital constituent of the services offering and basically addresses two questions:
• What do the buyers get when they purchase the product?
• What business are we in?

It is the bare minimum of a particular service without any frills or specific features and is the heart of the service. Thus, schools solve the need to provide basic education to children, airlines solve the need to move a person from one location to another, and a hotel provides a clean room for the night. Exhibit 2.1 discusses the core product offered at Flipkart as being a one stop online destination for a range of products and providing convenience of ordering, payment, and receiving of the products ordered by customers, and if need be, convenient replacement of the same.

Exhibit 2.2 **Spa Time**

The spa industry is going the greeting cards companies' way. In a bid to attract people, spas are creating packages around an occasion and marketing it as a product. So there are spa cuisines, spas with couple suites and four-hand experience (two masseurs working on an individual), and even Raksha Bandhan packages that can be gifted to one's sister on this special occasion. To make spa treatment a holistic experience, various spas have introduced meditation sessions, yoga sessions, and spa cuisine. While the spa at the Leela Kovalam Beach Resort, Kerala, offers its guests three Ayurvedic packages to choose from and it includes among others a free online consultancy for three months after departure (The Leela Kovalam 2013). One can experience the romance of a spa at Ananda in Uttaranchal, which is a destination spa. The Couples Connect package costs ₹24,500 for the couple for three nights stay and includes 4 spa sessions, daily activities, fitness sessions, and a special candlelight dinner with customized menu and a bottle of house wine. Also popular among travellers is the Kairali Ayurvedic Health Resort, Kerala, which received the 'Best Luxury Destination Spa' by World Luxury Spa Award 2012. Kairali has been awarded 'Health & Wellness Award 2012' by FIT Reisen at ITB, Berlin, Germany. Government of Kerala, India has awarded Kairali with Green Leaf Certification (The Highest Level of Classification for Ayurveda Centres).

Hotels, which cater to business travellers, also see a big opportunity in spas with a margin as high as 95%. Though ayurvedic products rule the market, Thai and French products are also used by various spas. To create a niche in the market, spas are launching their own product lines. The revenue generated by the Indian spa industry in 2013 was ₹11,000 crore (Mirza 2013) and is growing at a rate of 20–30% annually (Hospitality India 2013).

Source: Based on Talreja (2006); Mirza (2013); Hospitality India (2013); The Leela Kovalam (2013); Ananda Spa (2013).

Augmented product

According to Lovelock and Wirtz (2006), the core product and the supplementary services together constitute the augmented product. However, according to Kotler et al. (2006), the accessibility, atmosphere, customer interaction with the service organization, customer participation, and customers' interaction with each other along with the core and supporting products create the augmented product. In 1977, Lynn Shostack gave the molecular model for the augmented product. For example, Shostack's molecular model for airline services explains how vehicles, and food and drinks form the tangible elements of the airlines while the service frequency, transport, in-flight service, and pre- and postflight services form the intangible elements of the airlines product. For instance, in an economy hotel, supplementary services consist of check-in and check-out whereas in a first class corporate hotel, it consists of check-in, check-out, telephones, restaurant, valet service, etc. By adding more of supplementary services, the service provider can charge a higher price for the product. For example, the spa industry creates packages around an occasion and markets it as a product. So, there are different offerings in the spa category (see Exhibit 2.2).

Delivery process

This component consists of the manner in which the core and supplementary product is delivered to the final customer. Since the delivery of services involves constant interaction between the service provider and the customer, the delivery process must

Luxury hotels offer an array of services to their guests.

be planned in detail—the prescribed procedures for delivery of various services, and how and where customers fit in. Exhibit 2.1 shows how delivery process was managed at Flipkart for a better customer experience and marketing success. The integration of these three activities—core product, augmented product, and delivery services—can be explained with the help of a packaged trip by a tour operator. For a packaged tour operator the core delivery process consists of designing the package, flight and hotel reservation, and scheduling stay at various places along with the people processing and customer role. The supplementary services include sightseeing tours, taxi reservations, recreational activities during the scheduled stay, organized activities for children, etc. These services and the manner in which all this is handled forms the delivery process.

Various Levels of Service Product

According to Kotler (2002), there are five levels of service product the marketer needs to think about. They are:

Core or generic product/service   This is the most fundamental product/service that customers purchase. For example, customers purchase transportation when buying airline tickets.

Basic product/service   This is how the marketer translates the core benefit into a service product.

Expected product/service   This includes the attributes, such as design, quality, packaging, etc., which customers expect when purchasing a service product.

Table 2.1   Product level and customer value in services

Level	Product/service level	Definitions	Orientation	Customer value
1.	Core or generic	This is the most fundamental product/service customer purchase.	Customer	• Transportation
2.	Basic product	This is how the marketer translates the core benefit into a service product.	Company and customer	• Safe and timely transportation • Comfortable seat
3.	Expected product	A set of attributes along with basic product buyers normally expect while purchasing a service.	Market and customer	When customers buy an airline ticket, in addition to a seat they expect: • Comfortable waiting area • Prompt in-flight service • Good meals
4.	Augmented product	Basic product and something different, which delights the customer and differentiates one's product from another, e.g., incentives, warranty, delivery, and service.	Company and customer	• Reliability • Responsiveness • Safety • Supply of food that suits customer's health
5.	Potential product	New ways of attracting and satisfying the customer, which have not been offered yet.	Company and customer	• Offering gifts, which 'wows' the customer and wins loyalty

Augmented product/service   This includes the supplementary services the marketer offers to differentiate their product offering from other players in the same market segment.

Potential product/service   This consists of new ways of attracting and satisfying the customers.

These five levels of the product constitute the customer value hierarchy (CVH). Taking air transportation by a customer as the backdrop for customer value, a brief explanation of the various levels is provided in Table 2.1.

Classifying Supplementary Services

If we study a variety of services we observe that the core product may differ widely as there are common supplementary elements such as billing, order-taking, problem-solving, etc. Lovelock classifies them as facilitating or enhancing services. He personifies the services as a flower and maintains that if a service is poorly or badly executed it is like an unattractive flower with missing, wilted, or discoloured petals (Lovelock and Wirtz 2006). Depending upon the nature of the product we can have different supplementary services along with the core product. Generally, people processing services and high-contact services have comparatively more supplementary services. For example, let us take the case of a budget hotel in India. A clean room with bath facilities, telephone, and television is a basic core offering. Any services such as transport, business centre, safekeeping, or travel desk are referred to as facilitating or enhancing services.

Availability of clean rooms is a core offering of this budget hotel in Udaipur, Rajasthan.

NEW PRODUCT DEVELOPMENT

In this section 'product' is being used as a reference to the service product. Every service product has a life cycle. It passes through different stages such as introduction, growth, maturity, and decline. The challenge for companies is to prolong the age of the service product. The task of the company is to keep introducing new products

Exhibit 2.3   Differentiating a Savings Account

Indian banking industry is regulated by the Reserve Bank of India (RBI). There are a host of private sector banks, public sector banks, and foreign banks catering to the Indian market. In October 2011, the savings account rate was deregulated by RBI. Kotak Mahindra Bank seized this opportunity and proved beyond doubt that services can be differentiated even with the help of the 'plain Jane savings account'. A savings account is a low involvement product from the customer's point of view but from the bank's point of view, it is the 'base on which most retail banking is built upon. Thus banks have to hard sell the savings bank product as creatively as possible.' Keeping this in mind and with an eye on the market—aiming to mop up the business, Kotak turned to 'better returns from the savings account' positioning by offering a rate of 6% when competition was offering just 4%'. The result was an increase in the customer base by 50%, along with the doubling of the savings deposits in eighteen months. Thus, change in the service offering helped the sales force build volumes.

before the decline in the sale of the old product in order to stay profitable. Today, the marketing environment is characterized by intense global competition and a fast pace of technological development, and this in turn pressurizes firms to develop new products to maintain profitability and market position (Ali 2000). Companies that have a new product strategy in place are more successful than those that do not. Exhibit 2.3 shows how Kotak Mahindra Bank developed its savings account and reaped benefits from the same.

New product development, in a conventional buying environment, is largely driven by the need to innovate. More profitable and faster growing firms are found to engage in sustained innovative activities (Vermeulen et al. 2005). Thus, product development is 'An essential process for competitive success, survival and renewal of organizations' (Brown and Eisenhardt 1995). Also, the company must understand how the old product ages and then change the 'Marketing strategies as it passes through the life cycle stages' (Kotler et al. 2006).

Kotler et al. (2006) state that a company can obtain new products either by acquisition of existing companies or by setting up a research and development department for new product development. New product refers to (i) original products, (ii) product improvements, (iii) product modifications, and (iv) new brands that firms develop.

Failure is an intrinsic part of innovation (Davis 1997). Firms introduce many new products but 50% of the products disappear within four years (Asplund and Sandin 1999). This occurs because sometimes the cost of developing a new product is higher or the competitors fight back more than expected. 'Successful new services result from an appropriately designed structure and a carefully orchestrated process and are rarely mere happenstance' (Scheuing and Johnson 1989).

Stages in New Product Development

New product development involves the conversion of novel ideas into viable and marketable products. It is a complex process, which involves a complex range of activities. With 'more Indians come online for the first time, they are increasingly looking for convenient ways to find information on the web. With many of them surfing the Internet using their mobile phones, without ever having used a desktop computer' (PTI 2013a). Google realized the potential for organizing the search engine and localizing it to provide simple search services to the Indian masses. The main stages are objectives and strategy, new service idea, idea generation, idea screening, concept development and testing, business analysis, budget development, market assessment, service process, design, development, testing, strategy formulation, marketing, HR, commercialization, review, and control.

With 'more Indians come online for the first time, they are increasingly looking for convenient ways to find information on the web. With many of them surfing the Internet using their mobile phones, without ever having used a desktop computer' (PTI 2013a). Google realized the potential for organizing the search engine and localizing it to provide simple search services to the Indian masses (Exhibit 2.4).

Exhibit 2.4   **Google Searching for India**

Google has launched a service in India that would simplify our search. According to the company, this service will simplify the Internet for Indian users. Google Search can give users instant answers to common queries, such as the weather or flight status, in the form of information cards that appear above search results.

As Chandigarh is one of the top cities when it comes to Internet usage, Google formally launched the service in Chandigarh first.

So the next time you want to search for something, simply log on to Google's inside search site and the required information will be available at a moment's notice. A range of information can be accessed—from weather to flights, restaurants, ATMs etc. For example, the weather tab apart from posting the weather also gives weather forecast for the coming week and also has added features like giving weather updates after every three hours, along with peak heat hours, when to carry an umbrella, etc. The flight tab gives the status of the flight—not only the arrival and departure time but the exact location of the flight as well. Simply type in details of the city and it offers exact and precise information about theatres where you can catch the next movie, restaurants where you can take a quick bite, and ATMs where you can withdraw cash from.

Customised search options relating to movie timings that adhere to one's busy schedules are also available. The panel includes a feature through which one can simply select the hour and day when one wishes to see the movie, whether early morning or late night. Also, one can just type in the cuisine that suits one's taste buds and a list of restaurants will be available, under the restaurants head. It also provides a research option using which you can search on any topic and get the latest information. Also, if you are weak in arithmetic, the site offers a calculator for difficult computations.

New service objective and strategy

This is important for a well-conceived and carefully implemented new service development process. Lack of formulation of objective is like lifting anchor without determining the desired destination. The company's objective can be high cash flow or it could focus on a particular market share. The environmental analysis and the corporate objectives, and the mission of the business influence these objectives and strategy. These in turn 'drive and direct the entire service innovation effort and instil it with effectiveness and efficiency'. For example, AT&T has redefined itself as being in the information management and movement business instead of telecommunications equipment and services.

Thus, it now concentrates on all aspects of information management and movement (Scheuing and Johnson 1989).

New service idea

The new service idea consists of new idea generation as well as screening of these ideas to come up with the most feasible option.

Idea generation   This is the systematic search for new ideas by an organization. Sometimes a number of ideas have to be generated to find a few excellent ones, which are compatible with the business. Now, there is a paradigm shift as to how companies generate new ideas for product innovation. In the old model of 'closed innovation', companies believed 'successful innovation requires control'. As one cannot be sure of the quality, availability, and capability of others' ideas, the innovative ideas must come from within the organization and they should develop, manufacture, market, and distribute the product/service themselves. Increasingly this approach to innovation is no longer sustainable and 'open innovation' is emerging in its place. Using open innovation, an organization can and should use the external and internal ideas and paths to market for new product development. Adding external sources of technology also increases the possible number of sources for innovation (Chesbrough 2004). New product development ideas can come from any of the following sources.

Internal sources   According to a study more than 55% of all new ideas come from within a company (Kotler et al. 2006). Internal search, consultation, and brainstorming can be some ways to generate ideas internally. Also, employees in direct contact with the customers, be it the marketing staff or the service personnel, can be excellent sources for new ideas. Companies are increasingly motivating their staff to be unconventional and encourage out-of-the-box thinking to generate innovation across products and services. This helps them to tap the collective innovation talent inside the company rather than isolating it to a particular department such as R&D.

Customers   Companies are increasingly focusing on customer involvement in new product development to reduce uncertainty and achieve a more favourable cost/time product development curve. They feel that customers are 'Sources of information and knowledge and their involvement can enhance product concept effectiveness' (Lundkvist and Yakhlef 2004). Bonner (1999) stated that, the higher the customer involvement in the new product development, the greater is the likelihood of product success.

Competitors   Many companies get new product ideas from their competitors or other players in the market in the same product category, in the same market, or other markets. Keeping an eye on competitors' activities is one way in which companies can adopt their strategies as well as be at par with the services being offered in the market segment. See Exhibit 2.5 for understanding how Max differentiated itself from competition.

Distributors and suppliers   Distributors are in constant contact with the customers. They are a valuable source of information for problems faced by consumers and the new features, facilities, and services the consumer is looking for. Studies suggest that supplier involvement in new product development can 'Help reduce cost, reduce concept to-customer development time, improve quality, and provide innovative technologies that can help capture market share' (Handfield et al. 1999). It is generally seen that during the process of new product development, many problems emerge, such as cost, performance, timing, quality, etc., which results in trade-offs and design changes. However, if the suppliers are involved in the product development right from the idea generation stage, then potential technologies can be assessed and breakthrough ideas can be achieved. The suppliers can also be used to gather information about the new products being developed by rival companies.

Exhibit 2.5 **Delivering Medical Services: The Max Way**

Hospitals are a dreadful place to be and the nauseating disinfectant smell just adds to the misery. Max India Chairman Analjit Singh was no different and felt the same 'rejecting fragrance' and dejecting overall experience. To overcome this feeling he ensured across all the eleven Max Hospitals that when a customer and/or visitor enters the hospital, they are welcomed by an aroma of coffee. There is a Coffee Shop normally towards the left when a visitor enters the hospital where coffee is brewed. To ensure a constant coffee aroma there are standing instructions that if no one asks for coffee in ten minutes, then a cup of coffee is thrown into the sink and drained with hot water. The employees are trained to ensure the delivery of services according to the three pronged values of the group – '*sevabhav* (feeling of service), excellence, and to build credibility.'

Employees are taught to deliver service so as to differentiate themselves from other hospitals. Thus, when the 'food is placed on the patient's pendant table (sliding table attached to bed), it is important the attendant must not turn his/her back' towards the patient while walking out. 'What if the patient, who can't speak properly, is trying to signal and say things like 'Shift the table to the left or right', or 'I don't want cold water'. Therefore the attendant is taught 'to deliver the tray and then walk out backwards so that eye contact is maintained with the patient.'

Source: Based on Mitra (2013), Max Healthcare website.

Other sources   Companies can get ideas through 'other sources like trade magazines, shows, seminars, government agencies, new product consultants, market research firms, university, and inventors' (Kotler et al. 2006). See Exhibit 2.6 for an understanding of how IT companies in India are looking for innovative ideas from outside the company.

Idea screening   Once a number of ideas are generated, the next step is to screen the ideas to 'separate the chaff from the grain', that is, to select more meritorious ideas from the less promising ones (Scheuing and Johnson 1989). A good idea could be too expensive for the company to produce. Therefore, it looks for new ideas that the existing workforce can produce in the existing assembly line, which are profitable for the

---

Exhibit 2.6 **Innovation at IT Companies**

Infosys, MindTree, Wipro, Cognizant, and Tata Consultancy Services were hunting for innovative product lines at the Nasscom event in Bengaluru in the last week of June 2013. The event saw a dozen technology startups pitched the products in front of the technology giants as these giants look for innovative tech products to offer to their clients. In order to innovate, the companies are looking for ideas from startups. For example, Wipro and Cognizant are looking at startups like Data-Weave 'which provides data analytics for e-commerce ventures. TCS is working with Mumbai based startup iKen Solutions for its artificial intelligence products to understand customers' online purchase behaviour. Cognizant has set up an emerging business accelerator that has incubated twenty ideas over the past 18 months' as they look for ideas from outside the company.

organization to produce, and fit in with the objective and strategy of the organization. Kotler et al. (2006) identified the following issues—the new product should:

- fulfill the company's mission
- meet corporate objectives
- protect and promote the core business
- protect and please key customers
- result in better utilization of existing resources
- support and enhance existing product lines.

Concept development and testing

The product ideas selected after screening all the new product ideas are then to be developed into a product concept. A product idea is a possible product that the company may launch in the market. A product concept on the other hand, is a detailed version of the product idea stated in meaningful consumer terms. It is a description of the potential new service. According to Scheuing and Johnson (1989), a typical concept statement includes:

- a description of a problem a prospect might experience
- the reasons why the new service is to be offered
- an outline of the features and benefits of the new service
- rationale for the purchase of the new service offering.

A successful services firm cannot market an untested product. It has to first test the service offering in a limited market to see the market response.

Once the product concept is developed, it is tested on the target customers to examine the buyers' response to the service concept. This can be done in the form of simple attitude surveys or by other statistical techniques. A concept test is a technique used in marketing research to assess the reactions of consumers to a new product or a proposed change to an existing product (*Oxford Dictionary of Business and Management*). It evaluates whether a prospective user understands the idea of the proposed service offering, reacts favourably to it, and feels it offers benefits that answer unmet needs (Scheuing and Johnson 1989).

Smaller organizations, however, move over directly from product idea to full implementation without going into concept testing. Ultimately, if the financial implication of the new service developed is enormous, it is always better to test the feasibility of the new service offering rather than regret a disastrous mistake later.

Business analysis

This represents an exhaustive analysis of the business implications, such as sales, costs, and profit projections, of the new product concept. It involves both market assessment and drafting of the budget for the development and launch of the new service. The purpose of business analysis is to develop recommendations for the top management as to how to implement the new service offering.

Service design and development

Till now the new product exists only as a concept. It must now be developed into a physical concept, an operational entity, which customers can perceive as an imperative service and which can be produced within the estimated budgeted cost. The core product for the market offering is developed when the service is designed. This is different from concept development as it involves the help of prospective users and customer contact personnel, who tell the company what customers desire in a new service. The service design and development on the other hand, is done with the help of the users and the operational staff who will deliver the service. While designing the service we also have to design the delivery process and the system. This should be instated, refined, and restructured in order to ensure smooth delivery upon introduction. Read Exhibit 2.7 to see how PVR developed its service to offer food along with films and generate revenue.

Test marketing   Once the product has been designed, marketing strategy worked out, and the personnel trained to handle queries for and delivery of the new service, the next step is to launch the product in the market. Test marketing field-tests the service product within a limited sample of customers. This allows the marketer to gain experience of marketing the product and in the process, to find potential problem areas, and determine how the service product can be refined and made 'irresistible' to the target market.

Strategy formulation

This stage involves the development of marketing strategy and training of employees.

Marketing strategy   Once the service has been developed, that is, the product of the marketing mix has been decided, the next step is to develop the marketing strategy for

Exhibit 2.7   PVR Offers Films and Food

The year 1997 witnessed movie goers in Delhi being introduced to the multiplex culture when Ajay Bijli, the chairman and managing director of PVR Cinemas, came out with a multiplex at Saket, New Delhi. In the quest to provide a unique cinematic experience to the moviegoers, Bijli launched the Director's Cut in the Ambience Mall, Vasant Kunj outlet in 2011. The PVR's Gold Class also has plush seats in the auditorium along with seat service. However, Directors Cut has given premium viewing a new high and provides 'a full-length experience' for the viewers. It is a high-end format with theatres, restaurants, books, and merchandise. Its tickets are priced up to ₹1,200 on a weekend and offers facilities such as in-cinema dining and movie on demand. The cinemas screen independent and rare films, besides the mainstream ones which are hard to find on the big screen. A bar, lounge, and fine-dining restaurant greets you at the entrance; as does a store with quirky film memorabilia and DVDs for sale. The four auditoriums are furnished with fully reclining seats and an airline-style remote to call a waiter. You can choose your drinks, main courses, and desserts from an in-theatre menu. The staff has been trained for discreet service'.

The year 2013 took PVR closer to its films and food concept when it launched its first restaurant, Mistral, right next to Directors Cut serving exotic grills from the European and Indian cuisines. The outlet is spacious and has multiple seating options ranging from sofas and low seating to high bar chairs. Moving to the movie theatre from the restaurant is seamless, with many exit points leading straight into the theatre. There are a number of eating and drinking options and customers can choose from salads, sandwiches, pizzas, pastas, grilled items, etc. along with seventeen varieties of beer and as many varieties of whisky, cocktails, etc.

the introduction of the product into the market. According to Kotler et al. (2006), the marketing strategy includes:

- the price, distribution, and marketing budget for the first year
- target market, product positioning and sales, market share, and profit goals for the first few years, and
- the planned long-run sales, profit goals, and marketing mix strategy.

Personnel training   To complete the design part of the new product development, the employees have to be familiarized with the elucidation and operational details of the new service. Personnel training is critical to the success of new product development as services have often failed due to lack of proper training of the personnel who sell and deliver the service (Scheuing and Johnson 1989).

Commercialization

Once test marketing has been carried out and the product has been fine-tuned to the market, the next step is to launch the new service in the entire market area.

According to Kotler et al. (2006) the following four considerations have to be made while launching the new service.

When: The first decision is, when is the right time to introduce the new service?

Where: The company must decide whether to launch the service in a single/multiple region or national/international markets. Since a lot of investment is required to launch the product nationally, organizations generally opt for a planned market rollout.

To whom: Once the service has been launched in the market, the management has to determine the profiles of prime prospects, that is, it has to look for early adopters, heavy users, and opinion leaders.

How: The company must develop the action plan and spend the marketing budget appropriately on the marketing mix.

Post-launch review

Even after carefully testing the new product idea before commercialization of the service, market conditions may require further modifications. For example, after introduction in the market, Courier Pak, the document delivery service of Federal Express, realized that the key purchase decision-makers for the new service were executives and secretaries rather than traffic managers and shipping clerks. Consequently, they had to develop a separate advertising and sales approach. Also, the pickup and delivery locations were different and required additional ground operations. After making these changes, Courier Pak became a successful new service venture (Scheuing and Johnson 1989).

PRODUCT LIFE CYCLE STRATEGIES

This section provides a detailed explanation of the various stages of the product life cycle, the marketing strategies adopted during each stage, and finally, the limitations of the theory.

Product Life Cycle Stages

Each product passes through a distinct stage. These stages constitute the life cycle of the product. There are four such stages (Kotler et al. 2006) in the life cycle of a product (Fig. 2.1). These are as follows:

Introductory stage This is the stage immediately after the launch of a new product in the market. This period is characterized by slow sales growth and negligible profit as heavy expenditure is incurred for introduction of the product. If the product introduced is really innovative, it is at an advantage as the competition is then minimized. Examples of services in the introductory stage are 3G services, search engine optimization services, etc.

Growth stage The growth stage follows the introductory stage. This stage is characterized by high sales growth rate and increasing profits. Due to the heavy marketing expenditure in the introductory stage, people increasingly accept the product and hence, the high sales growth rate. Since increasing profits marks this stage, it is the task of the marketing department to protract this period. For example, direct-to-home (DTH) television services in India are in their growth stage.

Maturity stage This stage arises when all the potential buyers have accepted the product and consequently the sales of the product have now reached a plateau. The waning of profits marks this stage, as expenses have to be incurred again in marketing the product. For example, cinema halls have reached their maturity stage.

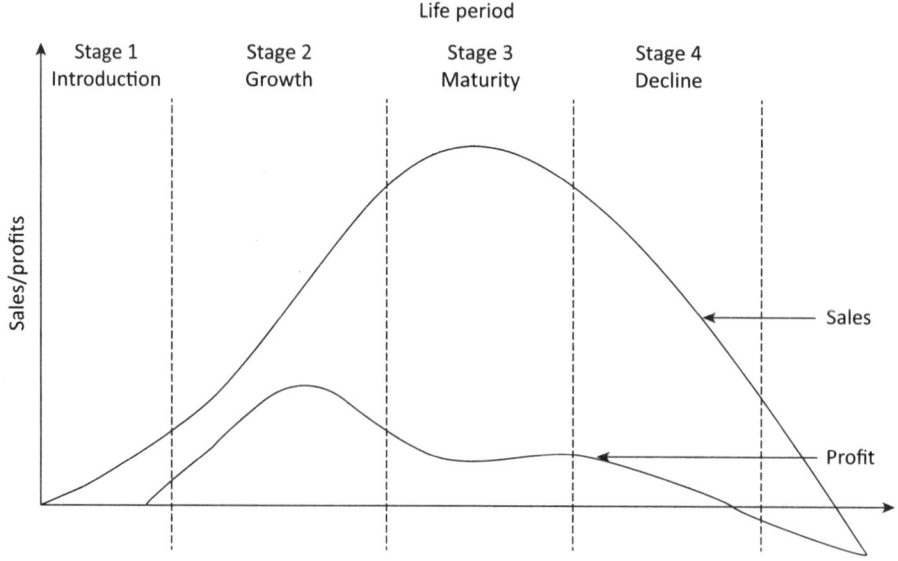

Fig. 2.1 Product life cycle

Source: Oxford Dictionary of Business and Management (2006).

Decline stage   This is the stage characterized by a fall in sales and hence, profits of the product and soon the firm incurs a loss. Services in the decline stage are post office services, rail transport, manual banking, etc.

This is the life cycle that most products follow. The understanding of this concept is essential as it guides the strategies to be made by an organization at various intervals of time. From this we can summarize that:

• Products have a life and they pass through different stages, as in a life cycle.
• Sales of the product pass through distinct phases and each phase is characterized by unique challenges, opportunities, and problems.
• Profits vary with the stage of the life cycle.

Different strategies are required during the different life cycle stages for the products to stay profitable for a longer duration.

It has been observed that three other types of patterns of the product life cycle are possible. They are as follows.

Growth–slump–maturity pattern   This pattern is characteristic of services, which pass through the introductory sales and maturity cycle and then instead of the decline there is a constant demand for the service; for example, life insurance products in India.

Cycle–recycle pattern   This pattern is characteristic of the hospitality industry where initially when a new property comes up, there is a demand represented by the initial cycle. However, later as the sales decline, efforts are made to push the sales with increased marketing strategies and this results in the second cycle, which is lower in magnitude and duration than the first.

Scalloped product life cycle   Here, the product passes through the succession of life cycles based on discovery of new service features/characteristics, uses, or users. For example, the insurance sector in India received a boost due to the different features it introduced from time to time. It has different products such as basic insurance plans, Term Assurance Plans, Unit linked plans, Pension Plans, Health plan, etc. Life Insurance Corporation (LIC) is one of India's leading service brands with '78 per cent market share in the life insurance space while servicing 28 crore individual policies besides covering more than 9 crore people under group insurance/superannuation schemes and more than 3 crore families under social security scheme' (Chamikutty 2011).

Marketing Strategies

We have seen that a service/product passes through different phases in its lifetime. Each stage has unique characteristics and needs to be handled differently so that (i) the product can develop a competitive advantage, (ii) it can stay profitable, and (iii) resources can be allocated properly.

See Exhibit 2.8 to understand some of the strategies adopted by Jubilant to ensure Domino's success in the Indian market.

Exhibit 2.8 Jubilant about Domino's

Jubilant Foodworks Limited operates Domino's Pizza brand in India and has exclusive rights for operating the brand in Nepal, Bangladesh, and Sri Lanka as well. With more than 500 stores in 131 cities Domino's has made Jubilant one of India's largest and fastest growing food service company. It 'commands 50% share of the pizza market'. India is the third largest base for Domino's outlets outside US and UK.

Fast food chain	India debut	Total number of outlets	Average outlets opened in a year
Dominos	1996	500	31
Yum India (Pizza Hut, KFC)	1995	399	23
McDonald's	1996	271	17
Global franchise architects (Pizza Corner, Coffee World, etc.)	1999	95	7
Nirula's	1935	80	1

Jubilant has worked constantly so as to enhance its market size and grow the category. Some of the strategies adopted are given here.

In 2004 it reinforced its 'delivery in 30 minutes or take your pizza free' which helped cut clutter and become the cynosure of the customer's eyes.

In 2008 it introduced a ₹39 entry-level pizza which helped it grow volumes by 20–25%.

Domino's started on a delivery centric model but keeping in mind that Indian families prefer to eat out, the last 200–300 stores in tier II and tier III cities are such that can accommodate the dine-in clientele. Last few stores are bigger 'and can take 100 people. This has helped Domino's grow 46–47% from 2005–2011; improve operating margins from 12.6% to 19.1%.'

Source: Based on the data from Domino's (2013), *The Economic Times* (2012), and Sarkar (2011).

The detailed strategies for a product as it passes through its different stages are elaborated in this section.

Introduction stage

The introduction phase is very important for services marketing because it is during this period that customers or consumers, on the basis of initial experimentation with the service, form their opinions about the service. If the introduction phase is not appropriately handled, the service introduced may be 'nipped in the bud', as it will lead to negative word-of-mouth publicity. Since in this phase the service is launched for the first time, logistics or other difficulties may emerge. This is a learning phase where staff skills have to be developed and systems have to be redesigned on the basis of experience (Lazer and Layton 1999). Thus, this stage is marked by frequent service modifications. Hence, the more carefully thought out the new service is in the planning stage, the less difficulty it will encounter in the introductory stage leading to the successful launch of the service. According to Michael (1971), quality has the largest impact on sales in this stage followed by advertising and price. Advertising is done mainly to create awareness among customers and can be accompanied by sampling and couponing.

Growth stage

If the introduction of the service is successful, that is, customers accept the offer and have a favourable experience, it will result in positive word-of-mouth followed by hectic sales activities. Service firms can review their strategies at this stage and can:

- get customer feedback as to how to further improve the service offered
- develop customer loyalty
- re-price the product to achieve market penetration
- strengthen distributor network
- shift from product awareness to product preference advertising.

This stage is marked by an expanded number of services and frequent modifications in the services. Advertising is done primarily to build awareness and interest in the mass market.

However, the sales promotion followed in the introductory stage is reduced to take advantage of the heavy demand. For example, the life insurance penetration in India is about 4.4% of the country's gross domestic product (GDP) in terms of total premiums underwritten annually, according to the Insurance Regulatory and Development Authority (IRDA). The penetration is quite less in India as against its peers and hence, the Indian insurance market provides ample opportunities to domestic and international players to harness the profitable avenues in the same (IBEF 2013). There are 23 life insurance companies operating in India and the insurance sector is huge and 'growing at a speedy rate of 15–20%. Together the banking and insurance services add about 7% to the country's GDP' (IRDA 2013).

The sector has been growing exceptionally since liberalization with the introduction of new investment type unit-linked insurance plans. The total premium underwritten by the life insurance industry has grown from ₹34,898 crore in 2000–01 'to ₹84,501.75 crore (during the April–February period of 2012–13 fiscal).

Private insurers together raked in ₹23,796.29 crore (US$4.33 billion) in these 11 months' (IBEF 2013).

Maturity stage

This stage is marked by slow sales. In this stage most of the consumers have tried the services, competitors have come up with similar services, and profits are constricted. The sales slowdown leads to overcapacity in the market, which further intensifies the competition. If the service providers have managed their growth period sales well and have been able to deliver 'customer delight', they will be in a better position to sustain sales in the maturity period. Most of the price-insensitive buyers have already tried the product; so this stage is marked by frequent markdowns, increased advertising, and sales promotion budget (to encourage brand switching), and aggressive selling so that the weaker competition withdraws and the dominant firms take over.

Decline stage

The final stage in the product life cycle is that of decline. This stage is marked by plummeting sales. At this stage, again it is the quality of service that is important and price cuts have virtually no impact (Michael 1971). However, a decline in sales does not necessarily mean that the service has left the maturity stage. Vyas (1993) has recommended a strategy, whereby the product sales can be enhanced by replacing the service with the enhanced version of the same service or by eliminating the service.

Step 1: Periodic review meeting (product portfolio)   During the scheduled meetings (can be monthly or bi-monthly depending upon the policies adopted by different organizations) product improvement opportunities, availability of new technologies, competitors' activities, and feedback from customers and channel partners is reviewed. New ideas for enhancement of service are identified. The product portfolio is reviewed in totality and with relation to its market segment.

Step 2: Product review   When the product portfolio is reviewed in totality, it leads to detection of new product ideas or opportunities and weak performing products are differentiated from performing products. The improved service ideas are detected and feasibility plans are prepared, which include development cost, sales/profit estimates and ROI analysis, etc. The new product is then developed as per the stages of new product development discussed earlier. Along with the identification of new product opportunities, the existing products are also reviewed to identify the products that are not performing as per expectations. During this stage the external environment is also reviewed for identification of potential forces, which may affect the performance of services in the future.

Step 3: Performance analysis   Performance analysis is done to identify the reasons for the drop in sales in the service product. The forces (both external and internal) that can contribute to the weak performance of services identified in Step 2 are evaluated. Some of the external forces can be government policies, change in national or international standards, change in specifications by key customers, major change in technology, and competitor strategies. The internal forces are loss/transfer of key personnel, design deficiencies, service delays, etc. The product performance is then studied keeping in mind the current performance vis-à-vis the future conditions (both internal and external) in which it has to perform. The various factors are then analysed to identify the major reasons for the drop in sales.

Step 4: Evaluation   In this step the evaluation of the service product is done to identify if the reasons for service sales failure can be controlled so that the sales continue to grow. Evaluation of different service options is carried out. This can be a simple or complex phenomenon depending upon the service, experience, and perceptions of individuals involved, bargaining, conflict, resource allocation, nature of costs, etc. Evaluation is carried out to determine the service product failure, reasons for loss in sales, and various options available, such as outsourcing, personnel review, branding, etc., to decide about the future course of action for the service product.

Step 5: Decision Product elimination suggestions are scrutinized thoroughly. If there is no market demand for the service and hence, no substitute product is required, the product is eliminated. However, a number of factors have to be considered before this decision can be finalized, such as whether the generic sales for the service category exists, the industry growth rate, customer feedback, channel partners feedback, sales and marketing personnel feedback, impact on organizations image, effect on product mix, etc. (discussed in Steps 2, 3, and 4). On the basis of the analysis of these factors organizations can go in for a service replacement decision instead of a service elimination decision. Thus, this step is the most difficult and several iterations may occur among Steps 3, 4, and 5 before the final decision can be made.

Step 6: Implementation This is the final implementation of the decision taken in Step 5. The decision taken is relevant if it is completed within a specific timeframe.

It is clear from this discussion that the marketing environment keeps on changing and companies have to review their strategies at regular intervals to match their competitive positions (Lazer and Layton 1999). Table 2.2 illustrates how organizations can match their characteristics, objectives, and strategies with the product life cycle to gain a competitive edge by effective resource allocation. In order to survive in the long run, organizations should introduce a new service before the complete decline in sales of the previous service so that the overall growth curve remains constant. According to Modis (1994), the rule of thumb is that 'When 90% saturation level of the old process is reached the new wave should be at 1% of the way into its own growth process'.

Table 2.2 Summary of product life cycle characteristics, objectives, and strategies

	Introduction	Growth	Maturity	Decline
Characteristics				
Sales	Low sales	Rapidly rising sales	Peak sales	Declining sales
Costs	High cost per customer	Average cost per customer	Low cost per customer	Low cost per customer
Profits	Negative	Rising profits	High profits	Declining profits
Customers	Innovators	Early adopters	Middle majority	Laggards
Competitors	Few	Growing number	Stable number beginning to decline	Declining number
Marketing objective	Create product awareness and trial	Maximize market share	Maximize profit while defending market share	Reduce expenditure and milk the brand
Cash flow	Negative	Moderate	High	Moderate
Focus	Non-users	New segments	Defend share	Cut costs
Differential advantage	Service quality	Brand image	Price and service	Service quality and price

(Contd)

Table 2.2 *(Contd)*

	Introduction	Growth	Maturity	Decline
Strategies				
Product	Offer a basic product/service	Offer service extensions, service, and warranty	Diversify brands and services	Phase out the weak
Price	Charge cost-plus	Price to penetrate market	Price to match or best competitors	Cut price
Distribution	Build selective distribution	Build intensive distribution	Build more intensive distribution	Go selective: Phase out unprofitable outlets
Advertising	Build product awareness among early adopters and dealers	Build awareness and interest in the mass market	Stress brand differences and benefits	Reduce to level needed to retain hard core loyals
Sales promotion	Use heavy sales promotion to entice trial	Reduce to take advantage of heavy customer demand	Increase to encourage brand switching	Reduce to minimal level
Organization				
Structure	Team	Market focus	Functional	Lean
Focus	Innovation	Marketing	Efficiency	Cost reduction
Culture	Freewheeling	Marketing led	Professional	Pressured

This denotes that for a particular service industry, the initial introduction phase is composed of services with shorter life cycles (in accordance with the low growth phase the service is in), the growth phase has services with relatively longer life cycles (in accordance with the high growth period), and again at maturity, the services life cycles are short showing a decline in the marketability of the service organization. If in the same service level, all organizations have a short life cycle, it might reflect a changing social pattern. If we consider the life cycles of a number of unrelated services and products and observe a general shorter life cycle for all, it may reflect a global economic recession.

Weaknesses of Product Life Cycle Concept

Even though the product life cycle concept is very important in the marketing of services, Doyle (2002) has listed the following weaknesses in the product life cycle concept.

Product/service oriented The marketing concept focuses on the customers, their needs and wants, and how best to satisfy them. However, the focus of the life cycle concept is the product/service. If managers focus on the product, they lose their customer orientation, which might be the other reason for the product to inevitably fall in the product life cycle stages of maturity and decline.

Undefined concept As there are different driving forces for demands, technologies, product categories, etc., there is no agreement as to the level of aggregation the concept refers to.

No common shape   As is evident from the discussion, there are different shapes for the life cycles of different types of products/services, so there is no standardization as to the common shape for the services.

Unpredictability   How long a particular product or service is going to stay in a particular phase of the product life cycle cannot be predicted. Some services might stay in a particular stage for a few months while others can be there for generations.

Unclear implication   Even where a life cycle pattern can be identified, the implications are not clear. For example, a service shows a decline in sales and is put in the mature phase of the product life cycle, whereas this decline in sales can be associated with some production problem at the service providers end or may be due to lack of effective service providing personnel.

Internal   Product life cycle is often a result of management actions and their implications rather than outside market forces. When sales become flat, there can be a number of internal problems relating to distribution, production, product, etc. Thus, it is the task of the management to identify the source of low turnover and take remedial actions instead of passing it off as the life cycle stage.

RESEARCH INSIGHT

Customer Involvement and Service Development

Pilar Carbonell, Ana I Rodriguez-Escudero, and Devashish Pujari (2012), 'Performance effects of involving lead users and close customers in new service development', *Journal of Services Marketing*, vol. 26, issue 7.

Customer involvement has been recognized as a key factor for successful service development. One important aspect affecting the outcome of new service development (NSD) projects in whose development customers are involved is the choice of the appropriate participating customer. This study examines the effect of two customer characteristics (relational closeness and lead-userness) on four indicators of new service performance.

SUMMARY

This chapter discussed in detail the concept of the product in services management. Along with the definition and nature of services it discussed the different levels of the service product, which is crucial as before discussing the different management techniques for services we need to be clear about the product and its various levels. The chapter also discussed the different levels involved in the development of a new product. The various strategies used in different product life cycle stages were discussed along with the limitations of the same. This gives a comprehensive understanding of the service product and forms a basis for discussion of strategies for the management of the same.

KEY TERMS

Augmented product   Additional consumer services and benefits sold with a core product. The augmented product can be a critical factor in the success of the core product.

Commercialization The stage in the development of a new product during which a decision is made to embark on its full-scale production and distribution.

Concept test A technique used in marketing research to assess the reactions of consumers to a new product or a proposed change to an existing product.

Core product The problem-solving service or core benefit that a consumer is really buying when purchasing a product.

Idea generation The systematic search for new product ideas.

Idea screening Screening new product ideas in order to identify and develop good ideas and drop poor ones as soon as possible.

Marketing strategy A plan identifying what marketing goals and objectives will be pursued to sell a particular product line and how these objectives will be achieved in the time available.

New product development A marketing procedure in which new ideas are developed into viable new products or extensions to existing products or product ranges.

Product life cycle The course of a product's sales and profitability over its lifetime. The model describes stages, each of which represents a different opportunity for the marketer.

Service product An offering that includes both tangible and intangible offerings, which satisfies customer needs through an integrated approach and at the same time contributes to societal welfare.

Test marketing A procedure for launching a new product in a restricted geographical area to test consumers' reactions.

EXERCISES

Concept Review Questions

1. Discuss what a service product is and how is it different from the traditional product.
2. Enumerate the different components of service offering with the help of examples.
3. What is new product development? How would you develop a new product for the tourism industry in India?
4. Critically discuss the product life cycle. Discuss with the help of examples from the Indian hospitality sector.
5. Evaluate the different strategies in the growth phase of the product life cycle.
6. What is the cascading life cycle? Critically discuss with the help of examples from any services sector.

Critical Thinking Questions

1. You have to introduce a new Italian restaurant in the Indian market. What steps are you going to take and why?
2. Discuss the different components of a product for the education sector.
3. You have to introduce a new airline in the Indian market. What strategies are you going to adopt initially, after a year, and after five years to market your airline?

Project Assignments

1. Identify any two new firms in a similar service industry. What are the similarities and differences in the product offering?
2. Visit the site for a service firm and try to identify which product life cycle stage it is in.
3. Identify a service firm, which has been launched within the past two years in India. Identify a similar one in China. Critically evaluate their strategies for the marketing of their service product. Can any similarities be drawn?

CASE STUDY 1   CCD 'Lounge'—Reconnecting with the Youth*

The Indian café market was worth around ₹880 crore in the year 2010 and is growing at a robust rate of 15–20% annually, fuelled by the aspiring urban youth and their rising disposable incomes. India's per capita coffee consumption is a low 85 grams which also offers great potential for coffee retailers to expand. Major players in coffee retailing include Café Coffee Day, Barista, Costa Coffee, Gloria Jean's Coffees, and Aromas. Other than this, entry of coffee retailing behemoths such as Starbucks and Dunkin Donuts has further fuelled competition in this sector. Café Coffee Day (CCD) is owned by the Amalgamated Bean Coffee Trading Company Limited which operates five divisions—Cafe Coffee Day, Coffee Day Xpress, Coffee Day Beverages, Coffee Day Fresh and Ground, and Coffee Day Exports.

CCD began its operations in the year 1996. Initially it was cautious in expansion as coffee culture was new to Indians, in fact it had opened only 25 stores in initial three years. But as its format gained customer acceptance, subsequent years saw a fast paced expansion with 250 stores being opened in 2011 alone. The company plans to cross the 2,000 store mark by the year 2014. The company's expansion plans for its retail business estimated at ₹200 crores will be funded by internal sources as well as private equity infused from the parent company. The company does not believe in the franchise model for expansion, hence, it will bear the entire cost of opening the new outlets. The cost is ₹30–40 lakh for a regular café and ₹70 lakh for a Lounge. Worth ₹1,000 crore, CCD is currently enjoying all the benefits of being a first mover as well as market leader in this category. Of the 2,000 cafes currently in India 1,200 are owned by CCD include the more premium Lounge and Square. Besides this, it also operates around 900 kiosks that cater to the takeaway segment. The success in India encouraged CCD to set up outlets in Vienna and Karachi as well.

Entry of coffee behemoths   The policy changes in retailing have resulted in many International food retailers setting up base in India. This too has influenced CCD's decision to revamp the Lounge. The Seattle headquartered Starbucks entered India in 2012 setting up the first store in Mumbai. Starbucks tied up with Tata Coffee, a subsidiary of Tata Global Beverages for its Indian foray. Tata Coffee will provide the coffee beans as well as open around 50 stores in the first year as a part of the joint venture. Another global major Dunkin Donuts also entered India in 2012 through the franchise route with Jubilant Food works which also distributes Domino's Pizza. To appeal to the Indian consumers that are not too accustomed to the doughnut, Dunkin Donuts has customized its offering to suit the Indian palette. While Starbucks' positioning strategy is more towards premiumness, Dunkin Donuts in contrast is more of an all-day coffee cum fast food joint (Shashidhar, A. 2012). CCD is thus flanked on both sides by very strong brands, one premium and the other regular. Hence, the company's decision to have presence in all segments.

The Lounge

CCD retails coffee in three different formats—the regular café which is the CCD outlet, the Lounge which is 20% more expensive than a CCD outlet, and then there is the premium 'Square' format that is even more expensive and exclusive than the Lounge and offers single origin coffees targeting coffee connoisseurs. The Lounge is positioned midway between the other two formats. CCD in an attempt to reconnect with its consumers who began moving up the economic ladder in the last few years, decided to give a new upmarket look to its Lounge outlets. The new format is designed to appeal to urban youth in the age group 25–30 years that are economically independent and have expanding wallets.

*Dr Swati Singh, Faculty, Bharatiya Vidya Bhavan's Usha and Lakshmi Mittal Institute of Management, New Delhi. Used with permission.

The Lounge is a more premium format than the CCD outlets offering beverages along with gourmet cuisine as opposed to fast foods offered at CCD. The cuisine at the lounge is European styled and offered in a manner that allows them to customize the food items such as bread and pizza. The company has targeted at high streets, premium malls, and airports to set up its lounge outlets. The coffee price is several times that of a regular CCD outlet. The coffee beans used are the same Arabica grown by the parent Amalgamated Bean Coffee Trading Co. in its estates at Chikmagalur and supplied across India.

The difference lies in the brewing techniques used as well as the exquisite ambience and extensive international menu. The Lounge provides better top as well as bottom line to the company although at a little higher rentals. A Lounge outlet offers 1.8 to 2 times better top line than the regular cafes. All the stores of the company are self-managed and take 18–24 months to forecast how an outlet is going to perform. To differentiate the Lounge, the company has brought exclusive global trends of coffee brewing to these lounges. The Lounge specifically targets the coffee connoisseur willing to indulge in revitalizing a cup of coffee prepared from globally renowned brewing methods. The format is designed to allow customers to experience a cup of coffee prepared from well-known brewing methods of select countries right at his table. The Lounge offers a wide array of starters, salads, dressings, burgers, pastas, even biryanis, palak paneer with paranthas, other than sandwiches and pizzas. The various alternate coffee brewing methods up for display at the Lounge include:

The Siphon Also referred to as 'Vacuum coffee method' which has its origin in Japan. The Siphon brew comprises of a complex setup which is brought at the customer's table, and the brewing is performed in front of the customer using select coffee beans. The coffee is brewed utilizing two glass pots placed one above the other with a flame placed below the lower pot. The vapour pressure and vacuum together produce a light coffee with rich flavor in just seven minutes. The coffee produced by the Siphon method is capable of indulging all five senses.

The French Press The French method true to its name is of French origin and utilizes coarsely ground coffee beans. The coffee and water are put together in a jar, stirred and allowed to brew for four minutes, and then the plunger is gently pushed to trap the coffee powder at the bottom of the jar leading to the preparation of another light coffee.

The Pour Over This method has its origin in USA and makes use of a very fine variety of coffee powder. The powder which is in a pouch is placed over a glass and hot water is poured gradually over the pouch slowly at an interval of few seconds. The result is a strong concoction which is both bitter and strong.

Mixology The mixology comprises of a range of 'Coffeetinis' that are primarily mocktinis served in classic martini glasses.

Connecting with youth The company chose an exquisite way to promote its Lounge concept through its 'Lounge Journals'. The Lounge Journals are a series of tête-à-têtes between city youth and select celebrities from various fields. It focuses on topics such as photography, creative writing, painting, animation, and sculpting to channelize the youth energy towards creativity and fruitful expression. The company invited Kuchipudi dancer Yamini Reddy at its outlet in Hyderabad to conduct an interactive session on classical dance (Staff Reporter 2012). The second series of the Lounge Journals was conducted in Chandigarh in August 2012, where television actress and show host Jassi as well as DJ Sameer came to interact with the customers and share their passions and hobbies (Puri, M. 2011). The Lounge journal made its debut in Mumbai in January 2013. The customers interacted with celebrated musician Luke Kenny. The musician discussed techniques related to music and performance. He also shared how the music industry has evolved as well as the opportunities it offers the youth (Indiainfoline 2013). A unique way of promoting the Lounge concept, the 'Lounge Journals', primarily aim at building positive WOM and consumer loyalty.

Conclusion

CCD wants to ensure that its format continues to evolve as its consumers progress in age and up the economic ladder. It has therefore positioned all three formats to appeal to different moods, clients, and occasions. The entry of foreign players that have deeper pockets and greater experience in coffee retailing has raised the bar further for CCD which is to be credited for establishing coffee retailing in India. Experts are however of the opinion that by expanding into the premium segment, CCD is stretching itself too thin and is likely to attract unwanted competition by more competent brands. The company has managed to stay in top till now and only time will tell how it continues to appeal to its target group and wards off competition both domestic and international.

Questions

1. What are the key factors influencing the revamping of The Lounge?
2. Which stage of the PLC do you think CCD and its various formats are at? Give reasons for your answer.
3. Do you think CCD is justified in its strategy of having three different formats for coffee retailing?

CASE STUDY 2 Growth of Insurance Sector in India: The 'Insurance Product' of LIC

Life insurance in India made its debut well over 100 years ago. In our country, which is one of the most populated in the world, the prominence of insurance is not as widely understood as it ought to be. What follows is an attempt to acquaint readers with some of the concepts of life insurance, with special reference to LIC. Life insurance is a contract that pledges payment of an amount to the person assured (or his/her nominee) on the happening of the event insured against. The contract is valid for payment of the insured amount during (i) the date of maturity, or (ii) specified dates at periodic intervals, or (iii) unfortunate death, if it occurs earlier.

Among other things, the contract also provides for the payment of premium periodically to the corporation by the policyholder. Life insurance is universally acknowledged to be an institution, which eliminates 'risk', substituting certainty for uncertainty, and comes to the timely aid of the family in the unfortunate event of death of the breadwinner. By and large, life insurance is civilization's partial solution to the problems caused by death. Life insurance, in short, is concerned with two hazards that stand across the life path of every person (i) that of dying prematurely leaving a dependent family to fend for itself, or (ii) that of living till old age without visible means of support.

The 'Life Insurance Product'

Contract of insurance A contract of insurance is a contract of utmost good faith technically known as 'uberrima fides'. The doctrine of disclosing all material facts is embodied in this important principle, which applies to all forms of insurance.

At the time of taking a policy, the policyholder should ensure that all questions in the proposal form are correctly answered. Any misrepresentation, non-disclosure, or fraud in any document leading to the acceptance of the risk renders the insurance contract null and void.

Protection Savings through life insurance guarantees full protection against risk of death of the saver. Also, in case of demise, life insurance assures payment of the entire amount assured (with bonuses wherever applicable), whereas in other savings schemes only the amount saved (with interest) is payable.

Aid to thrift Life insurance encourages 'thrift'. It allows long-term savings since payments can be made effortlessly because of the 'easy instalment' facility built into the scheme. Premium payment for insurance is monthly, quarterly, half-yearly, or yearly. For example, the salary saving scheme, popularly known as SSS, provides a convenient method of paying premium each month by deduction from one's salary. In this case, the employer directly pays the deducted premium to the insurance company. The SSS is ideal for any institution or establishment subject to specified terms and conditions.

Liquidity In case of insurance, it is easy to acquire loans on the sole security of any policy that has acquired loan value. Besides, a life insurance policy is also generally accepted as security, even for a commercial loan.

Tax relief Life insurance is the best way to enjoy tax deductions on income tax and wealth tax. This is available for amounts paid by way of premium for life insurance subject to income tax rates in force. Assessees can also avail of provisions in the law for tax relief. In such cases, the assured in effect pays a lower premium for insurance than otherwise.

Monetary needs A policy that has a suitable insurance plan or a combination of different plans can be effectively used to meet certain monetary needs that may arise from time to time. Children's education, start-in-life, marriage provision, or even periodical needs for cash over a stretch of time can be less stressful with the help of these policies. Alternatively, policy money can be made available at the time of one's retirement from service and used for any specific purpose, such as purchase of a house or for other investments. Also, loans are granted to policyholders for house-building or for purchase of flats (subject to certain conditions).

Insurance for women Prior to nationalization (1956) of life insurance, many private insurance companies would offer insurance to women with some extra premium or on restrictive conditions. However, after nationalization, the terms under which life insurance is granted to female lives have been reviewed from time to time. At present, women who work and earn an income are treated at par with men. In other cases, a restrictive clause is imposed only if the age of the female is up to 30 years and if she does not have an income attracting income tax.

Medical and non-medical schemes Life insurance is normally offered after a medical examination of the person to be assured. However, to facilitate greater spread of insurance and also to avoid inconvenience, insurance companies, such as LIC, have been extending insurance cover without any medical examination, subject to certain conditions.

With profit and without profit plans An insurance policy can be 'with' or 'without' profit. In the former, bonuses disclosed, if any, after periodical valuations are allotted to the policy and are payable along with the contracted amount. In 'without' profit plan the contracted amount is paid without any addition. The premium rate charged for a 'with' profit policy is, therefore, higher than for a 'without' profit policy.

Key man insurance Key man insurance is taken by a business firm on the life of key employee(s) to protect the firm against financial losses, which may occur due to the premature demise of the person.

Life Insurance Corporation of India

The Parliament of India passed the Life Insurance Corporation Act on 19 June 1956, and the Life Insurance Corporation (LIC) of India was created on 1 September 1956, with the objective of spreading life insurance much more widely and in particular to the rural areas, with a view to reach all insurable persons in the country, providing them adequate financial cover at a reasonable cost.

LIC had 5 zonal offices, 33 divisional offices, and 212 branch offices, apart from its corporate office, in the year 1956. Today, LIC functions with 2,048 fully computerized branch offices, 100 divisional offices, 7 zonal offices, and the corporate office. LIC's wide area network covers 100 divisional offices and connects all the branches through a metro area network. LIC has tied up with some banks and service providers to offer online premium collection facility in selected cities. The company's ECS and ATM premium payment facility is an additional customer convenience. Apart from online kiosks and IVRS, info centres have been commissioned at Mumbai, Ahmedabad, Bangalore, Chennai, Hyderabad, Kolkata, New Delhi, Pune, and many other cities. With a vision of providing easy access to its policyholders, LIC has launched its Satellite Sampark offices. The satellite offices are smaller, leaner, and closer to the customer. The digitalized records of the satellite offices will facilitate 'anywhere' servicing and many other conveniences in the future.

LIC continues to be the dominant life insurer even in the liberalized scenario of Indian insurance and is moving fast on a new growth trajectory surpassing its own past records. LIC has issued over one crore policies during the current year. It had crossed the milestone of issuing 10,132,955 new policies by 15 October 2005, posting a healthy growth rate of 16.67% over the corresponding period of the previous year.

From then to now, LIC has crossed many milestones and has set unprecedented performance records in various aspects of the life insurance business. The same motives which inspired our forefathers to bring insurance into existence in this country inspire LIC to take this message of protection, to light the lamps of security in as many homes as possible, and help people to provide security to their families.

Mission and vision of LIC

The mission of LIC is to 'Explore and enhance the quality of life of people through financial security by providing products and services of aspired attributes with competitive returns, and by rendering resources for economic development'. The company's vision is to be 'A transnationally competitive financial conglomerate of significance to societies and pride of India'.

Products offered by LIC

LIC offers a number of products, which have been divided into—insurance plans, pension plans, unit plans, special plans, and group schemes.

Insurance plans Keeping in mind the different requirements of different individuals, LIC offers a number of insurance plans with unique options that can fit into different requirements. The company has a number of options under children's plans, plan for handicapped dependents, endowment assurance plan, plan for high worth individuals, money-back plans, special money-back plans for women, etc.

Pension plans These plans provide customers with financial stability in old age. The different pension plans offered are Jeevan Nidhi, Future Plus, Jeevan Akshay IV, New Jeevan Dhara I, and New Jeevan Suraksha I. They thus provide annuity for life with the return of purchase price on the death of the annuitant.

Unit plans These are investment plans that help to realize the worth of hard-earned money. These plans yield rich benefits and also help to save tax even if a person does not have a consistent income. Thus, they provide the twin benefits of investment and insurance cover.

Special plans LIC's special plans are not plans but opportunities that the company offers at a point in time. These plans are a blend of insurance and investment. Currently, LIC offers the Golden Jubilee Plan under Bima Gold and New Bima Gold; Special Plan with Bima Nivesh 2005; and Jeevan Saral.

Group schemes These are life insurance schemes for groups of people and are ideal for employers, associations, societies, etc. They allow individuals to enjoy group benefits at really low costs. One can choose from a number of group schemes and social security schemes (LIC 2006).

LIC as a brand

LIC has been one of India's most recognizable brands. The company's ratings shot up at a time when several parts of the country were wrecked by natural disasters, most notable being the tsunami. In fact, LIC's handling of the situation earned it recognition in the Manila-based Asia Insurance Review. LIC visited the tsunami-affected areas with a list of policyholders, set up camps, and settled the claims immediately.

LIC has targeted both the urban and rural market. For the urban market it has increased emphasis on value-added services through its online portal and allowed for premium collection through ATM machines and ECS.

With 50% of the agents based in rural areas, LIC concentrates on personal selling in these regions. LIC has covered one crore below poverty line or marginally above the poverty line families with the help of its social security fund.

Questions

1. Comment on the different services being offered by LIC.
2. Which stage of the product life cycle is LIC in? Why?

REFERENCES

Abrar, Peerzada and Harsimran Julka (2013), 'IT cos snapping up startups to innovate product lines: Keen on partnership, infy, TCS, Cognizant, Wipro and MindTree begin talks', *The Economic Times*, New Delhi, 3 July, p. 1.

Adcock, R. and Halborg (2001), *Marketing Principles and Practices*, 4th edn, Prentice Hall, Harlow.

Ali, A. (2000), 'The impact of innovativeness and development time on new product performance for small firms', *Marketing Letters*, vol. 11, no. 2, pp. 151–163.

Asplund, M. and R. Sandin (1999), 'The survival of new products', *Review of Industrial Organization*, vol. 15, no. 3, pp. 219–223.

Bapna, Amit (2013), 'The colour of money', *The Economic Times*, Brand Equity, p. 3, 27 March.

'Back in the High Life' (2006), Brand Equity, *The Economic Times*, 15 February.

Bonner, J.M. (1999), *Customer involvement in new product development: Customer interaction intensity and customer network issues*, PhD thesis, Graduate School of the University of Minnesota.

Brown, S.L. and K. Eisenhardt (1995), 'Product development: Past research, present findings and future directions', *Academy of Management Review*, vol. 20, no. 2, pp. 343–378.

Chesbrough, H. (2004), 'Managing open innovation', *Research Technology Management*, vol. 47, no. 1, pp. 23–26.

Davis, S.M. (1997), 'Bringing innovation to life', *The Journal of Consumer Marketing*, vol. 14, no. 5, pp. 339–353.

Doyle, P. (1976), 'The realities of the product life cycle', *Quarterly Review of Marketing*, vol. 16, Summer, pp. 1–6.

Doyle, P. (2002), *Marketing Management and Strategy*, 3rd edn, Pearson Education, Essex, Chapter 5.

Economic Times (2012) 'Slump temporary, We'll open 100 outlets this year: Domino's Boss', *The Economic Times*, 31 August, p 4.

Ellwood, I. (2002), *The Essential Brand Book*, Kogan Page, London.

Gibney, Frank Jr and Belinda Luscombe (2000), 'The redesigning of America', *Time*, vol. 155, issue 11, pp. 66–75.

Gordon, G.L., R.J. Calantone, and C.A. Benedetto (1993), 'Business to business service marketing—How does it differ from business to business product marketing', *The Journal of Business and Industrial Marketing*, vol. 8, no. 1, pp. 45–57.

Grönroos, C. (1998), 'Marketing services: The case of the missing product', *The Journal of Business and Industrial Marketing*, vol. 13, no. 4/5, pp. 322–336.

Handfield, R.B., G.L. Ragatz, K.J. Petersen, and R.M. Monczka (1999), 'Involving suppliers in new product development', *California Management Review*, vol. 42, no. 1, pp. 59–82.

Keller, K.L. (2003), *Strategic Brand Management*, Pearson, Delhi.

Kotler, P. (2002), *Marketing Management*, Prentice Hall, New Delhi.

Kotler, P., J.T. Bowens, and J.C. Makens (2006), *Marketing for Hospitality and Tourism*, 4th edn, Pearson Education Inc., New Jersey, Chapter 9.

Kotler, P. (2003), *Marketing Management*, Prentice Hall, London.

Lazer, W. and R.A. Layton (1999), *Contemporary Hospitality Marketing—A Service Management Approach*, Education Institute of American Hotel and Motel Association, Michigan, Chapter 10.

Levine, M. (2003), *A Branded World*, John Wiley, New Jersey.

Lovelock, C. and J. Wirtz (2006), *Services Marketing*, 5th edn, Pearson Education, New Delhi, Chapter 4.

Lundkvist, A. and A. Yakhlef (2004), 'Customer involvement in new service development: A conversational approach', *Managing Service Quality*, vol. 14, no. 2/3, pp. 249–257.

Michael, G.C. (1971), 'Product petrification: A new stage in the life cycle theory', *California Management Review*, vol. 14, no. 1, pp. 88–91.

Modis, T. (1994), 'Life cycles: Forecasting the rise and fall of almost anything', *The Futurist*, vol. 28, no. 5, pp. 20–25.

Nicholls, A. (2004), 'Fair trade new product development', *The Service Industries Journal*, vol. 24, no. 2, pp. 102–117.

Ojha, A (2013), 'Service, selection and price are the three pillars', *Business Standard*, The Strategist, New Delhi, 18 February, p. 3.

Oxford Dictionary of Business and Management (2006), 4th edn, Oxford University Press, New Delhi.

Rampal, M.K. and S.L. Gupta (2002), *Service Marketing: Concepts, Applications and Cases*, Galgotia Publishing Company, New Delhi, Chapter 14.

Rao, R.M. (2005), *Services Marketing*, Pearson Education, Delhi, Chapters 1 and 7.

Ries, A. and L. Ries (1999), 'World-class brands', *Executive Excellence*, vol. 16, no. 3, p. 11.

Rio, A.B., R. Vazquez, and V. Iglesias (2001), 'The role of the brand name in obtaining differential advantages', *Journal of Product and Brand Management*, vol. 10, no. 7, pp. 452–465.

Sarkar, R. (2011), 'New dough for jubilant', *Business Standard*, 26 August, p. 10.

Scheuing, E. and E.M. Johnson (1989), 'A proposed model for new service development', *The Journal of Services Marketing*, vol. 3, no. 2, pp. 25–34.

Shetty, M. (2006), 'India moves to no.17 in global life insurance biz', *The Economic Times*, New Delhi, 20 July.

Shostack, G.L. (1977), 'Breaking free from product marketing', *Journal of Marketing*, vol. 41, no. 2, pp. 73–80.

Simoes, C. and S. Dibb (2001), 'Rethinking the brand concept: New brand orientation', *Corporate Communications: An International Journal*, vol. 6, no. 4, pp. 217–224.

Singh, S. (1997), *Right Brain Positioning in Strategic Marketing*, Indian Institute of Management, Calcutta.

Singhal, A. (2004), 'Creating and preserving brand', *Strategic Brand Management*, vol. 3, no. 5, pp. 18–21.

Talreja, V. (2006), 'Spa time: A massage for every occasion', *The Economic Times*, New Delhi, 7 August.

Verma, R., G.M. Thompson, W.L. Moore, and J.J. Louviere (2001), 'Effective design of products/services: An approach based on integration of marketing and operations management decisions', *Decision Science*, vol. 32, no. 1, pp. 165–193.

Vermeulen, P.A.M., J.P.J.D. Jong, and K.C. O'Shaughnessy (2005), 'Identifying key determinants for new product introductions and firm performance in small service firms', *The Service Industries Journal*, vol. 25, no. 5, pp. 625–40.

Vyas, N.M. (1993), 'Industrial product elimination decisions: Some complex issues', *European Journal of Marketing*, vol. 27, no. 4, pp. 58–76.

Wasson, C.R. (1968), 'How predictable are fashion and other product life cycles', *Journal of Marketing*, vol. 32, no. 3, pp. 36–43.

Wasson, C.R. (1978), *Dynamic Competitive Strategy and Product Life Cycles*, Austin Press, Austin.

Weber, J.A. (1976), 'Planning corporate growth with inverted product life cycles', *Long Range Planning*, vol. 9, no. 5, October.

Ananda Spa (2013) http://www.anandaspa.com/ananda-packages/inr/ananda-getaways/Couples-Connect.html, accessed on 1 July 2013.

CCD (2013), available from http://www.cafecoffeeday.com/thelounge/, accessed on 5 July 2013.

Chamikutty, P (2011), 'Most trusted brands 2011: LIC retains number 1 spot in life insurance category', available from http://articles.economictimes.india-times.com/2011–09–28/news/30212778_1_sbi-life-lic-clia-scheme, accessed on 11 July 2013.

Chowdhry, Seema (2013), 'Lounge Review: Mistral, Ambience Mall, Vasant Kunj, New Delhi', available from http://www.livemint.com/Leisure/5H45hc0Xa4SZ0eb0ix3O1O/Lounge-Review--Mistral-Ambience-Mall-Vasant-Kunj-New-Del.html, accessed on 5 July 2013.

Dominos (2013), available from http://www.dominos.co.in/about-us, accessed on 5 July 2013.

Economic Survey 2007–08, 'Insurance and pension funds', http://indiabudget.nic.in/es2007–08/chapt 2008/chap56.pdf>, accessed on 29 April 2008.

Express News Service (2013), 'Google launches 'start searching India' campaign, latest feature to show exact location of flights' available from http://www.indianexpress.com/news/google-launches--start-searching-india--campaign-latest-feature-to-show-exact-location-of-flights/1130348/, accessed on 27 June 2013.

Flipkart (2013), available from http://www.flipkart.com/about-us, accessed on 7 July 2013.

Ghose, Anindita (2011), 'Lounge Review, Cinema Eclipsed', available from http://www.livemint.com/Leisure/x9FFFN0PT7oMcjRiFM2uhP/Lounge-Review--Cinema-eclipsed.html, accessed on 5 July 2013.

Ghosh, D. (2010), 'Cafe Coffee Day aims for 100 'lounge' outlets', available from http://www.financialexpress.com/news/cafe-coffee-day-aims-for-100-lounge-outlets/712809, accessed 4 July 2013.

Hospitality India (2013), available from http://the-hospitalityindia.com/hospitality_brochure.pdf, accessed on 27 June 2013.

http://www.kotak.com/, accessed on 28 May 2014.

http://www.licindia.com/history.htm, accessed on 2 April 2008.

http://www.maxhealthcare.in/, accessed on 6 June 2014.

http://www.tanishq.co.in/tanishq_aboutus.html, accessed on 28 April 2008.

IBEF (2013), 'Insurance sector in India; available on http://www.ibef.org/industry/insurance-sector-india.aspx, accessed on 11 July 2013.

Indiainfoline (2013): 'Café Coffee Day introduces "The Lounge Journals" in Mumbai', http://www.indiainfoline.com/Markets/News/Caf%C3%A9-Coffee-Day-introduces-The-Lounge-Journals-in-Mumbai/5600590996, accessed 6 July 2013.

IRDA (2013), 'History of insurance in India', available from http://www.irda.gov.in/ADMINCMS/cms/NormalData_Layout.aspx?page=PageNo4&mid=2, accessed on 11 July 2013.

Jalali, Osama (2013), 'A move beyond movies', available from http://www.thehindu.com/features/metro

plus/Food/a-move-beyond-movies/article4814445.ece, accessed on 5 July 2013.

Jaypee sports (2013), available from http://www.jaypee-sports.com/aboutus.shtml, accessed on 5 July 2013.

JPSibrochure (2013), available from http://buddhinternationalcircuit.in/#, accessed on 5 July 2013.

Kanal, Nishtha (2013), 'Google launches campaign to help India use Search better', available from http://m.tech2.com/news/web-services/google-launches-campaign-to-help-india-use-search-better-/896592, accessed on 5 June 2014.

LIC (2011), available from http://www.licguru.in/profile-of-lic-of-india.html, accessed on 11 July 2013.

Mathews, Prince (2012), 'PVR vs Cinepolis: The Show (Down) Is On', available from http://forbesindia.com/article/boardroom/pvr-vs-cinepolis-the-show-down-is-on/32838/0#ixzz2Y92KpAhY, accessed on 5 July 2013.

Mirza, Sana (2013), 'A big challenge in the Indian Spa industry is lack of skilled workers', *Indian Hospitality Review* (online), available from http://www.indiahospitalityreview.com/interviews/big-challenge-indian-spa-industry-skilled-workers, accessed on 27 June 2013.

Mitra, S. (2011), 'CCD to bank on Lounge format to drive growth', http://www.mydigitalfc.com/news/ccd-bank-lounge-format-drive-growth-060, accessed 4 July 2013.

Pande, Bhanu and Ravi Tej Sharma (2011), 'Why Jaypee invested $400 million in F1 race when the project will make the group lose $35 million every year', available from http://articles.economictimes.indiatimes.com/2011–09–22/news/30189274_1_jaypee-sports-international-formula-one-management-buddh-international-circuit, accessed on 5 July 2013.

Prasanna, A. (2010), 'Cafe Coffee Day redesigns its lounge format', http://www.business-standard.com/article/companies/cafe-coffee-day-redesigns-its-lounge-format-110050600064_1.html, accessed on 3 July 2013.

PTI (2013a), 'Google launches "Start Searching India" campaign', available from http://www.thehindu.com/sci-tech/technology/internet/google-launches-start-searching-india-campaign/article4823575.ece, accessed on 6 July 2013.

—(2013b), 'Uttarakhand disaster: LIC asked to relax norms', available from http://businesstoday.intoday.in/story/uttarakhand-disaster-lic-asked-to-relax-claim-norms/1/196168.html, accessed on 7 July 2013.

Puri, M. (2011), 'Cafe Coffee Day introduces "The Lounge Journals" in Chandigarh', available from http://www.buzzintown.com/venue-review--cafe-coffee-day-introduces-the-lounge-journals-chandigarh/show--full/id--3733.html, accessed on 4 July 2013.

Rathore, V. (2013a), 'Jaypee owned Buddh Circuit rakes in big bucks as rich folks vroom their Ferraris, Maseratis', available from http://articles.economictimes.indiatimes.com/2013–05–01/news/38958254_1_gautam-singhania-buddh-international-circuit-oberoi-group, accessed on 6 July 2013.

—(2013b), 'PVR planning to take its luxury format Director's Cut to Thailand, Singapore and Hong Kong', *The Economic Times*, dated 8 May, available from http://articles.economictimes.indiatimes.com/2013–05–08/news/39117004_1_pvr-ltd-l-capital-major-cineplex-group, accessed on 5 July 2013.

Roy, Vilasini (2013), 'PVR's latest venture plays a summer romance', available from http://www.timeoutdelhi.net/restaurants-caf%C3%A9s/reviews/mistral, accessed on 5 July 2013.

Shashidhar, A. (2012), 'Changing The Brew', http://www.outlookbusiness.com/article_v3.aspx?artid=280761, accessed 4 July 2013.

Staff Reporter (2012), 'Café Coffee Day on a creative mission', http://www.thehindu.com/features/friday-review/dance/caf-coffee-day-on-a-creative-mission/article3691472.ece, accessed 4 July 2013.

Taj (2013), available from http://www.tajhotels.com/Special-Offers.aspx, accessed on 27 June 2013.

The Leela Kovalam (2013), available from http://www.theleela.com/locations/kovalam/offers/special-offers/ayurveda-at-the-leela, accessed on 27 June 2013.

CHAPTER
3
Managing the Services Brand

OBJECTIVES

After reading this chapter you will be able to understand the

- relevance of branding in services
- building of a brand
- building of brand loyalty
- management of a services brand
- management of a portfolio over time

BharatMatrimony Online 'match'ing

Indians have long relied on family, friends, temples, brokers, etc. for finding the right match. It took the foresight of an individual to leverage the power of the net and revolutionized the manner in which matches for life partners were made. It was on 14 April 1997 that Murugavel Janakiraman took an initiative to conceptualize, develop, and design a community portal for Indians working and living abroad. Features included matrimony, greeting cards, discussion forum, making friends, etc. Within two years Murugavel tasted success and in 1999 found his own life partner Deepa through his creation—BharatMatrimony. Forecasting a bigger opportunity in the Indian matrimony sector, BharatMatrimony opened its first office of 300 sq. ft in Chennai. Realizing that matches are sought within the community, he launched 10 regional websites in the year 2000. In 2001, it expanded its operations and opened up offices across India.

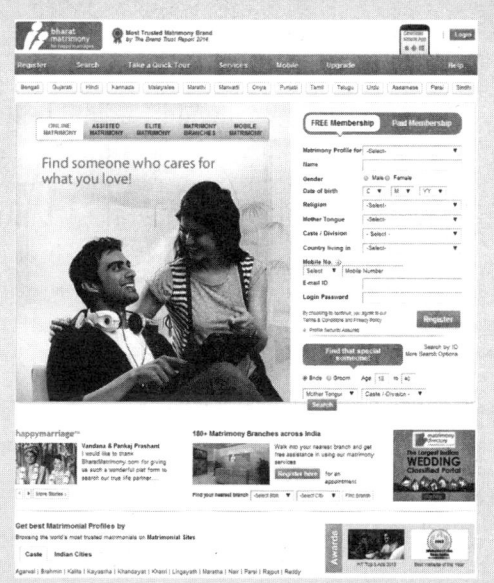

Source: Reprinted with permission from BharatMatrimony.

BharatMatrimony has come a long way since then and 'is celebrated as the Most Trusted Matrimony Brand combining tradition and technology with a network of 15 regional portals and over two crore members'. It has 179 offices spread across different locations in India and abroad such as UK, US, and United Arab Emirates, etc. Some of the brand-building strategies that have helped it reach this status are as follows:

- BharatMatrimony launched Matrimony Directory, the one stop portal to get everything needed to plan a perfect wedding. Astrology Religious Services, Beauty Grooming, Travels Tours, Hotel Accommodations, Decorators, Jewellers, and Wedding Cards are to name a few.
- BharatMatrimony joins hands with LinkedIn. Now members can display career details along with their personal details in their matrimony profile. This will enhance the credibility and improve the response to the member's profile.
- BharatMatrimony is available on iPhone, iPad, Android, Blackberry, and Nokia. Now members can explore partner search by downloading BharatMatrimony Mobile Apps that comes absolutely free with iPhone, iPad, Android, Blackberry, and with select Nokia phones as inbuilt Apps.
- BharatMatrimony has become the only matrimony site in the world with 100% verified mobile numbers. Profiles who have not verified their mobile numbers will not be part of the site any more. All profiles are reachable through mobile.

Thus, through sustained innovative marketing efforts and by providing technological platforms to connect with customers, BharatMatrimony.com was able to build itself from scratch into a global brand.

After going through the chapter, you will be able to answer the following questions:

1. Discuss the product being offered by BharatMatrimony.com.
2. Discuss the strategies adopted by the company to build its brand over the years.

Source: http://www.bharatmatrimony.com/successful-years.php, accessed on 20 August 2013.

BRANDING THE SERVICE PRODUCT

The biggest challenge for marketing professionals is their ability to create, maintain, and enhance brands. Branding is a major issue to be tackled in product strategy, as successful branding is one of the most potent tools for businesses to create and preserve value (Singhal 2004; Rio et al. 2001). Branding is an immensely challenging process, which requires intensive investment, building an element of trust with consumers, and delivering promises made to the consumer. The opening example of BharatMatrimony showcases how value can be added to the service of matchmaking. The journey of BharatMatrimony over the years shows how it has consistently delivered on its promise of facilitating marriages. This shows that it takes many years of efforts and investments to create global brands. The American Marketing Association defines a brand as, 'a name, term, sign, symbol, or design, or a combination of them, intended to identify the goods or services of one seller or group of sellers and to differentiate them from competitors' (Kotler 2002). Some of the notable brand names are Coca-Cola, Colgate, Disney, Goodyear, Heinz, Kellogg's, and Kodak. According to Ries and Ries (1999), 'marketing is branding' or branding is the glue that holds the marketing functions together. The concept of 'selling' is being replaced by 'purchasing' due to the rise of brands and so branding is important as it 'pre-sells' the product or service to the customer. Thus, branding is the most important activity for companies to become more profitable and more powerful. Branding helps marketers to be competitive in a fluctuating environment. Market conditions force marketers to adopt innovative branding strategies. Brand orientation is seen as a powerful tool for creating shareholder and long-term value (Simoes and Dibb 2001). A brand can convey up to six levels of meaning (Kotler 2002).

Attributes   There may be features/attributes associated with the brand. For example, a bank may list the services offered in its portfolio such as loans, savings accounts, demat account, online transactions, etc.

Benefits   A brand represents functional and/or emotional benefits. For example, a bank may offer a 24/7 service or ease of transactions or an unforgettable experience as mentioned by some airlines.

Values   These relate to the product/service values. For example, 'Made in Switzerland' for watches or 'Made in Japan' for electronic products evoke feelings of trust. For example, the 'Incredible India' campaign promotes unique Indian cultural aspects as a pull factor for foreign tourists.

Culture   A brand represents a culture. For example, Sony and Toyota represent Japanese precision and quality.

Personality   A brand may project a personality of the consumer. For example, a Diner's card is evidence of a customer's long association with the bank.

User   A brand points out the categories of users. For example, tour operators specifically target age groups of customers when they advertise travel packages such as family destinations, honeymoon couples, girls-only groups, etc.

Levine (2003) remarks that branding is a complex process, but its goal is simple. It is the creation and development of a specific identity for a company, product, commodity, group, or person. According to him, branding is the process by which a brand comes to be. Marketing communications play an important role in building brands. Advertising has been used to create mass awareness about the products or services. The role of public relations in creation of a brand has been overlooked in conventional literature.

Uses of Branding

A brand connotes a certain service offering and the choice of a branded service assumes a certain level of service. Consumers feel that service providers would like to uphold the brand and will honour their commitment. This reduces risk because a brand inspires confidence in the mind of the consumer. For example, when one chooses Marriott as a brand, a certain service assurance comes with it. It also reduces search cost as a customer is assured of specific standards. To sum up, a consumer associates a brand with the following aspects (Keller 2003):
- identification of source of product
- assignment of responsibility to product maker

- reduction of risk
- reduction of search costs
- promise, bond, or pact with the maker of the product
- symbolic device
- signal of quality

The brand helps manufacturers or service providers by helping them create a unique positioning for themselves, legally protecting the features, associating a distinct quality expectation, source of competitive advantage, and distinct returns. It also acts as barriers to entry for other brands. Investing in brands is also beneficial as these can be bought and sold as assets.

Brand Equity

A brand name not only imparts recognition to a product but gives it an identity. In the same product/service class, products of different firms can have different meanings for consumers. Thus, in the same product class, the product of one firm can mean quality, of another, value for money, yet another company's product can mean fun and good times, etc. The question is how do consumers associate these different meanings to different brands? This is because a brand name adds value to a product beyond the brand elements and the value added depends on the customer perception and hence, can mean differently to different customers. This value added to the product is brand equity and how this equity is built by customers is important as the customers' evaluation of the brand is influenced by this understanding. Keller (2004) defines brand equity from the customer's perspective as 'the differential effect the brand knowledge has on consumer response to marketing of that brand'.

Brand equity can be built by 'creating the right brand knowledge structures with the right consumers'. The entire brand-related contacts (whether personal or marketer-initiated) act as building blocks (Kotler and Keller 2006). As marketers, how do we influence customers that they seek the brand whenever they need to make a purchase in that category and across categories also? This can be answered by building a strong brand that positively influences the customers and by understanding the sources of brand equity for the customers. The various factors that lead to building brand equity are as follows:

Brand Knowledge

Brand knowledge is the understanding that the consumers have about a brand. The brand knowledge can be understood on the basis of two components—brand awareness and brand image (Keller 1993, 2003).

Brand awareness

It is the ability of customers to identify the brand under different conditions. To recognize the brand under different conditions, thus, highlights the importance of the two parameters—brand recognition and brand recall. A person is said to have high brand awareness when he/she is able to recognize the brand when given a clue about the brand (i.e., brand recognition) and is able to recall the brand when the needs related to the product category are to be fulfilled (i.e., brand recall).

Brand image

This is broadly the perception that the consumers have about a brand. These perceptions lead to the development of a representation of a brand in the mind of the consumers. Over a period of time, people can have more than one perception of the brand and all these lead to the formation of a brand image. The brand image and attitude are to be created first in order to achieve brand equity (Faircloth, Capella, and Alford 2001)

Brand Associations

These are 'anything that connects the consumers to the brand' (Aaker 1991, Aaker and Joachimsthaler 2000). People can have more than one connection and all these act as building blocks that lead to developing brand equity. Thus, if we talk about Big Bazaar, then associations like 'value for money', 'variety of products', 'fashion trends for the youth', etc. come to mind.

Big Bazaar provides 'value for money' offers

Perceived Quality

According to Aaker (1991), the quality of the brand as perceived by the consumers also leads to brand equity and defined it as 'customer's perception of the overall quality or superiority of a product or service with respect to its intended purpose relative to alternatives'. This is also a brand association but the relative importance has led to the elevation to a separate dimension of brand equity.

Brand Loyalty

The importance of brand loyalty as a construct of brand equity has been delineated by Aaker (1991) and treated it as a behavioural dimension. However, brand loyalty as an attitudinal dimension has also been identified and is defined as 'the tendency to be loyal to a focal brand, which is demonstrated by the intention to buy the brand as a primary choice' (Yoo and Donthu 2001).

Company Image

Keller (2003; 2005) identified the image of the company to be an influencer on brand equity. The image the organization has in the mind of the consumers is bound to impact on the brands launched by the organization due to the halo effect.

Brand Community

This includes the people associated with the brand such as users or representatives of the firm marketing the brand (Berthon, Holbrook, and Hulbert 2003).

Brand Elements

Brands can be identified and differentiated with the help of small brand identities that can be trademarked. These brand equity drivers are called brand elements. The brand elements need to be strategically chosen so that they are easily remembered and invoked for the product class. Some of the major brand elements are as follows:

Brand name Brand name is the central theme or key association of the product. It should be simple so that even a small child can remember it.

Logos and symbols Logos are used to visually represent 'origin, ownership, or association' (Keller 2004). Logos can be in the form of word-marks, pictorial (non-word) marks, or a combination of both (Keller 2004). Word-marks are corporate names written in a distinct form or style, such as Kit-Kat, Cadbury's, Yahoo!, etc. Non-word mark logos are also called symbols and are abstract logos that are unrelated to the corporate name, like the swoosh of Nike. Over time, the logo, symbol, and brand 'may become inseparable and increase memorability, aid recall, and help sales' (Ramaswamy and Namakumari 2009).

Characters 'These are brand symbols that take on a human or real-life characteristic' (Keller 2004). They can be animated like 'Tiger for Britannia biscuits', 'Tony the Tiger and Coco the monkey of Kellogg's' or live figure forms like Ronald McDonald (of McDonald's), Colonel Sanders (of Kentucky Fried Chicken), etc.

Slogans Research suggests that slogans of brands are effective keystones in building brand equity (Mathur and Mathur 1995). These are short phrases used to position the organization's offering.

Jingles These are musical messages of the brand and are used for advertising purposes to communicate the benefits of the brand (Keller 2004). They are different from slogans as they are musical.

Packaging Packaging includes wrappers or containers in which the product is sold. It does not directly contribute as an ingredient of the product performance but characterizes the product. It facilitates in transportation, storage of the product at the retailer's outlet, acts as a silent salesman on the shelves, carries a lot of information, aids in the consumption process, can be used as an in-home storage for the product, and after the product has been consumed, as a storage for other items (if it is reusable).

Through Corporate Societal Marketing

Corporate societal marketing is when organizations use their resources to undertake at least one marketing initiative that has a non-economic objective. This is due to the realization that consumer's perception of the company and its role in society can significantly affect brand equity (Hoeffler and Keller 2002).

Joint Branding Programs

An organization can tie up with another brand (either own or belonging to some other organization) to leverage their own brand. It has been studied that companies can create, communicate, or deliver value in a better manner when they partner with other companies.

Distribution Channels

The channel of distribution or where the brand is being sold also transfers value to a brand. Different retail outlets have their own perceptions in the mind of the consumers which is rubbed on to the brand being retailed at their outlets (Keller 2003; 2005).

Country of Origin Effect

The world has become a global village and increasingly products from other countries are fighting for shelf space with the local brands. Country of origin stands for the country in which the product is made and the consumer's perception of the product or the assessment of the product on the basis of this is called the 'country of origin effect' (Samiee 1994).

People

Endorsements are when well-known people and celebrities associate with the brand to promote it (Keller 2003; 2005). They can be famous personalities in different fields, acclaimed sportspersons, actors, etc.

Things

Things like events, causes, and third-party sources can also be used to build brand equity (Keller 2003; 2004; 2005). Events such as sporting, cultural events, etc. can be used to increase the brand awareness.

Types of Brands

Brands can offer different value propositions and so can be categorized into the following (Tybout and Carpenter 2006; Ramaswamy and Namakumari 2009):

Functional brands   These brands highlight the features and efficient performance of the brand, for example, the low-cost airlines highlight the functional benefit of transportation at an affordable price.

Image brands   These brands build on the brand image and emphasize the brand value. Credit card companies emphasize on the image created when customers use it to make payments.

Experience brands   These brands project the experience customers will get in order to create value. Thus, amusement/water parks focus on the experience they provide to customers.

Branding Challenges

Kotler (2003) has enumerated various branding challenges faced by a marketer.

To brand or not to brand   There are instances in service segments such as home loans and credit collection agencies, which work for leading banking brands, such as ICICI and HDFC. On their own, they would find it difficult to sustain their operations.

Brand sponsor decisions   These decisions are about whether the brand would be a manufacturer's brand, distributor's brand, or licensed brand. Firms such as Wills Lifestyle have opened their own stores for retailing its brand of clothes. Superstores, such as Marks and Spencer's, retail products using their own brand names. Certain firms, such as Disney Stores, sell their products under licence.

Brand name decisions   These decisions are related to whether individual names, blanket family names, separate family names, or company trade names should be combined with an individual product name. The idea of having the same name for different product in blanket family names or separate family names or corporate name combined with individual product name is that organizations can add sub-brands to these brands and offer more options or choices for the consumers to choose from. With individual names again, organizations can keep adding more brands to their portfolio.

Brand strategy decisions   These are related to brand positioning decisions.
    The challenge for the service provider is how to place the brand in the mind of the consumer. These questions have been addressed in detail in Chapter 6. Four strategic questions need to be addressed:
1. Who am I? (corporate identity, endorsement)
2. What am I? (category-related, benefit-related, usage, and time)
3. For whom am I? (segmentation)
4. Why me? (unique attribute, competitor)

    Brands are important because they act as the communication tool between increasingly physically separated businesses and consumers. According to Ellwood (2002), a brand is the area that surrounds a product or service that communicates its benefits and differentiates it from the competition for the consumer. The seven Ps of marketing must be integrated well to give the right perception of the brand product—price, place, promotion, place, people, process, and physical evidence. Ellwood (2002) has discussed the 'brand DNA' model. He relates DNA with brand proposition, brand personality, emotional benefits, and rational benefits. This has an impact on business culture, consumer culture, social image, and self-image.
    Singh (1997) has discussed about the brand's competence and its relationship with the external world. It is the relationship which dictates competitive advantage. The consumer choices of a brand are governed by numerous factors. These could be the

attributes, emotions, and price factors, among others. Brands help consumers to arrive at decisions as they simplify the decision-making process. Choosing a commodity is far more complex than choosing a brand. This is because in case of selecting a commodity, the decision is based on logical deductions and evaluation of rational attributes and parameters, necessitating volumes of data collection, assimilation, and comparison. Brands come with certain attributes and expectations that are clearly mapped. Brands allow consumers the luxury of engaging in emotional experiences. Singh (1997) postulates that brands have barely exposed the tip of a customer's emotional iceberg, using primarily three key emotions—warmth, humour, and fear.

Most marketers adopt the logical route to branding and benefit communication. The brand is positioned in the left brain offering a rational explanation of its key attributes, how they work, and the results they produce. As a result, the consumers respond to these with greater rational reasoning, which results in their minds ruling their hearts. If the marketer influences a consumer's right side of the brain, as frequently done in the fashion and fragrance industries, the brand is able to emotionally connect with the consumer. Once the consumer is bonded to the brand, faith in functional superiority follows, because emotionally the consumer is convinced of its benefits and quality. It is possible to impact the consumers' decision-making process through the route chosen to enter their mind space. How can the brand enter the consumer's right brain first? This can be done either by enhancing the intrinsic worth, that is, helping them to feel better about their own selves or through enhancement of their extrinsic worth (by helping them look better to the world around them). When a brand employs its core capability to enhance the consumer's intrinsic or extrinsic worth, it accomplishes a successful right brain entry.

Singh (1997) quotes the Plutchik's emotion solid scale where the range of emotions, such as adoration, ecstasy, terror, amazement, grief, rage, vigilance, loathing, disgust, sadness, fear, anger, surprise, apprehension, distraction, pensiveness, boredom, or annoyance, could be targeted. It is essential that some of the following factors be considered for successful brand building in the service industry. Each of these is explained in detail in this section.

Evoke feeling of trust

Service industry is primarily a people-oriented industry. The challenge for the service firms is to ensure uniformity of experience event after event. In order to ensure this, it is essential that adequate investments be made in the training of employees and experience as per the expectations that are built in the consumers. Unlike products, wherein there are quality certifications, a consumer perceives a higher level of risk especially in high-involvement and high-priced service categories such as buying time-share options, travelling to a particular country, or making financial investments. The consumer needs to be assured of a pleasant experience and endorsements by other consumers could evoke feelings of trust. Exhibit 3.1 illustrates the concept further.

Trained manpower

Employees of the firm are the face of the company as they communicate a lot about the service culture of the firm. Well-dressed employees with polite behaviour as well as

---

Exhibit 3.1 | **Life Insurance Corporation of India**

A case of an Indian brand, which evokes an element of trust in consumers, is Life Insurance Corporation of India (LIC). It is a public sector organization that has received numerous awards. Some of the awards received in 2012–13 are as follows:

- NDTV Profit Business Leadership Award
- Consumer Superbrand Award
- Outlook Money Award for Best Life Insurer 2012
- Excellence in Financial Services Award by Dainik Bhaskar 2012–13
- ABCI Award for Best Online Campaign
- CNBC TV Award for Outstanding Financial Professional 2012
- Power Brand Award 2012
- CNBC TV 18 Award Overall Leading Insurance Company 2012

In 2005 the company's profit was ₹5,800 crore. The business has been operating for the last 50 years. Life insurance in its modern form came to India from England in the year 1818. Oriental Life Insurance started by the Europeans in Calcutta was the first life insurance company on Indian soil. All the insurance companies established during that period were brought up with the purpose of looking after the needs of the European community. The Parliament of India passed the Life Insurance Corporation Act on 19 June 1956 and LIC was created on 1 September 1956 with the objective of spreading life insurance, particularly in rural areas. Despite so many multinationals operating this domain, LIC still has a leading market share in the life insurance segment. With the corporate office in Mumbai, at present, LIC has 8 zonal offices, 100 divisional offices, 2,048 branch offices, and close to 1,002,149 insurance agents called 'producers'.

Source: Based on the data from Life Insurance Corporation of India (2008), Newspaper reports.

---

product knowledge go a long way in developing relationships with the consumers. Taj Hotels connotes a luxury brand in India. Premium pricing strategy and attention to details, such as the ambience of the rooms, further reinforce the image of luxury.

Service blueprint

The service processes should be mapped and the flow of activities from one stage to another should be well thought of. In a service operation, critical time for each activity needs to be assessed and respected.

Physical evidence

Tangible cues help to create a high degree of confidence in consumers. Well-groomed employees, well-maintained building and ambience, visual imagery created at contact points, usage of state-of-the-art equipment, all contribute to creating a pleasant experience for the consumer (Exhibit 3.2). Great promises and advertisements devoid of tangible evidence do not influence customers for too long.

Mechanisms for consumers to reach the service provider A service firm needs to redress consumer grievances. More importantly, it should be able to anticipate consumer requirements and deliver services, which exceed consumer expectations. Obstacles,

| Exhibit 3.2 | **Tanishq—India's Largest Jewellery Brand** |

Tanishq is India's largest, most desirable, and fastest growing jewellery brand. The brand is the jewellery business group of Titan Industries Ltd and is promoted by the TATA Group. Tanishq had retail sales worth ₹1,200 crore in 2007 and is expected to hit ₹10,000 crore in 2013–2014. Continuing to expand, at present there are 150 and Tanishq plans to open 30 more showrooms in A, B, and C category cities across India.

Tanishq is prominent in the form of stand-alone boutiques. Each outlet has a distinct ambience with chic lighting and green plants. The sales staff wears uniforms and as soon as consumers enter an outlet, they are escorted by staff members and directed to a counter depending on their requirements. Beverages are offered to consumers and there is an air of professionalism. Tanishq promises pure gold jewellery and certifies the quality of the precious/semi-precious stones in writing. It offers the most modern, scientific, and non-destructive process to measure the exact purity of the gold jewellery using a karat meter. The entire process and experience that a consumer goes through right from entering to leaving the boutique signifies trust.

which inhibit consumer access to the service firm, need to be removed. The feedback and research process initiation should not be undertaken because it is politically correct to do so, but because they help consumers to voice their concerns and suggestions. This in turn helps the firm to continuously improve itself.

Connecting to consumers Marketers deploy various strategies to reach out to consumers. Advertising, sales promotion, personal selling, and public relations (PR) are some of these ways. However, PR could be deployed very meaningfully and be used as a tool to create a bonding with the consumer. Therefore, it was a win-win strategy for both the company and the farmers. Similarly, the Body Shop, a retail firm based in UK, associated itself with social and environmentally active groups and initiated a campaign for banning testing of cosmetics on animals. This led to an instant bond with over six million European consumers who participated in a signature campaign. When firms stand up for a right cause, a lot more is achieved than by simple advertising initiatives.

CREATING A BRAND

A brand is not a name or an accessory added at the end of the production process. It is a value that needs to be considered at each and every step of the creation of the product (Kapferer 2009). Any commodity can be made into a brand by adding value. The value can be in the form of differentiation added to the product. The product can be imbibed with images and this along with the values added form the brand halo. 'The brand is not what we create in factories' but as Alvin Achenbaum (a marketing guru) observed 'Ultimately a brand resides in the minds of the consumers' (Parameswaran 2010). Let us now try to gain an understanding of how successful brands are created and then successfully maintained over a period of time. Figure 3.1 highlights how brands can be built and then managed over time to create iconic brands (e.g., see Exhibit 3.3).

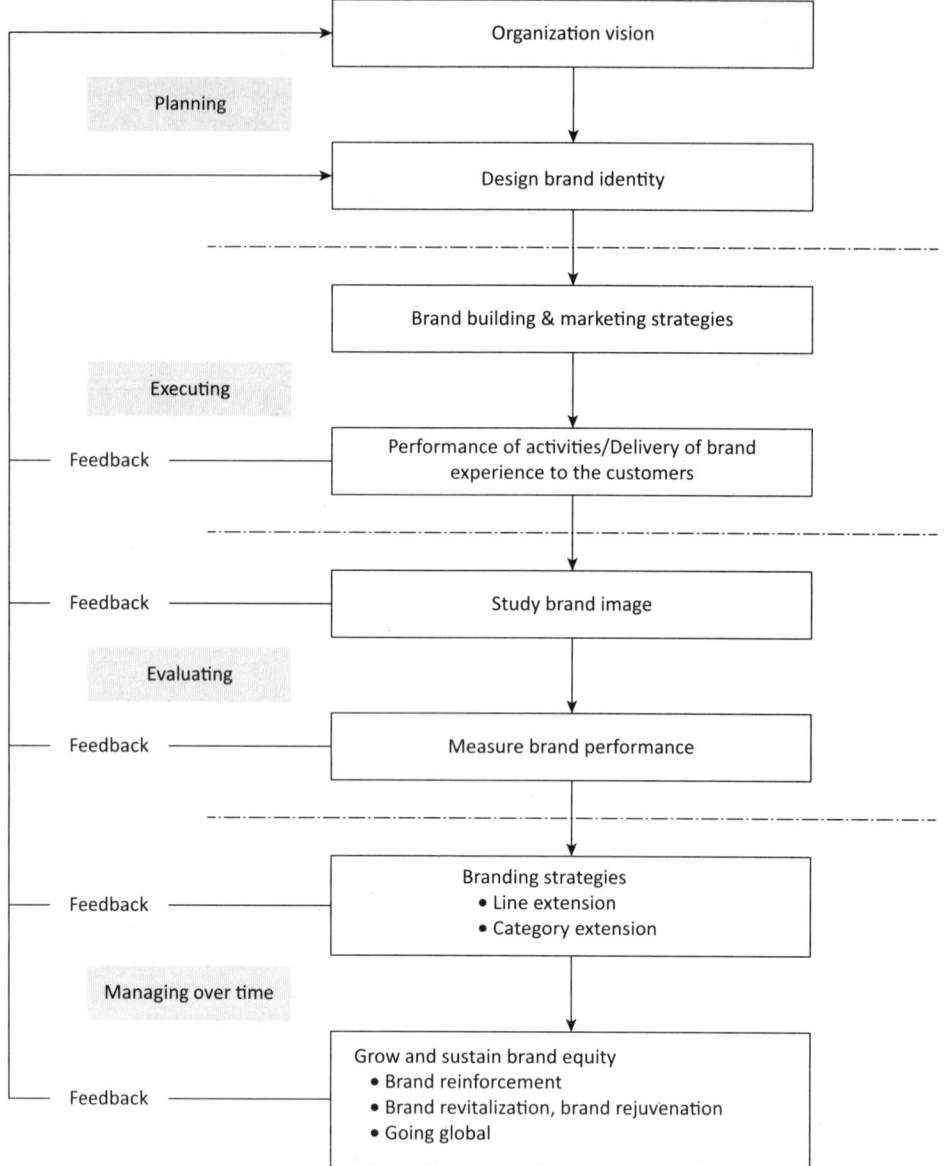

Fig. 3.1 Building and managing brands

Zara has benefitted immensely from its brand mantra of offering 'affordable, copycat versions of the latest fashions and making them available to shoppers in double-quick time'. The price tag is comparable to premium brands in India.

However, the consumers prefer the brand as at the same price it is trendier than other brands. Inditex keeps the merchandise as per the local tastes and preferences and styles that are not popular within a week of launch are quickly removed from the shelves. The popular designs are also replaced with new designs so that there is no reorder and

Exhibit 3.3 **Building Zara in India**

Zara is a Spanish apparel brand that globally belongs to Inditex and is known as a fast-fashion brand. It enters India through a joint venture with Tata Group's Trent (its retail arm). A look at Table 3.1 ('Zara—Weighing with competition in India') shows that in its three years of operations in India, it has left behind established apparel retailers such as Louis Philippe and Benetton in per-store sales. The ₹45 crore sales per store in 2012–2013 saw it leaving behind 'country's largest apparel brand Louis Philippe' far behind at ₹7 crore sales per store and brings it 'at par with the country's largest jewellery chain Tanishq'.

Table 3.1   Zara—Weighing with competition in India

Brand	Type of store	Annual sales (₹ Crore)	Store count	Average size (sq. ft)	Sales per year (each store) (in ₹ Crore)
Zara	Apparel Store	405	9	16000–22000	45
Benetton	Apparel Store	1050	600	1500	1.75
Louis Philippe	Apparel Store	1106	150	2000–3000	7
Reliance Fresh	Supermarket	5256	453	2000–5000	11.6
Shoppers Stop	Department Store	2256	55	50000	41
Tanishq & Gold Plus	Jewellery	8107	179	5000–15000	45

Note: All figures as of 31 March 2013

hence no requirement for warehousing. Inditex Trent plans to open 18 more stores in smaller cities such as Surat, Mangalore, Indore, etc in the period 2013–2016.

The reading highlights the fact that the Inditex's 'approach to fashion—creativity, quality design, and rapid turnaround to adjust to changing market demands—has allowed it to expand internationally at a fast pace and saw it retailing Zara in 86 countries through 1763 stores' (Inditex 2013). The brand marketing strategies it adopted was to provide the latest fashion at affordable prices in a short time period to the customers. The brand experience delivered is also in line as the customers know that if they do not purchase the design, then it might not be available the next time they visit the store.

Organization Vision

Organizations need to build the brand as per the 'soul' of the organization. It should flow from the vision and mission of the organization and should be able to capture the strengths of the organization. The competitive advantage of the organization needs to be uncovered and understood along with the weaknesses of the organization so as to frame a realistic brand strategy. The organizational culture is another important aspect that needs to be considered while performing the internal analysis. An organizational culture that directs the employees towards providing a consistent brand experience at various levels of interaction should be encouraged. The organization thus needs to look at the strengths of the employees as a whole. They then need to decide how they can leverage this and create a unique brand experience for the customers. For established brands, the brand heritage or how the brand came into being and the current image of the brand, both need to be understood for building the brand identity.

Designing Brand Identity

Brand identity is 'a vision of how the brand should be perceived by its target audience. It is a vehicle that guides and inspires the brand-building program. If the brand identity is confused or ambiguous, there is little chance that effective brand building will occur' (Aaker and Joaschimsthaler 2000). To broaden the scope of identity conceptualization, the framework provided by Aaker (1996) can be considered. This framework helps conceptualize the brand on the following perspectives:

Brand as product

The most important aspect for an organization is to consider the brand as a product for the formulation of the brand identity. This is because a product is directly linked with a brand and for the common consumer, the brand and the product are one and the same thing. Thus, if the product is good, it will be considered in the choice decisions of the consumer and will impact the user experience.

Brand as organization

According to this perspective, the organizational attributes are highlighted rather than the product or the other attributes. Thus, organizational factors such as innovation and trust can be highlighted to strengthen the brand identity.

Brand as person

This includes the brand personality dimension and the customer relationship dimensions. Brand personality is 'a set of human characteristics that can be associated with the brand such as gender, age, and personality traits such as warmth, honesty, integrity, etc.' The creation of a brand identity is discussed in the brand personality section of brand identity.

Brand as symbol

Consideration of the brand as a symbol is helpful in 'giving strength and structure to the brand identity.' It is also beneficial in aiding the customers to have a high recognition and recall about the brand. Brands can be symbolized through visual imagery or by highlighting the brand heritage.

A brand can choose any one of these or a combination of any of these to create an identity. A company need not focus on all of these to build their brand identity but should consider only those that effectively communicate what the organization wants to say about the brand or what the organization wants the consumers to remember or think of about the brand.

Brand Building and Marketing Strategies

Once the brand identity is decided, it needs to be operationalized through the other brand building and marketing strategies of the organization. The strategies that need to be aligned with the brand are the product strategy, pricing strategy, promotion strategy, distribution strategy, and online strategy. The product has to be the best and as per the needs and wants of the customer. It should satisfy some need and want of the customer, backed by a high perceived value. An organization that spends time and money in building a brand does not want the consumers to have a negative perception about the brand due to a poorly designed product or a product that is lacking in the attributes the consumers are looking for. It needs to be priced appropriately so as to add value to the brand. A brand needs to be 'available at the right place and right time' for consumers to purchase the brand and so how it is distributed is important. Also, consumers need to be communicated about the added values endowed to the brand by the company. This helps them in forming the required positioning of the brand in their mind that leads to consumer preference for the brand.

Performance of Activities/Delivery of Brand Experience to the Customers

The employees perform their activities and the experience of the brand is delivered to the customers. The appropriate performance of activities is essential for delivering the brand experience. Faulty executions can harm the brand and result in contradiction of brand values. For example, the inability of PricewaterhouseCoopers (PwC) to deliver on its brand values of 'teamwork, excellence, and leadership' came to the fore in the year 2009 when it was unable to 'spot a 7-year, 10 figure super fraud' at Satyam where 'several senior managers forged invoices and bank statements to the tune of more than $1 billion.' On being questioned by the authorities, PwC admitted that due to the problem of understaffing, it could not audit Satyam's accounts. It had outsourced this work to a local firm of accountants who had shared their Bengaluru office. Despite the claim that 'its very special kind of leadership demands "courage, vision, and integrity"', it still signed off the undeclared outsourced work of accounts each year. By not delivering on the brand values, PwC's brand image was damaged globally during the 10 months of media outrage that followed subsequent to the scandal (Ritson 2009).

Study Brand Image

The consumers through the various interactions and 'moments of truth' with the brand develop a perception about the brand. All the brand associations that a consumer holds in the memory help in forming the perception that is known as the brand image (Keller 2004). Brand association is any information that is linked to a brand in the memory of the consumer (Aaker 1991). These associations can denote a physical attribute, functional benefit of a brand, or a symbolic aspect of a brand (Kressmann et al. 2006). For the marketers, these brand associations differentiate the brand. Developing a positive feeling about the brand and a favourable attitude towards the brand is done by highlighting the benefits of consuming a brand. This further helps in positioning and extending the brand. For consumers, brand associations help them to organize information bits together to form a definite perception, organize, and to retrieve information at the time of purchase decision-making. For a brand, the brand associations can be multidimensional (Aaker 1991) and an understanding of the various brand elements is necessary. The customer on evaluation of the brand forms a perception or image of the brand. This brand image can be either similar or dissimilar to the brand identity set by the organization. If the image is similar to the identity, then the brand meets the customer's expectations, the customer is satisfied, and the brand becomes a preferred brand of the consumers leading to the creation of a strong brand. If on the other hand, the brand image is not as per the brand identity, it leads to creating a brand gap wherein the customers are confused as the brand promise is not met. Take the example of Reliance Telecommunications when, a few years back, the Dhirubhai Ambani scheme was launched. The brand promised to be affordable but the consumers on using the plan realized that there were a number of hidden costs and the offer was not as lucrative as was being communicated by the organization.

Measure Brand Performance

The brand that has been established in the market has some customer following and recognition. The performance of the brand needs to be measured to understand if the financial performance of the brand is as per the projected performance or not. This financial performance of the brand can be compared with the financial performances of the other brands in the market to gain an understanding of the standing of the brand in the marketplace. An understanding of the financial measures is not sufficient in itself. They need to be backed with an understanding of the customer loyalty and the perception of the customers toward the brand. A brand with a loyal customer base and with a brand image consistent with the brand identity is bound to be successful sooner or later. This understanding is also important to identify as it can provide input in the further revision of the brand strategies.

Branding Strategies

Organizations can use the equity of an existing brand to leverage the new product which is called as brand extension (Keller 2004). The new brand so launched is called the sub-brand and the existing brand is called as the parent brand. If the parent brand name has already been used in various product lines, it is also called a family brand (Kotler and Keller 2006). Brand extension can be either of the following:

Line extension When a new product is added to an existing brand in the same product category, it is called as line extension. Thus, Taj Exotica, Taj Exotica Resort and Spa, and Taj Safari are all line extensions of Taj in the same product category of hotels.

Category extension When an existing brand name is used to launch a new product in a different product category, it is called category extension. It is called as brand franchise extension (Tauber 1988) or brand extension (Sarkar and Singh 2005; Verma 2009). Thus, Taj SATS Air Catering Ltd that provides airline catering service in South Asia, as a joint venture between Taj and SATS (formerly known as Singapore Airport Terminal Services) uses both the established brand names for offering brand in another segment than hotels.

This understanding helps the organization to create brand architecture strategy for the organization and they can position themselves anywhere on the spectrum between a 'branded house' (where the same brand name is used to represent all the product offerings of the organization, for example, Virgin Atlantic Airlines, Virgin radio, etc.) and 'house of brands' (where an organization has a number of brands and all these are stand-alone brands that are independent of each other).

Growing and Sustaining Brand Equity

Brand equity needs to be grown and sustained over time. The brand needs to reinvent itself and stay young so that the current generations do not feel the brand is dated and is not meant for them. For growing and sustaining brand equity, brand challenges also need to be met over time and can be done by

Brand reinforcement   The brand needs to constantly remind the customers about its benefits, needs it satisfies, and the value proposition it offers. The customers' response to the marketing activities needs to be gauged and this should be considered for formulating new marketing strategies. The customers then need to be made aware about these activities and this will result in the achievement of the desirable brand image leading the brand to reposition itself as a desirable brand in the minds of the consumers. Such a brand will be 'current' and 'relevant' in the mind of the consumers and they will want to purchase it and be associated with it.

Brand revitalization   This includes rejuvenating and renewing the brands for consumers so that they feel that the brand is 'their' brand and not the brand of the generation(s) gone by. This can be done by managing the brand portfolio that is discussed later.

Brand going global   Till now, we have been discussing the various strategies that can be adopted by an organization to build a sustainable brand, worth high equity. The organization can leverage this brand and come out with strategies that help in penetrating the market and gaining high market share. Once the opportunities in the market have been utilized, the question is 'what next?' What does the organization do now to enhance its sales and profitability? The organization then needs to look beyond its current market to greener pastures. It needs to look at opportunities available in other countries/markets and try to exploit these as well. While going global, a brand can adopt any of these strategies.

Global brands   Companies can treat the world as one market and offer one brand globally. This leads to the development of a few global brands in the brand portfolio, which then becomes easier for the organization to manage.

Local brands   Companies can customize the brand according to the markets and come out with local brands in different country markets.

Feedback from various stages of planning, execution, evaluation, and managing over time is important so as to guide the subsequent brand vision and help in designing brand identity as per changing consumer behaviour and market trends.

BUILDING BRAND LOYALTY

Customer loyalty is often associated with a brand (Mascarenhas, Kesavan, and Bernacchi 2006). The market is cluttered with a number of brands, be it manufacturer brand or retailer's own labels. A slight change in the market share has a significant financial implication and it is the brand loyal customers that ensure sales in such a competitive scenario (Datta 2003). A 5% increase in customer loyalty can enhance the profitability of the company by 40–95% (Kim, Morris, and Swait 2008) depending upon the type of industry. Brand loyalty is a measure of how attached the consumer is with a brand. It shows the likelihood of a consumer to shift to another brand when a new brand is launched or an existing brand makes a change in its marketing mix (Aaker 1991). Loyalty is defined as 'brand loyalty is the biased (i.e., non random) behavioural response (i.e., purchase), expressed over time by some decision-making unit, with respect to one or more alternative brands out of a set of such brands, and is a function of psychological (decision-making, evaluative) processes' (Sheth, Mittal, and Newman 1999). Loyalty is both behavioural and attitudinal and can be expressed at the following five levels (Aaker 1991):

Brand switchers   These consumers form the lowest level of the brand loyalty ladder and are indifferent to the brand name. The buying decisions are based on price, availability, etc., and do not attach any importance to the brand.

Habitual buyers   Such types of customers are satisfied with the brand and are characterized by the absence of any kind of dissatisfaction with the brand. They are habitual buyers but can also switch over to another brand when provided with the stimulations by the competitors. It is a task to reach out to such type of customers as they have no reason to be on the lookout for alternatives.

Switching-cost loyals   These customers are similar to habitual buyers as they are also satisfied with the brand. They are different in the aspect that they have a switching cost as well which can be in the form of 'time, money, or performance risk associated with switching.' These customers can be induced to switch by offering a benefit that is large enough to compensate the risks involved.

Friends of the brand   These consumers really like the brand and consider it as a friend. They prefer the brand, have a liking for the brand, and are emotionally attached to the brand.

Committed customers   These types of customers form the top level of the brand loyalty ladder. They are committed towards the brand and feel the brand helps in expressing them or the functional use of the brand is extremely important to them. They take pride in the brand and even recommend it to the others.

These five levels are indicative and there can be overlaps and combinations of levels. For example, there can be customers who like the brand and have a switching cost as well. Other exceptions can also be there, for example, there can be customers who are dissatisfied but due to non-availability of alternatives (for instance, earlier in the Indian aviation sector, even dissatisfied fliers had to fly in Indian Airlines or Air India in the absence of any competing airlines) or switching cost is high, etc. The ultimate output of brand consumption is to create brand loyalty.

Companies benefit from brand loyalty as it

a) lowers vulnerability to competitors' marketing strategies (Keller 2004)

b) increases marketing communication effectiveness and reduces marketing costs (Keller 2004; Rundle-Thiele and Bennet 2001)

c) allows companies to charge higher margins (Keller 2004)

d) increases the probability of success in brand extension and licensing opportunities (Keller 2004)

e) means that customers are less price-sensitive (Krishnamurthy and Raj 1991), therefore they do not readily shift over with a change in prices by competitor brands

f) can induce loyal customers to buy more of the brand than they normally would when it is promoted, while non-loyal customers are likely to purchase the promoted brand only in small quantities (Cataluna et al. 2006)

g) has more influence on purchase decisions than price promotions (Cataluna et al. 2006)

Research shows that a 1% increase in customer loyalty equals 10% cost reduction, and a 5% increase in customer loyalty increases the profitability of the company by 40–95% (Kim, Morris, and Swait 2008). Also, the cost of attracting a new customer is five times more than the cost of retaining an existing customer (Reichheld and Sasser 1990). Thus, maintaining brand loyal customers is both beneficial and profitable for organizations.

MANAGING THE SERVICE BRAND PORTFOLIO OVER TIME

Brands are built over time through carefully thought-out strategies. Human effort, time, and money are required in abundance to build a brand from scratch. Once the brand is established and doing well, companies realize that to stay competitive and to tap other opportunities in the market, they need to come out with more products to attract consumers. Brands are the assets of a firm and can be used to leverage the entry of the firm in the same or different product categories. Hence, the new services product can be branded under the existing brand or the organization can give an entirely new brand name to the same. These decisions are strategic and have implications for the organization as a whole. Thus, over a period of time, a company can have a number of brands in its basket of offering for consumers in the same or different product categories. This is called brand portfolio and includes all the brands and brand lines that a company has to offer in the market.

For example, the Taj Resorts and Palaces has come a long way since 1903 when it opened its first property and has since become an iconic brand envied by many. This does not mean that it was a smooth ride or the brand did not face its share of problems. On the contrary, brand managers need to constantly ensure the success of their brands, otherwise, once successful brands can ride into oblivion. Brands that are successful in a product category invite competition. This leads to entry of other players and competition heats up. The brand therefore needs to reiterate, remind, and reinforce itself to the customers, so that they are constantly reminded about the brand benefits, the needs it satisfies, and how it is superior to other brands in the same category. The success ratio for a new brand launch is only 5%. According to the Black Eye Ratio, if 10 brands are launched in a year, then only two survive and do well in 24 months and this comes down to one brand in 70 months (Pinto 2010). This shows that for an organization to have a strong brand in its portfolio, it requires effort not only prior to the launch, but post-launch as well.

The brand has to consistently deliver in an environment that is dynamic—be it consumers, competitors, or political and legal environment. There can be a number of challenges that have to be managed on the path to success for a strong brand. Organizations need to ensure good quality, keep in mind the changing consumer trends, effectively and consistently communicate with its target audience, and keep the customers feeling excited about the brand. There are various examples of brands that were once prominent and performing well but could not maintain the same performance over a period of time. To manage brands, brand knowledge of consumers for each of the brands needs to be studied. This brand knowledge of the consumers can be positive or negative. The positive knowledge and attitude needs to be enhanced through brand communications and the negative knowledge and attitude needs to be changed through repositioning of the brand. The brand also needs to create new associations that position it as the brand that connects with the target audience. The brand elements, personality, endorsers, etc. need to be studied, so that it is relevant and creates appropriate imagery for the user. While all these lead to the brand being 'current' and 'relevant' for the customers, it results in the brand being able to retain its loyal customers, and at the same time helps in attracting new customers (see Exhibit 3.4).

Exhibit 3.4 **Bata Retailing for Success**

Bata was launched in 1894 by 'Tomas Bata, in Zlin (a small town in erstwhile Czechoslovakia, now the Czech Republic)', and the Bata Shoe Company set up store in India in 1932 (Superbrands 2009). In the year 2012, 40% of the ₹25,000 crore footwear market in India (growing at a 'compounded annual growth rate of 10% a year') was organized and Bata commanded 30% of the organized footwear market. This considering the fact that the year 2004 saw sales dropping to ₹693 crore from ₹720 crore sales in 2001 (a substantial drop of 62%). The reasons were many. The market was being flooded by well designed Chinese footwear, the consumers were looking for more than just value for money, its huge stores were more like warehouses 'which did little to welcome' footfalls. As a creative director with one of the Top 5 advertising agency says, 'The product became downright boring. There was nothing on offer for the brand conscious youth. Bata had become a brand for their grandfathers'.

The company took a stock of things and when the management changed in the year 2005, a number of other things changed as well. It wanted 'to become a brand attractive to the youth and to the fashion

(Contd)

Exhibit 3.4   (Contd)

conscious.' It became a 'value for experience' brand rather than 'value for money' brand. It worked on its product designs and brands. It engaged services of known designers like Malini Ramani to design exclusive collections for Bata. This is to be followed up by engaging 3–4 designers every year to design exclusive lines for Bata. In 2012, it had 20 sub-brands in its portfolio including premium brands such as Hush Puppies, Marie Claire, etc. Concentrating on stores that were more than 3,000 sq. ft, it changed its store format. Large store meant a better merchandise display. Also, the consumer could be serviced better. The smaller stores were to be slowly phased out, existing ones moved to larger facilities in the same vicinity. The store ambience is 'more inviting and comfortable with neatly stacked racks, attractive décor, friendly yet unobtrusive sales people.' Customers can also place online orders and 'if the shoe of their choice is not available at a particular store, the company will ensure home delivery in two days.' The impact on sales was also evident and Bata moved from a loss of ₹62.7 crore in 2004 to making profits of ₹47.44 crore in 2007 and ₹95.35 crore in 2010. 'The Bata scrip gained 40% in 2011. This was among the highest gains for BS-200 companies.' According to Sushmul Maheshwari, CEO, Rncos, 'The reason Bata has been able to accomplish the turnaround is primarily due to the fact that the company has accepted that it needs to change with time.' (Garg 2012).

Companies with successful brands in their portfolio can extend them over a period of time and have a number of strong brands that need to be managed by an organization. The brand architecture helps in managing these brands strategically as it helps in listing the various brand elements being used by the organization and provides clarity for use of these brand elements. This rationalization helps in maintaining brands that have a positive brand equity and are in sync with the consumers. Also, the brands left in its portfolio of brands are according to the current demands and need trends of the market. Brand managers need to ensure the smooth and successful running of business operations for strong brand equity. If they are not able to manage the brand, they need to rationalize so that they can maintain profitability in the marketplace. If they are not being profitable or able to retain business, then they need to take corrective action and ensure the success, otherwise the brand is lost. However, this is a cyclical process and the brand managers need to consistently check that the brand is able to perform in the market. To ensure success, brand has to satisfy consumers and have features according to the current needs of the customers (see reading Music World is out of Music). The performance of these various brands needs to be monitored over time, so that organizations can effectively rationalize their brand portfolio. In the rationalization of brands, companies decide on the brands to be retained after the necessary pruning of its portfolio of brands.

Rationalization can be done using any of the following ways (Sarkar and Singh 2005):
- liquidation
- merging
- selling
- milking
- elimination
- consolidation

Liquidation is when the firm terminates business and uses its assets to discharge its liabilities. If the brand is important and the firm wishes to retain it, then it can also be *merged* with another brand. *Selling* the brand is another option and Cadbury's sale to Kraft is an example. Deriving maximum sales and *milking* the brand is another option for the firm. However, if the firm feels that selling and merging are not possible, it can *eliminate* the brand. Also, if the brand is doing well, it can further *consolidate* the brand, that is, build it further. The brands of the company are evaluated and placed on one of the lists identified before. The non-performing brands are placed in any of the first five categories and the well-performing brands are placed in the last category for consolidation. The enhancement of core brands is a well thought-out strategy and it is these brands that the company should focus on as growth drivers for the organization.

So over a period of time, brands can be revitalized by the following methods:
- Reinforce positive brand attitude by reminding factors leading to strong brand equity
- Change negative brand knowledge and attitude by repositioning
- Create new brand associations
- Increase the frequency of brand consumed
- Ensure more consumption per service
- Use line and category extension to come out with new and relevant brands for consumers
- Rationalize the brand portfolio by removing brands that are no longer relevant for the consumers

All these activities will ensure a brand that is relevant and current for the consumers.

RESEARCH INSIGHT

Significant Components of Service Brand Equity in Health Care Sector

Hardeep Chahal and Madhu Bala (2012), 'Significant components of service brand equity in health-care sector', *International Journal of Health Care Quality Assurance*, vol. 25, issue 4, pp. 343–362.

The purpose of the study is to examine three significant components of service brand equity, that is, perceived service quality, brand loyalty, and brand image—and analyze relationships among the components of brand equity and also their relationship with brand equity, which is still to be theorized and developed in the health care literature.

The findings of the study support that service brand equity in the health care sector is greatly influenced by brand loyalty and perceived quality. However, brand image has an indirect effect on service brand equity through brand loyalty (mediating variable).

The study establishes a direct and significant relationship between service brand equity and its two components, that is, perceived service quality and brand loyalty in the health care sector. It also provides directions to health care service providers in creating, enhancing, and maintaining service brand equity through service quality and brand loyalty, to sustain competitive advantage.

SUMMARY

Branding is a key issue and challenge that decides the longevity of the service in the marketplace. To be successful a brand should be able to create a differential advantage so that customers want to consume it. Strong brands connect with the customers and add value to the service. Consumers take cues about the brands from different sources that act as building blocks in developing brand equity. Factors such as brand knowledge, brand elements, and brand community contribute towards brand equity.

With so much time, effort, and money spent on building a brand, the brand needs to be nurtured over time so that benefits can be reaped for a longer period. A new service launched by the company can use the existing brand name and thus get benefits of the established brand name even at the time of launch. The portfolio of brands so developed by the services firms needs to be managed with the help of various strategies such as liquidation, merging, and selling to keep the brand revitalized.

KEY TERMS

Ambush marketing   Gaining public attention during an event and diverting attention from the official sponsors of the event.

Brand   A name, term, sign, symbol, design, or a combination of them, intended to identify the goods or services of one seller or group of sellers and to differentiate them from competitors.

Brand associations   The various cues/factors that connects the consumers to the brand.

Brand awareness   It is the ability of the consumer to recognize or recall the brand as a member of a particular product class category.

Brand elements   The brand identities used to identify and differentiate the brand.

Brand equity   Brand equity is the added value (positive or negative) endowed to a product or service due to the perception of customers towards the brand.

Brand image   The perception that the consumers have about a brand.

Brand loyalty   Brand loyalty is having a particular brand as the primary choice while making a purchase.

Brand reinforcement   Reminding consumers about the brand benefits, the needs it satisfies, and how it is superior to other products in the same category.

Brand revitalization   Rejuvenating and renewing the brands for the consumers.

Co-branding   Bundling a brand with an existing brand of the same organization (i.e., parent brand) or the existing brand of another organization to leverage the brand.

Global brand   A brand that uses a uniform marketing strategy and marketing mix in all the market it serves.

Local brand   A brand that is available in one country or a limited geographic area.

Relative perceived product quality   This refers to the customer perception of the product quality in comparison to the other products available at a given price point.

EXERCISES

Concept Review Questions

1. What are the prerequisites for the success of a services brand?
2. Evaluate the decisions that need to be taken when branding services.
3. Discuss how a services brand can be built.
4. Write a short note on brand equity. How can an organization build the equity for its brand ?
5. Discuss the need for revitalizing the brand in services organizations.

Critical Thinking Questions

1. Is it important to have brand loyal customers? Discuss the importance of brand loyalty for a services product.
2. What revitalizations strategies would you recommend to a services brand that is a market leader in its category (such as banks, airlines, quick service restaurants, fine dining restaurants, etc.)?
3. How are brand equity and brand loyalty different when both are responsible for increased sales of the service's brands?

Project Assignments

1. Identify any two new firms in a similar service industry. What are the similarities and differences in the brand offering?
2. Visit the site for a service firm and try to identify the various brand elements being used to build brand equity.
3. Identify a service firm, which has been launched within the past two years in India. Identify a similar one in China. Critically evaluate their strategies for branding their service product. Can any similarities be drawn?

CASE STUDY 1   Radio Mirchi: Riding the Music Waves*

Introduction

Radio Mirchi was launched in the year 2001 by Entertainment Network, an arm of India's largest media house, Times Group. The channel which is the pioneer in the FM space has revolutionized music listening in India. Right from the outset, Mirchi has been a pioneer and has had many a firsts to its credit. It is the only channel to have the highest number of licences; that is, 32 cities of which 14 cities have a population over two million as well as a cumulative listenership of over 25 million nationwide in 2008 (*Pitch* 2008). The channel has retained the top position in almost all the cities in which it operates through interesting programming, hiring of the right talent, and a relentless thirst for new ways of reaching and entertaining the listener.

Creating a Mass Appeal

Ever since its launch, the channel has attempted to please segments across various demographics. From catering to the spiritual with 'bhajans' early in the morning to keep the office goers entertained from 7 to 11 am in the morning and 5 pm to 9 pm in the evening. Catering to the needs of the savvy woman from 11 to 5 pm and ringing in nostalgia with old Hindi classics from 9 pm to late at night every day. The channel has programs to cater to all tastes and age groups. Over the years, the channel has achieved numerous firsts with respect to the wide variety of programs it has offered. From characters like 'Sudharshan aka Sud' and 'The Ab surds'

which bind the listener and prevent channel surfing with their riddles during breaks to the hilarious 'Mausam Mausi' who not only provides the weather updates, but also mocks the news makers. The channel has utilized innovative mediums to reach its target audience, be it the Mumbai Dabbawallas to target office goers or student clubs to gain insight into the thought process of the youth.

Launching Morning Show by Collaborating with the Dabbawallas

Radio Mirchi came up with another attractive alliance to promote its morning show 'Hello Mumbai' by collaborating with Mumbai's Dabbawallas renowned world over for their expert delivery to over 2,00,000 people per day. The channel saw a goldmine of marketing database available to the Dabbawallas which could be tapped to enhance listenership. The idea to deliver a direct mailer along with each tiffin was executed in a unique way. The channel sent out a *mirchi* (dried red chilly) to spice up the lunch with each tiffin and a sticker was pasted on the dabba stating 'For more spice tune into Hello Mumbai with RJ Harsh and get to know what's hot in Mumbai'. The four-day activity covered key areas of the city and garnered tremendous response from listeners.

Student Clubs to Tap Youth

Taking a different route to garner listenership, Radio Mirchi Chennai chose to target college goers

---

*Dr Swati Singh, Faculty, Marketing at Bharatiya Vidya Bhavan's Usha and Lakshmi Mittal Institute of Management, New Delhi. Used with permission.

by creating clubs for them rather than the more tried and tested events and road shows. The clubs christened 'Mirchi Links' provide the target audience an 'opportunity to experience' the brand as opposed to the older methods (events and road shows) that serve to provide a mere 'opportunity to see' the brand. To make the club aspirational, a number of selection steps were put into place which also served to build consciousness. As a part of the selection procedure, students had to participate in a group discussion and personal interview. The whole idea was to ensure that the members chosen fit the required profile, that is, 'a 20-year-old trendy, witty, outspoken, fun loving, intelligent, flirtatious, smart, comfortable-with-self individual who also engages in a host of extra-curricular activities, and is also socially aware.' The club took in new members after every six months and membership was restricted to first and second year students only. The presence of Mirchi Links across colleges has provided Mirchi with a continuous presence through its brand ambassadors. The members of the Mirchi Links organize a host of activities across their colleges providing the non-members with the opportunity of experiencing the brand. This in turn builds loyalty for Radio Mirchi that gets the opportunity to observe changes in the tastes and preferences of the youth first hand and adapt accordingly. Other than this, the activity has also provided Mirchi with a rich and vast database of college goers that can be utilized by brands to target this group. The channel has always utilized any opportunity that came its way either through joint promotions with other brands or by developing contests of its own to target its listeners better (Srinivasan 2004).

Promotional Alliance with Brand Leaders

The high listenership of the channel along with its thirst for experimentation has led a number of reputed brands to collaborate with it to reach their target group more effectively. In 2010, Tata DoCoMo chose Radio Mirchi for a promotional alliance to organize a unique talent hunt 'Talent Ekdum Loaded' across six cities in Maharashtra. The contest was an attempt to promote the 'Ekdum loaded' recharge launched by TATA Docomo during the same time. The contest primarily targeted the youth which are the logical target group (TG) for both the brands and therefore was conducted across 36 colleges and eight malls. The contest provided a platform to the youth to showcase their talent. Other than the opportunity to display her talent, the winner of the contest was given an opportunity to intern with Radio Mirchi for three months. The event subsequently has become an annual affair for colleges in the region thereby increasing consumer loyalty towards Radio Mirchi (Ramsay 2010).

While Tata Docomo chose to target the youth, ICICI Prudential chose the Mirchi platform to reach out households. ICICI Prudential along with Radio Mirchi organized a first of its kind fitness contest in residential societies across Mumbai, Delhi, Ahmadabad, Bengaluru, Hyderabad, and Chennai. The Chairperson, Secretary, and the winning family from the society, obviously the healthiest amongst those participating, were then invited to Radio Mirchi studios of their respective cities where they were awarded the healthiest family trophy. Prior to the beginning of the campaign, Radio Mirchi Activation shortlisted societies from across the participating cities. The criteria for selecting society were a minimum of 125 flats and a common area where the activities could be conducted. Residents were then invited for an interactive session with a leading dietician who then conducted a BMI (Body Mass Index) check. Other than this, 2–4 members of the participating families then underwent a number of fitness tests, which included games such as balancing one's body on one leg, weight lifting, skipping, push ups, etc. The winner of each game received a Har Ghar Healthy goody bag. While the activation on ground helped generate a lot of positive buzz, Mirchi build up the excitement by carrying news of the campaign and encouraging societies to participate in the event. Mirchi took the entire activity to another level by introducing a character called 'Health Havaldaar' quite dissimilar to the regular pot-bellied havaldar aka policeman that we are so used to. The task of this healthy havaldar was to identify people indulging in unhealthy eating and hand them a Healthy goody bag (Indiatelevision 2008). In an attempt to target the channel's listeners, Investors' Clinic launched an interesting contest in the year 2013. As a part of the contest the winning participant was gifted a flat and hence, the contest was appropriately called 'Flat 983'. As a part of the contest, contestants were quizzed on their knowledge on Delhi by RJ Naved. Other than the flat, the winner also got the opportunity to meet popular cricketer Yuvraj Singh at a gala ceremony organized by Radio Mirchi in Delhi. The campaign received overwhelming response to the contest with over one lakh SMS and phones being received within just 10 days of the campaign launch (RnM Team 2013). Not far behind, Kerala Tourism also realized that Mirchi was an appropriate vehicle to market the state during the monsoon.

Searching for fresh talent with RJ Hunt

Radio Mirchi began the RJ hunt, a contest to promote entry of fresh talent into the Radio industry in 2003. The contest provided the contestants with an opportunity to show case their wit, humour, passion, and personality in front of listeners who would then vote for the contestant they felt had the winning voice and charm. As a part of the contest, candidates above the age of 18 years submitted their voice samples at Mirchi Mobile studios stationed outside various malls in the city. Radio Mirchi has not only entertained listeners by these contests, but also absorbed and groomed the winning contestants. RJ Harsh, winner of the 2003 contest, hosts the morning show 'Hello Mumbai' while RJ Rohit who won the contest in 2005 hosts 'Style BHai' and 'You and I' in Mumbai. Delhi's prized possession is RJ Naved, winner of the RJ hunt in 2004 (Media Release 2006).

Awarding Advertising Excellence with Mirchi Kaan Awards

Another interesting activity to increase consumer engagement was initiated in the year 2004. The awards termed 'Mirchi Kaan Awards' were launched by Radio Mirchi with the intention of awarding excellence in radio advertising. The awards served to showcase as well as acknowledge innovative radio advertising across as many as 17 categories. The organizers received as many as 300 entries across 15 categories in 2012. Over the years, the reputation of the awards have grown in stature to make it a much coveted award and a sought after event by the advertising fraternity. Moreover, it has introduced a new sense of seriousness towards the previously neglected radio advertising (exchange4media 2013).

Heralding a New Concept with Radio Films

Another first introduced into the programming mix by the channel was the concept of radio films. The channel used the backdrop of satire and comedy to bring home public interest messages and issues that have riddled the listener. The first movie was 'Kuch Kuch Sunta Hai', a satirical spoof on films being shot on historical locations and resulting in damaging of the locations/monuments in the process. The idea behind the two hour film that was shot on location with a live audience was to highlight the apathy of the government officials in protecting these sites. Radio Mirchi managed to gain entry into the Limca Book of Records with this film. This was then followed up by another film titled 'Bijli Ki Khoj'. This radio film highlighted the electricity crisis regularly faced by Delhi and attempted to take up the issue with concerned authorities (Joshi 2006).

Entering into CSR with Audio Films

In the year 2008, Radio Mirchi in association with Mirchi Movies announced a path-breaking initiative referred to as 'Listen to my movie', wherein a childrens' movie by Mirchi Movies titled 'Hari Puttar—A comedy of terrors' was converted into an audio film for the visually impaired. The music of the same film was also released nationally and promoted across various cities in the form of special 'amplings', an audio equivalent to movie screenings (exchange4media 2008).

Digital Radio with Telecom Providers

In 2010, Radio Mirchi entered the digital media space by launching Mirchi Mobile with Bharti Airtel. The success of this venture led the channel to form alliances with Vodafone, Idea, Reliance, Docomo, BSNL, and MTS. The Mirchi Mobile enables people to stay connected to their respective cities even after they migrate to different cities upon dialling a specified number. It allows them to listen to the radio in their mother tongue. The first in this series was Mirchi Bhojpuri created to cater to a large segment of Bhojpuri-speaking audiences from Uttar Pradesh and Bihar that have migrated to other states.

Extending Innovation to Annual Reports

The channels' continuous pursuit for excellence did not stop at programming but extended into the designing of its annual report too. Unlike the normally boring and cumbersome annual reports the industry has been used to, Radio Mirchi set a precedent here too by fitting a radio set right on the cover of the report. The channel from its initial years has been known for its annual reports that are more of design statements. Its report titled 'Reimagining Radio' for the year 2011–2012 is more of a creative's delight. It won Mirchi the much coveted Gold Midas at Midas Awards, World's Best Financial Advertising for this report. The report served the purpose of a direct mailer to its shareholders explaining to them its next strategy—of going digital. It describes the channel's new drawn strength in enhancing consumer engagement across platforms such as radio, mobile, and Internet. The awards do not end here in the year 2012, the channel also won a number of other prominent industry awards such as Popular Radio Channel of the Year at Global Awards for Brand Excellence, Merit at Designomics Awards for Digital Innovation Using Technology for an on-air contest called Mirchi Music Housie, and a Bronze at Big Bang Awards (Ad club B'lore) for Excellence in Communication & Media for the Purani Jeans Direct Mailer. Besides this, its RJs happen to have the highest recall as well as fan following (Kohli 2013).

The Way Forward

A clear leader from the start, the channel has never rested on its laurels. It has continuously reinvented itself to match the ever-changing tastes and preferences of its target audience. Its brand ambassadors and the RJs have not confined themselves to the comforts of the studio but have moved out and beyond to listener's homes, exhibitions, malls, movie theatres, and college campuses to mingle with the audience and a get a real feel of what the country wants to hear. Survival in the radio space is not an easy task, the presence of numerous players, short attention spans of the listeners, and the basic nature of the industry and its guidelines that make breaking even an onerous task, all make the future challenging for Mirchi. How it will continue to spice up the air waves remains to be seen.

Questions

1. How has Radio Mirchi managed to keep track of the pulse of the target audience?
2. Which according to you have been the major brand-building activities that have enabled Mirchi to rise above competition?
3. What are the key strengths of Mirchi that have enabled it to be a preferred promotion partner for other brands?

CASE STUDY 2   Music World is out of Music

Music World brand of retail stores were launched by the RP-Sanjiv Goenka group when they opened their first store in Chennai in 1997. It revolutionized the way music was retailed in India. Customers were invited to step in, listen to hit numbers, and then pick the album. Music lovers enjoyed the experience so much that it grew to a hundred stores spread across West Bengal and the four southern states (Hindu Business Line Bureau 2013). It was a premium speciality store and retailed 'audio CDs, DVDs, gaming consoles and software, other music accessories and also home videos of leading brands'. Once it established itself it followed the franchise route in 2003 to grow further (Moitra 2012). The largest of the stores was based in Kolkata on Park Street. It was a crowd puller and this reflected in its revenues which were the highest among all the Music World retail outlets, according to Sandip Roy (Editor, Culture for Firstpost.com).

'Music World was all about the customer. An expansive 3,800 sq. ft of retail space. CDs neatly displayed for browsing. There were listening stations. Obsequious attendants in uniforms hovered around offering shopping baskets and suggestions until you told them to leave you alone. Best of all, it had air conditioning which alone probably accounted for half its foot traffic in a city as muggy as Kolkata. It was an excellent rendezvous point', according to the Telegraph Bureau. Since Suchitra Mitra inaugurated the store on 30 March 2000, the Park Street address next to Flurys has played host to the likes of Aamir Khan and Hrithik Roshan, Kareena Kapoor and Preity Zinta, provided a CD-DVD platform for all major Tollywood films, and been the favoured meeting point on Park Street for friends and family.

All was well but then the sales started to decline from 2009 and company reported losses of ₹20 crore in 2009–2010 (Moitra 2012). According to Mr Sanjay Gupta, Corporate Head, Marketing, RP-Sanjiv Goenka Group, '...The medium of delivery of music has changed. There has been a shift to digital format from the physical CDs and DVDs. The onset of digitization of music and shift in consumer preferences towards music and video downloads has rendered the business model unviable'.

According to Achille Forler, Managing Director, Universal Music Publishing 'The compact disc technology is reaching the end of its cycle. The CD player and even the iPod are being replaced by multimedia terminals like the smartphone or the tablet while the hi-fi system is being replaced by docking stations that are affordable, less bulky, and delivering acceptable sound' (Telegraph Bureau 2013). This is further evidenced by the fact that in the current business scenario, 'Kolaveri Di breaks records on YouTube and more albums are downloaded compared to those sold over-the-counter' (Hindu Business Line Bureau 2013).

All these factors had a toll on sales at Music World and dire measures were called for.

'Music World had aptly summed up its predicament in its 2010–2011 directors' report: Music industry continues to face challenges of growth in view of strong movement of digital technology. Sale of music in physical form continues to show declining trend. The company has taken various steps including shutting down of non-performing stores as well as resizing of stores to minimise loss. Exercise to further rationalize manpower and cost is being undertaken. The company is evaluating the option of repositioning itself in the changed business scenario to minimise losses.' In the year 2012, it merged the bleeding music stores chain Music World with Spencer's Retail (Moitra 2012). It reduced its stores from 100 to seven (all in West Bengal).

The steps taken by the group to turnaround the store sales, it seems, was not enough. 'Revenues dipped to ₹35–40 lakhs a month in 2013 from ₹70 lakhs a month in 2012' (ET Bureau 2013). 'Sanjiv Goenka, Group Chairman, had in May (2013) said that his overall loss in the retail segment—Spencer's, Music World, and other retail operations—stood at over ₹100 crore for the year ending March 2013. In 2011–2012, the retail operations segment reported a loss of nearly ₹238 crore (Hindu Business Line Bureau 2013). So in 2013, it decided to down shutters on all the Music World retail outlets with the Park Street flagship store being the last one to down shutter in the end of June, 2013. The retail space for the outlets was taken on lease and so the company could easily down shutter without being saddled with idle real estate. However, the company decided to retain the brand name of Music World due to the strong brand equity associated with the brand name in the mind of the consumers (ET Bureau 2013).

Questions

1. Comment on the services brand of Music World.
2. At what step of building and managing brands was Music World not able to sustain itself?
3. Check the comments of the consumers online about the closing of the store and try to evaluate what level of loyal customers can you identify for Music World.

Source: Based on the data from ET Bureau (2013), Moitra (2012), Hindu Business Line Bureau (2013), and Roy (2013).

REFERENCES

Aaker, D. (1991), *Managing Brand Equity: Capitalizing on the Value of a Brand Name*, The Free Press, New York.

Aaker, D. (1996), *Building Strong Brands*, The Free Press, New York, .

Aaker, D.A. and E. Joachimsthaler (2000), *Brand Leadership*, The Free Press, New York.

Berthon, P., M.B. Holbrook, and J.M. Hulbert (2003), 'Understanding and managing the brand space', *Sloan Management Review*, vol. 44, issue no. 2, pp. 49–54.

Business Standard (2012), 'Madras HC orders shutdown of Subhiksha: Verdict follows retail chain's failure to repay ₹40 crore to Kotak Mahindra Bank', BS Reporter, 1 March, p. 2.

Cataluna, F.J.R., A.N. Garcia, and I. Phau (2006), 'The influence of price and brand loyalty on store brands versus national brands', *International Review of Retail and Distribution and Consumer Research*, vol. 16, issue no. 4, pp. 433–52.

Datta, P.R. (2003), 'The determinants of brand loyalty', *The Journal of American Academy of Business, Cambridge*, vol. 3, issue no. 1/2 pp. 138–44.

de Chernatony, L. (2001), 'A model for strategically building brands', *Journal of Brand Management*, vol. 9, issue no. 1, pp. 32–44.

Economic Times Bureau (2013), 'Out of Tune, Music World to shut shop', *Economic Times*, New Delhi, p. 4.

Ellwood, I. (2002), *The Essential Brand Book*, Kogan Page, London.

Faircloth, J.B., L.M. Capella, and B.L. Alford (2001), 'The effect of brand attitude and brand image on brand equity', *Journal of Marketing Theory and Practice*, vol. 9, issue no. 3, pp. 61–75.

Garg, Swati (2012), 'In step with the times: Bata is aiming to be a brand attractive to the youth and to the fashion conscious', The Strategist, *Business Standard*, New Delhi, 30 January, p. 1.

Hoeffler, S. and K.L. Keller (2002), 'Building brand equity through corporate societal marketing', *Journal of Public Policy and Marketing*, vol. 21, issue no. 1, pp. 78–89.

Jevons, C., M. Gabbon, and L. de Chernatony (2005), 'Customer and brand manager perspectives on brand relationships: a conceptual framework', *Journal of Product and Brand Management*, vol. 14, issue no. 4/5, pp. 300–09.

Kapferer, J.N. and V. Bastien (2009), 'The specificity of luxury management: turning marketing upside down', *Journal of Brand Management*, vol. 16, issue no. 5/6, pp. 311–22.

Keller, K.L. (1993), 'Conceptualizing, measuring and managing customer-based brand equity', *Journal of Marketing*, vol. 57, pp. 1–22.

Keller, K.L. (2003), *Strategic Brand Management*, Pearson, Delhi.

Keller, K.L. (2004), *Strategic Brand Management: Building, Measuring and Managing Brand Equity*, Prentice-Hall of India Private Limited, New Delhi.

Keller, K.L. (2005), 'Choosing the right brand elements and leveraging secondary associations will help marketers build brand equity', *Marketing Management*, vol. September–October, pp. 18–23.

Kim, J., J.D. Morris, and J. Swait (2008) 'Antecedents of true brand loyalty', *Journal of Advertising*, vol. 3, issue no. 2, pp. 99–117.

Kotler, P. (2002), *Marketing Management*, Prentice Hall, New Delhi.

Kotler, P. (2003), *Marketing Management*, Prentice Hall, London.

Kotler, P. and K.L. Keller (2006), *Marketing Management*, 12th Edition, Prentice-Hall of India, New Delhi.

Kressmann, F., Sirgy, M. J., Hermann, A., Huber, F.; Huber, S. and Lee, D J (2006), 'Direct and indirect effects of self-image congruence on brand loyalty', *Journal of Business Research*, vol. 59, pp. 955–64.

Krishnamurthi, L. and S.P. Raj (1991), 'An empirical analysis of the relationship between brand loyalty and consumer price elasticity', *Marketing Science*, vol. 10, issue no. 2, pp. 172–83.

Levine, M. (2003), *A Branded World*, John Wiley, New Jersey.

Malviya, Sagar (2013), 'At the sales counter: Indians can't have enough of Zara', *Economic Times*, New Delhi, pp. 4.

Mascarenhas, O.A., R. Kesavan, and M. Bernacchi (2006), 'Lasting customer loyalty: a total customer experience approach', *Journal of Consumer Marketing*, vol. 23, issue no. 7, pp. 397–405.

Mathur, L.K. and I. Mathur (1995), 'The effect of slogan changes on the market values of firms', *Journal of Advertising Research*, vol. 35, issue no. 1, pp. 59–65.

Parameswaran, A.M.G. (2010), 'You can make a brand out of any commodity', *The Economic Times*, New Delhi, 22 November, p. 4.

Pinto, V.S. (2010), 'India sees three brand launches a day, but only 5 per cent survive', *Business Standard*, 17 July, p. 1.

Ramaswamy and Namakumari (2009), *Marketing Management*, Macmillan.

Reichheld, F. and W.E. Jr. Sasser (1990), 'Zero defections: quality comes to services', *Harvard Business Review*, vol. 68, issue no. 5, pp. 105–11.

Ries, A. and L. Ries (1999), 'World-class brands', *Executive Excellence*, vol. 16, issue no. 3, p. 11.

Rio, A.B., R. Vazquez, and V. Iglesias (2001), 'The role of the brand name in obtaining differential advantages', *Journal of Product and Brand Management*, vol. 10, issue no. 7, pp. 452–65.

Ritson, M. (2009), 'When a firm pays price for brand contradiction: scandals involving PwC in India and the US could well harm its global brand', *The Economic Times*, New Delhi, 3 November, p. 4.

Rundle-Thiele, S. and R. Bennet (2001), 'A brand for all seasons? A discussion of brand loyalty approaches and their applicability for different markets', *Journal of Product and Brand Management*, vol. 10, issue no. 1, pp. 25–37.

Samiee, S. (1994), 'Customer evaluation of products in global market', *Journal of International Business Studies*, vol. 25, issue no. 3, pp. 579–604.

Sarkar, A.N. and J. Singh (2005), 'New paradigm in evolving brand management strategy', *Journal of Management Research*, vol. 5, issue no. 2, pp. 80–90.

Sheth, J.N., B. Mittal, and B.I. Newman (1999), *Consumer Behavior*, Harbor Drive, Orlando, Dryden.

Simoes, C. and S. Dibb (2001), 'Rethinking the brand concept: New brand orientation', *Corporate Communications: An International Journal*, vol. 6, issue no. 4, pp. 217–24.

Singh, S. (1997), *Right Brain Positioning in Strategic Marketing*, Indian Institute of Management, Calcutta.

Singhal, A. (2004), 'Creating and preserving brand', *Strategic Brand Management*, vol. 3, issue no. 5, pp. 18–21.

Superbrands 2009, Superbrands: An insight into India's strongest consumer brands, Volume III, Superbrands India Private Limited, Gurgaon.

Tauber, E.M. (1988), 'Brand leverage: strategy for growth in a cost-controlled world', *Journal of Advertising Research*, vol. 28, issue no. 4, pp. 26–30.

Tybout, A. M. and G. S. Carpenter (2006), *Creating and Managing Brands in Kellogg on Marketing*, Wiley India, New Delhi.

Verma, H. (2009), *Brand Management Text and Cases*, 2nd Edition, Excel Books, New Delhi.

Yoo, B. and N. Donthu (2001) 'Developing and validating a multidimensional consumer-based brand equity scale', *Journal of Business Research*, vol. 52, issue no. 1, pp. 1–14.

exchange4media (2008), 'Radio Mirchi's CSR initiative to make visually impaired "listen" to Hari Puttar', available from http://www.exchange4media.com/news/story.aspx?Section_id=7&News_id=32342, accessed on 12 July 2013.

exchange4media (2013), 'Radio Mirchi invites entries for 10th edition of Kaan Awards', available from http://www.exchange4media.com/51347_radio-mirchi-invites-entries-for-10th-edition-of-kaan-awards.html, accessed on 12 August 2013.

Hindu Business Line Bureau (2013), available from http://www.thehindubusinessline.com/companies/music-world-falls-silent/article4807599.ece, accessed on 3 August 2013.

http://www.bharatmatrimony.com/successful-years.php, accessed on 20 August 2013.

http://www.licindia.com/history.htm, accessed on 2 April 2008.

http://www.tanishq.co.in/tanishq_aboutus.html, accessed on 28 April 2008.

http://www.tajhotels.com/About-Taj/Company-Information/Default.html, accessed on 19 December 2014.

Indiatelevision (2004), 'Radio Mirchi partners with Dabbawallas', available from http://www.indiantelevision.com/mam/headlines/y2k4/july/julymam38.htm, accessed on 20 August 2013.

Indiatelevision (2008), 'Radio Mirchi 98.3FM and ICICI Prudential Health Solutions announces winners of Har Ghar Healthy', available from http://www.indiantelevision.com/release/y2k8/mar/marrel69.php, accessed on 21 August 2013.

Inditex (2013), available from http://www.inditex.com/en/who_we_are/concepts/zara, accessed on 20 August 2013.

Joshi, P. (2006), 'Radio's creative notes', http://www.business-standard.com/article/beyond-business/radio-s-creative-notes-106122301016_1.html, accessed on 12 July 2013.

Kohli, A. (2013), 'In pursuit of excellence and innovation: Mirchi's Prashant Pandey,' available from http://www.adgully.com/exclusive-in-pursuit-of-excellence-and-innovation-mirchi-s-prashant-pandey-52961.html, accessed on 12 July 2013.

Law, Abhishek (2013), 'Music World to shut down operations', available from http://www.thehindubusinessline.com/companies/music-world-to-shut-down-operations/article4807138.ece, accessed on 15 August 2013.

Media Release (2006), 'Radio Mirchi 98.3 FM presents RJ Hunt', available from http://www.afaqs.com/news/company_briefs/index.html?id=7512_Radio+Mirchi+98.3+FM+presents+RJ+Hunt, accessed on 12 August 2013.

Moitra, S. (2012), 'CESC to merge Music World, Spencer's', available from http://www.dnaindia.com/money/1665623/report-cesc-to-merge-music-world-spencers, accessed on 3 August 2013.

Pitch (2008), 'India's top 50 service brands: Radio Mirchi: singing supreme!', available from http://pitchonnet.com/blog/2008/10/06/pitch-5th-anniversary-2008-indias-top-50-service-brands-radio-mirchi-singing-supreme/, accessed on 4 August 2013.

PTI (2013), 'Tanishq eyes for 27% growth in revenue', *Economic Times*, available from http://articles.economictimes.indiatimes.com/2013-07-01/news/40307860_1_jewellery-business-tanishq-vice-president-marketing-sandeep-kulhalli, accessed on 21 August 2013.

Ramsay, S. (2010), 'Mirchi Activation and TATA Docomo present Talent Ekdum Loaded', available from http://www.eventfaqs.com/eventfaqs/wcms/en/home/news/Mirchi-Activation-and-TATA-Doc-1287030183868.html, accessed on 12 July 2013.

RnM Team (2013), 'Radio Mirchi announces Aliziya Elvi as the winner of contest FLAT 983', available from http://www.radioandmusic.com/content/editorial/news-releases/radio-mirchi-announces-aliziya-elvi-winner-contest-flat-983, accessed on 14 August 2013.

Roy, Sandip (2013), 'Goodbye Music World: A confession of embarrassed nostalgia', available from http://www.firstpost.com/business/goodbye-music-world-a-confession-of-embarrassed-nostalgia-868689.html, accessed on 10 August 2013.

Srinivasan, S. (2004), 'Radio Mirchi to drive loyalty with students' club', available from http://www.thehindubusinessline.in/2004/06/22/stories/2004062200770900.htm, accessed on 12 July 2013.

Telegraph Bureau (2013), 'Virtual logs out real music store: Curtains for Park Street landmark,' available from http://www.telegraphindia.com/1130613/jsp/calcutta/story_17002459.jsp#.Ugoaf9IsCfl accessed on 10 August 2013.

4 Marketing Research

OBJECTIVES

After reading this chapter you will be able to understand the

- concept of marketing research
- importance of marketing research for management
- influence of the Internet on marketing research
- developments in the Indian and global marketing research industry
- problems in marketing research
- upcoming trends in marketing research over the next decades

What's Your Competitor Doing?

Market research now has a new dimension. It is competitive intelligence (CI), that is, knowing what your competitors are doing about their business and customers, as well as yours. It is a fact that the competition is always looking to get your customers, while you want to retain yours and get theirs. It's the need of the hour for market agencies to provide hard 'intelligent' facts to their companies. Strategic intelligence is about knowing 'why' and 'how' the market affects you. Facts state that market data and information are available to most companies but 80% of it is unstructured. Thus, this data may not be relevant and remain unprocessed. What is important now is to convert this data into intelligence, analyse it, and arrive at an actionable strategy.

It is extremely crucial for companies nowadays to pick up relevant information regarding their customers, market movements, changes in technology and trends, competitors, their strategy, their customer feedback, and so on. This process is ongoing and needs to be updated time and again.

This will, in turn, help a company to become proactive and not reactive to market changes. Indian firms are considered short-sighted and seem more interested in working towards immediate goals. They currently do not feel the need for CI because there is room for everyone. However, in about 8–10 years, market penetration is going to be deep, leading to 90% saturation.

It is time for companies to realize the need for CI-based marketing and strategy as these are going to be the key to survival of companies across industry sectors.

After going through the chapter, you will be able to answer the following questions:
1. How does listening to customers help an organization?

2. What are the benefits of marketing research?

INTRODUCTION

The discipline of marketing begins and centres on customer needs. The domain of marketing extends to numerous areas such as researching for development of new ideas for product development; various elements of marketing mix such as product, price, place, promotion, after-sales services, and channels related to setting up customer relationship processes. Marketing research covers all such areas of research related to the domain of marketing. As issues of return on investment become increasingly important, firms compete fiercely for a space in the customer's choice criterion. As the competition becomes intense, they compete with each other to discover the parameters that can keep them ahead of others. Marketing research provides insights into customer and market dynamics.

Marketing research is evolving as a discipline. The most profound effect on marketing research has been the advent of the Internet, globalization (Struce 1999–2000), newer forms of data collection, and developments in data analysis and predictive tools. This chapter presents an overview of marketing research and leads to an understanding of why marketing research is important for service providers.

The American Marketing Association defines marketing research as follows: 'Marketing research is a function that links the consumer, customer, and public to the marketer through information—information used to identify and define marketing opportunities and problems; generate, refine, and evaluate marketing actions; monitor marketing performance; and improve understanding of marketing as a process. Marketing research specifies the information required to address these issues, designs the method of collecting information, manages and implements the data collection process, and analyses and communicates the findings and their implications'.

As Aaker et al. (1998) have elaborated, this definition highlights the role of marketing research as an aid to decision-making. Too often, marketing research is considered narrowly as the gathering and analysis of data for someone else to use. Firms can achieve and sustain competitive advantage through the creative use of market information. Hence, marketing research is defined as an information input to decisions, and not simply the evaluation of decisions that have been made. Market research alone does not guarantee success; the intelligent use of marketing research is the key to business achievement. A competitive edge is more the result of how information is used than of who does or does not have the information (Boughton 1992).

As the name suggests, marketing research signifies research in the area of marketing. Research per se signifies the scientific technique of data collection, analysis, and presentation of information. When a research technique is applied to the area of marketing, it signifies research pertaining to the following—identification of consumer needs, development of product as well as decisions related to the product, namely, packaging, branding, positioning, pricing strategies, distribution aspects, promotion potential estimation, demand forecasting, customer analysis, monitoring performance, competition analysis, and after-sales feedback. The scope of marketing is the scope for marketing research.

Parasuraman et al. (1985) defines marketing research as a set of techniques and principles for systematically collecting, recording, analysing, and interpreting data that can aid decision-makers involved in marketing goods, services, or ideas. This definition stresses on both the techniques and principles of marketing research. It also emphasizes the importance of data collection and analysis. It suggests that marketing research is an aid to decision-makers.

MARKETING RESEARCH AND MANAGEMENT

Marketing research can be viewed as playing three functional roles—descriptive, diagnostic, and predictive (McDaniel and Gates 1999). The *descriptive role* is about gathering facts and figures, such as, what are the sales for various product categories? What do people buy? How much investment is made on education in urban and rural areas? The second role of research is the *diagnostic function* wherein the data or actions are explained. What happened when pricing was changed? What was the effect of change of the size or shape of the product? What was the impact on demand when the new promotions were launched? The third role is the *predictive function* of research. This helps policy makers to make decisions about the products or service offerings based on data collected and analysis of the same.

Marketing research is an expensive exercise and requires commitment of funds on the part of the marketer. New product development especially is a long drawn process and the success rate is very small. The challenge for service providers is, therefore, to decide the attributes or operations related aspects that should be included in the services, which could lead to higher acceptance by the consumers.

Marketing research could help service providers understand the customers' perception of quality. 'Return on quality' is important for service providers. It is the management objective based on the twin principles—(1) that the quality being delivered is the quality the target market desires; and (2) that quality must have a positive impact on the profitability. The key to making returns on quality work is marketing research. It is the mechanism that enables organizations to determine what types and forms of quality are important to the target market. Marketing research can sometimes force marketers to abandon their cherished beliefs.

In a research quoted by McDaniel and Gates (1999), 'United Parcel Service had always assumed that on-time delivery was the paramount concern of its customers; everything else came second. Before long UPS's definition of quality centred almost exclusively on the results of time and motion studies. Everything else came second. Knowing the average time it took elevator doors to open on a city block and figuring how long it took people to answer their doorbells were critical parts of the quality equation. So was pushing drivers to meet exacting schedules. The problem was UPS's marketing research was asking the wrong questions. Its survey asked customers if they were pleased with delivery time and whether they thought delivery could be faster.

On further probing, it was discovered that the clients were not as obsessed with on-time delivery as it was thought. On the other hand, the customers wanted more interaction with the drivers—the only face-to-face contact any of them had with the company. If drivers were less hurried and more willing to chat, customers would get some practical advice on shipping.' This means 'listening to customers' is an important part of managing services.

LISTENING TO CUSTOMERS

'Listening to customers' means that a company must try to reach the customer. Prevalence of social media makes customers vocal and they do not hesitate to voice their opinions. It is also essential to reach out to as many customers as possible. In services, a business is contingent on satisfying and knowing the customers. Additionally, corporates need to ensure that customers do not slip between cracks.

Without customer feedback, a service company could not possibly meet the service needs of the customers. Consequently, this would impact both the bottom line of the company and its customer base. A well-structured customer survey can act as an indicator that the company is willing to listen to them. There are times when the customer wishes to be heard. He/she may have issues about a particular aspect of a company. Not all customers wish to abandon the company and many of them wish to give a chance to the company to improve things. They therefore wish to voice their opinion how things can be improved. A service company therefore needs to understand why the customers are trying to contact it. It is imperative that as a company it should connect with the customer's emotional status and provide a service that creates a critical emotional connect with the customer's personal circumstances. An easy way for a service company is to engage a set of customers through surveys to help it formulate a strategy that could help it to

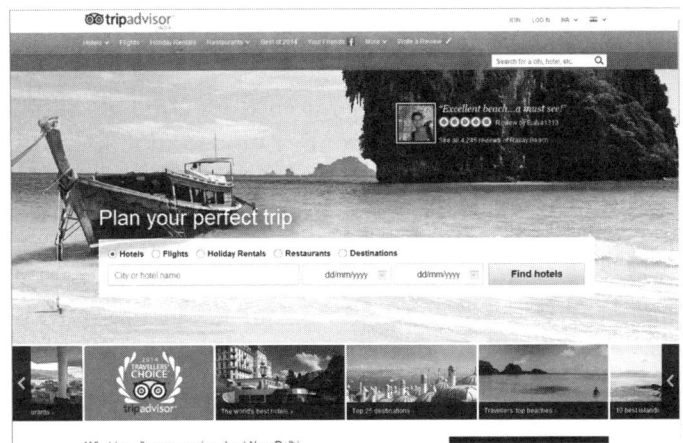

The reviews on tripadvisor.com are an important source of information for travellers.

Source: Tripadvisor LLC (2014). All rights reserved.

meet and exceed customer expectations. It would be wise for the company to listen to its customers and get a feedback because in addition to their opinions they also at times give some great out-of-the-box ideas. If a high percentage of customers suggest a similar thing then it would benefit the company to incorporate these suggestions and satisfy its customers as well those who have not spoken out so far. Many a time a company may need to draw attention to itself by reaching out to its customers through market surveys.

Service companies use various traditional and non-traditional methods to reach out to their customers.

Significance of Customer Feedback in Services Industry

Let us now try to understand the importance of customer feedback in services.

Determining customer requirements   This is especially true for those service companies such as airlines, hotels, banks, or utilities that would want to introduce new products. They often use techniques to classify people, objects, or variables into more homogeneous groups. Additionally, these techniques allow deeper understanding of the market. And therefore, greatly aid messaging and new product development by targeting homogeneous groups.

Benchmarking   As a service company it is vital to understand how your company's products and services excel or fall short as compared to its alternatives in the market. This would help the service company to further fine-tune or do away certain tangible or intangible product features.

Evaluating how your employees treat your customers   A function most overlooked in a large number of customer surveys is the way the company employees or representatives treat and behave with customers. A service company would do well to fill in the gaps created by deficient personnel interactions with the client through sensitivity training, knowledge proficiency of the employee, training in crisis management skills, and empowering the employees. It would further be extremely prudent to weed out those employees who do not have the right attitude or are found lacking in customer care.

Customer retention   Customer retention is an extremely important need of the service companies, especially when it is becoming more and more difficult to attract clients in a current market scenario. This makes it all the more important for the companies to carry out surveys on/about lost customers to identify the reasons as to why they have left the company with the aim of winning back the customers' trust and business. These surveys can help a service company to (i) segregate the product offerings, (ii) identify deficiency in bundling of services, (iii) offer features like 'pay for what you use', and (iv) identify the gaps or opportunities to introduce new complimentary products and services.

Identification of technological trends among the consumers   It would benefit a service company to keep itself posted about the emerging technology trends that are affecting current and prospective clients, especially if your service segment is sensitive to such technological innovations. Industries like hospitality, which are known for their old-world charm and human touch can do better if they are able to connect with the emerging new generation traveller who is looking for both privacy and pampering. It is not surprising that a lot of hotel properties have started to find a new balance between gracious charm and cutting-edge technology for the discerning customer of the new generation.

Until recently, majority of the messages from customers' complaints and queries on social platforms, could not be responded to by the service companies owing to the functionality gap in 'social listening' platforms, because of which service companies could not respond to the complaint in real time. Of late, numerous online social listening tools have opened up this space for the service to optimally exploit the service markets. Tools such as Social Dynamix, LiveOps Social, Salesforce Social Hub, Social Media Spaces by Moxie Software, Social CRM by Parature, etc., are now becoming part of the everyday lexicon of service providers.

A study published in Harvard Business Review suggests that customers do not tolerate a rushed and inconvenient service, and instead, they look for a satisfying experience. This study further quotes that customers are more likely to prefer knowledgeable frontline workers and on *call-and-done* interaction above all other factors and dimensions. Therefore companies that could provide this experience will win in the end. Additionally, aspects such as involvement, speed, courtesy availability, satisfaction, can-do attitude, honesty, skilled service, and appreciation can go a very long way in customer retention (Dougherty and Murthy 2009).

In order to appreciate customer's experience, a manager should draw upon different sources of information such as behavioural data gathered through self-service channels, customer satisfaction surveys, and recorded customer-agent interactions.

According to Honomichl (1996), the factors that influence a manager's decision to use research information are (i) research quality, (ii) conformity with prior expectations, (iii) clarity of presentation, (iv) political acceptability within the firm, and (v) challenge to the status quo.

Additionally, companies must rework practices to give company representatives, both call centre or otherwise, the authority to expedite individual customers' requirements and create satisfactory and positive customer experience.

Benefits of Marketing Research

Marketing research enables an organization to get insights into the dynamics of the markets, measure the impact of business environment changes, get perspectives on the service elements mix, and enable service providers to evaluate their strategies, monitor sales patterns, customer behaviour, and future ideas for new service offerings (Exhibit 4.1). The findings of the research may help organizations to take decisions about further investments in products and markets. It may give clues on initiating new interventions for managing their customers better. Market research provides answers to numerous questions such as:

- What will be the demand for my service?
- What should the service features be?
- What price will be able to generate higher sales?
- What should be the target market?
- What are the geographical areas which my firm should target?

Exhibit 4.1 **The Scope of Marketing Research**

The scope of marketing research extends across the following domains:

Sales analysis
- Measurement of market potential
- Determination of market characteristics
- Market share estimation
- Emerging buying trends
- Geographical analysis of sales

Sales methods and policies
- Evaluating alternate ways of reaching the consumer
- Effectiveness of direct selling
- Effectiveness of e-selling

Service product management
- Are the current service options enough?
- What are the consumer preferences?

Processes measurement
- Do the delivery processes need to be altered?
- What would make the delivery schedules faster and more effective?
- What should be the delivery time for each critical activity in the entire service delivery process?

Pricing-related research
- What should be the prices of various services?
- Can price bundling be initiated?
- What would be the impact of changing the prices on the mind of the consumer?

People management
- How do consumers perceive the service level of the employees?
- How do consumers perceive the service delivery?
- How has the people factor been a criterion in the choice of their decision?

Place-related issues
- What should be the mix of real-time service delivery options and the online delivery options?
- Are consumers happy with the use of technology in service delivery?
- What new interventions could be initiated to make the service more user-friendly?
- How many new outlets should be opened?
- Which new areas should be targeted for expansion?

Promotion
- Which combination of promotion techniques should be used?
- Which one is more effective?
- What is the potential of sales through online channels?
- How effective is the promotional strategy? What kind of images are created in the mind of the consumer?

Physical evidence
- To explore moments of truth for the consumer.
- What were the positive aspects about the point of consumer contact?
- Which areas of service delivery location need to improve?

- What media should I use for promoting my products?
- How satisfied are the customers with our services?
- How many customers stop using our services every month?
- How many new customers are added?
- What impact will the new technology have on the usage pattern of our services?

The above indicated areas are very valued by the customer and hence it is important that firms make investments in marketing research.

Marketers also need to study the cultural dimensions of their service delivery. For instance, McDonald's studied the religious and cultural practices in India and initiated the 'Navratra week' wherein no non-vegetarian meals are served in any of their outlets. Radisson Hotels, a Carlson brand, started a new fine-dining restaurant in India named, 'The Great Kebab Factory'. This concept became an instant success and thereby, franchising operations started for this chain both as a standalone restaurant in India, as well as the Middle East. The idea, based on research conducted in various culinary traditions across various states in India, was to serve kebabs either as a non-vegetarian or vegetarian option and continuously service numerous helpings.

TECHNIQUES OF MARKETING RESEARCH FOR SERVICES FIRM

In the services industry customer satisfaction depends directly on how immediately a service encounter is managed and monitored by the service provider. It is therefore imperative (as mentioned in this chapter) that complex organizational and strategic issues must be resolved if the service delivery is to be effective. Weiner (1985) concluded that people often engage in 'spontaneous causal thinking' especially in the cases of negative (service) encounter. Weiner, attributed this behaviour to three dimensions namely—locus (who is responsible for the event?), control (did the responsible party have control over the cause?), and stability (is the cause likely to recur?). It is therefore not surprising that over the period of time, service companies have become obsessed with what the consumer thinks before, during, and after the service encounter.

However, in addition to the traditional market research techniques, which have been tried and tested over a long period of time, the new buzzword in service research is 'big-data'. It has also caught the fancy of the service marketers, who often talk about being 'data-driven'. Simply put, big data is a universal term for a collection of data set(s), which are very large and complex. These are therefore difficult to process by using traditional tools of database management or existing data processing applications.

Big data should however not be confused with business intelligence, which uses descriptive statistics with high information density data to measure or detect trends. Instead, big data uses concepts from non-linear system identification and inductive statistics to infer laws (regressions, non-linear relationships, and causal effects) from large data sets to reveal relationships, dependencies, and perform predictions of outcomes and behaviours.

Besides numerous government agencies, research development organizations, ICT, and development technology companies, private sector, especially the services sector (e.g., eBay, Facebook, and Walmart), real estate sector, and fraud detection systems around the world have taken to this concept.

Numerous big data software include Platfora-Platfora Inc, Hadoop-Apache foundation, SAP HANA-SAP AG, Datameer-Datameer Inc., FICO® Blaze Advisor®-FICO, Spark-Apache Foundation, Splunk-Splunk Inc., Tableau-Tableau Inc., Aster–Teradata Inc., HPCC-Lexis Nexis, and HP Vertica – HP.

However, data is useless if proper techniques are not used and the expected outcomes are not achieved.

The following market research techniques are at the disposal of a marketer.

Conjoint-analysis/choice modelling   It is a statistical technique used in market research to determine how people value different features that make up an individual product or service.

Structural equation modelling (SEM)   It is a series of statistical methods that allow complex relationships between one or more independent variables and one or more dependent variables.

Factor analysis   It is a process in which the values of observed data are expressed as functions of a number of possible causes in order to find which are the most important.

Discriminate analysis   A statistical process that links the probability of default to a specified set of financial ratios.

Price sensitivity measurement (PSM)   It is a market technique for determining consumer price preferences. It was introduced in 1976 by Dutch economist Peter van Westendorp. The technique has been used by a wide variety of researchers in the market research industry.

Perceptual mapping/or multidimensional scaling   It is a diagrammatic technique used by asset marketers that attempts to visually display the perceptions of customers or potential customers. Typically, the position of a product, product line, brand, or company is displayed relative to their competition.

Simple and multiple regression analysis   It is a statistical technique that predicts values of one variable on the basis of one or more other variables.

Cluster analysis   It is the task of grouping a set of objects in such a way that objects in the same group (called a cluster) are more similar (in some sense or another) to each other than to those in other groups (clusters).

Each of these techniques has its unique features and can be used variously for price elasticity, customer satisfaction and loyalty studies, predicting market behaviour based on demographics and psychographics, etc.

Marketers often use various statistical methods to interpret collected data such as frequency distribution, descriptive statistics, comparing means or statistical testing, cross tabulation or pivot tables, correlations, linear regression, and text analytics. Marketers effectively use technology to automate the management of large and complex market data tables and forecasts in order to enhance competitive advantage and capture the customer base, besides achieving long-term sustainable growth. Techniques and associated analytics provide incisive business insight into emerging trends and shifting consumer behavior to marketers.

Let us look at Exhibit 4.2 to understand the current trends in marketing research.

Exhibit 4.2   **How Companies Use Market Research to Pivot Their Businesses**

A company pivots when it changes some aspect of its business in a fundamental way. Sometimes, a company will simply pivot by stressing a new feature on the same product. Other companies shift focus on an entirely new customer base. Still others change their entire business overnight. Successful pivoting is about leveraging the good elements of the company and doing away with the bad. The best pivots reveal the great research and innovation behind a misdirected initial bet. Bad pivots try to justify doomed businesses that simply need to admit failure. As always, staying on top of market research, even as the company grows and develops, is the key to identify if and when there is a need to pivot. Given below are a few famous examples of successful pivots, and the market research that helped make the decision.

Twitter: pivoted from Odeo   In 2005, Evan Williams and Biz Stone designed a platform to create, browse, and share podcasts. They were betting that podcasting would become a mainstream medium for sharing news and broadcasting opinion. They would eventually be proven correct, but not before Apple launched podcast support for iTunes in June. Williams and Stone took a step back and researched the new market, exploring user adoption rates, technology, and customer acquisition costs. They concluded that they had no real chance of competing against Apple. Crucially, however, they did not simply give up. They realized that the platform they had built had tremendous scalability and potential. Suppose they doubled-down on simplicity, and just made a portal where people could share what they were up to. They looked at existing social networks like Facebook, and researched customer dissatisfaction. Users loved Facebook for photo-sharing and friend-snooping, but often found the news feed to be overwhelming and cluttered. In this space, their new venture, Twitter, would provide a back-to-the-basics feed of information, with a focus on news and celebrities. It seemed crazy, but they pulled it off, accomplishing one of the most successful pivots of the 21st century.

Instagram: pivoted from Odeo   Kevin Systrom and Mike Krieger put a full year of work into a new location-based, check-in app called Burbn, even developing a full-fledged iPhone app. After releasing the app, the team wisely chose to re-evaluate the market. Systrom felt that 'it felt cluttered and overrun with features'. He and Krieger also faced the reality that they were late to the game in a trendy space already dominated by Foursquare. They removed almost all of their features, leaving only photos, commenting, and liking. They rebranded their business as Instagram. By looking closely at the market, understanding their strengths, and researching competitors, they were able to make the right call. The rest is history. Facebook bought Instagram in late 2012 for nearly three quarters of $1 billion in cash and stock.

YouTube   YouTube began as a video dating site called Tune In Hook Up. Founders Chad Hurley, Steve Chen, and Jawed Karim were disappointed with limited traction, but then they had another idea. After the Janet Jackson Super Bowl fiasco, they realized that finding proper videos online was surprisingly difficult. In addition, even when you could find one, the sites were buggy and unreliable. In addition, sharing a video was a chore as video email attachments were unreliable and most sites failed to provide dedicated video links.

The trio set out to solve these problems, instead of trying to compete in an already-crowded space. They researched the market and determined that they had a great shot at solving online video better than anyone else. In 2006, Google bought YouTube for $1.65 billion.

Before taking a decision to shut down the business or spend years trying to make a dying business work—it is better to step back, take stock of the market, do more research, and determine whether a pivot can save the company. It just might be the smartest decision ever made.

WHEN SHOULD A SERVICE FIRM NOT CONDUCT MARKET RESEARCH?

There are situations when market research should not be carried out. These could be related to the following situations:

1. The decision related to the service has already been taken and research is being done in order to be politically correct. This is merely a waste of resources.
2. There is ambiguity about the objectives of conducting research.
3. The data collected is not put to much use. Data collection is an ardous exercise and if this is not used, then resources should not be wasted on data collection efforts.
4. In case the sample does not represent the desired population aimed to be covered by the study, it will result in erroneous outcomes.

Mistakes Made by the Marketer

Following are some of the mistakes made by marketers:

- Jumping to conclusions: The biggest sin marketers commit is jumping to a conclusion first and then commissioning research to back up the idea. This attitude can lead to inherent bias and the research questions may be geared to give marketers precisely the answers they want to hear. The very purpose of research is thus negated.
- Lack of clear cut objectives for conducting research: There may be a situation wherein the objectives are not very well defined. In this context, the scope of research will not clearly map out the domain of the areas which need to be covered and hence, there may be a lot of ambiguity in conducting the research. In the end, when action needs to be taken on the research conducted, then information on some aspects may be missing.
- Misconception: Research findings are entirely different from what the marketer wants to believe. For example, in India, the misconception was that the beauty products market was essentially targeted at the female segment, whereas the male segment has emerged as a key user in this market.
- Identification of wrong market: Many marketers falter by ignoring category research before specific research. It makes sense to understand the dimensions of a category research clearly.
- Single research exercise: The other common hurdle in the way of effective research is trying to cover too much area in a single research exercise.
- Instrument: The instrument selected may be flawed and may have numerous errors. The sequence may not be correct or it may have double-barrelled questions, which use words such as 'and' or 'or', that may yield responses to number of questions and the conclusions drawn would not be appropriate. For example consider the following question:

    Were you happy with the food and the service when you dined at the restaurant?
1. Yes   2. No   3. Neutral

    Here there will be an ambiguity in the question as we are asking both for quality of food and service at the same time. If a closed-ended response is required, we would not know whether the person referred to food or service. The person may be happy with the food but not with the service or may be happy with service but not food.

- Flaws: The sampling method may be flawed and the sample may not represent the true population.
- Size: The size of the sample also matters. Choosing smaller samples may result in erroneous conclusions.
- Techniques: The data analysis tools have to be used with care. Using wrong techniques, wherein basic assumptions of testing are not met, may reflect in wrong analysis of the whole situation.
- Giving a general brief without quantifying the specific areas that need to be checked. The marketer is unable to decide what he/she actually wants to get researched. Thus, the brief tends to point in too many different directions, which may lead to inadequate outcomes.

INFLUENCE OF THE INTERNET ON CONDUCTING MARKETING RESEARCH

The Internet is a major phenomenon in the world. As the use of the Internet spreads, e-commerce will also increase. It is important for firms to understand the nature and characteristics of business conducted through the Internet. The conduct of business using online technologies depends on the infrastructure available in a region or country, as well as aspects such as the availability of PCs, bandwidth, and education profile, among other factors. Figure 4.1 provides an indication of the Internet penetration by region across various parts of the world. As it can be observed from the figure, the penetration of Internet is the highest in North America as compared to other parts of the world.

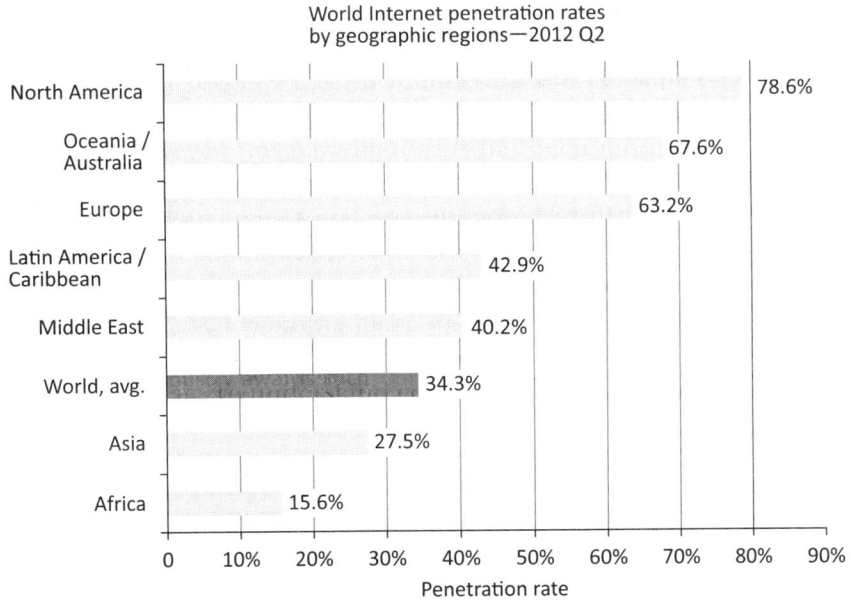

Fig. 4.1   Internet penetration by region in 2012 Q2

Source: Internet world stats—www.internetworldstats.com/stats.htm

The mobile sector has witnessed high growth rate especially in the emerging markets, which are the major engines of mobile connection and subscriber growth—in particular, Asia Pacific will add nearly half of all new connections between now and 2017 (1.4 billion) and will remain at just under 50% of both global connections and subscribers. Latin America and Africa combined will add the next 20%, representing 595 million new connections (AT Kearney 2013).

If one looks at the number of main telephone lines per 100 inhabitants, in 2013, USA had 57.15 lines, Japan had 51, Germany had 65.07, and China had 27.51, as compared to India which had 3.36 lines (World Bank 2013). This certainly has implications on the methodologies adopted by the marketing research firms to conduct marketing research. In a country where the reach of telecom and the Internet is still low, the use of such technologies will also be lower. The reliance will be more on more personal surveys. The connectivity in rural areas is still low and to reach nearly 50% of the population will not be possible if the reliance is only on online technologies.

Despite impressive growth in the number of Internet users and the availability of personal computers (PC), India still remains on the wrong side of the divide. The number of Internet users is still a negligible fraction of India's total population. Per capita availability of PCs is also very low.

The typical questions that online marketing research attempts to answer are—What are the purchase patterns for individuals and groups? What factors encourage online purchasing? How can we identify the real buyers from those who are just browsing? How does an individual navigate—Do consumers check information first or do they go directly to ordering? What is the optimal web page design? (Turban and King 2003).

Online market research methods range from e-mail, moderated focus group discussions, and surveys on the websites, to tracking of customers movement on the web. These days service providers can also look at Internet blogs to get an insight on what consumers feel about their products and services. Any negative reactions need to be looked into and addressed.

Online Market Research Tools

Web surveys   These are becoming popular among companies and researchers. Free software is available to conduct such surveys; for example, zoomrang.com (Turban and King 2003). Survey sites such as SurveyMonkey are also popular among marketers.

Online focus groups   These are conducted using Internet technology. They offer the advantage of reaching to widespread consumers at lower costs.

Tracking consumer movements   These are tracked using cookie files.

Transaction logs   The customers enter their information and knowledge about how they shop and clickstream behaviour can be monitored.

Cookies and web bugs   These can supplement transaction logs. Cookies allow a website to store data on the user's PC which can be used to find what the customer did in the past when they return to the site. Cookies are combined with the web bugs, tiny graphic files embedded on e-mail messages and on websites.

The feasibility of conducting online research offers numerous advantages such as saving time, lower costs, wide coverage, global samples, etc. However, the response rates may be lower than the conventional mail surveys. Also, it is more arduous to fill the forms online in case of lengthy questionnaires. Other issues could be assessing the correctness of the demographic variables and connectivity.

Marketing Research in India

The first form of formal research started in India in the year 1965 with the Operations Research Group (ORG). In 1971, HTA created IMRB to handle research for clients who were demanding it. Earlier, margins were low and were to the tune of 5–10%.

Today marketing research activity is not limited to FMCG marketers. At present, their share is down to 60% of the total spend. The active areas where a lot of research is being undertaken are—pharmaceuticals, media, financial services, and automobile industry.

The Indian entertainment and media (E&M) industry is on the cusp of a strong phase of growth, backed by rising consumer payments and advertising revenues across all sectors. Total advertising revenues are expected to increase at a healthy rate of about 14% CAGR from ₹322 billion in 2012 to ₹619 billion in 2017 (CII-PWC 2013). Additionally, India's wired Internet advertising market is expected to increase at a robust CAGR of about 28% from ₹21 billion in 2012 to ₹71 billion in 2017 (CII-PWC 2013). In October 2013, the total ad-time on News TVs across India shrunk to 12 minutes per hour owing to the guidelines set by the Telecom Regulatory Authority of India (TRAI).

Reducing viewerships of the news channels due to the viewers opting out of news channel subscription after digitization combined with restricted ad-time and high rate of failure has made marketers more careful about the ad-films' content and impact, with marketers now checking the films at each stage. One has to ensure that communication is working for the brand and the company image (Annuncio 1998).

Growing influence of the social media has opened up new avenues of research. Researchers across a wide range of disciplines in social sciences have been increasingly drawn to different online research methods. Market researchers harness the reach of the social media to develop unique insights into consumer and societal segments and gain an 'emotional' measure of a population on issues of interest. Online research methods or ORMs are ways through which researchers collect data via Internet and other social media by using tools such as online ethnography, online focus groups, online qualitative research, online interviews, online questionnaires, web-based experiments, online clinical trials, research through social media, etc. Additionally, Internet has also stimulated research by ordinary citizens. Although they may find it difficult to catch up with the professional researchers, they cannot be ignored, especially in these times of disengagement from the established political and economic systems. Then there is always the need to simplify the access to information, which is gaining more and more prominence as the search engines such as Google and Yahoo go into an overdrive to open up the world for the ordinary researcher.

India is gradually turning into the research outsourcing hub of the world owing to its increasing global expertise in market research and a large and evolving data base. Additionally, increasing number of pure-plays, full service firms, and KPOs have positioned Indian research outsourcing firms for higher value services.

PROBLEMS IN MARKETING RESEARCH

The industry is beset with a lot of problems. Some of these are as highlighted in this section.

- The population is large and heterogeneous. There is a diversity in languages that are used. This certainly has implications in terms of the level of skills required by the employees. The numbers to be surveyed are large, and cultural and linguistic diversity calls for even greater difficulties in adapting research to the local needs.
- There is a whole set of infrastructure problems. There is still a lot of automation that is required. This lack results in lots of delays in the data analysis and compilation.
- There are a whole set of problems with respect to manpower, methodology, and attitude. The industry requires manpower with a good conceptual understanding of the issues, diversified skills relating to understanding of different cultures, analytical skills, and ability to put in a lot of hard work. Currently, there are individuals working in Indian marketing research firms who are merely graduates, or professionals who have moved into research after working for a few years in the corporate sector. Most of the learning takes place on the job. Common sense is the most sought-after trait. There are no specific institutes that offer specialized training in these particular areas. Marketing research, as a discipline of study in the management institutes, is also not very popular, with very few professionals available who are well-versed in the technique of carrying out research.
- Most Indian organizations do not spend a great deal of the money on market research. Indian organizations are price conscious and it hurts them to pay colossal amounts on research. They still rely more on intuition rather than on the results of formal research.
- There is also a problem of carrying out industry-specific research in certain cases. For instance, there are certain industries that are dominated by two or three large players, as a result of which syndicated research does not make much sense on account of economies of scale. For instance, just two major players dominate the Indian soft drinks industry. There is also a problem of too many players in the field, as a result of which there is a paucity of requisite skilled manpower. Also, research is a process that requires lot of finance. As a result of small size, there is often a problem of handling bigger projects. Again, organizations often subcontract the fieldwork, which results in little control over the research process, resulting in erroneous results.
- There is also a serious problem of data fabrication. Probably, when organizations do take decisions based on these results, they discount this aspect. If an organization subcontracts the jobs, it is important to check the credentials of the research undertaken.

- There is also a lack of professionalism. The delays and lack of sufficient facilities in terms of manpower do contribute to that. In fact, there has been a mushrooming of firms that are characterized by lack of knowledge and experience.
- The turnover rate of employees is also very high. There are too many organizations and a dearth of good people, as a result of which people keep switching jobs for financial gain. Finding an overseas assignment is also seen to be lucrative.
- There are also problems of wrong identification of the problem. The client carries a preconceived notion as a result of which the entire research design is oriented towards a wrong problem. The research briefs given by the client are also sometimes very fuzzy, which further complicate the problem.
- The reports that are generated are often bulky, as a result of which decision-making is not easy. Often, they also lack in adequate recommendations.
- There is also a problem of information databases as a result of which a lot of time is wasted in collecting basic information. Database-building in India is still to develop adequately. There is no detailed information on retail audits and cultural studies, as a result of which there have been many problems of wrong positioning of the products.

Trends in the coming decades   This section discusses the trends that seem to emerge from the analysis.

Marketing in India is all about having to deal with tens or hundreds of millions of consumers. For the market researcher, therefore, there is no escape from the tyranny of enormous numbers. When we talk of marketing research, we talk of understanding through marketing research, a population of about 1.5 billion in the year 2020. In the coming decades the consumer in the rural areas will have adopted a far wider range of products and the rural marketing will not be an add-on, but the main event. There will also be shifts in the incomes of the consumers. The number of branded products will increase, but the diversity in the branded consumer base will increase equally. (See Exhibit 4.3 for more on the top research and competitive trends.)

- There is also going to be a massive market for the rural segments.
- There will also be a shift in the cultural paradigm that has been quite alien to the Indian culture. There will be an increase in hedonism without guilt—a case of, 'I'm doing it because I want to do it'. There will also be a significant increase in consumer spending on products that are low on functionality and high on indulgence.
- There will also be a change in the decision-making systems. There is going to be a shift in the traditional power balance systems. Children will influence many product purchases.
- There is going to be a greater accuracy in data collection and a decline in the traditional door-to-door interviewing methods where findings are totally dependent on the researcher's stimulus and consumer's response. There is going to be a greater amount of data capture through gadgets that will be more objective, and there will be less reliance on human intervention.
- At the level of industry, there is greater likelihood of consolidation. Additional use of sophisticated gadgets will mean capital investment, which means that the industry could end up being dominated by a few, may be only 2–3 large players who have the financial and infrastructural clout.

Exhibit 4.3   Research and Competitive Trends in 2014 in India

More strategic research   In recent years, many large companies (especially multinationals in India) have built internal strategy teams. It is becoming fashionable to hire strategy consultants from leading consultancies such as McKinsey, BCG, Bain, etc. Such consultants tend to be very data focused and will drive spend on research. A corollary will be increased sophistication of research definition (KIQs/scope) and data needs.

Emphasis shifts to small towns   With incomes and consumption rising faster outside of metros and Tier I cities, research focus is also shifting. The FMCG, white goods, and consumer electronics multinationals are ahead on this curve. There will be a rising interest in researching small-town and rural Indian markets, with demand being driven by health care, financial services, building materials, retail, auto, and several other consumption-led businesses.

Focus on channels   It is well known that in India's large and heterogeneous market, distribution and access are huge barriers. For companies such as Hindustan Unilever and ITC, distribution and reach across India are one of their biggest competitive advantages. Such networks take time and effort to build, and acquisitions are expensive. Adding to the problem, third party distribution is relatively unorganized, localized, and fragmented. There will be a rising interest in research to understand channel dynamics in local markets, and this will be a big growth area in 2014 and beyond.

Outward bound   Indian companies are trying to become global and several high-profile acquisitions in the past decade underline this trend. Besides mergers and acquisitions, there will be a new focus on organic growth in overseas markets, especially by small- and mid-sized companies. Increasingly, this will trigger rising demand for market research in non-India geographies. This demand will largely be driven by IT, knowledge services, pharma, minerals and metals, auto, and engineering.

SME's more open to research   In the past, spending on market research or competitive intelligence was limited to multinationals or the very large Indian companies. This is set to change, with SME's becoming more professionalized and ambitious. The realization that better decision-making depends on better information is now sinking in. However, most of these companies have not commissioned research before, and their managers are not always familiar with research. Client education, budgets, scope definition, and expectation setting will be big challenges for research providers. Interestingly, a lot of SME driven research will be related to diversification efforts, as traditional family-owned businesses look at new-age growth options. Research interest will be across sectors, but high growth areas will include hospitality, health care, restaurants, education, KPO, non-conventional energy, etc.

Best-of-breed providers   As companies mature in their understanding and application of research, the trend towards best-of-breed vendors will accelerate. No longer will they be happy with an existing vendors to serve all their needs, but would look towards specialized firms, especially those who can offer customized solutions and have proven methodologies for brand measurement, sales effectiveness, market sizing, competitive benchmarking, channel checking, etc.

In-house analyst teams   This trend was earlier prevalent amongst IT companies and multinationals but is now spreading to more Indian companies. It is partly driven by stronger in-house strategy teams. Challenges will arise due to small teams and incomplete set of competencies. Knowing what to do in-house and what to outsource is a big challenge/learning that will take time to sort out.

Realism about analytics   This trend mirrors a global phenomenon, as people jump into big data or analytics solutions driven by the hype. 2014 will bring a realization that though big data analytics will grow enormously,

(Contd)

Exhibit 4.3   (Contd)

it will not answer all our questions. We still need better definition of problems, data needs, and analysis. Overall, however, this learning will lead to growing maturity and an understanding that certain questions may be better answered by small sets of proprietary or external data, typically gathered or collated by conventional market research methods.

Adoption of smartphone/mobile technologies   Companies with large sales forces (typically in consumer goods) have long struggled with leveraging their sales force to collect real-time, on-the-ground data. In the past, multinational FMCG, and pharma companies have implemented technology solutions that typically include a hand-held device with proprietary software. This is costly and often not feasible for smaller companies. However, the proliferation of smartphones and relevant apps now offers low cost solutions for distributed data collection and this will be a big trend 2014 onwards.

Source: Arun Jethmalani, 2 January 2014. Reprinted with permission.

- The other trend could be a sharper polarization of the market research industry in terms of the services it offers. At one end there will be data suppliers, and on the other hand, there will be professionals whose role could centre round just the delivery of quick, cost-effective data. There will be a breed of value adders cast in the consultancy mode, to make sense of the data.
- Specialization in market research is moving away from the qualitative–quantitative divide, towards industry categories. There is a greater likelihood of having more financial market researchers, pharmaceutical market researchers, and automotive researchers, than focus group or product testing experts.
- Qualitative research budgets are being pumped up. Hindustan Unilever Limited (HUL) now sets aside a third of its budget for qualitative research.
- The marketing research agency is seen as a partner in growth and an extension of the marketing arm of the company. Earlier, the marketing research agency was hardly involved in decision-making. Today, because of the width of experience and knowledge base, clients expect the marketing research agencies to attend the strategy meetings.
- At the same time, one must accept that research can at best be a decision support system; there are a whole host of factors that have a bearing on the success or failure of a brand.
- Financial institutions, automobiles, public sector companies, media, and real estate are also taking on intensive studies to examine growth possibilities in the Indian market. Worldwide, government, finance, trade, pharmaceuticals, and media are some of the biggest sources of revenue (Chakraborty 1998).

Though the industry has evolved over a period of time, there is a great deal of potential and changes that are foreseen which have been deliberated upon. There will be a phase of consolidation, sharper polarization in the nature of services that are being offered, and increase in the syndicated research. Marketing research agencies will be seen as partners in the organization's growth and there will be a greater sophistication in the data analysis procedures. Time pressures on the industry are going to be immense; as a result, there will be greater emphasis on the sophisticated techniques of data collection and analysis. Visit the online resource centre to know more about the marketing research process.

RESEARCH INSIGHT

Conducting Market Research using the Internet: the Case of Xenon Laboratories

Lockett, Andy and Ian Blackman (2004) 'Conducting market research using the Internet: the case of Xenon Laboratories', *Journal of Business & Industrial Marketing*, vol. 19, issue 3, pp. 178–187.

The way market research is conducted has changed dramatically over the past 30 years, as a result of both the development of the prevailing view of best practices and the state of technology available to researchers. While it is clear that the Internet will increasingly be used as a medium for conducting market research, the full implications of this new channel are not yet fully understood. This paper examines the potential for an Internet-based financial services firm (Xenon Laboratories) to analyse the conduct of market research by using the web. The case demonstrates that, by employing a novel approach to market research, Xenon Laboratories is in a unique position to understand the charging structures in its market and the market for international payments using credit or charge cards. In doing so, the paper highlights the opportunity to unobtrusively gather market information from an international group of customers by providing Internet-based value-added services.

SUMMARY

This chapter delves upon the concept of marketing research. Marketing research is about extending the research to the domains of marketing—need analysis, product, price, place, promotion, process, people and physical evidence, and customer feedback. It is a systematic approach to research. With changing market dynamics and economic environment, market research is considered even more important. As firms expand globally, there are even more challenges in understanding consumers and markets. Marketing research could be used for describing, diagnosing, and predicting various aspects related to consumers and markets. There are numerous advantages for firms to engage in the marketing research, which range from a better understanding of markets to consumers. It helps to channelize investments, and customize and improve upon the service offering. Marketers should be careful to avoid making mistakes related to the research process. A systematic knowledge about the research process is extremely helpful.

The chapter also deals with the influence of the Internet on marketing research. As consumers begin to use Internet extensively, marketers will increasingly use this mode. However, the important aspects to be considered are the access to the Internet in an economy, and the kind of product category for which research is being conducted. Online market research methods range from e-mail, moderated focus group discussions, and surveys on the websites, to tracking of customer movements on the web. Online research techniques offer several advantages such as saving time, lower costs, wider coverage, and global samples.

KEY TERMS

Data analysis The process of systematically applying statistical and logical techniques to describe, summarize, and compare data.

Database An organized collection of information on a computer.

Internet An international network of computers, connected by modems, dedicated lines, telephone cables, and satellite links, with associated software controlling the movement of data. It offers facilities for accessing remote databases, transfer of data between computers, and e-mail.

Marketing research The systematic collection and analysis of data to resolve problems concerning marketing, undertaken to reduce the risk of inappropriate marketing activity. Data is almost always collected from a sample of the target market, by such methods as observation, interviews, and audit of shop sales. Interviews are the most common technique, and can be carried out face-to-face, by telephone, or by post.

Primary data The first hand data collected by an individual researcher. This involves personal surveys, interviews, telephonic surveys, online surveys, focus group discussions, Delphi studies, observation techniques, mystery shopping techniques, etc. A firm may use one or a combination of these techniques to obtain the data.

Process A specific, structured, and managed set of work activities, with known inputs, designed to produce a specific output.

Questionnaire A structured set of questions designed to generate the information required for a specific purpose, especially in marketing research. The questionnaire can make use of multiple-choice questions, with a series of formal questions designed to produce limited responses; alternatively, it can use more open-ended questions, giving respondents an opportunity to air their views. The latter types of questions are often used with small samples to provide the basis of questionnaires for larger samples.

Research design The master plan of the research to be undertaken. The function of the research design is to ensure that the requisite data in accordance with the problem at hand is collected. It is a blueprint for the research study, which guides the collection and analysis of data.

Sampling The process of selecting a group of items or individuals from a population to represent the characteristics of the population as a whole. Samples are often used in market research because it is not feasible to interview every member of a particular market.

Secondary data The data which could be obtained from published sources such as books, journals, magazines, newspaper, Internet websites, databases, annual reports of the firms, industry reports, industry association publications, government reports, white papers, etc.

EXERCISES

Concept Review Questions

1. Evaluate the scope of market research.
2. What are the mistakes made by marketers in conducting market research?
3. Explain the important steps in conducting market research.
4. How has the use of the Internet influenced the use of market research?
5. What are the challenges in conducting market research?
6. What elements should be considered while designing a questionnaire?
7. What are the various sampling techniques deployed in conducting research?
8. What are the challenges faced by small and medium firms in conducting research?

Critical Thinking Questions

1. In an airline, it was observed on a particular route, that 40% of the passengers did not finish their meals. When the formal feedback was taken it was found that the passengers just rated the meal quality to be average but no further details could be found.
   (i) Please suggest a strategy for research to find the reasons for non-consumption of the meals on the flight.
   (ii) Design a suitable questionnaire to measure consumer preferences for meals in context of the aforementioned case.
   (iii) Please indicate the data analysis techniques, which you could use with the questionnaire developed in the question above.
2. There is a need for businesses to adopt green practices for conserving the environment. Please suggest the appropriate research design to carry out this study for the hotel industry in India.
3. A bank in India wanted to carry out a customer satisfaction survey and find out whether the customers were happy with the services offered to them. It has 300 branches, with 150 in urban

areas and 150 in rural areas. To measure customer satisfaction, it carried out the survey randomly with 100 respondents each in the four metros, namely, Delhi, Mumbai, Chennai, and Kolkata as well as 30 respondents each in Bangalore, Ahmedabad, and Nagpur. Critically evaluate the sampling procedure chosen for the research study.

Project Assignments

1. Make a team of four students and conduct a market assessment of factors influencing the choice of mobile phone in the age group of 18–25 years in India. Identify the objectives, develop an appropriate research design, collect the data, and make an appropriate analysis.

2. Evaluate the Internet usage habits of college students with regard to working on their academic projects.

CASE STUDY   Population Growth and the Urban Poor*

According to the Organisation for Economic Cooperation and Development (OECD) estimates, by the year 2050, India will be the world's third largest economy. The population of India is expected to increase from 1,029 million to 1,400 million during the period 2001–26, an increase of 36% in 25 years the rate of 1.2% annually (Census of India). According to the Government of India's projections, urban population in the country, which was 28% in 2001, is expected to increase to 38% by 2026. The urban growth will account for over two-thirds (67%) of total population increase by 2026. Out of the total population increase of 371 million during 2001–26 in the country, the share of increase in urban population is expected to be 249 million. Delhi, for example, will have the highest growth of 102% during 2001–26. States such as Himachal Pradesh, Punjab, West Bengal, Orissa, Andhra Pradesh, and Karnataka will have a projected growth in the range of 20–30%. In states such as Haryana, Rajasthan, Uttar Pradesh, and Madhya Pradesh, the increase is projected to be 40–50% by 2001–26, which is above the national average of 36%. Of the projected increase in population of 371 million in India during 2001–26, 187 million is likely to occur in the seven states of Bihar, Chhattisgarh, Jharkhand, Madhya Pradesh, Rajasthan, Uttar

Pradesh, and Uttaranchal. It is interesting to note that nearly 54% of 554.8 million mobile users in India reside in the villages, as of 2013 (IDR 2013). Table 4.1 shows the rural market share of various mobile operators in India.

Rural Marketing in India

The Indian rural market is and will be difficult to ignore. It is true that the heart of India still resides in its villages. It reflects a lot of potential. Table 4.1 indicates that in categories such as mobile phones, rural markets have been gaining on the charts. Today, rural markets are critical for every marketer, whether it is branded shampoos, automobiles, soaps, or colour television. The size of the rural market is pegged at more than US$100 billion by 2025. The time has gone when marketers thought that van campaigns, cinema commercials, and a few wall paintings would be sufficient to entice rural folks to their folds. Thanks to television, today a customer in a rural area is quite aware about myriad products that are on offer in the marketplace.

It is true that all individuals in rural India have the same needs, wants, desires, and aspirations that anyone in urban India has, but the buying behaviour demonstrated by the rural Indian differs tremendously when compared to the typical urban

*Mirchandani, R., *Rural Marketing in India*, Aries Flash Online, http://business.vsnl.com/ariesagro/rural951.html, accessed on 17 November 2008. Reprinted with the permission of Dr Rahul Mirchandani, Executive Director, Aries Agro Limited, Mumbai, India.

Table 4.1   Rural market share of telephone operators in India

New rural ringtone			(in million)
Operator	Total subscribers	Rural subscribers	Rural market share (%)
Bharti	191.48	85.90	24.47
Reliance	125.73	30.14	8.58
Vodafone	155.03	84.01	23.93
BSNL	97.99	33.78	9.62
Tata	64.63	21.85	4.02
Idea Cellular	124.97	68.73	19.58

Source: TRAI March–June (2013).

Indian. Further, the same values, aspirations, and needs of the rural people vastly differ from that of the urban population. Basic cultural values still remain the same in rural India, where buying decisions are still made by the eldest male member, whereas even children have started influencing buying decisions in urban areas. Further, buying decisions are highly influenced by social customs, traditions, and beliefs in the rural markets. Many rural purchases require collective social sanction, unheard of in urban areas.

Another contrasting feature is the precision in the assessment of purchasing power of the consumers. In urban markets, income levels are generally used to measure purchasing power and markets are segmented accordingly. However, this measure is not adequate to define the purchasing power in rural areas because of the fact that rural incomes are hugely underestimated. Farmers and rural artisans are paid in cash as well as in kind. However, while reporting their incomes, they report only cash earnings, which in turn, affects the calculation of their purchasing power. This is the main reason why marketers are often surprised to find that their products exist in the households of people who, according to their surveys and estimates, do not have the purchasing power for this. Hence, it is important for every marketing manager to make an attempt to understand the rural consumer better so that the strategies are decided in a manner that they produce the desired results.

Rural Marketing Mix

The prices-sensitivity of a consumer in a village is extremely important to marketers. Rural income levels are largely determined by the vagaries of the monsoon and hence, the demand forecast is not easy. Apart from increasing the geographical width of their product distribution, the focus of corporates should be on the introduction of brands and development of strategies specific to rural consumers. Britannia Industries launched the successful Tiger biscuits especially for the rural market. It clearly paid dividends. Its share of the glucose biscuit market has increased from 15% to 38%. Unfortunately, most marketers of today try to extend marketing plans that they use in urban areas to the rural markets, which is a devastating strategy. They should adopt a strategy that appeals individually to the rural audience, such as price sensitivity and separate annual plans, and sales targets for the rural segment should be formulated. The marketing mix elements such as price, place, product, and promotion, should be customized for the rural market. If corporate marketers start designing goods for the urban markets and subsequently push them in the rural areas, they are bound to face problems.

The unique consumption patterns, tastes, and needs of the rural consumers should be analysed at the product planning stage so that they match the needs of the rural people. Companies such as Hindustan Unilever have successfully used strategies to influence the rural market for its shampoos in sachets. The sachet strategy has proved so successful that, according to an ORGMARG data, 95% of total shampoo sales in rural India is by sachets. The company had developed a direct access to markets through the wholesale channel and created awareness through media, demonstrations, and on-ground contact. This changed the attitude of the villagers. Today, the young and the educated in the villages are already large in number. And this number is increasing. Already, over 40% of all those graduating from colleges are rural youth. They are the decision-makers and are not very different in education, exposure, attitudes, and aspirations from their counterparts, at least in smaller cities and towns.

In rural India, annual *melas* organized with a religious or festive significance, are quite popular and provide a very good platform for distribution. Rural markets come alive at *melas*, days with religious significance, and festivals such as Diwali, Holi, Navratras, etc. People visit these fairs to make several purchases. According to the Indian Market Research Bureau, over 8,000 such melas are held in rural India every year. Besides these melas, rural markets have the practice of fixing specific days in a week as market days when exchange of goods and services are carried out. This is another potential low cost distribution channel available to the marketers. Also, one satellite town, where people prefer to go to buy their durable commodities, generally serves every region consisting of several villages. If marketing managers use these towns, they will easily be able to cover a large section of the rural population.

While planning promotional strategies in rural markets, marketers must be careful in choosing the right vehicle to be used for communication. It is worth noting that rural people want increasingly more information with circulation figures of many vernacular papers crossing 50% in rural India. Although television is undoubtedly a powerful medium, the audio-visuals must be planned, keeping them in mind, so as to convey a right message to the rural folk. The marketers must try and rely on the rich, traditional media forms such as folk dances, puppet shows, etc. with which the rural consumers are familiar and comfortable, for high impact product campaigns.

Questions

1. Based on the aforementioned case on rural markets, what should service providers, such as telecom firms, be doing?
2. Can service providers in India ignore rural markets? Critically analyse this, based on the data provided in the case study.
3. What are the buying preferences for consumers in rural areas in India?
4. As a marketer, if you were to offer health care consulting services to rural areas, what aspects would you consider while marketing the same?

REFERENCES

Aaker, A.D., V. Kumar, and G.S. Day (1998), *Marketing Research*, John Wiley, New York.

Ahluwalia, T. (1995), 'Polarisation in market research', Brand Equity, *The Economic Times*, 4 January.

Annuncio, C. (1998), 'Monitoring the mindset', *Outlook*, New Delhi, 13 July.

Bijapurkar, R. (1996), 'The traps in advertising research', *The Strategist Quarterly*, January–March, vol. 1.

Boughton, Paul (1992), 'Marketing research partnerships: A strategy for the 90s', *Marketing Research: A Magazine of Management and Applications*, 4 December, pp. 8–13.

Chakraborty, A. (1998), 'The new research agenda', *Business India*, 27 July–9 August.

Churchill Jr., Gilbert A. (1999), *Marketing Research*, Dryden Press, New York.

Fielding, Nigel G., Raymond M. Lee, and Grant Blank (eds.) (2008), *The SAGE Handbook of Online Research Methods*, London, Sage Publication Ltd.

Gaur, A. and S. Nagi (1995), 'Re-engineering marketing', *The Economic Times*, 4 January.

Gupta, I. (1996), 'Mapping your brand', *The Strategist Quarterly*, January–March.

Halve, A. (2007), 'Advertising in changing India', *The Marketing Whitebook 2007–2008*.

Honomichl, J.J. (1996), '1996 Business Report on the marketing research industry', *Marketing News*, 3 June.

Honomichl, J.J. (2005), 'Top 50', *Marketing News*, 15 June.

McDaniel, C. and R. Gates (1999), *Contemporary Marketing Research*, South-Western College Publishing, New York.

Parasuraman, A., V.A. Zeithaml, and L.L. Berry (1985), 'A conceptual model of service quality and its implications for future research', *Journal of Marketing*, vol. 49, no. 4, pp. 41–50.

Rakesh Kumar (2003), 'Analyzing marketing strategy for broadband services of BSNL', Dissertation for Post Graduate Diploma in Business Management, MDI, Gurgaon.

Sharma, S. (1995), 'Push button marketing', *The Economic Times*, 4 January.

Simon, J.L. (1969), *Basic Research Methods in Social Science: The Art of Empirical Investigation*, Random House, New York.

Struce, Doss (1999–2000), 'Marketing research's top 25 influences', *Marketing Research*, Winter/Spring.

Turban, E. and D. King (2003), *Introduction to e-commerce*, Prentice Hall, New Jersey.

Uchil, D. (2008), 'What's your competitor doing?', *The Hindustan Times*, New Delhi, 1 May, p. 30.

Weiner, Bernard (1985), 'An attributional theory of achievement motivation and emotion', *Psychological Review*, vol. 92(4), October, pp. 548–573.

AT Kearney (2013), *The Mobile Economy 2013 PDF—AT Kearney*, www.atkearney.com/documents/.../The_Mobile_Economy_2013.pd, accessed on 6 March 2015.

Business Standard (2006), available from http://www.businessstandard.com/strategist/storypage.php?tab=r&autono=260362&subLeft=3&, accessed on 8 April 2008.

CII-PWC (2013), India Entertainment and Media Outlook 2013, PwC India, www.pwc.in/india-entertainment-media-outlook/index.jhtml, accessed on 6 March 2015.

Confederation of Indian Industry, available from http://cii.in/menucontact.php?menu_id=629, accessed on 5 April 2008.

Dougherty, Dave and Ajay Murthy (2009), What Service Customers Really Want, available from http://hbr.org/2009/09/what-service-customers-really-want/ar/1, September, accessed on 11 June 2014.

http://blog.marketresearch.com/blog-home-page/bid/334826/How-3-Companies-Used-Market-Research-to-Pivot-their-Businesses, accessed on 8 January 2014.

http://data.worldbank.org/indicator/IT.NET.USER.P2, accessed on 8 January 2014.

http://www.internetworldstats.com/stats3.htm, accessed on 8 January 2014.

http://www.icmis.net/ictbm/ictbm13/proceedings/pdf/C3111-done.pdf, accessed on 8 January 2014.

http://www.valuenotes.biz/top-ten-research-competitive-intelligence-trends-2014-india/, accessed on 8 January 2014.

http://www.coolage.in/2013/12/23/indian-ad-world-emotions-are-the-new-rational/, accessed on 8 January 2014.

http://www.indiadigitalreview.com/news/india-has-5548-mn-mobile-users-1432-mn-internet-users-study/14350, accessed on 8 January 2014.

http://www.trai.gov.in/WriteReadData/PIRReport/Documents/Indicator%20Reports%20-01082013.pdf, accessed on 8 January 2014.

http://www.sourcingnotes.com/content/view/279/54/, accessed on 8 January 2014.

http://www.mediapost.com/publications/article/206652/global-marketing-research-holds-its-own.html, accessed on 8 January 2014.

http://www.vendorseek.com/listen-to-your-customers-through-market-research.asp, accessed on 11 June 2014.

International Telecommunication Union, available from http://www.itu.int, accessed on 3 May 2009.

'India to be global hub for market research', available from http://in.rediff.com/money/2007/may/05india.htm, accessed on 5 April 2008.

Merinews (2007), available from http://www.merinews.com/catFull.jsp?articleID=125367&catID=7&category=Lifestyle&rtFlg=rtFlg, accessed on 15 May 2008.

NASSCOM (2007), available from http://www.nasscom.in/upload/55199/Bharatmatrimony.pdf, accessed on 15 May 2008.

Rediff (2004), available from http://www.rediff.com/money/2004/may/18bpo.htm, accessed on 5 April 2007.

The Hindu (2001), 'Rural market—A world of opportunity', available from http://www.hinduonnet.com/2001/10/11/stories/0611000c.htm, accessed on 5 May 2005.

The Hindu (2008), available from http://www.hinduonnet.com/2001/10/11/stories/0611000c.htm, accessed on 1 June 2009.

The Hindu Business Line (2006), available from http://www.thehindubusinessline.com/catalyst/2006/08/17/stories/2006081700250400.htm, accessed on 1 June 2007.

—(2007), 'Market research firms must offer insights too', available from http://www.thehindubusinessline.com/catalyst/2007/02/08/stories/2007020800190200.htm, accessed on 15 July 2008.

—(2008), available from http://www.blonnet.com/2008/01/27/stories/2008012751080100.htm, accessed on 1 June 2008.

—(2008), available from http://www.thehindubusinessline.com/2008/01/27/stories/2008012751080100.htm, accessed on 1 June 2008.

VSNL Business (2006), available from http://business.vsnl.com/ariesagro/rural951.html, accessed on 1 June 2008.

World Bank (2013), *World Development Indicators* 2013, The World Bank, http://data.worldbank.org/sites/default/files/wdi-2013-ch5.pdf, accessed on 6 March 2015.

CHAPTER

5 Understanding Consumer Behaviour

OBJECTIVES

After reading this chapter you will be able to understand the

- basics of consumer behaviour
- process of consumer decision-making
- factors influencing buying behaviour of consumers
- concept of relationship marketing
- meaning of the term customer delight
- concepts relating to customer loyalty
- meaning of consumerism

Pester Power

Children in India constitute 18.7% of the world's kids' population and one-third of India's population is under the age of 15 years. This surely indicates that kids are a huge market and can play a very important role as influencers in brand purchase. According to the Cartoon Network New Generations study (2012), kids do influence household decisions of purchase when it comes to white goods with an average of 22% parents definitely considering their kids' opinions and an average of 44% parents who may consider them. Apart from watching programmes, kids also view a lot of advertisements, thus making them better consumers for advertising. A fact that is being considered by most brands is that, since a child's mind is not as cluttered as an adult's mind, they absorb messages faster, and this receptiveness to messages leads to what we know in marketing as a kid's 'pester power'.

Chota Bheem, a popular cartoon character in India

An interesting study by Millward Brown and IMRB (2008) showed that kids influence decision-making on categories not just meant for kids. It suggests that recognition of corporate logos happens at the age of six months. The brand name requests start at the age of three and differentiating between brand values happens by the age of 10, and brand loyalty starts at 11. Capitalizing on these facts, 'catch them when they are young' is the new mantra. If a teenager gets glued to a brand, she may be a consumer for life.

Children in middle-class India take important decisions at home, contributing substantially to household budget contours (Mallick 2012).

The popular logistics company DHL hopes to create brand recognition through toys; when a kid sees a yellow delivery truck—synonymous with DHL—on the road, children will definitely make the association. Brands such as Chota Bheem feature regularly in advertisements for chips, kids'

perfume, and thus ensuring an association and quick recall.

Experts peg the market for products and services in which kids play the role of an influencer at an astounding $100 billion (₹4,50,000 crore). In India, the advertising spend per year on products for kids, but purchased by parents, is 12 to 15% of the total ₹38,000 million; the rate is about 8% for products bought by kids themselves, like chocolates. Therefore, whether it is the Frooti ad or car advertisements for Maruti, or life insurance/mutual fund ads, brands are increasingly using innovative tactics to utilize the pester power of kids.

After going through the chapter, you will be able to answer the following question:

Analyse why kids' pester power is an important element in parents' decision-making.

Source: Based on *Live Mint* (2008), Malik (2012), Animation Express (2012).

INTRODUCTION

Consumer behaviour is an inter-disciplinary science that investigates the decision-making activities of individuals in their consumption roles. It describes the reasons for development of consumer behaviour as an academic discipline and an applied science. It is pertinent for marketers to understand the dynamics of consumer buying and consumption patterns to continuously improve their service offering. The service industry is dynamic and hence, it is important to understand the trends and customize the service offering appropriately. Schiffman and Kanuk (1997) define consumer behaviour as the behaviour displayed by consumers in searching for, purchasing, using, evaluating, and disposing of the products, services, and ideas, which are expected to satisfy their needs. It includes understanding questions such as the what, why, where, how, and when of consumer behaviour. Consumer behaviour is an integral factor in the flow of business.

This chapter gives an overview of consumer behaviour in the context of the service industry. It gives an insight into the dynamics of consumer behaviour and the decision-making processes, and delineates the factors affecting consumer behaviour. It also explores the concept of relationship marketing and consumer loyalty and discusses a case study on rural marketing in India. Consumer behaviour helps managers to:

- design the service mix
- segment the marketplace
- position and differentiate the product

- perform environmental analysis
- develop market research studies
- improve the personal ability of an individual to be a more effective consumer
- understand human behaviour and impact the policy decisions in public and organizational domains.

RELEVANCE OF CONSUMER BEHAVIOUR

Consumer behaviour has emerged as a separate area of specialization. Consumer aspirations change with the dynamics of the changing business environment. There is a need to document and understand differences in behaviour, buying, and usage patterns across various countries. There may be a change in the needs, personality, and lifestyle pattern of consumers. The product life cycle is also becoming shorter, and environmental concerns are becoming important. The ethical issues related to service marketing and consumption, and recycling, also need to be understood. Consumer behaviour draws inputs from various disciplines such as psychology, sociology, social psychology, cultural anthropology, economics, and strategic management.

The techniques used to target consumers have changed over the various time cycles. Prior to World War II, companies were production oriented, wherein the focus was on intensive distribution and mass production. The service element was not a consideration. There was then a shift to product orientation, wherein there was greater focus on the product features. For instance, when competition intensified, features such as the best quality, better performance, and maximum number of features, became key selling points. This obsession with product features rather than the assessment of the market need was known as marketing myopia (Levitt 1967). Later there was a shift to sales orientation, wherein the capability to sell predominated the market need. The next focus was on identifying the consumer need and offering a product/service, which satisfied those needs, while at the same time engaging in societal welfare. However, this paradigm shift has been more visibly seen in the case of developed economies. In the services sector, the service offering is decided based on the maturity of the service category and sophistication level of the consumers. Hence, in emerging economies, a sales orientation is still predominant. However, with the opening up of economies, and higher access to media and communication channels, consumers are becoming more discerning. As a result, marketers are making efforts to offer contemporary services in various sectors, such as telecom, ITES, railways, hospitality, etc. To understand consumer behaviour, one needs to appreciate the following aspects:

Consumer behaviour is a process that includes many activities.

- It is motivated.
- A consumer may adopt many roles.
- It is influenced by external factors.
- It varies for different people.

The Consumer Behaviour Process

It is important to develop a cause and effect relationship with the customer with regards to services. Additionally, it is also imperative to understand the relationship between service characteristics and its effect on search and evaluation behaviour of the customer. Further, it is important for the companies to understand that customers are essentially concerned about the 'process as experienced in service delivery' and also that 'customers want a unique customer experience'.

The customer inputs therefore spur the companies to innovate services and produce non-standard products. Depending upon the type of properties that a service possesses, marketers need to find the most suitable way to market it.

Marketing scientists view goods as possessing three types of properties—search property, experience property, and credence property. In a seminal study of these aspects, Nelson (1970), coined the term 'search qualities' to describe those qualities of a brand that 'the consumers can determine by inspection prior to purchase' and 'experience qualities' to refer to those that are not determined prior to purchase. He substantiated his claim by giving an example of 'style of a dress for search quality and a taste of a brand of canned tuna fish as an experience attribute'. Darby and Karni (1973) extended this concept further and said that 'certain qualities can never be verified by an average consumer'. They called these qualities 'credence properties'. According to them, these properties come into play when a consumer does not possess requisite competence to evaluate service quality and technical knowledge of services like medical procedures, financial expertise, etc. In such situations, the customer is unable to assess the true performance of the service, or possess the competence to simultaneously diagnose and fulfil her requirements. Additionally, there are few divergent processes that are dependent on the expert opinion of the service provider. In such case the evaluation has to rely on expert opinions. As an exception, therefore, these services are high on credence properties. Similarly manufactured goods and services also have their fair share of experience, search, and credence properties in various combinations.

Search properties   Experts have defined search properties as those characteristics of a product which a customer can evaluate and compare before purchasing a product. These properties assist a customer to identify the best service before purchasing. Customers often gather information prior to purchasing products or services through various objective or subjective measures. An example of search properties would be how students search for specific colleges and courses to enroll in or how customers compare and contrast different product features of refrigerator or a television set or for that matter various food items for their nutritional value.

Experience properties   These are those product qualities that are purely experiential and can only be evaluated only after a product is purchased by the customer. These properties cannot be gauged before the purchase of the product. These qualities are often described by the product companies in the advertisement of the product. For example, a company in the logistics sector may perceive its services to be excellent, but a customer really needs to experience its services before he/she could evaluate its quality and efficiency. Similar is the case of other services, namely public utilities, hotels, banks, home builders, theme parks, etc., where a customer cannot to do a reasonable assessment of the 'product' characteristics without actually experiencing what is being offered.

Indian Railways aims to provide better service to its passengers

Credence properties This characteristic is related to the credibility of the product offering. Usually a customer relies on the evaluation of 'experts' in the area, because these characteristics cannot be easily evaluated even after experiencing the product. A typical customer does not have enough understanding or competence to make an accurate evaluation. Customers, therefore, rely on the opinion of so called 'experts', who provide an appraisal and make comparisons. For example, how does an engineer know that he or she has been competently trained? How does a client know that she has hired the best contractor? How does the client of a consulting firm know the consultant's recommendations are the best? In all these situations, the customer mainly has to take the company's word for it, or the word of other so called experts.

Consumer behaviour can be understood by understanding the processes at three levels.

- Stage I: Pre-purchase activities
- Stage II: Purchasing activities
- Stage III: Post-purchase activities

The consumption can be analysed during different phases of—acquisition, consumption, and disposition. The acquisition phase analyses the factors influencing the choice exercised by the consumers. The consumption phase analyses the factors affecting their consumption patterns. The disposition phase analyses the consumers' disposition after they have consumed the services. There are three levels of analysis of consumer behaviour—(1) individual level of analysis; (2) micro-environment (interpersonal and situational influences); and (3) macro-environment (culture, subculture, social class, and economic conditions).

Decision-making Process

An individual consumer is a complex person who is influenced by numerous factors, which affect his decision-making process. One such model, which gives an insight into the customer decision-making process, is explained in this section.

EKB model

A comprehensive model of consumer decision-making, the Engel, Kollat, and Blackwell (EKB) model maps out a five-step decision process during which a range of internal and external variables continually intervene to influence the final purchase. The model maps out the complex mix of factors that affect the consumer decisions. It identifies five distinct aspects of consumer decision-making—(1) inputs; (2) information processing; (3) decision process; (4) decision process variables; and (5) external influences.

Inputs   The consumer experiences numerous stimuli, which are driven by the marketer, such as advertisements, road shows, technical literature, personal selling, or selling, through a network of friends/acquaintances.

Information processing   The consumer absorbs the information and tries to collect more information on the various options available. The information processing progresses in stages, such as exposure to information, capture of attention, comprehension of the information, acceptance of the information, and retention of the information by the consumer.

Decision process   At any given time, the consumer is exposed to various stimuli through the media and interactions with peer group, family, and friends. These different options vie for the consumer's attention. This information is then comprehended and processed, and the consumer retains the relevant data. The decision process also involves numerous steps. It is a five-step process as outlined below.

Need/problem recognition   During this stage, the consumer identifies his/her own needs and attempts to look for solutions.

Information search   The consumer searches for information on alternatives available in the marketplace. He tries to find more information from various sources on the features of various options. The time spent on information search will depend on the nature of the investment made.

Alternative evaluation   The consumer evaluates the alternate possibilities and tries to find the option that yields the best outcomes. Alternative evaluation is influenced by the beliefs, attitudes, and intentions of the consumer.

Choice   The consumer zeroes in on an option, which best meets his/her requirements after having evaluated various options.

Outcome of the decision   The outcome of the decision results in purchase or consumption.
   After the customer has made a choice, he/she may sometimes have a negative evaluation about the purchase. This is known as cognitive dissonance. The attempt of the service provider is to reduce the element of cognitive dissonance.

Decision process variables   There are numerous variables that influence the decision-making process. These are motives, evaluation criteria, lifestyle, and informational influence.

External influences   It refers to cultural and reference groups. Also included in this category are the unanticipated circumstances, which could have an influence on the decision-making processes.

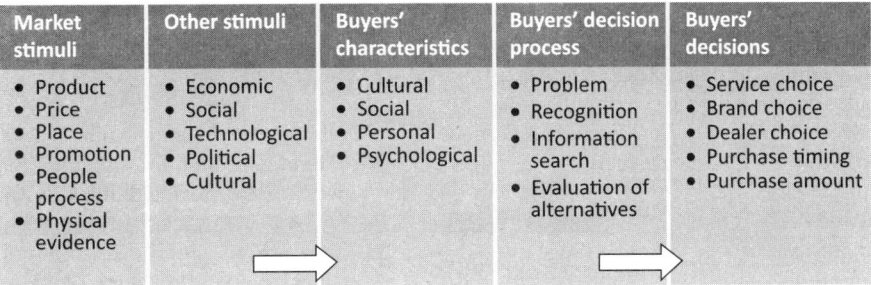

Market stimuli	Other stimuli	Buyers' characteristics	Buyers' decision process	Buyers' decisions
• Product • Price • Place • Promotion • People process • Physical evidence	• Economic • Social • Technological • Political • Cultural	• Cultural • Social • Personal • Psychological	• Problem Recognition • Information search • Evaluation of alternatives	• Service choice • Brand choice • Dealer choice • Purchase timing • Purchase amount

Fig. 5.1   A buyer's behaviour

There are different categories of consumer decisions. There are some decisions where the consumer buys on impulse, while there are others where he/she weighs various alternatives as in the case of health care, insurance, or investment in real estate.

CONSUMER BEHAVIOUR MODELS

There are numerous models for understanding consumer behaviour. A consumer is continuously exposed to market stimuli, which affect her decision processes. There are numerous factors that influence buyer behaviour. The stimuli along with buyer characteristics and behaviour result in a buyer's decision (Fig. 5.1).

CHANGING DYNAMICS OF INDIAN CONSUMERS

As the Indian economy grows, consumption patterns are witnessing a lot of changes. Some of these changes, such as income growth, increase in disposable income, an ever expanding female workforce, as well as the increased spending on entertainment, education, and health care are discussed in this section.

Income growth   The income levels of the consumers have been steadily rising.

Increasing disposable income   As income grows, expenditure on services and goods, which make life easy, is also increasing. Spending on domestic help and other services such as laundry, eating out, etc. is also increasing.

Women participating in workforce   As more and more women join the workforce, spendings on health care, beauty services, banking, the Internet, and convenience services will increase.

Education and health services   People are spending on health insurance and health care services are growing. People have started investing in preventive health checkups. The spending on education is increasing as people look for good quality education. So, a lot of international schools and institutions dedicated to higher education are being set up.

Entertainment   People are spending larger amounts on entertainment. There is increased spending on restaurants, malls, and movies.

Comfort with technology   Online shopping is increasing and consumers are making investments in high-tech products.

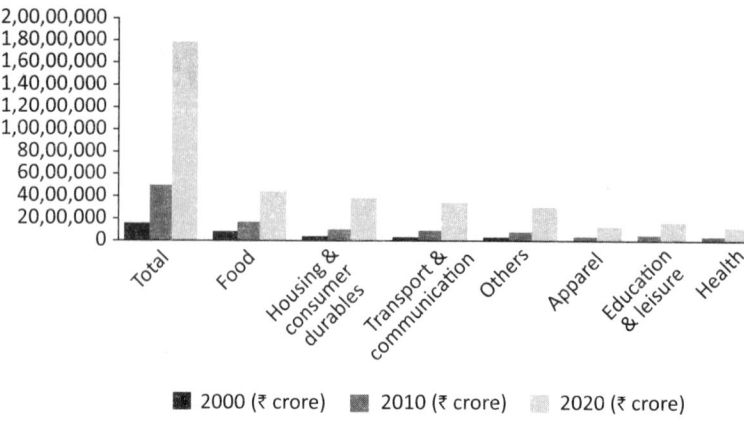

Note: All figures in ₹ crore
Source: Based on the data from BCG India Consumer Survey 2010

Fig. 5.2 Spending pattern of Indian consumers across segments

Source: Based on the data from *The Marketing Whitebook 2013–14*.

Figure 5.2 provides an insight into the current spending pattern of Indian consumers along with a projection of spending in the year 2020. The table details the percentage share of total consumption for nine categories.

The KSA Technopak survey on Indian consumers classifies consumers into four segments—(1) technology babies; (2) impatient aspirers; (3) balance seekers; and (4) arrived veterans.

Technology babies This segment in the age group of 8–19 years is estimated to be around 17 million in number. These are the post-liberalization kids with tremendous exposure to satellite and cable network, as well as familiarity with gizmos and computers. They are technology savvy and have a high degree of western influence. With 45% of India's population below 20 years, this segment is very attractive to marketers.

Impatient aspirers They belong to the age group of 20–25 years and are about 16 million in number. They are young and a wide number of career and education opportunities are available to them. They are more open to experimentation and are able to experiment with unconventional career opportunities. They spend on eating out, books, music, consumer durables, etc.

Balance seekers At around 41 million, this segment, in the age group of 26–50 years, spends on lifestyle goods due to their rising purchasing power. Looking good is important for this segment. They spend money on vacations and household goods as well. The marketing opportunities exist for entertainment avenues, home decor services, personal grooming chains, and bill payment services.

Arrived veterans This segment comprises nine million consumers in the age group of 51–60 years. The big spends are on children—their education, settling them, and

Exhibit 5.1   **Insights on Indian Consumers**

As per an ACNielsen survey, India is supposed to be the most optimistic country in the world. More and more Indians seem to have a positive outlook on job prospects and personal finances. While about 66% Indians are excited to try new products and services, ever-increasing disposable incomes are the drivers of increasing consumption. This will put India into the premier league of the world's consumer markets. By 2015, it will be almost as big as Italy's consumer markets. By 2025, the per capita spending will increase to ₹48,632, which is triple the current per capita spending.

Today, despite their lower incomes, rural households, due to their majority share of the population, are collectively India's largest consumers. They constitute 57% of the current consumption in rural areas as compared to 43% in cities.

Today, the largest category of spending (42%) is in food, beverages, tobacco, transportation, and housing. By 2025, this would have dropped to 25%, while transport and health will remain second and third biggest markets respectively. Communication which accounts for only 25% today will be among the fastest expanding categories with growth of over 13% a year on aggregate basis. India's relative share of world markets will rise in virtually every product and service category.

their marriage. Health care is another area of expenditure. This age group spends the maximum money on vacationing.

Exhibit 5.1 illustrates the trend of increased spending by Indian consumers.

FACTORS INFLUENCING BUYING BEHAVIOUR

There are numerous factors, which influence consumers' buying behaviour. These can be classified as cultural, social, personal, and psychological factors.

Cultural Factors

Taylor (1871) defined culture as a complex whole, which includes knowledge, belief, art, morals, customers, and any other capabilities and habits acquired by man as a member of society. Culture can be understood in numerous ways. According to one framework, culture can be analysed by understanding internal and external material culture.

External material culture   It refers to the external objects, which we experience in our day-to-day living, such as art, music, leisure, sports, buildings, etc. Use of technology has an impact on external material culture. Festivals are an integral part of the Indian culture. Leisure activities in India revolve around shopping, eating out, and watching movies. The Indian film industry, through its films, reflects the place of music and dance in our society. Indians are avid cricket lovers and companies use promotions and advertisements during cricket matches to target consumers. During various festivals, companies come out with special offers, which lead to increased spending by consumers. In India, the festivities begin with the Navratras, wherein the Mother Goddess is worshipped. This is followed by Dusshera, Diwali, and Id, during which gifts are exchanged.

Internal material culture   This refers to the ideas and points of view shared by most members of a society. The most prominent of these include knowledge systems (language, sciences, and objective descriptions of the material culture), belief and value systems (such as religions, political, or social philosophies), and the social normative system. The Indian society is driven by values such as family, respect for elders, and children. Children are the key factor around which families revolve.

However, environmental factors have an impact on the external and internal material culture. These evolve over a period of time. The marketing campaigns initiated by various service providers are also a depiction of the mindset of Indian culture.

Subculture   Each culture consists of many subcultures that help marketers identify consumer consumption trends. India, with its rich cultural diversity, is a melting pot of different subcultures. Northern and southern India have some distinctively different consumption patterns. In India, the food habits and consumption patterns differ across various states. North India, for example, is primarily wheat-consuming while south Indians primarily eat rice. The dress, colours, and fabrics used in south India are very different from those used in north India. For example, in Rajasthan (a state in north-west India), the food habits and colours seen are very different as compared to other parts of India. Exhibit 5.2 illustrates the trends in coffee consumption in India.

The infrastructure availability and the level of development in a country also affect the habits of consumers. People in various states prefer movies in their own regional language. The regional channels also reflect the use of the local language. Cultural factors can also be seen across various services. The general perceptions on consumers may be different from the reality.

Social Class

According to Kotler (2002), different societies exhibit different social classification. He elaborates, 'Social classes are relatively homogeneous and enduring divisions in

Exhibit 5.2   **Trends in Coffee Consumption in India**

Coffee consumption in India is on a steady rise. From being a traditional beverage consumed mainly in south India, it has a national presence now and is available in various formats. The consumption increased spending by 6–7% since 2007 due to better availability and improved market-driven strategies by the Coffee Board of India. Coffee consumption is expected to reach 125,000 tonnes this year from 85,000 tonnes in 2006. As far as facts are concerned, the domestic consumption of coffee is increasing, but out-of-home coffee shows an impressive increase of 12–13%. Specialist coffee outlets, such as Barista, Café Coffee Day, and Starbucks, have been driving sales of coffee, according to the Coffee Board. It estimates that around 50% of growth is from the non-coffee producing regions such as north India. The northern region of India is traditionally tea consuming, while south India accounts for more than three-fourths of the total annual coffee consumption.

The share of coffee consumption in restaurants and cafes is now 85% of the total out-of-home segment, according to the Coffee Board. However, per capita consumption is still low compared to other developed countries. Per capita consumption in Austria is 10 kg, the US is 4.095–6 kg, in the UK it is 3.03 kg, and in Japan it is 3.41 kg, while in India it is only about 80.600 grams.

Source: Based on the articles from *Business Standard* (October 2013), ET Bureau (1 January 2013), ET Bureau (22 October 2011), Indian Coffee Board (2007).

a society, which are hierarchically ordered, and whose members share similar values, interests, and behaviour'. Social classes give indications on spending patterns, recreation patterns, values, attitudes, lifestyles, and occupations. For example, in India there are a range of services targeted at the affluent segment of the society. With the economy growing every year and with increased job opportunities, the number of rich Indians is also growing every year. Exhibit 5.3 illustrates the strategies used by marketers to target the affluent Indian consumer.

Exhibit 5.3   **Lufthansa—How to Fly Premium Passengers?**

Lufthansa offers the services of a small private jet, which can fly passengers to over 1,000 airports all over Europe. And, the interesting fact is that, this is not the case with only European passengers; major Indian business houses are used to travelling in company planes in India and expect the same service when in Europe. The Private Jet, in fact, is one instance of how Lufthansa is aiming at the high-end traveller, whether in India or elsewhere.

Over the past few years, Lufthansa has been rolling out a lot of initiatives to attract more and more business class passengers by providing them with premium service. There are some compelling reasons as to why Lufthansa decided to attract the premium segment. This airline, which was once controlled by the German government, was badly hit by low-cost airlines such as Ryan Air and Easy Jet. The unfortunate part for the German airline was that even its loyalists began migrating to these low-cost airlines and it was left with the option of either climbing up the value chain or becoming cost competitive. Since legacy carriers such as Lufthansa can never compete as low-cost, the former was a more suitable option. So, Lufthansa started to brand itself as a premium airline that offered a quality flying experience. Unable to shield itself from the low-carrier business, German wings was set up in 2002 as a separate service, offering low-cost services.

With the new branding, Lufthansa began by improving the quality of food and service, which are two of the most important factors remembered by the customers. A seven-course menu and bone-china cutlery are among the services included. Only a few months ago, the exclusive Lufthansa First Class received top marks in the Skytrax Star Ranking, and now the experience is even more exclusive with new culinary highlights. On flights from Germany, Lufthansa has introduced 'Culinary Delights'. Taking the carrier's popular Star Chefs concept to a higher level, this new concept features menus created by chefs who have earned at least two Michelin stars or a comparable distinction. These menus will also change on a bi-monthly schedule. In addition, First Class passengers can now enjoy the exclusive caviar service as a separate course on day and evening flights. As appetizers, flights attendants will be serving a variety of canapés instead of a single option. In addition, the in-flight menus will be served on newly designed, high-end tableware, and include elements such as individual salt and pepper shakers for each passenger, a small bowl of olive oil, and elegant glass carafes for fresh water.

The Private Jet came as a strategy to reduce the connection times at Munich or Frankfurt for the business class passengers. The extremely luxurious First Class Terminal enables guests to drive up to the foyer and relax in the luxurious brown toned terminal. Transit passengers can sleep in private rooms, have a bath, and eat a gourmet meal, among other things. They can also be driven directly to the aircraft in a Mercedes S-Class or a Porsche Cayenne. The frequency of flights to India has increased and there are plans to expand it further to East India. This strategy clearly is an example of how analysing consumer behaviour can help a brand to provide the services that suit the consumers.

Source: Based on *The Strategist* (2006), Lufthansa deluxe in-flight service for premium guests (2013).

Social Factors

Consumer behaviour is influenced by social factors such as reference groups, family, social roles, and status (Kotler 2002).

Reference groups A person's reference group consists of all the groups, which have a direct or indirect impact on the individual. The reference group may be the family, friends, neighbours, and co-workers with whom the person interacts fairly. The family plays an extremely important role. The chapter-opening exhibit illustrates the influence of children on the purchase behaviour.

Family The family plays a very important role in influencing consumer buying behaviour. This may vary across cultures. However, in India, as in other Asian economies, the family influences buying patterns to a great extent. The choice of service providers for telecom, IT, transport, power, travel, resort destinations, etc., are more often family decisions rather than individual decisions.

Personal Factors

These factors can be understood by evaluating factors such as, age and stage in the life cycle, occupation, economic circumstances, lifestyle, personality, and self-concept. Age and stage in the life cycle are important determinants for purchase decisions. For example, in case of a higher age group, the spending increases on services such as health care, vacation, and travelling. Another case in point is Sony's strategy to target PlayStation at an older and more affluent audience (Exhibit 5.4).

Roles and status

A person's position in each group can be defined in terms of role and status. Marketers need to cater to the demands of different categories of consumers. For example, premium consumers expect better quality and wider range of services whereas, low-income group consumers may desire a no-frills, low-priced service. Occupation also determines the choice of service product. For example, the Life Insurance Corporation (LIC) of India has targeted the consumers from the underprivileged segment by providing micro finance for their business needs. Similarly, MicroGraam has initiated a number of small village level ventures to enable entrepreneurial development at the micro-level (Exhibit 5.5).

Consumer lifestyle

Lindquist and Sirgy (2005) have defined lifestyle as a constellation of individual characteristics that reflect certain behaviours, such as participation in social groups and relationships with significant others, commitment to certain behaviours, and a central life interest. This may vary according to socio-economic characteristics. Psychographics attempt to analyse and measure consumer lifestyle. To obtain a psychographic profile of consumer segments, marketers examine various aspects of personality and behaviour.

- Personality traits and concept of self
- Attitude towards brand and product class
- Activities, interests, and opinions
- Value systems

Exhibit 5.4   **Sony—Shifting Focus**

Marketing images in the past have often been of very young people but they are not seen as cool by those who are a lot older. They want to see people they can relate to—attractive yes, and a little older, people that 'age well'. With this very though in mind, the Victoria and Albert Museum in London has displayed an innovative sculpture soon and this has been designed by 3D, a rapper from Massive Attack and Sony's PlayStation video games business. This move from Sony clearly points to the fact that it is now targeting a different audience as well. The company has created artworks that allow people to interact within the gallery, or through the Internet using PlayStation. There seems to be an expansion—youth-oriented marketing as well as attracting older consumers. The company believes that after evolving the PlayStation brand prominently through close associations with youth-oriented activities, such as music, community football, etc., the brand is big enough to encourage a wider range of people, especially the older consumers. It is time now that the older audience starts recognizing Sony PlayStation as a broad-based entertainment brand willing to engage with culture and not just computer games. Even Nintendo, another video game brand, is targeting consumers aged 35 and above to highlight 'brain training' games designed to boost mental agility and memory.

Even other brands, such as Levi's and L'Oreal, which focus on youth-oriented marketing, are now moving towards targeting a wider market. It has been found out that many people start feeling ignored as they get older, though the fact is that it is the older, not the younger consumers who are the growth market in both numbers and purchasing power. According to the EU, the senior citizens market will grow by 81% from 2005 to 2030 while the 18–59 year old market will only increase 7%. One of the most active groups online are those over the age of 65. They compare prices, go to sites like TripAdvisor, and listen to other people online on things like YouTube. One of the most successful YouTubers has been a man over the age of 80 posting comments on life every day. He has had many millions of views.

Some brand consultants fear that such a strategy may lead to repulsion from some of the audience, who may not find the brand interesting anymore. To this, PlayStation's Christopher says, 'This strategy definitely does not mean to abandon youth marketing completely; they plan to run it parallel to each other, while constantly introducing new lively products.'

Source: Based on Carter (2006), Dixon, Patrick (2013).

The activities, interests, and opinions (AIO) inventory is used to measure lifestyles of consumers (Wells and Tigert 1971).

There is another framework, which is known as the VALS™ framework. SRI International's Values and Lifestyles is an available psychographic segmentation system, which has gained worldwide acceptance (Kotler 2002). VALS™ is a marketing and consulting tool that helps businesses worldwide to develop and execute more effective strategies. The system identifies current and future opportunities by segmenting the consumer marketplace on the basis of the personality traits that drive consumer behaviour. VALS™ applies in all phases of the marketing process, from new product development and entry-stage targeting, to communications strategy and advertising. Based on the personality traits of consumers, which can be measured, they are classified into various categories.

VALS™ framework   The SRI International Values and Lifestyles Framework gives a detailed insight into the VALS™ typology (The VALS™ Segments 2008).

Exhibit 5.5   MicroGraam's Micro Ventures

MicroGraam is an innovative microcredit lending platform that enables deserving students, farmers, and micro entrepreneurs to avail credit from social investors.

MicroGraam works with over 23 rural NGOs in Karnataka, Tamil Nadu, and West Bengal to connect borrowers to sources of equitable credit. MicroGraam borrowers use their loans for a wide range of activities from employability training programs, farmers, and micro-entrepreneurs. In Micro Ventures, a micro-entrepreneur and a micro venture capitalist enter into a revenue sharing agreement, which enables the two partners to create a micro to small enterprise (MSE). Although traditional microcredit provides the essential service of access to credit, entrepreneurs who are willing and able to undertake larger business ventures are unable to do so under the current paradigm.

MicroGraam has created Micro Ventures to address this underserved niche market of entrepreneurs who require a larger loan size but cannot obtain them from commercial financing. Micro Ventures provide flexibility and cost savings, which can only arise from long-term financing. In this model, the micro venture capitalist provides the full upfront cost to starting the business, and the two parties agree to share a percentage of the profits or losses. The two parties agree upon how to share the profits or losses (50–50, 60–40, etc.) and the number of years the micro venture capitalist will be involved. MicroGraam acts as the facilitator in the transaction and helps the entrepreneur with their business model.

The first micro venture facilitated by MicroGraam was a Dairy Farm in Kolar district of Karnataka. MicroGraam facilitated equity capital of ₹300,000 from six micro venture capitalists in July 2010. The dairy farm was set by the members of the Self-Help Group and the group members jointly managed the dairy farm. Micro venture capitalist hold 40% stake in the dairy farm and 60% is held by the SHG group. In two years, micro venture capitalist have been able to exit fully with an annual ROI of 11%. The latest micro venture initiative supported by MicroGraam is a 'water shop' in northern Karnataka. The micro-entrepreneur, Sikander, received financing from three micro venture capitalists to the tune of ₹300,000. He recently opened shop to provide clean drinking water to the surrounding area with 500+ households. This social business leverages sustainable business practices to address the public health need for safe water. Access to clean water and sanitation facilitates are pressing conditions in rural India and Micro Ventures has enabled this social cause to become a viable social business. In order to achieve long-term, sustainable development in rural India, financial models beyond traditional loans and saving are essential. MicroGraam continues to develop innovating financings for the needs of its borrowers, and it is looking forward to helping.

MicroGraam services a riche segment

Source: MicroGraam.

Innovators They are successful, sophisticated, and have high self-esteem. Image is important to them, not as evidence of status or power, but as an expression of their personality.

Thinkers Motivated by ideals, thinkers have moderate respect for the status quo institutions of authority and social decorum, but are open to new ideas.

Achievers They lead a goal-oriented lifestyle, motivated by the desire for achievement. They have many wants and needs and are very active in the consumer marketplace.

Experiencers Self-expression is the prime motivator of experiencers. Young, enthusiastic, and impulsive consumers, they quickly become enthusiastic about new possibilities but are equally quick to cool. These avid consumers are high spenders.

Believers These are conservative and conventional people with concrete beliefs based on tradition. Opting for familiar products and established brands, the believers are predictable consumers.

Strivers Trendy and fun loving, strivers are motivated by achievement. They are also concerned about the opinions and approval of others and like to demonstrate their ability to win over peers.

Makers They are practical people who are motivated by self-expression. Makers have constructive skills and value self-sufficiency. They are suspicious of new ideas and big businesses.

Survivors Leading narrowly-focused lives, survivors are cautious consumers. They represent a very modest market for most products and services.

Psychological Factors

An individual's buying behaviour is influenced by psychological factors such as perception, beliefs and attitudes, learning, and motivation.

Perception

Perception is the process by which an individual selects, organizes, and interprets information inputs to create a meaningful picture of the world. People can perceive the same object on account of perceptual processes—selective, attention, selective distortion, and selective retention. It is important for service providers to create the right perceptions. Consumers' interpretations of perceptions about products can be examined in several areas—consumer categorization, consumer attributions, product/service quality, perceived value, etc.

Beliefs and attitudes

A belief is a thought that a person holds about something. These may emanate on account of his/her conditioning, culture, religion, etc. An attitude is a person's favourable or unfavourable evaluation, emotional feelings, and action tendencies towards an object or an idea (Krech et al. 1962).

Organizations use a variety of techniques to mould consumer attitudes. For instance, marketers have spent considerable amounts on advertising to create health consciousness among Indian consumers. It has taken many years for firms such as Reebok and Nike, to create a positive disposition towards health. People's perception about the Tata Group is that of reliability. Reliance Industries is associated with big projects.

Learning

Consumer researchers have treated the theme of consumer learning from three perspectives—probability theory, behaviour analysis, and cognitive theory (Lindquist and Sirgy 2003).

Probability theory treats learning as formation of habits. There are numerous models which have been designed to study brand loyalty, brand acceptance, brand switching, and new product forecasting. Behaviour analysis focuses on how certain behaviours could be reinforced or modified. Cognitive theory is another alternative that emphasizes the thinking, rather than the doing, of learning. It involves a four-stage process (Hach and Deighton 1989):

- Formulation of hypotheses
- Exposure
- Encoding
- Integration

The consumer develops a hypothesis about the brand and then tests it. If it works, it reinforces her belief. Eventually, by seeking more information from diverse sources and experience, the consumer's information horizon widens.

Then her experience is encoded in the memory and new information is processed based on prior experience. Established marketers need to reinforce the positive elements of service experience. They could block the strategy and explain why they offer a superior service. For a new service provider, the strategies deployed could be disruption of existing competition and attempting to facilitate a trail by the consumers.

Consumer motivation

Research indicates that consumers who are motivated to process information are likely to do so at deeper levels of memory. For the service industry, depending upon the impact of the service on the consumer, the motivation to choose a service provider will be different. For instance, in the insurance sector, LIC is the market leader as consumers feel more secure investing with a public sector firm. The underlying motivation is security of the investment. Similarly, for health care services, reliability and genuine care are higher degree of concerns for deciding on a hospital or clinic. On the other hand, a choice of a multiplex theatre may be governed more by convenience, and membership of a polo club or a vacation destination may be governed by self-esteem needs. So, there may be diverse motivation factors, which are at play when a consumer makes a buying decision. Human element being an important factor in the services sector, reliability, tangibility, experience, and trust may become important factors rather than the motivation factors listed in Maslow's or Herzberg's framework.

The implication for marketers is to provide information that consumers would retain. The repetition and emotional content of the message makes a difference. The packaging, advertising, and display cues should be such that they assist memory retrieval.

INDIAN SHOPPING HABITS

The retail trade set up in India is changing drastically and it is extremely important for the storeowners to assess their store, and compare the relative development in each country, and usage of private labels. Exhibit 5.6 provides an insight into Indian shopping patterns.

Exhibit 5.6 **Shoppers' Trends**

This exhibit features excerpts taken from a study by ACNielsen. Shopper trends offer an analysis of the changing behavioural patterns of shoppers globally. The study considers when, where, and how often people visit key retailers and provides insights into these changing patterns. It allows the storeowners to assess their stores. Below is an interesting list of key drivers that drive the consumers towards them. Another find is that the number of stores visited has reduced, implying that people are settling down to their own brands and have stopped experimenting, the loyal shoppers have increased, and hence, the average number of stores visited has gone down.

Top choice driver	Rank
Convenient to get to	1
Close to home	2
Attractive and interesting promotions	3
Food and groceries are good value for money	4
Always have what I want in stock	5
Everything I need in one store	6
A place where it is easy to quickly find what I need	7
Low prices for most items	8
Good range of fresh products	9
Better selection of high quality brands and products	10
Staff provide good service	11
Good quality instant cooked food	12

Another advantage of the modern retail format is that the convenience factor is the most important one, followed by good promotions, and value for money items.

The marketing research conducted by ACNielsen has some interesting pointers regarding the trend of online shopping. More than 85% of the world's online population has used the Internet to make a purchase; this is about 40% increase in the past two years. This trend shows that online retail has become an integral part of modern-day life. The following are some findings of the new research on the online market in India.

(Contd)

Exhibit 5.6 (Contd)

About 78% of Indian respondents surfing the Internet have used it to make a purchase.

About 73% of Indians have purchased online tickets/reservations, highest in the Asia Pacific region. This category is quite suited because of its ability to provide efficient and comprehensive access to a wide range of comparable information.

Most Indians prefer to make payment via credit card, with 84% opting for this.

Most Indian online shoppers are loyal to the sites they make purchases from and do not experiment much. About 54% opt for the same site every time.

As Indians are extremely price sensitive, 48% of the online Indians are influenced by special offers on the sites. This is followed by general surfing (40%), personal recommendation (31%), online advertising (26%), and search engines (22%), which are some of the other factors that influence online shoppers in India.

Indians love networking with people. While they are one of the heaviest users of mobile phones, being online helps them to keep in touch with family and friends. According to Research and Markets (2013) over 130 million Indians are connected to the Web through fixed and mobile broadband. Social media usage is highly active among young urban Indians. There are millions of registered Indians on Facebook and millions on LinkedIn and they log into these sites for networking.

Apart from these online trends, grocery store shopping is also one of the most important activities of the Indian household. With the entry of numerous big players, such as Big Bazaar, Subhiksha, Reliance Fresh, Spencer's Retail, etc., competition has become fierce. Some of the trends observed from the ACNielsen (2007) survey of about 26,486 Internet users in 47 markets from Europe, Asia Pacific, the Americas, and the Middle East were as follows.

Good value-for-money is the most important criterion for Indian consumers while choosing the grocery shop. Due to this reason, players, such as Big Bazaar and Spencer's advertise themselves as being the cheapest and the best value-for-money destinations.

The second most important factor is better selection of high-quality brands and products (79%), followed by location (54%), and available parking space (54%).

Price, promotions, and perceptions allow customers to arrive at the perception of value.

64% of Indians research and compare prices to decide which store offers good value for money, while 58% decide on the basis of word-of-mouth information.

A study by Ipsos (2013) states that everybody, be they from lower household income (82%), middle (80%), or high household income (74%) are likely to spend time looking for a good deal.

Source: Based on the data from ACNielsen (2008), Ipsos (2013).

RELATIONSHIP MARKETING

The market dynamics are changing at an astounding pace. With increasing competition, consumers certainly have a wider choice. In the light of these changes, consumer focus assumes a lot of importance. Marketers are now looking at building long-term relationships with the consumers rather than analysing isolated transactions with them. The whole paradigm of marketing is witnessing a sea change whereby the following shifts are taking place (Table 5.1).

Success, as mentioned earlier, is being measured by lifetime market share and lifetime profits. For instance, a single cigarette could cost just a few rupees, while the lifetime value

Table 5.1 Shifting marketing paradigm

1980s	Current
• Mass marketing	• Personal
• Passive consumer	• Participative
• One-off, short-term	• Lifetime, long-term
• Limited use of technology	• Widespread use of technology
• Serve customers well	• Serve customers differently
• Success measured by current market share	• Success measured by lifetime market share
• Success measured by current profits	• Success measured by lifetime profits

of one cigarette smoker is ₹1.10 lakh over a 10-year period, which is roughly 7,000 times the value of a single pack of cigarettes. Another estimate points out that the value of all the consumer products and services, which one could personally use over the next 25 years, would be worth ₹1.4 crore. The customer becomes important because companies lose roughly 15% of their customers every year, and in three years the company would be left with only half the customers it started with.

Relationship marketing shifts the focus of marketing exchange from transactions to relationships (Foss and Stone 2001). Some organizations have realized the importance of relationship marketing and have tried to cash in on the opportunity. Citibank has launched a product called life-stage marketing wherein it recognizes the needs of the customers, as they grow older. As a student, a customer may need a loan for higher education, a few years into his job he/she will need money to get married, and then, a loan to buy a house.

Future Group has taken great pains to devise a consumer friendly programme when it found that while consumers knew its different brands they did not know all these belonged to the same group. Additionally, Future Group and Payback, one of India's largest and Europe's most successful multi-partner loyalty programmes, entered a strategic tie-up to bring out a dedicated, single loyalty card that could be used for the company's various brands. The 'one-card-several-benefits' concept now allowed the company to have 'crisper' consumer insight and a better personality engagement. In just 10 months since the PayBack programme began, the company has got 8 million customers.

Every week since then, the group has added more than a lakh consumers to its loyalty programmes. Like most marketers, Future Group by initiating relationship marketing, has built up a database of its consumers. For instance, according to September 2012 data of the company, almost 45% of the group level billing has come through customers engaged in the loyalty programme. For Pantaloons, specifically, 70% of the billing comes from loyalty programme customers. It has further perfected its programme by closely following up on the customer within the first three months. After a customer has picked up the card, the company communicates to them about the working of the system, and how it can benefit them. There are offers to woo the customer to actually come to the store and experience the ease of use. Once the concept sticks with her and she understands the 'value' of the loyalty card, the retailer starts tracking her shopping behaviour—what are the common items on her purchase list, does she come midweek from office or on weekends to shop, and so on. Future Group offers a mix of rewards to its loyalty programme customers that include free parking, a separate cash counter, free home delivery, no fee on exchange offers, premiere passes for films, to name a few.

This process is in lines with when General Motors hired McCann to generate a list of 50,000 potential buyers. At the click of a mouse, General Motors can get an idea about how much each of these people earn, the kind of electronic gizmos they possess, how large their families are, what cars they own, and where they holiday. Glaxo has a database of 2,30,000 doctors. It initiated a relationship marketing programme through its Care and Aid programme for medical practitioners and started communicating with each one of them 3–12 times a year.

Appropriate market segmentation is also essential for a right strategy. For that, one needs to answer some of the following questions.
- Do all my customers have the same service needs and expectations?
- If not, can I regroup them into a few manageable clusters?
- Does it leave me with enough communality so that I will have a basic common offer?
- Who belongs to which segment?

Hear Music, a record and CD music chain in California, segments its market. It identified four service segments—passive consumer (interested in only top hits); eclectic (wide tastes, a little bit of jazz and classical); specialist (knows more than the sales people about their selections); and collector (looks for masterpieces). The marketer needs to respond to these segments through appropriate training of service personnel. Relationship marketing entails a lot of effort on the part of the marketer but sustained efforts certainly ensure loyal customers, which is definitely worth all the effort.

CUSTOMER DELIGHT

The new age customer is very different; the expectation has increased, he/she has become more knowledgeable and is aware of multiple options to satisfy her needs, and switches over to newer brands for better value for money. There are increasing number of competitors, both domestic and global, offering higher value-added products and processes through innovation. Although achieving customer satisfaction has long been identified as the heart of the entire marketing concept, most companies pay greater attention to their market share than to their customers' satisfaction. This is surely a big mistake as the market share is a backward-looking metric, while customer satisfaction is a forward-looking metric. If customer satisfaction starts slipping, then market share erosion will hit the brand in a big way.

Although meeting customer expectations can satisfy customers, the emotional response, such as an element of surprise, can delight the customers. Even satisfied customers can indulge in brand switching. Thus, not just satisfaction, but the emotional response to satisfaction is what customer delight is all about. All companies need to monitor and improve their level of customer satisfaction, as satisfied customers truly constitute the company's relationship capital. Every hotel provides lodging facilities along with food and beverages, but what leads to a customer base is customer delight. The emotional feeling of being attached to a brand results in higher levels of customer loyalty.

Hence, it is important to note that customer satisfaction is a necessary but not sufficient goal. Customer satisfaction only remotely predicts customer retention in highly competitive markets because companies regularly lose some percentage of their satisfied customers. Thus, companies should aim to delight customers, not simply to satisfy them.

'Customer delight is conceptualized as an emotional response, which results from surprising and positive levels of performance. As such, it could provide an explanation for the observed variation in the intentions and subsequent loyalty of customers reporting the same level of satisfaction' (Journal of Service Research 2005). Customer delight, thus, is more than just a very high level of satisfaction. It involves surpassing the standards of service that a customer has thought of, and requires focusing on what is currently unknown or unexpected by the customer. A research conducted by the University of Auckland, New Zealand and Vanderbilt University, UK, analysed that delight is a function of three components:
- Unexpectedly high levels of performance
- Arousal (for example, surprise, excitement)
- Positive effect (for example, pleasure, joy, or happiness)

Satisfaction by contrast, proved to be a function of only disconfirmed expectations (better than expected) and positive effect (Lovelock 2001).

There are various ways in which a company can delight its customers—surpassing (not just meeting) the needs of the customers, keeping word for advertising and sales, and providing the best customer experience. In services especially, word-of-mouth promotion is extremely crucial. It is also important that companies that receive high satisfaction scores should advertise it (Kotler 2003). A high rating ensures that the prospective customers trust the brand and its service; for example, handling of crisis situations arising in the travel and hospitality sector. It is important to manage customers in a way that is consistent with the service promises. The delight of customers is beyond the stated needs and the expected offering. For example, Holiday Inn ran a campaign a few years ago that promised 'No Surprises'. Guest complaints were so high that the slogan 'No Surprises' was mocked, and Holiday Inn quickly withdrew the slogan. The 'moment of truth' in a service offering can make or destroy the customer's perception of a service.

The point to note here is that customer delight does not necessarily mean to raise the expectations of the customers to a never-ending level. The trick is to understate, but over deliver. A close relationship does exist between customer loyalty and high levels of customer satisfaction (customer delight). As customer satisfaction becomes customer delight, customer retention, and loyalty increase. A delighted customer (as compared to a merely satisfied customer) is more likely to remain loyal in spite of attractive competitive offerings and a small negative experience will be covered up by an extremely positive one previously.

CUSTOMER LOYALTY

Customer loyalty in a business context has been used to describe a customer's willingness to continue patronizing a firm over a long period of time, purchasing and using its goods or services on a repeated and preferably exclusive basis, and voluntarily recommending the firm's products to friends and associates (Lovelock 2001). Reichheld and Sasser (1995) have discussed the relationship of profit per customer, with the number of years the customer has been with the service business. These profits may emanate from—(1) increased purchases; (2) reduced operating costs; (3) referrals to other customers; and (4) price premium.

Dick and Basu (1994) have proposed four conditions related to loyalty, namely, loyalty, latent loyalty, spurious loyalty, and no loyalty. Loyalty signifies relative attitude and repeat patronage. Latent loyalty is associated with high relative attitude and low repeat patronage. Spurious loyalty represents a low relative attitude with high repeat patronage. No loyalty is associated with low relative attitude combined with low repeat patronage.

Categorization of Customer Loyalty

Rowley (2005) has categorized loyal customers into four different categories— (1) captive; (2) convenience seekers; (3) contented; and (4) committed. The customers in each of these categories respond differently to triggers to switching. Their behaviour and attitudes also vary.

Captive All stores have some customers in this category because they have no real choice. These customers have few opportunities for switching. For example, when markets open up and competition increases, certain consumers continue to remain captive, and remain inert in attitude and behaviour because they perceive decision-making associated with switching to be something in which they do not wish to engage.

These customers could be poached by competition by reducing switching costs and barriers. Bank loans for housing in India is a case in point. Inter-bank transfers and minimal paper-work have made it easier for customers to switch home loans. These customers have neither positive behaviour nor attitude, and have a low involvement with the brand.

Convenience seeker A range of convenience factors drives this loyalty. Here, convenience on account of location or timings or brands may be a reason. Distribution network becomes important in this case. Where convenience is a significant factor, customers may switch even when they are satisfied with their existing service provider. Convenience is particularly important in the context of low involvement, routine purchases.

Contented Contented loyals have a positive attitude towards a brand but are inertial in their behaviour. This means that they continue to expand as a customer but do not extend their involvement with the brand by subscribing to additional services. For example, a Citibank card holder may be a loyal credit card user but may not avail of the company's services such as overdraft facility or personal loans. Such customers may be particularly vulnerable to service or product failure and strong recovery strategies may be an opportunity for sustaining the loyalty of this group.

Committed   These customers are positive in both attitude and behaviour. They are delighted with the brand and can be depended upon for repeat purchases. They make a positive contribution to the ambience of the service experience. Such customers are resistant to competitors' attempts to entice them.

Loyalty, Switchers, and Stayers

Wangenheim and Bayon (2004) have studied the differences between stayers and switchers, and their impact on loyalty. The results of the study confirm that the switchers differ from stayers in their higher levels of active loyalty and lower levels of reactive loyalty, as well as more positive word-of-mouth publicity. Referral switchers differ from other switchers with respect to their higher satisfaction, active loyalty, and more positive word-of-mouth publicity. Exhibit 5.7 discusses customer loyalty initiatives in the Indian context.

Exhibit 5.7   **Loyalty Gains**

Loyalty programmes, such as loyalty cards, free parking, free gifts/coupons, and point redemption schemes, have become commonplace among both service providers as well as manufacturers. All these companies know the importance of a loyal customer.

Shoppers Stop on realizing that men would pick up only a handful of products from its outlets started informing them about bulk deals in the men's category. It has further developed a special app for smartphone users to help track 'personality types' of its customers to integrate it with the loyalty programme.

The loyalty programme strategies mentioned previously play a pivotal role in engaging the customer and encouraging him/her to spend on the products and services more often.

Market analysts believe that loyalty programmes are not just about winning over the customers with gifts; they should be built and developed in a way to create affinity and closeness to the brand. Many coalition loyalty programmes, such as the tie-up between the Delhi Metro and Citibank card, and ICICI and Tata group, also help create loyalty and identification. Retail chain Shoppers Stop started its loyalty programme (First Citizens) way back in 1994 and has over 630,000 members. The salespersons indulge in continuous communication with their customers and reward them with points and gifts. Airlines, such as Go, Air, Jet, and Air India, have frequent flyer programmes where the loyalists are upgraded to first class with frequent flyer points.

The biggest advantage of loyalty programmes is that they help to retain customers at value and thus, no company wishes to lose an opportunity to make their customers feel special. The question that arises here is, are not these loyalty schemes a drain on the company's funds? The answer is no, because it is an investment. Redemption of points against a minimum purchase is an advantage as it indicates the fact that more and more customers see value in the programme and are willing to spend more on the brand.

The challenge is not to consider this as a cost and be patient with the results. It is very important to make the customer feel comfortable and important. It is also important to convert invisible customers into active customers.

Source: Based on the articles from *Business Standard* (2006), Rewards of Loyalty (2012).

CONSUMERISM

This section discusses consumer rights and responsibilities in the Indian context.

Although the marketer's slogan has long been 'customer is king', it remains a vocal pledge. The concept of 'caveat emptor' or 'let the buyer beware' is still the motto of many. Hence, there was a need to protect the consumers. The consumer movement was started and what we see now is that 'consumers are more powerful than at any other time, and their power is increasing. One survey revealed that a typical business hears only 4% of its dissatisfied customers. The other 96% just quietly go away and 91% will never return' (Groucutt et al. 2004). This indicates how important it is to keep the customers happy and satisfied.

There is no single definition of consumerism. 'It is generally accepted as being any organized group pressure on behalf of customers or users of a product or service. This may be specific to an individual organization such as a "user group" or aimed at protecting consumers in general from organizations with which there can be exchange relationships' (Adcock et al. 2001). As the consumer movement has gained momentum, customers can raise their voice against an injustice and are increasingly able to communicate with organizations.

The real consumerism, as we know today, started in the US. Consumers today have 'consumer rights' to protect them from any exploitation.

RESEARCH INSIGHT

An Exposition of Consumer Behaviour in the Financial Services Industry

Antony Beckett, Paul Hewer, and Barry Howcroft (2000), 'An exposition of consumer behaviour in the financial services industry', *International Journal of Bank Marketing*, vol. 18, issue 1, pp. 15–26.

Deregulation and the emergence of new forms of technology have created highly competitive market conditions which have had a critical impact upon consumer behaviour. Bank providers must, therefore, attempt to better understand their customers in an attempt not only to anticipate but also to influence and determine consumer buying behaviour. The paper accordingly presents and develops a model which attempts to articulate and classify consumer behaviour in the purchasing of financial products and services. The theoretical insights generated by this model are then used to examine qualitative research data gained from focus group discussions on consumers' attitudes to their financial providers and their financial products. Finally, these findings are examined for the potential insights they provide to bank providers attempting to identify appropriate strategies which are conducive to increased customer retention and profitability.

SUMMARY

The chapter introduced the concept of consumer behaviour. It is fundamental to understand the behaviour of the consumer before the company launches its products. Consumer behaviour can be understood by understanding the processes at three levels—pre-purchase activities, purchasing activities, and post-purchasing activities. Consumption can also be analysed during different phases—acquisition, consumption, and disposition. There are three different levels of analysis of consumer behaviour—individual, micro, and macro environment. To understand consumer behaviour, an understanding of the decision-making process and the factors that can influence the decision, is important. The steps that a consumer follows when arriving at a decision are need/problem recognition, information search, alternative evaluation, choice, and outcome of the decision. The EKB model for consumer decision-making has also been discussed in detail. The framework for understanding consumer behaviour, which includes market stimuli, and buyers' characteristics, decision-making process, and decisions, has also been enumerated.

The chapter also gives insights into the changing dynamics of Indian consumers. Indian shopping habits have been highlighted. The convenience factor is the key for consumers in India, followed by promotions and other factors. The chapter also gives insights on online shoppers in India. Travel reservations in India are increasingly being done online. As the penetration of personal computers and the Internet increases, consumers will increasingly go online. The survey on Indian consumers has also been included. The factors influencing consumer behaviour—cultural, social, personal, and psychological—have been discussed in detail.

The concept of relationship marketing has also been discussed. Relationship paradigm looks at the lifetime value of a customer rather than a transaction-based approach. The deployment of relationship requires infusion of IT in various domains and this is a resource-intensive investment.

The chapter also enumerates on the concept of customer loyalty. Customer loyalty has been categorized as captive, convenience seekers, contented, and committed. The reasons why customers switch have also been discussed.

The concept of consumerism has been elaborated on. The section traced the evolution of consumer rights in India and discussed the consumer rights.

KEY TERMS

Attitude The way in which an individual views and evaluates something or someone. Attitudes determine whether people like or dislike things, and therefore, how they behave towards them. Attitude is traditionally divided into cognitive, behavioural, and affective components, although the main emphasis now tends to fall on defining attitude in terms of affect—the person's feelings towards the object, brand, etc.

Consumer behaviour The buying behaviour of individuals and households who buy goods and services for personal consumption. A number of different people, playing different roles, have been identified in the decision to make a specific purchase, that is, initiator, influencer, decider, buyer, and user.

Consumerism An organized movement of citizens and government agencies to improve the rights and power of buyers in relation to sellers.

Culture A complex whole, which includes knowledge, belief, art, morals, customers, and any other capabilities and habits acquired by man as a member of society.

Customer delight This is conceptualized as an emotional response, which results from surprising and positive levels of performance.

Customer loyalty A customer's willingness to continue patronizing a firm over a long period of time, purchasing and using its goods or services on a repeated and preferably exclusive basis, and voluntarily recommending the firm's products to friends and associates.

Decision-making The act of deciding between two or more alternative courses of action.

Motivation The mental processes that arouse, sustain, and direct human behaviour. Motivation may stem from processes taking place within an individual (intrinsic motivation) or from the impact of factors acting on the individual from outside (extrinsic motivation); in most cases these two influences are continually interacting.

Perception The process by which an individual selects, organizes, and interprets information inputs to create a meaningful picture of the world.

Reference groups Groups to which consumers belong and which influence their behaviour. Reference groups serve as direct (face-to-face) or indirect points of reference, providing comparisons that help to form a person's attitudes or behaviour.

Relationship marketing Marketing activities aimed at building long-term relationships with parties (especially customers) that contribute to a company's success. The goal is to ensure long-term value to customers, producing enduring customer satisfaction.

Social class A system for classifying the population according to social status.

EXERCISES

Concept Review Questions

1. Discuss the factors, which influence consumers' buying processes.
2. How does lifestyle affect the service provider's promotion strategy?
3. How do service providers target consumers in different social categories? Enumerate with different examples.
4. Discuss the Indian consumer's orientation towards shopping.
5. Discuss the future of the Indian consumer's spending pattern through online channels.
6. How does the family influence buying decisions? Discuss with appropriate examples.

Critical Thinking Questions

1. A very reputed cosmetic manufacturer, which retails its brand under the brand name Lakmé, has also started operating its salons under the brand name of Lakmé Salon. Please study the consumer response to Lakmé Salons in the age group 16–25 years. How does the same compare with other beauty salons operating in your region?
2. Please identify the influence of kids on the choice of various services such as cable vs satellite channels, music stores, restaurants, and multiplexes.

Project Assignments

1. Browse through the website of two telecom service providers. Discuss how effective their strategy is on the website, to attract potential customers.
2. Compare the loyalty programmes of Radisson hotels vis-à-vis Marriott hotels by accessing data available on their websites.
3. Compare the online shopping portals of Indiatimes with Yahoo India. Which one is more consumer-friendly?
4. Prepare a short write-up on consumerism practices in India using Internet-based research.
5. Is relationship marketing really practised in India? Discuss critically.

CASE STUDY | Realities of Rural Market Segmentation*

Introduction

There are a number of myths and realities regarding the immense potential of the Indian rural market. There is no doubt that the rural market presents a huge untapped opportunity as nearly 70% of the population lives in rural India. However, marketers need to explore growth indicators and key strategic tools for successful exploitation of this untapped market. The article focuses on segmentation, targeting, and positioning strategies for rural markets with some success stories of MNCs in the background.

Half a dozen religions, 33 languages, 1,650 dialects, and diversity in castes, sub-castes, tribes, culture, and subculture characterize rural India. So rural marketers need to have an open mind and sensitize themselves to understand the rural consumer. Apart from this, communicating in the language that the rural consumer comprehends is a challenge most marketers face. Creative approaches to providing a satisfactory offering in terms of adaptation to consumer needs through differentiated product offering and the advertising message used are absolute essentials to achieve success through effective segmentation and implementation.

In the changing business environment, even the rural customer is very active and quality conscious.

* Shivaraj, B. and T.P. Mohan Kumar (2006), 'Realities of rural market segmentation', *Marketing Mastermind*, October, ICFAI University Press.

Companies have been moving from traditional marketing to modern marketing; hence, marketing calls for more than developing a product, pricing, promoting, and making it accessible to target customers. Technology has also played a key role in transforming marketing. These developments have enriched the field of marketing management. Although there is a greater integration of business functions, unfortunately marketers are yet to understand the full impact of these developments.

Urban markets are increasingly becoming competitive and perhaps, getting saturated. Consider the case of toiletries, packaged tea, dry cell batteries, and even entertainment products and services. For most of these products, the demand seems to be increasing. This situation leads to the search for new markets for growth and satisfaction to both organization and consumers.

Rural markets are new markets, which are opening for consumer goods. Companies that have expanded in these areas have found that they have been able to ward off competition, generate a new demand, and in turn, increase their sales or profits. Many companies have already taken a lead in establishing their products in rural markets. Products of Hindustan Lever Limited (soaps, detergents, etc.) are made available in all rural markets through stockists, wholesalers, and retailers. Bisleri mineral water is available in some rural markets. Bournvita and Horlicks are served in small restaurants in prosperous rural areas. Marico's Parachute hair oil has already entered the rural market. Philips and BPL have become household names in the consumer durable market in rural areas. HMT watches are still preferred in rural markets. Mahindra's jeeps and tractors are very popular with farmers. Proctor and Gamble has introduced its shampoos in small sachets. Similarly, coconut hair oil, biscuits, toothpastes, and cosmetics, are all available in small packs and sachets for rural consumers.

Profile of the Indian Rural Market

Of the 121 crore Indians, 83.3 crore live in rural areas while 37.7 crore stay in urban areas, according to the Census of India's 2011 report.

The number of young educated people in rural India has increased from 58.7% in 2001 to 68.91% in 2011.

According to a study done by IBEF, the total rural FMCG market size in 2012 was 33% of the total FMCG market, while the market size of consumer durables has grown at a health rate of 10.3% from FY03–12.

According to TATA strategic group management team 2013, close to a third of both FMCG and durable sales is contributed by rural markets. Recent data shows that rural consumption has grown faster than urban in the last two years. Rural penetration of key durables has seen a significant upward trend. TV penetration has moved from around 31% in 2007 to 39.8% in 2010 and motorcycles/scooter penetration from 9.5% to 13.9% in the same period.

According to CRISIL 2012, discretionary spending of a typical rural Indian household rose to ₹24,000 in 2009–10, from ₹14,000 in 2004–05, growing at about 11% per annum, which is faster than the inflation rate of nearly 6% per annum over the same period.

There are nearly 42,000 rural supermarkets (haats) in India. The number exceeds the total number of retail chain stores in the US (35,000).

One-third of the total number of luxury goods is sold in rural India.

Two-thirds of the middle-income households are in rural India.

If the rural income goes up by 1%, purchasing power of rural India will go up by ₹10,000 crore. According to WSJ 2013 report, the rural mean household incomes have gone up by 6% in 2012.

Of the 893.15 million BSNL mobile phone connections, 340.60 million are in rural India.

Of the 20 million who have signed up for Rediff mail, 60% are from small towns.

Twenty-four million Kisan credit cards (KCC) issued in rural areas exceeds the 17.7 million credit and debit cards issued in urban India. A whopping ₹52,000 crore has been sanctioned under the KCC scheme.

The number of middle and higher income families (having ₹70,000 plus annual income) in rural

India is 21.7 million and the number in urban India is 24.2 million, which is nearly the same.

Of the six lakh odd villages in the entire country, 5.85 lakh villages or 98.5%, had a village public telephone (VPT) as of March 2011.

Out of the total population of India around 70% lives in rural areas; hence, 'rural India is real India'. India is now seeing a dramatic shift towards consumption and prosperity in rural households. The rural people differ from their urban counterparts on a large number of attributes. Their buying behaviour is also bound to differ and that has important implications for marketers. With the increasing consumption and discretionary incomes in rural India, there has been an upward thrust on measures to develop a marketing framework to exploit opportunities in widely scattered rural markets of the country for effective implementation of market segmentation and targeting.

Potentiality of Rural Markets in India

- The size of India's rural market stated as a percentage of the world population is 12.2%. It means that 12.2% of the world's consumers live in rural India. In incremental terms, spending in rural India during the period 2009–2012 rose by US$69 billion to urban India's US$55 billion.
- The rural market offers a great opportunity for different branded goods and services to target a large number of potential customers. HLL estimates that out of five lakh villages in India, only one lakh have been tapped so far, which goes to indicate the market potential of the rural market.
- Rural consumption of certain durables and non-durables is more than that in urban areas. Some of the products for which the demand in rural areas is more than in urban areas are sewing machines, radios, wristwatches, bicycles, etc. It is estimated that for durables, the annual growth rate is 25%, which is outstanding by any standards.
- There is also an increase in the average number of working days in a year. This has resulted in an increase in rural income in terms of absolute value.

- Accessibility to rural markets has become easy through improved infrastructural facilities such as transportation, communication, TV penetration, and information technology.
- The urban market is getting saturated and many companies are now targeting the rural market.
- Rural lifestyle is changing. Almost every household has at least one member living and working in a city.

Common Marketing Myths about the Rural Market

There are some myths about rural markets and rural consumers.

Rural market penetration is not beneficial   Some people feel that rural consumers are not worth bothering about and can be neglected because they tend to buy unbranded products rather than the branded variety.

In reality, the study conducted by MART reveals that there is a high preference for branded products among rural consumers. It indicates that there is a potential for branded products if a company can fulfil the requirement of the consumers through effective market segmentation and targeting strategies.

Rural consumers will take just what is given to them   Another myth that marketers believe is that if the company has solid sales in rural areas, its product is safe and secure.

In reality, the rural sales of Iodex and Amrutanjan are high due to lack of choice. It is true that rural consumers are quite loyal to some brands, such as chyavanprash or toothpaste brands such as Colgate, which have made efforts to build their brand names in rural areas. However, as toilet soaps demonstrate, brand building is required because of a wide choice available to customers. Therefore, rural consumers cannot be counted as blindly loyal. Price also plays a vital role; the higher the price, the more cautious rural consumers will be. They will search for new brands. Where the price is low, they are happy to shop on impulse.

Rural consumers will only buy really cheap mass-market brands   One of the important misconceptions about rural consumers is that they are more sensitive to price and purchase low- priced products. Low-priced brands, such as Nirma, are obviously in the lead. However, another startling revelation is that penetration of premium products is being reported even among the poorer sections of the masses.

One family one brand Marketers often expect rural households to be homogeneous in consumption. Marketers make the mistake of thinking that the entire household prefers to use only one brand.

In reality, many families prefer multi-brand usage. The fact is that, rural households are not homogeneous especially when it comes to soaps, detergents, and tea. Even when price differences exist, privileged consumers such as the heads of families or favoured sons, insist on a superior brand of soaps, tea, or washing powder for their use.

Distribution drives rural sales Another misconception is that rural marketing is only about distribution. However, in reality, distribution is clearly the key to rural marketing, but it is wrong to imagine that distribution is all that matters. Rural consumers are not cocooned from the urban world as they are increasingly getting access to markets in towns, either directly or indirectly. Whatever the means are, rural consumers are eager to consume. If marketers do not capture the opportunity to satisfy the needs of rural consumers, then rural consumers will search for other alternatives to fulfil their needs.

Rural market is an extension of the urban market One of the misconceptions is that the marketing campaigns in rural areas are akin to those in urban areas. Hence, marketers believe that the same marketing campaigns will embrace the brand and product preference of the rural market too.

In reality, rural markets possess dynamics that are distinct from their urban counterparts by virtue of their genesis, size, and target audience. Brands and products need to be presented and promoted in a manner that caters to local cultural and social sensitivities. It is also important to introduce features in the product that holds significance for rural consumers.

Size of the market The size of the market can be estimated based on an analysis of current product penetration levels and sales volumes. Even limited acceptance of the product translated into a potential market can bring profits. In reality, limited acceptance in a rural area does not imply that the product has market potential. Such an assumption might cause increased product mortality as a greater number of competing firms flood the market with their products while the actual demand may be very low.

Perception and attitude of rural people are the same It is a myth that the attitude, values, and purchasing behaviour of consumers in rural areas in one region is the same as that in another region. Marketers may also adopt a 'one size fits all' approach for promoting a product. In reality, the rural markets in India are a complex montage of cultural and social mindsets, which greatly influence the local lifestyles. Often purchase decisions are made collectively, with people seeking advice from influential members of the village. Despite education, employment, and income levels being major factors in product preferences, the social, and cultural mindset acts as a key to purchase decisions and this mindset differs from one region to another. Hence, it becomes imperative for marketers to use a multi-level approach for product promotion and to keep the distinct regional dynamics in mind before planning a marketing strategy.

Rural Market Segmentation

The aforementioned myths and misconceptions regarding the rural market indicate that there is a need for effective rural market segmentation. In fact, the rural market satisfies the prerequisites for market segmentation such as measurability, accessibility, differentiability, and substantiability. Marketers should evaluate the segment opportunity with reference to their short-term and long-term objectives. If a company's objective is to achieve long-term sustainable sales volume by expanding its consumer base, then it has to go rural instead of expecting consumers to come to urban markets to purchase products and services. Companies, such as Asian Paints, HLL, and Colgate-Palmolive, which reach rural homes with their products, demonstrate this. Companies should also examine their resources and capabilities for serving rural markets. They should conduct small pilot projects, which will provide an opportunity to evaluate the target segment behaviour towards the product or service being offered. Smart marketers in rural areas, such as HLL and ITC, initiated pilot projects named Shakti and e-Choupal, which were later transformed into mega rural marketing models.

Rural consumers are influenced by rationality, personal experience, the level of utility that is derived from the consumption, etc. The clever, gimmicky advertisements do not work with rural consumers. Their buying behaviour is influenced by the experience of their own friends, relatives, and family members. Above all, quality of the product and its easy availability are the primary and vital determinants of consumer buying behaviour. The techniques of bombarding product messages have a limited influence. Rural consumers are very much attached to and influenced by the touch and feel aspect of any promotional activity. It is imperative that the marketing experts understand the mindset of rural consumers for every product, in any specified region. Hence, it is necessary that more research studies on the rural market, especially on segmentation, targeting, and positioning strategies should be undertaken. The research will help marketers understand the rural consumers better and generate more reliable data with particular attention to product-specific, region-specific, group-specific, and seasonal-specific information, for effectively segmenting the market. It is also important that language and regional behavioural variations should be given due attention while developing the rural communication strategy. In order to taste success, the aim of marketing agencies must be to 'feel the local touch'. Rural distribution of the products automatically paves the way for the next big market revolution in rural areas. The structure of competition in rural market is very complex and is not uniform. The competition dynamics change from one village to another; this is visible in the form of new local or regional brands on the shelf competing with other national brands.

Rural Marketing Strategies

Marketers can make consistent attempts to innovate tools and strategies to overcome the challenges they face in the business arena. Business innovations are broadly classified under two heads—product/service innovation and process innovation.

Marketers need to design creative solutions to overcome challenges typical of the rural environment, such as physical distribution, channel management, and promotion and communication. Corporate India and government bodies alike have made several efforts to bridge the gap between rural and urban India. The urban–rural divide in FMCG consumption is being bridged rapidly. In the case of some high volume consumables, such as toilet soaps, washing powders, packaged tea, biscuits, and detergent cakes, the penetration and usage in urban and rural markets is comparable, because companies now segment their customers into similar clusters in order to market specialized products and services to each group. Initially, marketers in India concentrated on segmenting only the urban market. But with the saturation of urban markets in recent years, and the simultaneous growing demand in rural markets, the need to segment the rural market is increasingly being felt. More and more companies are moving away from the assumption that rural consumers are a homogeneous mass with little or no differences. Firms are beginning to divide the rural market into homogenous segments in order to reach out to each segment more effectively.

Today, rural marketers have become more focused on consumer choice and requirements. This calls for segmenting, targeting, and positioning (STP). Since the rural market in India began to grow rapidly in the post 1990s, marketers needed to evolve different strategies for different customer groups to tap the rural markets effectively. Creative segmentation can help a company get closer to its customers by developing the appropriate differential marketing mix for each segment through changes in one or more of the four Ps of the marketing mix, that is, product, price, place, and promotion.

Effective Segmentation and Targeting—Success Stories of Rural Market Segmentation

Earlier the rural market in India was considered a homogeneous mass. HUL was the giant and undisputed market leader in detergents (Surf) in India. However, it suffered significant losses at the hands of a new and small organization called Nirma Chemicals. The latter's washing powder, Nirma, very quickly caught the attention of the middle- and lower-income customers, who were finding it difficult to make both ends meet with their limited monthly income.

Nirma was the lowest priced branded washing powder available in grocery and cooperative stores. The middle-class segment was happy as they could now choose a lower priced washing powder against Surf, which was beyond their budget. Nirma also had an impact on upper middle-class and higher-income families, who chose Nirma for washing their inexpensive clothes. In the year 1984, HUL decided to take a fresh look at the market. Research conducted across the country revealed that different income groups of consumers had varying expectations from detergents and washing powders. Thus, to counter the attack from Nirma, HUL launched Sunlight (yellow), Wheel (green), and Rin (blue) detergent powders for different market segments. This strategy of segmenting the market helped HUL win back part of its lost market. HUL ended FY 2012–13 with ₹25,810.21 crore (US$4.15 billion) in revenue.

Similarly, T-Series introduced audio cassettes at unbelievably low prices and took away a huge share from the then market leader HMV. These initiatives taught the big firms valuable lessons on the importance of segmenting the market.

Market segmentation offers several benefits over mass marketing. Segmentation helps distinguish one customer profile from another within a given market, and it facilitates in understanding the needs of the target buyers. The company can create more fine-tuned product offerings and price them appropriately for the target segment. 75% of people in rural India are engaged in agriculture, but they cannot be clubbed under one category. There are large farmers, medium farmers, small farmers, marginal farmers, and agricultural labourers. Their income levels, lifestyles, and behaviour are different. Therefore, there is a need to classify rural consumers under different segments. Further, the remaining 25% of the rural population is engaged in non-farm activities, which could be segmented as self-employed labourers, daily wage labourers, salaried employees, traders, micro entrepreneurs, etc.

Those families in rural areas with some members residing in urban areas tend to have a different level of exposure to the outside world, which in turn affects their aspirations and lifestyles. Access to mass media (television or radio) also varies widely in rural areas, which affects consumer behaviour. Hence, these factors need to be considered while segmenting rural customers.

Brooke Bond Lipton India Ltd (now part of HUL) decided to expand its branded tea into the largely unbranded loose tea segment in the rural market. The company explored the buying, consumption, and other habits of all tea consumers in order to identify a cross-section of people united by common behaviour traits. Only after conducting extensive research did HUL conceive the idea of A1, a new brand of tea for the rural market. A bundle of benefits were designed to meet the needs of the rural segment.

HUL began by collecting photographs and video clips of people across the country, who buy loose tea, in order to study their lifestyles in general, and their tea preparation and tea drinking habits in particular. It studied the number of times people drink tea during the day, the time they drink tea, how they serve it, and the family members who are regular tea drinker. Alongside, HUL tracked other items of food and drink that these people consumed, the soaps and detergents that they used, and how they spent their leisure, so as to understand just where tea and its consumption stood in their matrix of needs. The objectives were to understand exactly what bases of segmentation could be used to differentiate consumer groups. It would have been too simplistic to use just price as a factor to define the segment. As a result of this elaborate exercise, HUL found a simple but highly effective idea that it could use to define its segment—all who desire a strong cup of tea. Cutting across geographical, cultural, income, and age groups, this need emerged as a unifier for many tea drinkers. So, HUL used this as the one overriding characteristic that would distinguish its chosen niche from the rest of the market.

Conclusion

Different marketers have attempted multiple segmentation approaches in the rural market. It seems clear that one cannot rely on a specific segmentation approach. Rather, one needs to explore and understand customers through behavioural research or by undertaking pilot projects in rural areas to be able to identify well-defined segments.

Only effective segmentation will help in reaching the target customers by using the appropriate positioning platform. Merely the adoption of urban segmentation, targeting, and positioning (STP) strategies for rural markets cannot be helpful in winning frontiers in the ever-changing and growing rural market.

This is one area where a lot more work needs to be done by research agencies, advertising agencies, and marketers alike, to develop a holistic STP and understanding of the rural market, as there is a huge potential for the Indian rural market to reap maximum benefit. The challenges of rural market segmentation need to be evolutionary and not revolutionary. It has to be considered as an investment today for a better future tomorrow. Organizations should focus on nurturing the rural markets and should have a long-term perspective rather than concentrating on achieving short-term objectives.

The greatest problem is that the rural market is still evolving in efficient dissemination of information and there is no set format for understanding consumer behaviour. A lot of research is still to be conducted in order to understand the rural market. The future is certainly bright for the Indian rural market through its effective implementation of STP strategies, which will create more room for all players including consumers, marketers, investors, and others in the market. As the market matures and deepens further, one can really hope to see the fortune day very soon by providing a benchmark for traders worldwide, especially in fast moving consumer goods (FMCG), where India is the major consumer as well as a producer. As rightly put by C.K. Prahalad, 'The future lies with those companies who see the poor as their customers'.

Questions

1. Discuss the role of consumers in the context of rural markets in India.
2. How can service firms tap the rural markets in India? Does it make sense for them to customize the service offerings in light of the profile of the consumers at the bottom of the pyramid?

REFERENCES

Biwalkar, M. (2006) 'Loyalty gains', *The Strategist, Business Standard,* New Delhi, 17 October.

Business World (2005), 'Kids' pester power', *The Marketing Whitebook,* pp. 140–141.

Business World (2005), 'The evolving Indian family', *The Marketing Whitebook,* pp. 168–170.

Business World (2008), *The Marketing Whitebook* 2012–13, ABP Pvt. Ltd, New Delhi.

Carter, M. (2006), 'Growing up', *The Strategist, Business Standard,* New Delhi, 24 October.

Darby, M.R and E. Karni (1973), 'Free competition and optimal amount of Fraud', *Journal of Law and Economics,* vol. 16, April, pp. 67–88.

Dick, A. and K. Basu, (1994), 'Customer loyalty: Towards an integrated framework', *Journal of the Academy of Marketing Science,* vol. 22 (2), pp. 99–113.

Foss, B. and M. Stone (2001), *Successful Customer Relationship Marketing*, Kogan Page, London.

Hach, S.J. and J. Deighton (1989), 'Managing what consumers learn from experience', *Journal of Marketing*, April, vol. 53, p. 3.

'Is majority of India non-vegetarian?', *The Times of India*, New Delhi, 19 October 2006.

Joshi, P. (2006), 'Cinemas as impulse buy', *Business Standard*, New Delhi, p. 11, 12 October.

Kotler, P. (2003), *Marketing Management: The Millennium Edition*, Prentice Hall, New Delhi.

Krech, David, R.S. Crutchfield, and L.B. Egerton (1962), *Individual in Society*, McGraw-Hill, New York.

Lindquist, J.D. and M.J. Sirgy (2003), 'Shopper, buyer, and consumer behaviour', *Biztantra*, New Delhi.

Lovelock, C. (2001), *Services Marketing*, Addison-Wesley Longman, Delhi.

Nelson, P. (1970) 'Information and Consumer Behaviour', *Journal of Political Economy*, vol. 78, March–April, pp. 311–29.

Nichenametla, P. (2006), '3,256 complaints, 0 penalties', *Business Standard*, New Delhi, 12 October.

Reichheld, F.J. and W.E. Sasser Jr (1995), 'Zero defections: Quality comes to services', *Harvard Business Review*, vol. 73, pp. 59–75, September–October.

Rowley, J. (2005), 'The four Cs of customer loyalty', Marketing Intelligence and Planning, Bradford, vol. 23, no. 6/7, p. 8.

Sarkar, K. (2006), 'Micro finance now on LIC agenda', *Business Standard*, New Delhi, 25 October.

Schiffman, L.G. and L.L. Kanuk (1997), *Consumer Behaviour*, 6th edn, Prentice Hall, London.

Swami, M.R. (2006), 'High flyers', *The Strategist*, *Business Standard*, 24 October.

Tylor, Edward B. (1871), 'The origins of culture and religion in primitive culture', *1873 edition of Primitive Culture*, vols I and II, Harper & Brothers, New York.

Wangenheim, Florian V. and Tomás Bayón (2004), 'The effect of word of mouth on services switching: Measurement and moderating variables', *European Journal of Marketing*, vol. 38, issue 9/10, pp. 1173–1185.

Wells, W.D. and D.J. Tigert (1971), 'Activities, interest and opinions', *Journal of Advertising Research*, vol. 11, no. 4, pp. 27–35, August.

Cherian, C., N. Dasgupta, and A.G. Doreswamy (2007), 'Effect of marketing on society', Paper presented at the International Marketing Conference on Marketing & Society, 8–10 April, Kozhikode, available from http://dspace.iimk.ac.in/bitstream/2259/320/1/657-663.pdf, accessed on 14 May 2008.

'Consumer protection as a barometer of India's democracy', available from http://www.consumer-voice.org/independenceday.asp, accessed on 8 May 2008.

http://articles.economictimes.indiatimes.com/2011-10-22/news/30309786_1_coffee-consumption-amalgamated-bean-coffee-trading-ccd, accessed on 20 December 2013.

http://articles.economictimes.indiatimes.com/2013-01-01/news/36094011_1_cafe-coffee-day-coffee-makers-coffee-capsules, accessed on 20 December 2013.

http://businesstoday.intoday.in/story/pester-power/1/10554.html, accessed on 20 December 2013.

http://pitchonnet.com/blog/2012/08/21/how-well-do-indian-marketers-understand-the-indian-youth/, accessed on 20 December 2013.

http://services.byu.edu/sw/doku.php?id=usb:unit9:sbp9a

http://timesofindia.indiatimes.com/business/india-business/Household-income-in-rural-India-grew-11-per-annum-in-5-years-Report/articleshow/17309532.cms, accessed on 20 December 2013.

http://timesofindia.indiatimes.com/business/india-business/Indian-consumers-show-both-impulsive-and-compulsive-buying-behaviour-Ipsos/articleshow/24195067.cms, accessed on 20 December 2013.

http://www.acrwebsite.org/search/view-conference-proceedings.aspx?Id=6817

http://www.animationxpress.com/index.php/latest-news/cartoon-network-unveils-new-generation-2012, 6 Dec 2012, accessed on 18 June 2014.

http://www.business-standard.com/article/management/growth-markets-in-rural-india-113020400032_1.html, accessed on 20 December 2013.

http://www.business-standard.com/article/markets/coffee-consumption-to-touch-125-000-tonnes-113101300197_1.html, accessed on 20 December 2013.

http://www.business-standard.com/article/specials/the-rewards-of-loyalty-112102200040_1.html, accessed on 20 December 2013.

http://www.changemakers.com/powerofsmall/nominations/micrograam-marketplace, accessed on 20 December 2013.

http://www.globalchange.com/marketing-to-older-consumers.htm, accessed on 20 December 2013.

http://www.mckinsey.com/insights/asia-pacific/the_bird_of_gold, accessed on 20 December 2013.

http://www.mcommerce.io/mcommerce-sales-rise-by-136-year-on-year-18072013/, accessed on 20 December 2013.

http://www.microfinanceindia.org/uploads/news_attachments/20130724120608_state-of-the-sector-report-2012.pdf, accessed on 20 December 2013.

http://nikitamalik.com/2012/11/22/childs-play-a-systematic-review-of-pester-power-in-india/, accessed on 20 December 2013.

http://www.researchandmarkets.com/, accessed on 20 June 2014.

http://www.researchandmarkets.com/research/w9x47k/impact_of_social, accessed on 20 December 2013.

'Internet the new pit stop for Indian shoppers?', available from http://in.nielsen.com/news/20080201.shtml, accessed on 10 May 2008.

Jayashankar, P. (2008), 'In pursuit of youth', *The Hindu Business Line*, available from http://www.thehindubusinessline.com/catalyst/2004/09/09/stories/2004090900090200.htm, accessed on 10 May 2008.

SRI Consulting Business Intelligence (2008), 'The VALS segments', available from http://www.sric-bi.com/VALS/types.shtml, accessed on 11 May 2008.

www.ibef.org, accessed on 20 December 2013.

'Youth to drive e-commerce growth in India', IAMI summit news, available from http//www.domain-b.com/ebusiness/general/20060119_commerce.html, accessed on 10 May 2008.

6 Segmentation, Targeting, and Positioning for a Services Firm

OBJECTIVES

After reading this chapter you will be able to understand the

- impact of segmenting, targeting, and positioning on the marketing mix
- process and bases of targeting, and the different targeting strategies
- various positioning strategies and the importance of competitive advantage in marketing

Mobile Money Transfer

Bharti Airtel and Vodafone are the major players in the Indian Telecom sector and together account for 51.52% of the Indian market customers (Cellular Operators Association of India 2013). They both have come out with mobile money transfer facilities for their customer base.

Airtel's mobile wallet solution Airtel Money, has two types of accounts—the Express account and the Power account. Express account is free and has a daily limit and a maximum account balance of ₹10,000, whereas the Power account has a charge of ₹50 and an enhanced daily limit and maximum account balance of ₹50,000. Airtel Money allows users to make utility payments and purchase rail/flight tickets on various online portals.

The Power account provides additional benefits of ability to pay for movie tickets, shopping, and other extras such as the ability to pay for insurance premiums, subscriptions, and donations. Users with

Power accounts can also transfer money to other Airtel Money customers as well any bank account through NEFT transfer. There are no minimum balance requirements. Minimum amount that can be spent is ₹5 and minimum amount that can be transferred to a bank account or Airtel Money customer is ₹10.

The scarcity of banking outlets in Indian villages (less than 5% villages have a banking outlet) and the need for financial inclusion are the main drivers of Vodafone's 'M-Pesa'. Through M-Pesa, Vodafone plans to service the unbanked, underserviced sections in India. People, especially in the remote areas, can transfer money to any mobile phone, remit money to a bank account, make payments for utility bills, and deposit and withdraw cash from designated outlets, and make payment to recharge mobile, DTH service subscription, and shop at select shops.

M-Pesa provides two kinds of services—Mobile Wallet and Mobile Wallet and Mobile Money account. To avail the M-Pesa services, users need to pay a minimum initial amount out of which ₹100 is deducted as a one-time account activation fee and the remaining is credited to the user's account as balance. For fund transfers, the maximum limit per transaction is ₹5,000, which is also the daily fund transfer limit. The maximum limit for prepaid recharges is ₹2,500. ICICI Bank and Vodafone also charge a fee when the user sends money to a registered or unregistered user or bank account. This fee depends on the transaction value.

After going through the chapter, you will be able to answer the following questions:
1. Who are the target audience for Airtel Money?
2. Discuss the target audience for M-Pesa by Vodafone.

INTRODUCTION

The market consists of numerous customers who are geographically scattered and have specific needs and buying practices. A company needs to market its products to this vast sea of customers to remain profitable. Segmentation, targeting, and positioning are strategic fundamentals of marketing used to generate competitive advantage, which can be translated into business opportunities that form the success stories of organizations. Defining a market is the basis of segmentation. Originally, a market was defined as a physical place where buyers and sellers gathered. From time to time, different subject/area experts have given different definitions of a market. To a marketing professional, a market constitutes all the actual and potential buyers of a product or service. It is up to the professional to create a competitive advantage and capture the market share.

Service firms vary widely in their abilities of servicing. It would, then, not be wise to compete in an entire market. Instead, organizations should focus on the set of customers they can serve best. In 1974, Sinner defined focus as 'A narrow product mix for a particular market segment'. According to Johnston (1996), 'Focus is to understand the needs of a specific market and to focus all the efforts of the plant on achieving them through the use of proven technologies'. Thus, it can be said that the focus for a service organization should be a group of buyers who exhibit similarity in their needs, purchasing manners, purchasing situations, consumption styles, lifestyles, etc. For a service organization, the company's focus can be described on two dimensions—the service focus and the market focus. Taking the two variables of services offered and the market served, organizations can be grouped into four types—(1) unfocused; (2) service focused; (3) market focused; and (4) fully focused.

An *unfocused organization* is unformulated at the service concept level. Hence, it tends to serve a wide market with a wide range of services. The idea is to provide a range of services so as to cater to any need of a wide variety customers. For example, AIA is the 'largest independent publicly listed Pan-Asian life insurance group in the world and has a heritage of over 90 years in the Asian insurance market. It has wholly-owned main operating subsidiaries or branches in 14 markets in Asia Pacific.' In India, Tata-AIA Life

Insurance Company provides a wide range of commercial, personal, and life insurance products through a variety of distribution channels (Tata 2012).

A *service-focused organization*, on the other hand, provides a narrow range of services to a wide market. For example, Café Coffee Day, India's only vertically integrated coffee company, is the largest café chain. The mission statement, 'To be the best café chain in the country by offering a world-class coffee experience at affordable prices', is thus an example of a service-focused organization, as its focus is providing excellent coffee. Café Coffee Day includes 2000 cafés (which includes the more premium Lounge and Square) and 900 coffee kiosks (Shashidhar 2012). The company has opened two cafés in Austria and fourteen cafés in Czech Republic (CCD 2013). Its menu ranges from hot and cold coffees to several exotic international coffees, food items, desserts, and pastries.

A *market-focused organization*, while concentrating on a narrow market segment, provides a wide range of services. For example, Shahnaz Hussain, a pioneer in herbal beauty care in India, provides a wide range of ayurvedic skin, hair, and body care treatments for women.

This proposition of many services being provided by a single organization may seem convenient for individual customers who want a one-stop shop, but as far as corporate clients are concerned, this might not prove to be a very profitable proposition as purchases for different services may be made by different people or sometimes different departments altogether.

A *fully-focused organization* provides a very limited range of services to a specific market segment; for example, low-cost carriers work on the premise that a segment of customers needed the core service of quick transportation without the service frills and at reduced fares.

If we consider the traditional MBA programme in India, it is slowly becoming a mass programme with the mushrooming of different business schools, but MBA specialization in retail, hospital management, and agriculture is now catering to a certain segment of professionals and students (Kumar 2006). According to Kotler et al. (2006), marketing has passed through the following different stages—mass marketing, product-variety marketing, target marketing, and micro marketing.

Mass marketing   In this form of marketing, the seller mass produces, mass distributes, and mass promotes one product to all buyers. The idea is to achieve the lowest costs and prices, and create the largest potential market. For example, Haryana Tourism has opened thirty motels in Haryana, which are similar in appearance and have a uniform level of service.

Product-variety marketing   In this form of marketing, the seller produces two or more products/services having different features, styles, quality, and size. The argument is that different consumers have different tastes and, therefore, a single product might not satisfy their wants. For example, McDonald's offers different types of burgers, such as hamburgers, chicken burgers, veggie burgers, etc., to cater to a variety of consumer tastes. Gujarat Tea Processors and Packers that sell Wagh Bakri brand of tea is promoting 'tea drinking culture of India' through their Tea Lounges where they serve more than 50 varieties of teas such as organic tea and iced tea. They plan to come up with 50 more Tea Lounges in the coming three years (2013–15) (*The Economic Times* 2013).

Target marketing   The seller identifies market segments, selects one or more, and develops products and services tailored to the selected segments in this form of marketing. Today, this concept is well accepted in most industrialized nations. For example, Singapore's population is made up of Chinese, Malay, and Indians, and rice is the staple diet of these three ethnic groups. In order to cater to their palates, McDonald's has added rice burgers and fried beef slices served between two pressed rice cakes to its menu in Singapore. McDonald's was buoyed by the success of its rice burgers in Taiwan (it sold five million rice burgers in six months) and added it to its menu in Singapore (Reuters 2006). Today, more and more companies are looking at target marketing to drive their sales (Exhibit 6.1).

Fast food chain segment is growing steadily in India

This adaption makes sense for a market like India where 'organized fast food chains also called the Quick service restaurants (QSR)' are growing at a steady rate of growth. The size of the QSR market has increased from $1,500 crore market (in 2009–10) to $3,400 crore in 2012–13 and is expected to grow at CAGR of 27% and reach $7,000 crore by 2015–16. Quick service restaurants are now spreading their business in Tier II cities or smaller towns of India. Currently global brands are dominating in QSR formats with a total share of 60%, which includes Domino's (20%), Subway (12%), McDonald's (11%), KFC (9%), and Pizza Hut (8%) (Crisil Research 2013).

Micro marketing   The Internet and database technology have helped companies to cater to small segments with distinctive needs. Today, buyers are looking for speciality in the product and service they purchase. Hospitality companies are pursuing this by maintaining databases of regular customers and finding creative ways to serve them with personalized marketing.

Exhibit 6.1   **Global Fast Food Chains Think Local for Growth**

Foreign fast food chains such as KFC, McDonald's, and Domino's are realizing that localizing the menu to suit Indian tastes is extremely important. Kentucky Fried Chicken (popularly known as KFC) started its operations in India in the mid-1990s but was forced to shut down. After years, it has reopened its operations in the country, branding itself as KFC and not reminding customers about Kentucky Fried Chicken. These global companies found that Indians mostly eat out in groups and at least one member of the group is a vegetarian; hence, the vegetarians have definite reservations regarding places such as KFC. To counter this, KFC has included a number of vegetarian options in its menu, although only 15% of the revenues are earned from this.

Domino's, the world leader in the pizza delivery market is positioning itself in several non-metro cities as a dine-in restaurant. It is a fact that in smaller cities, going out to the market and eating out is an integral part of family life; thus, positioning oneself merely as a convenience home delivery store does not make sense. Most Domino's outlets are built bigger and designed to accommodate 25–30 customers. While about 65% of Domino's revenues come from home deliveries, this segment will grow further. But in smaller cities, dine-in outlets will drive growth.

McDonald's, the world's fastest fast food chain is immensely popular among children, teenagers, and family alike. The menu is highly localized and it also has low-priced burgers and ice-creams to attract new consumers to the brand. While in metros, McDonald's is seen as a convenience outlet, in smaller cities like Jaipur, it is still an aspirational brand. Hence, McDonald's strategy is to make the brand available to a larger market.

This clearly shows that positioning locally is very important for companies, especially in the food and hospitality sector.

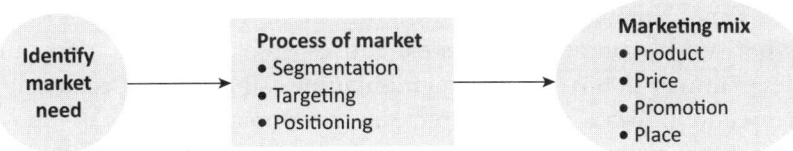

Fig. 6.1   Market need versus segmentation, targeting, and positioning

The three major steps in focused marketing are—segmentation, targeting, and positioning (Fig. 6.1). Normally, markets are born with a first brand that creates the division. If this category is profitable, another competitor, sensing a good opportunity, enters this category. As more and more competitors enter, it becomes increasingly difficult to capture the attention of the customers. What do marketers do then? They choose a subgroup of persons in the market and address their product directly to them. This is the crux of segmentation.

According to Kotler and Bes (2003), 'Renounce attacking the whole market. Show yourself as the most efficient option for a subset of the market and you can become the leader of that segment. It is better to be the head of the mouse than the tail of the lion'.

It is not realistic for a firm to appeal to all the potential buyers in a market. Marketing professionals can, therefore, choose a segment of the market and then direct all their marketing efforts towards them in order to get the maximum benefit. How they choose the segment to be served forms the basis of targeting. Hence, targeting measures the attractiveness of the segment and then selects the segments to be served. Once these segments are chosen, the next step is to tell this segment audience that you are the best choice for them. This is done by highlighting those qualities in the product, which are important to the target customers, and this is known as positioning. Positioning consists of choosing how the company wants its products to be regarded by the customers. According to Kotler and Bes (2003), the advantages of segmentation, targeting, and positioning are:

1. It fragments the market and at the same time makes it bigger, because once the customers find their needs better covered they tend to increase their consumption.
2. A new player can generate a competitive advantage for itself by following this strategy.
3. By segmenting the market and taking out products for each segment, a market leader can create barriers to competition by discouraging the entry of new competitors.

SEGMENTATION

Market segmentation is defined as the process of dividing the market into distinct groups that share common characteristics, needs, purchasing behaviour, or consumption patterns. These groups may react to the marketing mix in a similar manner. Market segmentation is a marketing strategy that recognizes the need for 'specialization' to suit the needs of a segment of the market rather than trying to be 'all things to all people'. For example, English news channels in India, such as NDTV, NDTV Profit, Headlines Today, Times Now, CNN-IBN, and CNBC, are devoted to business news targeted at business persons, corporate business executives, stock-market traders, and money market dealers (Kumar 2006). Market segmentation is important because it leads to efficient and effective utilization of resources, improves manageability of the market by dividing the markets into smaller parts, and helps to improve the company's ability to satisfy customers. According to Cadeaux (2004), market segmentation has both strategic and operational dimensions.

The strategic decision involves the determination of characteristics and the number of segments to be served, and the development of distinct marketing programmes for a product market entry. The operational decision involves allocation of resources across the segments chosen, so as to optimize some objective such as profit or sales.

Market segmentation helps the firm to more effectively and/or efficiently use its resources. It also helps to design the marketing strategies around the target segments. Thus, there is a closer alignment between the customer needs and the organization's product or service offering. This also leads to enhanced customer satisfaction and loyalty, and hence a stronger competitive advantage leading to superior financial performance (Hunt and Arnett 2004). We can summarize the objectives of segmentation as follows:

1. Identify the similarity of needs of potential buyers within a segment and pursue them with tailored products or services supported by appropriate market mix strategies.

2. Identify the difference between needs of buyers among segments and try to cater to these different needs. For example, the Taj group of hotels, while catering to the luxury and leisure segment, has opened Ginger Hotels to cater to business budget travellers.

3. Once the specific segment has been chosen for the marketing efforts, the organization is more focused in its efforts and there is potential for increased return on investment.

4. Even before the marketing efforts are carried out, marketers can study the feasibility of their actions, which saves a lot on operational costs and time later.

5. It is simpler for the marketers to assign the buyers to different segments on the basis of a number of parameters and is highly cost-effective.

Market Segmentation

Different segmentation variables can be used to segment a market. There is no single way and a marketer has to try different variables. Some principal segmentation variables can either be based on the consumer or the buying situation. Consumer-based segmentation can be further segmented by geographic, demographic, or psychographic means.

Geographic segmentation

In this type of segmentation, the marketer divides the market into different geographic units such as regions, nations, states, countries, cities, and neighbourhoods. For example, India can be divided into different regions such as north, south, east, west, and central. Each region has its own staple diet; for example, in the north, wheat and pulses form an integral part of the diet, in south India rice forms a vital part of the different dishes, and in east India sea food is more prevalent. Hindustan Unilever Ltd, keeping these local preferences in mind, launched its Annapurna Aata in some select markets in the south where it charged a premium owing to subdued competition.

Geographic segmentation permeates knowledge of customer preferences endorsing companies to modify the product offering accordingly. For example, in India, fast food brands such as Domino's, Pizza Hut, and Café Coffee Day are all looking at Tier-II cities for their next growth phase. According to Ajay Kaul, CEO, Domino's India, eating out in cities such as Bhubaneswar and Baroda is considered in a more integral way, so Domino's plans to have a larger format in these cities, with dine-in arrangements. Café Coffee Day, with a number of stores in India, has presence on highways and temple towns. According to Sandeep Kohli, MD India, Yum! Restaurants International, Pizza Hut, has city-specific promotions, which has helped the brand to gain popularity. All these chains also consider reducing the prices by 5–10% as compared to metros and customizing their menus, which are suited to the diner in the different cities they plan to target (Vyas 2006). Banks are also using geographic segmentation; for example, the Gramin Bank concept is intended to give credit and other services to people living in villages in India. ITC has targeted rural farmers with its e-choupal, enabling farmers in the rural hinterland to get the best price for their produce. Exhibit 6.2 discusses how car dealers in China have to come out with differentiated strategies for customers visiting their car showrooms.

Exhibit 6.2   **Car Dealers in China**

China has a number of first time car buyers who have a limited knowledge of cars and these customers visit the showroom a multiple times to look at the cars. On these multiple visits they also bring along family and friends for their opinion and also to negotiate the price. Therefore, the car dealers in China are more patient with these customers and are also working out strategies for these multiple visits from customers to make them feel special and welcomed. There are more than 100 car brands available in China and dealers have to ensure creative ways for return visits. In Shanghai's Pudong district, Ford Motor Showroom provides in-house manicurist and shoe-shiner. Singers perform at barbeques for customers and periodically the dealers hold drawings for gifts such as iPads and TVs. In Foshan, a city in southern Guangdong provinces, a Honda Motor outlet holds talks on feng shui, shows recent hit films from Hollywood and Chinese studios, and offers massage chairs for relaxation. The three-story Mercedes Benz dealership in Shanghai's Putuo district has a 12 seat theatre (often showing movies that feature Mercedes vehicles), a cigar room for repeat customers, a library, a fitness centre, and a game room that includes pool tables and driving games. At lunch there is a buffet with five different meat and vegetable dishes, and a full-time tea artist brews various types of Chinese tea.

Demographic segmentation

This consists of dividing markets into groups based on demographic variables such as age, life cycle, gender, income, occupation, education, religion, race, and nationality. This variable is most commonly used for segmentation because of the following reasons:

- Customer preference and the number of times they are going to use the particular service product varies closely with this variable.
- These variables are easy to measure and lots of secondary data is usually available.
- It helps to assess the size of the market and reach it efficiently.

Some demographic factors that can be used to segment the markets are discussed in this section.

Age and life cycle stage   Consumer preferences change with age. A child may want toy cars, a cricket bat, and candies at the age of five, but at the age of ten, the same child may want a cycle, and at the age of eighteen a two-wheeler, mobile, iPod, laptop, etc. Thus, targeting the customers according to their age is a strategy followed by marketers. In India, marketers are increasingly targeting their goods at children keeping in mind the pester power of children. The term *pester power* is increasingly being used in marketing to denote a child's influence on the buying process of parents and relatives (Catlin 2004). Children are becoming increasingly sophisticated consumers in their own right and mobilized by advertising, promotional materials, and peer pressure, seek to influence their parents' spending power and household purchases. The scenario of both working parents, who treat their children to non-obligatory items to compensate for having less time to spend with them, further facilitates this.

Children are an active segment of the market. A high exposure to media and the ever-increasing purchase ability have resulted in children moving up the value chain. This category of consumers plays a very strong role in households relating to purchases such as apparel, footwear, accessories, etc. An example of how marketers are developing their marketing communication keeping this segment of kids in mind is McDonald's. It added a coupon in the shape of a ball with the Disney Adventures Magazine (a children's magazine) offering a free Soft Serve with every Happy Meal. Thus, when the children buy this magazine and get the coupon, they are bound to influence their parents to take them there. This is an example of how kids are being considered as major influencers of buying decisions across various service categories such as fast food chains.

Many banks and financial institutions are using the age and life cycle stage to cater to customer needs. ICICI is catering to the need of a better shopping experience by getting strategic tie-ups with Visa, MasterCard, and with leading retailers such as Big Bazaar and Spencer's for its debit card. It has also launched services such as kid-e-bank for children, bank@campus for students, PowerPay for salaried employees, ICICI select for high net worth individuals, and business multipliers for business people (Raj 2006). The bank introduced iWish, its popular recurring deposit scheme for savings account holders, in 2012. If we consider the population distribution of different ASEAN countries, we see why developed nations are targeting India and China in Asia (Table 6.1).

iWish: ICICI's deposit scheme provides flexible options to customers

Source: ICICI Bank website

Table 6.2 shows the distribution of population by marital status and sex.

Gender segmentation   Marketers of products such as clothing, cosmetics, personal care items, jewellery, and footwear commonly segment markets by gender. However, gender segmentation is now being increasingly used in the hospitality business. The marketing implication is to choose characteristics that can appeal across rigid gender roles. As the number of women travellers has increased, hotels have added hair dryers, fitness facilities, child care services, and safe deposit boxes. In India, five-star hotels offer a range of services to make women guests feel welcome and secure. With facilities such as women butlers, exclusive fitness centres, customized diets, spa therapists flown in from abroad, designer room appurtenances, and whole floors crafted specially for lady travellers, the Indian hospitality industry is doing its utmost to pamper women guests. This trend is bound to pick up pace as more and more women join the workforce.

The twenty-third floor of New Delhi's ITC Maurya Sheraton has been christened Eva and reserved exclusively for women guests. ITC Grand Central Sheraton in Mumbai,

Table 6.1 Population of different ASEAN countries*

| Country | Age structure | | | | | | | | |
| | 0–14 yrs | | 15–64 yrs | | 65 yrs and over | | | |
	Male	Female	Male	Female	Male	Female	Total
China	124,773,577	107,286,198	509,458,015	481,717,081	60,597,243	65,753,724	1,349,585,838
India	187,236,677	165,219,615	413,334,440	385,521,792	32,992,850	36,494,985	1,220,800,359
Pakistan	3,774,720	31,967,787	61,600,152	57,643,155	3,877,418	4,375,636	193,238,868
Bangladesh	27,393,912	26,601,199	48,204,038	53,458,647	3,918,341	4,078,723	163,654,860*
Nepal	5,045,989	4,859,274	9,279,587	9,884,814	630,853	729,750	30,430,267

*as per July 2013 est.

Source: Based on the data from *World Fact* book.

Table 6.2 Per cent distribution of population by marital status and sex

State	Never married			Married			W/D/S		
	Total	Male	Female	Total	Male	Female	Total	Male	Female
India	48.7	53.5	43.8	46.2	44.2	48.2	5.1	2.3	8
Andhra Pradesh	42.3	47.9	36.7	50.9	49.9	52	6.8	2.2	11.4
Assam	54.4	58.8	49.7	41	39.4	42.7	4.6	1.8	7.6
Bihar	54.7	58.9	50.2	41.7	38.8	44.8	3.6	2.3	4.9
Chhattisgarh	47.8	51.5	44.1	46.8	46.1	47.6	5.4	2.5	8.3
Delhi	50.2	53.2	46.6	46.5	45.1	48.1	3.3	1.7	5.2
Gujarat	45.2	49.3	40.9	49.7	48.1	51.4	5.1	2.7	7.7
Haryana	49	54.1	43.2	46.9	43.8	50.4	4.2	2.1	6.5
Himachal Pradesh	45.9	51.3	40.7	48.2	46	50.3	5.9	2.6	9.1
Jammu & Kashmir	54.5	57.9	51	41.5	39.7	43.4	4	2.4	5.6
Jharkhand	52.5	57.3	47.6	43.5	40.7	46.5	3.9	1.9	6
Karnataka	45.9	52	39.8	47.3	46.2	48.4	6.8	1.8	11.8
Kerala	42.5	49.4	36.1	50.6	49.1	52	6.9	1.5	11.9
Madhya Pradesh	49.5	53.3	45.5	46	44.1	47.9	4.5	2.6	6.6
Maharashtra	44.3	49.7	38.7	50	48.3	51.7	5.7	1.9	9.7
Odisha	47.3	51.7	43	46.9	45.8	47.9	5.8	2.5	9.2
Punjab	47.4	52.2	42	47.6	45	50.5	5	2.8	7.5
Rajasthan	49	53.1	44.6	47	44.9	49.2	4	2	6.2
Tamil Nadu	42.6	48.2	37	50	49.3	50.8	7.4	2.5	12.3
Uttar Pradesh	54.7	58.8	50.3	41.1	38.3	44.2	4.1	2.9	5.5
West Bengal	45.1	50.3	39.6	49.5	48.1	51	5.4	1.6	9.4

Source: Based on the data from the Census of India 2011a.

unveiled 15 women's-only rooms. The Taj group offers a special butler service. Women guests can use their assistance for making dinner reservations, booking appointments at the parlour or spa, arranging shopping expeditions, or procuring reading material. The hotel's kitchen occasionally customizes dishes to suit a woman guest's diet plan—Atkins, low-carb, no-sugar, or high-fibre. According to the 2011 Census, the gender-wise population of the 20 states/union territories is given in Table 6.3.

Income Marketers have long used segmentation on the basis of income and class. Table 6.4 illustrates the broad demographics of India on the basis of income and psychographics.

The hospitality industry has long used income segmentation. The high bracket income group serves as a target for luxury hotels. When Taj's first hotel, the Taj Mahal Palace and Tower, Mumbai, was inaugurated in 1903, it was perhaps the only place where a British viceroy could rub shoulders with an Indian maharajah. Keeping an eye on the growing segment of the business budget travellers, the Indian Hotels Company

Table 6.3 Gender-wise distribution of population of top 20 states/union territories

State/union territory	Total population		
	Persons	Males	Females
India	1,21,01,93,422	62,37,24,248	58,64,69,174
Uttar Pradesh	19,95,81,477	10,45,96,415	9,49,85,062
Maharashtra	11,23,72,972	5,83,61,397	5,40,11,575
Bihar	10,38,04,637	5,41,85,347	4,96,19,290
West Bengal	9,13,47,736	4,69,27,389	4,44,20,347
Andhra Pradesh	8,46,65,533	4,25,09,881	4,21,55,652
Madhya Pradesh	7,25,97,565	3,76,12,920	3,49,84,645
Tamil Nadu	7,21,38,958	3,61,58,871	3,59,80,087
Rajasthan	6,86,21,012	3,56,20,086	3,30,00,926
Karnataka	6,11,30,704	3,10,57,742	3,00,72,962
Gujarat	6,03,83,628	3,14,82,282	2,89,01,346
Orissa	4,19,47,358	2,12,01,678	2,07,45,680
Kerala	3,33,87,677	1,60,21,290	1,73,66,387
Jharkhand	3,29,66,238	1,69,31,688	1,60,34,550
Assam	3,11,69,272	1,59,54,927	1,52,14,345
Punjab	2,77,04,236	1,46,34,819	1,30,69,417
Chhattisgarh	2,55,40,196	1,28,27,915	1,27,12,281
Haryana	2,53,53,081	1,35,05,130	1,18,47,951
NCT of Delhi	1,67,53,235	89,76,410	77,76,825
Jammu & Kashmir	1,25,48,926	66,65,561	58,83,365
Jharkhand	3,29,66,238	1,69,31,688	1,60,34,550

Source: Based on the data from Census of India (2011b)

Table 6.4 Income levels and psychographics of Indian consumers

Category	Annual household income	Sub-category	Population (people) (%)	Consumer trends	Major consumption areas in descending order	Total consumption (%)
Affluent	Above ₹9,11,310; $18,500	Professional affluent	2 (4 million)	Well educated, mid to large businesses or good jobs, with sufficient income to allow indulgences	Transportation and communication, health, food, apparel, education, leisure, housing, and consumer durables	16
		Traditional affluent	4 (9 million)		Transportation and communication, food, health, apparel, education, leisure, and housing	8
Aspirer	₹3,64,524–9,11,310; $7,400–18,500	Urban aspirers	8 (19 million)	Consumers are educated, have mid-sized businesses or stable jobs, with income sufficient to live comfortably as well as indulge a little	Food, transportation and communication, health, education, leisure, apparel, and housing	11
		Rural aspirers	6 (14 million)		Food, transportation and communication, health, education, leisure, housing, and apparel	8
Next billion	₹1,62,558–3,64,524; $3,300–7,400	Large town next billion	6(14 million)	Have basic education, have small businesses or low paying jobs, income level allows them to sustain a basic lifestyle	Food, health, transportation and communication, apparel, housing, education, and leisure	7
		Small town next billion	24 (58 million)		Food, transportation and communication, health, education, leisure, apparel, and housing	24
Struggler	Less than ₹1,62,558; $3,300	Struggler	50 (121 million)	Illiterate with limited education, jobs are manual labour with very low income, generally daily wage.	Food, health, transportation and communication, apparel, housing, education, and leisure	26

Source: Based on the data from BCG and CII, 2012; *Business World* 2013.

launched Ginger. ITC also had Fortune hotel properties spread throughout India to cater to the same segment. Keeping this income segmentation in mind, Air Deccan launched its low-cost, no frills airline carriers in India. Paramount Airlines offers business class experience at higher-end economy fares. It targets the corporate travel segment; customers who are not eligible for business class on full service carriers and do not have time to shop for cheap fares, and the higher end of the leisure market (Kumar 2006). Nirav Modi, diamond jewellery designer who clocked a sales of around $250 million (approximately ₹1,600 crore) in 2012–13 has a 'private clientele of the uber-rich'. He aims to open 5–10 stores in India and approximately the same number in cities such as London, New York, Dubai, and Hong Kong. His salon in Mumbai 'caters to high-end clients, mostly industrialists.' At present his pieces cost more than ₹10 lakh and he plans to introduce pieces at ₹5 lakh price points in his upcoming stores (Rathore 2013).

Psychographic segmentation

This segmentation variable divides buyers on the basis of social class, lifestyle, and personality. The income levels and psychographics of Indian consumers is given in Table 6.4.

Social class Almost every society is made up of social class structure. These social classes are relatively ordered divisions and are of importance to marketers as people from a social class exhibit similar behaviour. They show distinct similarities in product and brand behaviour in areas such as travelling, leisure activities, and food habits. A hotel targeting a social class is more successful than a hotel where different social classes are present, as it breeds dissatisfaction among the consumers. Marketers also use both social class and income to segment the market.

Lifestyle Companies are now trying to understand the customer's lifestyle in a comprehensive manner to design their service to suit their needs. NDTV's website is a classic example. The company has understood the lifestyle of the customers and designed its services for them. If viewers log on to the site to look at the share prices, and want to look at the past financial history of various companies, they can do so at the same site. If they want to book tickets for a vacation abroad, they can use the same site to book air tickets in a link called, Travel. Hotel reservations can also be made from the same site. Apart from this, they can also book movie tickets and do some shopping from the same site (Raj 2006). *The Marketing Whitebook 2013* classifies the Indians into five segments and identifies opportunities waiting to be tapped.

Personality It is the unique psychological characteristic that leads to unvarying and lifelong responses to the environment. Personality is an important segmentation variable as people tend to make purchases according to their personality. Thus, Southwest Airlines has been specializing in humour for a long time and the airline's growing army of flight attendants—now numbering 7,000—includes a few actors, a stand-up comic, and hundreds of skilled amateurs. Thus, people who apart from seeking a low airfare, are fun-loving opt for this airline (Exhibit 6.3). It has achieved a growth rate of 8% over the last decade, making it the only profitable major airline (Suskind 2003).

Exhibit 6.3   **Southwest Airlines**

'Ok people, it's open seating, just like at church—saints up front, sinners in back', Yvonne LeMaster said into the flight attendant's microphone, as chuckling passengers filed from the ramp past the cockpit and tiny galley kitchen. 'Remember, this isn't a furniture store. You're only renting this seat for an hour.'

On Southwest Airlines Flight 639 from Baltimore/Washington International airport to Cleveland, LeMaster's shtick marks a small milestone. Southwest's flight attendants, famous for their airborne stand-up routines, are cracking jokes again.

Co-founded 31 years ago by Herbert Kelleher, a Harley-Davidson-riding iconoclast, Southwest has been specializing in humour for a long time. Over the past decade, as the airline has experienced 8% annual growth and has come to employ 35,000 people, generating laughs has become an official corporate goal, even a part of recruitment. 'Have you ever used humour to solve a workplace problem?' is a question asked in job interviews.

All of this corporate levity worked beautifully through the devil-may-care 1990s, as Southwest— a 'people mover' discount carrier that is now one of the only profitable major airlines—mined and enriched deposits of humour.

Then came 9/11. The laughter stopped on Southwest. No memo from headquarters was needed, though some were sent. 'It is evident that the usual Southwest humour should temporarily play a lesser role in our lives', said a memo dated 18 September 2001. The memo also included a list of cancelled activities, such as Halloween costumes on flight attendants and some regular gags played with passengers. In other words, humour was out of the question until further notice.

Last Spring, letters started to trickle in to the carrier's Dallas headquarters. Passengers said they missed the jokes. Southwest President Colleen Barrett decided the airline should wade in slowly. A memo distributed in late May last year read that, 'based on customer feedback and our take on the national mood, we think it is appropriate to resume the optional use of humour'. Beneath were listed guidelines, such as 'know your audience'—a 'friday night planeload to Las Vegas' compared with a 'weekday morning between business centres'. She also urged the crew to 'use common sense and good judgment', such as 'avoid references to politics, religion, bodily functions, and changes in the airline business since 9/11'. But it was not until after Thanksgiving that Southwest got back its groove.

In 16 A, Mark Rafferty, a 45-year old architect and fellow frequent flier, talked about how, on one recent Southwest flight, everyone laughed at a couple of good ones and then just started talking to each other. 'You could see it, row by row', he says. 'The plane was positively noisy, and it wasn't from the engines'.

Then the two men, both converts to Southwest, swapped in-flight favourites across the seat back. 'Oh yeah, there was a great one a few years ago', Rafferty said, a bit later, 'They told everyone on the plane's left side, toward the terminal, to put their faces in the window and smile so our competitors can see what a full flight looks like.'

Behavioural segmentation

In this type of segmentation, buyers are grouped on the basis of their awareness, approach, and use of a service. On the basis of this, buyers can be segmented on the basis of—special occasion, benefits, usage, loyalty, and buyer readiness.

Special occasion segmentation   Buyers are divided into groups on the basis of circumstances when they make a purchase or use a service. This helps firms to build the service use. For example, for a weekend dinner a person might take his/her family to a neighbourhood restaurant, but if the occasion is a birthday or an anniversary celebration, they might go to a fine-dining restaurant such as 360°, Travertino, Bukhara, etc. to celebrate. Airline advertisements aimed at the business traveller often highlight discounts on the spouse's tickets, convenience, and on-time departure. Umaid Bhavan Palace, Jodhpur, a hotel managed by the Taj group, has used the special occasion of Holi festival to target prospective clients. People specially come to Umaid Bhavan Palace to celebrate the festival of Holi here with the present Maharaja, Gaj Singh and his family.

Benefits sought   Marketers having an idea of the benefits the customers seek in the service can develop service features that match the benefits their customers are seeking and can communicate the same more effectively to the consumers. Keeping this in mind, various banks, insurance companies, and financial institutions are providing a complete set of financial solutions to cater to different financial needs of the customers. Banks are offering different types of services such as loans for higher studies, housing, computer, and automobile; insurance; pension schemes; kiddy bank (small) savings, etc. (Raj 2006).

Usage rate   Customers can be grouped into light, medium, and heavy users. For example, mobile service providers, such as Vodafone and Airtel, provide different plans according to the usage rate of their service. They also provide corporate connections where, at a minimum number of connections, they provide free incoming calls among the group and reduced rental plans. Many airlines provide frequent flyer programmes to ensure the continued patronage of their clients.

Loyalty status   Segmenting on the basis of loyalty is very useful for organizations as they can then specifically target these customers to make them their brand advocates, that is, people who are loyal and recommend the brand to friends. Also, if they know about the loyalty status of the customer, they can specifically target the marketing strategies to move them up the loyalty ladder. Thus, customers who are brand loyal to Taj hotels will try to stay in a Taj hotel in the cities they visit.

Buyer readiness stage   This implies the readiness of the customer to purchase a particular service. A customer might be unaware of the service, some are informed but are not in need of the service at a particular point of time, some want the service, and some are willing to buy it. It is the task of the marketer to move the consumers up this ladder to ultimately purchase the service. For example, at Pragati Maidan, Delhi, different fairs such as book fairs, job fairs, and financial fairs are organized. Various banks and financial institutions market different loans and financial services during such fairs. The idea is to inform customers about their presence and to move the prospective customer up the buyer readiness stage.

Effective Segmentation

The market is replete with great ideas turning into failures. For example, a few years ago, Videocon launched its picture-in-picture (PIP) concept, targeting it at the higher-end television segment in India. This allowed viewers to watch multiple channels at the same time. However, it did not take into account the limitations of the human brain, that is, registering only one message at a time, and failed (Kumar 2006).

As is evident from the above discussion, there are many ways to segment a market but all are not equally effective for different services provided by different service owners. For a market segment to be useful it should have the following characteristics:

Measurable   This implies the degree to which the segment's size and purchasing power can be measured. The segmentation variable chosen should be easy to measure. For example, we have a lot of data available on demographics (see Tables 6.1, and 6.2) and for a marketer targeting say, the women segment, it is easy to determine the segment size.

Accessible   It implies the degree to which the segment can be reached and served. Thus, a market, which can be easily accessed, is more lucrative for a marketer to target.

Sustainable   The segments should be large and profitable enough to serve as a market. For example, Pizza Hut planning to open its chains in Tier-II cities of India intends to reduce the price by 5–10% as compared to its prices in metropolitan cities of India. This is because it knows that smaller cities have the required consumers with the spending capacity in a particular range and hence, wants to cash in on this segment.

Actionable   The segment should be large enough and feasible for the company to design programmes to attract and serve it. If the segment is small, then the cost dynamics involved will not make the action profitable.

Keeping the discussion on segmentation in mind, it can be concluded that there is no single way to segment the market. A marketer can also use a combination of more than two ways to segment the market.

TARGETING

Once the market has been segmented, the marketers need to decide which segment they are going to focus their activities on. Thus, targeting is the choice of a single segment or group of segments that the organization wishes to select. Thus, it is actually a target sub-market or target segment (Masterson and Pickton 2004). Companies can evaluate and select market segments on the basis of—segment size and growth, segment structural attractiveness, or company objectives and resources. For example, Exhibit 6.4 shows how Longchamp is focusing on targeting customers for its stores. Once the segments have been evaluated, the market to be targeted can be selected on the basis of—undifferenti-ated marketing, differentiated marketing, or concentrated marketing. For companies, the next step is to decide the market coverage strategy for the markets to be targeted.

Evaluating Market Segments

The study of segment size and growth, segment structural attractiveness, and company objectives and resources help us to evaluate market segments.

Segment size and growth   Before entering a segment, a company must first collect information on the current segment sales, growth rate, and expected profitability of

> **Exhibit 6.4** **Longchamp Grows during Lull Times**
>
> French company Longchamp, known for its folding nylon LePliage handbags, is adding more stores and clocking in revenue growth faster than rivals like Louis Vuitton. In 2012, when the luxury industry grew at 10%, 'LVMH Moet Hennessy Louis Vuitton SA's fashion and leather goods division' grew at 14%; Longchamp 'advanced to 16% to €454 million ($615 million)' in the same period. In 2013, its revenue growth is expected to come down to less than 10% but it needs to be highlighted that the luxury sector will grow at 5% in the same period. According to its Chief Executive Officer, Jean Cassegrain, one of the brand's strength lies in offering value for money. In 2013, it planned new stores in Tel Aviv, Rome, Sao Paolo, and Abu Dhabi, and in 2014 it plans to open stores in Barcelona and Munich.
>
> Revenue growth is expected to be fulfilled through stores in Europe's most visited cities. These cities attract travellers from America, Asia, etc. and therefore business is drawn from not only these tourists but locals as well. According to Cassegrain 'sales to non-Europeans are rising faster than sales to Europeans, who account for a larger share of the total.'

various segments. So, if a firm has the skill and the resources, it can target a segment which has a higher sales, growth rate, and profitability. For example, the quick service restaurants (QSR) in India stands at ₹5,500 crore in 2013 and is expected to reach '₹16,786 crore by 2018' as per Technopak advisors. According to another study by Rabobank, the QSR segment is growing at 30% annually till 2015 (Bailay 2013). All these show that even though there are a number of players in India, it is still an attractive destination for QSR formats and has attracted US burger chain Johnny Rockets to set up shop here.

Segment structural attractiveness A segment having a desirable size and growth may still not offer attractive profits. This depends upon a number of factors. Applying Porter's five-forces model, we can say the segment structural attractiveness depends upon:

Nature and number of competitors present If the competitors are strong and aggressive, the segment is less attractive.

Substitute products The presence of a number of substitute products may limit prices and profits, say, the presence of a number of motels may reduce the room rate of a hotel.

Bargaining power of buyers If the buyers in a segment have a strong bargaining power relative to suppliers, they may demand more quality services at a lower price and set competitors against each other.

Bargaining power of suppliers If the suppliers are powerful, that is, they are large and concentrated with few substitutes available, or the supplied product is an important ingredient of a dish, then the market is less attractive.

Threat of new entrants If a segment size and growth is attractive, there is always the potential threat of new entrants.

Company objectives and resources After collecting the information on the different segments, a company must match it with its own objectives and resources.

Segments may be tempting, but if they do not match with the long-term objectives of the firm, they must be discarded straight away, otherwise they may divert the company's attention and resources from the main goal. If the segment fits the company's objectives but the company lacks the resources to compete effectively in the segment, it should not enter the segment. The company should enter a segment only if it can gain a sustainable advantage over its competitors. Therefore, US Burger chain Johnny Rockets planned a new outlet in Select Citywalk mall in Delhi and Ambience mall in Gurgaon during Christmas period of 2013. The format in India will be the same it is known for, that is, the song and dance routines by its staff to entertain guests. The company is making an extra effort to train employees so that they know the proper moves. A team will visit India from the US to train the employees here (Bailay 2013).

Selecting Market Segments

After evaluating different segments, the next step is for the company to select the target market, that is, decide which and how many segments to serve. There are three types of market coverage strategies.

Undifferentiated or mass marketing   This concentrates on the common needs of the buyers rather than the differences. Hence, it ignores the market segmentation differences and goes for the entire market with a single offer. For example, in the early 1990s Airtel and Essar promoted mobile services for the entire market without coming up with the different plans that are prevalent today.

Differentiated or segmentation marketing   In differentiated marketing, a company targets several market segments while designing separate offers for each. For example, ITC has a chain of luxury hotels such as Maurya Sheraton and Towers on the one hand, and a chain of business budget hotels on the other, with a different marketing mix for each group.

Concentrated or niche marketing   In this type of marketing a company goes for a large share of a small market instead of going for a small share of a large market. It is specifically appropriate for companies with limited resources and has proved beneficial for hospitality companies, as they have gained a strong marketing position due to a greater knowledge of the segments' needs. For example, Mahanagar Telephone Nigam Limited launched a mobile promotional plan called 'Trump Vidyarthi Plan' in 2007 to cater to the needs of students.

Customized or micro marketing   In this type of marketing, the individual customer preference is important as the marketer specifically focuses on the needs of the individual customer and how to best satisfy these needs. For example, the business process outsourcing (BPO) industry caters to the specific requirements of different clients by deputing a specialized workforce. The advantages and disadvantages of the different market coverage strategies are summed up in Table 6.5.

Market Coverage Strategy

The target market selection involves the dynamic process of matching the changing variety of products and services with the changing variety of customer wants (Cadeaux 2004).

Table 6.5 Advantages and disadvantages of different targeting strategies

Targeting strategy	Advantages	Disadvantages
Undifferentiated targeting	• Cost economies and so potential savings on production/marketing costs • Low market research and product development cost	• Unimaginative product offering • Chances of failure high in today's competitive environment • Heavy competition
Differentiated targeting	• Greater financial success as compared to undifferentiated targeting • Economies of scale in production/marketing	• High costs for marketing, marketing research, forecasting, sales analysis, promotion planning, and advertising • Cannibalization
Concentrated targeting	• Concentration of resources • Can better meet the needs of a narrowly defined segment • Allows some small firms to better compete with larger firms • Strong positioning	• Segments too small or changing • Large competitors may more effectively market to niche segment

According to Cadeaux (1997), the selection of target markets is a strategic and entrepreneurial process. Companies need to consider several factors while choosing a market coverage strategy. Some of these are described in this section.

Company's resources When a company has limited resources, concentrated marketing makes the most sense.

Degree of product homogeneity Products that can vary in design are more suited to differentiation or concentration whereas undifferentiated marketing is more suited to homogeneous products.

Product life cycle stages When a firm introduces a new product, it may be practical to launch only one version and then undifferentiated or concentrated marketing makes more sense, whereas in the mature stage, differentiated marketing is more feasible.

Market homogeneity If buyers have the same taste, buy a product in the same quantity, and react similarly to marketing efforts, undifferentiated marketing is an appropriate strategy.

Competitor's marketing strategies When a competitor uses segmentation, undifferentiated marketing can be suicidal. Conversely, when competitors are pursuing undifferentiated marketing, a firm can gain advantage by using differentiated or concentrated marketing.

POSITIONING

The concept of positioning coined by Jack Trout and Al Ries in 1969, came into prominence when they elaborated on it in 1972. In their famous treatise, *The Positioning Era Cometh,* the authors emphasized that positioning is the battle for a place in the consumer's mind. According to Ries and Trout (1981) (cited in Festervand 2004), positioning should not be confused with strategy, even though the two are inextricably related.

'Positioning starts with a product. A piece of merchandise, a service, a company, and institution, or even a person. Positioning is not what you do to a product. It is what you do to the mind of the prospect. That is, you position the product in the mind of the prospect.'

Theodore Levitt (1980) argued that all goods and services are differentiable and there is no such thing as a commodity. All marketing strategies involve a search for a competitive advantage (Hunt and Arnett 2004). Rosser Reeves has defined positioning as 'The art of selecting, out of a number of unique selling propositions, the one which will get you maximum sales.'

Scanlon (1994) (cited in Festervand 2004), defined positioning as, 'The act of defining the product's image and value offer so that the segment's customers understand and appreciate what the product stands for in relation to its competitors.' Kotler (1984) defined positioning as 'Arranging for a product to occupy a clear, distinctive, and desirable place in the market, and in the minds of target consumers'. Thus, we see that all the experts treat positioning as the image of the product in the mind of the consumers as well as how they are unique or different from the competitors.

Consumers are overloaded with information about products and services. A product's position is the way it is defined by consumers on important attributes—the place the product occupies in consumer's minds relative to competing products. Therefore, Johnny Rockets (US Burger chain) to differentiate its offering from competitors will be 'positioning itself as an upscale rival to McDonald's chain. The burgers will be priced at ₹275 to ₹375 compared with ₹25 and ₹110 excluding taxes at McDonald's' (Bailay 2013). Marketers do not want to leave their product's position to chance. They plan positions that will give their products the greatest advantage in selected target markets and then design marketing mixes to create the planned positions. According to Kotler and Bes (2003), positioning creates differentiated brand personality even within the same market and also allows the brand to be positioned differently in different markets. Positioning can be related to logical, functional, symbolic, and experiential aspects of the service provided. There are three steps to effective positioning:

1. Identify a set of potential competitive advantages to exploit.
2. Select, define, and refine the most appropriate set of product attributes.
3. Effectively communicate the product's position to the desired market.

Positioning Strategies

A brand manager has an entire range of differentiating strategies to decide on the position of his/her service. He/she must choose a strategy, which holds a niche in the market and serves a competitive advantage. These strategies revolve around different aspects of the brand and according to Sengupta (2003), this can be expressed as four strategic questions.

1. Who am I?   3. For whom am I?
2. What am I?   4. Why me?

Who am I?   This concerns the corporate credentials of the brand. The prospect thinks of the brand in terms of the stable from which it comes, which can give the brand a competitive advantage. For example, the UB group extended the name of its bestselling beer Kingfisher to its airline and got a competitive advantage.

What am I?   The functional capabilities of the service are related to in this aspect. The strategies in this can be grouped as follows:

Category-related positioning   When an existing category is crowded, the same service can be positioned in another category. For example, Haryana Tourism offers a set of hotels in Haryana and has categorized them based on adventure, pilgrimage, and golf. Adventure tourism has been further classified as parasailing, rock climbing, canoeing, etc.

Benefit-related positioning   A service, which offers more than one benefit, is bound to attract more customers. Thus, we have business hotels that offer conferencing and banqueting facilities too. But if the benefits are large, it might leave a vague and diffused imprint on the customer's mind.

Positioning by usage, occasion, and time of use   A good usage positioning has accounted for the success of many services. Banking firms have come up with different types of loans keeping this in mind. For example, State Bank of India (SBI) offers different types of loans for different household items. SBI organizes loan melas for farmers at the time of purchase of seeds for sowing. The bank thus uses a positioning strategy based on occasion. The time of use has resulted in banks setting up special counters for deposits of income tax during the last dates of filing of returns.

Price–quality positioning   This concept occupies great importance in developing economies such as India. Within the last few years a number of low-cost carriers have positioned themselves on the basis of price–quality.

For whom am I?   This involves positioning the service according to the target segment. Thus, it would apply to all the consumer-based segmentation variables discussed.

Why me?   This tells the consumer why he/she should choose a particular service over the other alternatives present in the market. This allows a company to tell the consumers how they are best suited for them.

Physical attribute differentiation   The heritage hotels in Rajasthan, which are conversions of old forts into hotels, differentiate themselves on the basis of their physical attributes. Taj Lake Palace at Udaipur, built in the seventeenth century and run by the Taj group of hotels, is an example of physical attribute differentiation wherein an elegant fantasy in white marble rises out of the turquoise waters of the Pichola Lake.

Service differentiation   Providing services that benefit the target market can also provide a competitive advantage. Unwanted differentiation occurs when a company consistently provides terrible service. Many commodity companies are also realizing the importance of service differentiation. For example, Maruti Suzuki has lately positioned itself as

Exhibit 6.5 **Branding Toddler Education**

Today's competitive times are witnessing the emergence of a number of branded pre-school educational centres. This is also due to the availability of huge incomes and parents looking at pre-school education more seriously. As more and more organized chains enter the market, the focus on branding and positioning is bound to gain importance. Eurokids has 450 playschools and will add another 200 by next year. Kidzee, a Zee Network venture, has 418 operational and 120 signed-up play-schools. Apart from these national big players, there are regional players such as Kangaroo Kids in Mumbai, Shamrock in Delhi, and Apple Kids in Tamil Nadu.

According to the managing director of one of the national chains, since this is a service industry, branding is vital as it creates and builds confidence. Today, the choice of a pre-school is a detailed and well thought out selection by parents, which makes competitive positioning all the more important. Since there is no pre-scribed syllabus for pre-school education, there exists a huge opportunity for these chains to differentiate themselves. It is also true that they basically offer the same thing and end up copying each other. But Kidzee and Eurokids insist that they have uniquely positioned themselves in the market. Eurokids positions itself as 'the pre-school specialist' and Kidzee claims to 'identify and nurture the unique potential in the child'.

These pre-school chains have to advertise in order to create differentiated competitive positioning in the market. Eurokids spends about 10% of its revenues on marketing, and usually uses women's publications such as Femina, Woman's Era, and Good Housekeeping for its print advertisements. The advertising takes place at a national (to promote the brand) and local level (to promote the branch or admissions). Association with shows, such as Sa Re Ga Ma Pa Little Champs, also gives them huge visibility. The fees range from ₹300 per month for lower-end to ₹3,000 per month for the higher-end segment. There is no doubt that this sector is going to become more intense as the expectations of parents increase and competition reaches a higher level.

having the largest number of service stations in India. Exhibit 6.5 shows how a number of pre-school educational centres brand toddler education.

Personnel differentiation   Hiring and retaining better people than the competitors can provide a strong competitive advantage. This also includes training the staff so that they are polite, forthcoming, and respectful. They must understand the customer needs and respond quickly to them.

Location differentiation   Location can provide a strong competitive advantage. Hotels located on the main road on any hill station are at a competitive advantage but Green Breeze Resort, Barlowganj, Mussoorie presents its location of being away from the crowded mall, as a competitive advantage. For example, Taj Exotica and Cidade De Goa (facing the Arabian Sea) use their location as a competitive advantage.

Image differentiation   Image provides a competitive advantage for a product or a service by creating a unique image in the mind of the consumer. The image builds a distinct perception of the product/service in the consumer's mind. For example, there are a number of hotels built in old palaces in Rajasthan, but Umaid Bhavan Palace, Jodhpur, run by the Taj group, differentiates itself as the largest residential palace wherein the present maharaja still resides, and if the guests are lucky they can interact with him, making their experience an interesting one.

Selecting the Right Competitive Advantage

An organization may have several competitive advantages. For example, Taj Exotica, Goa may have a location advantage, personnel advantage, and service advantage, but it has to select the one on which to build the positioning strategy. Exhibit 6.6 shows how Airtel is positioning its services. However, a company can choose more than one competitive advantage too. Rosser Reeves was of the opinion that companies should identify only one unique selling proposition and project itself as number one on that attribute. It is very important that a company also delivers what it proclaims. If it is able to do this, it will get good word-of-mouth recommendations and repeat patronage. Some companies may opt for more than one competitive advantage for their positioning, the advantage being that they can attract customers for each category. However, the disadvantage can be that it may confuse the customers. In general, there are some positioning errors a company must avoid. These are:

Under-positioning When companies fail to position their services it is referred to as under-positioning. For example, stand-alone restaurants in India never position themselves.

Over-positioning When companies project a very narrow picture to the buyers it is referred to as over-positioning.

Confused positioning When a company tries many ways to position its services leaving the customer confused as to what ultimately it stands for, it results in confused positioning.

Distinguishing a Brand from Its Competitors

Hunt and Arnett (2004) have grounded the market segmentation strategy and the competitive advantage in the resource–advantage theory. The theory maintains that competitive advantage leads to superior financial performance and this competitive advantage can be obtained by providing more value in the market offering at a lower cost.

According to Hunt and Arnett (2004), competition is the constant struggle among firms for comparative advantage in resources that will yield competitive positions in the

---

Exhibit 6.6 **Positioning Airtel**

Airtel has long used the friendship platform to position itself. Starting with 'har ek friend zaroori hota hai' to 'joh tera hai who mera hai', it has maintained the youth focus and friendship aspect to the core. The new campaign shows a woman is waiting at the bus stop with her daughter on a rainy day and a visibly 'working' woman comes along and tries to connect with her phone and is unsuccessful. The first lady hands her, her own phone but the offer is rejected with a rebut that the lady wants to send an email. The first lady says that email can be sent and then there is a visible change in the attitude of the second lady. The campaign speaks of Internet access at a flat rate of ₹1 for services ranging from email, Facebook, music, and films. Therefore, Airtel positioned its Internet facilities on the mobile at an all-inclusive prices point of ₹1 to encourage 'snacking' by the rural subscribers who have a 'data capable phone but were unwilling or use these services'.

marketplace, and hence, superior financial performance. Considering the competitive matrix for a segment, a firm will have an advantage in the marketplace if the market offering has:

1. superior perceived value as compared to rivals' marketing offer at a cost lower than the competitors
2. superior perceived value as compared to rivals' marketing offer at the same cost as rivals
3. perceived value equal to rivals' marketing offer at a price lower than the rivals.

These positions of competitive advantage lead to enhanced financial performance. A firm is at a disadvantage if it produces a market offering that has:

1. lower perceived value as compared to the rivals' marketing offer at the same cost as rivals
2. lower perceived value as compared to the rivals' marketing offer at a cost higher than the rivals
3. value equal to the rivals' marketing offer but at a cost higher than the rivals.

At these positions the firm is at a disadvantage and this leads to inferior financial performance. Apart from these positions of advantage and disadvantage, two further positions are possible. These are when the firm produces a market offering, which has:

1. lower perceived value compared to the rivals' market offerings at a cost lower than the rivals.
2. superior perceived value as compared to the rivals' market offering at a cost higher than the rivals.

In these two marketplace positions the firm's financial performance depends upon the ratio of resource produced value to resource costs of its market offering as compared to those of its rivals. A firm whose ratio is higher than that of rivals will have superior financial performance in contrast to firms whose ratio is lower. Similar competitive analysis can be done for different products in different market segments.

According to Kotler et al. (2006), the characteristics of a good competitive advantage can be:

Important   The difference delivers a highly desired benefit to the target buyers.

Distinctive   The competitive advantage is unique or more distinguished than that of the other competitors.

Superior   The competitive advantage is a cut above the other options available to a customer in the same category.

Communicable   The difference is easily communicable and noticeable to the buyers.

Pre-emptive   Competitors cannot easily copy the competitive advantage.

Affordable   The buyers should be able to easily pay for the difference.

Profitable   The company should be able to introduce the difference and still be profitable.

Some competitive advantages may be too insignificant, too costly, or not in agreement with the company profile. Thus, the competitive advantage must be chosen with great care. If the company keeps the above points in mind vis-à-vis the objectives and goals of the company, it can choose a competitive advantage that makes the most sense.

Perceptual Mapping

Each brand has a set of competitive advantages, the effective communication of which helps the consumers form a mental image of the product and is thought of as occupying a certain position in the consumer's 'perceptual space'. The favourite means of describing this image is perceptual mapping.

Perceptual mapping is a means of exhibiting in two or more dimensions, the place the product or brand occupies in the consumer's mind. It generally refers to techniques used to represent this product space graphically. We can create a number of maps from the same data, using a different pair of dimensions. Hence, each such map will represent a different context (Semon 1994). In general, marketers have two broad objectives in mind when undertaking perceptual mapping. These are to:

- determine where a target brand is positioned versus the competition
- help identify product attributes, which are the key determinants in influencing customer choice for the product class.

Determinant attributes are those that are important to customers, and also exhibit differences across brands. Even if a product attribute is very important, if brands are not perceived to differ on that attribute, then the attribute will not be influential in customers' choice decisions. Often, the determining aspects of a product are latent, unobservable constructs, which include a number of manifest, observable attributes. Perceptual mapping techniques can be very useful in uncovering these latent dimensions (Kohli and Leuthesser 1993).

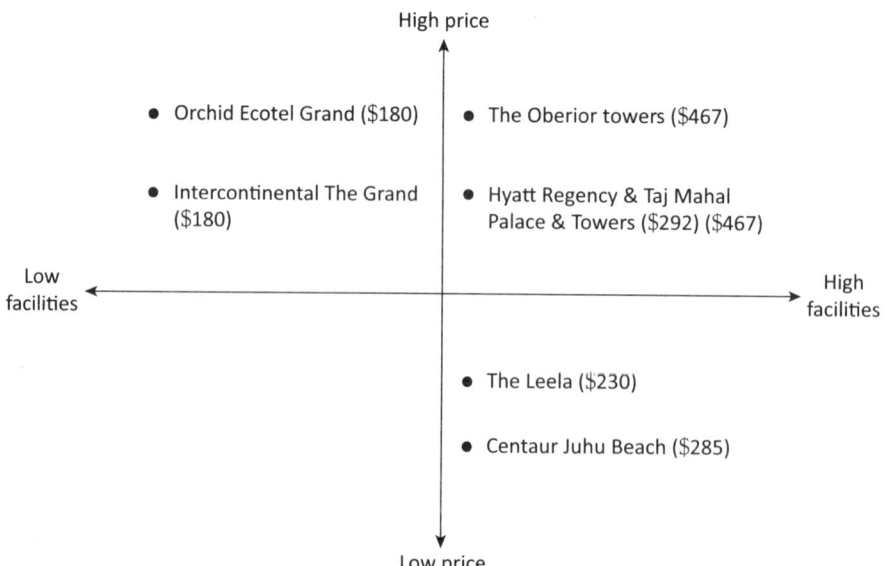

Fig. 6.2 Perceptual map of five-star deluxe hotels in Mumbai, India*

* The information on rates and facilities available were collected from the websites of the various hotels.

Exhibit 6.7   **Meaningful Re-positioning**

Information technology (IT) companies in India are experiencing a lot of re-positioning activities. This is mainly due to falling dollar rates, increased pressure on prices, and the impact of globalization. Hence, to stay ahead of others, companies will have to reinvent and remap their positioning. While they have to compete heavily on price factors, they may not want price to become the differentiator for their customers. Being typecast as addressing a niche can also become a problem as the company may be seeking to address new industries as they grow. The domestic IT sector in India offers a lot of opportunities and new businesses can be reached if the clients have clarity on the service provider's expertise and offerings. The problem that growing companies face is that they are themselves unclear about their own positioning strategies and end up giving varied internal communication that reflects on to the external world. Mastek re-positioned itself around verticals, such as insurance and government, which turned out to be a good move as about 70% of the company's business comes from these domains. Citrix is re-positioning itself for enterprise-level services. Sify changed its name to Sify Technologies and implemented a new logo with new colours, as it wanted to be known as a technology company providing IT services, beyond the Internet and e-commerce capabilities. Thus, these IT players are reinventing themselves, finding new ways to insulate themselves against the fluctuating market dynamics. The ones who win the race will have to create sustainable brand and intellectual property.

The perceptual mapping of the five-star deluxe hotels in Mumbai has been illustrated in Fig. 6.2. On this map, the positions are essentially neutral. Hence, one location on the map does not necessarily have to be better or worse than another position (Kotler et at. 2006). Increased competition can make a re-positioning strategy necessary. Changing situations also warrant a re-positioning strategy by firms (Exhibit 6.7).

Another example of re-positioning is McDonald's restaurants in Europe. To counter the fast food, drive-through image and create a more sit-down eating experience, McDonald's conducted an experiment in a German hamlet 15 miles south of Munich. The sales of this two-storey restaurant, where the makeover finished, have grown 22%. According to Michael Heinritzi, owner and operator of 30 McDonald's franchises in southern Germany including this one, the customers like the new concept and clients now include businesspeople who drop by in the morning for a coffee. McDonald's has revamped 2,000 of its 6,400 eateries across Europe, which is the second biggest market outside North America. According to Denis Hennequin, 'Re-imaging is important in the fast-moving competitive world of retail' (Sekhri 2007).

RESEARCH INSIGHT

Assessing the Implementation of Market Segmentation in Retail Financial Services
Meadows, Maureen and Sally Dibb (1998), 'Assessing the implementation of market segmentation in retail financial services', *International Journal of Service Industry Management*, vol. 9, issue 3, pp. 266–285.

Market segmentation is widely regarded as a panacea for a variety of marketing ailments. Yet research in the financial services market highlights a number of significant barriers to the implementation of segmentation schemes. These barriers range from weaknesses in customer data and inappropriate organizational structure, to lack of marketing orientation and difficulties in obtaining a fit within the existing distribution structure. While the marketing literature acknowledges that these difficulties exist, there has been little formal analysis to capture the characteristics of these barriers. This problem is compounded by the considerable size and diversity of the sector which make it difficult to generalize about the implementation problems. This means that the extent of any barriers may vary in different areas of the financial services market and even in different organizations, and that this variation may feasibly translate into different levels of segmentation usage. This research uses four short financial services case studies to examine the application of segmentation and consider the implementation barriers. Although the case studies cover a range of financial services companies, the analysis focuses on the provision of charge/credit cards by these organizations. The growth rate and increasing importance of the charge/credit card business make this a particularly pertinent area to analyse and allow a comparison with retail banking services more generally. The findings support the notion that a range of barriers to segmentation exists and shows how the importance of these barriers varies in different organizations.

SUMMARY

To be successful, an organization should focus on the target market's needs and requirements. It should shape the product offering based on this analysis. Segmentation, targeting, and positioning helps to focus on the needs of the market and align the company's resources to get the competitive advantage in the market. For a firm to have a longer and profitable innings in the market, the marketing mix should be based on the above mentioned strategies. If marketers indulge in this activity at the inception level, then the whole marketing plan is clear and leads to profitable courses of action. However, this needs to be reviewed at periodic intervals to cater to changing customer preferences, new competitions in the market, and new opportunities available. Segmentation, targeting, and positioning are extremely important for a company to become profitable.

KEY TERMS

Differentiated marketing   A marketing exercise in which the marketer selects more than one target market and then develops a separate marketing mix for that segment.

Mass marketing/undifferentiated marketing   The type of marketing where the producer produces in bulk, distributes in bulk, and promotes the same to all consumers.

Micro marketing   Databases and the Internet have allowed sellers to target small needs of individual customers. The marketing for these small segments with distinctive needs is known as micro marketing.

Positioning   After targeting a segment, the marketer needs to position the product or service in the customers' minds. It refers to the battle for the target consumer's mind space.

Product variety marketing   In this type of marketing, the seller produces two or more products or services having different features, style, quality, etc.

Segmentation   The process of dividing the market into distinct groups having similar characteristics, needs, purchasing behaviour, geography, psychographics, etc. These people tend to react to the marketing mix in a similar manner.

Targeting   This step follows the segmentation strategy and means choosing a single segment or group of segments, towards whom the marketing mix will be targeted.

Target marketing   In this type of marketing, the seller segments the market, targets a particular segment, and develops products and services for this segment.

EXERCISES

Concept Review Questions

1. List and define the three stages of target marketing.
2. Discuss the different levels of market segmentation.
3. Explain how companies identify attractive market segments and choose a market coverage strategy.
4. Differentiate between segmentation and positioning.
5. What is positioning? Discuss its importance in the success of a firm.
6. In the competitive position matrix, when is a firm at an advantage in the marketplace?
7. Discuss perceptual mapping and its role in marketing strategies.

Critical Thinking Questions

1. You have to market a low-cost air carrier in India. Choose your market segmentation criteria giving reasons for the same.
2. You have to market car loans in India. Which targeting strategies are you going to use and why?

3. You are launching a new budget hotel chain in India. What will be your target market and how will you position the hotel vis-à-vis the competitors present in the market?
4. You are in the insurance sector. How will you segment the Indian market for the sales of children's policies?

Internet Exercises

1. Collect information from the Internet and conduct a demographic segmentation for selling insurance policies in China. (You may choose the type of insurance policy you want to market.)
2. Download details of a business budget hotel's chain in India. Do the perceptual mapping for the same. What conclusions can you draw from it?
3. Visit the websites of two banking organizations. Compare how they have positioned themselves. What suggestions can you give them to improve their market performance?

CASE STUDY   Bharat's Visa

Visa, the financial services provider, has long been talking to the urban audience in India. Its memorable campaign of 1996 showed Sachin Tendulkar talking about the Visa Power and advocating 'go get it'. The non-metro India figured in the 2006 campaign 'starring Richard Gere but as an exotic tourist destination.' Around that time the market shifted from credit to debit cards. Thus, 2008 saw Vinay Pathak explaining the benefits of the card as a rickshaw driver to his passenger. This did not work as the card was positioned for use at the point of sale environment (retail outlet) for cashless transactions but it did not cut ice as India has an 'anaemic' point of sale environment.

The year 2011 saw Visa shift attention from India to become the 'payment gateway for Bharat'. The urban Indians had 'limitless propensity to spend' but Bharat—'the non-urban India had affordability but

no access.' Visa then opted to become the financial enabler for Bharat. It launched 'Dream to advance' campaigns where it showed that location was immaterial and people can realize their dreams through the use of payment gateways. The rate of use of debit cards for online payments is twice the rate of use for payments at physical stores. Visa, therefore, came out with a TV campaign in September 2012 where a man in Kashmir procures engineering parts online (through the use of Visa) to make a cycle generator and solve the electricity problem in the village so that the children could study at night. This saw a complete shift from urban and semi-urban to rural and small town people. The campaign has touched Datiya (a small town in state of Madhya Pradesh), Siddipet (a small town in state of Andhra pradesh), and Sirsa (in Haryana), where people did not know that the debit cards could be used online as well.

Another latest Visa campaign shows a woman in a remote village in Rajasthan procuring sewing machines through the Visa card online, and using it to stitch alphabets on girls clothes who have no time to go to school as they are busy fetching water from several kilometers away. This shows the company's shift towards Bharat but the main focus is trust that is highlighted through the use of the card in an online setting and both the urban and rural customers need to have trust in the brand to use it in the online medium. It is important that it does not lose focus of the urban consumers as '70% of its volume is driven by the top metros.'

Mainline advertising is not the only strategy Visa is using to reach its target audience. It has 'tied up with Aadhar initiative to ensure each of the UID (unique identification) number holders gets a bank account and a Visa debit card'. It has also 'joined hands with Tinkle, a monthly comic publication to have four pages in each of the issues focusing on financial nuggets by getting a favorite character like Suppandi to talk about basic nuances of banking and finance' (Bhatt 2013). This shows that Visa is trying to reach out to the rural consumers in more ways than one.

Questions

1. Discuss the positioning strategy of Visa over a period of time.
2. Has Visa selected the right competitive advantage to position itself? Why or why not?

REFERENCES

Aulakh, G. (2013), 'Vodafone to woo migrant workers with money transfer service', *The Economic Times*, New Delhi, 22 August, p. 4.

Balakrishnan, R. (2013), 'Friends forever', Brand Equity, *The Economic Times*, 4 September, p. 3.

Bailay, R. (2013), 'US Burger chain Johnny Rockets to sing and dance its way into your heart', *The Economic Times*, New Delhi, 4 October, p. 4.

Bhatt, S. (2013), 'Who's got the power?', Brand Equity, *The Economic Times*, New Delhi, dated 25 September, pp. 2–3.

Boomberg (2013), 'Longchamp outpaces Vuitton with value for money luxury', *The Economic Times*, 3 October, p. 4.

Business World, 'The income pyramid', *The Marketing Whitebook 2007–08*, pp. 31–33.

Business World, The Marketing Whitebook (2005).

Business World, The Marketing Whitebook (2013).

Cadeaux, J.M. (1997), 'Counter-revolutionary forces in the information revolution: Entrepreneurial action, information intensity, and market transformation', *European Journal of Marketing*, vol. 31, no. 11/12, pp. 768–785.

Cadeaux, J.M. (2004), 'A commentary on Hunt and Arnett's paper—Market segmentation strategy, competitive advantage, and public policy: Grounding segmentation strategy in resource-advantage theory', *Australian Marketing Journal*, vol. 12, no. 1, pp. 26–29.

Catlin, Jenny (2004), 'Marketing to children', *Marketing Mastermind*, February, pp. 45–51.

Lamb, Charles, Joseph Hair, and Carl McDaniel (2004), *Marketing*, Thomson South-Western, Singapore.

Cherian, John (2000), 'The red carpet all the way', *Frontline*, New Delhi, vol. 17, no. 7.

Disney Adventures (2007), 'Promotional offer insert McDonald's', *Disney Adventures*, vol. 1, no. 4.

Economic Times (2013), 'Wagh Bakri to set up 50 tea lounges in three years', New Delhi, 19 September, p. 4.

Festervand, Troy A. (2004), 'Industrial recruitment and economic development: A comparative analysis of competing South-eastern cities using perceptual mapping', *Journal of Business and Industrial Marketing*, vol. 9, no. 7, p. 460.

FH&RA India, 'Indian hotel industry survey, 2004–2005', *HVS International*, New Delhi.

Ganguly, Dibyendu (2006), 'Makeover mania', *Economic Times*, New Delhi, 10 November.

Ho, A. and T. Ying (2013), 'Why Chinese have shiny nails after a vist to a car showroom', *The Economic Times*, New Delhi, 28 August, p. 4.

Hunt, Shelby D. and Dennis B. Arnett (2004), 'Market segmentation strategy, competitive advantage, and public policy: Grounding segmentation strategy in resource-advantage Theory', *Australian Marketing Journal*, vol. 12, no. 1, pp. 7–21.

Jain, S. (2008), 'Meaningful re-positioning', *Hindustan Times*, New Delhi, 1 May, p. 30.

Johnston, Robert (1996), 'Achieving focus in service organizations', *The Service Industries Journal*, January, vol. 16, no. 1, pp. 10–20.

Kohli, C.S. and L. Leuthesser (1993), 'Product positioning: A comparison of perceptual mapping techniques', *The Journal of Product and Brand Management*, vol. 2, no. 4, pp. 10–19.

Kotler, Philip and Fernando Trias de Bes (2003), *Lateral Thinking*, John Wiley and Sons, New Jersey.

Kotler, Philip, John T. Bowen, and J.C. Makens (2006), *Marketing for Hospitality and Tourism*, Chapter 8, Pearson Education Inc., New Jersey.

Kumar, V.V. Ravi (2006), 'The niche marketer', *Marketing Mastermind*, May, pp. 29–32.

Lovelock, Christopher and Jochen Wirtz (2006), *Services Marketing*, 5th edn, Pearson Education, New Delhi, Chapter 3.

Masterson, Rosalind and David Pickton (2004), *Marketing: An Introduction*, The McGraw-Hill Companies, Berkshire, Chapter 4, p. 110.

Mehra, Puja and Sandeep Unnithan (2005), 'Airborne Indians', *India Today*, 11 July.

Mohnot, S.R. (2002), 'Market forecasts and indicators 2002–2012: Emerging market in India 2002–2012, The explosive decade', Industrial Techno-Economic Services Pvt Ltd (INTECOS), in association with the Centre for Industrial and Economic Research, New Delhi.

Porter, M.E. and V.E. Millar (1985), 'How information gives you competitive advantage', *Harvard Business Review*, vol. 63, no. 4, July–August 1985.

Raj, T.V. Ram (2006), 'Brand indispensability—An innovative branding strategy', *Marketing Mastermind*, May, pp. 15–20.

Rathore, V. (2013), 'Jewellery designer Modi plans strong of retail stores', *The Economic Times*, 19 September, p. 4.

Ray, Nayantara (2006), 'On the ginger trail', *Business Standard*, 22 March.

Reuters, *Economic Times*, New Delhi, 3 January 2006.

'School goers: Playful pretenders, corporate climbers, cautious planners, the home makers', *Business World, The Marketing Whitebook 2007–2008*, pp. 195–223.

Sekhri, Ravi (2007), 'McDonald's makeover in Europe increases sales', *The Economic Times*, New Delhi, 28 June, p. 13.

Semon, Thomas T. (1994), 'Classification and perceptual mapping are different tasks', *Marketing News*, 6 June, vol. 28, no. 12.

Sengupta, Subroto (2003), *Brand Positioning: Strategies for Competitive Advantage*, Tata McGraw-Hill Publishing Company Ltd, New Delhi.

Suskind, Ron (2003), 'Humour has returned to Southwest airlines after 9/11 hiatus—Flight attendants try hard to amuse the passengers', *Wall Street Journal*, 13 January.

Turakhia, S. (2008), 'Branding toddler education', *Hindustan Times*, 2 May, p. 28.

Vivek (2006), 'Global fast food chains think local for growth', *The Economic Times*, New Delhi.

Vyas, Suchi (2006), 'Hungry kya? Idli-pizza vie for plate space', *The Economic Times,* 15 May, p. 4.

BCG and CII (2012), available from http://www.bcgindia.com/documents/file107199.pdf, accessed on 5 June 2013.

CCD (2013), available from http://www.cafecoffeeday.com/austria-stores-locator, accessed on 10 November.

Cellular Operators Association of India (2013), available from http://www.coai.com/Statistics/GSM-Subscriber-Figure-Report, accessed on 10 November.

Census of India (2011a), available from http://censusindia.gov.in/Census_And_You/age_structure_and_marital_status.aspx, accessed on 14 November 2013.

Census of India (2011b), available from http://www.censusindia.gov.in/2011-prov-results/prov_results_paper1_india.html, last accessed on 8 October 2014.

Crisil Research (2013), available from http://crisil.com/pdf/CRISIL%20Research_Article_QSR_17Sep2013.pdf, accessed on 11 November.

http://www.asiahotels.com/hotelinfo/InterContinental_The_Grand_Mumbai_Hotel/, accessed on 27 May 2006.

http://www.asiahotels.com/hotelinfo/Orchid_Ecotel_Hotel_Mumbai, accessed on 27 May 2006.

http://www.cafecoffeeday.com/aboutus.htm, accessed on 19 July 2007.

https://www.cia.gov/library/publications/the-world-factbook/geos/np.html, accessed on 12 November 2013.

http://www.finanznachrichten.de/nachrichten-2006-01/artikel-5806353.asp, accessed on 28 April 2008.

http://haryanatourism.com/adventure/rock_climbing.asp, accessed on 3 May 2006.

http://www.indiastat.com/india/ShowData.asp?secid=391136&ptid=12977&level=3, accessed on 15 May 2006.

http://www.laterooms.com/de/hotel-reservations/4300_centaur-hotel-juhu-beach.aspx, accessed on 20 May 2006.

http://www.mumbairegency.hyatt.com, accessed on 27 May 2006.

http://www.shahnaz-husain.com/treatments.asp, accessed on 17 May 2006.

http://www.tajhotels.com, accessed on 31 May 2006.

http://www.tajhotels.com/Palace/Umaid%20 Bhawan%20Palace,JODHPUR/default.htm, accessed on 13 May 2006.

http://www.tajhotels.com/Resevation/default. aspx?disprooms=H00073/India/Mumbai/The%20 Taj%20Mahal%20Palace%20%26%20Tower, Mumbai/, accessed on 27 May 2006.

http://www.tata.com/indian_hotels/media/20060322_ ginger.htm#, accessed on 12 May 2006.

http://www.tata.in/company/releases/inside.aspx? artid=shnvQkbCax8=, accessed on 10 November 2013.

http://www.theleela.com/mumbai/room_only. asp?resident=no, accessed on 20 May 2006.

http://www.tourismofindia.com, accessed on 1 May 2006.

http://www.travelmasti.com/oberoi_mumbai.htm, accessed on 27 May 2006.

http://www.utdallas.edu/~tskim/Lecture%20Note% 206.pdf, accessed on 1 May 2006.

Kotler, Armstrong, http://www.armstrong/Kotler, Marketing, accessed on 15 September 2006.

Lal, Neeta (2005), 'Making room for the ladies', *The Week*, 21 August, http://www.the-week.com/25aug21/ lifestyle_article5.htm, accessed on 18 May 2006.

http://www.censusindia.gov.in/vital_statistics/srs/ Chap_2_-_2010.pdf last accessed on 8 October 2014.

IANS (2013), available from http://indiatoday.intoday. in/story/vodafone-india-launches-mobile-money-transfer-with-icici-bank/1/300737.html, accessed on 10 November.

PTI (2012), available from http://articles.economic times.indiatimes.com/2012-02-23/news/31091208_1 _airtel-money-bharti-airtel-mobile-wallet-service, accessed on 10 November 2013.

PTI (2013), available from http://articles.economic times.indiatimes.com/2013-08-21/news/41433319 _1_mobile-money-transfer-service-vodafone-part-ners-payment-service accessed on 10 November 2013.

Saxena, A. (2013), available on http://gadgets.ndtv. com/telecom/news/vodafone-india-launches-m-pesa-mobile-wallet-with-icici-bank-355406, accessed on 10 November.

The Hindu (2013), available from http://www.the-hindu.com/business/Industry/vodafone-icici-launch-mpesa-money-transfer-service-in-bihar/ article4995614.ece, accessed on 10 November.

7 Customer Perceptions of Service

Understanding 'Young' Customers

Social trends largely influence the manner in which consumers generally behave. Therefore, when Housing Development Finance Corporation Limited (HDFC Ltd) launched its online protection plan, Click2Protect, its task was cut out to promote insurance online and appeal to a younger audience. The motive was to make the consumers realize the need for a protection plan as young people like to live in the present and most do not worry much about the future. Five different commercials were made depicting different life situations that require a man to secure his family, in case he meets with death so as to make the potential customer 'feel concerned'. Needless to add that the entire campaign was in line with the positioning strategy of 'sar utha ke jiyo'.

Click2protect makes sense given the fact that the online term insurance space has a 5% share (in terms of premiums) and India's life insurance segment collected new business premiums worth ₹11,742.7 crore for April–May 2013. Indian insurance companies collected a combined ₹1,07,010.7 crore worth of new premiums for FY2012–13, according to data released by IRDA. Also, the young population that has been targeted is spending considerable time online and is also comfortable purchasing insurance policy online.

Apart from HDFC, the other online players for term insurance are Aviva Life's i-Life, Aegon Religare's iTerm Plan, ICICI Pru Life Insurance's iCare, etc. The biggest hindrance in selling term insurance is the perception that these products do not pay anything at the end of the policy term. Also, most consumers are still driven by tendency to seek returns from their investments in life insurance products and hence tend to look at endowment-linked products as semi-protection products.

After going through the chapter, you will be able to answer the following questions:

1. What is the customer perception regarding term insurance plans?

2. Who are the various players providing online term insurance plans?

3. How did HDFC plan to impact the motives of customers?

INTRODUCTION

In the current business environment, the customer is the focus of all marketing activities. Organizations can provide the best services to their utmost capabilities but if the customer does not perceive them to be of quality, all is in vain. Thus, it is very essential for the service provider to understand how customers can perceive the service as a quality service and carry a euphoric feeling. However, not all customers are alike and what might be pleasing to one may not be so to others. It is the task of the marketing team to understand the factors affecting customer perception, service quality, and satisfaction to have a competitive edge, and to create a perceptual difference. If all these are considered and the service provider targets the customers with a total service experience, the customer perceives the service as quality service, spreads positive word-of-mouth, and will reconsider the service provider when he/she next makes a purchase.

CUSTOMER PERCEPTION

'Perception is defined as the process by which an individual selects, organizes, and interprets stimuli into a meaningful and coherent picture of the world. This is a highly individual process based on each person's needs, values, and expectations' (Schiffman and Kanuk 2002). According to them, individuals exercise selectivity in the perception of the environment to which they are exposed and this selection depends upon two major factors:

1. Expectations in cases of first experience with the service and previous experience in case of repeat purchases as it affects expectations, and
2. The motives (needs, desires, etc.) at that particular point of time

Expectations are a pre-conditioned set of notions or ideas that individuals have regarding any activity. If service providers build hype around a product or service, people have high expectations, and if these are not met, it leads to disillusionment and ultimately dissatisfaction with the service. Thus, at the time of market entry it is always better to create few expectations so that they are easily met and surpassed.

Motives are the needs or wants of a person at a point of time. Thus, motives change from time to time. If an individual is very hungry he/she would probably notice the amount of time taken to serve the meal, leading to dissatisfaction if the time taken is long. However, if the urgency of food is not great, the same person would notice the way the meal was served and then the outcomes of perception would be completely different. The concept of fast dining and fine-dining restaurants came up to cater to these different motives. Similarly, insurance companies have developed different types of policies and banks have devised different ways of cash dispersal. See the opening case to understand how HDFC targets to affect the motives of the customers.

Perceptions can be related to the service (as in the service product), or the service delivery and the service provider (as in the organization). It is important to note that perceptions are not fixed but change with time. However, it takes a number of experiences to change quality judgments. In services marketing, it is the perception regarding the service provider that is important whenever a new service is launched. All organizations have two types of customers—internal and external. Perceptions and further approaches are related to both sets of customers. The opening case studies the customers' perceptions of investment in life insurance products.

SATISFACTION VERSUS SERVICE QUALITY

Customer satisfaction can be attained not only by providing the best possible product and services, but also by creating a whole experience, which satisfies the customer. If this experience is satisfactory, customers may even overlook minor details. For example, if an upscale beauty salon provides a beautiful ambience, has attentive attendants, and serves refreshments to waiting clients, then even if the styling outcome is not to the customer's satisfaction, the whole experience is so exhilarating that the client feels cosseted and wants to return. If on the other hand, in a beauty salon with highly-trained staff who would do a good job of styling, but are busy talking to each other and do not focus on the client, the client may feel neglected and not want to return (Schiffman and Kanuk 2002). Thus, satisfaction is a broader concept that includes perceptions of service quality, price, situational factors, and personal factors.

CUSTOMER SATISFACTION

Customer satisfaction is the affable notion of customers if they perceive the service experience to be in line with their expectations. Generally, if a service satisfies the needs and wants of customers, it results in customer satisfaction. The higher the level of fulfilment, the higher is the satisfaction. Since marketing focuses on the needs and wants of customers, one of the prime marketing objectives should be to maximize customer satisfaction. Zeithaml and Bitner (2003) enumerate the following factors that affect customer satisfaction.

Product and service features The service features are the prime determinants of customer satisfaction and cause high levels of satisfaction if they satisfy the customer's needs and wants.

Customer emotions Emotions are a state of the mind and depend upon the customer's feelings at a point of time. They are reflected in the customer's attitude. If the customer is in a happy state of mind, she will look at things positively, and is not easily irritated or excited.

Attributions for service success or failure   This includes the perception of the sequence of events that lead to the success or failure of the service. If the customer perceives the sequence to be one-off and out of control of the service provider, say, a computer error, it leads to less dissatisfaction in comparison to an error, which is repetitive and can easily be controlled.

Perceptions of equity or fairness   If the customer feels she has been treated at par with other customers, or that she has received her money's worth, it leads to positive perceptions towards satisfaction.

Customer satisfaction is important because a customer is the one and only judge of service quality. Customers have a set of expectations, and on experiencing a service they examine the service on the basis of the service features, and draw favourable or unfavourable conclusions about the service provided. The conclusion drawn is of prime importance to the service provider as it can provide important insights on how to improve their service processes (Swaddling and Miller 2002).

SERVICE QUALITY

Kasper et al. (1999) defined quality as 'The extent to which the service, service process, and the service organization can satisfy the expectations of the user'. Since services are a series of activities and the 'product' is 'missing' (Grönroos 1998), the service quality forms an important aspect in the perception of services. It can be used as a tool for differentiation and can provide a competitive edge. It is important to study service quality as it impacts organizational profits because it is directly related to customer satisfaction, customer retention, and hence customer loyalty (Mohsin 2005). Kandampully (2000) states that the service quality is crucial for the success of any service organization. At the time of service delivery, customers interact closely with the service providers and get an inside knowledge of the service organization. This knowledge gives them an opportunity to critically assess the service provided and the service provider. Thus, service quality plays an important role in adding value to the overall service experience.

Perceived Service Quality

Grönroos (1988) described how service quality and perception were linked and the factors that constitute service quality. This section discusses perceived service quality on the basis of experienced quality and expected quality.

Experienced quality   Due to its innate characteristics, services can also be defined as an experience. Intangibility of services leads the customer to perceive the quality on the basis of the image of the company, which can either be the corporate image, local image, or both. Further, this image is the result of technical quality and functional quality.

- Technical quality is the 'outcome dimension'. It relates to 'what' the customers receive on interacting with the firm and is an important dimension in quality assessment. This quality reflects the basic design of service, namely, its blue printing and execution. This forms the first impression of customers and this can be controlled to some extent by focusing on the basic product and standardizing the service manufacturing procedures.

- Functional quality is a 'process-related dimension'. It comes into play only when the customer has a positive impression of the technical quality and comes for product trial or re-purchase. It relates to 'how' the service is meted out to the customer at the time of service delivery. This is highly subjective and can depend upon a number of factors such as appearance and behaviour of employees, what they say, and how they say it.

If the organization has a positive image, the customers are willing to overlook minor mistakes, but if its image is negative then even minor mistakes can prove fatal for the organization.

Expected quality This is related to customer expectations when they purchase any service. Customer expectations may be based on market communication, organization's image, word-of-mouth referral, and customer needs as described below:

Market communication The information provided by organizations regarding their products and services. It is directly controlled by the organization.

Image of the organization Image of proven skills, innovativeness, ability to handle problems, performance, etc. It can only be controlled partly by the organization.

Word-of-mouth This is an informal, influential communication done voluntarily by the consumers based on their own knowledge and experience with the service. A positive word-of-mouth communication is favourable for the organization, but if the customer is dissatisfied he/she can adversely affect the image of the organization by creating negative word-of-mouth communication. Due to the intangibility associated with services, customers tend to attach more significance to word-of-mouth communication in the purchase of services.

Customer needs Customer needs at a particular point of time influence the quality perceptions. Customers who are hard-pressed for time will expect a prompt response in a beauty salon, but if they have ample time they will expect to be pampered and indulged.

If the customer experience is not as per his/her expectations it will result in dissatisfaction and a negative word-of-mouth communication. Thus, while communicating the image of the organization to the market, it is important not to unduly create impressions about the services, which the organization may ultimately not be able to fulfil. If the expected quality matches the experienced quality, it will result in customer satisfaction. However, if the customer experience exceeds the customer expectations, it leads to customer delight. The idea is to move from customer satisfaction towards customer delight. There are different models for measuring service quality, such as SERVQUAL, Gap model, and service encounters.

Dimensions of Service Quality—The SERVQUAL Instrument

The most eminent instrument in attempting to systematize the service quality is the 'gap model' of service or SERVQUAL that was developed by Parasuraman et al. (1985).

This conceptual framework was developed initially to measure customer perception of service quality for the financial services sector, but was later deployed to measure customer satisfaction in other services sectors such as hospitality, telecommunications, and health care.

SERVQUAL assumes that service quality is crucially determined by inconsistency between expectations and perceptions of customers (Gupta et al. 2005). According to Parasuraman et al. (1988), service quality includes dimensions of service such as reliability, responsiveness, assurance, empathy, and tangibles. These five elements are explained in detail in this section.

Reliability This is the consistent ability to perform the promised service both steadfastly and accurately. This means that the service provider provides the service in the same manner, without making errors, and on time. Reliability is very important to consumers' decision-making process, as they need to be confident that the promise the service organization is making will be fulfilled. For example, if an organization has to send an important consignment, which has to reach its destination in a particular time period, then it is bound to choose an organization which scores highest in reliability. Thus, it is a criterion on which the purchase decision is based.

Responsiveness This is the willingness to help and to provide timely service to consumers. All the employees who are dealing with customers need to be sensitive to the customers' needs and should contribute to creating a 'memorable' experience for them. If a customer is kept waiting for the service he/she requires, it creates inevitable negative perceptions of quality which could otherwise have been avoided. Say, for example, if a person's car repair is taking longer than expected, serving complementary drinks or providing some form of entertainment to the customer can turn a potentially poor customer experience into a favourable one.

Assurance This is based on communication, trustworthiness, capability, courtesy, and security. In other words, the organization is keeping the customer informed; they are creating feelings of credibility and honesty, and are showing that they have the knowledge and the skills to perform the services well. During this whole process the service providers have to give due courtesy and respect to the customer, and generate feelings of security that his/her interests are safe in their hands. For example, financial companies, such as banks and insurance providers, need to consistently assure their customers that their best interests are being looked into. Punjab National Bank uses the tag line of 'the name you can bank upon'; ICICI uses the tag line 'khayal aapka'.

The Life Insurance Corporation (LIC) of India links its advertisements to the 50 years it has been in business and says, 'Fifty years of insuring lives, fifty years of ensuring smiles'. Union Bank of India claims to be 'Good people to bank with'. In e-business, where the customers are not sure about the credibility of the organizations, the organizations' assurance by providing a consumer rating point can be used to generate feelings of trust and credibility. For example, www.bizrate.com provides ratings for the organizations, which use BizRate to carry on their business. BizRate carries out these ratings by collecting customer reviews (a minimum of twenty reviews in the past ninety days) and conducting statistical analysis on the same. This gives a significant rating of a store's performance and not just the opinion of a handful of customers (BizRate 2006). Similar ratings are given for all the stores present at the BizRate site.

Empathy   This involves the provision of caring and providing individualized attention to the customers. The employees should be approachable, sensitive to the needs of the customers, and make an attempt to understand their needs. The aim is to make the customers feel unique and special. In industrial selling, smaller organizations can provide more personalized service and are hence preferred in comparison to larger organizations. For example, in the airline transportation business, it is not uncommon to see a customer's baggage missing in transit. If at that point, the airline staff is able to show empathy and make the customer feel that his/her needs are being given utmost importance, it could take the sting out of a bad experience.

Tangibles   These include the appearance of the physical facilities, equipment, personnel, and communication materials. These provide evidence of the care and attention to detail that is exhibited by the service provider. Service companies, especially in the hospitality sector, focus on the tangibles to show their differential advantages. For example, the ITC ad focuses on the environment and sends across the message that to experience the environment, which soothes the five senses, visit an ITC Hotel and experience how it feels to sleep like a baby again. The advertisement of The Grand Hyatt, Mumbai, coaxes you to 'feel the Hyatt touch' and shows the different tangibles such as the room, conference hall, etc.

This SERVQUAL model is used to measure service quality and there is general agreement that it is a good predictor of service quality. However, Sureshchandar et al. (2003) argue that all the factors deal only with the element of human interaction in service delivery; however, other factors such as service product or the core service, standardization of service delivery, the non-human element, and social responsibility, are equally important.

SERVICE ENCOUNTERS AND MOMENTS OF TRUTH

Service encounter is the situation when the customer or consumer is experiencing the service and the service providers are fulfilling all they promised through their different advertisements, and on direct contact with the customers. This concept was introduced by Normann (1983) and literally means 'the time and place, when and where, the service provider has its opportunity to demonstrate to the customer the quality of its services. In the next moment, the situation is over, the customer is gone, and there are no easy ways of adding value to the perceived quality. If a quality problem has occurred it is too late to take corrective action and to do so a new moment of truth has to be created' (Grönroos 1988). If in these service encounters the service providers are able to keep or surpass the services promised, it leads to positive perceptions by the customers. These are referred to as 'moments of truths' because at these points customers are able to differentiate between promises and performances, get a view of the service quality of the service provider, and make judgments about use of that service again in the future. Zeithaml and Bitner (2003) identified three types of service encounters.

Remote encounters   This occurs when there is no direct human contact with the service provider. Examples of remote encounters are cash transactions through ATMs; communication through mail (billing statements); new schemes and incentives, or any

---

Exhibit 7.1 **SBI to Open ATMs at Railway Stations**

The SBI has entered into a deal with the railways to install 681 automated teller machines (ATM) at railway stations across the country. The majority of these will have an Internet kiosk to book railway tickets. The railway property has been a prized location eyed by banks, as these are places with maximum traffic. Some years ago, the railways allowed banks with the highest bid to set up ATMs at suburban stations in Mumbai. In addition to this, banks have also witnessed transactions from third-party banks, thus generating additional income. Banks have been lobbying for ticket issuing facilities at the ATMs, which was resisted by the railways in order to avoid outsourcing of ticket issuance.

The State Bank group has the largest ATM network in the country with about 26,000 ATMs (SBI 2013), with many machines in rural and semi-urban areas. The group is also the largest debit card issuer in South Asia with more than 17 million ATM-cum-debit cards on the Maestro platform of MasterCard International. Apart from the standard facilities of cash withdrawal, balance enquiry, and mini-statement, the bank's ATMs facilitate temple trust donations, tuition fee payments, payments of JMET and GATE fees, utility bill payments, and mobile top-up.

---

form of corporate communication; use of the Internet to order for services, gain information regarding service product, or price; etc. For example, after finding that opening an ATM at railway stations was very profitable, SBI is planning to install more ATMs, which will also have an Internet kiosk alongside to book railway tickets (Exhibit 7.1).

Phone encounters The most convenient and frequent type of customer interaction occurs through the telephone. Since most of the customers make inquiries through the telephone, the service personnel handling the call can, by showing the appropriate knowledge and skills, convert an enquiry into a confirmed order. However, service organizations, which outsource their tele-services, cannot control the quality of the services and most of the time this leads to customer queries not being resolved, thus leading to customer dissatisfaction. This causes a detrimental effect towards the perception of service organizations. For example, to get a billing correction made on the bill received for mobile services used, a customer had to make several calls to the service provider's customer care number, but the issue was not resolved in spite of continual reminders.

Face-to-face encounters This occurs when a customer is in direct contact with the employees. When a person is in direct contact with the service provider, both verbal and non-verbal forms of communication are important, and understanding service quality becomes more complex. It is at this point that all the tangible cues become important.

CUSTOMER PERCEPTION, SERVICE QUALITY, CUSTOMER SATISFACTION, AND PURCHASE DECISIONS

Customer perception is dynamic. It is influenced by a number of factors and changes with each interaction with the service provider. For a marketer, this is a cyclical phenomenon, which affects the purchase decision each time the customer purchases the services (Fig. 7.1).

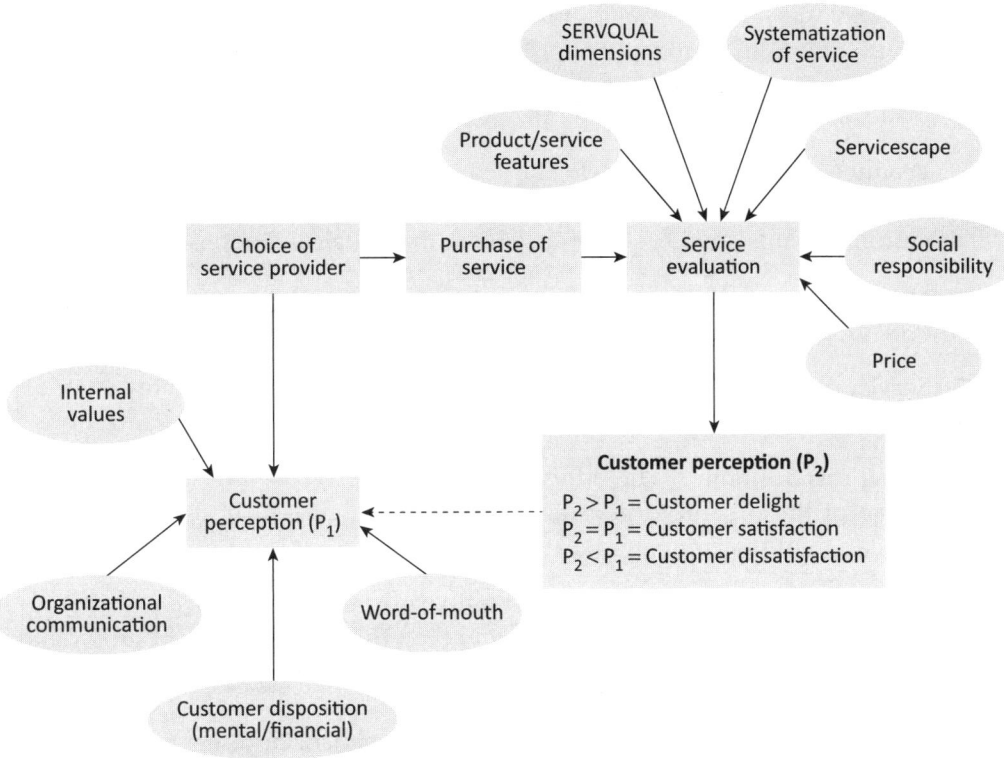

Fig. 7.1 Customer perception, service quality, and customer satisfaction affecting service purchase decision

When consumers purchase a service product for the first time they are influenced by the following factors.

Internal values The needs and desires of individuals are fulfilled on the basis of their internal values which are influenced by a number of factors such as culture, social group, etc.

Perception Their perception of the organization based on the different communications by the organization affect customer perception.

Disposition at the point of time This includes the money which they can afford to spend at that point of time and who are they experiencing the service with (for example, a person may eat at any restaurant when he/she is alone but may choose the eating place differently depending upon the company he/she is dining with and the level of impression he/she wants to create). This also includes the mental disposition of the person at the time of purchase. For instance, a person who is not in a mood to venture out will like the meal to be home-delivered, and so he/she would consider only those restaurants, which provide such a facility.

Word-of-mouth communication One of the main factors affecting customer perception is the feedback they get from their peer groups or relatives who have experienced the service, or have some information on the service.

Based on all these considerations consumers perceive different service providers and then choose the service provider they would like to consider for the current purchase. When they purchase the service and experience it themselves, a mental evaluation is made about the services rendered. This depends upon a number of features:

Product/service features   Do the features of the service match the requirements of the customers at the point of time? Are they what the customer was looking for? Say, a customer wants good food but he/she realizes that the food is not to his/her taste.

Systematization of service   This includes the non-human dimensions, such as processes, procedures, systems, and technology, used by the service providers.

Servicescape   This includes the tangible facets of service quality such as machines, equipments, employee appearance, and the ambience of the organization.

Social responsibility   The ethical practices observed by the service provider build the image of the organization as a good corporate citizen. It also affects the customers' evaluation of the company.

Price   The price of the service in comparison to other service providers is important versus the service product. If a customer feels that he/she is not getting value for money in spite of spending more on the service than he/she would otherwise have spent, it affects the customer's evaluation of the service.

Based on the customer's evaluation of the service, customer perceptions are formed about the service provider and the service rendered. If this perception matches with the perception the consumer had when he/she set out to make the purchase, it leads to customer satisfaction. If this is below the customer's expectations, it leads to customer dissatisfaction. However, if the customer experiences a service, which is more than what he/she had expected, it results in customer delight. This experience of the customer affects the purchase decision when he/she has to purchase the service at a later date. Thus, the customer perception is a cyclic ongoing phenomenon, which affects the service purchase and is influenced by each purchase he/she makes. Thus, it is the task of the service provider to deliver good quality service each and every time a customer is making a purchase.

MANAGING E-SERVICE AND E-SERVICE QUALITY

Internet penetration in India is growing by the day. In June 2012 there were 1,37,000,000 Internet users in India, which translates to 11.4% penetration. India had 6,27,13,680 Facebook subscribers, by the end of 2012, which translates to 5.2% penetration (Internet World Stats 2013). Online market in India is approximately $12 billion (Singh 2013) and above all it allows two-way communication between the service provider and consumer. All this highlights the attractiveness of the web for service providers. Exhibit 7.2 highlights how companies are leveraging the power of the net to reach out to customers. Each interaction on the web is a moment of truth for the customers and so companies need to manage these moments to enhance their brand image. Service providers can use the web broadly to provide accurate and prompt service, enhance quality

Exhibit 7.2   Delivering Music Online

Saavn (South Asian Audio Video Network) delivers music streaming services online. They started off as a 'third-party licensor of indian music for the US-focused music services'. According to Vinodh Bhat (CEO and Co-founder of Saavn) the idea was generated in 2006 when their friends told them about the lack of Indian content on Apple's iTunes store. Realizing an untapped opportunity existed for Bollywood music followed by regional music, they started working towards the technology for music streaming. By mid 2010, they had launched their first consumer product with approximately 1.5 lakh songs. Within the first six months they were able to attract a million users. In 2010 they also launched their Saavn app for android.

Saavn has invested and worked on streaming technology, user experience, and delivery. For instance, Saavn streams dynamic audio bitrate adjustment for better streaming on any connection so that the user experience is not marred when there is a network switch while streaming content. The search algorithms are such that users can always find the music they are looking for through the proprietary phonetic search that capably understands what a user is looking for, disparate spelling notwithstanding. Also they have linked worldwide deals with music companies so that customers can access music from any country. To ensure the comfort of the user with the technology they send regular updates to their apps as they do not want to overwhelm the users with the backend technology. To ensure a good experience their website has songs listed as per language, moods, weekly top 15, and have also started a radio service where services are featured on the basis of different requirements such as chartbusters, party, and romance.

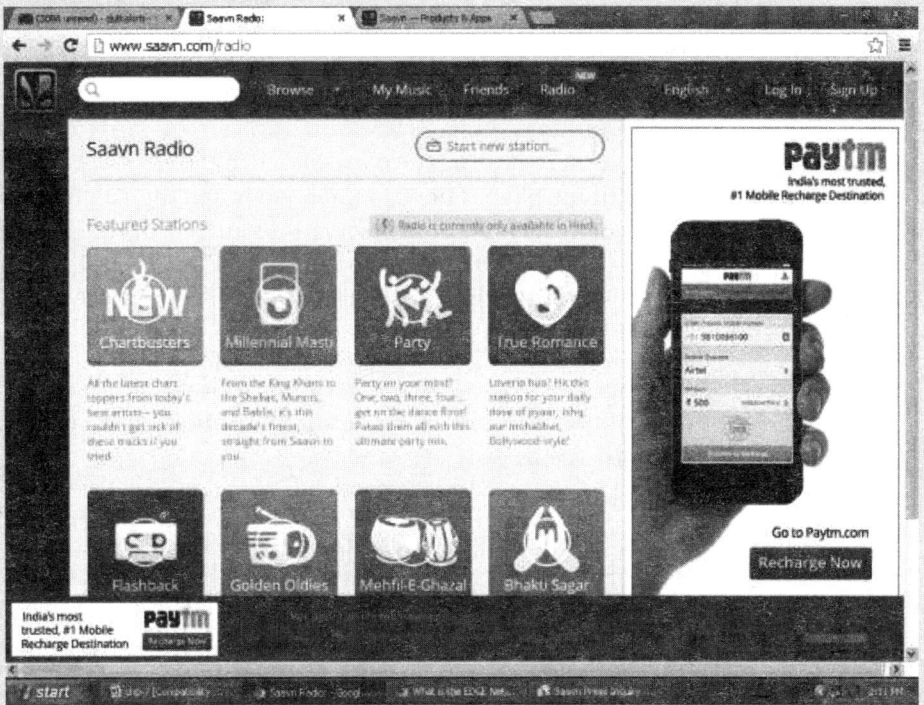

Saavn delivers online music streaming services

Source: http://www.saavn.com/

of service and connect both with internal and external audience (Asgarkhani 2005). More specifically the power of the web can be leveraged for the following:

1. Reach a number of people for their services
2. Photos and virtual tours of service outlets can be added to overcome the aspect of intangibility
3. Post ads, sales promotions, and other communication related messages online
4. Post testimonials of other customers to provide word-of-mouth for prospective customers
5. Communicate with suppliers (through passwords) and strengthen backend
6. Communicate with employees (through employee specific passwords) and so increase internal marketing
7. Use the website for existing customers and do relationship marketing
8. Use the website for customer services such as payments, making claims, and after-sales service.
9. Use it for selling the service
10. Enable customers to customize the service
11. Create organizational image through its brand history and the 'about us'
12. Digitalize the products (for example software, music, etc.) and deliver them on the net to overcome the aspect of inseparability
13. Hire people
14. Get customer feedback
15. Use it for recovery strategy

According to Van Riel, Liljander, and Jurriëns (2001), e-service offerings should include:

Core service   The information regarding the core service that the service provider offers should be provided on the home page. Therefore, if it is a hotel, then all the services they are providing should be evident such as room reservations and corporate business venue.

Facilitating service   The various facilitating services (for a hotel), for example providing pictures of the location, a virtual tour of the place, search facilities, online account, etc.

Supporting services   Support service (for a hotel in corporate business) can include meeting halls, dining facilities, etc., while for leisure travellers, services may include room service, sightseeing trips, etc.

Complementary services   This would include (for a hotel) a site map, information on local places of importance, weather conditions, etc.

User interface   This is 'through which the customer accesses the service'. The website in this case should be designed in a manner so that it is easy to use, easy to find information, should be downloaded quickly, etc.

It further needs to be highlighted that the online strategy needs to be integrated with the offline strategy and both should be aligned so that it does not create any confusion regarding the brand image. e-service quality can be evaluated for both new and routine buys and for recovery of services online on the basis of these factors (Ribbink et al. 2004, Parasuraman et al. 2005, Raman et al. 2008, Lee and Lin 2005, Swaid and Wigand 2009, and Ojasalo 2010).

Reliability   This includes how much the customers can rely on the website to provide accurate information about the kind of service promised (for example, delivering the promised quality or delivering in the promised time), the product features, etc.

Responsiveness   How quickly the consumers received a response (immediate, within 1–2 working day/s, within a week, etc.). This also includes the information related to product returns, how the problems posted by customers were handled, information about misplaced packages, defective items, etc.

Access   Ability to reach the website quickly, how the company can be reached when needed by the customers, etc.

Ease of use   How easy it is for a consumer to navigate between the various pages on the website and get the desired information.

Efficiency   It includes the ease and speed of accessing and using the site, that is, if a customer wants to purchase online, how much time it took to reach the site and complete the entire process online.

Assurance and trust   This includes the trust the website is able to generate in the customers on the basis of its reputation, truthful information presented, etc.

Security   The ability to make customers believe that it is safe and secure to transact on the website, that is the information provided by the customer (for example for online purchase) is safe and protected.

Clarity of pricing   There is complete knowledge about the prices that are going to be charged (for example for shipping, delivery of the product, etc.) and there are no hidden charges or surprises for the customers.

Personalization/customization   The extent to which the site can be customized for customers' shopping experience. This includes customization of the online purchase and can also include their previous online history, shopping preferences, etc., so that the customer does not have to feed the same information repeatedly.

'e-scape' or the e-servicescape includes the appearance of the site and the use of visual appeal to provide a good experience to the customers. This includes appearance of the site—use of colour, images, music, etc; layout of the website; etc.

Contact   How the customers can contact the service providers, that is, through telephone, online chat, etc.

Compensation   This includes the information related to compensation provided to the customers in case there are any problems related to purchases such as delay in delivery and return of products.

Perceived value   The perceived value of purchasing from the site, for example, how economical it was to purchase from the website, feeling of being in control, overall value for money, etc.

GAP MODEL OF SERVICE QUALITY

Zeithaml et al. (1988) developed the Gap model to analyse quality problems and to help managers understand the ways of improving service quality. The model is divided into two parts—one relates to customers and the other relates to service providers (Ham et al. 2003, Zeithaml et al. 1988, Zeithaml and Bitner 2003, and Grönroos 2000).

Gap 1 (Management Perception Gap)

The first gap occurs due to a difference between customer expectations and the management's perceptions of consumer expectation. Thus, we can say that the management's perception of the customer expectations was inaccurate. This gap is more prominent in service organizations than in firms producing tangible goods, and can be caused by marketing research orientation, communication, levels of management, relationship marketing, and service recovery.

Marketing research orientation

Marketing research involves collecting information from customers regarding their expectations in this particular instance. It is the key vehicle for understanding consumer expectations and perceptions. The following points are some of the important considerations leading to misconceptions by the organization as far as customer expectation is concerned.

Market research focus   The organization is conducting market research but is not focusing on the customer expectations.

Qualitative and quantitative issues in data collection   The organization focuses on customer expectations for conducting marketing research, but the information collected is insufficient or inaccurate.

Data interpretation   The organization collects sufficient data, which is appropriate to the task at hand, but this data was not interpreted extensively or accurately.

Management orientation   The information collected is appropriate and is interpreted correctly, but is not used by the service firm. The firm believes that the operational aspect is more important and does not pay due importance to the marketing aspect or the customers.

Communication   This is the exchange of ideas between service providers and customers. The degree of communication facilitates the transfer of opinions and feelings of the customers to the service providers and hence, helps them in reducing the gap between the customer perceptions and the expected service. Factors, such as external communication, internal communication, quality of communication, and medium of communication, are considered to provide superior customer service.

External communication   This is the communication flow between service organizations and customers. This involves all communications with any of the staff of the service provider, say, from the bell porter to the manager in a hotel. The conduct of all the personnel who are in direct contact with the frontline staff is responsible for widening or reducing the gap. Since the top management is responsible for the policy formulations, it is very important for them to get feedback about customer expectations and perceptions. However, the more the number of layers in the organization, or the bigger the organization, the further the top management is from their target customers. Thus, it is advisable for them to interact with the customers on a continual basis and experience the service.

Upward (internal) communication   Instead of, or, in addition to interacting with the staff, many top managers also get the desired information in the form of regular feedback from the frontline staff. This information can be obtained by going through formal reports or by informal interaction with the staff.

Quality of communication   The extent to which the inputs are sought at the time of communication constitutes the quality. Only when there is quality interaction can the management get a clear perspective of what the customers want.

Medium of communication   The medium of communication is important. Direct contact is preferred over written media, as complex and ambiguous messages can also be communicated.

Levels of management   Even when the top management makes extra efforts to understand the customers, it is generally seen that the more the layers or tiers of management in an organization, the larger the size of this gap. This occurs because of the communication gap that occurs when the information flows through the layers of the organization.

Relationship marketing   This involves building strong relations with the customers instead of just treating them as one-time shoppers. The stronger the relations, the lesser the gap, and the customer becomes more loyal in the process. Along with focusing on attracting new customers, the organizations should focus on the changing needs of the existing customers so as to build customer loyalty.

Service recovery   Often, when customer services are not up to customer expectations, customers complain. The handling of this complaint is crucial for organizations as this is the moment they can make up for their flaws and satisfy the customer. At the time of service recovery, the service provider gets an insight into the customer perceptions and this helps in reducing the gap. Implementation of these service recovery strategies helps to minimize the gap.

Customer satisfaction is important to create positive perceptions about the organization. Lack of proper understanding of consumer expectations can result in company decisions that are not as per the customer needs. Service recovery strategies are the last resort and are possible only if the customers complain. Instances are observed when a customer experienced a service failure but did not complain about it. Thus, at this instance, service recovery is not possible and the customer carries these notions, which can negatively impact the organization.

Gap 2 (Service Quality Specification Gap)

The second gap is the service quality specification gap between the company perceptions of consumer expectations and the customer-driven service designs and standards. The organization has an understanding of what it thinks the customer expects, but is receptive to translate this into specifications for the employees to adhere to. These factors are the standards the customer expects in the service delivery that are visible to and measured by the customers. They confirm to the customers priorities rather than to the company requirements of productivity or efficiency. Thus, service design (as per the customer expectations) and its excellent execution are critical for customer satisfaction. The different reasons contributing to this gap are management commitment, internal quality programmes, service design, and perception of feasibility.

Management commitment   The policies and organizational culture flow from top to bottom. If the top management is committed towards customers and cherishes them, they make policies and plan the service experience around customers. Managers just have to follow these policies to create customer delight. However, Gap 2 occurs if the top management lacks commitment, which can be due to any of the following factors.

Resource commitment to quality   If the management shows indifference to the needs of the customers, this results in less or no resource allocation towards improvement of quality that the customers consider vital.

Management orientation   If the management is profit-oriented, it will be interested in maximizing profits and will be unwilling to spend money on something that does not contribute towards improving the efficiency. These organizations have a product-based approach to quality rather than a user-based approach.

Internal quality programmes   The personnel have to follow an internal quality programme and the customer expectations might not fit into them.

Service design   A poor service design can result in Gap 2 because:
- New service development is unsystematic.
- Service designs developed are ambiguous and unidentified, leading to confusion among the employees, which reflects in their delivery of the service.
- Service design does not confirm to the overall positioning.

Perception of feasibility   Often, organizations feel that what the customers expect is not feasible and do not make an effort in that direction. This lack of feasibility can be due to lack of funds on the part of the service provider or due to some physical constraints such as unavailability of trained personnel. Thus, the greater the management perception that the gap cannot be fulfilled, the larger the gap.

Customer defined standards   In organizations the personnel performance is measured over a period of time for different purposes, such as increments, rewards, bonuses, etc. The organization can have any of the following:

Lack of properly defined standards   If the management does not incorporate customer expectations in its defined standards it will also not be incorporated in measuring the staff performance. Thus, even if an employee makes an effort to meet customer expectations, it will not be measured in his performance appraisal and thus, demotivate him from making the extra effort. This will affect the service delivery, and hence, the perception of the quality by the customers.

Absence of process management to focus on customer requirements If the process managers are not giving due importance to quality as perceived by customers, it will reflect in their performance, and to create a differential advantage it is important to focus on what the customer feels is important rather than on what the organization feels is important.

Formal process of setting service quality goals It is of prime importance that the frontline staff also gives due importance to customers' needs. The staff should be made aware of this and a formal service quality goal should be set by the planners and the management, by taking the staff into confidence. The staff will then realize the importance of customer satisfaction, feel the importance of his role, and be committed to creating a better experience for the customers. However, if the management just lays down rigid specifications for the staff to follow, employees will feel stifled and may not feel motivated to take initiatives to develop customer satisfaction (which is also reflected in Gap 3).

Physical evidence and servicescape These include the tangible elements of service. The servicescape includes the physical setting where the service is delivered. It includes all the tangibles such as business cards, reports, presentations in hard or soft form (say, the use of a laptop in making the presentations), equipment, materials used for service delivery, the appearance of service staff, the uniforms, etc.

The service personnel use the service quality design and standards as benchmarks for service delivery. A flaw in the service design is bound to affect the customer satisfaction, as it would be mirrored in the performance of the personnel. Thus, the management should be very careful in designing the standards for service quality. Organizations can use service blueprinting for reducing this gap.

Gap 3 (Service Delivery Gap)

This gap occurs due to the difference in the service delivery standards and the actual service delivery by the employees. This means that the quality specifications laid down for the staff to follow were not met at the time of service production and delivery process. This can be due to:

Problems in specifications The specifications were too complicated or rigid and hence, could not be followed by the staff.

Employees not fulfilling the roles It is the role of the employees to cater to the effective and efficient delivery of service. An employee not delivering a service to the customer requirement can be doing so due to:
- Inability to perform the job, which would be a reflection on the human resource policies of the organization.
- Technology–job fit, that is, the tools and technologies used for performing the job are wanting or inappropriate.

- The extent to which an employee works as a team is important. If the personal disposition of the employee hinders this, he/she will not get along well with his/her colleagues and superiors, which again, will affect the service delivery of the employee.

Customers not fulfilling the roles Customers are an intrinsic part of service delivery and play an important role in the service quality delivery. Gap 3 can result if the customers are not aware of the roles and responsibilities they play in the service delivery.

Failure to match demand and supply The gap in service delivery can occur if the service providers are not able to match the demand and supply. Services cannot be inventoried and so, if there is an under-demand for their service, it results in a loss, as these cannot be stored for later use. On the other hand, if there is an over-demand for the service, the service organizations again lose sales, and hence revenue.

Deficiencies in human resource policies The human resource policies are ineffective or not clear and these result in either choosing the wrong person for the wrong job, or affecting the motivation level of the employees by creating inappropriate policies. The HR policies can show the following deficiencies:

Ineffective recruitment The person recruited is not appropriate for the job specifications demanded.

Role ambiguity The job description is not clear and this results in confusing the employees about what is expected from them.

Perceived job control Employees should not feel restrained by rules and regulations. They should have the leverage to modify their job roles to suit the customer's needs. This is also important at the time of service recovery.

Inappropriate evaluation and compensation If employees feel that the evaluation of service rendered and hence, compensation offered is not as per or close to their expectations, or is not at par with what the other employees are offered, it will create feelings of resentment.

Problem with service intermediaries Service intermediaries refer to the retailers, franchisees, agents, and brokers responsible for the delivery of the service. The service organization has only a limited control over them and cannot control the service delivery of these intermediaries who represent them and interact with the customers on their behalf. These service intermediaries have their own goals and in times of conflict they are bound to safeguard their own interests. As they are the first point of contact for the customers, and represent the organization itself, customers are bound to evaluate the service quality on the basis of their interaction with these intermediaries. It is thus, up to the service organizations to motivate the intermediaries to meet the company goals and provide a satisfying experience to the customers.

Services are the product in themselves. If the delivery of service is not as per customer expectations, needs, or wants, it will turn away customers. The strategies to manage the role of employees, intermediaries, and the demand and supply, are covered in the subsequent chapters.

Gap 4 (Market Communication Gap)

The market communication gap occurs when the service delivered is not as per the expectations created by the communication made by the organization. The communication includes sales force interaction, and advertising and promotions of the organization. When the communication strategy does not match the services provided, it creates feelings of dissatisfaction. The gap can occur when there is:

Planning problem or lack of integrated services marketing communication   When the operations people are not involved with the marketing communication campaigns, then the promises made by the communication tend not to be realistic or accurate, but can be exaggerated. The customer who forms his expectations on the basis of these promises may be in for a rude shock when he visits the service organization, leading to a gap. This can occur when:
- There is a tendency to view each external communication as independent and not integrating it with service operations.
- The communication is not based on interactive marketing. The service product is delivered by the people and so it is not consistent in behaviour. Customers should be made aware of this fact so that they can form realistic assumptions.
- A strong internal marketing programme is absent.

Execution problem or ineffective management of customer expectations   This occurs due to the following reasons:
- Service organizations are not able to manage the customer expectations through communications.
- They are not able to adequately educate the customers.

Over-promising   In order to sell the services, marketing people can get carried away and promise more than they can execute. Over-promising can be done through:
- advertisements
- personal selling
- physical evidence cues.

The extent to which firms are pressurized to create new business or meet the business of competitors, also affects the extent to which they over-promise. The second reason to over-promise is the industry norm or the extent to which they think the competitors are over-promising.

Inadequate horizontal communications within the organization can increase this gap. These communication gaps can be between:
- sales and operations
- advertising and operations
- differences in policies and procedures across branches and units.

These communication gaps can cause the sales and advertising people to promise more services than the operations people can deliver. The sales people may even price the service inaccurately due to failure in understanding the factors involved in the service delivery. Also, different branches and units of the same service organization may be pursuing different policies due to lack of communication with each other. A customer who visits one facility may expect the same service level from the other, which can again result in a gap.

All the activities of marketing, sales, operations, and communications should be integrated. When the operations people are involved in the communication strategy it results in realistic communication. This leads to higher levels of motivation and commitment among the operations staff. They can also give ideas for services, which may not have occurred to the marketing staff. The strategies for overcoming this gap are discussed later in Chapter 14.

Gap 5 (Perceived Service Quality Gap)

This gap results when the perceived or experienced service is not as per the expectations of the customers. This results in:
- negative quality perceptions
- bad publicity and reputation
- a negative impact on the organization's image
- lost business due to all the negative perceptions.

All the gaps studied are with the assumption that the gap always occurs negatively. The gap can be positive too; for example, when the service quality designs are more than what is expected by the customers, or the service delivered is better than what was promised in the communication and the perceived service quality is more than the customer expectations.

The gap analysis is used to:
- identify inconsistencies between the quality of service provider and customer expectations
- identify the reasons for creation of these quality problems
- develop processes to close these gaps
- improve the perception of the service quality in the customers and create a quality image for customer satisfaction.

Customer perception is very important in the customer decision-making process for services. If the service provider can understand how the customer is going to perceive the service, he can channellize the energy and the resources to match these customer perceptions, and create a better service quality impact on the customers.

RESEARCH INSIGHT

Hospital Service Quality: A Managerial Challenge

Rose, Raduan Che, Jegak Uli, Mohani Abdul, and Kim Looi Ng (2004), 'Hospital service quality: A managerial challenge', *International Journal of Health Care Quality Assurance*, vol. 17, issue 3, pp. 146–159.

While much is known generally about predictions of customer-perceived service quality, their application to health services is rarer. No attempt has been made to examine the impact of social support and patient education on overall service quality perception. Together with six quality dimensions identified from the literature, this study seeks to provide a more holistic comprehension of hospital service quality prediction. Although 79% of variation is explained, other than technical quality the impact of the remaining factors on quality perception is far from constant, and socio-economic variables further complicate unpredictability. Contrary to established beliefs, the cost factor was found to be insignificant. Hence, to manage service quality effectively, the test lies in how well health care providers know the customers they serve. It is not only crucial in a globalized environment, where transnational patient mobility is increasingly the norm, but also within homogeneous societies that appear to converge culturally.

SUMMARY

Customer perception is very important for customer decision-making in the services sector. If the customer does not perceive the services to be good, then all the efforts and the money spent by the service provider will be futile. The marketers thus need to understand what customer perception is and how best to influence this. This has been discussed in this chapter. The chapter further gives an overview what customer satisfaction is and how the service quality can impact customer satisfaction. The service quality has been discussed in the light of the SERVQUAL instrument. It is discussed that the customer is influenced by the service encounters and how these 'moments of truth' can be managed for a better customer experience.

The next section focuses on how customer perception is linked to service quality, which impacts customer satisfaction and hence, their purchase decision.

Since most of the organizations now have an online presence, the e-service quality is also discussed and also how it can be leveraged for delivering services. This section further delineates how e-service can be evaluated for new and routine buys and for recovering services online. To further help the marketers in influencing the customer perception, the next section talks about the Gap model. This model delineates the various gaps that can occur in the customer expectation and the service provider's delivery of service. The section emphasizes the reasons for the occurrence of the gaps and the implications of the various levels of these gaps. If the service provider can understand how the customer is going to perceive the service, he/she can channelize the energy and the resources to match the customer perceptions, and synergize to create a better service quality impact on the customers.

KEY TERMS

Customer perception   A cyclical phenomenon, which affects the purchase decision each time the customer purchases the services.

Customer satisfaction   The degree of satisfaction provided by the goods or services of a firm as measured by the number of repeat customers.

E-SERVQUAL   Measures how the service quality can be determined when services are delivered online.

Gap model   A model to analyse the quality problems and to help managers to understand how the service quality can be improved.

Purchase decision   A plan to purchase a particular product or service in the future.

Service encounter   The situation when the customer or consumer is experiencing the service and the service providers are fulfilling all they promised through their different advertisements, and by direct contact with the customers.

Service quality   The extent to which the service, service process, and the service organization can satisfy the expectations of the user.

SERVQUAL   This model supports the assumption that service quality is crucially determined by inconsistency between the expectations and perceptions of customers.

EXERCISES

Concept Review Questions

1. What is perception and why is it important for an organization to know the customer's perception?
2. What is customer satisfaction and how is it different from customer's perception of service quality?
3. What is service quality? Discuss the various factors affecting service quality.
4. Discuss critically the relationship between customer satisfaction and service quality.
5. How can marketers ensure good service quality online?
6. What is the Gap model? Critically discuss the various gaps in service delivery.
7. How does the Gap model contribute to effective service delivery?

Critical Thinking Questions

1. Identify a recent visit to a restaurant. What were your expectations prior to the visit, your experience of the services rendered by the restaurant, and your perception after the visit?
2. During a visit to a bank did you feel any of the gaps in services discussed in the Gap model? How would you like the organization to overcome the gap?

3. Discuss the quality of the service rendered to you during your last visit to get your car serviced or your last visit to a beauty salon.
4. Pick any two well-known restaurants in your locality. Discuss the perceptions about these restaurants and identify points of similarities and differences. What service quality improvements would you recommend to them?

Internet Exercises

1. Visit the website of your bank. Try to make an online transaction. Identify the factors that lead to your satisfaction/dissatisfaction. How is this different from your experience at the local branch you generally visit?
2. You have to plan your vacation to a hill-station in India. Identify two hotels on the Internet in the same geographic region. Visit their websites and identify your perceptions about the hotels on the basis of information available. Which hotel would you prefer and why?
3. Visit the websites of two hospitals and try to identify how they have addressed the various aspects of service quality and customer satisfaction.

CASE STUDY 1 **BlueStone: Managing Customer Perceptions Online**

It is no secret that India is the world's largest market for gold jewellery. The domestic gems and jewellery market in India stood at roughly $30.1 billion in the year 2013 (PTI 2013). Over the years as customers have increasingly become net savvy and shifted to purchasing products online, the jewellery space has also witnessed a spurt in online jewellery business. Although initially the focus was more on artificially jewellery and semi-precious stones, but now even silver gold and diamond jewellery sales have picked up online. eBay in India, sells trinkets every four minutes, while solitaire sales are ranked third just behind mobile phones and wrist watches (IANS 2012). Jewellery buyers in India have always relied on the tried and trusted family jewellers to purchase gold, silver, and diamond ornaments. People in India prefer to touch, feel, and try out the ornaments before indulging in the purchase. This resulted in online jewellers launching a host of facilities to manage customer perceptions by dealing with issues such as variety, after-sales services, payment methods, and delivery to not only build

*Dr Swati Singh, Faculty, Marketing at Bharatiya Vidya Bhavan's Usha and Lakshmi Mittal Institute of Management, New Delhi. Used with permission.

sales volume and gain wider expectance, but also to encourage sale of big ticket ornaments.

Taking the Plunge

The penchant of Indian consumers to purchase online has seen a number of companies enter into the online jewellery retailing space. One such venture BlueStone.com commenced operations in the year 2012. The venture launched by Vidya Nataraj and Gaurav Kushwaha with an initial investment of $5 million from venture capital firm Accel Partners as well as entrepreneur Meena Ganesh. The website offers the young Indian women and men a wide range of products across an array of price bands. The varied selection of gemstones and metals offered by Bluestone are difficult to find particularly in traditional jewellery stores across Tier II and Tier III cities. Keeping in mind consumer's requirement for purity and trust, the company provides international third party certification for all the products offered. Other than this to re-instil confidence in the purchase, the company also offers 30-day money-back guarantee. To facilitate the consumer in choosing the products the company has ensured that the jewellery browsing experience is pleasurable. The website was designed to provide a 360-degree experience using the latest technology to enable customers to make an informed choice. Other than this, the company provides toll free calling and live chat to enable customers to get their queries answered. The company also included product reviews and consumer testimonials to further empower consumers. Other than this the company also began offering buying, gifting, and wedding guides to enable consumers compare products and help the consumer decide. Understanding that buying jewellery is an intimate experience for which the buyer requires multiple suggestions and guidance, as a part of its wedding guide, the website provides guidelines to a first time buyer on how to choose an engagement ring. It also explains simple things such as fix the budget, ensure right size, and the 4Cs of buying a diamond. Other than this, the website provides guidance in helping consumers care for their jewellery.

The company recently also launched a wedding bespoke model. Under this model, the company connects consumers to stylists that enable them to create customized jewellery for their wedding. One of the major hurdles, in purchase of jewellery in India is the consumers' desire to touch feel the product prior to purchase. The company launched two initiatives to deal with this constraint. The first was to launch guide stores in Mumbai, Delhi, and Bengaluru. The stores feature a selection of new pieces and all-time favorites besides providing styling advice. The other effort made by the company was enabling consumers to try out jewellery in the comfort of their home without the pressure of making the purchase. This service first initiated in Bengaluru was later extended to Delhi, Mumbai, Chandigarh, Chennai, and Hyderabad.

The company also began offering investment plans where buyers put in certain instalment while the company contributes the remaining instalment. For the 11-month plan, consumer pays for 11-months while company pays the 12th instalment, in the 16-months plan consumer pays for 16-months and subsequent two are paid by company while for the 21-month plan, the company contributes subsequent 3 instalments.

The company boasts of excellence in services. It ensures this through transit insurance, free returns, and lifetime exchange. The pre-sales services ensure timely delivery to the customer. The packaging used by the company ensures safe delivery of the products. In case consumer is not happy with the purchase, the free exchange policy is extremely responsive and customer friendly. In case of returns, the company keeps customer informed both through email and phone. The product is collected by the company's courier at a time and date appropriate to the customer and the money is deposited in the customer's bank account by the date specified by the customer sales representatives.

The company initially relied on heavy presence on the Internet to spread awareness and encourage adoption. However, in 2013 the company also launched a TVC to spread awareness. Other than that, the company makes use of opportunities throughout the year to bring out numerous collections and promote their products ranging from collection for shivratri, divali, janamastami, and an 'afrah' collection to mark Eid-ul-Fitr. Other than that, the company also engages in a number of sales promotions to build traffic and sales.

Competition Galore

The online jewellery space does not have dearth of competition. Others in the fray include CaratLane, the online jewellery store which was founded in the year 2008 and is based out of Chennai. The portal's website receives 5,00,000 page views each month and has recorded up to 1,000 transactions per month. Its revenue in 2011 was as high as $10million, with average transactions ranging anywhere between ₹1 lakh to 18,000 (AAK 2012). Just like BlueStone, CaratLane too found it hard to convince cautious shoppers to purchase high end jewellery online. Primary worries centered around genuineness of the jewellery and the safety of the transactions. The company addressed these issues by outsourcing logistics to well known courier companies and ensuring that gems and jewellery were authenticated by independent international agencies. Another problem faced by the company that hindered large ticket sales was that only 1.5% of Indians own credit cards. To tackle this, the company had to allow payment in instalments (IANS 2012). Intangibility of the online space have been addressed by most online jewellers through the offline route. Just like Bluestone, CaratLane has opened up outlets across metros in an attempt to allay the fears of cautious Indian customers and give them a feel of the products as well as build trust into the system. While CaratLane opened 'Solitaire Experience Lounge' in Delhi to offer personalized services, Juvalia & You, an online retailer for exquisite fashion jewellery incubated by Springstar GmbH in collaboration with the Smile Group has also adopted the offline model to engage customers and gain trust. It set up temporary kiosks in malls across Delhi, Punjab, and Haryana. The company also uses multilevel marketing which uses 5,000 odd registered stylists or agents to sell the company's products. The company used the online model as a catalogue for its offline model (Samal 2012).

Way Forward

The future for companies such as BlueStone and CaratLane is encouraging. As consumers are riddled with lack of time and their need for convenience in shopping continues to rise, online jewellers can be guaranteed of a long haul. A report by Associated Chambers of Commerce and Industry of India (Assocham) has estimated that India's online retail market is poised to reach ₹70 billion by 2015 from ₹20 billion in the year 2011 (Samal 2012). The online jewellers need to be cautious of changing trends and keep focus on the consumer's pulse.

Questions

1. How is BlueStone attempting to change consumer perception about purchase of fine jewellery?
2. How has BlueStone attempted to address the various aspects of service quality though its website?
3. How have online jewellers used customer perceptions to design their marketing strategies?

CASE STUDY 2   Indian Beauty Business: A Focus on Shahnaz Husain*

The Beauty Industry in India

The beauty services industry in India, largely unorganized, and pegged at over ₹12,000 crore by some observers (others peg it as low as ₹2,000 crore), is slowly but steadily taking the organized route to do business. The emergence of players such as

* Based on Dutta, Kirti (2009), 'Case study on Shahnaz Husain', in Vinnie Jauhari and Charla Griffy Brown (eds), *Women, Technology and Entrepreneurship: Global Case Studies*, Reference Press, New Delhi.

Marico's Kaya Skin Clinic, Lakmé Beauty Salon, VLCC, Shahnaz Husain Herbals, CavinKare's Limelite and Green Trends, Keune, and Jawed Habib Hair and Beauty, can be attributed to this trend, say observers. According to industry estimates, the organized and semi-organized beauty services industry in the country is about ₹1,500–₹1,600 crore (some peg it as high as ₹6,000 crore). Clearly, the scope for conversion from unorganized to organized is high, say observers. The organized beauty segment is growing at about 25–30% per annum, which only highlights how fast the rate of transformation is, say analysts. According to Vineet Gupta, Chief Executive Officer, Jawed Habib Hair and Beauty, 'In the next five years, there will be a marked shift from the unorganized to organized segments in the industry. This implies a turnaround for the business' (*Financial Express* 2006).

Pricing

At the moment the prices of services rendered depend on the type of treatment and the provider offering the service, though the accent these days is on high quality at a reasonable price. For instance, the average consumer spend in a Kaya Skin Clinic, Shahnaz Husain Herbal Salon, Lakmé Beauty Salon, or Limelite, works out to about ₹1,000 per month (Green Trends in comparison, is Cavin Kare's budget parlour targeted at the family, where the spend is about ₹300 per month per person). Hair specialists, such as Jawed Habib's, on the other hand, may price their hair solutions higher to that of its beauty services (Jawed Habib's haircuts and styles, for instances, have a premium price tag, though beauty services are moderately priced).

In contrast, Keune, which is a hair care brand from Holland, marketed by Brushman India through exclusive, company-owned, branded salons and retail outlets, has services modestly priced at about ₹300–450 for men's and women's haircuts, while applying hair colour costs about ₹600–1,250 per person, according to Brushman MD, Kapil Kumar. Given the burgeoning beauty market, international salon chains are eyeing the Indian marketplace keenly, with the French player Jean-Claude Biguine (JCB), for instance, looking to set up operations in the country shortly.

Distribution

Pantaloon Retail has also taken its first tentative steps in the beauty services segment with the launch of its budget parlour, Star and Sitara in Bengaluru, in May 2006. 'We are targeting BigBazaar and Central malls for the launch of our parlours', says Kishore Biyani, Managing Director, Pantaloon Retail. 'A second parlour is due to be launched in Ahmedabad in the next few days', he added. All this action implies more competition for existing players, who are ramping up operations quickly. Kaya Skin Clinic, for instance, which closed the last financial year with a turnover of ₹44 crore on the back of 43 company-owned outlets in 15 locations in the country, will increase the overall number to 50 this fiscal. In the Middle East, where it has three clinics in Dubai and Abu Dhabi, the company will add a few more centres, says Rakesh Pandey, Chief Executive Officer, Kaya Skin Clinic. The plan is to achieve a turnover of about ₹60 crore this fiscal by pitching its flagship skin solutions to customers, though the company does not rule out an entry into the hair care segment too. 'We are currently test marketing a hair loss treatment in Bengaluru', he said.

Meanwhile, close rival Lakmé Beauty Salons, which has over 85 franchisee controlled outlets in over 34 cities, is keeping its focus on a select few metros and mini-metros. These include Mumbai, Delhi, Baroda, Kolkata, Jaipur, Ahmedabad, and Kochi among others, says a company spokesperson.

Service standardization and training

VLCC, Keune, Shahnaz Husain (barring some seven to eight outlets in Delhi, all Shahnaz Husain parlours in India are franchisee owned), and Jawed Habib's, are all ramping fast, though the pressure of maintaining a standard format and level of service goes up significantly as outlets increase, especially the franchisee run ones. 'Yes, the pressure of standardization is there', says Shahnaz Husain, proprietor of Shahnaz Husain Herbals, 'but we handle this by providing regular inputs on products and services to our partners'. Lakmé, on the other hand, has a franchisee model, where five company-owned salons act as centres of excellence and training for its associates. 'The aim is to not only to provide brand saliency, but also equip our partners with the latest trends and techniques', says a company spokesperson (*The Financial Express* 2006).

Training, in fact, is a need stressed by all players in the organized beauty segment given the dearth of quality professionals in the industry. 'That is the most important element of the business', says Sandeep Ahuja, Chief Executive Officer, personal care, VLCC, which has five professional training academies in the country apart from 100 slimming-cum-beauty-cum-fitness centres, and a division catering to the manufacture of herbal skin care and body care products.

Modus operandi

The format or mode of operation is another area critical to a player, with VLCC, for instance, embedding its beauty regimen within its weight loss and fitness programme. Lakmé, in contrast, plays on its exclusive beauty and hair services; Kaya boasts of its scientific approach to skin problems; while Green Trends is all about affordable hair and skin solutions using natural products. 'Limelite is an upmarket salon-cum-day spa targeting a well-heeled audience', says Jagdish. 'Green Trends, however, is your neighbourhood salon', he adds.

The future competition

The US-based Regis Corp, the dominant group in the international hair salon segment with some 11,000 outlets in North America and allied locations, also has its sights on India. Not surprisingly then, its entry is being monitored closely by its nearest rival Toni & Guy with some 3,000 salons across the world, who is also believed to be studying the Indian marketplace (*The Financial Express* 2006).

Shahnaz Husain

Of all the players in the beauty industry, Shahnaz Husain in one of the oldest, most acclaimed players who can be credited with a number of firsts. She is a pioneer in herbal cosmetics and has won more accolades, awards, and mentions in the international press than any other Indian woman. *The Esprit* magazine of Germany has dubbed her as Asia's Helena Rubenstein, *Good Housekeeping* calls her Estee Lauder, and *The Daily Telegraph* has named her 'the uncrowned queen of Indian beauty therapy'. Today, she heads the largest organization of its kind in the world, with more than 400 franchise salons worldwide and ranges of natural formulations for skin, hair, and body care. Indeed, hers is the story of a truly successful entrepreneur who transcends geographical boundaries to reign over the world.

Ranges of specialized products

As leaders in product innovation, the Shahnaz Husain group has evolved more than 350 formulations for general care, treatment of skin and scalp disorders, health, and fitness. In fact, a characteristic feature of the group has been its dynamism, introducing unique concepts from time to time, and keeping abreast of the latest techniques in ayurvedic and herbal products cosmetology.

The products have grown out of clinical usage, based on massive client feedback, as an answer to precise and individual needs. Based on 'care and cure', the product ranges include entire lines of therapeutic formulations, which perform high level multiple tasks and reflect a deep understanding of the demands of protective, preventive, and corrective care. They have no exact equivalents in the market. Apart from the legendary Shahnaz Herbal Range, there are ranges for precise needs, as well as those based on specific extracts, such as Flower Power (of floral extracts), Neem Range, Honey Health, Himalayan Herb, Sun Range (sun-block products), Man Power, Kids Collection, Colour Magic (range of make-up cosmetics), Aromatherapy bar, and Shapet (ayurvedic formulations for pets). A line of ayurvedic health tonics, medicinal formulations (such as pain relieving balm, blood purifiers, cough syrup, Isabgol), food supplements, herbal drinks, herbal teas, immunity enhancers, medicines, ayurvedic slimming capsules, aromatherapy essential oils, as well as the medicines used in the ayurvedic centres, have also been launched, along with innovative accessories and gift items (Mahajan). The group has recently launched some revolutionary products in modern skin care, which include the 24-carat gold range, pearl cream and mask, oxygen cream, astro-gem therapy range, diamond collection, and a signature spa collection. Shahnaz also entered the mass market with Fair One, a natural fairness cream and plans to launch Shahnaz Forever this year, an entire range at affordable prices for all segments of the market (Shahnaz 2006).

Reasons for success

The undisputed queen of the world of beauty presented an exciting new level of botanical energy with her flower power collection. Rejecting the synthetic artificiality of the west, she portrayed the innocence of nature in her products. She started this herbal crusade single-handedly. As the saying goes, 'imitation is the best form of flattery', and the number of other people entering this niche segment was a compliment to her. But still, she is a force to reckon with and has earned the sobriquet of 'India's beauty ambassador' from none other than Barbara Cartland, for her tremendous contribution towards popularizing Indian products in the west.

One of the main reasons for her success is that since beauty care is an image-based business, she has become the brand ambassador herself. Basing her customized beauty care on the adage that 'external body condition is a barometer of internal health', Shahnaz came up with beauty care of the level of paramedical care, complete with diagnosis and prescriptions. It was this holistic trend that set the terms for her long innings as the 'Herbal Queen' (Bakshi 2005).

Another reason for her success is that she just did not concentrate only on make-up and doing hair, but proposed total skin care. Her company, showing an annual growth rate of 19.4% is not finance driven but emotion driven.

Current Stage of Business

Health and beauty products

Today, Shahnaz is described as Asia's Helena Rubenstein, exporting more than 400 'nature care and cure' products to 104 countries and having over 650 salons globally (Bhardwaj 2006).

Shahnaz has 400 formulations for general care, and treatment of skin and scalp disorders already on the shelves. She has outlets at prestigious stores such as Galleries Lafayette in Paris, Harrods and Selfridges in London, and Seibu Chain in Japan. Her products also sell at Bloomingdales in New York, La Rinascente in Milan, and El Certe Inglis in Spain, as well as in exclusive outlets and clinics worldwide. In fact, Shahnaz was the first Asian to enter Galleries Lafayette in Paris in herbal care, and the first Asian to be featured in the 18-foot shop window of the store. Hers is the first Indian herbal cosmetic company to have featured in Harrods and Selfridges (Shahnaz 2006).

Today, her products are selling globally from US to Japan, in Europe, Russia, Middle East, Africa, South-east Asia, Australia, and even in Iceland. (CNN 2004, Choong 2004).

Spas

Shahnaz Husain ventured in to the spa business by setting up the Medispa in the US island of Saipan, off the pacific coast, in collaboration with Hyakumata group of Japan to open a spa at their 24-hour golf course. This is now called Shahnaz Husain Ayurvedic Spa. She has incorporated holistic healing techniques such as yoga and meditation along with the spa experience. The spa has traditional ayurvedic treatments and soothing massages, anti-stress treatments, aromatherapy, specialized body packs, skin and hair treatments, supervised diets, yoga, meditation, etc. This spa received much success and was followed by spas in Toronto and Greece. Based on this success, Shahnaz is planning to launch a spa collection (Bakshi 2005). She is planning to set up a health resort at Dhauj (Haryana), just 45 km from Delhi. It is targeted at foreign tourists and city-dwellers who wish to get a healthy weekend getaway (Mahajan). Currently, the group is considering spa proposals for countries such as Saudi Arabia, Spain, Italy, and Australia.

Beauty training schools

Shahnaz is also the pioneer of vocational training in beauty in India. More than three decades ago, when only apprenticeship training was available, Shahnaz started her beauty institute, Woman's World International, to provide comprehensive training in beauty.

All the courses offered at these various institutes are in tune with international standards and students are taught the latest techniques in skin and hair care. These schools were the basis of the franchise-based enterprise (*Hindustan Times* 2006).

The franchisees

In 1979, Shahnaz started her first franchise clinic in Calcutta. This was the beginning of the worldwide chain. Shahnaz began to encourage ordinary housewives to open salons in their own homes. She had already shown them the way by opening her very first salon in her own house. Shahnaz trained them and offered the Shahnaz Herbal franchise (Rangoonwala 2001).

Shahnaz also adopted a highly successful method to promote the new franchise salons. She made it a point to attend their opening. She addressed press conferences, where she spoke on the benefits of herbal care and also gave free consultations. This not only attracted crowds to the inauguration of the salons, but also gave the new venture a real impetus. It was based on a personal interaction, where she would meet people, listen to their problems, and provide beauty solutions. Apart from training all the franchisees and therapists, refresher courses are also provided from time to time. An excellent feedback system is maintained and all new developments and techniques are communicated to the franchisees from time to time.

Shahnaz husain forever beautiful shops and ayurvedic centres

The success of the franchise system prompted the opening of Shahnaz Husain Forever Beautiful shops, based on a concept of lifestyle marketing. The wide and varied ranges, along with accessories, are housed under one roof, with exclusive shop design and efficient customer information system. Specially trained sales staff provide guidance and information regarding products. Shahnaz Husain ayurvedic centres, carrying out traditional treatments of panchkarma, dhara, and Kerala massage, have also been set up for the cure of various ailments. The centre employs ayurvedic physicians and professionally trained personnel to conduct the various treatments. An individualized approach, along with all necessary facilities have been made available, to provide a perfect environment for treatment (*The Times* 2003).

Research and development

Research and development have always received high priority in the group's two R&D units. To ensure the purity of raw material, a herb and flower farm has also been set up near Delhi. Thus, quality control is exercised right from the raw material stage. This is done through rigorous testing and research. The extraction of essential oils, infusions, decoctions, tinctures, and other extracts is carried out by the group itself. Various methods of soil culture and cultivation are followed, using superior natural composts and fertilizers, which actually contribute not only towards the purity and quality of the raw material, but towards actually creating a superior product. Various preparations are obtained from the herbs and flowers for use in the formulations, such as infusions, decoctions, distillates, essences, powders, tinctures, and so on, in keeping with the ayurvedic system. These are made under strict supervision, using the latest technology. Stringent quality control tests are carried out for various dilutions. Thus, by exercising control at each stage, high quality is ensured (Shahnaz press folder).

Shahnaz Husain Herbal has a large network of over 400 franchise and associate clinics in India and abroad, operating under the franchise system. The franchise clinics have extended not only to the cities, but even small towns all over India. Today, a countrywide zonal distribution network exists, with 40 distributors and more than 600 sub-distributors all over India. There are more than 500 outlets in India, which include the franchise clinics, Shahnaz Husain shops, and counters in leading stores, shops, and cottage industries emporia. Thus, the brand is ideally positioned in the herbal cure and care market. The year 2005 has been a remarkable year of global branding, setting up franchise clinics, shops, and spas, as well as launching products in Russia, Scotland, London, Manchester, Australia, Malaysia, and Indonesia.

Conclusion and lessons learnt

'What really matters in life is not what you want but how badly you want it. You can achieve any level of success if you want it that much', has been one of Shahnaz's guiding principles. She also says that, 'If I am walking towards the goal and if I feel the door is closed, I don't walk away, but open my own doors' (CNN 2004). Thus, having a vision, being passionate and focused about it, and trying to achieve it with a crusader's zeal, no matter what the obstacles, have been the reasons Shahnaz could find success in spite of coming from a conservative family and trying to sell a new concept to the world. The 66-year old entrepreneur says, 'you never fail until you stop trying. I never stop, so I never fail'.

Questions

1. What were Shahnaz's reasons for starting business? Relate it to customer perceptions prevalent at that time.
2. How did Shahnaz use customer perceptions to design her marketing strategies?
3. Critically relate Shahnaz's current businesses with the customer perceptions she has based them on.

REFERENCES

Bakshi, Veeshal (2005), 'Remaking the beauty business', *The Financial Express*, 5 February, p. 4.

Bhardwaj, Manali (2006), 'Padma Sundari Shahnaz Husain', *City Limits*, 15 February, p. 79.

Bhat, V. (2012), 'Digital consumption is growing the fastest in India', *The Strategist*, New Delhi, 26 November, p. 3.

Business Today (2006), 'The 25 most powerful women in Indian business', 12 March.

Choong, Renee (2004), 'Herbal products to enhance natural beauty', *The Star*, 10 March.

Cunningham, Jennifer (2005), 'Shahnaz Husain: Ayurvedic cosmetics manufacturer', *The Herald*, 20 June, p. 19.

'Estee Lauder of India', *Global Indian*, Middle East Edition, vol. 2, no. 11, p. 18.

Grönroos, C. (1988), 'Service quality: The six criteria of good perceived service quality', *Review of Business*, vol. 9, no. 3, pp. 10–13.

Grönroos, C. (1998), 'Marketing services: The case of the missing product', *The Journal of Business and Industrial Marketing*, vol. 13, no. 4/5, pp. 322–336.

Grönroos, C. (2000), *Service Management and Marketing: A Customer Relationship Management Approach*, 2nd edn, Chapters 4 and 5, John Wiley and Sons, Chichester.

Gupta, Atul, J.C. McDaniel, and S.K. Herath (2005), 'Quality management in service firms: Sustaining structures of total quality service', *Managing Service Quality*, vol. 15, no. 4, pp. 389–402.

Ham, C.L., W. Johnson, R. Plank, A. Weinstein, and P.L. Johnson (2003), 'Gaining competitive advantage: Analysing the gap between expectations and perceptions of service quality', *International Journal of Value-based Management*, vol. 12, no. 2, pp. 197–203.

Kandampully, J. (2000), 'The impact of demand fluctuation on the quality of service: A tourism industry example', *Managing Service Quality*, vol. 10, no. 1, pp. 10–18.

Kasper, Hans, P.V. Helsdingen, and W. De Vries (1999), *Services Marketing Management: An International Perspective*, Chapter 5, John Wiley and Sons, England.

Khicha, P. (2012), 'Budgeting for the uncertain times: the new campaing for HDFC Life Insurance's online term insurance is aimed to make the potential consumer "feel concerned"', *The Strategist*, New Delhi, 6 February, p. 4.

Kurian, Anupa (2003), 'A truly beautiful woman must have inner beauty', *Gulf News Tabloid*, 8 May, pp. 1–2.

Lane, Winsome (2000), 'Secrets of eternal beauty', *Standard*, Hong Kong, 27 February, pp. 6–8.

Lee, G.G. and H.F. Lin (2005), 'Customer perceptions of e-service quality in on-line shopping', *International Journal of Retail & Distribution Management*, vol. 33, issue 2, pp. 161–176.

Mahajan, Prarthana, 'India is naaz of Shahnaaz', *Inside Fashion*, vol. 2, no. 7, p. 18.

Majumdar, Pallavi (2005), 'Shahnaz Hussain goes mass market', *Business Standard*, 19 January, p. 22.

Mohsin, Asad (2005), 'Service quality perceptions: An assessment of restaurant and café visitors in Hamilton, New Zealand', *The Business Review*, Cambridge, vol. 3, no. 2, pp. 51–57.

Normann, R. (1983), *Service Management*, John Wiley, New York.

Parasuraman A., V.A. Zeithaml, and L.L. Berry (1985), 'A conceptual model of service quality and its implications for future research', *Journal of Marketing*, vol. 49, no. 4, p. 47.

Parasuraman A., V.A. Zeithaml, and L.L. Berry (1988), 'SERVQUAL: A multiple-item scale for measuring consumer perceptions of service quality', *Journal of Retailing*, vol. 64, no. 1, pp. 12–37.

Parasuraman, A., V. Zeithaml, and A. Malhotra (2005), 'E-S-Qual: A multiple-Item scale for assessing electronic service quality', *Journal of Service Research*, vol. 7, issue 3, pp. 213–233.

'PSBs score in traditional products', *The Economic Times*, New Delhi, 4 September.

Raman, M., R. Stehenaus, N. Alam, and M. Kuppusamy (2008), 'Information technology in Malaysia: E-service quality and uptake of internet banking', *Journal of Internet Banking and Commerce*, vol. 13, issue 2, pp. 1–18.

Rangoonwala, Yousuf (2001), 'Herbal queen', *The Telegraph in Schools*, 19 July–1 August, p. 11.

Ribbink, D., A.C.R. van Riel, V. Liljander, and S. Streukens (2004), 'Confort your online customer: quality, trust and loyalty on the internet', Managing Service Quality, vol. 14, issue 6, pp. 446–456.

Sakhuja, Latika (2005), 'Herbal beauty care franchising pioneer', *The Franchising World*, vol. 6, pp. 48–50.

Schiffman, G. Leon and Leslie L. Kanuk (2002), *Consumer Behaviour*, Chapters 6 and 7, Prentice Hall, New Delhi.

Sengupta, Hindol (2003) 'From bloody fingers to hands decked with diamonds', *Mid Day*, Delhi, May 6.

Sherman, Elizabeth (1990), 'India's queen of beauty', *Harpers and Queen*, September, pp. 274–277.

Singh, Kishore (2002), 'In the parlour of the diva of potions', *Business Standard*, 13 February, p. 14.

Sinha, Vimmy (2006), 'Guts and glory', Delhi Times, *The Times of India*, 14 April, p. 11.

Success (1996), 'India's beauty queen', *Success*, June, pp. 37–38.

Sureshchandar, G.S., C. Rajendran, and R.N. Anantharaman (2003), 'Customer perceptions of service quality in the banking sector of a developing economy: A critical analysis', *The International Journal of Bank Marketing*, vol. 21, no. 4/5, pp. 233–241.

Swaddling, David C. and Charles Miller (2002), 'Don't measure customer satisfaction', *Quality Progress*, vol. 35, no. 5, pp. 62–67.

Swaid, S.I. and R.T. Wigand (2009), 'Measuring the quality of e-service: Scale development and initial validation', *Journal of Electronic Commerce Research*, vol. 10, issue 1, pp. 13–28.

The Times (2003), 'Amazing success story of Shahnaz Husain', Kuwait, 15–31 August.

Van Riel, A.C.R., V. Liljander, and P. Jurriëns (2001), 'Exploring consumer evaluations of e-service: A portal site', *International Journal of Service Industry Management*, vol. 12, issue 4, pp. 359–377.

Zeithaml, Valarie A. (1988), 'Consumer perceptions of price, quality and value: A means-end model and synthesis of evidence', *Journal of Marketing*, vol. 52, no. 3, pp. 2–20.

Zeithaml, Valarie A. and M.J. Bitner (2003), *Services Marketing*, Tata McGraw-Hill Publishing Company Limited, New Delhi.

Zeithaml, Valarie A., Leonard L. Berry, and A. Parasuraman (1988), 'Communication and control processes in the delivery of service quality', *Journal of Marketing*, vol. 52, no. 2.

AAK (2012), 'India's online jewellery business: Culture and clicks', available from http://www.economist.com/blogs/schumpeter/2012/05/indias-online-jewellery-business, accessed on 4 December 2013.

Asgarkhani M. (2005), 'The effectiveness of e-service in local government: A case study', *The Electronic Journal of e-Government*, vol. 3, issue 4, pp. 157–166, available from www.ejeg.com.

Financial Express (2006), 'Armed for the beauty market', available from http://www.financialexpress.com/inc/index.html, accessed on 2 September.

http://www.financialexpress.com/fe_full_story.php?content_id=1 15954, accessed on 1 September 2006.

http://www.shahnaz-husain.com, accessed on 1 September 2006.

Husain, Shahnaz (online), available from http://www.shahnaz-husain.com, accessed on 1 September 2006.

IANS (2012), 'More shoppers buying jewellery online', available from http://businesstoday.intoday.in/story/jewellery-shopping-online/1/23800.html., accessed on 4 December 2013.

IBEF (2013), available from http://www.ibef.org/industry/insurance-sector-india.aspx, accessed on 23 November.

Internet World Stats (2013), available from http://www.internetworldstats.com/stats3.htm#asia, accessed on 23 November 2013.

IRDA product (2013), available from http://www.irda.gov.in/ADMINCMS/cms/frmGeneral_Layout.aspx?page=PageNo584&flag=1&mid=Products%20offered%20%3E%3E%20Life%20Insurers, accessed on 23 November.

Ojasalo, J. (2010), 'E-service quality a conceptual model', *International Journal of Arts and Science,* available from http://www.academia.edu/1003804/E-Service_Quality_A_Conceptual_Model, accessed on 23 November 2013.

PTI (2013), 'Indian gems and jewellery market worth $30.1 billion: Report', available from http://articles.economictimes.indiatimes.com/2013-04-18/news/38647110_1_market-share-jewellery-market-coloured-gemstones, accessed on 4 December.

Rangaraj, R. (2005) 'Shahnaz Husain launches Fair One', *Chennai Online*, available from http://www.chennaionline.com/fashion-lifestyle/Fashiontips/2005/05elder.asp, accessed on 20 September 2006.

Rediff Books (2006), available from http://books.rediff.com/bookstore/, accessed on 2 September 2006.

Samal, I. (2012), 'Jewellery e-commerce players taking offline route to woo customers', available from http://www.business-standard.com/article/companies/jewellery-e-commerce-players-taking-offline-route-to-woo-customers-112100400133_1.html, accessed on 3 December 2013.

SBI (2013), available from https://www.sbi.co.in/user.htm?action=print_section&lang=0&id=0,10,75, accessed on 24 November.

Singh, S. (2013), 'Can Amazon crack Indian e-commerce market?', available from http://timesofindia.indiatimes.com/tech/tech-news/internet/Can-Amazon-crack-Indian-e-commerce-market/articleshow/23111026.cms, accessed on 24 November.

The Economic Times (2006), 'SBI to open ATMs at railway stations', 5 August, available from http://economictimes.indiatimes.com/articleshow/1855597.cms, accessed on 19 September 2006.

8   Customer Expectations

Building Expectations for Naukri

The website www.Naukri.com was launched in March 1997 and it heralded the online job search market in India. It virtually brought the job seekers and job providers together. The idea to launch Naukri.com came to Sanjeev Bikhchandani while he was working for HMM (now Glaxo SmithKline) when he saw his colleagues lapping up editions of *Business India* magazine that had appointment ads for managers and contained 35–40 pages of appointment ads in every issue. While his colleagues had no intention of leaving their current jobs, they would still look at all the offers and discuss the openings earnestly. Apart from this, a few job consultants would call every week with job offerings. He estimated that there must be '100 head hunters with 4–5 clients' and these jobs were not listed in *Business India* or elsewhere. It did not take him long to figure out that the job market was huge and highly fragmented. They decided to aggregate the jobs making it easier for various applicants to search for their dream job. They got a lot of publicity as they were the first site targeting Indians in India, whereas others such as rediff.com, *Khoj*, and *Samachar* were all targeting Indians in the US. Journalists in India had begun to write about Internet and were looking for Indian examples to talk about. With only 14,000 people accessing the Internet then, they had to ensure that they kept coming back and so the customers were allowed to log on for free. The website was rudimentary then but its ads in the TV drove traffic to the website and the 'Hari Sadu' ad was an instant hit with the masses. The website has now evolved and you can search for jobs, post resumes, search by sectors, search for PSU/Government jobs, premium jobs, and also international jobs. If you create login details, Naukri.com builds expectations by informing that you can get connected with over 45,000 recruiters, there would be thousands of jobs posted daily on the website, so a number of opportunities daily. Customers can create a number of job alerts for themselves and target the kind of jobs they want. Also, they can get relevant jobs on their mobile phones or online as well. The ease of process is accentuated by the fact that they can apply for a job in just one click. To ally the concerns of their customers, they are also informed that they can block their current employment organization from viewing their profile. They can also apply to the jobs while keeping their resume hidden from recruiters. Customers can also mark themselves as 'passive jobseeker' if they are not actively looking for a job.

After going through the chapter, you will be able to answer the following questions:
1. Trace the customer insight that lead to the creation of naukri.com.
2. How did naukri.com ensure that customers kept coming back to its website?

INTRODUCTION

Service providers exist because of customers who are the ultimate judges of the services rendered by an organization. It is important for service providers to know the level of customer expectations in order to meet and even excel them to gain maximum customer satisfaction. As customer expectation is an important criterion for post-consumption evaluation, it is also important for the service providers to manage the customer expectations so that customers do not develop expectations that are difficult for the service providers to satisfy. The opening case corroborates this fact. The success over the years of naukri. com shows that it was able to create and manage customer expectations successfully.

The term 'expectation' is used differently in the service quality literature and consumer satisfaction literature. In the consumer satisfaction literature, expectations are predictions about what is likely to happen in a forthcoming transaction. In the service quality literature, expectations are what customers ideally want. They are customers' expressions of what they believe the service provider should offer, rather than would offer (Parasuraman et al. 1988). The service provider's time and effort are both wasted if the customer's expectations are different, as expectations influence the customer satisfaction at the time of service delivery (Coye 2004). According to Zeithaml et al. (1993), 'Expectations are viewed as predictions made by customers about what is likely to happen during an impending transaction or exchange'.

Expectations can be defined as, 'The preconceived set of ideas consumers have, that function as a point of reference against which performance is evaluated or judged'. Parasuraman et al. (1985) studied the different expectations a customer might have related to a service and gave the 'determinants of service quality' (Chapter 7 has already elaborated on customer perception). Kandampully (1998, 2000) stated that service quality is crucial for developing loyal customers and is hence responsible for the success of any service organization. At the time of service delivery, the customers interact closely with the service providers and get an inside knowledge of the service organization. This knowledge gives them an opportunity to critically assess the service provided and the service provider. Thus, service quality plays an important role in adding value to the overall service experience. Also, customers seek organizations that are service loyal, that is, aim to provide consistent and superior quality of service for the present and in the long-term, and organizations aiming for this are bound to get customers' loyalty (Kandampully 1998).

A survey of the Indian banking sector in Delhi and National Capital Region (NCR) showed that there was a difference between the customer expectations and perceptions about the service quality offered by the different banks (Fig. 8.1). It was observed that there was a significant difference between customer expectations and perceptions in the public sector banks, while the foreign banks fared well with a low difference.

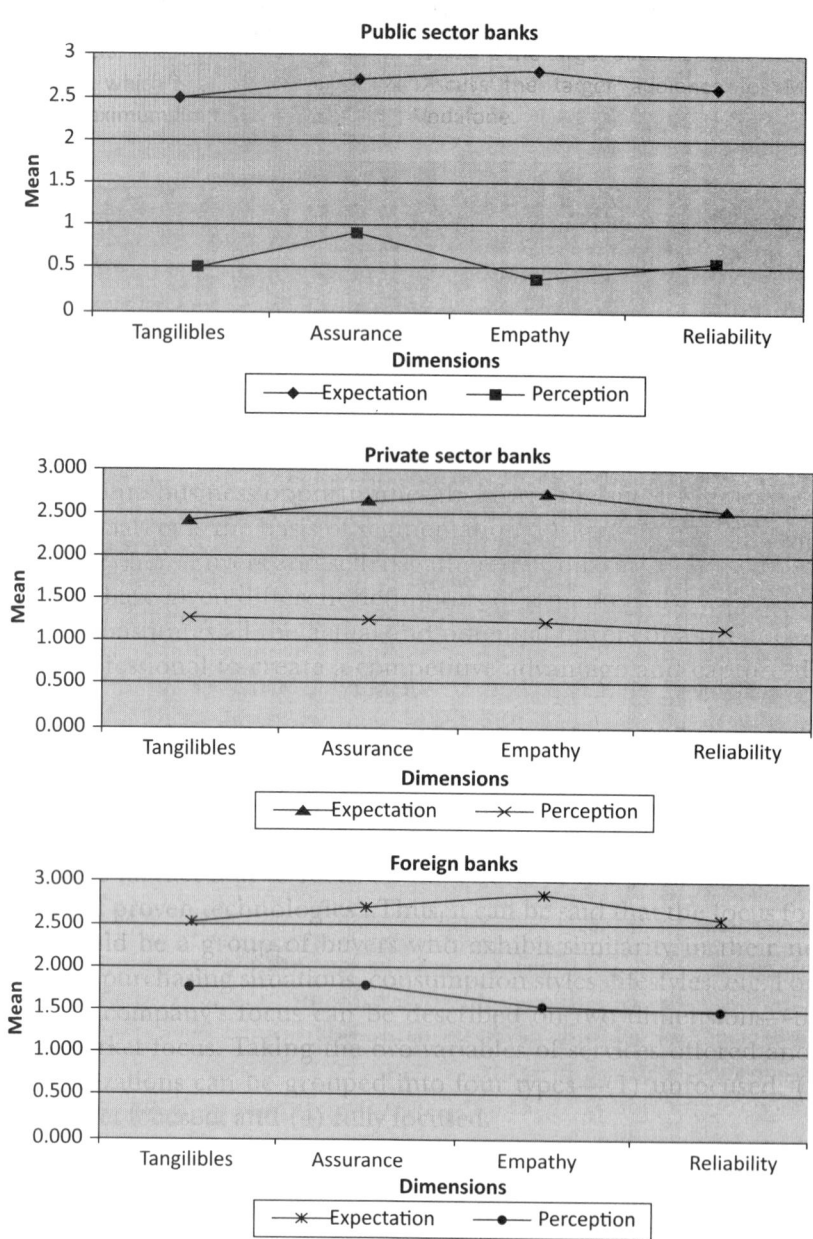

Fig. 8.1 Customer expectations and perceptions regarding different banks

Source: Based on Dutta and Dutta (2007).

TYPES OF CUSTOMER EXPECTATIONS

Zeithaml et al. (1993) specified three different types of customer expectations of service—desired service, adequate service, and predicted service.

Desired service is the service customers want or 'hope to receive'. For example, if a person signs on to www.naukri.com, he/she expects to find a job as per his/her specifications, with a desired salary, in a particular locality. It is a combination of what the customer believes 'can be' and 'should be'.

Adequate service is the standard of service the customers are willing to accept. For example, the customer knows that he may not find a job to suit his profile, or that he may have to compromise on salary, or, if both the profile and salary meet his expectations he may have to relocate. Thus, adequate service is the lowest level of service that the customer is willing to accommodate (Zeithaml et al. 1993).

Predicted service is the level of service customers believe is likely to occur in a given situation. Predicted service expectations are lower than desired expectations and are the 'will' expectations of the customers (Boulding et al. 1993). These services can lie anywhere between the adequate and desired service levels for the customer to have a positive opinion about the service provider, so as to motivate the customer to try their services. However, predicted and desired services can be equal if the customer feels that the service provider is excellent (Hamer 2006).

A zone of tolerance separates desired service from adequate service. This zone of tolerance is 'the extent to which customers recognize and are willing to accept variation in the delivery of service' (the heterogeneity characteristic of services) (Zeithaml et al. 2011). Considerable variation has been found in customers' tolerance zone, which was likely to be different in different situations, and also differed from customer to customer. The closer the delivery of the service to the desired level in the zone of tolerance the lesser the dissonance and customer is happy but the closer the delivery of service to adequate level the more the dissonance and customer is dissatisfied. If the delivery of service lies anywhere between the zone of tolerance (other than the ends as mentioned above), the customer does 'not particularly notice service performance'. For example, if you order food, then the time taken to deliver the food by the service provider can be twenty minutes and these twenty minutes might not seem long if you are not very hungry but if you are feeling extremely hungry then these twenty minutes wait might seem very long.

However, it is to be observed that the levels of adequate and predicted service levels vary for the different dimensions of service quality (see details on dimensions of service quality in Chapter 7 on Customer Perceptions of Service'). Therefore, customer's level of expectations is more for reliability, followed by responsiveness, assurance, empathy, and tangibles in the same order (Berry, Parasuraman, and Zeithaml 1994). So if the food that is delivered to you in twenty minutes is consistent to the level of quality expected but the washroom is not as clean as always, then the customer might still be satisfied compared to a situation in which it is vice-versa, that is, the food is not up to the mark but the washroom is clean as always.

Factors Influencing Customer Expectations

Expectations can be formed by a variety of reasons (Zeithaml 1993 and Boulding et al. 1993). Some of these have been elaborated in this section.

Beliefs of the individuals   Expectations formed due to the beliefs of individuals can be classified as—descriptive, informational, and inferential (Coye 2004 and Grönroos 1988).

Descriptive   Expectations formed as a result of direct personal experience with the service provider are descriptive expectations. For example, if an initial contact with the front desk employee was pleasant, the customer would expect a similar treatment during the next visit too.

Informational   Expectations formed on the basis of information collected by the customer directly or indirectly through attention to information provided by others. For example, if Domino's Pizza promises to deliver its pizza in 30 minutes, the customer expects to receive the pizza within the stipulated time.

Inferential   Inferential expectation is when the customer draws an inference (expectation) about a future interaction on the basis of a prior belief. For example, on the basis of a pleasant exchange with the front desk employee, a customer feels that the room service staff is also going to be well-mannered and polite.

Customer's personal philosophy about a product or service   This influences the 'should be' aspect of expectations.

Customer's personal needs and wishes   Expectations are based on what the customer needs at that particular point of time. For example, if a customer needs a low calorie diet, he/she expects to find such dishes on the menu irrespective of the other lavish cuisines the outlet can offer at that particular time.

Service provider's image and reputation   Factors such as image of proven skills, performance, etc. which can be partly controlled by the organization also influence customer expectations. For example, the Shangri-La hotel advertisement carefully builds the customer's expectation by telling her that the cuisine is from China, Japan, and Thailand, and indicating the cost and the time she can expect to spend to dine at 19 Oriental Avenue.

Service provider's promises   The promises due to staff interaction, advertising, and other marketing communications can create problems when service providers over-promise at the time of sale. If the service provider's promises, through staff interaction and advertisements, create expectations that are easily met, it leads to repeat patronage. Exhibit 8.1 illustrates how online mother and baby store, hopscotch.in is able to record one lakh customers a month.

Exhibit 8.1 **Successfully hopscotch.in**

India provides a number of marketing opportunities for babies as it is the second most populous country in the world. As on 4th March 2014, India's population stood at 1,262 million (approximately) (World population statics 2014). The market for 'baby, kid, and maternity products' is further made attractive by the fact that there are '27 million recorded births a year' and has market size of ₹42,000 crore growing at 20–25% annually.' To serve this segment, Rahul Anand along with his ex-colleague founded hopscotch.in in October 2012.

Realising that 'many of his friends always sought to buy baby brands from the west Anand decided to set up an online shopping company that would get international brands for babies, kids, and new mothers from around the world' and that too at unbeatable prices. Starting from 50 brands it has now scaled up to about 500 brands dealing in apparel, accessories, shoes, stationery, toys, stationery, etc. for children upto 13 years of age. They keep the excitement going by offering different brand every day. It also has 'boutique sale of select brands that aren't available at stores in India and it lasts for 3–7 days. All registered users are sent mails on boutiques or about 20 brand offerings for a period.' Therefore, by living up to its promise of bringing international brands at competitive prices it has been able to clock one lakh customers a month.

Implicit service promises, such as price and tangibles, associated with the service It is generally observed that people associate a higher price with a higher quality, and hence, their expectations are going to rise if the price is high in comparison to other service providers.

Word-of-mouth communication Positive word-of-mouth communication from other customers, family, and friends, etc. raise customer expectations and due to the intangible characteristic of services, this aspect holds more significance in the purchase of services.

hopscotch.in: The successful online store for mothers and children

Prior experience with the service provider   The perceived service quality delivered by a service organization forms an important basis for the customers to revise their expectations when they next visit the service organization.

Perception of service alternatives   Alternatives include the other service providers for the same service category from whom the customer can obtain services. If there are a number of service alternatives, customer expectations for the services are bound to be higher than when there are few alternatives available. For example, when only Indian Airlines and Air India were operating in India, and customers did not have any other option, their expectations were different; but with the advent of other players, the customer expectations for air travel services are more varied.

Managing Customer Expectations

Once the service provider is aware of the customer expectations, the next step is to manage the customer expectations. Customer expectations can be managed by controlling the different factors that influence them.

Consumer education   The expectations of consumers can be managed by educating them about the services that the service providers offer. This can be done by different contact methods.

- Through call centres, when customer care executives call to provide information about a service that is to be offered
- Educating the customer when he/she makes an inquiry prior to a purchase
- Using publicity to promote the products.

A case in point is when many service providers offer loyalty points for spending money on their services, but customers realize that after spending so much, the return was negligible. i-mint, India's first coalition loyalty programme was launched to counter this, so that customers get a better deal for the same money spent (Exhibit 8.2).

By providing customer education, companies can manage individual beliefs and philosophy of the customer. Also, by providing this education at the time of service delivery, they can mould the expectations for the next service interaction with the customer.

Corporate communication   Through their various communication tools, organizations can provide cues to the customers about their service quality and thus help them to build realistic expectations. These expectations are based on the service provider's image and reputation, which can be partly controlled by the service organization.

Service delivery   Managing customer expectations at the time of service delivery is easier said than done. The delivery of services is a crucial aspect due to the different characteristics of services and the presence of the customers as part of the delivery process. If customer expectations are not met, they can be managed only if the customer complains to the service provider. Chapter 17 provides a more elaborate discussion on service recovery. The delivery of the service in the initial experience of the customer should focus

Exhibit 8.2 **How to Get More for Your Loyalty**

Loyalty programmes have become commonplace among huge retail chains, such as Shoppers Stop, Lifestyle, and Pantaloons, as well as airlines, restaurants, etc. But the fact remains, that the rewards one gets, even with a loyalty card are minuscule. For example, getting a discount of ₹100 after spending ₹10,000 is no motivation at all. To change this, coalition loyalty programmes are being introduced, in which different companies get together to offer a single loyalty programme and collectively reward their customers.

The Nectar Card, one such coalition loyalty card in the UK, has about 55% of Britons as its members. The benefit is that the customer gets an advantage of various stores through a single card and the points accumulated are higher, thus leading to higher rewards. In India, i-mint introduced coalition loyalty, the first of its kind in India in June 2006. Companies partnering it included ICICI Bank, HPCL, Airtel, Lifestyle, etc. Consider the supreme advantage; if one pays one's bill via an ICICI credit card and fills petrol from HPCL, one gets rewarded by all these companies. Also, the customer is able to redeem the points at any of these six companies within a timeframe of six months.

In June 2010, PAYBACK has taken a controlling stake in i-mint and so i-mint is now PAYBACK. Payback program itself was launched in the year 2000 in Germany by Alexander Rittweger along with Deutsche Lufthansa AG and Roland Berger. Within a month of its launch, it acquired more than one million customers. In India its partnering with i-mint was strategic as it was the leading loyalty programme and in the year 2009 had generated ₹120 billion of sales through its cards and had a strong partner portfolio of 1,500 companies. i-mint on the other hand benefitted as it gained access to 'Payback's IT tools so as to bring advanced data mining solutions' so that customers could be targeted with more relevant personalized offers.

on individual beliefs and try to align them with the service organization's service delivery. They will also form an input for the service quality expectations formed by the customer for subsequent re-purchases. If the service delivery matches or exceeds customer expectations, it results in positive word-of-mouth feedback by the customers and vice-versa.

Service guarantees It can be provided to manage customer expectations as the customer feels that if the expectations are not met, there is some compensation attached, and it also gives him/her an added reason to complain to the service provider about any unmet expectation. In the pre-purchase stage, they also act as a reassurance to the customer that if their needs and wishes are not met, there is some compensation attached. Service guarantees also provide a differential advantage to organizations when other competitors in the industry are not following them, and may influence the customer to purchase from the service provider who is offering such guarantees.

Price policy One of the factors affecting the customer's perception of the service quality is the price. Thus, organizations should choose their pricing policy with great care so as to affect the customer expectation in a manner that meets the quality to be delivered by the service organization.

Positioning Another way of managing customer expectations is by positioning the services in the mind of the customers to give a realistic direction to the service expectation.

Positioning can create a differential advantage for the firm vis-à-vis other service providers. The positioning strategy should be in line with the pricing strategy so that there is complete harmony in the marketing communications.

Mission statement This gives the customers the long-term vision and values of the organization. Mission statement can be used as a tool to inform customers about the organization's strategy and reason for existence, so that they can form realistic expectations. They help the customer to form the image of the organization and hence, their expectations from the organization.

Service quality Customer expectations can be met and managed by managing the service quality and training, and motivating the staff to follow the best practices.

Related concepts On the basis of all the cues discussed earlier, we can manage customer expectations. As discussed in the Gap model in Chapter 7, a gap occurs when customer expectations and perception of service delivery do not match. We can say that the experience of the delivery of services causes expectations to be as follows (Afthinos et al. 2005 and Hamer 2006):

Confirmed When the performance of the service organization is as per expectation, then expectations are said to be confirmed.

Disconfirmed When the perceived performance of the service organization is not as per customer expectations, services are said to be disconfirmed. Services can be:

Negatively disconfirmed When the customer's perception of service delivery by the service organization is below expectation, disconfirmation is said to be negative.

Positively disconfirmed When the customer's perception of service delivery by the service organization is better or exceeds expectations, disconfirmation is said to be positive.
    Consumers who perceive a positive disconfirmation will perceive the service provider as being higher in quality than a consumer who experiences negative disconfirmation. Therefore, exceeding expectations is preferable to failing to meet, or meeting expectations. According to Hamer (2006), exceeding low expectations results in the same level of quality perceptions as exceeding high expectations. As discussed in the section on factors affecting customer perception, the prior experience of customers with the service provider affects their expectations when they next visit the organization. If a firm delivers services that show positive disconfirmation, that is, exceed the customers' initial expectations, they tend to revise their expectations upwards. These revised expectations form the basis of customer perception of service quality when he/she next visits the service organization, who will then have to deliver a higher level of service to keep up with the expectations and this cycle is repeated every time the customer comes to it for a repurchase.
    If the organization under-promises but over-delivers, this will create a problem where the customers form an initial low perception of service quality and may not even want to try the services initially. Thus Hamer (2006) expounded that the best option is to create

'realistic expectation setting' (as proposed by Bitner et al. 1997) by promising realistically and delivering consistently. Rust et al. (1999) by their longitudinal experiment showed that if the customer expectations are exactly met, it results in a positive preference shift. Even not quite meeting customer expectations may still increase the preference for the service provider, as the customer has experienced the service and so there is shrinkage in the variance of predictive service delivery in the next transaction. Thus, the experience leads to decreased risk and this leads to greater preference for the service provider.

If we consider the Gap model as discussed in Chapter 7, we see that the service quality delivery gaps occur initially due to the difference between the customer expectations and the management's perception of the customer expectations. Thus, the first step to managing customer expectations is to conduct market research and analyse what customers actually expect from the service organization. Managers should not only make an effort to understand the customers' needs and expectations, but also communicate this information to all the front-level employees so that they can manage better and cater to those customer expectations.

Customer expectations affect the perceived quality of services. If the communication tools of the company raises the customer expectations, then even if the quality of service delivered is high, it may not match with the raised customer expectations and lead to a lower perception by the customers. The importance of managing expectations is further supported by the study that if the perceptions are held as fixed, it is observed that higher the expectations, the lower is the perceived quality (Boulding et al. 1993).

PROCESS MODEL OF CUSTOMER SERVICE EXPECTATION MANAGEMENT

Managing customer expectations is crucial for an organization's success. As discussed earlier, we have different strategies proposed for managing expectations. Since services involve continuous interaction between the customers and service providers, we can manage expectations at two levels:

- When the customer is not in direct contact with the service provider—pre- and post-service encounters.
- When the customer is in direct contact with the service provider—during the service delivery process.

We have studied that customers have their set of expectations when they enter the process of service delivery. These expectations are affected by the controllable cues (which are directly controllable by the service organization such as price, marketing communication, etc.) and uncontrollable cues (which are not under direct control of the organization such as publicity, word-of-mouth communication, etc.). All these have been discussed in detail in the section on managing customer expectations. When the customer enters the service delivery process with such expectations, it is the role of the service provider to manage the customer expectations while providing the services, so that it results in a positive service quality perception by the customer. These can be provided in the form of planned cues and by responding to the unplanned cues. Planned cues are provided with the deliberate intention of raising, lowering, or making relevant initial expectations. They include the planning of tangibles such as facility, design, employee behaviour, delivery of services, client-to-client interaction, etc. If the service provider believes that the initial expectations are unrealistically high, then it is important to modify these expectations to fit closely to what it can deliver. This can be identified by the nature of service request, which if unrealistic can trigger service providers to clarify these unrealistic expectations. For example, if a medical practitioner faces an unrealistic expectation from a client, she can provide standardized responses, and if they do not suffice she can then provide customer specific responses to modify the customer expectations realistically. In the practitioner's office, the display of her various certificates of degrees and achievements are all cues that she is providing to the customers, to form or modify their expectations.

Unplanned cues are the environmental cues provided to the customers within the service delivery scenario and can be in the form of interaction with other customers, observing the service delivery to other clients present, etc. For example, if while waiting for a dental treatment the patient hears other clients complaining about the pain, he may be demotivated. The service provider's role here is then more of damage control. She will have to reassure the patient that his treatment will be different and hence less painful than that of other patients. It is thus important for the service provider to be aware of the types of cues the customers may react to and try to overcome them, either explicitly or covertly. By managing both the planned and unplanned cues, the aim is to modify the customer expectations and make them more realistic. In case the customer does not respond to the cues and expects to experience the same service he had anticipated initially, it is up to the service provider to try and provide cues so that there is minimum gap between the expected and the desired services. One way can be to manage the services product. Keeping in mind the customer expectations, service providers should try to modify the service 'product' the best they can, so that some of the customer's requirements are met. Exhibit 8.3 illustrates how Myntra plans to clock ₹1,800 crore sales in 2014–15 and ₹6,000 crore in early 2016.

Influenced by the cues, the customer experiences the service provided and may feel that the expectations are either met or unmet, or a combination of both. Based on the levels of expectations met by the service provider, customers form their perception of the service quality, which ultimately impacts the satisfaction level of the customer with the service provider. If the cues at the time of service delivery are managed well, the chances are that the customer forms realistic expectations, which are most likely to be met at the time of service delivery, leading to a favourable perception of the service provided and hence higher level of satisfaction with the service provider (Coye 2004).

However, it is sometimes observed that the customers are themselves not clear about their expectations. They may have fuzzy, implicit, or unrealistic expectations. Fuzzy expectations refer to expectations by customers when they are not clear about what they want from the service provider. They may feel that something is wrong or lacking but are themselves not clear about what the change should be. When customers experience the service, fuzzy expectations remain fuzzy and so they do not feel satisfied. The task of the service provider is to focus on the fuzzy expectations and by initiating a dialogue with the customer, try to make the expectations more precise and the customer

Exhibit 8.3   **Myntra's Shopping Assistant on Your Cell Phone**

Shopping through mobile phones is a global phenomenon and mobile payments are expected to grow to '$721 billion worth of transactions' by the year 2017 'with more than 450 million users according to Gartner' (Thomasson 2014). comScore's report of the year 2013 shows that over 35% of consumers in top 50 ecommerce sites were accessing them only through mobile devices. According to Mukesh Bansal, co-founder, Myntra, '80% of growth in the past here months has come from mobile. A quarter of the company sales is coming from mobile users and by the end of 2014 it is expected to increase to 40%.'

To reach its target of ₹1,800 crore in sales in the year 2014–15 and ₹6,000 crore in early 2016 Myntra decided to cater to this mobile segment and optimize their offering for them. The mobile screen is limited in size and hence it is 'not possible to list 50 product options on this small screen'.

The solution will be to make 'navigation easier and more predictive.' Myntra plans to do this by making its mobile application interactive through 'an artificial intelligence powered chat-based personal shopping assistant which will hand-hold the consumer through the browsing session.

It is, in fact, being considered as a service offered in order to serve the needs of the ever-increasing bloggers' community.

more convinced of the type of change they are looking for so that on experiencing the service they are clear about their expectations, and hence there is a higher probability of trying to satisfy them.

Implicit expectations refer to those elements of the service that are so evident that customers do not think about them consciously and so do not take into account the probability of them not materializing, and are more common when the service provider and the customer have a long history of mutual dealing. However, the problem arises when these expectations are not met. Hence, it is the task of the management to reveal the implicit expectations of the customers in order to make them explicit. If the customers do not make them explicit, then the expectations are not met, and hence will be self-evident in the next transaction, as implicit services cause a negative surprise when they are not met but do not cause any positive surprise when they are met. When the service provider does not meet such expectations, it gives the customers reason to complain and be unhappy about the service provided.

Unrealistic expectations are expectations that are highly unlikely to be met by any service provider; for example, an organization wants a recruitment agency to find a type of person who is difficult to find. The customers themselves cannot meet such unrealistic expectations. Such expectations can be managed by calibrating the unrealistic expectation. Defining the problem, and executing the solution and the effects of the solution can often achieve this. By calibrating the expectations, customers are made aware at the onset of the service process that their expectations are unreal and hence, cannot be met. This also creates dissatisfaction in the customers but the degree is less than it would have been if the customers had been made to realize this later in the service delivery process, when more time and money had been invested. Fuzzy, implicit, and unrealistic expectations are more common in professional services such as consultancy, recruitment services, etc. (Ojasalo 2001).

RESEARCH INSIGHT

A Confirmation Perspective on Perceived Service Quality

Lawrence O. Hamer (2006), 'A confirmation perspective on perceived service quality', *Journal of Services Marketing*, vol. 20, issue 4, pp. 219–232.

The paper seeks to provide a theoretical and empirical investigation of the relationship between consumer expectations and consumer perceptions of service quality.

The principal finding is that consumer expectations are positive predictors of perceived service quality (i.e., higher expectations lead to higher perceptions of quality). Another finding is that the relationship between expectations and perceived service quality is much stronger than prior literature suggests.

The practical implication of this study is that practitioners should seek to actively manage their customers' expectations to increase those expectations. This paper is valuable to practitioners who are seeking to use expectations to achieve higher perceptions of quality among their customers. It is also valuable to researchers who are seeking to understand the relationship between expectations and quality perceptions.

SUMMARY

At the time of purchase of services, customers have a perception about what the service providers 'should' offer rather than 'would' offer. This expectation further helps the customer in evaluating the purchase decision leading to customer satisfaction (if expectations are met) or dissatisfaction (if expectations are not met). Expectations that are in line with the delivery of services require the least effort to deliver a satisfactory experience for the customer. The marketers should thus be aware of the various types of customer expectations—desired, adequate, and predicted. If they are aware of the various factors influencing the customer expectation, they can influence and manage them better.

The chapter thus discusses this issue first and then delineates the various factors influencing customer expectations and how to manage them, so that they are as realistic as possible. This is done holistically by not only focusing on customer education but also on other factors such as service guarantees, promotional campaigns, corporate communication, price policy, etc. A model has been proposed to manage customer expectations during the service delivery process so that the customers perceive the service quality positively. Thus, managing customer expectations is important as the perceptions of service quality are measured against these. Perception of service quality is the basis of customer satisfaction and, in turn, builds strong customer relationships.

KEY TERMS

Customer expectations The preconceived set of ideas consumers have, that function as a point of reference against which performance is evaluated.

Fuzzy expectations These expectations are when the customers are not clear about what they want from the service provider.

Implicit expectations Elements of the service that are so evident that customers do not think about them consciously and so, do not take into account the probability of them not materializing.

Unrealistic expectations Those expectations that are highly unlikely to be met by any service provider.

―――――――――――――――― **EXERCISES** ――――――――――――――――

Concept Review Questions

1. Critically discuss the importance of customer expectations in the role of service delivery.
2. Discuss the different types of customer expectations and their relative importance to a service marketer.
3. Critically discuss five factors influencing customer expectations, which according to you are most important.
4. Discuss any three marketing strategies, which can be most effective in managing customer expectations.
5. Explain fuzzy and unrealistic expectations and how the services marketer can overcome them.

Critical Thinking Questions

1. Consider your recent services purchase, and identify your expectations for the purchase and the factors responsible for forming these expectations.

2. Discuss instances in your service purchases when your expectations were not met. Try and evaluate the reasons for your unmet service expectations.
3. Discuss instances when your service expectations were surpassed. How did this affect your future expectations and interactions with the service organization?

Internet Exercises

1. Visit the website of an organization in the aviation sector and try to form your expectations based on the information available.
2. If given an opportunity to make changes to the website of your favourite hospitality firm, what changes would you recommend to influence the expectations of the customers, and why?

CASE STUDY 1 Expectations from Zomato

About the Company

Zomato was founded in July 2008 out of a living room in Delhi. As on 15 April 2014, there were 650 people working for it in 12 countries representing 21 nationalities with a presence in 41 cities across 12 countries. The idea behind this was to 'help people find and connect with great places to eat around them. 'It is a restaurant discovery website and mobile app. It lists information on restaurants—menus, photos, reviews curated for credibility and contact information' (Sruthijith 2013) for restaurants in various countries.

Deepinder Goyal and Pankaj Chaddah started Zomato (Foodiebay, in an earlier avatar) while still working as consultants at Bain & Co. in Delhi. By the latter half of 2009, the website gained some traction and user feedback was excellent. It was then that they both quit their jobs and took up Zomato full time.

The Business Model

It makes its money from ads restaurants place on their pages. Restaurants advertise with Zomato because of better targeting. They can pay only to be displayed when someone is searching for a location—'Colaba', for instance—and further narrow it to be displayed only for 'take-outs in Colaba'. According to Goyal, Zomato revenues in 2013 were approximately ₹3 crore each month (Sruthijith 2013).

Zomato, which claims nearly 15 million users visit its website every month, earns about 65% of its revenue from India while the rest comes from markets such as the United Arab Emirates, the United Kingdom, the Philippines, and South Africa. (Julka 2013). All the money comes from the website as they had not monetised the mobile app. Since only the website has been monetized, let us see how they are managing customer expectations on this.

Managing Expectations on the Website

Once you log on, a page comes which clearly mentions the cities for which information can be accessed at Zomato. It further builds expectations by talking about the '225,600 listed restaurants in 12 countries'.

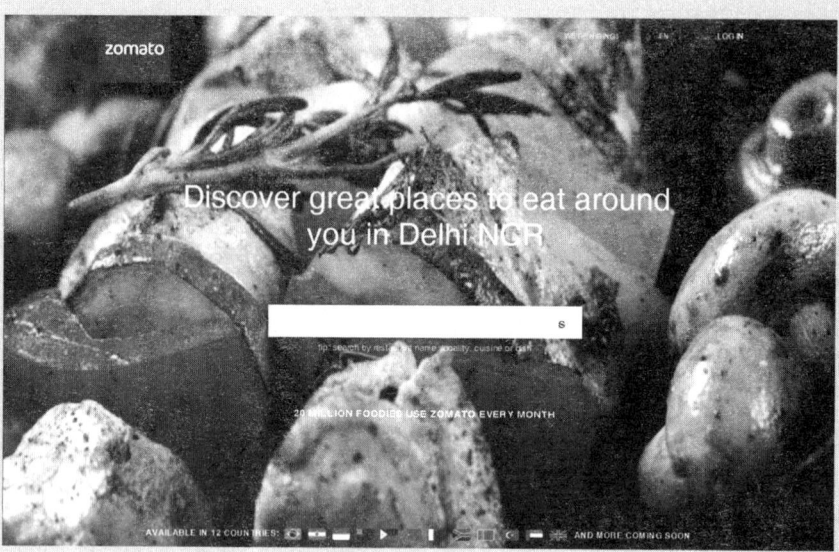

Zomato for Delhi NCR
Source: www.zomato.com

There are mobile apps that can be downloaded on the mobile phone for convenience of the customers.

The moment you click on a particular city (say Delhi NCR) the following page opens up:

The page builds expectations by talking about discovering great places to eat and there is a search engine for easy search. It also talks about 16 million foodies using Zomato every month thus building confidence of the web page visitor. The flags of the 12 countries where Zomato is present is also highlighted, which gives the website a global touch. There are a number of login options given like Facebook (recommended and mentioned that they will not post anything without permission), Google +, and email.

The website is very user-friendly and the moment you click on the search engine, it prompts various options in a dropdown menu such as get home delivery, go out for a meal, go out for drinks. etc. The moment you select an option, it prompts you to type a location name. It can even detect your current location. On choosing a particular location (say Khan Market in New Delhi), the restaurants are listed in the order of highest ranking first.

The search can further be refined on the basis of cuisine and cost for two people. More filters can also be applied such as happy hours, pure veg, etc.

Therefore, overall, it is very easy to search for information on Zomato. Also, if you click on a particular restaurant you can read all the reviews in detail, post comments on other reviews, and even leave your own review and rating. The rating is on a scale of 1–5 and has options like 1, 1.5, 2, 2.5,...4.5, 5, where 5 is excellent.

Conclusion

Keeping in mind the customer friendly site, ease of navigation, wealth of information available, and peer reviews; it is not surprising that Zomato has entered the ₹1,000 crore club in five years post-launch. It has managed the customer expectations and perceptions well to reach the elite club.

Questions

1. What are your expectations from a site like Zomato?
2. Visit the website and post a review. How easy or difficult was it?
3. What further recommendations would you give to Zomato so that they can further manage customer's expectations?

CASE STUDY 2 Distance Learning Programmes

Introduction

The world is witnessing strong winds of change. Global boundaries are vanishing giving rise to the concept of the 'global village'. Rapid transformation in business and industry has revolutionized the executive mindset and education is emerging as the most powerful platform to progress in this world without boundaries. The concept of education is itself changing. It is no longer a static, regimented process confined to the formative years of childhood or adolescence, but is a dynamic, continuous, and ongoing process that extends throughout an individual's professional career. To provide the opportunity of learning along with maintaining a professional career, many institutes have come up with the concept of distance learning programmes. These programmes not only provide higher education without the constraints of location and time, but also give professionals the opportunity of academic enhancement, which reflects in their professional recognition.

Distance learning is being propagated as the education of the twenty-first century. Moving with the e-business, the education sector also plans to accomplish more by changing focus from 'brick-and-mortar' to 'click-and-mortar'. A number of institutes in India are providing distance learning programmes along with regular options of classroom teaching. Some of them are Symbiosis Centre for Distance Learning, Narsee Monjee Institute of Management Studies, HughesNet Global Education, and IMT Distance and Open Learning Institute.

The impact of the rapid pace of transformation in business and industry has triggered a metamorphosis in executive mindsets. This has made it imperative for graduates, aspiring business persons, and professionals to equip themselves with the latest know-how and best practices. Versatile management training is indispensable as it provides the requisite skill sets to withstand the emerging challenges of the corporate world and successfully leverage career opportunities.

Higher and Technical Education

The importance of education, especially higher education, has been constantly growing and knowledge-based industries are now occupying centre stage in development. Though the modern higher education system in India is almost 135 years old, its growth has been much faster after India became independent.

Over the past 50 years, there has been a significant growth in the number of new universities and institutions of higher learning in specialized areas. There are now 273 universities/deemed to be universities (including 18 medical universities and 40 agricultural universities) and 12,300 colleges (of which 4,683 are in the rural areas) (Table 7.1).

Table 8.1 Number of institutions of higher education, enrolment, and faculty

Year	Number of colleges	Number of universities*	Students (in '000)	Teachers (in '000)
1950–51	750	30	2,63,000	24,000
1990–91	7,346	177	49,25,000	2,72,000
1996–97	9,703	214	67,55,000	3,21,000
1998–99	11,089	238	74,17,000	3,42,000

Note: * includes institutions that are deemed to be universities, but excludes other institutions.
Source: UGC Annual Report 1996–97 and 1998–99 and selected educational statistics, Ministry of HRD.

Ninth Plan

The Ninth Plan reiterates the objectives/policy directions of the National Policy for Education, 1986, and the Programme of Action, 1992.

Broadly, the Ninth Plan emphasizes the following strategies to improve the higher education system:

- consolidation and expansion of institutions
- development of autonomous colleges and departments
- redesigning of courses
- training of teachers
- strengthening of research
- improvements in efficiency
- review and monitoring, etc.

The Ninth Plan period saw the emergence of separate universities for science and technology, and health sciences; autonomous colleges with the freedom to design curricula; evolution of new methods of teaching and research; framing of admission rules and conducting of examinations; as well as the creation of centres of excellence and the National Assessment and Accreditation Council (NAAC). There are also institutions of higher learning recognized as deemed to be universities with their own sources of funding, in addition to government grants. The major emphasis in strategies relating to higher education during this period has been on an integrated approach, with an emphasis on excellence and equity, relevance, promotion of value education, and strengthening the management systems. Autonomous centres have been set up within the university system to provide common facilities, services, and programmes to universities, and for the promotion of quality.

It is increasingly recognized that in the context of major economic and technological changes, the system of higher education should equip students with adequate skills to enable their full participation in the emerging social, economic, and cultural environment. Universities are thus witnessing a sea change in their outlook and perspective. Also, information and communication technology is leading to fundamental changes in the structure, management, and mode of delivery of the entire educational system.

Many universities have already recognized the strategic significance of open and distance learning and offer correspondence courses. At the beginning of the decade, there were 64 universities offering courses through correspondence. The developments in the field of information technology and expansion of infrastructure for communication all over the country has created an unprecedented opportunity to serve the needs of continuing education, and also to meet the demands for equal opportunity for higher education. The Indira Gandhi National Open University (IGNOU), established in 1985, has 1.2 million students on its rolls and offers 72 programmes. The university has created a countrywide network of student support structures, with 46 regional centres and 765 study centres. It has also created a media network and teleconferencing system to electronically link all distance teaching institutions in the country. Many departments of correspondence courses in various universities were converted into independent open universities during the Ninth Plan period. There are, at present, nine open universities in the country, all started by different states during the 1990s.

Tenth Plan—Objectives, Key Issues, and Focus

The main objective in the Tenth Plan is to raise the enrolment in higher education of the 18–23 year age group from the present 6 to 10% by the end of the plan period. The strategies would focus on increasing access, quality, adoption of state-specific strategies, and the liberalization of the higher education system. Emphasis would also be laid on the relevance of the curriculum, vocationalization, and networking on the use of information technology. The Plan would focus on distance education; convergence of formal, non-formal, distance, and IT education institutions; increased private participation in the management of colleges and deemed to be universities; research in frontier areas of knowledge; and meeting the challenges in the area of internationalization of Indian education.

The issues of access and equity are central to the university/higher education system. Only about 6% of the estimated population in the 18–23 age group is currently in the university system. Measures to increase enrolment, including that of the disadvantaged sections, will thus be given attention during the Plan.

Quality Improvement/Academic Reforms/Relevance of Curriculum

The basic issue of quality improvement will be addressed through the modernization of syllabi, increased research, networking of universities and departments, and increased allocation of funds. Networking through local area network (LAN), wide area network (WAN), and information and library network (INFLIBNET) will also lead to increased academic activities and research. The university system will be expected to utilize the autonomy it enjoys for innovations in teaching and for pursuing high-quality research. The emphasis will be on conferring autonomous status on more colleges, provision of the means to interact across geographical boundaries of institutions, improving the infrastructure, more rationalized funding of research, integration of teaching, research and evaluation, and mutual collaboration and cooperation among universities for optimum utilization of available resources. There is a pressing need to improve the management and governance of universities to better enforce financial and administrative discipline. Decentralization of the university system, greater powers to faculty departments and nomination of students to university bodies on the basis of merit/excellence are therefore, issues, which will receive attention. The accreditation process should be made more transparent, time-bound, and be progressively freed of government regulations and control, leading to a situation when the whole procedure would be based on a system of public appraisal/acceptance.

Under the ongoing scheme of strengthening scientific research, the UGC will continue to assist university departments, which have achieved excellence in research in different disciplines of science, especially in the emerging areas of biotechnology, biomedicine, genetic engineering, nuclear medicine, social science, humanities, etc.

In view of the resource crunch faced by the UGC and the higher education system, it is proposed to give incentives to universities/ colleges, which make efforts to increase/raise internal resources.

Distance Education and IGNOU

The non-formal system (distance and open learning) accounts for only 13% of the total enrolment in higher education. Out of 7.7 million students enrolled in universities and colleges, the distance education/correspondence courses cover only one million students. The distance and open learning system provides flexibility in terms of combination of courses, age of entry, pace of learning, and methods of evaluation. The coverage of open universities will, therefore, need to be extended to the backward regions, remote inaccessible tribal areas of the northeast, and some of the eastern states. At present, there are nine state open universities and 64 institutes of correspondence courses and Directorates of Distance Education in conventional universities. The enrolment of distance learners in the open and distance education system is expected to rise significantly in the Tenth Plan period. IGNOU has expanded its regional centres and network of study centres in the Ninth Plan period. It now has 46 regional centres and 691 study centres. It has been vested with the twin responsibilities of acting as an open university and offering need-based education, training, and extension programmes, with special focus on the disadvantaged sections of the society, and acting as the national nodal agency to determine and maintain standards in distance education.

IGNOU has established the Distance Education Council (DEC) to act as the nodal agency for the distance education system at the tertiary level. The university has adopted an integrated multimedia instructions strategy consisting of print material and audio–video programmes, supported by counselling sessions at study centres. It manages a dedicated 24-hour satellite TV channel, Gyan Darshan, which beams educational programmes from school to tertiary level, 24 hours a day. Preparations are on to launch 40 FM educational radio channels (known as Gyan Vani) under a memorandum of understanding with Prasar Bharati. During the Tenth Plan, IGNOU will set up open universities in states where none exist at present, and expand the activities of Gyan Darshan and Gyan Vani. The target is to extend the coverage of the open learning system to the backward regions, remote inaccessible areas of the northeast, and low female literacy blocks in some of the eastern states.

In April 2002, the government constituted the Committee on Promotion of Indian Education Abroad (COPIEA) under the chairmanship of Secretary, Department of Secondary & Higher Education. With globalization of the Indian economy, student mobility across national boundaries has increased phenomenally in the higher, technical, and management sectors. A large number of foreign educational institutes have also established their presence in India and there is immense potential for Indian educational institutions to set up campuses abroad. The COPIEA will monitor all activities aimed at promoting Indian education abroad and will regulate the operation of foreign educational institutions to safeguard the interests of the students and the larger national interest as well. To this end, a system of registration will be introduced under which institutions will have to furnish information on operations and adhere to certain guidelines relating to publicity, maintenance of standards, charging of fees, granting of degrees, etc. The COPIEA will, over a period of time, develop a sectoral policy on foreign direct investment in the education sector.

Symbiosis

Symbiosis Centre for Distance Learning (SCDL) started in 1994, as a 'correspondence section' of Symbiosis Institute of Management Studies (SIMS) for defence personnel and their dependents. In the year 2001, SCDL was established as a separate institute offering courses through the medium of distance education, providing an opportunity to thousands of students to enhance their careers and lives. The vision of SCDL is to create a 'world campus' where anyone is able to learn and achieve their dreams for higher education and enhanced career. The mission of SCDL is to provide every student with a means for 'self-paced, self-styled learning' anywhere, anytime.

SCDL has grown exponentially in the last four years, attracting students from all states of India and from more than 20 foreign countries. Today, SCDL has an active student strength of over 60,000. It has introduced new courses each year and established facilities, services, and technologies to assist the student community. In the past three years, SCDL has gained tremendous popularity not only amongst fresh graduates seeking higher education, but also among working professionals from the corporate and administrative sectors. The emphasis on improving the quality of education and students services has been the main reason for this popularity. SCDL diplomas are widely recognized and accepted by the industry, and in fact, SCDL has become the 'preferred education provider' for several top companies nationwide such as IBM, Cognizant, Wipro, Spectramind, Sahara Group, Reliance Infostreams, CSC India, etc.

Learning methodology

Symbiosis follows blended learning, that is, combining various forms of learning.

- Customized study material books for self-study.
- Online learning/e-learning to enhance understanding of key concepts through interactive e-learning modules.
- Monthly classroom lectures at the corporate premises—faculty based learning to promote peer-interaction.
- Students address their specific academic queries via e-mail to SCDL, to which an in-depth reply is sent by an expert faculty within 2–3 days (e-mentoring).

Narsee Monjee Institute of Management Studies

In order to meet the growing demand for management education, Narsee Monjee Institute of Management and Higher Studies (NMIMS) was established in 1981. The institute commenced its activities with a master's degree programme in management studies. It later started the distance learning programme under the Department of Distance Learning and offers various courses.

Learning methodology

The programmes include study material, self-evaluatory quizzes, discussion questions, and personal contact programmes (PCPs). Students can interact with designated NMIMS faculty via e-mail for clarification of doubts.

HughesNet Global Education

HughesNet is a premier, satellite-based education and training service for corporates and working professionals. The HughesNet Global Education platform seeks to redefine the next generation of education—real time interactive onsite learning (IOL). The platform seamlessly integrates the strengths and advantages of the traditional method of education with the latest in technology. Using a very powerful interface, HughesNet Global Education enables a student to have highly interactive sessions with students and instructors all over the country, using video, voice, and data.

Over the last two years, over 4,750 students have successfully completed a programme on this platform, thus demonstrating its efficacy and effectiveness. Best of all, these programmes are convenient, accessible, and targeted to suit the continuing education needs. With 50 classrooms in 34 different cities in the country, HughesNet Global Education has made higher education simpler than ever before. It has tied-up with premier institutes in India (and abroad), which include names such as the IIMs, XLRI, NMIMS, etc.

IIM Kozhikode

In May 2002, IIM Kozhikode became the first management institute in India to offer a management programme (Executive Management Education Programme—e-MEP) over the Hughes DirecWay platform. Over 500 professionals have taken up the 10-month programme.

IIM Calcutta

In November 1961, the Government of India established the Indian Institute of Management, Calcutta (IIMC) as the first national institute for post-graduate studies and research in management. It has been playing a pioneering role in professionalizing Indian management through its post graduate and doctoral level programmes, executive training programmes, and research and consulting activities.

For example, if you log on to IIMC for a general management programme for IT professionals, the programme delivery is shown as follows. The sessions will be delivered on HughesNet Global Education's Interactive Onsite Learning platform. The heart of the platform is a powerful user interface that enables a large number of geographically distributed students to have a highly interactive 'one-to-one'/'one-to-many' exchange with a central faculty. The system incorporates live broadcast video, and two-way audio and data interactivity to enable students to watch and interact with the faculty live on their PCs.

IIM Bangalore

The Indian Institute of Management, Bangalore (IIMB) was established in 1973. Today, IIMB is recognized as India's best business school. Its world-class infrastructure provides the foundation for its programmes of teaching, research, consulting, and other professional services.

XLRI Jamshedpur

XLRI Jamshedpur, one of India's premier management institutes, announced the launch of a Post Graduate Certificate in Business Management (PGCBM) in August 2002. This programme is designed for high potential, mid-career managers moving up to the next level in business management.

IIFT Delhi

One of the top 10 management institutes in India, IIFT Delhi offers working executives one of its most sought-after programmes on the HughesNet Global

Education Interactive Onsite Learning platform, namely, Executive Masters in International Business or EMIB.

Manipal University

This, the largest private education initiative in India, will offer a one-year executive MBA programme on the HughesNet Global Education platform. Other Courses offered are MBA-FS and PGDBM.

Narsee Monjee institute of management studies (Deemed university)

Better known as NMIMS (Deemed University), it is one of the top ten business schools in India with excellent brand value, intellectual capital, infrastructure, and focus towards growth (*Business India* 2002). PGDGM offered by NMIMS is a 14-month programme designed specifically for working executives and is tailor-made for all those who want an edge without quitting their current job and without compromising on the faculty or the institute from which they would like to acquire the necessary knowledge.

Apollo university

Apollo International, in cooperation with Hughes Escorts Communication Limited (HECL), is making US-accredited Western International Universities (WIU) degrees accessible to Indian students supported by HECL satellite technology. Students go through a 14-month course in international business, and are enrolled directly with the Apollo University.

Loyola institute of business administration

Loyola Institute of Business Administration (LIBA) had its origin in the year 1979. Located in the sprawling campus of scenic and idyllic Loyola College (established in 1925), LIBA is one of the most prestigious management institutes in south India. It has attained an enviable ninth position among management schools in India. To retain its status as a premier business school, LIBA relies heavily on a two-way interaction with business and industry.

Conclusion

Thus, we see that a number of institutes are offering distance learning programmes by adopting a variety of standardized programme delivery methods. The question arises that with these standardized programmes being offered to a vast majority of students in different parts of the country, with varied academic standings, and hence, requirements, how do these universities cater to the expectations and needs of the different customers. How do they make sure that the needs of the students for the academic quest are being fulfilled? To what extent are the customer expectations being achieved and what are the customer expectations from such institutes? These are some of the issues that need to be discussed.

Questions

1. What according to you are the customer expectations in the distance learning programmes?
2. What are the ways in which the distance learning programmes are imparting knowledge to the students in the different institutes covered?
3. Critically discuss the programme delivery methodology adopted by the different institutes and give suggestions for future delivery of courses.

REFERENCES

Afthinos, Yanni, Nicholas Theodorakis, and Nassis Pantelis (2005), 'Customers' expectations of service in Greek fitness centres', *Managing Service Quality*, vol. 15, no. 3, pp. 245–258.

Berry, L.L., A. Parasuraman, and V.A. Zeithaml (1994), 'Improving service quality in America: Lessons learned', *Academy of Management Executive*, vol. 8, No. 2, pp. 32–52.

Bitner, Mary Jo, William T. Faranda, Amy R. Hubbert, and Valarie A. Zeithaml (1997), 'Customer contributions and roles in service delivery', *International Journal of Service Industry Management*, vol. 8, no. 3, pp. 193–202.

Boulding, William, Ajay Kalra, Richard Staelin, and Valarie A. Zeithaml (1993), 'A dynamic process model of service quality: From expectations to behavioural intentions', *Journal of Marketing Research*, vol. 30, no. 1, pp. 7–27.

Coye, Ray W. (2004), 'Managing customer expectations in the service encounter', *International Journal of Service Industry Management*, vol. 15, no. 1, pp. 54–71.

Daftari, Irshad (2006), 'How to get more for your loyalty', *The Economic Times*, 4 September, p. 13.

Dutta, Kirti and Anil Dutta (2007), 'Customer expectations and perceptions of service quality in the banking sector: A study of India', 3rd International Conference on Services Management, Pennsylvania State University.

Frewin, Angela (2006), 'Travelodge hits out at "misleading" ads', *Caterer & Hotelkeeper*, vol. 196, no. 4408.

Grönroos, C. (1988), 'Service quality: The six criteria of good perceived service quality', *Review of Business*, vol. 9, no. 3, pp. 10–13.

Hamer, Lawrence (2006), 'A confirmation perspective on perceived service quality', *Journal of Services Marketing*, vol. 20, no. 4, pp. 219–232.

Julka, Harsimran (2013), 'Zomato raises ₹227 crore from Sequoia, InfoEdge for overseas expansion', *The Economic Times*, New Delhi, 7 November.

Kandampully, Jay (1998), 'Service quality to service loyalty: A relationship which goes beyond customer services', *Total Quality Management*, vol. 9, no. 6, pp. 431–444.

Kandampully, Jay (2000), 'The impact of demand fluctuation on the quality of service: A tourism industry example', *Managing Service Quality*, vol. 10, no. 1, pp. 10–18.

Kangis, Peter and Vassilis Voukelatos (1997), 'Private and public banks: A comparison of customer expectations and perceptions', *International Journal of Bank Marketing*, vol. 15, no. 7, pp. 279–287.

Nair, R. (2014), 'Myntra plans to offer chat-based shopping assistant', *The Economic Times*, New Delhi, p. 6, 14 April.

Ojasalo, Jukka (2001), 'Managing customer expectations in professional services', *Managing Service Quality*, vol. 11, no. 3, pp. 200–212.

Parameswaran, Maheswaran (2006), 'Jalandhar topping for Mac', *The Economic Times*, 18 September, p. 4.

Parasuraman, A., V.A. Zeithaml, and L.L. Berry (1985), 'A conceptual model of service quality and its implications for future research', *Journal of Marketing*, vol. 49, no. 4, p. 47.

Parasuraman, A., V.A. Zeithaml, and L.L. Berry (1988), 'SERVQUAL: A multiple-item scale for measuring consumer perceptions of service quality', *Journal of Retailing*, vol. 64, no. 1, pp. 12–37.

Parasuraman, A., V.A. Zeithaml, and L.L. Berry (1991), 'Understanding customer expectations of service', *Sloan Management Review*, vol. 32, no. 3, pp. 39–48.

Pratap, Rashmi (2006), 'Soon, blog from your cell phones: Reliance first operator to launch moblogging', *The Economic Times*, 10 October.

Robledo, Marco Antonio (2001), 'Measuring and managing service quality: Integrating customer expectations', *Managing Service Quality*, vol. 11, no. 1, pp. 22–31.

Rust, Roland T., Jeffery J. Inman, Jianmin Jia, and Anthony Zahorik (1999), 'What you don't know about customer perceived quality: The role of customer expectation distributions', *Marketing Science*, vol. 18, no. 1, pp. 77–92.

Shangri-La advertisement (2006), *The Economic Times*, 3 November.

Sruthijith, K.K. (2013), 'How Deepinder Goyal's Zomato entered into the ₹1,000-crore club', *The Economic Times*, New Delhi, p. 5, 12 November.

Zeithaml, Valarie A. and Mary Jo Bitner (2003), *Services Marketing*, Tata McGraw-Hill Publishing Company Limited, New Delhi.

Zeithaml, Valarie A., Mary Jo Bitner, D.D. Gremler, and A. Pandit (2011), *Services Marketing*, 5th edition, Tata McGraw-Hill Publishing Company Limited, New Delhi.

Zeithaml, V.A., L.L. Berry, and A. Parasuraman (1993), 'The nature and determinants of customer expectations of service', *Journal of the Academy of Marketing Service*, vol. 21, no. 1, pp. 1–12.

http://www.cityofahmedabad.com/nmims/, accessed on 7 November 2006.

Hughes (2006), http://www.hughes-ecomm.com/services/global_services.htm, accessed on 6 November 2006.

Moneylife (2007), available from www.rediff.com/money/2007/jan/24inter.htm, accessed on 12th April 2014.

my.naukri.com, accessed on 13 April 2014.

Narsee Monjee Institute for Management Studies (2006), www.nmims.edu, accessed on 7 November 2006.

Planning Commission (2006), Vision 2020, Planning Commission, Government of India, http://planning commission.nic.in/plans/planrel/fiveyr/10th/volume2/v2_ch2_5.pdf, accessed on 6 November 2006.

Sahay, Arvind (2005), 'naukri.com' available from www.vikalpa.com/diagnosis/2005/oct_dec_147_161.pdf, accessed on 4 June 2006.

Saraswathy, M. (2014), 'Grabbing eyeballs no kids' stuff', *Business Standard*, New Delhi, p. 2, 7 April. payback.net/press-in/information/story, accessed on 14 April 2014.

Symbiosis Centre for Distance Learning (2006), http://www.scdl.net, accessed on 6 November 2006.

Thomasson, E. (2014), 'Retailers too step into crowded mobile payment market', *The Economic Times*, New Delhi, p. 6, 7 April.

www.hopscotch.in, accessed on 14 April 2014.

www.infoedge.in/corporate-quick-facts-milesotnes.asp, accessed on 1 May 2013.

www.naukri.com, accessed on 12 April 2014.

www.naukri.com, accessed on 14 January 2014.

www.payback.net/en/press/press-releases/jpress-releases/article/payback-expandiert-nach-indien/, accessed on 14 April 2014.

www.worldpopulationstatistics.com/population-of-india-2014/, accessed on 14 April 2014.

www.zomato.com, accessed on 15 April 2014.

www.zomato.com/india, accessed on 15 April 2014.

9   Pricing Strategies for Services

OBJECTIVES

After reading this chapter you will be able to understand the

- factors influencing pricing concerns of a firm
- various pricing objectives
- various methods of pricing services
- factors involved in marketing-oriented pricing
- methods of estimating value to the customers

Sky Wars

India is supposed to have the cheapest air fares in the world and the competition is intensifying. In June 2013–2014, the arrival of AirAsia saw an intense fare war yet again. The official carrier Air India offered tickets starting at ₹100 on several routes. Needless to say, such was the response that the website crashed. AirAsia India, as part of its inaugural promotion, offered tickets ranging from ₹600 to ₹1,900 on select routes. GoAir, a budget airline, had tickets on sale starting from ₹1,599. Spice Jet too joined the fare war and dropped prices even before the AirAsia bookings started. AirAsia aims to offer tickets that are 30% lower than its rivals in the sectors that it operates in.

Discounted tickets help an airline to generate cash through advance bookings. However, the picture is not all that rosy for most airlines as they are losing money, constrained by rising fuel prices, high airport infrastructure charges, and price wars.

If the costs were constant, low fares would have increased revenue and contribute towards the bottom line. When an airline offers promotional fare, other carriers have no choice but to match or undercut the new fares to stay afloat. The full-service carriers too slashed their fares; however, their cost of operations are way beyond the low-cost carriers. The gap in fares between full-service and low-cost carriers narrowed to just over 10% in the quarter. The strategy of full-service carriers to slash fares to match up to low-cost airlines is not followed anywhere around the globe. In most countries, where both low-cost and full-service carriers operate on the same routes, the price differential is well marked and the products are clearly well established. In India, following the losses, most carriers have increased fares by 15–25%.

After going through the chapter, you will be able to answer the following questions:

1. Have the customers gained by fare wars?

2. What are your views on air price wars? Do you think business suffers even when there is a short-term increase in revenues?

Sources: Based on Choudhury (2014), Rai (2014), and Das Gupta (2013).

INTRODUCTION

A service manager is often on pins and needles when it comes to pricing his/her service offering. Needless to say he/she has to identify an optimum price for the service. He/She is essentially required to create a pricing model that is inclusive of (a) profit and (b) cost of creating and delivering services. A service manager, however, can use some of the product pricing guidelines to calculate his costs and operating expenses along with the target profit in setting the price for services. This strategy is usually a mix of 4Ps, economic patterns, service characteristics, and market demand and competition. It is also about increasing profit and revenue generation. Additionally, the success of a service business besides pricing strategies, also depends upon absolute clarity on market conditions, along with an understanding of what the consumer desires and the amount that he/she is willing to pay.

This chapter gives an overview of the pricing concerns of a firm. It also gives an overview of alternate pricing strategies adopted by service firms. The categorization of service strategies is done in three broad areas—cost-oriented pricing, competitor-oriented pricing, and marketing-oriented pricing.

Pricing the services is an immensely challenging task. The attributes of services are very different as compared to manufactured products. The attributes of intangibility, inseparability, perishability, and heterogeneity make the task complicated. Services also vary on the experience and credence attributes, which create psychological costs such as anxiety, and mental and physical effort (Lovelock 2001). Lovelock indicates the following four non-financial costs:

1. Time expenditures (time spent on finding out about prices and attributes of a service offering)
2. Physical effort (such as fatigue and discomfort)
3. Psychological burdens (such as mental effort and negative feelings)
4. Negative sensory burdens (unpleasant sensations affecting any of the five senses).

There may be numerous considerations for pricing services. These can be listed as follows:

- Revenue oriented—the concept of costs and profits may be important.
- Capacity oriented—this is to meet the available supply.
- Demand oriented—this is to maximize demand
  - recognize the paying potential
  - offer different modes of payment.

Pricing decisions can have a great impact on profitability, assuming that the service, which is being delivered, meets the customer needs. Pricing is one of the elements of the service mix and needs to complement the other elements of the service mix.

Demand plays an important role in an economist's approach to pricing. In certain cases, the pricing pattern may depend on the demand. However, the regulatory framework and market conditions may determine the pricing strategies of a firm.

PRICING OBJECTIVES

There may be numerous objectives, which a service firm may deploy before choosing a pricing strategy (Avlonitis and Indounas 2005):

- maintenance of existing customers
- attraction of new customers
- customers' need satisfaction
- cost coverage
- creation of prestige for the firm
- long-term survival
- service quality leadership
- achievement of satisfactory profits
- sales maximization
- market development
- achievement of satisfactory market share
- determination of fair prices by customers
- profit maximization
- sales stability in the market.

For instance, power supply is the domain of state governments and the government sets the tariffs. Similarly, the concerned ministry sets railway fares in India. The government regulates the supply and prices of LPG. The fee charged by government schools is regulated. Market conditions such as monopoly, monopolistic, or oligopoly market structures may influence pricing decisions. In a monopoly environment, a single player holds a major market share. He may or may not be free to set prices if the market is regulated. For instance, when the telecom sector in India was not deregulated, the government decided the STD/ISD tariffs. With deregulation, private players have a higher degree of autonomy to decide the pricing strategies.

METHODS OF PRICING SERVICES

Shapiro and Jackson (1978) have identified three methods used by managers to set prices:

1. Cost-oriented pricing
2. Competitor-oriented pricing
3. Marketing-oriented pricing

Cost-oriented strategy is an internally driven strategy. Competitor-oriented pricing is driven more by competitors' strategies. Marketing-oriented pricing focuses on the value that the customer places on the service being driven.

Cost-oriented Pricing

This strategy aims to recover some of the costs incurred in offering the services to the consumer. There are four methods, which reflect this ideology:

1. Full cost pricing
2. Marginal cost pricing
3. Target return pricing
4. Contribution analysis

Full cost pricing This method prices the services after taking into account the fixed as well as the variable costs (direct costs). The issue with this approach is that it is not market driven. The sale may be determined by the demand and the paying capacity of the market.

Marginal cost pricing This strategy aims at pricing the service in a manner that direct costs can be recovered and the full costs may be recovered after a certain period of time. The price is set below total and variable costs so as to cover marginal cost (Palmer 1994). This strategy is adopted specially in the services sector, as they are perishable. When occupancy levels in a hotel are low and when an aircraft is flying with unoccupied seats, prices are lowered so that some costs may be recovered, rather than losing the entire cost.

This strategy has a bearing on reducing the impact of excess capacity. Also, in certain services sectors like telecom, where private players are operating, the break-even timeframe is larger, but the service provider looks in at larger volumes to achieve the profitability scenario.

Target return pricing Here, the price is determined at the point that yields the firms' target rate of return on investment (McIver and Naylor 1986; Meidan 1996).

Contribution analysis This is the deviation from the break-even analysis where only the direct costs of a product or service are taken into consideration (Bateson 1995).

Empirical research indicates that many service companies in the US have followed the cost plus method. This takes care of all the costs and also includes a profit margin. Zeithaml et al. (1985) in their study of the pricing behaviour of 323 service companies in 13 different sectors in the US, found that 63% of these companies had adopted the cost plus method.

Competitor-oriented Pricing

There are two forms, which service providers may adopt:
1. Going rate pricing   2. Competitive bidding

Going rate pricing

In this scenario, the pricing is done as per the competition in the market. However, marketers may like to use price differentials to differentiate their service offering to the consumers. The prices may, however, be similar to that of the competition (Palmer 1994; Zeithaml and Bitner 1996).
- The pricing may be below that of competitors (Payne 1993; Zeithaml and Bitner 1996).
- Pricing according to dominant price in the market—the leader's price that is adopted by the rest of the companies (Kurtz and Clow 1998).
- The pricing may be above that of the competition. Exhibit 9.1 explains pricing above the competition.

Competitive bidding

In this particular case, the bid is offered to the lowest bidder. Bidding is a complex task, especially in the case of large service firms and contracts. For instance, building of flyovers or privatization of airports require complex pricing procedures with complex

Exhibit 9.1   **Hotel Rates Sky High at Delhi and National Capital Region (NCR)**

Room rates in India are at an all-time high. The rates in Delhi and NCR will rise by 30–40% in the future, making India one of the most expensive destinations in Asia. The hike in Delhi and Mumbai has overtaken Bengaluru. The rates of an average five-star hotel room was about ₹10,000–12,000, but has now reached about ₹16,000. As India suffers from a lack of rooms, 150 hotel projects are under active development. A factor for this rise is attributed to the increase in inbound business travellers. A major disadvantage of this rise in rates is that India might lose a lot of its inbound tourists due to very expensive costs. They may end up choosing alternate destinations for travel.

Source: Based on Awasthi and Dey (2006).

documentation. The building of power plants, offering telecom services, and privatization of railways, etc. are all complex cases where bidding is used to allocate business. The most usual process is the drawing up of a detailed specification for a process and putting the papers up for tender.

Many service firms also offer bidding prices on products. For instance, India Times shopping invites bidding for airline tickets. These may be to invite new price conscious consumers into the ambit of the service provider.

Marketing-oriented Pricing

This strategy takes into account a much wider range of factors. Jobber (2001) has discussed 10 factors, which could influence marketing-oriented pricing strategy:

1. Marketing strategy
2. Price–quality relationships
3. Product line pricing
4. Negotiating margins
5. Political factors
6. Costs
7. Effect on distributors/retailers
8. Competition
9. Explicability
10. Value to the customer

Please see Exhibit 9.2 on how the accommodation sector in India needs to adopt a marketing oriented approach to pricing.

Marketing strategy

The marketing strategy has a considerable influence on the pricing strategy of the firm. The target market and its characteristics, demand, positioning, strategy, and nature of competition, all have a bearing on the marketing strategy.

The service provider may opt for different pricing strategies. It may be penetration pricing (low pricing strategy) or may be 'skimming-the-cream' strategy (charging premium for the service offering). The penetration-pricing strategy aims at generating volumes, whereas the premium-pricing strategy looks at higher profits from smaller numbers. Some service providers offer multiple service brands to map the complete market.

For example, Fruchter and Rao (2001) in their research have discussed the 'optimal-pricing strategy' for a provider of network services. The researchers propose that the

Exhibit 9.2   **Pricing vis-à-vis a Competing Tourist Destination**

The Indian tourism sector needs to mend its ways; otherwise smaller destinations such as Tunisia, Reunion Island, and Uzbekistan, among others, will start pinching the huge number of European travellers that India gets. France is India's second largest market and contributes about 28% to India's total inbound tourists' figure. The latest travel market show, TopResa in France, displayed a few realities of the tourism market in India. The Indian Tourism Board at TopResa was bland and lacked life, as compared to those of Sri Lanka and Mauritius. According to one tour operator present at the show, a big reason was that India has become too overpriced. Reservations at a luxury hotel like Maurya Sheraton are at about $500 for a standard room. This in fact is more expensive than a 304-day trip at Reunion Island or Tunisia. The operators also feel that the hotels in India try and upsell the hotel rooms. They try to sell the premium category rooms even when the regular rooms are available. Some close observers feel that increase in the number of inbound tourists is mainly due to the business travellers, because the number of leisure travellers has actually gone down. It is not wrong to say that rooms in New York are cheaper than those in India!

Source: Based on Sharma (2006).

optimal-strategy consists of penetration strategy for a membership fee, low at the beginning, increasing with network size, and a skimming strategy for the usage price, starting high and declining later.

Other examples of such a pricing strategy include Internet access, web-based services such as financial and other business services, telecommunication services, and other growing membership-based services. For example, for Internet services, if usage demand is decreasing in the network size, the optimal policy is one of penetration in membership fee and skimming in usage price. If on the other hand, the usage demand is increasing in the network size, the optimal policy is one of penetration not only in membership fee, but also in usage price.

Price changes   With regard to demand, Rathmell (1974) observed that the demand for professional services is usually price inelastic on the downward size. Reducing the price of a professional service is not likely to increase primary demand or expand the size of the market served by 'small' service businesses. The search, credence, and experience characteristics of the service product influence consumer demand (Darby and Karni 1973).

Rhymer (2001) has raised the issues of price raise and its timing. She remarks that many service providers fear losing customers when prices are raised. The secret is to explain to the customers the reason behind the price change. The timing of the price change also may matter. For example, parking lots in Gurgaon (NCR) charge much more on weekends than on weekdays.

In order to target various consumer segments simultaneously and to save loss of revenue, the demand of the service across various segments is also taken into consideration. For instance, service upgrades illustrates the concept further (Exhibit 9.3).

Exhibit 9.4 gives an insight into managing variable demand.

Exhibit 9.3 Service Upgrades

Service providers operating in sectors such as airlines, train services, hotels, sports stadiums, and performing art companies, typically offer different service classes (e.g., first class, business class, and economy class). Biyalogorsky et al. (2005) have suggested a model that considers the use of upgrades as a contingent mechanism to ameliorate situations in which the realized demand for upper-class service is lower than allocated capacity. Providers typically struggle between two alternative strategies—advance selling first class units at a reduced price, or reserving them for sale at a full price. The first strategy eliminates the opportunity to sell first class units at the full price if such a demand occurs later, but the second strategy is risky because demand uncertainty may lead to valuable units not being used.

The managers could issue upgradeable tickets. These tickets provide a way to ensure that first class capacity can always be used, allowing the provider to capture more potential value. Compared with advance selling first class units at discounted prices, employing upgradeable tickets allows a service provider to sell first class units at a full price whenever feasible.

The managerial guidelines to improve allocation of upper class capacity include the following:
- Use upgradeable tickets to increase profits, if the probability of obtaining full price for first class is sufficiently high.
- When using upgradeable tickets, reserve more first class units for sale at full price compared to the units reserved without upgradeable tickets.
- Advance selling is the most profitable policy and reserving is the least profitable, if the probability of selling first class at full price is very small.
- Offering upgradeable tickets is the most profitable policy and reserving is the least profitable, if the probability of selling first class at full price is intermediate.
- Offering upgradeable tickets is the most profitable policy and advance selling is the least profitable, if the probability of selling first class at full price is sufficiently high.

Source: Based on Biyalogorsky et al. (2005).

Exhibit 9.4 Option-based Approach for Pricing Perishable Service Assets

Option pricing is used to develop an alternative model for pricing services that have fixed availability and expiration. Pricing of hotel rooms is used to demonstrate this in a marketing context.

Use of the option model approach   The model is based on a binomial option model for discrete time. Finch et al. (1998) have proposed a method of price cut option, allowing us to predict and manage revenues in a more dynamic way. Such a calculation assumes an appreciation of market price elasticity (wherein price change affects sales), information about consumer price sensitivity, and sufficient margin to make the price cut option practical. Finch et al. (1998) propose that the option to cut prices works best where a high priced service is involved. High prices and key margins allow greater flexibility in pricing.

Availability of service has a bearing on choosing the option pricing strategy. Option to cut prices is a strong one where alternatives are far off. There should also be a means of informing consumers about the price changes. Internet and other multimedia equipment provide greater opportunities for such communication. Effective revenue tracking and accounting systems enable the option-pricing strategy to work for the firm.

Source: Based on Finch et al. (1998).

Price changes over the service life cycle   Avlonitis et al. (2005) have discussed the pricing objectives over the service life cycle. They have pointed out that a comprehensive review of literature on services marketing reveals that the model of the life cycle has not been examined as thoroughly as in the case of physical products. In their research on 170 companies operating in six different sectors in Greece, they have pointed out the following:

'The service firms have a hierarchy of pricing objectives. They aim at sustaining customer relations along with attracting new customers in order to achieve satisfactory rather than maximum financial results, and ensuring the firms' long-term position in the market. It was found that transportation and shipping companies emphasize on managing capacity and assets, while insurance companies are interested in satisfying their customers' and distributors' needs and developing the market. Information technology companies focus on high quality service, while airlines are interested in maintaining and expanding their customer base.'

According to a research conducted by Avlonitis and Indounas (2005), it is pointed out that service firms in the sample, paid very little attention to adopting customer-oriented methods, perhaps due to the difficulty in determining their customers' demand and needs. The sample of the research includes 170 service firms operating in Greece. Their research covers banks, insurance companies, transportation and shipping firms, airlines, information technology business, and medical services.

Price–Quality relationships

Consumers consider price as an indicator of quality; for example, first class or business class options advertised by full-service airlines in India. In the case of telecom operaters price comparisons are used as a basis for helping consumers to make choices.

The case of Lufthansa is different. Here, the firm mentions categorically that 'there is no better way to fly'. The firm also mentions prices to attract consumers to international destinations.

Product line pricing

This pricing strategy offers different levels of services at different prices. There may be different offerings to the consumer based on differentials in pricing; for example, economy and business class rooms offered by a hotel. Some service firms offer different brands in order to offer services at different price ranges; for example, Carlson offers Radisson, Country Inns and Suites, and Park Plaza to map consumers who are willing to pay different prices for different service categories.

Differential pricing is a widespread strategy in the services sector. The method is widely accepted in almost every sector of the economy. The basic concept of differential pricing involves charging different prices to different consumer segments for the same service. A simple example can be medical services, where the health-care fee is subsidized for poor people, while other patients are required to pay a standardized fee. Also, some services such as transportation, airlines, and railways are subsidized for senior citizens. This general fact of differential pricing has been accepted and customers do not complain when senior citizens are being charged less. People understand that many senior citizens are on fixed incomes and may not be able to afford the services at the standard rate. Providing differential advantage may ensure higher profits for the company in general, as it ensures that the services are available to the maximum number of people.

Negotiating margins

In some firms, customers expect a price reduction. The price paid by the customer is very different from the list price. The difference may be on account of order size discounted, competitive discounts, or fast case payment discounts. For example, for institutional usage of Internet or travel services, firms may offer special rates.

Political factors

When pricing policy acts against public interest, the government may intervene. For example, the railways in India are not privatized, and government decides the pricing, which is not based on market factors. Similarly, the prices of LPG and basic telephony or Internet services are influenced by government policy.

Costs

The strategies have already been discussed in the previous section under cost-based pricing.

Effect on distributors

Distribution systems play a key role in certain service categories such as travel and hotel reservations. Their margins must be adequate for them to push the production. However, online bookings directly with the service providers are changing the dynamics of interaction with the distributor network. Many airlines in India offer online bookings and charge lower fees if the consumer books directly, ahead of the date of travel. The booking of tickets through travel agents is more expensive. Hence, the online options are redefining the role of distributors. Today, online portals such as makemytrip.com and cleartrip.com offer more attractive options for booking travel through them.

Competition

The service firm may make comparisons on product features. Refer to the discussion under competition-based pricing in an earlier section, where examples have been provided.

Explicability

The service provider in this case should be able to explain the price differentials on its service offerings logically. For example, SOTC and Thomas Cook holiday advertisements in India. These tour operators offer various family tours to different locations in Europe. Depending on the number of destinations covered, number of nights, food, and entry fees to different destinations, different prices are charged for different tours to similar destinations.

VALUE TO THE CUSTOMER

This pricing strategy assesses the pricing decisions from a consumer's perspective. The target market, demand, and economic factors in a market, may influence the decision to price service. For example, India is a price conscious market. Variables operating in India have budget airlines, such as GoAir and IndiGo, which offer apex fares and compete with rail travel over long distances. The air travel by domestic consumers has greatly increased.

The second aspect is that the consumer has become solution oriented. She does not look at individual services but a combination of services, which offers her convenience. Guiltinan (1987) has elaborated on some of the strategies, which marketers have adopted in offering bundled services. Bundling is the practice of marketing two or more products/services in a single 'package' for a special price. Some examples are given here.

- Some banks offer special programs in which customers with large deposits are offered locker facilities, overdraft, and credit cards at no annual fees.
- Hotels offer special packages with complimentary nights and sightseeing.
- Hospitals build in complementary tests with some packages for medical check-ups.

Jobber (2001) has discussed four methods of estimating value to the consumers.

Buy response method This estimates directly the value that customers place on a product by asking them if they are willing to buy at various price levels.

Trade-off analysis It measures the trade-off between price and other product features so that their effects on product preference can be established.

Experimentation This pricing strategy attempts to place a service at scale, at different locations at varying prices. Test marketing may be used here initially to test the effect of services offered at varying levels. The customer satisfaction level may be monitored at various levels. After test marketing, changes may be made in the service offering. For example, when the Oberoi Group launched Trident as a brand, it was supposed to be a budget brand. When the demand started to increase and Oberoi's service was considered exceptional, the company raised the prices of its rooms and Trident is no longer a budget brand, but an upmarket brand. Testing helps the firm to calibrate its offering.

Analysis of the economic value to the customer If a firm can provide higher economic value to the customer, it can charge a higher price. This helps in building up revenues for more services provided.

Exhibit 9.5 explains value-to-customer pricing.

Pricing Based on Value to the Customer

There are two aspects of 'customer value' (a) perceived value (it is the benefit that the customer believes that he/she has received from the service after purchase of the service) and (b) desired value (it is the value that a customer desires in a service).

There are different levels at which customer values can be examined from (a) at lower level, they could be the perception of the attributes of a service or (b) at higher

Exhibit 9.5 **Value-to-customer Pricing**

Big hotel chains are finding the budget hotel segment very attractive, thus making things even more complicated for their smaller counterparts. The bigger hotels can afford and, hence, plan to acquire strategically located properties, or tie up with existing hotels and upgrade them. In the hospitality industry, small and medium enterprise (SME) hotels account for a sizeable turnover. These hotels are primarily one- and two-star hotels, with about 9,500 rooms and account for at least 260 hotels in the country. Most of them are in cities such as Haridwar and Jaipur.

The budget hotels are also known as 'no frills' hotels and about 4,300 rooms are expected to come up in 2014, of which 17% is expected to be for the budget segment. The disadvantage remains that the ever-increasing real estate prices may force the budget hotels to either increase prices or face a margin squeeze. Another roadblock for SMEs is funding, and as interest and land prices are going up, banks should be allowed to extend the term loan tenure to fund such projects. Such hotels have a high inflow of domestic travellers, unlike deluxe or five-star hotels with a large proportion of foreign travellers. An important factor in favour of budget hotels is that these hotels can operate at 50% occupancy and still make profits. The main reason for this is that these hotels have lower fixed costs as compared to deluxe or mid-segment hotels.

Source: Based on the articles from *The Economic Times* (2006); www.equitymaster.com.

level, it can be viewed as an emotional payoff or achievement of goals or desires. It would not be false to say that a customer derives value from the attributes of the service. They also derive value from attribute performance and also from the consequences of achieving desired goals after the use of the service.

While developing value-based pricing model, a service company often utilizes customer data, as well as various other features of the service in question. Additionally, a service company needs to conduct an analysis of competing services. This helps in identifying the other options that the consumer may have. If gathered efficiently, such data can tilt the balance in favour of the service company's bottom line.

There are many strategies that a service manager, depending upon the services he/she is in, takes recourse to:

Low value-based pricing In this kind of pricing, the price is a balance between what customers are willing to pay and the lowest price that a service company has to offer. Depending upon the value of the service in the eyes of the customers, a service company can modify the base price of the service. Value-based pricing strategies, therefore, are dependent on the value that the customer places on the service. For example, a company 'A' may reduce its costs (discount) without decreasing the value (benefits). Stores like the Big Bazaar or Walmart follow this pricing strategy. In addition to discount pricing services, companies exhibit actions such as odd pricing, synchro-pricing, and penetration pricing depending upon existing market situations.

Discounting It is often used by the services sector to refocus the customer attention to the services that they offer. Unlike other industries where there is a physical product that needs to be moved, the services sector uses the discounting strategy to (a) improve efficiencies within the service delivery at the organizational end and

(b) attract or bring back the straying customer back to the company. When a company launches its service wing for the first time, it is akin to breaking a new ground. It therefore needs that first client who could be the spokesperson of the services of the company, besides being a good referral source. During the initial period, payment terms for the service are also negotiated at an optimum rate suitable for both the clients and the company. These terms could be in the form of a discounted annual maintenance contract inclusive of a few parts replacement/discounted parts/or ancillary product replacement, etc.

Another method of giving discounts is the early payment discounts that are usually offered by the banks and property companies. Additionally, a lot of retail services like the utility companies also specify this fact on their invoices.

How much should the discount be—this is the moot question. Service companies often tag discount values to various scenarios. The first scenario is the trail discount—as given by the satellite TV companies to their customers for one month. Companies therefore should be able to identify their margins in this entire process of offering discounts to the customers and ensure that the value of the discount is worth the value that you wish to give.

Odd pricing   It is also known as odd-even pricing, charm pricing, and fractional pricing. It is defined as setting a price that are a couple of paise below an evenly numbered price such as ₹10. This can raise conversions up to a whopping extra 21–34%. This simple strategy encourages customers to place orders and raise the chances of people purchase. This has worked because of (a) the 'left-digit effect', that is, 9 is usually less than 10 and since the number is less, the customer perceives a saving in the purchase, (b) it is also psychological because a customer looks at prices from left to right, in most cases, and (c) memory process time or the right-digit effect. This effect is negative and acts as a counter to left-digit-effect strategy. Experts solve this problem by printing, for example, the 99 price in a larger font and the decimal or 0.99 price in smaller font. Such a strategy is for those customers that do not fall for 9.99 price tag, that is, to say that physical magnitude is directly related to numerical magnitude.

Synchro-pricing   Demand of many services, namely theatre and hotel bookings, airlines and other passenger transportation, utility services, tax services, etc. fluctuates seasonally. For services that see constrained supply at peak times, managers use various differentials such as time, pace, volumes, and prices to attract customers. Service managers therefore capitalize on the customer sensitivity by using prices to synchronize and manage demand and supply.

In terms of revenue management, synchro-pricing or differential pricing can often be observed when a service company tries to find a right balance between (a) prices charged, (b) segments sold, and (c) capacity used. Aspects such as these can be clearly observed in the hotel and airline industries.

Penetration pricing   It is a technique where most marketing firms set a very low entry price of the product. When extended to services, firms lower their charges for initial months of the service launch, in order to capture a large pie of the service segment.

This strategy works on the expectation that the target customer would switch to the new service because of the low price. This strategy hopes to increase the market share of the service along with sales volume. In all, this strategy leads to low production costs and higher service inventory turnover.

This pricing strategy works well in markets (a) where product demand is highly (price) elastic, (b) they are suitable for the mass market, and (c) there are economies of scale.

It is thus imperative that soon after the introduction of the service, it should not face stiff competition from other similar services. In fact it would be very favourable if the service company is able to gain the first mover advantage for itself. However, disadvantage of this strategy is (a) that the customer may leave the service once the price is increased and (b) the service company may not make any profit if the prices are kept very low.

Prestige pricing   Brands in the category of high end jewellery, perfumes, luxury cars, or haute couture are usually sold at a premium price. This pricing appeals to the aura of exclusivity because it is targeted towards a particular clientele. Such kind of pricing is also called prestige pricing or image pricing and it is solely based on the price of the product (which is kept at an artificially high level). It also encourages favourable perceptions among buyers who are upwardly mobile. This practice exploits the predisposition of buyers to assume that expensive items have distinctive quality and exceptional reputation.

Marketers create brand value for which customers are agreeable. These products are viewed by the markets as differentiated luxury products and come under a separate product category.

Marketers may use premium pricing as a competitive practice or as a marketing strategy depending upon the aspects that either influence the product sustainability or profitability. These aspects in brief are (a) information asymmetry, that is, buyers have no independent basis by which to verify the claims of 'exceptional quality' of a service or products and (b) the market dynamics, that is, level and degree of competition and entry barriers.

Skimming pricing or creaming   When a company employs skimming as its pricing strategy, it hopes to achieve a break-even at an early stage of the product launch as it needs fewer sales. Such products are sold a high price, the company therefore skims the market. A company usually sacrifices high sales to achieve high profits.

This technique is employed when immense resources have gone into research and these then are to be reimbursed as soon as possible. Usually, companies in the area of electronics and high end cosmetics employ this technique to gain the first mover advantage and to target the early adopters of products and services. It is assumed that because the early adopters have less price sensitivity towards the new products, their need to be the first far outweighs cost sensitivity or they may have very high disposable income. Then there could also be cases when this pricing is used when there is no substitute for the product or where there is a limitation on its production due to government policies.

This strategy is, however, employed for a very limited period of time to (a) recover the costs and (b) gain market share. However, this could leave the product vulnerable to the competition.

Value pricing   According to Cahill, 1994, when a fairly low price is set for a high-quality service, it is called value pricing. This term is applied when the prices of a product or service are based on customer's perception of the value of the product. A company thus decides the price of a product or services based on what the customer is willing to pay for it. An important component of the value pricing is the need to determine the value of the product or services for the customer. Firms therefore use the customer value model to determine the value that a customer associates with the product or services. Additionally, this concept calculates the economic benefits that a product or service can offer to the customer. The firms in the services sector aim at determining a price which is appropriate for the quality of the product. These firms maintain a consistent pricing over time and do not resort to tactics such as discounts and sale. Brands such as McDonald's, Domino's, and low-cost-no-frills airlines have been designed to work with low costs and therefore have the capacity to offer reasonable prices. They determine the price of the service/product by its cost of purchase and the benefit which will accrue to the company. Additionally, these firms often assemble a bundle of products/services that could be desirable to a wide group of customers and price them lower than they would otherwise cost.

Customers find these organizations attractive and trust the value of the products/services that they offer. They also prefer such a pricing because it helps them to find what they want and need.

Market segmentation pricing   It occurs when a service firm charges more than one price for its products and services, to different groups of customers. These products and services have been produced at the same time; however, they are marketed differently to customers who may perceive them to be of different quality. Additionally, service companies may use this segmentation to take advantage of disparities in pricing in different geographical regions. Theoretically, segmentation focuses on customers' product and price needs. Practically, it is a way by which similar requirements of a specific group of customers could be identified and satisfied within a market. A discerning service company therefore uses segmentation as an alternative to 'one size fits all' principle. It is also extremely effective if the service company has been able to identify clear difference in market requirements.

Price segmentation essentially is a marketing strategy for a company with a limited range of products/services, wherein it offers the same or different versions of the same product/service at different prices to different groups, thereby eliminating 'customer surplus' (it is the difference between what a customer is willing to pay for the product/service and what they actually have to pay). Regional and seasonal price variations are also a part of price segmentation, for example, peak- and off-season prices of hotel rooms and airline tickets always vary considerably, or gyms in the college areas offer student discounts and operate late nights in order to cater to the student community. Similarly gyms in residential areas offer senior citizen discount during the day in order to optimally utilize their facilities and generate profits. Restaurants and bars on the other hand designate particular weekdays for ladies and club discounts on food and beverages.

How can price segmentation improve?

Price segmentation can improve in the following ways:

1. By taking an outside-in approach, a service company can use the direct attributes such as sales spend and derived attributes such as the intensity of the competitive environment, product centricity, and customer sensitivity for price segmentation. Additionally, price segmentation can be further reviewed with the help of customer data so that internal constrains regarding customer classification could be removed.
2. A service firm needs to move from reviewing only customers and product and sales to leveraging transaction data. These data tell the company 'what the customers value', 'do they prefer your premium products or your discount products', 'what is their frequency of purchase', 'when do they purchase', etc. By looking into these data, a service company can get to the bottom of true value-based pricing and reconfigure segments based on what your customers buy and not by how your systems identify them.
3. Services industry usually classifies its customers; however, classification does not determine those attributes that are statistically most significant for the purpose of segmentation. These statistics do not explain the customer spend on the location and the reasons for their willingness to pay for a particular service. Statistical analysis should be therefore used as a tool for e-segmentation to determine 'not only what is important to customers, but also to determine the degree of important of the service to the customer'.

Price framing   Krishna et al. (2002) explained price framing as how an offered price is communicated to the customer. For example, if there is a reference price given along with the offered price or the price being communicated in percentage terms, or in rupees, or is the reference price credible. This framing effect could also be due to the description provided by the retailer in the form of a 'semantic cue' (SALE up to 50%), an offer of a free product, and/or a comparative pricing with other brands. Such an exercise is undertaken to support the given price and also attract a customer. The main aim of framing is to define the decision criteria and to influence customer's needs and biases. For example, a prospective customer of a hospitality product has a notion that what type of service would define their social status, a service personnel could easily frame the offer by ascertaining comparisons of public perceptions by providing different examples of various other services. In the absence of such a notion, a service personnel could define his offer in such a manner that the customer becomes convinced to purchase it. A customer usually carries around with himself a set of perceptions and biases along with a mental checklist that they refer to when weighing different aspects of a service or product, before taking the final decision. This can be influenced by the marketing team, which can add to or subtract the customer biases and thus push the customer towards purchasing the service or product from you. In marketing parlance you can create a positive context within which a customer is more likely to take a purchase decision.

Price bundling It is a part of product line pricing strategy, which has been defined by Guiltinan (1987) as an exercise by which two or more products or services are sold for a single price. Later in 2002, Stremersch and Tellis stated that bundling or tying a discount could contribute to buying larger quantities. They went on to say that it is a common marketing practice among marketers to put together two or more unrelated cross-category products. This usually happens when a marketing firm faces heterogeneous demand for an unsubstitutable perishable product and therefore hopes to interest the buyers to purchase at a price bundle, by breaking down different perceived values of more than two products. For example, a firm that produces products A and B sells them at a high prices as long as it can, they then bundle these products to maximize more profit. This gives incentive to customers who want to buy both products, especially when perceived values of the products are different for different consumers.

This strategy creates a win-win situation for both the customer and the sellers, because it is considered to be better than pure pricing. Additionally, it creates a reference price effect. Companies usually offer these in season tickets, computers and electronic producers, and accessory packages for automobiles.

An example of this bundling can be observed in the coffee shops of most hotels or in the happy hours of restaurants. They often bundle food items with beverages. A consumer can buy the bundle with a relatively cheap price, while the hotel/restaurants can maximize its profit.

Complimentary pricing It is a pricing method by which a complementary product is priced to achieve maximum sales volume without considering cost or profit to stimulate the demand of the other product. The aim is to create a level of profit that effectively takes care of the losses sustained by the first product. The first product which is necessary and is needed by the customer is priced very high.

There are three aspects to complementary pricing, which are as follows:

Captive pricing When a customer purchases a product, he/she wishes to enhance its value by adding accessories, services (insurance), and other products to enhance its appeal. Companies view this as an opportunity to peddle their add-on products and services with little or no costs both for themselves and also to the customer. This is also one of the ways with which to increase brand loyalty.

Two-part pricing Firms often divide the price into two parts (a) the fixed price that gives the customer with bare minimum service and (b) the additional add-ons that the customer may or may not choose to accept as features or services (like insurance cover for family and/or free paint job, etc.)

Loss leadership It is essentially to take the product/service desirable to the customer and to gain the market share. Retail outlets reduce the prices significantly but not without covering the transaction costs. Stores use this pricing in order to attract new customers and also those customers who are loyal to their competitors. There are risks in this strategy because it may cast aspersions on the quality of the product/service.

Results-based pricing It is based on the basis of the results or the outcomes of the services. It is used in atypical situations where the outcome is highly uncertain but very important. The most relevant aspect is outcome of the service. This type of pricing is common in law firms, where the client pays fees based on the performance of their lawyers and the total sum of money the lawyer is able to get or save on their behalf.

Results-based pricing is also known as *contingency pricing*, and it is another pricing option that can be used by firms to drive business. In the e-commerce and IT, this type of pricing is based on the quality-contingency model. According to this model, the customer is promised a refund if the products/services provided does not meet quality standards. In other words, the price of the product is contingent upon its quality as perceived by the consumer. Additionally, service firms find this pricing appealing when it has some performance data about itself, especially when it expects to perform better than perceived by the market. This enables it to increase profits and strengthen its market position in situations where no single price contract could provide positive outcome. In situations where a service firm faces only a limited competition, a firm that employs contingency pricing gains a competitive advantage, and captures a higher market share, thereby increasing profits at the cost of competing firms and the customer. Another aspect of results-based pricing is the commission-based approach that is taken by service firms. Agents of service firms are compensated for offering highest rates and services to clients. This approach motivates them to further the service firms' business.

The benefit of results-based pricing is that it helps the customer to avoid indecisiveness that acts a roadblock to paying for a service or for making a purchase, for example, a customer while making an online purchase is assured of the replacement/refund facility being available at all times on the net. This pricing assures a customer that they will be refunded all or a portion of their money if the satisfaction and quality standards are not met. This pricing is applicable across a whole range of goods and services that assures a certain level of performance.

RESEARCH INSIGHT

Heterogeneity of Consumer Demand: Opportunities for Pricing of Services

Taher, Ahmed and Hanan El Basha (2006), 'Heterogeneity of consumer demand: opportunities for pricing of services', *Journal of Product and Brand Management*, vol. 15, no. 5, pp. 331–340.

This paper fills a conceptual and practical gap for a structured review of the current state of knowledge about the pricing of services. It offers practical and solid advice and examples demonstrating the application of the different types of pricing strategies for service providers.

The purpose of this paper is to provide a framework to help marketers of services price their products by looking beyond costs and competitive forces. By analysing the value of information, consumers' price sensitivity, and transaction costs other than search costs, against the characteristics of their service, they could make more profitable pricing decisions.

According to the authors, services should be priced in a way to reflect the customers' price sensitivity, the nature of the transaction and its cost, and the value of information. The pricing should also reflect the four characteristics of services—intangibility, perishability, lack of standardization, and inseparability of production and consumption.

SUMMARY

This chapter gives an overview of the pricing concerns for service firms. It provides information on detailed strategies deployed by firms and also categorizes the strategies under three broad areas—cost-oriented, competitor-oriented, and marketing-oriented. Ethical issues in pricing are also discussed along with inputs on differential pricing methodology.

This chapter delineates the pricing objectives. These could be—maintenance of existing customers; attraction of new customers; customers' need satisfaction; cost coverage; creation of prestige for the firm; long-term survival; service quality leadership; and achievement of satisfactory profits among others.

There are numerous strategies that service firms adopt. These can be broadly classified in three categories—cost-oriented pricing, competitor-oriented

pricing, and marketing-oriented pricing. Under each of these categories, there are numerous strategies that the firm can deploy. The examples of the firms give an insight into how these strategies may be adopted, either in combination or isolation. The service firms should be able to judge the impact of business environment changes which are occurring and adopt appropriate strategies. The emerging economies offer immense opportunities for services that the mass market can adopt. Focusing on volumes while offering good value can be a very strong strategy for long-term sustenance of the firm. However, premium pricing strategies are used by firms to target niche markets. Their product design and communication strategies should resonate with the pricing strategy.

KEY TERMS

Cost plus pricing An approach to establishing the selling price of a product or service is estimated, and a percentage mark-up is added in order to obtain a profitable selling price. A variation to this approach is to estimate the costs of a particular stage, say, the costs of production only, and then add a percentage mark-up to cover both, the other overheads (including administration, selling, and distribution costs), and the profit margin.

Full cost pricing An approach to setting selling prices ensuring that the price of a good or service is based on all the costs incurred in its supply, including overheads. It usually involves an absorption approach to the costing of units.

Marginal cost pricing The setting of product selling prices based on charging only marginal costs to the product. The approach is only likely to be used in exceptional circumstances, such as when competition is intense, as its application to a complete range of

products is likely to cause the business to make losses by its failure to cover its fixed costs.

Mark-up The amount by which the cost of a service or product has been increased to arrive at the selling price. It is calculated by expressing the profit as a percentage of the cost of the good or service. The mark-up is used in retailing, both for setting prices and as a ratio for control and decision-making.

Price discrimination The sale of the same product at different prices to different buyers. Usually practised by monopolists, it requires that a market can be subdivided to exploit different sets of consumers and that these divisions can be sustained.

Pricing The setting of selling prices for products and services supplied by an organization. In many cases, selling prices will be based on market prices but in other circumstances, pricing will be based on costs using information provided by the management accounting system.

EXERCISES

Concept Review Questions

1. What role does pricing policy play in forming an opinion about the service offering?
2. Which method should the marketers deploy for pricing their services?
3. How do service upgrades take care of the limitations of demand supply mismatch?
4. Is the life cycle concept applicable for pricing services? What role does it play in deciding a pricing strategy?

Critical Thinking Questions

1. The hotels offer a specific price if bookings are made online. When a customer approaches the desk for extension of her stay in the hotel, she is offered the rack rate. The customer requests for an online rate, but the staff does not agree. She goes to a business centre and books the hotel online, and gets a confirmed reservation at a lower price. Please examine the pricing strategy of the hotel critically.

2. Should the service firm opt for cost plus pricing or value for money pricing? Please evaluate the statement and support with examples.

3. Compare the online prices offered for a hotel through various search engines. What is your advice to the consumer on the choices he should make for online reservation for a hotel?

Internet Exercises

1. Choose two website firms in India, which deploy the mechanism of auction pricing. Compare and contrast their offering for an airline reservation.

2. Select two tour operators. Compare a tour option between Delhi and Switzerland for the tours offered by them. Are there price differences? Are the differences in pricing strategy explained by the tour operators? Browse through their websites to arrive at logical conclusions.

CASE STUDY   Why does Differential Pricing Help the Poor?*

When consumers find out that a restaurant gives senior citizens a 10% discount off their tabs, the under-65 customers do not complain that they are 'subsidizing' seniors—being charged more so that seniors can be charged less. Nor do they complain that if the restaurant can charge seniors less, it can afford to charge everyone less. People seem to understand that many seniors are on fixed incomes and may not be able to afford as much as those under age 65. And, when parents taking their children to an amusement park pay half the adult price for a child's ticket, those patrons buying adult tickets do not demand the same discount, claiming it is unfair to charge adults more so that children can be charged less. Indeed, they seem to sympathize with the parents.

This is called 'differential pricing', and it is widely accepted in just about every sector of the economy—except in the market for prescription drugs.

What is Differential Pricing?

Differential pricing is the practice of charging some customers or clients more, while charging others less, for the same product or service. Virtually, every industry and most companies engage in some form of differential pricing. For example, the airlines have a range of fares they charge customers, based on when and how they make their reservation, whether they want to fly first, business class, or coach, or whether they are willing to stay over a Saturday night. And many passengers fly free by using frequent flier miles. Historically, health-care providers have also engaged in differential pricing. Doctors charge most patients their standard fee, but poor patients often pay a reduced amount—if they pay anything at all. Such doctors are not criticized, but commended for their charity and public service because they—not the patients paying full price—were perceived as bearing the loss.

Why do Companies Practise Differential Pricing?

Economists argue that companies engage in differential pricing in order to maximize sales and thus, profits. First, a company establishes a business model that anticipates a standard price for the product or service that should result in a profit if sales goals are met. The question then arises, 'Are there those outside the business model who may purchase the product if it costs less?' The answer is almost always yes, and so the company begins

*Matthews Jr, M. (2003), 'Why differential pricing helps the poor?', Insider Online, http://www.insideronline.org/archives/2003/may03/pricing.pdf, accessed on 12 August 2008. Printed with permission.

to look for ways to reach those individuals. It is the market's way of ensuring that more consumers get products and services at lower prices, and companies make higher profits—a win-win for both companies and consumers—unless, of course, you manufacture and sell a product that is politically sensitive, such as brand-name prescription drugs. For instance, the media, many politicians, and special interest groups have come to believe that differential pricing helps the drug companies while hurting the poor. In fact, eliminating differential pricing in prescription drugs will only hurt the poor.

Differential Pricing as a Social Benefit

Differential pricing permits companies and individuals to make their products or services available to people in a wider range of incomes. Take, for example, airlines. The airlines want to sell as many tickets to as many people as possible. Their most lucrative business model is to sell expensive tickets to business travellers who expense the costs to their company and so, are less sensitive to the price. But many people without such expense accounts are not willing to pay that price. Since the aircraft is making the trip anyway, and the 'marginal cost' of adding more passengers is virtually zero, the airlines devised a way to identify pleasure travellers by requiring a Saturday night stay—which many business travellers do not want—thus allowing millions of people with lower incomes or no expense account to travel to see family and friends.

Pharmaceuticals and Differential Pricing

Like most industries, pharmaceutical manufacturers too engage in differential pricing. And like most industries, differential pricing has allowed lower income people, both here and abroad, to have access to drugs they never would have had otherwise. In US, drug manufacturers provide billions of dollars in free or drastically discounted brand-name drugs to states and programmes that seek to provide care to the poor and indigent. In addition, several drug companies have implemented discount cards for qualified low-income seniors. Pfizer and Eli Lilly went a step further by allowing all qualified

low-income seniors to purchase any drug they sell for $15 and $12 per month, respectively. By identifying low-income seniors, drug companies are able to segment those who need help the most.

Differential Pricing and Other Countries

Drug companies are often criticized for selling bulk quantities of prescription drugs to foreign governments, especially Canada and Mexico, for prices lower than many Americans can purchase them. However, such practices are common and well accepted in other industries, and make sense from an economic standpoint. Canada's per capita GDP is about two-thirds that of the US—$19,170 vs $29,240 (1998, US dollars). Mexico's is a mere $3,840. Even automakers sometimes sell their cars for less in Canada, and some Americans have been crossing the border to buy those cheaper cars—spurring a backlash from US auto dealers, who lose sales as a result. But when drug companies discount their products or give them to impoverished countries, critics claim that such practices prove the companies are charging Americans too much and so they clamour for price controls.

They ignore the fact that the only reason doctors can afford to provide free services to some low-income people is that many others are willing to pay the full price. If no one pays the full price, no one can get a deeply discounted price.

Who does Differential Pricing Help?

If a company that sells a product for several different prices were told by the government that it could only sell at one price, the company likely would no longer be able to sell the product for the current lowest price. Higher income people who are willing and able to pay more would pay lower prices. And lower income people would be forced to pay more—precisely the opposite of what lawmakers intend by single-price legislation. Differential pricing helps low-income people get a product they could not otherwise afford. If the political party were to do away with differential pricing in the market for prescription drugs—for example, by forcing a drug company to sell to every purchaser at the lowest price paid by any purchaser—it would ensure that low-income people all over the world would pay more or could no longer get the drugs they need.

Conclusion

Providing the widest possible access to a product means permitting—even encouraging—differential pricing. Eliminating differential pricing ensures that low-income people will have little or no access to

the newest, life-saving drugs. It's a death warrant masquerading as social do-goodism.

Questions

1. What is differential pricing? Discuss with help of examples from various sectors.
2. How can differential pricing be used as a strategic tool to enhance consumerism?

REFERENCES

Avlonitis, G.J. and K.A. Indounas (2005), 'Pricing objectives and pricing methods in the services sector', *The Journal of Services Marketing*, vol. 19, no. 1, p. 47.

Avlonitis, G.J. and K.A. Indounas (2004), 'Pricing strategy and practice: The impact of market structure on pricing', *The Journal of Product and Brand Management*, vol. 13, no. 4/5, p. 343.

Avlonitis, G.J., K.A. Indounas, and S.P. Gounaris (2005), 'Pricing objectives over the service life cycle: Some empirical evidence', *European Journal of Marketing*, vol. 39, no. 5/6.

Awasthi, R. and S. Dey (2006), 'Hotel rates in Delhi & NCR move skyward', *The Economic Times*, 8 September, p. 4.

Bateson, J.E.G. (1995), *Managing Services Marketing Texts and Readings*, 3rd edn, The Dryden Press, Orlando.

'Bharti Airtel gives MTNL blues', *The Economic Times*, 27 October 2006.

Bhargava, Hemant K. and Shankar Sundaresan (2003), 'Managing quality uncertainty through contingency pricing', Proceedings of the 36th Hawaii International Conference on System Sciences.

Biyalogorsky, E.E. Gerstner, D. Weirs, and J. Xie (2005), 'The economics of service upgrades', *Journal of Service Research*, February, vol. 7, no. 3.

'Budget hotels offer rooms with a view', *The Economic Times*, 22 August 2006.

Darby, M.R. and Edi Karni (1973), 'Free competition and the optimal amount of fraud', *Journal of Law and Economics*, 16 April.

Finch, J.H., R.C. Becherer, and R. Casavant (1998), 'An option based approach for pricing perishable service assets', *The Journal of Services Marketing*, vol. 12, no. 6, p. 473.

Fruchter, G.E. and R.C. Rao (2001), 'Optimal membership fee and usage price over time for a network

service', *Journal of Service Research*, vol. 4, no. 1, August, pp. 3–14.

'Government slaps anti-dumping duty on recordable discs', *The Economic Times*, 10 October 2006, p. 10.

Guiltinan, J.P. (1987), 'The price bundling of services: A normative framework', *Journal of Marketing*, vol. 51, April, pp. 74–85.

Guiltinan, Joseph P. (1987), 'The price bundling of services: A normative framework', *Journal of Marketing*, vol. 51, no. 2, pp. 74–85.

Gupta, N.S. and H. Ramakrishnan (2006), 'Maruti and MNCs face transfer pricing rap', *The Economic Times*, 15 May, New Delhi.

Hasan Huseyin Ceylana, Bekir Koseb, and Mufit Aydin (2014), 'Value based pricing: A research on service sector using Van Westendorp Price Sensitivity Scale', *Procedia—Social and Behavioral Sciences*, vol. 148, pp. 1–6.

'Jet set fly', *The Economic Times*, 21 September 2006.

Jobber, D. (2001), *Principles and Practice of Marketing*, McGraw-Hill, London.

Khan, Uzma and Ravi Dhar (2010), 'Price framing effects on purchase of hedonic and utilitarian bundles', *Journal of Marketing Research*, vol. 47, no. 6, pp. 1090–1099.

Krishna, A., R. Briesch, D.R. Lehmann, and H. Yuan (2002), 'A meta-analysis of the impact of price presentation on perceived savings', *Journal of Retailing*, vol. 78, pp. 101–118.

Kurtz, D.L. and K.E. Clow (1998), *Services Marketing*, John Wiley, New York.

Lovelock, C. (2001), *Service Marketing: People, Technology, Strategy*, Addison Wesley Longman, New Delhi.

McIver, C. and G. Naylor (1986), *Marketing Financial Services*, 2nd edn, The Institute of Bankers, Canterbury.

Meidan, A. (1996), *Marketing Financial Services*, Macmillan Business Press, London.

Palmer, A. (1994), *Principles of Services Marketing*, McGraw-Hill, London.

Payne, A. (1993), *The Essence of Services Marketing*, Prentice-Hall, London.

Philip and Pratap (2006), 'BSNL cuts STD rates to Re 1/min', *The Economic Times*, 12 October, p. 5.

Philip, J.T. (2006), 'Cellcos need quality time', *The Economic Times*, 3 July.

Rathmell, John M. (1974), *Marketing in the Service Sector*, Winthrop Publishers, Cambridge.

Rhymer, J. (2001), 'Avoiding the pricing trap: Customers care up to a point', *Franchising World*, vol. 33, no. 8, p. 30.

Shapiro, B.P. and B.B. Jackson (1978), 'Industrial pricing to meet customer needs', *Harvard Business Review*, Nov–Dec, pp. 119–127.

Sharma, R. (2006), 'Incredibly overpriced India', *The Economic Times*.

Stremersch, Stefan and Gerard J. Tellis 2002, 'Strategic bundling of products and prices: A new synthesis for marketing', *Journal of Marketing*, vol. 66, no. 1, pp. 55–72.

'Tax on unbranded goods to help FMCGs in long run', *The Economic Times*, 2006.

Zeithaml, V.A. and M.J. Bitner (1996), *Services Marketing*, McGraw-Hill, Singapore.

Zeithaml, V.A., A. Parasuraman, and L.L. Berry (1985), 'Problems and strategies in services marketing', *Journal of Marketing*, vol. 49, no. 4, pp. 33–46.

Choudhury, Santanu (2014), 'India Airlines intensify fare wars', http://blogs.wsj.com/indiarealtime/2014/08/28/india-airlines-intensify-fare-wars/, accessed on 1 December 2014.

Das Gupta, Surajeet (2013), 'Fare wars land airlines in a mess', 18 November, http://www.business-standard.com/article/companies/fare-wars-land-airlines-in-a-mess-113111801112_1.html, accessed on 1 December 2014.

Hotels Sector Analysis Report, (2014), https://www.equitymaster.com/research-it/sector-info/hotels/Hotels-Sector-Analysis-Report.asp, accessed on 2 December 2014.

http://harrison8bal.hubpages.com/hub/Why-Odd-Pricing-Works-The-$999-Psychological-Illusion HubPages, accessed on 1 July 2015.

http://hbr.org/1998/11/business-marketing-understand-what-customers-value/ar/1, accessed on 14 December 2014.

http://timreview.ca/article/525, accessed on 14 December 2014.

Rai, Saritha (2014), 'AirAsia launches in India with $17 flight fare, sparks fare wars', http://www.forbes.com/sites/saritharai/2014/05/30/airasia-launches-in-india-with-17-flight-fare-sparks-fare-wars/, accessed on 1 December 2014.

Strategies for Promotion for Service Sector

OBJECTIVES

After reading this chapter you will be able to understand the

- ingredients of marketing communication
- need for marketing communication
- process of communication
- nuances of promotion planning and strategy
- different elements of the promotion mix and when are they selected
- importance of advertising
- dimension of sales promotion, personal selling, and direct marketing
- essentials of public relations and e-marketing
- importance of an integrated marketing communication

SOTC Promoting Tourism

India's outbound travel has been growing at a consistent rate and since 2001 the number of outbound departures have been twice that of inbound travel. Outbound travel has been growing at an annual rate of 9.4% and in 2011, 14.21 million Indians travelled abroad (Incredible India 2012). It has been estimated that by the year 2020, fifty million Indians would have travelled abroad (Manju 2012). Kuoni Travel (India) Private Limited's outbound division—SOTC had anticipated this way back in 1976 and by the year 2010 became India's No. 1 holiday brand with size twice as large as the nearest competitor.

SOTC has used 'both conventional media channels as well as below-the-line promotions'

to build awareness and promote its services. However, the 'most vociferous support comes from word-of-mouth endorsements from clients who have experienced SOTC's hospitality.' In conjunction with tourism boards it promotes destinations in shows called SOTC holiday bazaar. Various shows held across India such as Thailand Holiday Bazaar, Great Singapore Holiday Bazaar, Hong Kong Holiday Bazaar, etc. were very successful. They were the first ones to conceptualize a Holiday Bazaar where they offer attractive discounts and exclusive offers to customers. They also participate in various fairs and travel related events such as Times Travel Fair, Times Lifestyle Fair, India International Travel Mart at Mumbai, Times Utsav', etc. to connect with the customers (Superbrands 2009).

After going through the chapter, you will be able to answer the following questions:

1. Why is SOTC participating in various fairs, holding Holiday Bazaars, etc.?
2. Discuss the various initiatives taken by SOTC to promote itself.

INTRODUCTION

Today, with liberalization, the world has become a marketplace where local products rub shoulders with the best of national and international brands. The customer is treated as a king and has a number of options to choose from. In the consumer buying process we saw that the customer purchases a product or service from the awareness set, that is, the brands the customer is aware of, out of the total number of brands (total set) available to him/her. If the service meets the initial buying requirements of the customer, they form the consideration set and as the customer gathers more information, the strong contenders form the choice set from which the customer makes the final choice (Kotler and Keller 2006). If the customer is not aware of the service, it will not fall in the awareness set and consequently, will not form the final choice for purchase of services. Hence, it is of utmost importance to communicate to the customer the service that is offered by the organization and influence the customer so that the service organization is the final choice for purchase. As you can see in the opening case, SOTC is communicating with its customers through various channels so that they are the customer's final choice for purchase in the holiday segment. Once the communication has been initiated, it is important for the organization to continue the communication with the current and potential customers in different ways to cover pre-purchase, purchase and consumption, and post-purchase stages.

MARKETING COMMUNICATION AND PROMOTION

Promotion is the communication function of marketing and is defined as (Engel et al. 1987):

'Controlled, integrated programme of communication methods and materials designed to present an organization and its products to prospective customers; to communicate need-satisfying attributes of products to facilitate sales and thus contribute to long-run profit performance'.

Promotion includes all forms of marketing communication, which is the manner in which an organization communicates with other organizations and customers to facilitate exchange processes. However, an organization also needs to communicate with other organizations for procurement, distribution, and even sale of services. DeLozier (1976) gave the following definition of marketing communication:

'The process of presenting an integrated set of stimuli to a market with the intent of evoking a desired set of responses within that market set and setting up channels to receive, interpret, and act upon messages from the market, for the purposes of modifying present company messages and identifying new communication opportunities'.

This definition is important as it focuses on an 'integrated' approach and talks about 'setting up channels...from the market', that is, a feedback approach from the market. Fill (2002) gave a definition, as follows:

'Marketing communication is a management process through which an organization enters into a dialogue with its various audiences. Based upon an understanding of the audiences' communications environment, an organization develops and presents messages for its identified stakeholder groups, and evaluates and acts upon the responses received. The objective of the process is to (re)position the organization and/or its products and services, in the minds of members of the target market, by influencing their perception and understanding. The goal is to generate attitudinal and behavioural responses'.

This definition focuses on three aspects—dialogue, positioning, and cognitive response. *Dialogue* is the communication between the organization and the target audience. *Positioning* comes into play when there is more than one organization providing the same service in the given category. The marketing communication should focus on the perceptive position the organization wants to create about their service in the consumer's mind in relation to other services. *Cognitive response* is the response of the consumers to the marketing communication, which is revealed in the form of influencing the purchasing or organization related activities. Marketing communication promotes both the organization and its service offering, and effective communication is critical for the success of an organization. Marketing communication is generally taken as communication with the external audience, but good communication with the internal audience like employees is also vital for the success of an organization.

In light of the above discussion we can define promotion as, 'The managerial process of communication an organization has with its target audience to generate attitudinal and behavioural responses and facilitate exchanges for mutual benefit'.

The promotion mix consists of the following five modes of communication— advertising, personal selling, sales promotion, direct marketing, and publicity (Kotler 2006):

1. 'Advertising: Any paid form of non-personal presentation and promotion of ideas, goods, or services by an identified sponsor.
2. Personal selling: Face-to-face interaction with one or more prospective purchasers for the purpose of making presentations, answering questions, and procuring orders.
3. Sales promotion: A variety of short-term incentives to encourage trial or purchase of a product or service.
4. Direct marketing: Use of mail, telephone, fax, e-mail, or Internet to communicate directly with, or solicit response or dialogue, from specific customers and prospects.
5. Publicity: A variety of programmes designed to promote or protect a company's image or its individual products'.

In the service sector we can also talk about the following two factors, which play an important role in the promotion of services:

Word-of-mouth These include recommendations from other customers and are not directly under the control of the organization. Indirectly, the organization can control these communications by providing an experience that meets, or is above the consumer expectations, so that the word-of-mouth is always positive. This aspect is more important in view of the fact that less knowledgeable customers rely more on word-of-mouth to guide their decision-making (Lovelock and Wirtz 2006). A study by ACNielsen shows that it is word-of-mouth that affects the purchase choice of Indians the most. In developed countries, it is advertising that affects the purchase choice, but in developing countries, such as India and Indonesia, it is word-of-mouth that affects the purchase decision the most. Indians are a closely-knit society and are easily influenced by their peers, relatives, etc. This effect is most obvious in purchase of services such as holidays (see opening case) and loans, with the loan market being dominated by word-of-mouth rather than advertising. Even though the use of the Internet is widespread in India, the reliance on blogs for making buying decisions, though prevalent in the West, has not been greatly accepted in India (Vivek 2006).

Internet marketing or e-marketing Distribution of services information and promotion through electronic media is known as e-marketing or Internet marketing (Jobber 2001).

Need for Marketing Communication

The need to promote the product has been explained in this section.

Differentiate Marketing communication aims to differentiate the services, especially when there is no perceptible difference available. For example, not much differentiation is possible in the services provided by the banking sector—where Allahabad Bank, State Bank of Hyderabad (SBH), and Union Bank are all advertising their education loan. They all provide loans up to ₹7.5 lakh (for studies in India) and ₹15 lakh (for studies abroad), but Allahabad Bank focuses on a better career; SBH focuses on the right support; and Union Bank talks about the good future, education, and good people to bank with. Thus, with the help of advertising they have tried to differentiate their products to appear as unique in the minds of customers.

Remind Marketing communication involves promotion of the service, which reminds the consumers of the need they may have so that they can enter into a similar exchange. It also tries to reassure the consumers about the services being provided by the service provider, and is important, as it helps in retaining current customers.

Inform The communication about the services product helps in informing the target market about the services being offered, so that the same can be incorporated in the awareness set. When the objective is to inform, the advertising copy contains the details of the services being provided. For example, Jet Airways informing consumers about its e-ticketing facility and trying to build confidence about the same by informing about payment protection being used (VeriSign and Thawte) that is in line with the industry standard.

Persuade Communication attempts to persuade current and potential customers about the desirability of entering into an exchange relationship.

THE COMMUNICATION PROCESS

The communication process consists of a source, or the organization that intends to send a message to its audience. The organization decides what message it wants to convey to the customers, through which medium it intends to send the message, and how it wants to deliver (encode) the message. This message then reaches the target audience, which deciphers (decodes) the message and gives a feedback to the source in the form of either verbal communication or indirect communication, in the form of purchase of goods. The target audience deciphers the message in accordance with a number of factors such as beliefs, attitudes, needs, etc. In reality, there can be a difference in the message perceived by the audience and the message that was originally intended by the communicator. For example, the advertisement by United Colors of Benetton showing the hands of a white man handcuffed to those of a black man was accepted variably across different parts of the globe. In New York, for instance, there were a lot of complaints as people deciphered it as a black man under arrest. However, it was awarded the 16th Grand Prix for Best Poster. A goal-oriented communicator begins with the target audience and codes the message in coordination with their needs and perceptions so that the message deciphered is what was intended by the source.

PROMOTION PLANNING AND STRATEGY

Promotion planning and strategy is a sequential process and involves careful planning for an effective impact. The different steps involved in promotion planning are shown in Fig. 10.1.

Situational Analysis

Situational analysis is the current analysis of both the internal and external factors affecting the organization. The internal factors consist of all the factors internal to an organization and the external factors consist of market segment analysis, environmental analysis, and competitor analysis.

Internal analysis

Some of the factors to be considered while performing the internal analysis are:

Strengths and weaknesses   The company should list out the strengths and weaknesses of the organization. The idea is to cash in on the strength by focusing on it and conveying the same to the target audience and to work on the weakness and try to overcome them, and not highlight the weak areas in the marketing communication. The strengths and weaknesses of all the strategic business units/departments such as operations, finance, marketing, etc. must be carried out.

Service specifications   The service specifications or the services product must be worked out in detail so that there is no ambiguity regarding the communication of the offering to be made.

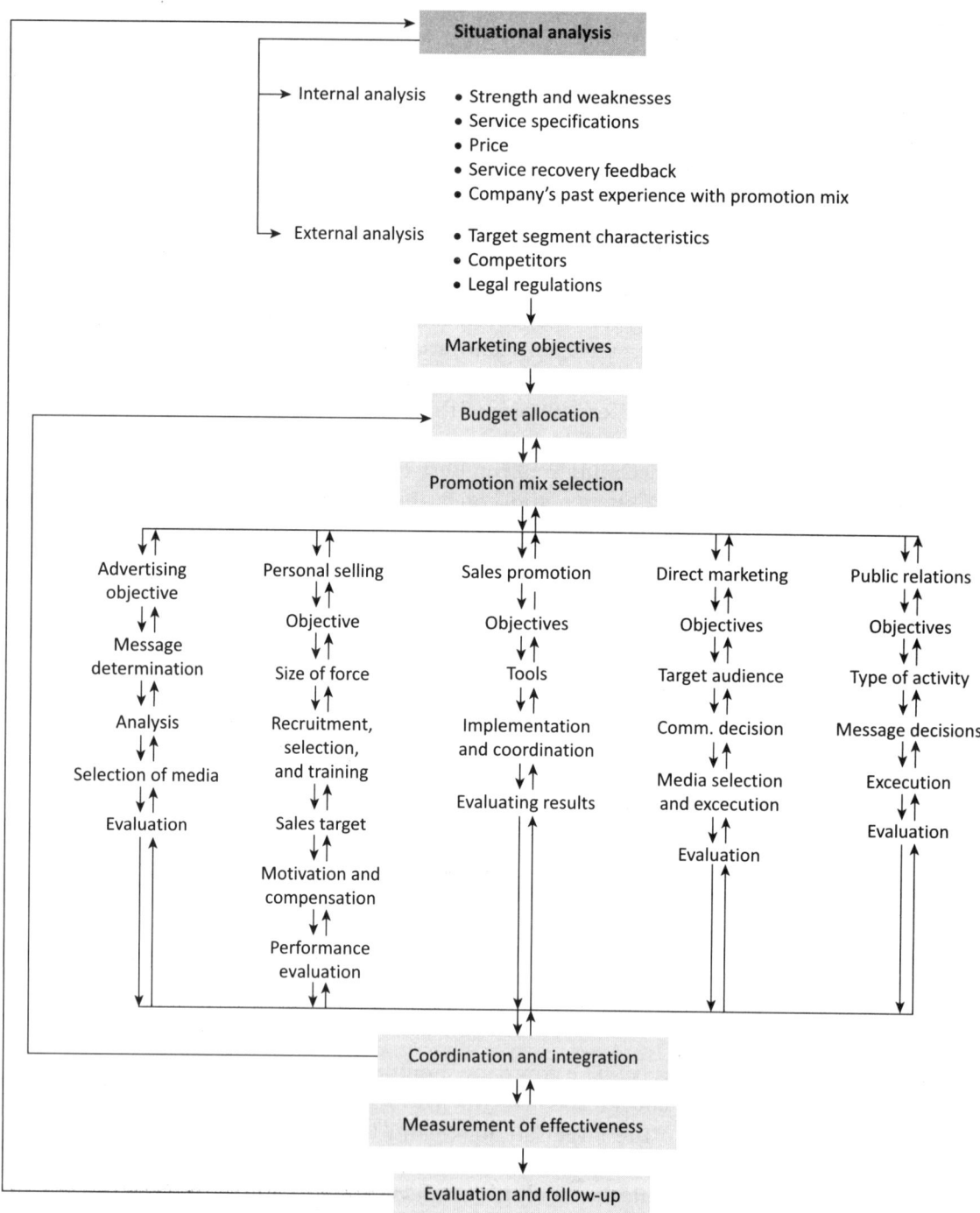

Fig. 10.1 Promotion planning strategy

Price Pricing is one of the four Ps of marketing and the price at which the service is offered is of utmost importance. It is also one of the considerations on the basis of which the customer sets his expectations about the quality of service offering.

Company's past experience with the promotion mix If the service organization has already worked on the promotion mix, the previous experience of the same (difficulties faced, outcome assessments, etc.) is bound to influence the mix to be selected.

Service recovery feedback Service recovery occurs due to a number of reasons, one of them being marketing communications (see Chapter 17). If the marketing communication creates expectations that cannot be fulfilled, and if any such issues are highlighted during recovery feedback, then they should also be taken into consideration.

External analysis

External factors are important while designing the promotion strategy. External analysis is important to understand the opportunities and threats existing in the market so that the opportunities can be exploited and threats can be worked out strategically, well in time. Some of these external factors are target segment characteristics, competitors, and legal regulations.

Target segment characteristics It is very important to study the segment identified to be the main focus for the marketing of services. If the service organization is aware of the needs, attitudes and beliefs, culture, etc., of the customers, it can tailor the promotion strategy on the basis of this knowledge and reduce the disparity between the organization message and customer perception of the same.

Competitors The promotional activity of the competitors affects the promotional strategy to be followed, namely, the budget allocation, the message, the media selection, etc.

Legal regulations The legal regulations governing the promotion mix in different countries have to be kept in mind while deciding upon the promotional strategy so that the promotion campaign does not run into any legal hassles later on. Different countries have different rules governing advertising and what is acceptable in one country might not be acceptable in others. In India, there are some regulatory bodies that control advertising and marketing communication. A voluntary and non-profit organization, the Advertising Standards Council of India (ASCI), ensures that all advertising is legal, decent, honest, and truthful along with a sense of social responsibility and encourages fair competition. The ASCI is legally recognized (since 2 August 2006) and all the TV commercials have to abide by the ASCI code. It encourages the public to complain against advertisements, which they consider to be false, misleading, offensive, or unfair. An independent Consumer Complaints Council (CCC) evaluates all complaints. The ASCI has also sought the support of the concerned associations, such as Indian Broadcasting Foundation (IBF), to persuade the TV channels to adhere to its code and implement the decisions of its CCC. The ASCI's service is free of cost to the public and further information can be obtained from the website www.ascionline.org.

(The Advertising Standards Council of India 2006). In May 2012, ASCI along with TAM Media Research launched National Advertising Monitoring Service (NAMS) so as to further reduce 'misleading ads that harm the interests of consumers'. 'It monitors all the newspapers and TV channels across the country in all languages for violation of the ASCI code'. Approximately 45,000 print and 1,500 TV ads are monitored on a monthly basis. Sectors covered are banking, health, education, telecom, real estate, etc. Any ad that is found violating the ASCI code is forwarded to ASCI on a weekly basis which 'then takes suo motu cognizance of potentially violating ads' (ASCI 2014). The Monopolies and Restrictive Trade Practices Act, 1969, also deals with unfair trade practices. It regulates any misleading, false, and wrong representation in writing (in ads, warranty guarantee, etc.) or oral (at the time of sale) even if no actual injury is caused. It also considers all business promotion schemes announcing 'free gifts', 'contests', etc., where an element of deception is involved. The department of consumer affairs is also working on legislation to curb misleading ads and communications. Under the new norms, if the advertised service or product fails to deliver as per its promise, it will attract a penalty. Also, the companies will now be responsible for any misuse of brands by fake marketers (Jha and Philip 2006).

Marketing Objectives

The marketing objectives to be achieved in the communication campaign should be clear from the outset. The ultimate aim of communication is to stimulate sales and increase profits, but the objectives have operational value, and can be related to sales (the buyer knowledge and buyer readiness stage) (Kotler et al. 2006) and distribution of the service. Some of the marketing objectives are as follows:

Brand awareness   When a service organization enters a market it, needs to make the consumers aware of their presence and the services they offer. Thus, when GETIT Infomedia launched its portal AskMe.com to create consumer awareness, it roped in youth icon Ranbir Kapoor as its brand ambassador to promote this all-in-one app. 'The campaign shows a girl in a new city and she is confused by the numerous apps on her mobile phone. Ranbir helps her by asking her to first delete all the other apps and just download the AskMe app, which will guide her with all the relevant information one requires'. Thus, the ad creates awareness about how AskMe.com is the 'father of all apps' as one does not have to go to different apps to look for deals, classifieds, local search, etc. Also, with the passage of time, to have a top-of-the-mind awareness recall, the service organization needs to constantly keep the customers aware of the services being offered. Thus, creating brand awareness is a never-ending process. For example, the advertisement encouraging tourists and making them aware of Goa as a tourism destination promoting adventure; beach; medical meetings, incentives, conference, and exhibitions (MICE); etc. Central Bank of India is creating awareness of the fact that, in spite of being in the market for generations, they still provide value service without a generation gap.

Brand knowledge   The purpose of awareness is to build brand recall and recognition, but often customers might not be aware of the different services being provided by a service provider. Thus, organizations frequently communicate with the target audience to make them aware of the services being provided. Radisson informs customers of the wedding services it provides. Similarly, IDBI informs customers about the various services IDBI Bank offers, be it corporate banking, retail banking, SME products, or agro products.

Brand attitude   Organizations can communicate with their various audiences to create a favourable attitude towards the brand. An attitude is developed when the customers assess the brand with the perceived ability of the service to meet the need under consideration. Depending upon the need at hand, the customers can develop a liking or a preference for the service.

Liking   It is important for the service provider to have a favourable attitude towards the brand. If not, the organization must try to identify the factors responsible for a negative attitude and try to remove these feelings. Bank of India is trying to develop a positive attitude in the customers' mind by stressing in their print, as well as TV and radio advertisements, that they value relationships and in their bank, along with banking services, relations are also developed.

Preference   If a customer likes a particular brand, the next step is to create a preference for the brand over other service providers. An organization can create preferences by trying to identify what they are good at and then try to promote these features to try to build preference in the target audience. For example, Hike was launched globally in December 2012 and added 'its first 5 million users in 9 months' and in 18 months it was able to cross 'the 20 million user mark' (Indian Express 2014). Innovative features like the ability to control the last seen, online status and ability to chat with friends even when they are offline, 'big file transfer' for up to 100 MB each that allows you to exchange documents, PDFs, MP3, etc. (get.hike.in 2014) drove the benefits clearly to the customers and helped them gain success in the instant messenger market which had established players like WhatsApp.

Conviction   Another aspect of communication is trying to instil confidence in the customers in order to motivate them to make the purchase. Favourable attitudes can be converted into conviction by marketing communication. The marketing communication of BSNL's Dataone broadband informs customers that it is India's number one Internet service provider and highlights the various features of its broadband service. UCO Bank's advertisement tries to convince the customers that it is the right option for carrying out business in the twenty-first century. It also ends with the tagline, 'Honours your trust'.

Sales   There can be a time lag between convincing the customers about the purchase and the actual act of purchase by the customer. To remove this time lag, the service provider can motivate customers to make purchases by offering schemes for a limited period. For example, the advertisement of Jet Airways and Etihad Airways offered 'LoFares Sales' of flat 20–50% off on flights in India and across the world to convince customers to purchase for 3 days only, ending on 27 July 2014. They also informed that customers would get double miles for booking on jetairways.com and etihad.com.

Distribution   The service organization can also communicate with its audience to search for franchisees or distributors for their services. For example, when Jay Retailing and Merchandizing Pvt. Ltd wanted to expand its retail chain 'The Loot', it placed double-paged advertisements in magazines highlighting the requirements the franchisee has to fulfil.

Budget Allocation

The following four methods for allocating the budget for marketing communication are generally used (Kotler and Keller 2006; Kotler et al. 2006; and Jobber 2001):

Affordable method   This is a simple method of identifying the amount of money the organization can afford to spend in a particular financial year. It is not related to the objective of marketing communication or the amount of money required to perform effective marketing communications.

Percentage of sales method   Some organizations fix a particular percentage of sales as the amount allocated for marketing communications. Supporters of this method find the following advantages related to it:
- Companies spend as much as they can afford.
- It encourages managers to correlate selling price, promotion cost, and profit per unit.
- Encourages stability, especially when the industry spends the same percentage.

   However this method has its limitations. These are:
1. It views sales as a cause of promotion rather than the result.
2. Budget allocation is on the basis of availability rather than based on opportunities.
3. If sales fall, then the communications also are limited, whereas more communication may be required to boost the flagging sales.
4. As the sales vary from year to year, the budget for communication also varies and makes long-term planning difficult.
5. There is no logical basis for choosing the percentage other than what competitors are doing or what the organization has already been doing.

Competitive parity method   This method allocates the budget for marketing communication on the basis of competitor's outlay. This method advocates that:
1. Competitor's budget represents the industry wisdom.
2. Spending what competitors spend prevents promotion war.
   However, it is seen that neither of the cases is necessarily applicable.

Objective and task method   Setting the budget on the basis of costs involved in performing specific tasks for achieving specified objectives is known as allocating budget on objective and task method. In this method the management decides beforehand what they want to achieve from their marketing communication, plans the tasks involved, and sets the budget accordingly, thus focusing on the objectives to be achieved rather than on what competitors are doing.

Promotion Mix Selection

The next step is to select the promotion mix based on the communication objectives and budget allocated. An organization can opt for a combination of mixes, say, advertising, sales promotion, and personal selling, or only sales promotion and personal selling, etc. All the different promotion mixes are studied in more detail in the communication mix. A summary of the advantages and disadvantages of the different communication mixes can be drawn here to give a comprehensive view (Table 10.1). A detailed discussion of the promotion mix follows in the subsequent portions of the chapter.

Table 10.1   Advantages and disadvantages of different elements of the promotional mix

S. no.	Promotional Tool	Advantages	Disadvantages
1	Advertising	• Informs customers about the services • Reaches mass audience • It reminds and reinforces the services offered • Can be used both for long-term image building and quick sales • Reaches geographically dispersed customers at low cost per exposure	• One-way communication • Impersonal and not as persuasive as some of the other promotion mixes • TV advertising requires a large budget and is faced by multiple channel options and channel switching • Advertising copy needs to be changed after regular intervals to continue generating consumer's interest
2	Sales promotion	• Gain attention for the service • Offers strong incentives to customers to purchase the service	• Effects are short-lived • Do not contribute to long-term brand value
3	Personal selling	• Most effective in building buyer preference, conviction, and purchase • Is interactive and can tailor presentations according to buyers' needs • Two-way communication can take place, where service providers also get insights into the customer's requirements for the services product • At the time of re-purchase, it provides service providers an opportunity for service recovery (if any) • The information provided is current • Helps in building customer relationships	• Is the organizations' most expensive promotional tool • Other promotional tools such as advertising and sales promotion can be stopped after a period of time but personal selling requires more commitment and cannot be varied easily
4	Direct marketing	• Can customize the message to individual requirements • The message will be more current as regards service details as the time period required for flow of information from service provider to customer is less in comparison to advertising	• The reach is limited and cannot reach mass audience with this method (except through Internet marketing)

(Contd)

Table 10.1 *(Contd)*

S. no.	Promotional Tool	Advantages	Disadvantages
5	Publicity	• Consumers believe publicity material more in comparison to advertisements • Can reach those customers also who avoid advertisements and sales force • Can reach a wider audience at negligible or low cost to the organization	Often negative publicity can also be created

The following factors influence the choice of promotional mix (Jobber 2001; Kotler and Keller 2006):

Resource available and cost of promotional tool The different communication mixes have varying costs associated with them. Advertising may require more money, whereas sales promotion and publicity might cost a lot less. Thus, resources available for the communication mix will affect the choice of promotion.

Market size and concentration Advertising is seen to be most effective when a mass market is present and if the market is also geographically dispersed. Internet marketing is also gaining prominence with more consumers getting online and the cost associated is also less compared to some of the other methods of promotion. If the target audience is small, reaching them through personal selling will be more feasible.

Customer information needs Personal selling is used if the service involved requires technical discussions or discussions of different options available, for example, in the sale of insurance policies—a cover can range from ₹30,000 to ₹25 lakh, and the advertisement encourages consumers to call and ask for more options. If not much technical information is required, customers can be satisfied by advertisements.

Push versus pull If the service provider is focusing on the channel intermediaries, it focuses on push strategy, which can be achieved through personal selling and sales incentives, but if the consumers are the focus, then service providers engage in pull strategies, which can be achieved by advertising and consumer promotion.

Product life cycle The stage of the life cycle the service is in affects the choice of promotion mix. For example, in the introductory stage, the organization will invest in both advertising and sales promotion, whereas in the decline stage, the investment in both the activities is reduced (Table 10.2). For a detailed discussion on the effect of product life cycle in promotion mix, refer to Chapter 2.

Buyer readiness stage The stage of the buyer in the purchase process affects the choice of the promotion mix. It is seen that in the awareness, interest, desire, action (AIDA) model of consumer purchase, advertising, and publicity help to raise awareness and create interest in the consumers, but are not very effective in encouraging consumers to take action. Sales promotion and personal selling are known to affect desire and inspire customers to take action and purchase the product.

Table 10.2   Effect of product life cycle on choice of promotion mix

	Introduction	Growth	Maturity	Decline
Advertising	Build product awareness among early adopters and dealers	Build awareness and interest in the mass market	Stress brand differences and benefits	Reduce to level needed to retain hardcore loyals
Sales promotion	Use heavy sales promotion to entice trial	Reduce to take advantage of heavy customer demand	Increase to encourage brand switching	Reduce to minimal level

Coordination and Integration

The whole marketing plan needs to be coordinated and the message displayed should be uniform so as not to confuse the customers about the services provided. It should also be in line with the services provided so that the customer expectations can be met easily and surpassed, as the case may be. Moreover, since a combination of promotion mix is used, which different departments handle (advertising by advertising department or agency, personal selling by the sales department, etc.), there can be issues when the message delivered may not be consistent. Say, the advertising department may position the service as premium, whereas the sales force may offer discounts giving a contrary notion.

Measuring Effectiveness

Measuring effectiveness of the communication helps the management to know about the outcome of the effort and the money spent on the communication strategy.

Effectiveness can be measured by conducting communication (advertising) research. Measuring recall and recognition of the services by the target audience, what features they recall, their perceptions about the service provided based on the marketing communication, and attitude formation or change (for a first time consumer or a re-purchaser of the service provided), all provide interesting knowledge and information to the managerial staff. Generally, what is targeted should be measured. Thus, if the objective of communication is sales, then the sales department should be the focus of research to measure the impact of advertisement on sales. The New York American Marketing Association in affiliation with Advertising Club Bombay started the EFFIE Awards in India. These awards measure the success of an agency in increasing the clients business across a variety of parameters. In 2013, Lowe Lintas won the trophy for the Effie Agency of the year. O&M won a Grand Effie for its Lifebuoy Roti campaign (Menon 2014).

COMMUNICATION MIX

As discussed, the communication mix consists of advertising, personal selling, sales promotion, direct marketing, and publicity. Let as now look at each of these methods of communication in detail.

Advertising

Advertising is a paid form of communication by the service provider with its target audience to facilitate exchanges (of services or information) with its stakeholders. An organization can either design the advertisement in-house (by creating a department) or it can outsource it from an advertising agency. In India, the advertising industry stood at ₹12,526 crore in 2013 (Pitch Madison Media Ad Outlook 2013). There are many advertising agencies, the most prominent being Ogilvy and Mather (O&M), Lowe, McCann-Erickson, Contract Advertising, FCB-Ulka, etc. In deciding the advertising programme, an organization has to look into the following five Ms of advertising (Kotler and Keller 2006):

Mission The mission is the objective the organization wants to achieve from the advertisement. The advertisers can have different missions such as to inform, to persuade, or to remind the customers, and hence the advertisement copy will defer depending upon which objective the advertiser wants to achieve.

Money This includes the money allotted for the advertisement (budget allocation).

Message This relates to the objective and positioning strategy. Organizations spend a lot of time and effort in finalizing the message they want to convey to the consumers. For example, the famous Vodafone network advertisement campaign showing a boy being followed by his dog was a very simple way of showing the area coverage of the service provider, and made a complete connection with the consumers.

Media Based on the reach of the target audience and costs involved, a number of media options are available for the service organization to choose from.

Measurement The measurement of the effectiveness of the advertisement can be done in the form of communication impact and sales impact.

Advertising Process

The advertising process consists of the steps shown in Fig. 10.2.

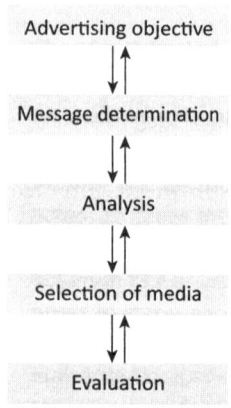

Fig. 10.2 The advertising process

Advertising Objective

Advertisements are most effective when they flow from a particular objective to be achieved. These objectives can be as follows (Jobber 2001):

Create awareness Advertisements are used to create awareness about the services amongst the consumers. For example, when educationtimes.com introduced its Dial-a-career services, the purpose of its ad was to create awareness about the services by giving details about how by following 3 simple steps (sms EDU2 <code> to 58888) they could connect to expert counselors and get free career related queries on fashion, chartered accountancy, BBA, MBA, etc. (*Times of India*, 25 July 2014).

Stimulate trial Advertisements can stimulate trial of the service, considering the fact that once the consumers try the service and are satisfied, they are bound to return. For example, the ad of Vijay Karnataka, the daily newspaper in Karnataka in its ad in Brand Equity profiles its reader 'Reshma Kulkarni, former Personal Secretary and soon-to-be professional baker, who will soon need a bigger kitchen. The ad says that if you want your brand to connect with lakhs of its readers like her, go to www.vijaykarnataka.com/aboutustoday'.

Position services   Product positioning is very important, as it shows how the customers perceive the service that determines their consumption of the same. The services can be positioned on the basis of the following:

Service characteristics and customer benefits   This is generally used in the hospitality industry where hotels are classified as luxury, budget, etc. on the basis of services being provided. Indigo Airlines offers business packages that include return flights, accommodation for one night, and breakfast. Their leisure packages include return airfare, hotel stay, airport transfers, breakfast, and sometimes sightseeing as well.

Price   Positioning services on the basis of price signifies value for money and quality services at low prices.

Service user   Services can be positioned on the basis of the target audience for whom they are meant. For example, the advertisement of Indraprastha Apollo hospitals positions the service—advanced heart check—on the basis of service user, that is, smokers. Clove Dental positions its services for people with yellow teeth and talks about 'dazzling white treatment for ₹1450 only'.

Service use   Services can be positioned on the basis of how they are going to be used by the consumer. Olx.in talks about how people can use it to sell their used goods. People can download the free app on Google play or go online to post a free ad and connect with people who want to purchase it.

Symbols   Symbols can be used to position services; for example, the golden arches of McDonald's and the logo of Punjab National Bank. Currently, Deutsche Bank is using the symbol depicted as inserted in the pocket/purse of famous personalities such as Sunil Gavaskar and Sania Mirza.

Competition   Positioning against well-known competitors increases effectiveness as they can be used as reference points. For example, Maruti released full-page advertisements in *The Times of India*, New Delhi, 14 August 2006, showing how Maruti provides unmatched value whether you buy it, run it, or sell it. The advertisement then went on to compare the mileage of various models of Maruti (800, Alto, Omni, etc.) with that of Tata Indica and Hyundai Santro. It also compared the maintenance cost and resale value. However, Maruti was forced to stop this ad when Hyundai lodged a complaint with MRTP saying that the ad was 'misleading and disparaging' and was a fit case of 'unfair trade practice' (*The Economic Times* 2006). Another example of positioning against well-known competitors is that of CNN-IBN proclaiming that it is the most watched English news channel, and providing comparative results with NDTV, another well-known Indian channel. Another very interesting advertisement of positioning against competitors is that of *Dainik Jagran*, which considers news channels as its competitors and has tried to position itself in relation to them.

Social context Positioning the service provider as a socially conscious organization is becoming relevant, especially in the current century. For example, ITC Hotels is advertising 'the warmth of our hospitality extends not just to you but to the planet as well.' The ad copy further states that 'at ITC Hotels, you do good every time you step in. With all our hotels being LEED® Platinum Certified, we don't just pamper you but also the planet, Welcome to the world of responsible luxury'.

Correcting misconceptions Advertisements can be used to correct misconceptions that exist about the services. For example, if at the time of service recovery, a service provider finds that certain misconceptions exist about the services that are creating expectations, which the service provider cannot fulfill, it should try to correct the same with the help of advertisements.

Remind and reinforce Vodafone and Airtel advertise constantly just to remind the customers about their presence and create top-of-the-mind recall so as to maintain their market share. Advertisements meant for reminding the customers are generally targeted at sales, so that the market share is retained.

Provide support to sales force Advertisements have a wide reach and make the consumers aware about the service provider, thus giving the sales force an edge when they make their sales call. An aware consumer is bound to be more receptive towards the sales force than a consumer who is not aware about the service provider. Also, contact numbers and e-mail addresses are given in the advertisements so that interested consumers can call. It then becomes easy for the sales force, as they need call on interested parties only. For example, see the ad of MTNL targeted at business clients; it states a contact number where interested parties can call and also provides an e-mail address.

When the promotion mix is being selected, the budget is allocated for the different promotion mixes to be selected. This defines the budget allocated for advertising, which can again depend upon the stage in the product life cycle—competition, frequency of advertisements, and differentiation of services product.

ITC announces the launch of its new hotel in Gurgaon

Message determination

The message to be conveyed to the consumers should be important for the consumers and should communicate the advantages that the service is going to provide to the customer. The message should be:

Simple   So that it can be recalled easily like, 'Punjab National Bank—The name you can bank upon', or 'BSNL—Connecting India'.

Focus on differential advantage   Ads should highlight how the service provider is different and how it can satisfy the needs and wants of the customers. For example, Finnair's advertisement highlights the lie-flat seat consumers can enjoy while travelling between Delhi and Europe.

Lifestyle   The advertisement can target a particular lifestyle and relate the service to it. For example, Punjab National Bank uses lifestyle to put forth the idea of its e-banking facilities by showing a couple eating fast food and working on a laptop. They also highlight facilities like tele-banking, Internet banking, and debit/credit cards.

Fantasy   This implies creating a wonder around the service provided. For example, the advertisement of Kerala Tourism tries to create fantasy by giving it a heavenly feel and the tag line, 'God's own country'.

Testimonials   They can also be used when a known celebrity endorses a service. For example, cellular phone service providers use four celebrities to endorse their products, while Rahul Dravid features prominently in ads of Bank of Baroda and Abhishek Bachchan endorses American Express. Table 10.3 provides a snapshot on celebrity endorsements. However, there is a trend of employing celebrity endorsers too. These are experts in their sphere of professional careers like chef Sanjeev Kapoor, beauticians such as Coleen Khan, Naina Balsavar, Jawed Habib, etc. (Vyas 2006). Number of Advertisers in 2013 with top celebrities are listed in Table 10.4.

Once the advertisement message has been decided, it is very important to put it forth in an attractive manner so that it grabs the viewers' attention. The following points must be given careful consideration before finalizing the advertisement:

Table 10.3   Celebrity endorsements on TV during Jan–June 2013

Category	Personality	% Share of overall Celebrity endorsement
Film industry [80%]	Film actor	40
	Film actress	40
TV industry [9%]	TV actor	4
	TV actress	5
Sports [11%]	Sportsmen	11

Source: Based on the data from AdEx India online (2014).

Table 10.4   Top celebrities with the maximum number of advertisers in Jan–June 2013

Celebrity	% share
Katrina Kaif	6.71
Shah Rukh Khan	6.67
Salman Khan	5.2
Aamir Khan	5.0
Kareena Kapoor	3.8

Source: Based on the data from AdEx India online (2014).

- illustration
- headline
- copy.

For example, the advertisement of Presidium, Proposed Secondary School, though illustrated in black and white and does not use any celebrity, draws attention because the message has been portrayed in such a manner. The headline is enticing as it makes the consumer want to read further and the copy or the main text is simple, yet strong and convincing.

Analysis and Selection of Media

Every day, as a country, time spent on media is 127 minutes (on an average) with the least being 114 minutes '(by 51–60 years of age working people and 20–30 years of age married and working people)' and maximum being 167 minutes '(by 20–30 years old non-working single people)' (Marketing Whitebook 2014). The advertising message can be presented before the audience through a number of media. The major ones for advertising can be categorized into print, electronic, and outdoor (also referred to as out-of-home).

1. Print: newspaper, magazine, letters
2. Electronic: radio, TV, cinema, e-mail
3. Outdoor: kiosks, billboards, street furniture, transport (neon lit high-tech mobile trucks, etc.)

Factors affecting selection of media

The major factors affecting the choice of media are as follows:

Media reach   The task of the manager is to select the media that has maximum reach for the target audience. Reach denotes the number of people that are being exposed to that medium. The media reach in Indian states is given in Table 10.5.

In India, TV has the maximum media reach; even more than press. This holds true for all the regions of India (*The Marketing Whitebook* 2014).

Type of service   The type of service being advertised also affects the choice of media. For example, hotel and restaurant ads are better shown in colour magazines and as coloured ads in newspapers. The glossy *Brand Equity* supplement of *The Economic Times* carries coloured ads of hotels and airlines such as Four Seasons and Emirates. VLCC uses sales promotion techniques such as discounts and free health check-ups in order to increase sales. Such initiatives are promoted heavily in radio (and some newspapers) during the period the offers are valid.

Cost involved   The cost involved in the particular media and its fit with the budget is also a major consideration. Even though television has high initial cost, the cost per thousand exposures is considerably less.

Table 10.5   Media reach in Indian states

Media	Reach (%)
Press	20.4
TV	52.8
Cable & Satellite	45.8
Radio	15.2
Cinema	3.2

Source: Based on the data from *The Marketing Whitebook* (2014).

Media

Advertising spend across media was ₹31,877 crore (in 2013) which is expected to grow at 16.8% to become ₹37,216 crore in 2014. The major contributor (₹5,000 crore) to this growth is the Lok Sabha Elections that were held in 2014 (IndiaTelevision.com 2014). The different media, such as television, print, and radio, are discussed in detail in this section.

Television Globally, TV accounts for more than 40% of advertising expenditure and contributed 41% to the total media ad market in India in the year 2006 (*Business World* 2008). TV formed 40% of the total media ad market in 2012 (Pitch Madison Media Ad Outlook 2012). 'The number of TV channels in the country has grown from 130 i n 2004 to 788 in 2014 and the sector has witnessed an exponential growth', 'India now has the third largest TV market with close to 154 million TV households, next only to China and the USA' (PTI 2014a). The money spent on advertising in television was ₹12,419 crore (in 2013) which is expected to grow at rate of 15% to reach ₹14,282 crore in 2014 (IndiaTelevision.com 2014). Also, year-on-year the time spent on watching TV ads is growing. In India 'television consumption starts at 99 minutes for 12–14-year-olds, peaks at 107 minutes for 20–30-year-olds, and steadily falls to 100 minutes for 60-year-olds (Marketing Whitebook 2014). Television has a distinct advantage over the other media as it uses both audio and visuals to create a dramatic effect, and is highly persuasive. The physical evidence of services can be brought about better with the help of this media. Moreover, it has broad acceptability and high believability. In India, it has a broader reach than even the newspapers. TV can also target the illiterate masses in rural areas.

Advertisements of products and services can be linked to events like cricket matches or FIFA World Cup when there are opportunities of targeting maximum viewers. A lot of money is spent in advertisements during the match intervals, both on ground and onscreen, where viewers are exposed to the brand messages (see Exhibit 10.1). For example, BSNL sponsors all the fours and sixes in cricket matches, and as soon as a four or a six is scored, it is announced as, 'BSNL four (or six)'.

Prime time charges are always higher in comparison to late night or other non-primetime slots. However, there are certain drawbacks associated with TV; the first being that the number of ads have increased from 86,000 in 2001 to 2,60,000 in 2005,

Exhibit 10.1 **Indian Premier League's Ad Spend—Season 7**

The extremely popular Indian Premier League (IPL) T20 Tournament, has over the years provided mileage to a number of brands. The seventh season saw the etailers also jumping on the bandwagon to build visibility for themselves. An on-air ad cost for a ten second spot was ₹4.75 to 5 lakh. Presenting sponsors like Vodafone and Karbonn Mobile have paid anywhere between ₹50–60 crore (and get airtime of 200 secs) and associate sponsors like Amazon, India, TVS, Havells, etc. have paid between ₹25–35 crore (and get airtime of 100 secs). Apart from Amazon India, other etailers like Flipkart and Go Daddy also advertised during IPL. Amazon launched its operations in India ten months prior to launching its first Indian television commercial during IPL 7.

and 200 channels have been added. Thus, along with the fragmentation of the media, there has been an increase in the number of adverts leading to ad clutter (the sheer volume of advertising that viewers encounter every day). Globally, the ad clutter is increasing and stands at 484 (TV ads every week). India ranks at number 32 with a clutter of 311 compared to US, which has a clutter of 789 (Krishna and Soneji 2006). With the launch of numerous channels, consumers have many options and channel switching is very common; hence, to capture the viewers' attention service organizations have to invest in many channels. Alternatively, organizations can segment the target audience and choose the channel accordingly. For example, to reach business people in the Hindi speaking states, advertisements can be aired on Aaj Tak or Zee News, the most popular regional news channels in the region.

Viewers get bored watching the same ad repeatedly. Thus, to generate interest companies have to change ad copy at regular intervals, which also involves costs. Getting viewers' attention is very difficult due to channel switching; thus, even if the ad is aired at prime time, there is no guarantee of audience viewership. Surprisingly, even though regional language channels enjoy maximum viewership, it is the mass entertainment channels that draw the maximum advertising revenue.

Press This includes both newspapers and magazines at national and regional levels. With the onslaught of TV and now the Internet, consumers have many distractions and the press has to compete very hard. This is combined with the fact that press can use only visuals, audio and motion appeal are both lacking; and 74.04% of the population is literate as per Census, 2011 (India TV News 2014). However, in 2012, it overtook TV marginally (TV contributed 40% and print 41.7%) to be the biggest contributor in the ad pie (Pitch Madison Media Ad Outlook 2012). Advertising in the print media has been growing steadily. Advertising in print grew at a rate of 4% in 2012, 10% in 2013, and 'is expected to grow by 17% to ₹15405 crore in 2014' (IndiaTelevision.com 2014). Advertisers are using this medium to reach out to the customers. In the year 2013 this media reported a growth of 10% with revenues totaling ₹13,167 crore. Sectors that contributed to this increased advertising on ratio include FMCG (12.3% of total ad pie); Auto (11.7% of total ad pie), and education (9.71% of total ad pie). Also 'at a national level Indians spend 36 minutes daily on print on average.' (Marketing Whitebook 2014).

Advertising in the print media has been growing steadily. Advertising in print grew at a rate of 4% in 2012, 10% in 2013, and 'is expected to grow by 17% to ₹15405 crore' (IndiaTelevision.com 2014). A look at the ad spend distribution by year from 1990 to 2004 shows that print constituted 70% of ad spend in 1990, which reduced to 51% in 2004 and became 41.7% in 2012 (Pitch Madison Media Ad Outlook 2012). Most of the cellular service providers and credit card companies mail promotional material of new schemes and services launched directly to existing customers.

Press offers opportunities to segment market demographically and psychographically, and gives credibility and prestige. The ads in the magazines or newspaper can be reviewed at leisure and referring back to an ad for information (say, phone number or address of the service organization) is easier. There is a good pass along readership. The quality of reproduction is also good in most of the magazines, for example, the ad for Singapore Airlines.

However, there are some weaknesses too, as readers can just gloss over advertisements (selective attention) thus ignoring the campaigns. If ads have been targeted in, say, auto magazines, then there is high competitive clutter. Moreover, there is a long ad purchase lead-time and the position is also not guaranteed in magazines.

Newspapers have the added advantage of immediacy and information on discounts and sales offers are best passed on by newspapers. However, it faces the issues of low quality reproduction and lacks colour quality. Moreover, doubling the size of the ad does not double readership but definitely doubles the cost.

Radio Radio, being cheaper than TV still lags behind in advertising penetration in India. In 2003, it contributed just 2% to the overall advertising revenue and is way behind the share of 6–7% in developing countries and 14% in US (*The Marketing Whitebook* 2005) and in 2012 it just rose to 3.2% (Pitch Madison Media Ad Outlook 2012). With the private sector allowed to enter, there are now a number of players in the FM channels. As per the Information and Broadcasting ministry 'while 245 FM Channels were launched in 85 cities since 2005, in the third phase 839 channels are proposed to be launched in 294 cities and added community radio is also a key thrust area. The number of operational community radio stations has increased from 64 in 2009 to 163 in 2014' (PTI 2014a). Advertising in this medium is growing and is expected to grow at '15.04% in 2014, with the total advertising spends adding up to ₹1,262 crore against ₹1,097 crore in 2013' (Pitch Madison report cited in IndianTelevision.com 2014). Time spent on radio varies according to the age of the listeners. The youngest listeners spend approximately 70 minutes (average basis); the 20–30 years age group listen for 83 minutes; the 51–60 years age group listens for 77 minutes and for 60 years age group it is 81 minutes (Marketing Whitebook 2014). Radio has the advantage of geographic localization and has the distinct advantage of being mobile. Radio is preferred by organizations as here you can give audio effects to the advertisement, the ad is cheaper to produce, and during traffic rush hours there is bound to be wider coverage. However, the drawback associated with radio is that there are no visuals and it has to rely on the audience's imagination.

Outdoor Outdoor advertising is getting a new look with newer technology upgrading the quality of the hoardings and availability of newer options such as bus shelters, kiosks, and mobile trucks.

In India, outdoor advertising has a long history and other than hoardings, ads painted on walls are a common sight especially on the highways. Apart from painted billboards, digital outdoor hoardings are also catching on along with advertising on taxis, auto-rickshaws, buses, etc. Outdoor spending on ads has increased from 2000 when it was 8% of ad expenditure to 8.5% in 2003 and came down to 6.5% in 2012 (Pitch Madison Media Ad Outlook 2012).

The guidelines and policies set for roadside advertisements were formulated in 1972, but the traffic population has faced a drastic change since then (See Exhibit 10.2).

Outdoor advertising is expected to grow at 6.2% in 2014 to become ₹1,977 crore (Madison report cited in Napier 2014). However, outdoor advertisements have limitations and they can serve as additional (reminder) ads but not as the sole medium

Exhibit 10.2 **Outdoor Advertising Policy**

'The guiding principles of the Outdoor Advertising Policy, 2008 are as follows:

1. The policy for outdoor advertising is driven, not by revenue imperatives, but by city development imperatives. Therefore, in its implementation, it will be clear that outdoor hoardings are permitted only if they are not a road safety hazard or if they support the city's public service development and enhance its aesthetics.

2. The policy will explicitly work to discourage visual clutter. This will be done by increasing the space between the billboards and in restricting large billboards to select areas of the city, like its commercial hubs.

3. The policy is designed to ensure that outdoor advertising is not hazardous to traffic. It will assume that there is a significant correlation between road safety and distraction because of roadside billboards, visible to the drivers. This will be done by allowing large size billboards only after significant distance from the traffic junctions and intersections, by providing significant space between the two billboards on roads, by completely banning billboards on pedestrian walkways, and in placing billboards at significant distance from the right of way of any road.

4. In addition, large size billboards will be completely banned on major city arterial roads, like the Ring road. The list of roads will be decided jointly between the MCD and the traffic police.

5. The policy will actively promote the large size billboards in commercial areas (defined as metropolitan city centre, district centre/sub central business district, community centre/local shopping centre/convenience shopping centre in the master plan) of the city. In this case, the agency will work to maximize the revenue gains, which can be used for city development.

6. The policy will promote the use of advertising in what is commonly known as street furniture. These are devices placed on public service amenities of the city such as railway carriages, buses, metro trains, commercial passenger vehicles, bus shelters, metro shelters, public toilets, and public garbage facilities, to name a few. This is done to improve the revenue viability of these public provisions. But it will be noted that the use of advertising space is not the primary function of the utility, it is its supporting function. Therefore, the city agency will ensure that the placement of the public utility is done keeping in mind its public purpose, not its advertising viability. In addition, the agency will ensure that the primary function of the 'street furniture' is being maintained and if not, then suitable punitive action must be taken against the advertising concessionaire.

7. The policy is judicious in ensuring that there is a differentiation between the use of commercial advertising and private advertising, where signage is used to identify the location of the owner of the building or the space within the building. The policy will do this by laying down clear lists of what is allowed and what is completely disallowed to guide members of the public.' (Delhi outdoor advertising policy 2008).

of advertising. They suffer from short exposure time, maybe a couple of seconds, are expensive, and are affected by environmental conditions.

Cinema Cinema was a weak medium of advertising with the ads placed during the start of the movie or during the interval when the audience viewership fell drastically. However, now innovative ways of placing products or services in the movies has opened up new vistas. It has been studied that consumers recognize a product more if they have seen it placed in a movie or a TV programme. Film placements, associative marketing, cross-branding, and integrated promotion with movie and TV serials, are increasingly becoming a part of the media budget.

The mega blockbuster *Kkrish* is a successful example of how Singapore tied up with the movie to promote tourism in Singapore. Cinema advertising is predicted to register a growth of 10.4% in 2014 and reach ₹167 crore (Madison report cited in Napier 2014). It formed only 0.53% of the ad pie spent in 2012 (Pitch Madison Media Ad Outlook 2012).

Internet Advertising on the Internet is rising in India as more and more consumers are going online for their needs. The growth can be gauged by the fact that it accounts for 8% of the money spent for advertising in various media (Pitch Madison Media Ad Outlook 2012). Age groups from 20–60 years spend 78–86 minutes on the Internet. It has become the third most preferred medium after Print and TV for advertisers. In 2013, it grew by 32.4% and in 2014, it is expected to grow at 29.5% to reach ₹3,950 crore from ₹3,050 crore in 2013. 'Of these display advertising will continue to have an upperhand compared to search with revenue totalling to ₹2,150 crore.' (IndianTelevision 2014 and Napier 2014).

There are a number of models available for advertising on the net, such as intromercials, ultramercials, and contextual advertising. With brick and mortar companies opting to advertise online, a number of dot com companies are using the traditional media of press and hoardings to reach the target audience. Naukri.com's famous Hari Sadu ad comes to mind, and Shaadi.com is another example to understand how the company is investing in a combination of media choices to build its presence in the market.

Internet advertising gains more importance considering the fact that consumers give up the time on TV to offset time spent on the Internet. Moreover, the Internet is eating into the prime time viewership as over half of all home Internet users log in between 6.00 p.m., and midnight. Another reason contributing to the success of this medium is the global economic recession that necessitated the judicious spends of money. 'Internet being a return on investment medium, it is becoming the preferred choice for them. The growth in online advertising is expected from FMCG, automobile and banking sectors'. (IndianTelevision 2014).

Evaluation

According to John Philip Jones, renowned advertising icon, 'Any advertising that does not deliver sales in the first seven days is completely ineffectual' (*The Economic Times* 2006). To gauge the effect of advertising programmes, they need to be evaluated constantly. The effect of advertising can be measured by measuring the ad recall or by measuring the sales effect. Ad recall can be measured by taking recall tests wherein consumers are asked to recall everything related to advertisers—the advertising message, brand name, etc. Sales effect of advertising is more difficult to measure than the ad recall as the sales are affected by a number of factors such as individual preferences, service features, and price. However, one way to measure the effect of advertising is to compare the sales vis-à-vis the advertising budget.

The short-term impact of advertising can be influenced by a 'good creative', whereas the medium (one year) impact can be affected by a combination of creative, ad spend, and media choice. Long-term effects of advertising can be measured by studying the penetration, purchase frequency, advertising intensiveness, advertising elasticity, etc.

It is seen that organizations often opt for a combination of media to get their message across. A case in point is Shaadi.com, which has chosen different media to convey its messages such as magazines, hoardings, TV, YouTube, etc.

Personal Selling

Personal selling involves selling the product of the service organization through the sales force. This involves maintaining a sales force and hence a sales department, the personnel of which are involved in direct contact with the customers. The maintenance of the sales people, their travelling cost while on sales calls, etc., all cost the organization a great deal. Thus, in the overall communication budget they are responsible for a major chunk of the money allocation. The sales force performs the following functions (Kotler et al. 2006):

Prospecting   This involves search for identification of prospective new customers.

Targeting   This involves allocation of time (fixing appointments) with the prospective customers and at the same time allocating time to servicing current customers.

Communicating   The sales employees communicate about the service organization's 'product' offering and try to answer all their queries.

Selling   After communicating about the services the sales personnel approach their main goal—closing the sale. To achieve this, they may make commitments, promises, offer discounts, and try to mould the service offering in the best possible manner.

Servicing   Certain services; for example, the sale of insurance, require the sales representatives to constantly assist the customers by getting all the forms filled, collecting the cheques and depositing them with the service organization, and delivering the documents to the customer.

Information gathering   Since the sales people interact continuously with the customers they can get the customers' feedback regarding service requirements, service delivery gaps, and how they can make improvements. The organization should decide what information they want from the customers and direct the sales people accordingly.

Allocating   During scarce delivery it is the task of the sales personnel to decide whom to allocate the resources to. For example, during the season when there is requirement for banqueting or conferencing from different sources, the sales people decide whom to allocate the same to.

Personal selling can be a challenging job as Akshara, the Kerala IT mission's e-literacy and enterprise programme implemented in association with local bodies, realized. When they had to market the idea of computer learning to fishermen, they realized that the fishermen never had the time, as they were mostly offshore. So Akshara hit upon an innovative idea of going on fibre boats to groups of fishing boats at sea. When the fishermen had cast their nets and were waiting for their catch, the Akshara team utilized this opportunity to inform them about e-learning, and the encouraging results speak for themselves (Exhibit 10.3).

Sales Force Management

The management of the sales force requires the following functions—objectives; the size of the force; recruitment, selection, and training; allocation of sales targets; motivation and compensation; and performance evaluation (Fig. 10.3).

Objectives

This involves the specific objectives for the sales force, that is, to achieve a market share of 15% from 12%, or to achieve a certain average rate of return (ARR). These targets can then be divided geographically or region-wise and further targets can be allocated to the sales personnel. This helps the management to also decide the number of personnel required in the department in a particular territory.

Size   The sales force can follow a geographic structure, product structure, or a customer-based structure. In the geographic structure, geographic areas are allotted to the sales force, and they are responsible for the sales of all the service products and the customer satisfaction in that particular area. In the product structure, the sales force is allotted specific service products and are responsible for the sale of that service product. For example, in the insurance sector, products, such as life insurance, general insurance, vehicle, or event insurance, can be allotted to different sales personnel. In a customer-based structure, the sales force is allotted customers on the basis of market segmentation, say, for booking rooms in hotels. The sales force can also be assigned as exhibition and fairs event managers, managers to handle different corporate accounts, etc. Once this is decided, specific requirements of the sales force are drawn for recruitment.

Recruitment, selection, and training   Once the job description is drawn, the next step is to identify sources from where the sales force is to be recruited. The human resource department can place an advertisement in the newspapers, place requirements with consultants, or draw from their network, etc. The list of prospective candidates are drawn and

Fig. 10.3   Personal selling process

interviewed. The short-listed candidates are then enrolled and passed through a train-ing programme where knowledge about the organization, its services, its competitor organization and their services, selling procedures, etc., is imparted to them.

Sales target allocation   Once the training is over, the sales personnel are informed about their sales areas (geographic, product-wise, etc.) and the targets (in line with the objectives set) they have to achieve.

Motivation and compensation   Once the sales force has been allocated targets, moti-vation is provided to them in the form of incentives, either monetary or otherwise. In some organizations the compensation or remuneration offered is itself linked to the sales in the form of commission.

Performance evaluation   At regular intervals (weekly, monthly, etc.) the performance of the sales force is reviewed. This helps the organization to keep a check on them. If a person has performed well, they reward him/her (e.g., employee of the month), or if the performance is not as per expectations, they try to find reasons for this—service product failure, sales force drawback, and try to overcome them. If at subsequent per-formance evaluations the employee is still not performing, he/she may be replaced.

The evaluation and control of the total sales force is done at the coordination and integration level. This is also required to make sure that the advertising and other pro-motion mixes are in tune with the promises and communications made by the sales personnel.

Sales Promotion

'Sales promotion consists of short-term incentives to encourage the purchase or sale of services' (Kotler et al. 2006). The potential of sales promotion can be derived from the fact that the promotional marketing industry in India (not including the market-ing of movies) is ₹500 crore and has shown a growth of about 50% in the past couple of years, and is expected to grow to ₹1,500 crore by 2008. FMCG companies have used this since long, but services industry such as insurance, financial services, health care, telecom, hotels, etc., are also using it increasingly. In the services industry, promotions are used to increase customer loyalty and to generate a buzz or excitement about their services (Kaushik 2003). For example, Pantaloons tries to create a buzz by offering 'buy 2 get 2 free on men's and kids' wear on purchases during the festive season. The ad further motivated by offering 'additional 5% cashback on Axis Bank debit and credit cards on purchase of ₹4500 and above. Maximum cashback of ₹2000 can be availed'.

Sales promotion can include coupons, rebates, price off, contests, demonstrations, etc.; it is most effective when used along with other promotion techniques. A good sales promotion can also result in publicity when it is talked about in the media; the vice versa also holds true. For example, 'Hilton HHonors, the loyalty programme of ten Hilton Worldwide Hotel brands in July, 2013 did a travel related stunt called "Travel is Calling You" in Chicago'. They had done a survey on spontaneity and according to the results, 80% of the Americans had said they would drop everything to get an all expense paid weekend getaway. So in August 2013, HHonors along with AT&T called

Exhibit 10.4 **Telcos Reducing Free Minutes to Increase Revenue**

Various telecom companies in India have gone through a 'prolonged period of cut-throat competition that left them bleeding and debt ridden.' Not wishing to increase data tariffs due to competitive pressure in the marketplace, telecom companies are working around various promotional offers to increase revenue. They have started reducing discounted or free calls. This helps them raise effective, or realize, call rates, thus boosting key parameters such as average revenue per user (APRPU)' For example 'Airtel hasn't hiked the tariffs anywhere in the country. They have reduced the validity period of voucher packs from 28 to 21 day. Similarly, Vodafone has also not hiked its tariffs but was simply changing promotion packs from time to time. Uninor as a part of its cleaning up drive has devised different mechanisms to ensure that the changes in the promotional packages didn't hurt a subscriber. In Maharashtra for instance if the validity of the pack was reduced from 28 to 20 days, then the minutes were increased from 100 to 150'.

lucky winners who had to answer the call of travel at that time to win'. 'Chris Pagnozzi, a Chicago Comedian would be at the other end of the line and when participants accepted the offer, salsa dancers would perform and a pedicab would pedal the winners to nearby AT&T store where they would receive an iPad Mini, small beach related gifts like flip-flops, and a towel. Apart from two free night certificates that they could avail at any of the 4,000 Hilton HHonors hotels and resorts in 90 countries worldwide, they also got two $500 American Airlines gift cards and a $500 American Express gift card to enable a spontaneous getaway' (Reuters 2013 and Newman 2013).Thus, for a successful promotion, ideation and implementation should be worked out in detail so that it achieves the desired results. The timeframe for running a promotion is also an important consideration in sales promotion. If a sales promotion runs for too long or too often, it becomes part of customer expectations and if it is then discontinued, it builds resentment in the minds of the customers, who even stop using that service provider. Also, running promotions for too long incurs cost to the company and eats into the profitability (see Exhibit 10.4). It is argued that promotion benefits customers who would have bought the product anyway and so a proportion of the money spent is wasted anyway.

There are different tools available for achieving the sales promotion, but first the objective has to be clear as to what has to be achieved from it. Sales promotion steps are shown in Fig. 10.4.

Setting objectives

Sales promotion is part of marketing communication and hence, the objectives would flow from the objectives set out for the same. In general, the objective of sales promotion is to increase short-term sales by attracting customers from competitors by providing them with some incentives. They can also be used for rewarding loyal customers or trying to hold on to new customers. It is important to note that the promotional objective should fit in with the brand values and the market segment being targeted should desire the offering.

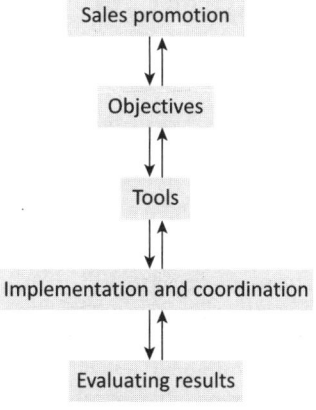

Fig. 10.4 Sales promotion process

Selecting the promotional tool

There are different tools that can be used for promoting sales. Some of them are elaborated in this section.

Coupons   Coupons allow a customer to gain some discounts on purchase of specified products or services. Coupons can be mailed to customers or they can be placed in ads in newspapers or magazines. They can even be inserted in newspapers, or as in the case of Domino's, they can be attached to the menu pamphlet and offer discounts on the next purchase (within a specific time period). As a case of joint promotion, Reliance distributed coupons (with discounts valid in specific places of other service providers) on the purchase of Reliance mobile services. Coupons can be used either at the introductory stage (as in the case of Reliance) or at a mature stage to boost the sagging sales.

Packages   Packaged tours are very much on the rise in India. There are a number of options for customers to choose from. Club Mahindra offers packages for different destinations. A visit to the company's website provides the details of the tariffs for complete holiday packages at different locations.

Reward points and premiums   Most companies provide reward points as an incentive to use their services more often. Most of the airline companies provide frequent flier programmes for their clients so that the next time they fly, they can use their services and gain points, which they can redeem by opting for the various promotional offers. For example, see the advertisement of Emirates, which states, 'Fly Emirates and earn up to 15,000 bonus skyward miles'. Credit card companies also offer reward points to encourage customers to use their cards more often. Every time they use their cards to make purchases, points are accrued which are collected and can be redeemed later when they can exchange points for merchandise.

Premiums are merchandise offered to customers as an incentive to purchase or use their service. The merchandise offered can be:

Free in the mail offers   Credit card companies are using this sales promotion technique clubbing reward points with other brands. For example, ICICI Bank credit cards offered Leather Passport Holder, Parker Pen Set, and Travel Organisers, against certain reward points.

Self-liquidating offers   These are offers wherein along with using reward points customers have to pay some cash also. For example, HDFC Bank offers books, DVDs, etc., against reward points and cash.

Deals   To sell their services, credit card companies also offer certain deals wherein other brands are offered for sale at discounted prices on payment of equated monthly instalments (EMIs). For example, HDFC offers a bouquet of discount vouchers as welcome gift apart from various discounts depending on the type of credit card. It also offers zero% interest on purchases from select outlets.

Price off   This is a big motivation for people who are ready to make the purchase decision. Advertisers generally make such offers for a limited period so as to influence the customers to purchase the product in a stipulated time. For example, the ad of yatra.com offers flat 25% off on hotel bookings and an additional 5% off on using the mobile app using promo code 'hotel' for the period between 28–31 July 2014.

Special offers   Organizations take out special offers, sometimes clubbing it with an anniversary celebration, etc., to promote their services. For example, VLCC on its 25th anniversary offered various price offs and special packages to celebrate the occasion. You could get flat 25% off on salon services or book a slimming or beauty package worth ₹25,000 and above and get salon services worth ₹20,000 absolutely free, etc. Special offers can be offered to boost sales. Oberoi Hotels and Resorts came up with a special offer of a complimentary third night or complimenatary additional rooms for two children up to 12 years of age for stays from 1st April to 30th September, 2014 (except for stays between 14–18 August 2014) in order to boost sales.

Live demonstrations and roadshows   Roadshows are organized to create awareness about the product and to attract the public, some competitions are organized and prizes announced. Aviva Life Insurance, as part of its initiatives to expand the customer base in India and build awareness about the importance of life insurance policies, kicked off a series of roadshows across 14 towns and cities in Kerala. Revolving around the theme of man's desire to predict the future, the roadshow designed several themes and attractions, including gifts for participants (*Business Line* 2006). Standard Chartered Bank held career-counselling sessions for children in Mumbai where they gave students a guided tour on the details of banking. They also organized a Harry Potter party at some of their branches along with games revolving around actual incidents in the Harry Potter story (Kaushik 2003). The roadshow organized by Airtel in Chandigarh for the launch of Airtel Magic I-card was organized to create brand awareness.

Kiosks and free service camps   Organizations frequently put up roadside kiosks where they offer information about their products and also offer free service for products purchased previously. For example, water purifier company, Aquaguard follows this practice as part of its customer service programme.

In-store competitions   This promotional activity creates a buzz for the service provider and gives the youth an impression that something is happening and they should be a part of it. For example, Barista organized a competition in its Delhi, Mumbai, Bengaluru, Pune, and Kolkata outlets where customers filled a five-word form on why they found coffee fashionable. Winners were flown to Delhi to get a makeover by Elite Modelling Agency and wardrobe by H2O Cue! design house. Café Coffee Day and Barista came up with different types of promotions during the football world cup in 2006 (Krishnan 2006b). Café Coffee Day tied up with sponsors to award prizes to weekly winners, while Barista tied up with ESPN to offer live feed in major metros and provided instant gratification to customers who predicted the correct outcome of the match.

Point-of-purchase material   Service organizations offer brochures and leaflets to dealers at their retail outlets providing information about their service products. For example, Tata Indicom and Bajaj Allianz provide brochures to their target customers.

Contests   Contests are also used as a sales promotion technique with rewards announced to attract customers. For example, Singapore is a successful example of how it tied up with the movie *Krrish* to promote tourism in the country. Later, Singapore highlighted the spots and even ran contests to attend the premier of the movie in Singapore. They also built a special package of four days and three nights and offered free T-shirts autographed by Hrithik Roshan and free tickets for watching the movie in Singapore. They offered tours of all the places where the film was shot (Exhibit 10.5). After the success of its promotional campaign of sunsilk-gangofgirls.com, Sunsilk plans to go international as well as rural where it will be re-christened Sunsilk Saheliyan. The site features gang games, blogs, parade ground, hot jobs, etc., in addition to advice on haircare, relationships, and astrology. The website has 2,50,000 registrations, 25,000 gangs or user clubs, and the site has registered 200 million hits and gets an average of 12–13 million page views every month (Coutinho 2006).

Scratch cards   Scratch cards are used to provide instant rewards to customers and are generally used by service providers to encourage customers to use their services. An example is of *Loksatta* newspaper whose marketing objective was to increase its circulation before the launch of its new supplement 'Viva'. The paper held Scratch2Win, a contest where readers had to scratch a coupon and if they were lucky, could win anything from a pen to a house. Public response to the communication was overwhelming and *Loksatta* was compelled to extend Scratch2Win by another month. During the campaign, the paper's circulation increased by a whopping 22%.

Implementation and coordination

Once the promotional technique has been identified, other decisions, such as the scale of implementation (in a city, metros, or all-India basis, etc.), time-duration for running the promotional offer, and management responsibility of the feature, follow. The consumers have to be made aware about the promotional campaign and different outlets/branches have also to be informed so that they can handle queries. A successful implementation and coordination is equally essential for the success of any promotional programme.

Evaluate the results

As always, the results achieved have to be measured so as to evaluate the effectiveness of the programme. This can be measured by keeping an eye on the sales figures before, during, and after running the promotional programme. Many times consumers prepone/postpone their programmes to avail of the promotional offer, thus accounting for some of the sales, but the long-run increase in sales denotes that new customers are also attracted by promotional offers.

Direct Marketing

Over the years direct marketing has assumed new meanings. Originally, direct marketing attracted customers by contacting them without involving any intermediaries. Thus, salespersons were also a part of direct marketing. However, with the introduction of media, such as telephone, television, and the Internet, the concept was redefined.

The Direct Marketing Association (DMA) defined it as 'An interactive system of marketing that uses one or more advertising media to affect a measurable response and/or transaction at any location' (Kotler et al. 2006).

Jobber (2001) defined it as, 'The distribution of product, information, and promotional benefit to target consumers through interactive communication in a way that allows response to be measured'.

Thus, direct marketing is usually short-term and allows an immediate measure of the programme response. With the growing use of Internet, there are a whole lot of opportunities for direct marketing. The general method adopted in direct marketing (see Fig. 10.5) is as follows:

Objective setting   The objective of direct marketing must be set in order to be clear as to what has to be achieved from the activity. The aim must be in line with the communication objective and can be marketing related (to generate enquires, acquire customers, etc.), communication related (to create awareness about the service, about any new service introduced, etc.), and finance related (to increase sales, ROI, etc.). Service providers can also target a combination of objectives such as providing information about a new service and at the same time trying to sell it too.

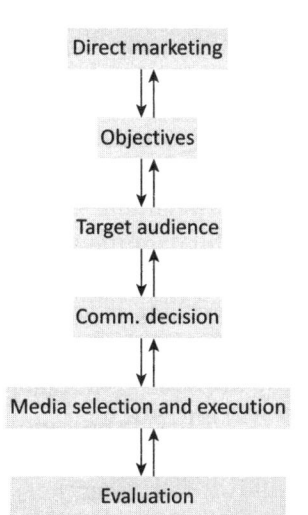

Fig. 10.5   Direct marketing process

Identifying target customers   Once the objective is decided, the next step is to draw a list of the target or potential customers based on the objective to be achieved. This list can include all the existing customers who are already purchasing from the service provider, customers who purchased in the past, a list of enquirers, and a list of prospective customers that can be drawn from a database (directories, yellow pages, paid databases available in the market, etc.).

Communication decision   Based on the objectives, the decision regarding the message to be conveyed is taken. For example, if the objective is communication and sales of a new service product, then what is to be communicated is decided.

Media selection and execution   How the message is conveyed is decided in media selection. The different media available for direct marketing are as follows:

Direct mail   Communication messages sent via post to prospective customers constitute direct mail. Dell Computers is an organization sending direct mails to corporates in India through brochures on laptops and computers with their specifications, price, etc. Direct mail allows messages to be personalized for customers. The initial cost can be high and the response received is generally 2% (Jobber 2001).

Telemarketing   Using telecommunications and information technology to communicate with customers is called telemarketing. With the growing use of telephones and mobile phones, and falling costs of call charges, telemarketing is increasingly being used by organizations to reach their audience. The use of toll-free numbers has also helped to increase inbound calls. Most noticeable are the finance companies offering loan facilities to their customers. Telemarketing also acts as a support to the sales personnel as the customers evincing interest can be asked for appointments so that the sales personnel can visit them. Telemarketing is preferred as it is less time-consuming than personal selling with the facility of a two-way communication. However, in telemarketing it is easier for a person to be negative, the non-verbal stimuli are missed out, and it is considered intrusive.

Catalogue marketing   The sale of products and services through catalogues distributed to agents and customers, or at the service provider's outlet, is known as catalogue marketing. Many agents sell holiday packages through catalogues. For example, catalogue of HDFC Kids Advantage account provides a communication address, which helps in the measurement of responses. The catalogue offers a free CD of the movie Hanuman on opening an account and urges prospective customers to hurry as the offer is valid till 31 December, i.e., for a limited period.

Inserts   Inserts are generally put in newspapers or magazines where they are clubbed with some promotional offer. For example, *Outlook*, *Reader's Digest*, etc. put inserts in their magazines for subscription to their magazines and offer different gifts for different periods of subscription ordered.

Evaluation   The measure of the effectiveness of the direct selling activities can be achieved by studying the response rate to the campaign, the sales affected as a result of the campaign, the enquiries generated, etc.

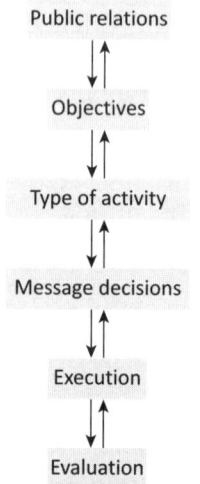

Fig. 10.6 Public relations process

Public Relations and Publicity

Management of the relationship with the various stakeholders such as employees, shareholders, and government falls under the management of public relations. Jobber (2001) defines public relations as, 'The management of communication and relationships, to establish goodwill and mutual understanding between an organization and its public'.

The management of public relations consists of the following steps (Fig. 10.6):

Setting objectives   Management of public relations can accomplish many objectives. Some of these are to advance the reputation, which in turn will help them to gain good employees and to sell, etc., overcome misconceptions, create goodwill with employees, customers, government, etc.

Major tools   Public relation activities include corporate advertising, seminars, lobbying, donations, publicity, etc. Publicity constitutes a major portion and involves communicating through news in the media without paying for it. Placement in the news gives the message more credibility and hence is a more delicate situation to be managed, as there is no control over the viewpoint expressed by the news supplier.

For example, Shahnaz Hussain, since the inception of business in 1970s relied on publicity to gain media attention. She attended conferences and featured regularly on BBC since 1977, talking about Indian herbs versus chemical treatments. During her launches abroad she made sure that enough buzz was created and was covered by the media.

The most popular way of dissemination of information is through a news release, which pleases editors and stands a greater chance of being used, and can be written using the guidelines given in message decisions. Other publications such as annual reports, newsletters, and magazines, also help to build company image and communicate news to target markets.

Organizing events (e.g., Lakme fashion Week) gives companies a chance to reach the target audience and draw attention to the company's name and products.

Message decisions   Deciding what has to be said and how it is to be said is a very important decision. Editors can reject press releases if they do not find them appealing. This can be overcome by making the headline factual instead of using ostentatious or grandiose language. The opening paragraph should be a brief summary of the release, content should also be factual, and the less important message should be towards the end as lower paragraphs have a higher probability of being cut. The news release should not be lengthy and the layout should have small paragraphs with lots of white space to show that it is easy to read.

Execution   The execution of the publicity or seminar, or donation should be in line with the other marketing communications made by the organization so that the image being portrayed is uniform and does not create any ambiguity in the mind of the consumers.

Evaluation   Kotler et al. (2006) identified the following three ways of evaluating the effects of public relations. These are:

Exposures   An easy way to measure public relations is to measure the physical space covered in the different media such as publications, radio, and TV and the average audience covered by the same. For example, 2,000 column inches of news covered in 100 publications with a circulation of 100 million. However, this is not a very satisfactory method, as presence in a media does not guarantee that the audience has read it or paid attention to it, or that they remember it.

Awareness/attitude change   An alternate way is to measure the awareness created or attitude change due to public relations. For example, how many people heard about the news or how many changed their views as a result of the news, etc.

Sales and profit contribution The change in sales before and after the campaign can be measured to evaluate its effectiveness. However, public relations is never done in isolation, but is always in coordination with other promotional tools hence, it is difficult to measure the individual effect of public relations on sales.

E-MARKETING

Internet is a global medium and the companies using it are potentially addressing global audience (Wymbs 2000). This is because the use of Internet is growing at a fast rate not only in India but also worldwide. What took the radio 38 years and TV 13 years, Internet did in five years, that is, reach an audience of 50 million users (Lagrosen 2005).The World Wide Web has revolutionized the communication process, be it information search, product purchases, etc. The Internet provides unlimited opportunities—many of them still unexplored—for the marketing of goods and services. The growing use of Internet across the globe adds to the opportunities offered by it. Companies start with a presence on the net—through their website—by providing corporate information; the second stage is the interaction stage where service providers interact with customers online; and in the progressive stages there is transaction of business and services online and further integration with the supply chain (referred to as e-business) (Levy and Powell 2002).

For customers to be attracted to a site it should take a few seconds to download or open, be attractive, user-friendly, and informative. Table 10.6 shows that after e-mails, it is information search that people devote maximum time to, and this pattern has been continuing over the years. The Internet allows organizations to connect to the masses at minimum cost, and remote customers can also be contacted, thus giving the organizations opportunities for direct marketing.

The overall Internet-using population in urban India has grown by 28% between April 2006 and April 2007 to reach 120 million in 2012.

'Time spent on the Internet by users in India rose 24% from 2010 to 2012, and more sophisticated categories of Internet use, such as e-mail/chat, social networking, and entertainment, grew more quickly than reading and browsing. Downloads of applications for mobile phones have multiplied eight times in two years, with social networking and music being the major categories. Social networking is the single biggest use for smartphones, after voice, with the number of Facebook users in India jumping from less than 10 million in 2009 to in excess of 50 million in 2012.' (McKinsey 2012)

Table 10.6 Popularity of online activities

Rank	Online activity	2010 (hours/month%)	2012 (hours/month%)
1	E-mailing/chat	7	9
2	Entertainment	2	3
3	Social networking	3	5
4	Read/browse	6	6
5	Research/purchase	2	2

The Internet has a limitation in marketing products, as consumers cannot physically see the product before purchasing. In services marketing, due to the different characteristics of services like intangibility and inseparability, Internet has an added advantage. Better quality of pictures can be placed on the website, giving a feel of the ambience and the services to be provided. For example, Taj View Hotel at Agra has given photos of its exterior, lobby, etc.

In India, various government organizations are also going online. An example is Indian Railways, which has provided train schedules, online reservations and bookings, and train planner, etc. Also see the number of advertisements—ICICI Bank, Citibank, NBC India.com—posted on this site.

Many organizations also send e-mails to prospective buyers to provide information. As this trend is increasing, customers have started treating it as junk mail and are spending less and less time on them. However, some traditional services such as computer programming can be directly delivered online. Some service industries have evolved to becoming virtual organizations where they provide services only through the net. In a more dramatic breakthrough, a heart specialist sitting in a Delhi clinic can perform even delicate surgeries, such as an open heart operation, on a patient in Bengaluru.

NEED FOR COORDINATION IN MARKETING COMMUNICATION

It is important for the marketing communication to deliver a uniform message so as to build a consistent brand image. This also enforces the message being sent to the target customers for them to form an opinion about the services provided. Coordination in marketing communication is required at two levels:
1. within the different marketing communications
2. between the marketing department and rest of the services.

Coordination within the marketing communication means that the different types of communications chosen (advertising, promotion, etc., and within advertising, print media, outdoor, electronic media, etc.) should be delivering a uniform message.

In Chapter 7, we have studied the importance of customer education through marketing communication. It is very easy to sell the services by making promises to lure customers but what happens when these promises are not met? Exhibit 10.6 gives a fair idea of the consequences a service provider may have to face, apart from bad publicity and word-of-mouth by the affected party.

Integration of marketing communication can be managed by focusing on factors such as the service promised, communication message, Internet communication, and guarantees.

Service promised The service promised in marketing communication should be in line with the services being delivered by the service provider and all the personnel in the organization must be aware of what services the customers expect.

Communicated message The message should be focused on educating the customers about the services to be provided so that the customer expectations are more realistic and in line with what is to be delivered to them. Thus, in various communications the

Exhibit 10.6 **Cruise Nightmare**

An elderly couple's holiday in Egypt turned into a nightmare. Their travel operator in Delhi failed to provide them with the services he promised and was asked to pay a compensation of ₹32,500 to the couple. The old couple had complained that the cabin allotted to them on the cruise was dark and dingy and they had to climb four floors to reach it. When these problems were brought to their notice, they were ignored. The complaints of the couple were accepted since, when any service provider advertises in a newspaper that the facilities being provided will be of five-star standard, it has to live up to it, without any deficiency. Failure to provide such service, entitles the consumer to receive compensation. While the tour operator continued to claim its international standards, the Court concluded that if the complainants had not suffered the trauma of the trip, they had no reason to approach the district forum at the expense of their time and money.

service provider should focus on the services to be provided so the customer has a fair idea of what to expect.

Internal communication   The flow of information within the organization should be at all levels—horizontal and vertical. For example, the operations department should know what the sales and marketing department has promised (either through advertising or through personal interaction) the customers, so as to manage customer expectations.

The operations department in isolation can also work at its best but it would not get the desired results if it is not in line with what the customers are expecting. Thus, the idea is that all the employees are aware of what has been promised by the organization so that they can all work towards the same goal.

Guarantees   Guarantees of 100% satisfaction build trust in the customers that the service organization will stand by their promises. For more details on guarantees refer to Chapter 17.

RESEARCH INSIGHT

Sales Promotion—A Missed Opportunity for Services Marketers?
Ken Peattie, Sue Peattie, (1995), 'Sales promotion—A missed opportunity for services marketers?', *International Journal of Service Industry Management*, vol. 6, issue 1, pp. 22–39.

'Below-the-line' sales promotion as part of the communication mix is virtually ignored within the services marketing literature, in comparison with personal selling and 'above-the-line' advertising. However, 'below-the-line' techniques have been growing in their extent, credibility, and sophistication during the last two decades. They have now reached the point where they deserve consideration in relation to other areas of marketing practice beyond their fast-moving consumer goods (FMCG) origins. The different tools which make up the promotional toolkit have also reached a point where they deserve individual consideration instead of being bundled together. This research seeks to demonstrate how one such tool, the promotional competition, represents a significant opportunity for services marketers. It also reviews the literature relating to sales promotion to build a case for the suitability of competitions for services marketing, and presents the findings of a survey of 188 services-sponsored competitions to explore the nature and extent of competitions' use in practice.

SUMMARY

Marketing communication is an important aspect of marketing and helps the organizations to communicate with their target customers. This chapter delineates the importance of marketing communication. There are different ways to develop marketing communication and a mix of promotional tools gives the service provider the opportunity to communicate with a wider target audience. A detailed discussion of the process of advertising gives a perspective on advertising of services and helps to decide which medium or combination of media to choose for advertising different services. An insight into the product placement in movies as an advertising tool is provided. The use of the Internet as an advertising media has been emphasized. It is important to note that with the introduction of subsequent media (say radio, TV, etc., and now the Internet), the previous media tools were not wiped out but each media has its pros and cons, and it is for the marketer to decide which media reaches the target audience best.

The elements of promotion mix are discussed. The promotion planning and strategies are discussed in the context of services industry.

Personal selling process and the functions being performed by the sales force are highlighted in the section on personal selling. The next section on sales promotion defines the same and various options available to manage sales strategically for the benefit of the organization. The section on direct marketing delineates how an organization can interact directly with the target audience and involves the use of a media. The section on public relations discusses how communication and relationships can be managed to establish goodwill between an organization and its public. The next section discusses the growing popularity of online activities and the need for an organization to manage this. The availability of different tools for the marketer highlights the need to have congruent messages. All the personnel of the service organization should be aware of the messages being communicated to provide maximum customer satisfaction.

KEY TERMS

Advertising A communication that is paid for by an identified sponsor with the object of promoting ideas, goods, or services. It is intended to persuade and sometimes to inform. The two basic aspects of advertising are the message and the medium. The media that carry advertising messages range from the press, television, cinema, radio, and posters, to company logos on apparel. Advertising creates awareness of a product, extensive advertising creates confidence in the product, and good advertising creates a desire to buy the product. Advertising is a part of an organization's total marketing communication programme.

Direct marketing Selling by means of dealing directly with consumers rather than through retailers. Traditional methods include mail order, direct mail selling, cold calling, telephone selling, and door-to-door calling. More recently telemarketing, direct radio selling, magazine and TV advertising, and online computer shopping have been developed.

Personal selling Person-to-person interaction between a buyer and a seller in which the seller's purpose is to persuade the buyer of the merits of the product, to convince the buyer of his/her need for it, and to develop with the buyer an ongoing customer relationship.

Promotional mix An organization's total promotional effort, including personal selling, advertising, publicity, public relations, and sales promotion. The promotional mix attempts to attain integrated marketing communications.

Publicity The technique of attracting the attention of the public to a product, organization, or event by the mass media. Publicity involves a third party, such as a newspaper editor or TV presenter, who determines whether the message is sufficiently newsworthy to publish and what the nature of the message should be.

Public relations Influencing the public so that they regard an individual, firm, charity, etc., in a favourable light compared to their competitors, as in business a good corporate image is an important asset.

Sales promotion An activity designed to boost the sales of a product or service. It may include an advertising campaign, increased PR activity, a free-sample campaign, offering free gifts or trading stamps, arranging demonstrations or exhibitions, setting up competitions with attractive prizes, temporary price reductions,

door-to-door calling, telephone selling, personal letters, etc.

EXERCISES

Concept Review Questions

1. What is marketing communication? What are the different decisions required to be taken in a marketing communication?
2. Critically discuss the relevance of marketing communication in a services organization.
3. Of the different promotion mix, which would you choose for a hospitality service provider and why?
4. Critically discuss the different media available for advertising. To advertise a restaurant, which media would you choose and why?
5. Differentiate between personal selling and direct marketing.
6. Evaluate the importance of coordinated marketing communications for service organizations.

Critical Thinking Questions

1. Discuss the need for marketing communication when the audience is well informed about the different services available.
2. Do you think it is important to have an objective of marketing communication at the start of the communication campaign?

3. What would you suggest—advertising or personal selling—for attracting new customers by an insurance provider?
4. What promotional tools can a marketing consultancy firm use to attract and retain customers?
5. Discuss the use of different promotion mixes at the time of launching a new restaurant.

Project Assignments

1. Visit the website of at least two banking service providers. Discuss the different promotional tools being used by them. Which one would you choose as a customer?
2. Visit the website of two renowned hospitality chains. Evaluate the sites in terms of marketing communication. Do these sites help in promoting or selling the services? Give reasons.
3. Enumerate the different sales promotion techniques being used by a travel industry service provider. What can you suggest to enhance their effectiveness?

CASE STUDY Communicating 'Yatra' Style*

Introduction

India is a promising country for e-commerce. 'According to IAMAI, there are over 2.5 crore online buyers and more than 21.3 crore Internet users (in 2014). The digital commerce market grew by 33% to ₹62,967 crore last year (2013) as against ₹47,349 crore during the corresponding period of 2012. Of the total digital commerce business last year, travel business accounted for 71% valued at ₹44,907 crore.' (PTI 2014b). There are a number of players operating in the area of online ticketing and travel booking such as MakeMyTrip, Yatra, Goibibo, Cleartrip, etc. Let us

take a look at how Yatra is communicating with its customers for marketing itself effectively.

About Yatra

Yatra.com was launched in the August 2006 and 'is a consolidator of travel products. It provides information, pricing, availability, and booking facility for domestic and international air travel, hotel bookings, holiday packages, and bus and railway reservations. It offers a host of travel services designed to make business and leisure travel easier'. Yatra has positioned itself through the tagline 'Creating

*Dr Kirti Dutta

Happy Travellers'. The company boasts of having done '20,000 domestic tickets and 5,000 hotels and holiday packages a day. It provides reservation facility for more than 12,000 hotels in India and over 400,000 hotels around the world'.

'Customers can access Yatra.com through multiple ways: through their user-friendly website, mobile optimised WAP site and applications, 24x7 multilingual call center, a countrywide network of Holiday Lounges, and Yatra Travel Express stores. Yatra.com provides booking facility for all the popular as well as exotic national and international destinations. Yatra.com is today ranked as the leading provider of consumer-direct travel services in India. Yatra.com over the years has emerged as the most trusted travel brand in India and has won the award for the 'Most Popular brand in Travel & leisure Category' by Matrixlab. It has also been voted 'Most Trusted Brand of India' in the online travel category by Brand Equity (in 2010). It won the 'Best Travel Website' award in IAMAI's 2nd Annual India Digital Awards (in 2012). It won the CNBC Awaaz Travel Award (for the third time in a row in November 2012). Yatra won three awards at the India Tourism Awards for its outstanding performance as a tour operator in 2012–13. Organised by the Ministry of Tourism, Government of India, Yatra.com was felicitated for 'Outstanding performance as a Domestic Tour Operator (Rest of India)', 'Outstanding performance as a Domestic Tour Operator in Jammu and Kashmir' and 'Outstanding performance as an Inbound Tour Operator—Cat C'.

'Yatra.com was certified by PCI DSS certification (Payment Card Industry Data Security Standard), the most stringent security standard for organizations that handle cardholder information. With this, Yatra has become one of the major Online Travel Agent's in India to receive this certification that signifies the highest levels of security for card transactions on its portal' in August 2012 (Yatra 2014).

Marketing Communication Strategies Adopted Over the Years

In January 2007, Yatra announced its promotional campaign of 'Kebab mein Haddee' in partnership with Bollywood Blockbuster 'Salaam-e-Ishq'. The customer had to simply do travel booking through its website to meet one of the 'six star couples (Salman Khan–Priyanka Chopra, John Abraham–Vidya Balan, Akshaye Khanna–Ayesha Takia, Anil Kapoor–Juhi Chawla, Govinda–Stephanie, and Sohail Khan–Isha Koppikar) from the movie. The television commercial (TVC) announcing the contest was aired on more than 12 entertainment and news channels including Zee TV, Zee Cinema, Zee News, MTV, Channel V, ETC, Sahara One, HBO, CNBC Awaaz, and CNN IBN'.

Speaking on this promotional offer, Dhruv Shringi, Co founder, Yatra.com, said, 'Yatra.com is extremely excited to partner with the first multi-starrer blockbuster of 2007 and getting associated with some of the biggest stars of Bollywood to spread awareness about Yatra.com. We are looking for innovative opportunities to interact with our customers to promote our brand, and we found Salaam-e-ishq as the most appropriate fit. The exuberance of the brand is also reflected in 'Salaam-e -ishq'.

It roped in Boman Irani as its brand ambassador with the tagline 'here we go'. In November 2007, it launched its 'Yatra Care Program' that includes Yatra Trip Guarantee (where it promised to reimburse ₹500 for every 4 hours of flight delay for customers who had booked through its site), Yatra Miles (its loyalty program), and My Yatra (where they will manage the complete record of every customer)'. In 2008, it announced a compensation of ₹200 for domestic flight delays of over 20 minutes to all air travellers irrespective of the fact where they had booked the tickets and not necessarily Yatra.com users (Money Control 2008a).

In January 2008, it launched its 'Yatra Fair Deal Promise' where 'every time a consumer buys an international air ticket, he would be assured of a "Fair Deal Promise" offering the most competitive prices for all international air tickets. He would also be entitled to receive free shopping vouchers worth ₹4,000 with every air ticket. Also, he can save additional 10% on the base fare if he is an owner of a Master Card. In addition to these savings, the customer has the flexibility to pay only 25% of the air ticket value and the balance amount can be paid at a later date through multiple payment options such as cheque, demand draft, or credit card at no additional costs. To save more money on the international trip, customer can plan his travel as per his budget with the Yatra airfare calendar, which shows the lowest airfares for the month (Business Standard 2009).

In 2008, it introduced another scheme for international travellers called the 'Best Fare Challenge'. As per the Scheme, after booking an international ticket from Yatra.com, if a customer finds a lower International air fare within 24 hours, that is available from either a travel agent or an online travel portal, he/she can avail of the 'Best Fare Challenge'. Under this challenge, Yatra.com will cross-check the fare, and if all the terms and conditions are met, then the customer will be paid double the difference between the fares' (Money Control 2008b).

In 2010, 'Yatra.com launched its new TVC campaign. In its ongoing endeavour to increase customer touch base, this campaign comprising of 3–4 TVCs each designed to focus on the best deal that Yatra. com is offering under various categories. Yatra.com initially had a stereotype image with (Yatra 2014) Boman Irani being their brand ambassador with the tagline 'here we go' and positioning Yatra as the best place for 'less expensive travel options including food, travel and stay' (Mera Event 2010). Keeping in mind, the target audience (youngsters between the age group of 21–30 years and earning less than 5 lakh p.a.), Yatra.com introduced a campaign which was an animated series and has been conceptualized by Rediffusion' (Yatra 2014).

In 2011, on completion of 5 years Yatra announced '30 free holiday packages' and a car as a part of its celebration month. The offer was valid from 1st August 2011 till 30th August 2011. To avail the offer the customers were asked to submit a slogan following a booking with Yatra.com. Every day, one lucky winner was rewarded with a free holiday for two to Goa on the basis of the slogan entries received on www.yatra.com/5years. Towards the end of the 30-day promotion, on 10th September 2011, one lucky winner with the best slogan was chosen for the Grand Prize—a car worth ₹8 lakh (Yatra 2014).

In 2011, Yatra repositioned itself with the campaign 'Creating Happy Travellers' through 'travel o dance', its unique dancing act which expressed the happiness when a customer travels with Yatra.

com and included a performance by the dance group—'Asma'.

In 2012, they launched their 'SBI holiday cum shopping card so that travellers could avail discounts across Yatra.com travel and holiday packages, exclusive previews to its deals and benefits including accelerated rewards on their purchases. Customers win reward points every time they use the card. So, the more they swipe their cards, the closer they get to their next dream holiday' (PTI 2012).

The year 2012 saw Yatra rope in Salman Khan in a double role: that of an investor and brand ambassador. He became Mr Yatra and featured in Yatra's multimedia ad campaigns 'with a marketing budget in excess of ₹30 crore' (Upadhyay and Dewan 2012).

On 11 June, 2013 it announced a '40% off' on last minute hotel bookings across 10,000+ hotels in India. The offer was open to bookings made either on the day of check-in or one day prior to check-in. The maximum discount which was offered through this deal was of ₹1,500/- or 40% of the booking price whichever would be lesser. The offer was valid till 31 July 2013.

On 28 November, 2013 it launched its 'e-gift cards in collaboration with QwikCilver, the pioneer in the gift card solutions category. The concept of gift cards is gaining prominence as being the ideal gifting solution for various occasions like birthdays, weddings, anniversaries, etc. These e-cards launched by Yatra.com will help customers make travel bookings and gift a wide range of flights, hotels and holiday packages to friends and family. The card can be personalised as per the traveller's requirements and preferences and is available in multiple denominations ranging from ₹1,000 to ₹10,000 and more'.

Yatra's Target for 2014

Yatra.com has targeted a 40% revenue growth in 2014–15. According to Yatra.com president Sharat Dhall, 'At present, hotel bookings constitute 15% of the business, holiday packages around 20% and flight bookings account for the rest. During the next financial year, we expect the hotel bookings and holiday packages to grow to around 45%. The company is going to focus on mobile applications. We see a significant traffic coming from mobile handsets. Currently, we are seeing 12% actual sales through channel. We expect this segment to grow tremendously going ahead,' he said.

The company is planning to push more and more products through mobile applications, like holiday packages and car, bus and train bookings in the next few months, he said. Currently, Yatra.com offers only domestic, international flight and hotel bookings through mobile application.' (PTI 2014c).

Other Strategies Undertaken

In 2014, Yatra announced 'a daily bonanza of gifts for a 14 day period starting from 13 February 2014. Travellers booking a domestic flight through Yatra.com could win a tablet, LED TV, or digicam. Under this offer, travellers making bookings starting at ₹10,000 and above would be eligible to participate in the lucky draw and three winners will be selected every day'.

In March 2014, Yatra tied up with Cafe Coffee Day (CCD) and offered customers 'discount coupons on making a purchase of ₹200 and above at any CCD outlet. The promotional code mentioned on the CCD bills could be redeemed online to avail

discounts of ₹300 through desktop & WAP and ₹500 through Mobile app (Android & iOS) on booking any domestic flight and a flat 20% off on hotel bookings.' (Yatra 2014).

In July (valid from 28–31 July) and August (valid from 4–8 August) Yatra.com announced flat 25% off on hotel bookings, with additional 5% off on using the mobile app (where customer had to use promo code 'hotel'). Consumers were informed about the free download of Yatra App on App store, Google play, and Windows store. Alternatively, customers could give a missed call at a number mentioned in the ad. The offer was valid on minimum booking of ₹3,000 and maximum discount offered was of ₹5,000. The print ad was taken out in the Times of India, New Delhi and the consumers were encouraged to log on to the website for more information.

Apart from the various strategies discussed above it also has a presence on Facebook (http://www.facebook.com/Yatra) and twitter (http://twitter.com/#!/yatraholidays). It also has a presence on sites like CouponDunia as can be seen from the following screenshot.

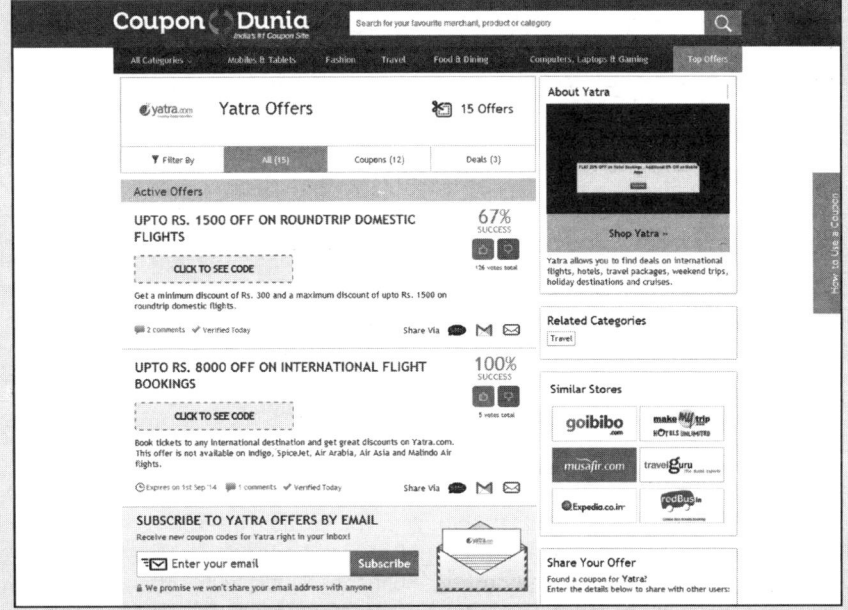

Yatra has a presence on CouponDunia
Source: http://www.coupondunia.in/yatra, accessed on 5 August 2014.

Conclusion

Yatra.com has its pulse on the consumers and has been marketing itself effectively over the years as is visible from their strong performance year-on-year. It has carefully merged its online and offline strategies to provide an integrated experience to its customers.

Questions

1. What is the basis of Yatra's positioning and subsequent repositioning strategy?
2. What different tools of marketing communication can be seen as applied by Yatra.com?
3. Critically evaluate the advertising strategy adopted by Yatra.com.
4. What sales promotion strategies have been adopted by Yatra.com?

Sources: PTI (2014b), 'Indian e-commerce market to clock higher growth in 2014: IAMAI', http://timesofindia.indiatimes.com/tech/tech-news/Indian-e-commerce-market-to-clock-higher-growth-in-2014-IAMAI/articleshow/34970852.cms, accessed on 4 August 2014.

Business Standard (2009), http://www.business-standard.com/article/press-releases/yatra-com-introduces-fair-deal-promise-scheme-for-the-international-travelers-109010501127_1.html, accessed on 5 August 2014.

Money Control (2008a), http://www.moneycontrol.com/news/business/yatracom-to-compensate-for-your-flight-delays_336791.html?utm_source=ref_article, accessed on 5 August 2014.

Money Control (2008b), http://www.moneycontrol.com/news/business/yatracom-intoduce-best-fare-challenge_338346.html?utm_source=ref_article, accessed on 5 August 2014.

PTI (2014c), 'Yatra.com eyes 40% sales growth in FY '15', http://articles.economictimes.indiatimes.com/2014-01-05/news/45882682_1_cent-revenue-growth-holiday-packages-yatra-com, accessed on 5 August 2014.

Upadhyay, A and N. Dewan (2012), 'Salman Khan becomes brand ambassador & investor for travel portal yatra.com,' http://articles.economictimes.indiatimes.com/2012-03-28/news/31249703_1_brand-ambassador-travel-portal-portal-yatra-com, accessed on 5 August 2014.

http://www.coupondunia.in/yatra, accessed on 5 August 2014.

http://www.meraevents.com/blog/2012/03/28/new-brand-ambassador-for-yatra-com-salman-khan, accessed on 5 August 2014.

http://www.yatra.com/fair-deal-promise-on-international-flights, accessed on 5 August 2014.

http://www.yatra.com/international/cheap-flights, accessed on 5 August 2014.

http://www.yatra.com/new-tvc-campaign.html, accessed on 5 August 2014.

http://www.yatra.com/press-releases-2014.html, accessed on 5 August 2014.

REFERENCES

Adenekan, Samuel Abiola (2007), 'Putting CSR into perspective', *Communication World*, San Francisco, vol. 24, no. 6, p. 48.

'Air Deccan anniversary offer', *The Economic Times*, New Delhi, 24 August 2006, p. 4.

'Amazing success story of Shahnaz Husain', *The Times*, Kuwait, 15–31 August 2003.

Anand, Sanjay (2006), 'Now, watch TV via MTNL phone lines', *The Times of India*, 13 October, p. 19.

Aupperle, K. D., A. B. Carroll, and J. D. Hatfield (1985), 'An empirical examination of the relationship between corporate social responsibility and profitability', *Academy of Management Journal*, vol. 28, no. 2, pp. 446–463.

'Avoid targeted ad war, MRTPC tells Maruti, Hyundai', *The Economic Times*, New Delhi, 13 October 2006, p. 4.

Baines, Paul, Chris Fill, Kelly Page, and Piyush Sinha (2013), *Marketing*, Asian Edition, Oxford University Press, Delhi.

Balakrishnan, Ravi (2006), 'Out-of-the-box, on the box, towards 360', Brand Equity, *The Economic Times*, 20 September.

Bird, R., A. D. Hall, F. Momente, and F. Reggiani (2007), 'What corporate social responsibility activities are valued by the market', *Journal of Business Ethics*, vol. 76, pp. 189–206.

Business World (2005), *The Marketing Whitebook*, 2005.

Chhabra, Rahul (2006), 'After cruise nightmare, Rs 32,500 compensation', *The Times of India*, November.

Cottrill, M. T. (1990), 'Corporate social responsibility and the marketplace', *Journal of Business Ethics*, vol. 9, no. 9, pp. 723–729.

Coutinho, Ashley (2006), 'Sunsilk's Gang of Girls goes global', *The Economic Times*, 17 November.

Dasgupta, P. M. (2014), 'E-tailers too jump onto IPL bandwagon for a big score', *The Economic Times*, New Delhi, 14 April, p. 6.

DeLozier, M. Wayne (1976), *The Marketing Communications Process*, McGraw-Hill Book Company, New York.

Dobhal, Shailesh (2006), 'TV fast losing its net worth', *The Economic Times*, p.1.

Doyle, Peter (1976), 'The realities of the product life cycle', *Quarterly Review of Marketing*, Summer.

Doyle, Peter (2002), *Marketing Management and Strategy*, 3rd edn, Pearson Education, Essex, Chapter 5, pp. 130–156.

Engel, James F., Martin R. Warshaw, and Thomas C. Kinnear (1987), *Promotional Strategy Managing and Marketing Communications Process*, 6th edn, Irwin, Chapter 1, Homewood, Illinois.

European Commission (2001), 'Promoting a European framework for corporate social responsibility', European Commission.

Hillenbrand, C. and K. Money (2007), 'Corporate responsibility and corporate reputation: Two separate concepts or two sides of the same coin?', *Corporate Reputation Review*, vol. 10, no. 4, pp. 261–277.

Husted, B. W. and D. B. Allen (2007), 'Corporate social strategy in multinational enterprises: Antecedents and value creation', *Journal of Business Ethics*, vol. 74, pp. 345–361.

Ibrahim, N. A., D. P. Howard, and J. P. Angelidis (2003), 'Board members in the service industry: An empirical examination of the relationship between corporate social responsibility orientation and directorial type', *Journal of Business Ethics*, vol. 4.

Incredible India (2012), *India Tourism Statistics at a Glance — 2011*, Department of Tourism, Indian Government, New Delhi, India.

'Internet and metros', *The Economic Times*, 16 November 2006, p. 4.

Israni, Naveena (2006), 'Infrequent flyer? Miles to go before you can redeem points', *The Economic Times*, New Delhi, 20 October.

Jha, Mayur Shekhar and Joji Thomas Philip (2006), 'Advertisers face penalty for misleading claims', *The Economic Times*, 11 August, p. 5.

Jobber, David (2001), *Principles and Practices of Marketing*, McGraw-Hill Publishing Company, Chapters 11–15, Berkshire.

Jones, Marc T. and M. Haigh (2007), 'The transnational corporation and new corporate citizenship theory: A critical analysis', *The Journal of Corporate Citizenship*, vol. 27, pp. 51–69.

Joyner, B. E. and D. Payne (2002), 'Evolution and implementation: A study of values, business ethics, and corporate social responsibility', *Journal of Business Ethics*, vol. 41, no. 4, pp. 297–311.

Juholin, E. (2004), 'For business or the good of all? A Finnish approach to corporate social responsibility', *Corporate Governance*, vol. 4, no. 3, pp. 20–31.

Kaushik, Neha (2003), 'The promise in promotions', *Businessline*, Chennai, 4 September.

Khan, A. F. and A. Atkinson (1987), 'Managerial attitudes to social responsibility: A comparative study in India and Britain', *Journal of Business Ethics*, vol. 6, pp. 419–432.

Kotler, Philip and Kevin Lane Keller (2006), *Marketing Management*, 12th edn, Prentice Hall of India Private Limited, New Delhi, p. 193.

Kotler, Philip, John T. Bowens, and James C. Makens (2006), *Marketing for Hospitality and Tourism*, 4th edn, Pearson Education Inc., New Jersey, Chapter 9.

Krishna, Sonali and Haresh Soneji (2006), 'TV ad clutter triples in India but not everyone's watching', *The Economic Times*, New Delhi, 5 September, p. 4.

Krishnan, Raghu (2006a), 'Coffee cafes kick off World Cup mood', *The Economic Times*.

Krishnan, Raghu (2006b), 'Innovation wins the day for Coffee Café', *The Economic Times*, 5 September, p. 4.

Lagrosen, Stefan (2005), 'Effects of the Internet on the marketing communication of service companies', *Journal of Services Marketing*, vol. 19, no. 2, pp. 63–69.

Levy, Margi and Philip Powell (2002), 'SME Internet adpotion: Towards a transporter model', presented at 15th Bled Electronic Commerce conference e-Reality: Constructing the e-Economy, Bled, Slovenia, 17–19 June 2002.

Lovelock, Christopher and Jochen Wirtz (2006), *Services Marketing*, 5th edn, Pearson Education, New Delhi, Chapter 5.

'Maruti advertisement', *The Times of India*, 14 August 2006.

Newman, A. A. (2013), 'Promotions celebrate those willing to just get up and go', *The Economic Times*, 12 July, p. 4.

'Overall ranking of top 25 ad agencies', Brand Equity, *The Economic Times*, New Delhi, 24 May 2006, p. 4.

Perrini, F., A. Russo, and A. Tencati (2007), 'CSR strategies of SMEs and large firms: Evidence from Italy', *Journal of Business Ethics*, vol. 74, pp. 285–300.

Pickton, David and Amanda Broderick (2001), *Integrated Marketing Communications*, Pearson Education Ltd, Harlow, Essex.

Ray, Michael (1973), 'A decision sequence analysis of developments in marketing', *Journal of Marketing*, vol. 37, no. 1, p. 31.

Razdan, (2006), 'Filmmakers are at advantage in Rs 13,000 crore advertising market', *The Economic Times*, 3 March.

Sacconi, Lorenzo (2007), 'A social contract account for CSR as an extended model of corporate governance (II): Compliance, reputation, and reciprocity', *Journal of Business Ethics*, vol. 75, pp. 77–96.

Scaria, (2006), 'Kerala fisherfolk finally discover how to use net', *The Economic Times*, 11 August, p.18.

Sharma, Samidha (2006), 'FIFA cup: Big boys' ad party', *The Economic Times*, New Delhi, 7 June, p. 4.

Sharma, Samidha (2006), 'Happily married: Brands, show biz', *The Economic Times*, 15 June, p. 4.

Silberhorn, D. and R. C. Warren (2007), 'Defining corporate social responsibility: A view from big companies in Germany and the UK', *European Business Review*, vol. 19, no. 5, pp. 352–372.

Singh, Sanjay K. (2006), 'Cops want key roads cleared of hoardings', *The Economic Times*, 10 November, p. 4.

Stanwick, P. A. and S. D. Stanwick (1998), 'The determinants of corporate social performance: An empirical examination', *American Business Review*, vol. 16, no. 1, pp. 86–93.

Stoll, M. L. (2007), 'Backlash hits business ethics: Finding effective strategies for communicating the importance of corporate social responsibility', *Journal of Business Ethics*, vol. 78, pp. 17–24.

Superbrands, (2009), 'Superbrands: An insight into India's strongest consumer brands Volume III', Superbrands India Private Limited, Gurgaon.

The Economic Times (2014), 'Telcos withdraw free minutes to boost bottomlines', *The Economic Times*, 16 April, p. 6.

'The effectiveness effect', *The Economic Times*, New Delhi, 20 November, p. 4.

The Marketing Whitebook, Business World, 2008.

'Value ad net gain', *The Economic Times*, 31 October 2006, New Delhi, p. 4.

Verma, Meenakshi and Mayur Shekhar Jha (2006), 'Multiplexes the new battlefield for ad wars', *The Economic Times*, 15 June 2006, p. 4.

Vivek, T. R. (2006), 'Nothing beats word-of-mouth in India', *The Economic Times*, 24 October, p. 4.

'Warne's hair ad violates British rules', *The Times of India*, New Delhi, 18 May 2006, p. 32.

Wasson, Chester R. (1968), 'How predictable are fashion and other product life cycles', *Journal of Marketing*, vol. 32, no. 3, pp. 36–43.

Wasson, Chester R. (1978), *Dynamic Competition Strategy and Product Life Cycles*, Austin Press, Austin.

Weber, John A. (1976), 'Planning corporate growth with inverted product life cycles', *Long Range Planning*, October.

Women in Management Review, (2004), 'CSR activities generate higher performance—official', *Women in Management Review*, vol. 19, no. 5–6, pp. 280–281.

Wymbs (2000), 'How e-comerce is transforming and internationalizing service industries', *Journal of Services Marketing*, vol. 14, pp. 463–478.

Zeithaml V. A. and M. Bitner (2000), *Services Marketing*, 2nd edn, Tata McGraw-Hill Publishing Company Limited, New Delhi.

Adex India Online (2014), http://www.indiantelevision.org.in/tamadex/y2k13/sep/tam16.php, accessed on 19 July 2014.

Amway India, http://www.amwayindia.com/htmls/BusinessOpportunity.html, accessed on 29 August 2008.

Amway India, http://www.amwayindia.com/htmls/BusinessOpportunity.html, accessed on 2 September 2008.

ASCI (2014), http://www.ascionline.org/index.php/nams.html, accessed on 19 July 2014.

Basu, Aparimita (2006), 'Media laws and overview', http://www.legalserviceindia.com/articles/media.htm, accessed on 28 November 2006.

Business Line (2006), 'Aviva roadshows across Kerala', http://www.blonnet.com/2006/09/16/stories/2006091 601 861 900.htm, accessed on 1 December 2006.

Business Standard (2009), http://www.business-standard.com/article/press-releases/yatra-com-introduces-fair-deal-promise-scheme-for-the-international-travelers-109010501127_1.html, accessed on 5 August 2014.

Delhi outdoor advertising policy (2008), http://www.cpcb.nic.in/upload/NewItems/NewItem_119_Delhi_outdoor_advt_policy2008.pdf, accessed on 26 July 2014.

Direct Marketing Association of India, http://www.directmarketing-association-india.org/DM_report_outline.asp, accessed on 18 August 2008.

Economic Times (2006), www.indiaontop.net, *The Economic Times*, New Delhi, 17 August.

educationtimes.com Dial-a-career ad (2014), *The Times of India*, dated 25 July 2014, p. 13.

Harjani, P(2011), 'India's tourist flock to Spain', http://travel.cnn.com/mumbai/life/indian-movie-boosts-spanish-tourism-694426, accessed on 3 August 2014.

http://get.hike.in, accessed on 3 August 2014.

http://www.adclubbombay.com/affiliates.htm, accessed on 12 November 2006.

http://www.bestmediainfo.com/2014/07/askme-ropes-in-ranbir-kapoor-to-launch-bapp-of-all-apps-campaign, accessed on 3 August 2014

http://www.coupondunia.in/yatra, accessed on 5 August 2014.

http://www.cuponation.in/yatra-coupons, accessed on 5 August 2014.

http://www.indiantelevision.com/tamadex/y2k8/apr/tam.14.php, accessed on 18 August 2008.

http://www.indiatvnews.com/news/india/india-s-top-states-with-highest-women-literacy-rate-31348.html, accessed on 25 July 2014.

http://www.itchotels.in/responsibleluxury/, accessed on 5 August 2014.

http://www.meraevents.com/blog/2012/03/28/new-brand-ambassador-for-yatra-com-salman-khan, accessed on 5 August 2014.

http://www.museedelapub.org/pubgb/virt/mp/benet-tion/pub_benetton.html, accessed on 15 November 2006.

http://www.time.com/time/magazine/article/0,9171, 9591 58,00.html, accessed on 16 November 2006.

http://www.time.com/time/magazine/article/09171 95591 5800.html, accessed on 16 November 2006.

http://www.tribuneindia.com/2003/20030404/chd.htm, accessed on 1 December 2006.

http://www.vgc.in, accessed on 30 October 2006.

http://www.yatra.com/fair-deal-promise-on-international-flights, accessed on 5 August 2014.

http://www.yatra.com/international/cheap-flights, accessed on 5 August 2014.

http://www.yatra.com/new-tvc-campaign.html, accessed on 5 August 2014.

http://www.yatra.com/press-releases-2014.html, accessed on 5 August 2014.

Indian Express (2014), Tech Desk, available from http://indianexpress.com/articles/technology-others/hike-messenger-claims-15m-users-powered-by-young-users, accessed on 3 August 2014.

Indian Television.com's AdEx India Analysis, http://www.indiantelevision.com/tamadex/y2k8/apr/tam14.php, accessed on 18 August 2008.

Juxt Consult, http://www.juxtconsult.com/syndicated_research/indiaonline2007/internet_report_mail.asp, accessed on 20 August 2008.

Lindstorm, Martin (2008), 'Inside Wal-Mart's sustainability program', http://www.adage.com/brightcover/lineup.php, accessed on 21 February 2008.

Madden, Normandy, 'Radio ad revenue grows 39 per cent', http://adage.com, accessed on 1 December 2006.

Manju, V. (2012), 'Indian outbound tourists on rise', *The Times of India* (online), available from http://articles.timesofindia.indiatimes.com/2011-07-21/mumbai/32776514_1_indian-arrivals-tourism-australia-indian-visitors, accessed on 4 August 2014.

McKinsey (2012), file:///C:/Users/windows/Downloads/Online_and_Upcoming_The_internets_impact_on_India%20(1).pdf, accessed on 3 August 2014.

Mehra, P. (2008), 'Products, even news bulletins continue to cash in on IPL', http://www.livemint.com/Articles/PrintArticle.aspx, accessed on 22 June 2008.

Menon, Rashmi (2014), 'Effie 2013: Lowe Lintas clinches agency of the year title', http://www.afaqs.com/news/story/39726_Effie-2013:-Lowe-Lintas-clinches-Agency-of-the-Year-title, accessed on 4 December 2014.

Money Control (2008a) http://www.moneycontrol.com/news/business/yatracom-to-compensate-for-your-flight-delays_336791.html?utm_source=ref_article, accessed on 5 August 2014.

Money Control (2008b), http://www.moneycontrol.com/news/business/yatracom-intoduce-best-fare-challenge_338346.html?utm_source=ref_article, accessed on 5 August 2014.

Napier, J. (2014), 'Madison world sees ad spends growing 16.8% this year', http://www.dnaindia.com/money/report-madison-world-sees-ad-spends-growing-168-this-year-1963566, accessed on 26 July 2014.

Pitch Madison Media Outlook (2012) (online), available from www.madisonindia.com/whatsnew/pdf/pitchmadisonmediaadoutlook202012.pdf, accessed on 5 September 2014.

Pitch Madison Media Outlook (2013) (online), available from www.madisonindia.com/whatsnew/pdf/pitch%20madison%20media%20ad%20outlook%202013.pdf, accessed on 5 September 2014.

PTI (2014a), 'No of TV channels has gone up to 788 now: I&B ministry', http://articles.economictimes.indiatimes.com/2014-02-19/news/47489920_1_fm-channels-tv-channels-community-radio, accessed on 25 July 2014.

PTI (2014b), 'Indian e-commerce market to clock higher growth in 2014: IAMAI', accessed from http://timesofindia.indiatimes.com/tech/tech-news/Indian-e-commerce-market-to-clock-higher-growth-in-2014-IAMAI/articleshow/34970852.cms, accessed on 4 August 2014.

PTI (2014c), 'Yatra.com eyes 40% sales growth in FY '15', http://articles.economictimes.indiatimes.com/2014-01-05/news/45882682_1_cent-revenue-growth-holiday-packages-yatra-com, accessed on 5 August 2014.

Radhakrishnan, S. (2008), 'Sri Lanka's Jetwing Hotels plans India foray', http://www.thehindubusinessline.com/2008/03/23/stories/2008032351110300.htm, accessed on 9 September 2008.

Reuters (2013), 'Stop, drop and get out of town: Hilton honors reveals America's spontaneity', http://www.reuters.com/article/2013/07/30/va-hilton-hhonors-idUSnBw305481a+100+BSW20130730, accessed on 26 July 2013.

Sheikh, Aminah (2008), http://in.rediff.com/money/2008/feb/20ipl.htm, accessed on 20 August 2008.

Taj (2008), http://www.tajhotels.com/AboutTaj/Careers/Corporate_Social.htm, accessed on 10 September 2008.

Taj Hotels, http://www.tajhotels.com/Leisure/Taj%20View%20Hotel,AGRA/facilities.htm, accessed on 29 August 2008.

TechDesk (2014), http://indianexpress.com/article/technology/technology-others/hike-messenger-claims-15m-users-powered-by-young-users, accessed on 3 August 2014.

The Advertising Standards Council of India, http://www.ascionline.org/five/recentdvpt.htm, accessed on 28 November 2006.

The Marketing Whitebook (2014), Business World.

UNESCO report, http://unesdoc.unesco.org/images/0014/001461/1461 92e.pdf, accessed on 29 August 2008.

United Colors of Benetton, http://www.benetton-group.com/40years-press/img_our_campaigns.html, accessed on 2 September 2008.

United Colors of Benetton, http://www.museede-lapub.org/ pubgb/virt/mp/benetton/pub_benetton.html, accessed on 15 November 2006.

Upadhyay, A and N. Dewan (2012), 'Salman Khan becomes brand ambassador & investor for travel portal yatra.com', http://articles.economictimes.indiatimes.com/2012-03-28/news/31249703_1_brand-ambassador-travel-portal-portal-yatra-com, accessed on 5 August 2014.

Vaid (2008), 'Brands that prick the conscience', http://www.moneycontrol.com/india/news/presse-lease/brands-that-prickconscience/20/34/259806, accessed on 11 September 2008.

Managing Distribution Channels in Service Industry

OBJECTIVES

After reading this chapter you will be able to understand the

- importance of distribution in services
- relevance of different channels in the distribution of services
- concept of distribution channels
- dimensions of a global distribution system

Booking Tickets with Indian Railways

Indian Railways known for its pioneering efforts in Internet-based ticket reservations did not rest on this laurel alone. In 2013 the 'e-ticketing site booked approximately 48% of the total reserved tickets on the Indian Railways network.' To take the e-ticketing experience to a new level and make train tickets available at the customers' doorstep, IRCTC revamped the site so that it could book 7,200 tickets per minute (as compared to 2,000 tickets per minute till then) and handle 1.2 lakh users as against 40,000 users earlier (PTI 2013a). 'To tap the potential of mobile phone market in India and thereby facilitate the common man, by providing him anywhere, anytime, and hassle free booking option' IRCTC launched the facility of booking tickets on 'non-Internet based mobile phones on 1 July 2013' through SMS (Indian Railways 2014). This was done keeping in mind the fact that 'less than 5% of India owns a smartphone among the 80% who own mobile phones in India' (Railnews 2013).

'IRCTC also took a slew of measures for smooth running of its system such as blocking of agents during the initial two hours of booking from 8–10 am and Tatkal ticket booking from 10 am to 12 noon respectively. It was done to prevent illegal booking through automated software by touts so as to make the system available only to the individual users during this period,' as this period draws the maximum rush. To facilitate the users further, IRCTC (along with Microsoft) 'developed an IRCTC App for Windows 8' so that there was 'a new channel of booking e-tickets in addition to the existing portal' (PTI 2013b) and SMS facility.

After going through this chapter, you will be able to answer the following questions:

1. Discuss the different strategies adopted by IRCTC to reach out to its customers and make ticket booking easier for them.
2. Discuss why IRCTC needs to take such initiatives.

INTRODUCTION

In marketing, the distribution of services holds an important place. Services are inseparable, that is, there is simultaneous production and consumption of services. Due to increased competition in the marketplace, there are a number of options available to customers. Thus, the distribution or place element of the services marketing mix is strategically important as the service providers need to be present at convenient locations when customers require them.

DISTRIBUTION

Distribution includes the flow of services from service provider to customer and can be performed by service providers themselves or by a service intermediary, such as a travel agent booking tickets on major airlines for customers. For example, a few years ago if one had to book tickets on Indian Railways, they had the option of going to the railway station and standing in queue or getting it from various agents. But IRCTC changed all that by providing a number of options for customers so that the tickets were available at their doorstep (see the opening example). In services, the customer has to be brought to the service provider rather than the service product being delivered to the customers. Thus, location is of prime importance; by occupying strategic locations the service provider can draw the customers. The different characteristics of services make the distribution of services more direct than distribution for physical goods. The network through which distribution takes place is known as the distribution channel and consists of independent organizations involved in the process of making a service available for consumption by customers. In Chapter 1, we studied the classification of services in relation to place and time. Accordingly, services can be of the following types (Lovelock 1983).

Customer goes to the service organization   This includes services such as hospitals, hospitality industry, and transportation services (such as bus, rail, and air).

Service organization comes to the customer   This includes personal services such as cleaning and laundry and repair services such as plumbing and electrical repairs.

Customer and the service organization transact at arms length (mail or electronic communications)   This includes broadcast services and communications services such as telephones and mobiles.

FACTORS AFFECTING CHOICE OF DISTRIBUTION CHANNELS

Distribution holds an important position in the purchase of all the three types of services. The distribution factors affecting their choice can be divided into:
- factors affecting the choice of service provider by customers
- factors affecting the choice of distribution channels by service providers.

Factors Affecting the Choice of Service Provider by Customers

The various factors are discussed in this section.

Outlet type   The type of service provided and its requirement by customers at the time of purchase, decides the selection of the service provider. For example, in medical services, if a person has a heart problem he/she will choose a hospital providing a cardiac specialist but if he/she is suffering from a common cold the choice of service provider will be different. The same is the case with the hospitality industry where a person wanting a Chinese meal will visit a service provider selling this instead of say an Italian cuisine provider. The distribution of these services requires their presence at convenient locations, which are easily accessible by the customers. The timing of the availability of the services is also equally important.

Outlet numbers   The number of outlets operated by the service provider also has an implication on the distribution because the more the number of outlets, the better distributed the service provider is, and so the chances of customers availing the services are also more. For example, McDonald's, one of the leading global food service retailers, has more than 35,000 local restaurants serving nearly 70 million people in more than 100 countries each day (McDonald's 2014). In India, McDonald's has opened its outlets at railway stations, airports, malls, etc. (Exhibit 11.1). Kentucky Fried Chicken has more than 18,000 restaurants in 115 countries and territories around the world (KFC 2014). In India there were 223 restaurants (in 2012) across 35 cities and KFC plans to have 500 restaurants across 75 cities by the year 2015 (KFC 2012) Thus, more the number of outlets, easier it is for the company to reach out to more number of people for its services delivery.

Accessibility   There are a number of service providers in the market and so there are unlimited choices for the customers. Thus, to be the first choice of the customer the service provider has to be easily available to the customers. For example, a number of banks are forming ATM sharing arrangements wherein the customer has the option of using ATMs of other banks for money transactions. From 16 banks who were members of the National Financial Switch (NFS)—Allahabad Bank, Andhra Bank, Bank of Baroda, Corporation Bank, ICICI Bank, IDBI Bank, J&K Bank, Karnataka Bank, Punjab National

---

Exhibit 11.1   **Now Mac Express at Stations and Airports**

McDonald's, the major American fast food joint, has launched a number of outlets in India since its first restaurant opened in New Delhi in 1996. This was followed by a Drive-Thru and a disabled friendly store in Noida (UP) in 1997. The year 1999 saw it launch an outlet in a mall (at Ansal Plaza, New Delhi) followed by a highway restaurant located at Mathura (UP).

In 2001 it launched the first thematic restaurant at Connaught Place (New Delhi). In 2002, its restaurant in a food court was launched at 3C's in Lajpat Nagar (New Delhi) along with its restaurant at the Delhi Metro Station and at Inter State Bus Terminus (New Delhi). In 2003 it launched a Dessert Kiosk at Faridabad (Haryana). It also started its Delivery Service in the year 2004 in New Delhi and in 2006 McDelivery on Bicycles was flagged off at Chandni Chowk (Delhi). The same year (2006) saw it open its 100th restaurant in India. In 2007 it opened its restaurant at Domestic Airport, New Delhi. In 2008 it launched its first 24 hours restaurant at Old Delhi Railway Station (McDonald's, 2013).

Source: Based on McDonald's (2013).

Bank, United Western Bank, Dhanalakshmi Bank, Tamilnadu Mercantile Bank, South Indian Bank, Oriental Bank of Commerce, Karur Vysya Bank, and Yes Bank in 2006 it has grown by leaps and bounds and there are 78 direct members, with 1,66,928 ATMs (National Payments Corporation of India 2014). The NFS allows the customers of these banks to use ATMs of other member banks for money transactions (*Times* 2006).

Location   The location of the service provider determines the type of services they are going to provide. For example, in the hospitality sector, a service offer targeting adventurous customers will be located in the mountainous region. This allows the service provider to offer options of trekking, paragliding, etc., and customers visiting hill stations can avail of these opportunities.

Factors Affecting the Choice of Distribution Channels by Service Providers

The various factors are explained in this section.

Resource considerations   When the distribution of the services is made directly to the customer, the number of outlets is important in order to capture a wider customer base. If the service provider has sufficient resources (financial, human resource, etc.) to monitor and supply quality services at multiple sites, they can directly open their branches at different locations. However, another option is adopting the franchisee route. In franchising, the service provider (franchiser) charges fees from the franchisee, and in return, allows the franchisee to sell the services under a fixed format (decided by the franchiser) and use the brand name. McDonald's has a strength of over 2,8400 franchisees and along with the use of the trademarks, it provides support in areas of operations, human resource and training, marketing, etc. (McDonald's Corporation 2014). Choice Hotels International markets more than 6,300 hotels across 3,540 countries. In India, the company is represented by four brands—Quality Inn, Comfort Inn, Clarion Hotels, and Sleep Inn and Cambria Suites. 'These brands offer an unbeatable choice—covering market segment from full service, upscale to limited service mid-scale hotels'. They franchise the Quality Inn and Comfort Inn brand hotels throughout India with hotels in Bengaluru, Ahmedabad, Amritsar etc. (Choice Hotels India 2007)

The major benefit to the franchiser is that it increases distribution of their services, expands the brand, and gets revenues from sales; but the disadvantages are that they have to manage the channels in the form of monitoring the franchisees to ensure consistency in delivery as per their standards, managing channel conflicts, etc. The benefit to the franchisee is that they get consultation and support from the franchisers in the form of operations, marketing support, etc., which helps them to set up the business faster. However, the disadvantages are that they have to pay fees and royalty to the franchiser, face restrictions in terms of products offered and services delivered, and the poor service delivery of a sister franchisee can adversely affect the reputation of the entire chain (Kotler et al. 2006).

Choice of intermediaries   There are different choices available to the service provider. These are shown in Fig. 11.1.

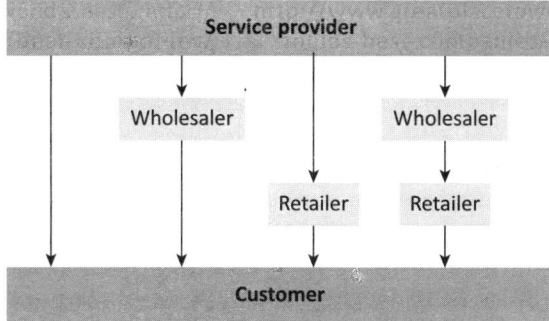

Fig. 11.1   Distribution channels in services

The service provider can directly supply the services to the customers without going through a channel intermediary. All the nationalized banks open their offices to directly cater to the needs of the customers.

The second option available is going through a channel intermediary—a wholesaler, who in turn sells to customers. An example is the different tour wholesalers offering assembled packages. The third option is again through an intermediary—a retailer. Most of the retail chains supply the products from the manufacturer to the customers. For example, Reliance retail chains and Big Bazaar retail chains in India. Reliance has set up rural business hubs in Punjab, Haryana, Himachal Pradesh, Uttaranchal, and West Bengal. These hubs act as procurement centres for grains and milk, which will give Reliance a cost advantage. Thus, Reliance plans not only to sell these through its retail chains, but also to supply to other retail players such as Big Bazaar (Monga and Philip 2006). In such a situation, Reliance is acting as a wholesaler and Big Bazaar is a retailer selling the products directly to the customers—the fourth option in Fig. 11.1. Service providers can also use a combination of different channels. For example, Vodafone and Airtel are selling through retailers and also providing services directly to customers through company-owned outlets such as Hindustan Petroleum fuel stations, and travel agents of which 200 agents are grocery sellers, small vendors, etc.

National and state tourist agencies are an excellent way to promote services related to tourism in a particular nation or state. For example, the Ministry of Tourism in India releases the 'Incredible India' advertisements promoting tourism to different states in India and the advertisements promoting tourism to Kerala sponsored by Department of Tourism, Government of Kerala (Kerala Tourism 2006).

Market need   An organization decides on the number of distribution outlets keeping in mind the need of the market. A case in point is Twenty Four Seven Convenience Stores (as the name suggests it is a retail store chain that is open 24 hours a day seven days a week). According to Samir Modi, president of Twenty Four Seven Convenience Stores 'It's now time to increase the footprint fast. The concept is there, the brand is there and there is demand for round-the-clock-shopping, be it emergency shopping, a hop-in option or for impulse shopping...the audience includes double-income households, busy professionals with no time during the day or youths seeking instant gratification.'

There are plans to increase the number of stores from 40 stores (in 2014) to 5,000 stores (by 2019). Of these about 500 outlets will be in Delhi alone, 100 in each metro, and 20 stores each in different smaller towns (Mitra 2014).

STRATEGIES FOR DISTRIBUTION

Distribution of services can be achieved in a number of ways as discussed in the earlier section. Keeping in mind the nature of the product, kind of image an organization wants to portray, and the coverage area, the organization can go for intensive, selective, and exclusive distribution.

Intensive distribution   This strategy enables the service provider to make available its services through as many service providers or outlets as possible. For example, if we look at the banking industry, the unique selling proposition of public sector banks is the number of branches present throughout the country. The postal system still has a number of branches in remote areas too. The services of Indian Oil, Bharat Petroleum, etc., can be availed through a number of petrol pumps located throughout the length and breadth of the country. Indian Railways, apart from its online presence, has a number of booking counters from where railway tickets can be booked. It has also tied up with the postal department and Indian Oil Corporation, so that a customer can also book railway tickets through these outlets. The opening exhibit shows that tickets can now be booked even through non-Internet based mobile phones simply by sending SMS.

Selective distribution   In this type of distribution, the service provider chooses some intermediaries to make available its services to the consumers. In this case, the organization does not have to worry about managing a number of service outlets and can have a greater control over the distribution system. For example, an airline can choose travel agents to sell its services from a number of travel agents present in a city.

Exclusive distribution   In exclusive distribution, the number of intermediaries is limited and as the name suggests, it involves sole dealing arrangements between the service producer and the intermediary/retailer. This is generally done to create an image of exclusivity and class. For example, Lladro, the Spanish luxury porcelain brand, has entered into exclusive shop-in-shop arrangements with Ethos Swiss Watch Studio in Chandigarh. It plans to open exclusive outlets in Indian metros. According to Anisha Gaur, Manager (Retail Operations), Lladro, 'The exclusive stores are flagship stores, which create a complete brand experience, including the perfect merchandise, music, and customer service. Our three-year plan for India will focus mainly on metros and mini metros and we will have our exclusive stores only in metros' (*Retailer* 2008).

Another strategy for distribution of services is *franchising*. The word is derived from the French meaning 'to be free from servitude'. The rapid development of franchising is attributed to the growth of services-sector activities. Franchising involves selling a business service to an independent investor who has working capital, but little or no prior experience. Services generally require business format 'package' franchising in which the franchiser transfers most elements necessary for the local entity to establish a business and run it profitably. This may include 'managerial assistance in setting up and running local operations', advertising and marketing support, research and development, etc. Companies such as Twenty Four Seven Convenience Stores (Mitra 2014), McDonald's, Pizza Hut, and Starbucks, follow this model (Hollensen 1998). Depending upon the intensive, selective, and exclusive distribution an organization is going for, it can choose the number of franchisees in a particular geographic area.

MANAGING DISTRIBUTION CHANNELS

Management of the channels lies with the service organization. Jobber (2001) gave the following issues to be addressed while managing channels:

Selection   This consists of the choice of channel members. The different candidates must be identified and selection criteria should be drawn so that all the channel members are at par. When distributing its products in Russia, Panasonic failed to take this into consideration and faced a major problem as is evident from Exhibit 11.2.

Motivation   Service organizations can motivate channel members to act as franchisees. For example, Mother's Pride advertisements motivate people to be a master franchisee and individual franchisees by focusing on love, respect, and trust.

They further motivate people to act as master and individual franchisees by highlighting the fact that by creating a unique educational landmark they would be known and respected in their town, that is, they would get name, fame, fortune, and goodwill.

Training   Most of the organizations train their franchisee to maintain the standards expected of them. McDonald's and KFC both focus on the training they provide to their franchisees. In KFC, which is a part of Yum! Brands, each brand has a franchise business coach (FBC) and/or franchise business leader (FBL) to provide business insight and instruction to the franchisees. As the franchisees move into steady-state operations, the FBC or FBL keeps them abreast of important business initiatives, organizes key regional training activity, and acts as the primary point of contact (KFC 2006). By providing training, organizations instil product knowledge in franchisees giving them the confidence to market their services (Jobber 2001).

Exhibit 11.2   **Russian Retailers Threaten Boycott of Panasonic**

Major Russian electronic retailers have threatened to boycott products from Japan's Panasonic in 2006. They had accused the Japanese company of selling goods to intermediaries who often paid no import duties, or lacked certification. A German retailer was found selling Panasonic flat televisions at hefty discounts to its customers. The Russian office of Panasonic denied all charges, but the situation was not easy to handle. According to them, the 'grey' imports charges are baseless. The retailers aim to solve the issue as a joint effort and also seem to be ready to sacrifice immediate profits to set rules that are in line with Russian practices.

Evaluation Evaluation of the distribution channel members at regular intervals is necessary to provide an insight into the functioning of the channel intermediary. The idea is to check for standard deviations in supply of service, identify the reasons for the same, and try to remove these so that the level of service is maintained. However, if after repeated efforts the channel intermediary shows no signs of improving, it is best to drop that channel member. Different criteria for evaluation can be sales performance, profitability, quality of service provided, etc.

Managing conflict The distribution process consists of a number of independent organizations working together for a common goal. Ideally, they should all work together keeping the best interest of all concerned in mind. However, individual members rarely take this view. They all try to maximize their own gain and then channel conflicts are bound to occur. Broadly, two types of channel conflicts are observed—horizontal conflict and vertical conflict.

Horizontal conflict This is the difference in opinion between channel members at the same level. For example, a McDonald's franchise in Delhi might compromise on the personnel employed for delivery of service to increase his/her profits, but this would in turn affect the quality of service and may dissatisfy the customers. This dissatisfaction would be against McDonald's and so would affect the perception of the customers towards all the McDonald's outlets. This would result in conflict among the franchisees and cause horizontal conflict.

Vertical conflict This is the result of disagreement between different levels of the same channel. For example, Reliance (wholesaler) might have a disagreement with Big Bazaar (a retailer) regarding delivery of products. This would result in a vertical conflict (Kotler et al. 2006).

As a service provider the onus for the amicable resolution of the conflict lies with them. They should think in terms of trying to create win-win situations for all. They can also try and avoid conflicts by organizing regular meetings with channel partners so as to create an environment of mutual trust and understanding. To avoid horizontal conflict, market partitioning can be done or areas may be allotted to different members for providing services. Jobber (2001) also lists coercion or use of force to garner compliance from channel members and the effective but expensive way of buying out the channel member (channel ownership).

ONLINE DISTRIBUTION

Internet penetration is growing at a phenomenal rate and has shown a tenfold increase from 1999 to 2013. The first billion Internet users were reached in 2005, the next billion (i.e., 2 billion figure) was achieved in 2010 and the three billion figure is expected to be reached by end of 2014. As of 1 July 2014, there were 2.92 billion Internet users, which is 40.4% of the world population (Internet Live Stats 2014). In India Internet penetration is 19.19% and accounts for 243 million Internet users. Compared to United States, which has 279.8 million Internet users representing 86.75% of the population with

Internet (Internet Live Stats 2014), there is a lot of opportunity waiting to be explored in India.

The e-retailing format has been successful in developed markets especially in categories such as books, durables, phones, and apparel. Many brick and mortar retailers have started e-retail operations in response to the growth of stand-alone e-tailers (Mulky 2013). Internet penetration in India was traditionally considered too low to support e-retailing, but the rise in the number of Internet users along with growing acceptability of online payments, proliferation of Internet-enabled devices, and favorable demographics are the key factors driving the growth of e-commerce in the country. The evolution of e-commerce in India can be divided into two phases based on emergence of various sub-segments. August 1995 witnessed the launch of Internet in India via dial-up in 6 cities. The years 1996–2000 account for the first phase of growth and saw launch of B2B portals, online matrimonial, and online job portals. The period 2000–2005 saw muted activity in this space' as the 'IT downturn in 2000 led to the collapse of more than 1000 e-commerce businesses in India. The year 2005 was marked with the entry of low cost carriers (LCCs) in the Indian aviation sector. This year was the beginning of the second wave of e-commerce in India and is continuing till now. People flocked online to search for travel related information and to book tickets. The ripple effect was that consumers were now comfortable shopping online and hence the growth of online retail (Ernest and Young 2013) from ₹91 billion in 2011–12 to ₹504 billion in 2015–16 (*The Hindu* 2014). Yet, it remains a nascent portion of the overall e-commerce segment in India where the travel business dominates with about two-thirds share. However, the equation is changing fast enough to pose a threat to brick-and-mortar retailers—not just of books, music, and electronics, but also apparel and grocery.

EFFECT OF THE INTERNET—GLOBAL DISTRIBUTION SYSTEM

According to Kotler et al. (2006), the Internet is an effective marketing tool for hospitality and travel companies. The Internet is an effective distribution system allowing for the purchase of services from any corner without visiting the store or service provider. The online payment system further facilitates the purchase of services. (For more details on Internet marketing, see Chapter 10 on Services Promotion). The distribution of services such as travel, airline reservation, hotel/rail/cruise/reservation, car rentals, etc., via the Internet deserves a mention of the global distribution system (GDS). In the 1960s, GDS was first developed by the airline industry to keep track of flight schedules, availability, and prices. The conceptualization of the Sabre system began in 1953 with a chance meeting between American Airlines President C.R. Smith and R. Blair Smith, a senior sales representative for IBM, on an American Airlines flight from Los Angeles to New York. Their conversation about the travel industry sparked the idea of a data processing system that would create a complete airline seat reservation and make all the data instantly available electronically to any agent, at any place. This idea became a reality six years later when American Airlines and IBM jointly announced a plan to develop a semi-automatic business research environment, better known as Sabre. 'The revolutionary system was the first real-time business application of computer technology. It enabled American Airlines to leapfrog from handwritten passenger reservation information in the 1950s, to an automated system. In 1960, the first Sabre reservations system was installed in Briarcliff Manor, New York. The mainframe system was state-of-the-art technology and processed 84,000 telephone calls per day. When the network was completed in 1964, it became the largest, private, real-time data processing system, second only to the US government's system. It became an integral part of AMR Corporation, saving American Airlines 30% on its investments in staff alone (Sabre Travel Network 2006).

However, the travel agents were spending excessive time in manually entering reservation details. To facilitate them, Sabre (owned by American Airlines) and Apollo (United) installed their proprietary internal reservation systems in travel agencies in the mid-1970s; they were among the first e-commerce companies facilitating B2B e-commerce. The automation of the reservation process for travel agents increased their productivity and made them an extension of the airline's sales force. There are currently four major GDS systems—Amadeus, Galileo, Sabre, and Worldspan. In addition, there are several smaller or regional GDSs, including SITA's Sahara, Infini (Japan), Axess (Japan), Tapas (Korea), Fantasia (South Pacific), and Abacus (Asia/Pacific) that serve the interests of specific regions or countries (Das 2002). Out of these, Abacus, Infini, and Axess are joint ventures with Sabre (Sabre Travel Network 2006). Exhibit 11.3 illustrates how Indian (formerly Indian Airlines) is using the GDS platform to compete against the low-cost carriers in India. The low cost carriers (LCCs) entry into the market in 2005 made air travel available for the masses which hitherto was a luxury meant for the rich and for corporate travel. To reach out to the people, LCCs in India used their own websites and the online travel agents (OTAs) to reach out to the masses. Airlines either sell their tickets directly to customers or through GDS and OTAs. GDS offer air and railway tickets, car rental information, and hotel rooms. This makes it compelling for OTAs to partner with them. OTAs also directly partner with airlines, hotels, railways, and bus services. (Ernst and Young 2013).

Exhibit 11.3   **Indian Goes Agro on Ticket Sales**

Now it is time for Indian to sign up for more global distribution system (GDS) platforms to take on increasing competition from low-cost carriers. According to analysts, this will help Indian to increase its distribution reach by adding another 15,000–18,000 booking terminals. This will also help Indian to bring more high yielding passengers from business class. Other domestic airlines such as Jet Airways and Kingfisher are already on various GDS platforms. In fact, airlines have been using the Internet extensively to sell tickets, giving them cost advantages.

Although the incremental cost of distribution and acquisition of new customers will be high for Indian, the new GDS platforms will help travel agents book Indian flights on the same system as other airlines, making it easier to compare and offer the best prices to the customers.

Distribution of Bank Services and Branch Location

Meidan, Arthur (1984), 'Distribution of bank services and branch location', *International Journal of Bank Marketing*, vol. 2, issue 3, pp. 60–72.

The author presents the major channels of distribution for banking services and the four main types of quantitative techniques available for bank branch location decisions—economic, spatial, bivariate, and multiple regression methods. He indicates the leading bank distribution strategies and attempts to assess the impact of new technology developments on the future of distribution of bank services and branch location.

SUMMARY

Distribution stands for place in the seven Ps and is one of the vital aspects of marketing. Services involve simultaneous production and consumption and they cannot be inventoried. Successful marketing of services is not possible unless it is made easily available to the customers for purchase. This chapter defines distribution and delineates factors affecting the choice of service outlet by the customer and also the factors affecting the choice of distribution channel by the service provider. Keeping in mind the factors affecting the choice of the customer, the service provider can choose their own distribution channel vis-à-vis their organizational strategy. Here, the different channels available for distribution have been highlighted. The strategies for distribution—intensive, selective, and exclusive have been discussed. The section on managing distribution

channel further talks about how the different distribution channels can be managed to distribute the services effectively and efficiently. Conflict management along with the various types of conflicts have also been distinguished. The Internet revolution has impacted the delivery of services. The last section in the chapter therefore talks about the same and discusses the global distribution system and the impact of e-commerce on the delivery of services.

Services require the customer to be present in the servicescape. Thus, if the service outlet is not located at a convenient place, then the whole process of designing and producing the services product is futile due to the absence of customers. Products on the other hand can be distributed from the factory (production unit) to the store where the customers can purchase them (retail outlet).

KEY TERMS

Distribution The allocation of goods to consumers by means of wholesalers and retailers.

Distribution channel The network of firms necessary to distribute goods or services from the manufacturers to the consumers.

Franchisee A licence given to a manufacturer, distributor, trader, etc., to enable them to manufacture

or sell a named product or service in a particular area for a stated period.

Retailer A distributor selling goods or services to consumers.

Wholesaler A distributor selling goods in large quantities, usually to other distributors.

EXERCISES

Concept Review Questions

1. Critically discuss the importance of distribution in the marketing of services.

2. Discuss the different types of distribution channels and their relative importance to a service marketer in the insurance sector.

3. What is channel conflict? Discuss giving different types of channel conflicts.
4. In the light of channel conflicts, which type of distribution channel is most effective in the marketing of services, and why?
5. Discuss the relevance of GDS in the distribution of travel industry services.

Critical Thinking Questions

1. Consider the recent purchase of mobile services by you or your family. Identify the different alternatives available for purchase of this service from a service provider. Which channel did you choose and why?
2. Identify two dissimilar services such as hospitality and mobile network services. Discuss the distribution channels for these and how they are similar or dissimilar.

3. Consider an instance when you faced unsatisfactory service delivery in a franchisee restaurant. How did this affect your perception about the restaurant chain? Discuss strategies you can suggest to the franchiser for managing such a situation.

Internet Exercises

1. Visit the website of any two no-frills, low-cost airline service providers. What are the different options available for booking their services? Compare the sites and evaluate which site delivers the service in a better manner and why?
2. You have to open an account in a bank (online). Of the different options available on the Net, identify any two to three service providers. Which service provider would you choose and why? (Focus the evaluation on the basis of delivery of services by the service provider).

CASE STUDY Selling Grocery Online in India

—Kirti Dutta

Standing at ₹21,60,000 crore (July 2014), India's grocery market is the sixth largest globally. Online grocery retail touted as the new kid on the block is slowly gaining mileage and will reach ₹60,000 crore by 2020, which will be 2% of the grocery market. This niche segment is expected to contribute 10–20% of overall e-commerce jobs with each warehouse of online grocery companies employing around 50–100 workers depending on the scale of operations, according to Randstand India (cited in Joshi 2014). The following are the key triggers for converting customers to online shopping.

- Organised grocery retail is under penetrated and unprofitable due to high rents and utility bills. As a result, finding a good store, which carries all of what a customer needs, is not always possible.
- The local kirana is too small, carrying only 1,000 SKUs, and hence does not always meet the needs of customers.
- Traffic, lack of parking, and frequent out-of-stock situations are some of the problems customers face when shopping through physical stores.

- Grocery buying is typically the same month on month. Hence, customers are very familiar with the products and do not feel the need to touch and feel a majority of the items. For fresh produce, this is an issue but easy return policies can convert customers.

Here are some of the players operating in the online grocery retail space.

Bigbasket.com Started in 2011 and is currently operational in Hyderabad, Bengaluru, and Mumbai as an online grocery supermarket. It carries 10,000 products and 1,000 brands and has fruits, vegetables, grocery and staples, spices, bread, bakery and dairy products, meat, beverages, personal care, imported and gourmet products, etc. They also have pesticide-free/organic fruits and vegetables apart from pre-chopped vegetables (Joshi 2014). They offer a time slot for home delivery as per the customers' convenience. The customers' orders are delivered in their signature vans and customers can pay by cash, card, or food coupons on delivery. For orders of ₹1,000 or above, the delivery is free. To build customer confidence they have an on-time everytime guarantee, that is, if a customer does not receive an order on time, then 10% of the order value will be credited to his BigBasket account that can be used towards the next order. The quality is also guaranteed through a no questions asked return policy and if the customer is not satisfied with the quality of the products delivered they can either return the products to the delivery personnel at the time of delivery or can contact the customer support team to do the needful. Customers can also download the BigBasket app on their mobile and place orders through the same.

LocalBanya.com   Set up on May 2012, it is another online supermarket retailing company that offers more than 8,000 products in categories such as fruits, vegetables, groceries, and kitchenware. They offer free home delivery anywhere in Mumbai on an order amount of ₹500 or more for next day delivery. If customers place an order before 10 am and want delivery on the same day, they can get it through express delivery, which is chargeable at ₹30 per delivery. The customers can pay for their purchases through cash or card on delivery or make online payments through credit/debit/net banking options. They have a Reserve Bank of Banya, that is the 'Banya points' for loyal customers. It allows customers to earn 1% points on their bills. Thus, a bill of ₹500 will be equal to 5 Banya points and each point is equal to ₹1, which can be used in the next purchase. They have a cancellation and return policy as per which broken, leaking, or expired goods can be returned. As per LocalBanya.com, 'Good once sold will not be taken back unless the product on arrival is damaged, expired, or faulty. Our supply crew checks the quality of all ordered products before they reach you. Products purchased on LocalBanya.com can be returned only if unopened and in resaleable condition'. As per this, bread/fruits and vegetables/eggs/ dairy products can be returned within 2 days of delivery. Non-food and packaged food can be returned within 5 days of delivery.

GreenCart.in   Greencart went live in the year 2013 with the objective of making the best quality and

the widest range of fresh produce (farm-o-fresh fruits and veggies) easily available to everyone. They offer more than 1,500 products in over 30 categories in select areas in Mumbai. They ensure the freshness of the fruits and vegetables through zero stock policy and just-in-time delivery. The prices are charged as per the price at which customers shop but if on the day of delivery the prices of the items fall then the same benefit is passed to the customers and they are charged a decreased rate. They offer free home delivery on a bill of ₹399 or more per day. They have a six day ordering system that enables customers to shop for six days in six minutes. The customers can order once a week but get their fruits and vegetables delivered daily, thereby saving them the headache of pilling up the week's quota in the fridge. They also have a 100% satisfaction guaranteed, whereby if the customer is not satisfied with the quality they can return the product at the time of delivery with no questions asked. Customers can pay for their purchase through cash on delivery or pay online through credit/debit cards or net banking or use ticket restaurant meal vouchers. They also roll out gift coupons and freebies from time to time for their loyal customers.

Ekstop.com   This is an online destination for all grocery and daily essentials home delivered in Mumbai except the border areas of Madh Island, Manori, Dahisar, Mulund, Vandi, and Mankhurd. Customers can buy groceries, beverages, toiletries, baby care, stationery, etc. at huge discounts. The customers can pay cash on delivery, Sodexo voucher, ticket restaurant voucher, and can also pay through secure online payment options net banking, credit/debit cards, etc. There is free home delivery on a minimum order quantity of ₹400. They also have a Super Fast EkSpress delivery (1–4 hours) with options to schedule the delivery. However, if the customer is not available and a delivery is rescheduled then a fee of ₹30 is charged.

All these players pay special attention to sourcing of products. Big Basket trains its employees for handling of the fresh produce and invests in freezing/chilling equipment to handle storage at its hub and in delivery vans. It also ensures that the produce spends only a few hours in the cold storage. With the help of technology they are able to predict the buying patterns of customers and through direct sourcing are able to deliver the produce fresh to the customers.

LocalBanya.com uses just-in-time inventory for produce that moves out to the customers as quickly as it arrives so that it is fresh on delivery. It also uses the warehousing for product management. Greencart.in also works on a zero inventory policy to maintain a minimum inventory level in case of packaged food products. For fresh produce it goes to the vendor directly—usually the farmer or in the case of imported fruits, the agricultural middleman. Greencart uses cellulose films for packaging to protect fresh produce from human touch and environmental factors. For leafy fruits/vegetables it uses customized cold storage boxes during transportation.

EkStop.com, to supply fresh produce, sources the perishables in real time through agricultural markets in Vashi (Navi Mumbai) and through wholesalers who serve as stock points within city limits. With 180 employees across four locations in Mumbai, it uses hub and spoke model for warehousing (Joshi 2014).

There are players like Aaramshop.com, who follow a near-hybrid, asset-light business model. It fulfils orders placed on the site via the preferred neighbourhood retailer closest to the customer, who will deliver at the consumer's doorstep within a couple of hours of placing an order. 'We are leveraging the existing last mile strength of the independent neighbourhood retailers and integrating it with the opportunities offered by the entire digital eco-system,' says Aaramshop CEO and MD Vijay Singh.

Singh feels that Aaramshop is not in danger of becoming a classifieds for *kiranas* as Aaramshop's revenue model is not based on specific transactions, but on premium services offered to brands (such as analytics, activations, coupons, and advertising) and subscription-based privilege services for retailers. The attempt is to enable engagement between retailers and customers, be it through walk-ins, phone-based orders, online orders, or even a mobile app (to be launched in August 2014). Aaramshop currently operates in 35 Indian cities with 3,500 retailers with an access to 2.5 million urban households (Joshi 2014).

Thus, we see that online distribution of groceries is catching up fast. It however remains to be seen whether these players can scale up and sustain themselves over a period of time.

Questions

1. Compare and contrast the distribution strategies being followed by the different online grocery companies.
2. Compare the distributions strategy adopted by Aaramshop with the other online grocery companies.

REFERENCES

Banerjee, Rajiv (2006), 'Subhiksha draws up carpet bombing plan', *The Economic Times*, 6 December, p. 4.

Business Standard (2002), 'Barista appoints new head for local operations', 5 August 2002.

Dey, Sudipto (2006), 'Indian goes agro on ticket sales', *The Economic Times*, 14 November, p. 4.

EH&C (2002), 'Barista coffee sets up new company in Sri Lanka', *Express Hotelier & Caterer*, 23 September.

Gooptu, Pradeep (2002), 'Barista coffee brews South Asian thrust, *Business Standard*, 3 December.

Gupta, Parul (2002), 'Multinational fast food majors outpace local peers', *Business Standard*, 4 October.

Gupta, Sanjeet Das (2002), 'Barista Coffee Company grabs IIM graduates' fancy in New Delhi', *Business Standard*, 22 February.

Hollensen, Svend (1998), *Global Marketing*, Prentice Hall, London, Chapter 9, pp. 235–263.

Jobber, David (2001), *Principles and Practices of Marketing*, Berkshire, McGraw-Hill Publishing Company, Chapters 11–15.

Joshi, D. (2014), 'Long way to go', The Strategist, *Business Standard*, dated 14 July 2014, p. 1.

Kaul, J. (2002), 'Nirula's plans to go national', *Express Hotelier & Caterer*, 26 August.

Kaul, P. (2003), 'Pizza Corner to take franchising route', *Express Hotelier & Caterer*, 20 January.

Kothari, D. (2002), 'The fast food boom', *Express Hotelier & Caterer*, 23 September, p. 11.

Kotler, Philip, John T. Bowen, and J.C. Makens (2006), *Marketing for Hospitality and Tourism*, Pearson Education Inc., New Jersey, Chapter 13.

Lovelock, Christopher H. (1983), 'Classifying services to gain strategic marketing insights', *Journal of Marketing*, vol. 47, Summer, pp. 9–20.

Monga, Deepshikha and Joji Thomas Philip (2006), 'RIL wants to play big in supply chain', *The Economic Times*, 26 September, p. 4.

Monga, Deepshikha and Meenakshi Verma (2006), 'Now Mac Express at stations and airports', *The Economic Times*, 8 December, p. 5.

Retailer (2008), 'Lladro plans to expand in tier-II cities', *Retailer*, New Delhi, vol. 3, no. 5, p. 14.

Reuters (2006), 'Russian retailers threaten boycott of Panasonic', *The Economic Times*, New Delhi, 8 December, p. 25.

Ritzer, G. (2000), *The McDonaldization of Society*, Pine Forge, New Delhi.

Scanlon, N.L. (1998), *Quality Restaurant Service Guaranteed*, John Wiley, New York.

Singh, Harsimran (2006), 'Battery glitch? Blame it on your mobile operator: Weak network stresses cell phone, reduces handsets life say experts', *The Economic Times*, 11 December 2006.

Times News Network (2006), 'Choice Hotels charts ₹750 crore expansion', *The Times of India*, 4 December.

Choice Hotels (2007), available from http://www.choicehotelsindia.com/company_profile.php, accessed on 5 July 2014.

Das, Samipatra 'Global distribution system in present times', http://www.hotel-online.com/News/PR2002_4th/Oct02_GDS.html, accessed on 14 December 2006.

Ernst and Young (2013), available from http://www.ey.com/Publication/vwLUAssets/Rebirth_of_e-Commerce_in_India/$FILE/EY_RE-BIRTH_OF_ECOMMERCE.pdf, accessed on 15 July 2014.

http://bigbasket.com, accessed on 15 July 2014.

http://economictimes.indiatimes.com/articleshow/1232731.cms, accessed on 14 December 2006.

http://www.barista.co.in, accessed on 7 October 2008.

http://www.domain-b.com/companies/companies_m/mcDonald/20070222_franchise.html). accessed on 27 February 2007.

http://www.ekstop.com, accessed on 15 July 2014.

http://www.expresshospitality.com/20080831/market21.shtml, accessed on 7 October 2008.

http://www.financialexpress.com/old/latest_full_story.php?content_id=132468, accessed on 7 October 2008.

https://www.greencart.in, accessed on 15 July 2014.

http://www.ibef.org/artdisplay.aspx?tdy=1&art_id=19321&cat_id=60, accessed on 6 October 2008.

http://www.keralatourism.org/index.php, accessed on 13 December 2006.

http://www.kfc.com/about/, accessed on 13 December 2006.

https://www.localbanya.com, accessed on 15 July 2014.

http://www.livemint.com/2007/11/28235623/Caf%C3%A9-Coffee-Day-eyes-overseas. html, accessed on 7 October 2008.

http://www.mcdonalds.com/corp/about.html, accessed on 14 December 2006.

http://www.mcdonalds.com/corporate/promise/vision/index.html, accessed on 5 August 2003.

http://www.mcdonaldsindia.com/supchain.htm, accessed on 7 March 2003.

www.McDonaldsindia.net/key-milestones.aspx, accessed on 3 March 2014.

http://www.pizzacorner.com/aboutus/, accessed on 3 October 2008.

http://www.sabretravelnetwork.com/about/history.htm, accessed on 14 December 2006.

http://www.thehindubusinessline.com/2007/01/23/stories/2007012302712300.htm, accessed on 6 October 2008.

http://www.thehindubusinessline.com/2007/03/02/stories/2007030203260500.htm, accessed on 6 October 2008.

http://www.thehindubusinessline.com/2007/03/02/stories/2007030203260500.htm accessed on 7 October 2008.

Indian Railways (2014), available from http://www.indianrail.gov.in/rtsms.pdf, accessed on 27 June 2014.

Internet Live stats (2014), available from http://www.internetlivestats.com/internet-users/, accessed on 5 July 2014.

KFC (2012), available from http://www.kfc.co.in/ accessed on 27 June 2014.

KFC (2014) available from http://www.kfc.com/about/, accessed on 27 June 2014.

McDonalds (2014), available from http://www.about-mcdonalds.com/mcd/our_company.html, accessed on 27 June 2014.

Mitra, S. (2014), 'The K K Modi Group-backed convenience chain is trailing Bharat Petroleum's In & Out at petrol pumps, but it is increasing the count of its standalone stores', available from http://www.business-standard.com/article/beyond-business/modis-unveil-24x7-store-105060301015_1.html, accessed on 5 July 2014.

Mulky, Avinash G. (2013), 'Distribution challenges and workable solutions', www.sciencedirect.com, accessed on 30 July 2014.

National Payments Corporation of India (2014), available from http://www.npci.org.in/nfsatm.aspx, accessed on 27 June 2014.

PTI (2013a), 'IRCTC books record 5.02 lakh e-tickets on single day', available from http://timesofindia.indiatimes.com/india/IRCTC-books-record-5-02-lakh-e-tickets-on-single-day/articleshow/18763783.cms?referral=PM, accessed on 27 June 2014.

PTI (2013b), 'IRCTC App for Windows-8 for e-ticketing', available from http://economictimes.indiatimes.com/articleshow/22491794.cms?utm_source=contentofinterest&utm_medium=text&utm_camplyJJaign=cppst, accessed on 5 July 2014.

Rail news (2013), available from http://www.railnews.co.in/how-to-book-railway-tickets-through-sms/, accessed on 5 July 2014.

Sethi, Sunil (2002), 'CEO-Speak vs employee per cent', *Business Standard*, 22 November, www.business-standard.com/archives/2002/nov30th accessed on 5 July 2014.

The Hindu (2014), available from http://www.the-hindubusinessline.com/features/smartbuy/crisil-online-retail-to-become-rs-50000cr-industry-by-2016/article5722525.ece, accessed on 15 July 2014.

12 Physical Evidence

OBJECTIVES

After reading this chapter you will be able to understand the

- concept of physical evidence
- importance of physical evidence in the management of services
- management of different elements of physical evidence

Starbucks India Cafes

From a single store in Seattle in 1971 to its entry to the Indian market in October 2012 Starbucks' journey has been highly successful. Though the Indian café chains' market is promising pegged at $300 million and growing at 20% annually, its global rivals such as Gloria Jean's Coffees and Costa Coffee are having a tough time here.

India is dominated by a tea drinking culture and drinking coffee in bars is through a sit-in concept. Here, consumers like to hang around the outlet for hours compared to the global phenomenon of grabbing coffee on the go from generally tiny outlets and kiosks. Thus, coffee chains in India have to maintain elaborate and plush outlets to attract Indian consumers (based on article by Bailay 2014).

Starbucks' research on the Indian consumers confirmed that for Indian consumers, coffee is not the primary reason for visiting a café. The consumers spend around 45 minutes in the café and use it to meet relatives and friends. Starbucks is therefore positioning itself as an aspirational brand, and is

Credit: IndiaPicture/Mahatta Multimedia Pvt. Ltd.

going over the top with its stores, and the stores are some of the most luxurious it has opened anywhere in the world. They believe that a coffee house should be a welcoming and familiar place for people to connect, and so the stores are designed to reflect the unique character of the neighbourhoods they serve. The stores are not as per the global design standard but each store has been designed to reflect the local touch to appeal to the consumers. For example, the store in New Delhi's Connaught Place has ropes and chatai on the walls and henna patterns on the floor, with pictures of Indian spices on its walls, while the Pune store has a rich display of antiques and copper. Along with its locally sourced coffee, the outlets offer an India-centric food menu too.

The flagship store in Bengaluru is spread across 3,000 square feet and embraces the architectural style, lush landscape, and greenery of Bengaluru. It is designed with antiques of that region. Thus, Starbucks is investing not only money but time and other resources as well while designing each store it opens so that it is unique in design and not a replica of another store.

After going through the chapter, you will be able to answer the following question:

Why does Starbucks need to pay so much attention to its outlet when it is retailing coffee and coffee is what the customer is going to consume?

INTRODUCTION

Convincing customers about the quality of the service prior to purchase can be a tricky affair for service providers due to the intangible nature of services. This difficulty is directly proportionate to the intangibility of the services. However, by supplying cues service providers can make it more tangible for the customer and hence easier to evaluate. Tangibility can be incorporated by managing the physical environment of services. Another characteristic of services that affects the physical environment of services is inseparability, or the simultaneous production and consumption of services. This aspect makes it inevitable for the customer to be present at the time of production and delivery of services. The physical evidence can affect the perception of the customer at the time of service delivery, especially for leisure and entertainment services such as upscale restaurants, theatres, resorts, leisure parks, etc. (Wakefield and Blodgett 1994). This implies that physical evidence also communicates with the customers along with the other aspects of marketing mix and needs to be managed carefully by the services organizations.

PHYSICAL EVIDENCE

According to Shostack (1977), customers are frequently searching for 'surrogates' or 'cues' to help determine the firm's capabilities to overcome the 'intangibility' of firms. On the basis of this reasoning, Booms and Bitner (1981) broadened the traditional four Ps into the seven Ps of services. Physical evidence was one of the Ps added for all the tangible cues along with the physical surroundings. According to Zeithaml and Bitner (2003), physical evidence is 'The environment in which the service is delivered and where the firm and customer interact, and any tangible components that facilitate performance or communication of the service'. Bitner (1992) introduced the nomenclature of 'servicescape' to the physical facility where the services are delivered or offered/performed.

Importance of Physical Evidence

'Environment is vivid because the stimulus a person receives from one source can generate multiple and unexpected sensations, images and ideas' (Greenland and McGoldrick 2005). In Chapter 7, we have already seen how physical evidence or service-scape affects the evaluation of services by the customers, and ultimately has an affect on the customer's perception of the service quality of the service provider.

The servicescape can be managed to get the following benefits:
- It helps to package the service offering for the customers.
- Servicescape can appeal to the emotions of a person and deduce a favourable response from the customers.
- It can act as a facilitator to shape customer behaviour and enable effective flow of activities.
- It can act as a differentiator to distinguish a service provider from its competitors. For example, fast food restaurants, such as McDonald's and KFC, differentiate their services on the basis of their standard designed servicescapes. Differentiation also allows the service provider to charge different prices for different services targeted at different customer segments.

It influences a customer's subjective perception of waiting time. Baker and Cameron (1996) identified how different physical evidences can be controlled to influence the customer's subjective perception of waiting time. They defined subjective time as 'How individuals perceive and feel about the length of a time duration'. This is important considering the fact that 'As the waiting time increases the customer satisfaction tends to decrease' (Baker and Cameron 1996).

Types of servicescapes

According to Bitner (1992) there are two types of servicescapes (i.e., environment in which service is delivered)—*lean* and *elaborate*. Services requiring a simple structure, relatively few elements, and few spaces to deliver the service are referred to as lean servicescapes. For example, a post office kiosk requires a simple structure for the delivery of service. The design of the physical evidence for a lean servicescape is simple, especially where there is no interaction between customers and employees. Services requiring a complex structure, with many elements and forms, is referred to as an elaborate servicescape. For example, a heart specialist will require an elaborate set-up with proper machinery for conducting different tests, an operation theatre, rooms, etc. when deciding upon the physical evidence.

The servicescape concept postulated by Bitner (1992), talked about the complexity of servicescape on the basis of presence of customers, employees, and presence of both (also discussed in Chapter 1 on Introduction to service industry while classifying services). There can be the following types of servicescapes:
1. If only the customer is present (i.e., self-service) the servicescape can be lean (like e.g., an ATM) or complex (e.g., a water park).
2. If only the employees are present (i.e., remote service) then also the servicescape can be lean (e.g., telephone mail order service) or elaborate (e.g., insurance company).

3. If both customer and employees are present (i.e., interpersonal services) then also the servicescape can be lean (e.g., hair salon) or elaborate (e.g., restaurant).

The service providers need to understand the kind of customer interaction at the servicescape they are using to deliver the service and design it accordingly so that the money is well invested and gets the desired returns. It has to be understood that the servicescape can be used to differentiate the services as well, for example, a hair salon and restaurant can be lean or elaborate keeping in mind the segmentation targeting and positioning of the same. Thus, a roadside dhaba has a lean servicescape whereas a restaurant in a five star property is very elaborate. Exhibit 12.1 shows how Club Mahindra has set up an elaborate servicescape to capture the market for vacation ownership.

MANAGING PHYSICAL EVIDENCE

The physical evidence comprises of a number of factors each of which has a bearing on the customer perception of the service provider. Services are intangible but they are accompanied by 'physical objects' that cannot be categorized as true product elements. The benefit of these objects is that they verify the existence or completion of a service, whereas a true product never requires evidence. For example, when travelling by any airline, the ticket confirms the service that the airline is going to provide and serves as an evidence of the service. This evidence is of two types—peripheral evidence and essential evidence. Peripheral evidence is actually possessed as part of purchase and has little or no independent value; for example, a debit card is useless without the funds it represents. On the other hand, the customer cannot possess the essential evidence, but it is so dominant in its impact on service purchase and use that it is considered an element on its own. For example, if a person purchases a credit contract (which in itself is a peripheral evidence), the bank that facilitates this has a strong impact on the service perception and is an essential element.

Whether essential or peripheral, service evidence forms the heart of the service image, and must be carefully designed and managed as a service in itself. This evidence provides clues and confirmations, and influences customer perceptions and expectations about the service (Danciu 2007). For example, try and remember the last time you walked out of a servicescape without availing the services of the service provider just because you felt the services provided would not be as per your expectations. The physical evidence has the power to turn away or generate an emotional appeal with the customers. According to Turley and Fugate (1992), the different broad categories to be considered while designing the physical evidence for a service are the:

- locational perspective
- atmospheric and image perspective
- operational perspective
- consumer use perspective
- contact personnel perspective.

Locational Perspective

One of the most important physical evidence affecting services is the location of the service provider (when there is direct contact with the service provider) or the facility from which the service is to be provided (for example, ATMs, drop boxes, etc.). A good strategic location does most of the work for the service provider, especially in the hospitality sector, retail outlets, banking services, etc. It has generally been observed that for day-to-day services, customers prefer services which are available conveniently; therefore, firms that are located close to where people work or live have an added advantage. However, if a person is going on a holiday they would prefer a location with scenic beauty and one that is away from the chaos of daily life. Whatever be the case, we see that location is an important factor, comes at a prime cost, and cannot be easily renovated or changed.

Physical evidence is an important part of the services

Atmospheric and Image Perspective

This includes the controllable factors of the internal and external environment that influence the customers. Customers use whatever cues are available in the servicescape to draw their perceptions of the service to be provided, and hence the atmosphere plays an important role in influencing customer's initial perceptions. Some of these factors are discussed in this section.

Layout/decor The layout or decor of the servicescape can affect the customer's perception of the service to be provided. This includes the layout of the service delivery, the parking, waiting area, etc. The layout and decor in an upscale restaurant would be more important than that of a roadside inn (*dhaba*). The furniture, colour concept, and central theme of the restaurant, will all be a part of the decisions to be considered while finalizing the decor.

Signage   The signage includes the signs, logos, style of decor, and personal artefacts used by the service provider. All these signs communicate the style statement of the service provider and influence the perception of the customers. These include signs for direction, communications of rules such as no smoking, etc., and the certificates displayed by a medical practitioner in the servicescape. Signs are important in forming the initial impression of the servicescape.

Ambience   It includes both the internal and external ambience of the servicescape. The external ambience includes landscaping, cleanliness of the external environment, scenic beauty, etc. Internal ambience includes factors such as air quality, temperature, noise, music, odour, etc. For example, if you go to a fair the brightly coloured tents, the bright, colourful, and jovial appearances of the performers, etc. all bring forth the fact that the customers are going to have a fun-filled experience. Oakes (2000) carried out a detailed study to see how the musicscape influences customers and found that music affects customer expectations, generates emotions by stimulating original memories with the music being played, and encourages behavioural response of repeat patronage.

The internal atmosphere of an organization can be altered by renovations, which is time-consuming and expensive (keeping in mind the actual cost involved in the renovations and opportunity cost of the customers who would have otherwise patronized the place). Thus, it is important to place initial close attention while planning the environment.

Operational Perspective

This includes both the production and delivery of services. Services are experiences and, therefore, require the customers to be present at the time of service delivery. The servicescape in such a scenario involves various factors.

Equipment   Use of technology to deliver a consistent service helps the service providers to reduce the heterogeneous characteristic of services. Technology also ensures that the service quality delivered across different locations is fairly uniform.

Signs for use of technology   Allocation of equipment is in itself not effective until it is used properly. Thus, at ATMs detailed instructions are provided for customers about the process for using the facility. The customers must be made to feel comfortable, and the technology should be easy to follow and use, for mass acceptance of the same.

Cleanliness   The other important factor to consider in the operations is the cleanliness of the servicescape. This also acquires importance depending upon the type of service delivered. For example, in the hospitality and health-care industry a lot of importance is attached to cleanliness, whereas a not so clean banking servicescape may still be acceptable to the customers.

Consumer Use Perspective

This aspect focuses on the degree to which a servicescape is designed around the customer rather than the operations. This includes factors as explained in this section.

Billing statement This involves the ease of understanding; for example, a mobile services bill has a number of sections, such as SMS charges, incoming calls, outgoing calls, and roaming charges, for the customer's information. Telecom service providers have the facility of call centres where customers can call and get clarifications for any queries.

Stationery This includes business cards, brochures, menus, etc. designed for the customer's use and easy referral.

Internet/web page Customers are increasingly using the Internet for information search. Thus, the Internet or web page should be such that it provides the information that customers may require regarding the services such as pricing, availability, booking option, etc.

Tickets Tickets are a part of the physical evidence and affect customer perceptions. Indian Railways through its Internet site allows customers to book tickets online and follows it up by delivering the tickets within 24 hours. IndiGo, a low cost, no-frills airline has the facility of providing tickets online, which customers could print from their own computer terminals and produce at the time of boarding, along with an identity proof. Facilities like these, which provide customer convenience, add favourably to customer perceptions (Exhibit 12.2).

Contact Personnel Perspective

The contact personnel are a part of the servicescape and also form a part of the services product. The appearance of the contact personnel—their cleanliness, dress code, demeanour, friendly, and smiling countenance—forms an initial and lasting impact on the customer's perception of the services*.

There are a number of factors affecting the customer's perception of the servicescape. All the factors are equally important and service managers have to make a trade-off depending upon the situational factors and the type of response they want to elicit from the customer.

CREATING THE SERVICE ENVIRONMENT

Both the organizational and customer perspective highlight the fact that the service environment plays an important role in the service experience of the customers. All the aspects discussed in these sections should be taken into consideration while designing the service environment. In a product category like hospitality, for example quick eating restaurants, the product can be common across organizations, but it is the service experience that includes the service environment that can be the differentiator. Lot of money is invested by organizations while designing their servicescape or the place where the service is consumed by the consumers so that it is appealing and makes the customers come back again and again. Studies show that the customer's perception about the attractiveness of the servicescape had a higher impact on their intention to revisit the service outlet than the quality of the

---

*Based on Turley and Fugate (1992), Zeithaml and Bitner (2003), Vignali and Davies (1994), and Vignali (2001).

> **Exhibit 12.2** **Travelling with Soft Copies of Tickets**
>
> Booking tickets for railways and airlines on the Internet has simplified life for many travellers. They just had to get a printout of the e-ticket so booked and produce it at the time of travel along with original identity proof. For railway travel customers were charged a fine of ₹50 per ticket if they were travelling without a printout of the ticket.
>
> Airline travellers could get a printout of their ticket by giving their PNR (passenger name record) number at the airport counter of the airline they were flying (Express News Service 2013). However, as a part of the green initiative of Indian Railway Catering and Tourism Corporation (IRCTC) to save paper in the year 2011, they have done away with the printout of the e-ticket and customers can travel by showing an SMS message of the ticket on their mobile phone or a screenshot of it on a laptop/iPad along with original identity proof to be shown to the ticket examiners (Philip 2011). Following their footsteps in 2013, the Bureau of Civil Aviation Security (BCAS), which is the nodal agency for civil aviation security, has issued orders for acceptability of soft display of tickets on laptops, tablets, and smartphones at the entry point of airport (PTI 2013).
>
> *Source*: Based on Philip 2011; *Express News Service* 2013, and PTI 2013.

merchandise, pricing, etc. and that in case of retail outlets store choice precedes brand choice (Darden et al. 1983 cited in Baker et al. 1992). Thus, the service outlet environment is important and needs due and careful attention for the desired impact.

Before creating the environment we need to understand how the environment impacts the consumers. Mehrabian and Russell (1974) studied that the stimuli in the environment that includes physical features such as lightning, colour, store layout, etc. impacts the emotional state of the consumers. The emotional states induced are feelings of pleasure and arousal. The extent of the feelings generated will then impact the consumer's level of willingness to move towards and explore the environment (e.g., propensity to buy) (Baker et al. 1992). Hence, if a customer visits a service outlet and feels excited and is happy in and with the environment of the outlet, then they might spend more time there and explore the outlet more, which might lead to more purchase then or at a later point of time when they might revisit the outlet again. However, if the consumer does not feel excited and happy in the outlet then they might not want to spend more time there, and if they feel unhappy with the environment, they might want to leave immediately leading to loss of sales. Since then a number of studies have been conducted in retailing to see how different environments influence the emotional state of consumers. It was found that pleasure induced in the store impacted willingness to purchase and arousal induced in the store impacted the willingness to spend more time in the store and interact with the sales personnel (Donovan and Rossiter 1982).

Taken together, these two can be represented on a two dimensional scale where the y-axis represents the extent of arousal (negative, i.e., sleepy to low to high) and the x-axis represents the level of pleasantness (negative, i.e., unpleasant to low to high). Thus, if a service outlet is arousing and pleasant (see image) it creates feeling of excitement in consumers. For example, theme parks, adventure tourism centres, etc. can all create feeling of excitement by highlighting these two constructs for their outlet. A service outlet can be pleasant and sleepy (that is negative arousal) to attract customers, for example, beauty parlours that want to be pleasant and relaxing at the same time so that consumers spend more time in their outlet. Thus, depending upon the type of outlet and the services provided, service sellers can moderate their environment to create a lasting impact on their customers. If the environment is unpleasant, it is better not to arouse the customers as it leads to distress. So if, for example, there is a demand supply gap and demand is high leading to overcrowding then it is better not to have an arousing atmosphere (for example loud music) as it would lead to distress among customers. On the other hand, if the environment is unpleasant and sleepy it is boring for the customers and again service providers need to take care so that they do not alienate the customers (Lovelock et al. 2010; Baker, Levy, and Grewal 1992).

Houseboats in Kerala aim to create a perfect service environment for tourists

Credit: IndiaPicture/Mahatta Multimedia Pvt. Ltd.

The servicescape concept of M.J. Bitner (1992) delineates the factors in the service environment that impacts the customer's perception of the servicescape. These factors are the ambient conditions, space/functionality and signs, symbols, and artifacts. These factors were found to impact not only the customers but the employees as well. Thus, the servicescape should be such that it improves the productivity and service quality delivered by the employees. Let us now see these factors in detail.

Ambient conditions The environmental factors that affect the five senses of human beings are referred to as ambient conditions. These factors include a number of elements in the servicescape that consciously or sub-consciously elicit psychological, emotional, or cognitive responses from the customers and employees. These include but are not limited to the following.

Temperature The temperature in the retail outlet can be controlled to draw the customers in. During hot and humid weather, the door should be left slightly open so that the cool wafts of air draw the customers in the store.

Scent Scent is also used in good measure to attract the customers. This is especially true for bakery products where the scent of fresh baked products entices the customers to make impulse purchases. Otherwise also a scent that might not be perceived by the customers or not related to a particular product is also found to impact the customers. Retail outlets should use a distinctive scent and it should not smell similar to a competitors or any other store as it will reduce the desired impact on the customers. Thus, managers can use a distinctive smell to differentiate their stores in the minds of the customers (Spangenberg et al. 1996).

The smell of freshly-baked bread invites customers to spend more in this bakery

Credit: Ibudgetphoto/Mahatta Multimedia Pvt. Ltd.

Colour The colour chosen for the retail outlet impacts the feelings of the customers. Colours have been classified into cool and warm with blue being the coolest and red the warmest colour. The other warm colours are yellow and orange and the other cool colours are green, indigo, and violet (Kusterer 2007 cited in Hyodo 2011). It has been suggested that colour associations were formulated early in the evolution of mankind where yellow colour was associated with sunlight and was arousing while blue colour was associated with night and so associated with passivity (Luscher and Scott 1969 cited in Hyodo 2011). Studies show that warm colours such as yellow and red are primarily responsible for drawing customers into the store than cool colours such as blue and green. However, once inside the store more stimulated purchases, fewer purchase postponements, and a stronger inclination to shop and browse were found in blue retail environments (Bellizzi and Hite 1992) as blue colour was rated as more positive, relaxed, and favourable on an evaluative factor. Thus, warm colours can be used more successfully in the store windows and entrances as well as buying situations associated with unplanned impulse purchases. Cool colours on the other hand can be used in outlets where considerable time is spent on the purchase deliberations as warm colours here would make shopping unpleasant for customers and may result in premature termination of the shopping trip (Bellizzi, Crowley, and Hasty 1983).

Music   The music in a service setting is shown to affect the perception of the store by the consumers and their behavior in the store. Shopping intentions were greatest when subjects were exposed to happy music that was liked (Broekemier et al. 2008). Studies also show that music can be used to increase arousal when the customers are recreational oriented in purchase and to decrease arousal when customers are task oriented in their purchase behavior (Kaltcheva and Weitz 2006).

Space/function   This includes the physical layout at the store, the furnishings, and equipment that contribute not only to the ambience but also help the service personnel in delivering the services to the consumers.

Layout   This includes the manner in which the space is allocated, the floor plan that ensures the adequate display of merchandise, and ease of movement at the store. The layout has to be such that whatever the kind of service outlet, the floor planning should ensure that the customers do not feel intimidated by the spatial layout, have no difficulty in finding their way in the store/items that they are looking for and that they can inspect the products properly. This makes the place less intimidating for the customers and helps them make decisions quickly and more comfortably (Vonderschmidt 2002).

Furnishings   These include the furniture, fitting, curtains, carpets, etc. that are used in the service outlet and impact the ambience and décor of the place. These can be used to help create a differential image of the service outlet. The comfort provided by the furnishings impact the customer satisfaction depending upon the kind of service outlet. For example, in a restaurant all these things are important for the customers who seek a comfortable and clean environment but if we talk about a bank, then the furnishings should be adequate but need not be lavish as primarily the customer is seeking service related to banking and it will not leave a negative impression on the customer if it is adequate.

Equipment   This includes the machinery and equipment used at the service outlet that facilitates the delivery and performance of the service. Thus, the equipment should be adequate and functional for appropriate delivery of the service. For example, there needs to be adequate number of billing machines at retail outlets so that customers do not have to stand in long queues for billing.

Signs, symbols, and artifacts   These are the facilitators at the service outlet that ensure smooth delivery of the service experience. They are the signals used inside or outside the service outlet that communicate with the customers about the layout of the store or the environment so as to guide them during the service process. These can be the symbols that indicate exit, elevator direction, direction to billing counter, directions to specific areas in the service outlet (such as ladies or men section and smoking/non-smoking sections), etc. Signage can also be used to educate the customers about the kind of service that is to be delivered to them, for example, numbering systems to collect orders, or display of token number in banks, etc. Signs, symbols, and artifacts assume more significance when the service staff is not present to guide the customers through the service experience.

MANAGING PHYSICAL EVIDENCE AS A STRATEGY

We have seen how physical strategy acts as a motivator to influence people for repeat purchases. It also affects the customer's initial purchase decision. Thus, strategic management of the physical evidence by organizations can influence their profitability (Fig. 12.1).

Corporate Vision, Mission, and Goal

The corporate vision, mission, and goal direct the organization in the type of service they want to deliver within a service industry. For example, within the hospitality industry, organizations may decide to open an upscale restaurant with a specific vision and mission for the same (Exhibit 12.3).

Corporate strategy This includes the strategic layout of the services keeping in mind the vision, mission, and goal of the service organization. This aspect is cross-functional and involves finance, marketing, HR, etc.

Clarify roles of servicescapes Once the corporate strategy for services delivery has been worked out, it is easier for the organization to work out the role servicescape plays in the delivery of the service (for example, lean or elaborate). This can further be classified according to servicescape usage such as self-service, interpersonal service, or remote service.

Planning the servicescape On the basis of the role of servicescape, the management can now plan (map) the different elements of the servicescape such as operational,

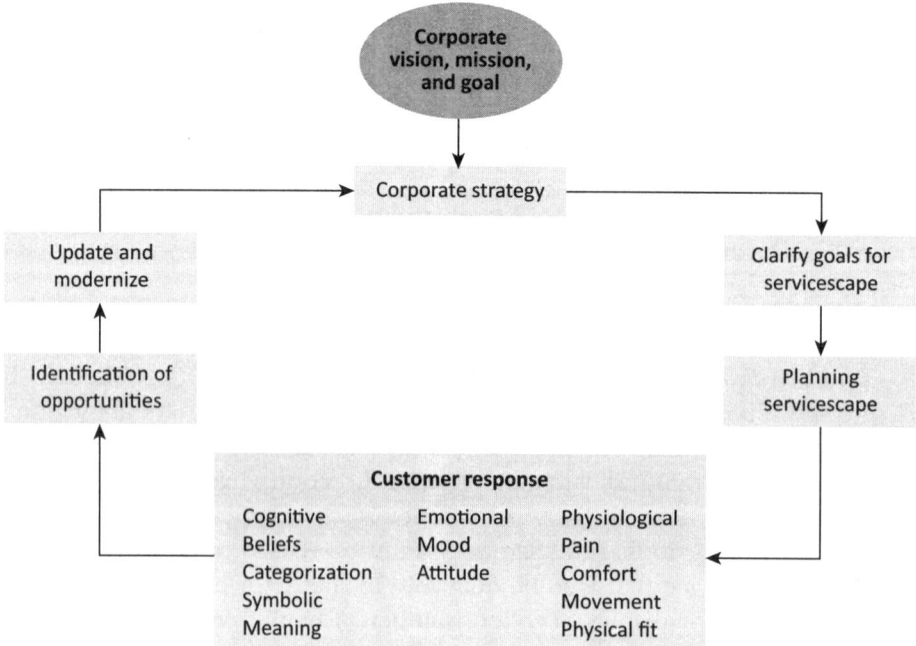

Fig. 12.1 Strategic management of physical evidence

Exhibit 12.3   **Metros Warming Up to Boutique Hotels**

Hotelier Vikram Chatwal, who owns Hampshire Hotels and Resorts, believes that Indian metros are not only ready for Manhattan style boutique hotels but also Hautel Couture. Chatwal, who has nine hotel brands in his portfolio, has recently opened one in Manhattan. He believes that the style conscious guests frequenting the city have an eye for design and detail. His core customers are business executives from media, finance, and technology industries, including celebrities who form 10% of the clientele. The Hautel Couture takes care of aspects such as location, design, logo, graphics, food, music, art, staff, and so on. The trend, which started with Morgan in Manhattan, has spread around the world. With extreme detailing for architecture and unusual designs, the aim is to provide a richer, unique, and more intimate experience. The concept in India is already quite popular in Rajasthan where many hotels offer a unique product and service mix. This concept is surely gaining a lot of popularity among the rich and famous, and is all set to be another innovative hospitality wave.

locational, atmospheric, etc. The brand name and logo can be planned in accordance with the image the service organization wants to portray. A detailed blueprint of the servicescape should be formed and all decisions thought out after much deliberation, as any oversight here will cost more later on, in the form of renovations, etc.

Customer response   Servicescape communicates with the customers and elicits a response from them. It is for the organization to monitor the customer response and check for gaps. This can be done with the help of various market research techniques. According to Bitner (1992), the type of response generated is cognitive, emotional, and physiological.

Cognitive response involves influencing the beliefs of the customers towards the service provider. This also helps the customers to categorize the service provider within that service industry; for example, restaurants are classified as fast food, elegant sit-down, etc. The emotional response generated involves two dimensions—pleasure–displeasure and degree of arousal. Customers are bound to go to a restaurant, which is high in pleasure and arouses excitement about the service experience. Physiological comfort is affected by factors such as noise, degree of temperature, lighting, floor space for movement, etc. All these factors act as 'surrogate indicators' in forming beliefs about the service quality. Thus, the service organization management should constantly monitor the effect of servicescape on the customers.

Identify opportunities   Based upon customer feedback and research, the organization should identify the problem areas or missed opportunities. For example, the marketing communication may not match with the image being portrayed by the physical evidence and so needs a revision in the marketing communication, which will be more cost-effective and deliver the desired effect.

Update and modernize   Once the different opportunities have been identified, the management needs to update and modernize the physical evidence. Also, time and fashion changes, and the depreciation of assets affect the decision to modernize or update the servicescape. The management should identify what needs to be done and the cycle is again repeated, starting from the corporate strategy.

RESEARCH INSIGHT

The Influence of the Quality of the Physical Environment, Food, and Service on Restaurant Image,
Customer Perceived Value, Customer Satisfaction, and Behavioral Intentions

Ryu, Kisang, Hye-Rin Lee, and Woo Gon Kim (2012), 'The influence of the quality of the physical environment, food, and service on restaurant image, customer perceived value, customer satisfaction, and behavioral intentions', *International Journal of Contemporary Hospitality Management*, vol. 24, issue 2, pp. 200–223.

The purpose of this study was to propose an integrated model that examines the impact of three elements of food and service quality dimensions (physical environment, food, and service) on restaurant image, customer perceived value, customer satisfaction, and behavioral intentions.

Data was collected from customers at an authentic upscale Chinese restaurant located in a Southeastern state in the USA through a self-administered questionnaire. Anderson and Gerbing's two-step approach was used to assess the measurement and structural models.

Structural equation modeling showed that the quality of the physical environment, food, and service were significant determinants of restaurant image. Also, the quality of the physical environment and food were significant predictors of customer perceived value. The restaurant image was also found to be a significant antecedent of customer perceived value. In addition, the results reinforced that customer perceived value is indeed a significant determinant of customer satisfaction, and customer satisfaction is a significant predictor of behavioral intentions.

SUMMARY

Services being intangible, create problems for both customers—who are consistently looking for cues to overcome this, and service providers—who want to elicit a favourable response from the customers. The service providers can overcome this by managing the servicescape. The process of strategic management of servicescape is a continuous process and needs to be updated constantly. Customers are present at the time of delivery of services. Physical evidence is thus an important aspect of the seven Ps of marketing. It communicates with the customers along with the other elements of the marketing mix and helps them evaluate the services, both 'prior to' and 'after' the service delivery.

The importance of physical evidence is further highlighted by the fact that it affects customer satisfaction too. The chapter brings forth the importance of managing physical evidence. It delineates the location, atmosphere and image, operations, consumer use, and the contact personnel perspectives for designing physical evidence. A model, which links the physical evidence with the corporate vision and strategy, and customer response, has been designed to manage physical evidence as a strategy. This is a cyclical process and allows the management to upgrade and modernize the facility with time. Thus, by effectively managing the servicescape, an organization can subtly influence customer perception, decision, and satisfaction while purchasing the services.

KEY TERMS

Atmospheric and image perspective   It includes controllable factors of the internal and external environment that influence the customers.

Consumer use perspective   This aspect focuses on the degree to which a servicescape is designed around the customer rather than the operation of the service.

Contact personnel perspective   This includes the appearance of the contact personnel, their cleanliness, dress code, demeanour, and friendliness, among others.

Locational perspective The location of the service provider or the facility from which the service is to be provided.

Operational perspective This includes both the production and delivery of services.

Physical evidence The environment in which the service is delivered, and the firm and customer interact, and include any tangible components that facilitate performance or communication of the service.

Servicescape This includes the tangible facets of service such as machines, equipment, employee appearance, and the ambience of the organization.

EXERCISES

Concept Review Questions

1. Critically evaluate the role of physical evidence in delivery of services.
2. Discuss the different ways in which a service provider can use physical evidence in affecting customer perceptions.
3. How can a service provider manage the atmospheric physical evidence? Explain by taking the example of any service provider.
4. Critically discuss the importance of managing the physical evidence by a service organization.

Critical Thinking Questions

1. Identify a recent visit to a restaurant. How did the physical evidence affect your perceptions? Give reasons.

2. What are the different physical evidences that a service provider of life insurance can plan?
3. Choose any service organization. Identify the current physical evidence they are using and suggest recommendations to enhance customer perception.

Internet Exercises

1. Visit the website of a travel service organization. Identify the different physical evidences that have been used to influence the customers.
2. Visit the website of your bank. How is it similar/dissimilar to the other forms of physical evidence provided by the bank?

CASE STUDY Physical Evidence—A Case of KFC

KFC Corporation

KFC Corporation, based in Louisville, United States, is the world's most popular chicken restaurant chain. Since Colonel Harland Sanders founded it in 1952, KFC has been serving customers delicious, already-prepared, complete family meals. There are over 18,000 KFC outlets in 115 countries and territories around the world.

Colonel Sanders, an early developer of the quick-service food business and a pioneer of the restaurant franchise concept founded KFC in Corbin. He began franchising his chicken business at the age of 65. Building on a foundation of family-orientation, quick service, high-quality food, and affordable prices, the Colonel signed up his first franchisee, Pete Harman, in 1952. Soon after, Colonel Sanders created the restaurant franchise concept and quickly expanded throughout the United States.

By 1964, Colonel Sanders had more than 600 franchised outlets for his chicken in the United States and Canada. That year, a group of investors bought KFC and is credited with growing the chain to its segment dominance. PepsiCo Inc. acquired the company in 1986 and in 1991 Kentucky Fried Chicken switched to KFC as its official identifier.

KFC has 223 restaurants across 35 cities in India and will have 500 restaurants across 75 cities by 2015 (KFC 2012).

The New Logo of KFC

In 2006 KFC changed its logo and the new logo depicted Colonel Sanders with his signature string tie, but for the first time, replaces his classic white, double-breasted suit with a red apron. The apron symbolizes the home-style culinary heritage of the brand and reminds customers that KFC is always in the kitchen cooking delicious, high quality, freshly prepared chicken by hand, just the way Colonel Sanders did 50 years ago. This is only the fourth time in more than 50 years that the logo has changed.

KFC Restaurant of the Future

After three years of testing different restaurant designs in the US and international markets, KFC revealed its restaurant look of the future. KFC's new global image is in the process of being rolled out in restaurants around the world.

The new global restaurant design is refreshing, contemporary, highly-differentiated, and helps keep KFC relevant with customers by giving them a higher quality, overall dining experience. The new design is based on thoughtful strategic tenets, which provide a strong brand image foundation, while being flexible for different international market needs. It communicates a progressive and energetic spirit for KFC and prepares the brand for future global growth.

Design features for the US include:

- Bright, and bold graphics on the restaurant exterior and interior that incorporate the Kentucky Fried Chicken name as well as KFC, communicate a fresh sense of brand pride. African American artist Charly (Carlos) Palmer took KFC's historical icons and gave them an updated, cool, and modern look.
- Graphics and pub signs that showcase the company's icons: '11 Secret Herbs and Spices', 'Finger Lickin' Good', and 'Sunday Dinner, 7 Days a Week'.
- Signature symbols (the Colonel, the bucket, Kentucky Fried Chicken) create distinctly KFC retail style shop front designs that invite customers inside with open glass.
- Heroic use of the signature red colour in a bold architectural way, and crisp white design accents to keep the brand youthful and fresh.
- Warm and contemporary interior designs with spacious and innovative seating help customers feel welcome and comfortable in groups or alone.
- Thoughtful interior and exterior lighting enhances the customer experience.
- A digital jukebox that is free of charge for customers to play the music they enjoy most.
- Southern-inspired brand new menu items, slow-cooked, and served fast to star alongside KFC's core products

Since the first Kentucky Fried Chicken restaurant opened its doors in Utah in 1952, the brand continues to enjoy growing popularity around the world. The company's top markets outside the United States are China, the UK, Australia, South Korea, Mexico, and Europe, including France, Germany, the Netherlands, and Holland. KFC is also tapping growth in important emerging markets such as India, Russia, and Brazil. Each new restaurant opening brings jobs and career opportunities along with economic vitality for that community.

KFC's enduring success and popularity is attributed to a relentless focus on great taste, high quality, and the nearly 500,000 talented employees focused on providing great service to the 4.5 billion guests who visit their restaurants around the world each year.

Questions

1. Discuss the different physical evidence factors being used by KFC.
2. Discuss the new logo of KFC. What are the different changes made and why? As a customer, compare your perceptions about the new versus the old logo.
3. Critically discuss the physical evidence features KFC is going to use in the upcoming outlets.

REFERENCES

Baker, J, M. Levy, and D. Grewal (1992), 'An experimental approach to making retail store environmental decisions', *Journal of Retailing*, vol. 68, no. 4, pp. 445–460.

Baker, Julie and Michaelle Cameron (1996), 'The effects of the service environment on affect and consumer perception of waiting time: An integrative review and research propositions', *Journal of Academy of Marketing Science*, vol. 24, no. 4, pp. 338–349.

Bellizzi, J.A., A.E. Crowley, and R.W. Hasty (1983), 'The effects of colour in store design', *Journal of Retailing*, vol. 59, issue 1, pp. 21–45.

Bellizzi, J. A. and R.E. Hite (1992), 'Environmental Color, Consumer Feelings, and Purchase Likelihood', *Psychology & Marketing*, vol. 9, issue 5, pp. 347–363.

Bitner, M.J. (1990), 'Evaluating the service encounters: The effects of physical surroundings and employee responses', *Journal of Marketing*, April, vol. 54, no. 2, pp. 69–82.

Bitner, M.J. (1992), 'Servicescapes: The impact of physical surroundings on customers and employees', *Journal of Marketing*, vol. 56, no. 2, pp. 57–71.

Booms, B. and M.J. Bitner (1981), *Marketing Strategies and Organizational Structures for Service Firms*, *Marketing of Services*, James H. Donnelly and William R. George (eds), American Marketing Association, Chicago, pp. 47–51.

Broekemier, G., R. Marquardt, and J.W. Gentry (2008), 'An exploration of happy/sad and liked/disliked music effects on shopping intentions in a women's clothing store service setting', *Journal of Services Marketing*, vol. 22, issue 1, pp. 59–67.

Donovan, R.J. and J.R. Rossiter (1982), 'Store atmosphere: An environmental psychology approach', *Journal of Retailing*, vol. 58, pp. 34–57.

Duttagupta, Ishani and Raja Awasthi (2006), 'Metros warming up to boutique hotels', *The Economic Times*, New Delhi, 6 July 2006, p. 4.

Greenland, Steve and Peter McGoldrick (2005), 'Evaluating the design of retail financial service environments', *The International Journal of Bank Marketing*, vol. 23, no. 2/3, pp. 132–152.

Hyodo, Jamie (2011), 'Can colours make me happy? The effects of environmental colour on mood: A meta-analysis', *Advances in Consumer Research*, vol. 39, pp. 858–867.

Kaltcheva, V.D. and B.A. Weitz (2006), 'When should a retailer create an exciting store environment', *Journal of Marketing*, vol. 70, pp. 107–118.

Lovelock, C., J. Wirtz, and J. Chatterjee (2010), Service Marketing: People, Technology, Strategy, 6th Edition, Prentice Hall, Pearson, New Delhi, Ch 10.

Lovelock, Christopher and Evert Gummesson (2004), 'Whither services marketing? In search of a new paradigm and fresh perspectives', *Journal of Services Research*, vol. 7, no. 1, pp. 20–41.

Mehrabian, Albert and James A. Russell (1974), *Psychology*, MIT Press.

Oakes, Steve (2000), 'The influence of the musicscape within service environments', *The Journal of Services Marketing*, vol. 14, no. 7, pp. 539–554.

Sharkey (2006), 'The super-rich spice up their jumbo jet voyages', *The Times of India*, New Delhi, 19 October, p. 38.

Shostack, Lynn G. (1977), 'Breaking free from product marketing', *Journal of Marketing*, vol. 41, no. 2, pp. 73–80.

Spangenberg, E.R., A.E. Crowley, and P.W. Henderson (1996), 'Improving the store environment: do olfactory cues affect evaluations and behaviours', *Journal of Marketing*, vol. 60, pp. 67–80.

'Spice up your life with bar-coded mobile ticket', *The Economic Times*, New Delhi, 13 October 2006, p. 5.

Turley, Lou W. and Douglas L. Fugate (1992), 'The multidimensional nature of service facilities: Viewpoints and recommendations', *The Journal of Services Marketing*, vol. 6, no. 3, pp. 37–46.

Vignali, Claudio (2001), 'McDonald's: Think global, act local—the marketing mix', *British Food Journal*, vol. 103, no. 2, pp. 97–108.

Vignali, Claudio and B.J. Davies (1994), 'The marketing mix redefined and mapped: Introducing the MIXMAP model', *Management Decision*, London, vol. 32, no. 8, pp. 11–16.

Vonderschmidt, G. (2002), 'Planning user friendly layouts', *Chain Store Age*, November, vol. 78, issue 11, p. 132.

Wakefield, Kirk L. and Jeffery G. Blodgett (1994), 'The importance of servicescapes in leisure service settings', *The Journal of Services Marketing*, vol. 8, no. 3, pp. 66–76.

Zeithaml, V.A. and M.J. Bitner (2003), *Services Marketing*, Tata McGraw-Hill Publishing Company Limited, New Delhi.

Bailay, R. and R. Bhushan (2013), 'Starbucks goes plush for India, gives its stores a local flavor', *Economic*

Times, New Delhi, available from http://articles. economictimes.indiatimes.com/2013-09-13/ news/42041703_1_tata-starbucks-unique-starbucks- experience-starbucks-plans, accessed on 14 May 2014.

Bailay, R. (2014), 'Coffee chain Starbucks expand- ing aggressively in India', *Economic Times*, New Delhi, dated 14 April, available from http://articles. economictimes.indiatimes.com/2014-04-14/ news/49126396_1_costa-coffee-cafe-coffee-day- coffee-chain, accessed on 14 May 2014.

Danciu, Victor (2007), 'Performance in service market- ing from philosophy to customer relationship man- agement', available from http://www.ectap.ro/ articole/237.pdf, accessed on 2 July 2008.

Express News Service (2013), 'Soft copies of e-tickets can get fliers through airport departure gates', available from http://www.ndtv.com/article/india/ now-show-soft-copy-of-plane-tickets-to-enter-into- airports-311853, accessed on May 14 2014.

http://home.businesswire.com/portal/site/google/ index.jsp?ndmViewId=news_view&newsId= 20061114005428&newsLang=en, accessed on 15 December 2006.

http://www.kfc.ca/home/en/news.html, accessed on 17 December 2006.

http://www.kfc.com/about/colonel.htm, accessed on 17 December 2006.

http://www.yum.com/about/brands.asp, accessed on 20 December 2006.

KFC (2012), available from http://www.kfc.co.in/history. php, accessed on 24 May 2014.

Mehrotra, K. (2014), 'Has this "Unique Third Place" captured the heart of the Indian consumer yet?', available from http://pitchonnet.com/blog/2014/04/ 16/unique-place-captured-heart-indian-consumer- yet-2/, accessed on 14 May 2014.

Philip, C.M. (2011), 'Now travel with just a soft copy of the rly e-ticket', available from http://timesofindia. indiatimes.com/city/chennai/Now-travel-with-just- a-soft-copy-of-rly-e-ticket/articleshow/10181485. cms, accessed on 14 May 2014.

PTI (2013), 'Now show soft copy of plane tickets to enter airports', available from http://www.ndtv. com/article/india/now-show-soft-copy-of-plane- tickets-to-enter-into-airports-311853, accessed on 14 May 2014.

Starbucks (2013), 'Starbucks Continues Expansion in India with the Opening of the Much Anticipated Flagship Store in the Beautiful "Garden City" of Bangalore', available from http://news.starbucks. com/news/starbucks-continues-expansion-in- india-with-opening-of-new-flagship-store-i, accessed on 14 May 2014.

Managing People in Service Industry

OBJECTIVES

After reading this chapter you will be able to understand the

- concept of internal and external labour markets and how do they impact people management issues in a service firm
- importance of service culture and its impact on customer satisfaction
- employee engagement and its impact on service culture
- people-related factors that contribute towards creating excellence in service culture in a firm
- relationship between customer satisfaction, employee satisfaction, and profitability of the firm

Excellence in Services

Raashi had taken a day tour from Tokyo to Mt Fuji, which also involved visit to Hakone and other neighbouring places, from one of the leading tour firms operating in Japan. The tour involved a departure at 7 a.m. from Tokyo and return at 7 p.m. It was an air-conditioned coach with the tour guide and about 40 travellers.

The tour began with the tour guide giving all details on sightseeing halts and meals. Raashi was excited as she had heard great things about Mt Fuji and the spectacular scenery of Hakone. The bus was about to arrive at Mt Fuji When it suddenly stopped. The driver and the guide made several attempts but could not restart the bus. There were angry customers, asking for a refund and grudging about a lost day and how they would not get this opportunity again. Near the base of the mountain was the café where the meals were to be provided. The guide tried to pacify the customers by announcing that the meal expenses for all passengers would be borne by the tour company. Finally, everything was sorted. The passengers had their lunch and a new bus was arranged. The tour went on as usual. The bus took the passengers to Hakone. They missed one of the rides committed but were safely brought back to Tokyo. The guide thanked the customers and the ticket money was refunded to every single customer on the tour the same day. Raashi was overwhelmed. She had a good time and other than two hours of halt at the base of Mt Fuji, everything was as per the itinerary. She was touched by the hospitality and the courtesies extended by the guide and the firm.

After going through the chapter, you will be able to answer the following questions:

1. What role do people play in delivery of a service experience?
2. What are the factors that play a role in people being able to deliver in a service firm?

INTRODUCTION

This chapter deals with the human perspective on services, that is, the effect people have on management of services. An overview of the labour market and how it affects people has also been discussed. The chapter also discusses service culture and its impact on customer satisfaction. The factors contributing to service excellence are examined along with an overview on the relationship between employee satisfaction, customer satisfaction, and the overall profitability of the firm.

The services industry is very strongly driven by the human factor. The nature of services industry is such that people become a very important component in the delivery of the services. The experience factor in consumption of a service contributes immensely to consumer loyalty.

For instance, good experiences while dining, travelling, and education stay with you forever and you will want to come back to re-live the same experience. Brands such as McDonald's, Disney Theme Parks, Domino's, Pizza Hut, and Four Seasons have won laurels on account of their unique experience and being able to live up to people's expectations.

In recent times, technology has acted as a driver to enhance the experience for the consumer, but the human factor cannot be eliminated. There are services sectors wherein the human element plays an important role in delivery of the experience such as education, consulting, beauty services, telecommunication, and insurance among other sectors. Human resources are the efforts, skills, and capabilities that people contribute to an employing organization (Leopold et al. 1999). Strategic human resource management helps to achieve competitive advantage through the development of a highly committed and capable workforce (Storey 1995). Culture and leadership styles become the important focus in the strategic human resource management approach (Towers 1994). Culture and human resources provides a distinctive edge to the services firm. It is human capability and commitment that distinguish successful organizations from the rest (Storey 1989). Jones (1997) agrees and argues that people and the way they are managed and deployed are the single-most sustainable source of competitive advantage.

Employees are the face of the firm. Hence, it is important that they are treated like internal customers. If employees are not treated well, they will not treat the customers of the firm well and that is very dangerous for the firm. Every unpleasant experience can lead to negative word-of-mouth, which will drive customers away from the firm. In the light of creating positive experiences for the customers, it is important to care for the employees in a firm just as one would treat customers. To understand people issues in a service firm, it is important to understand the following questions. This chapter tries to address these issues.

1. How does the external supply of manpower impact people management issues in a firm?
2. What constitutes the culture of a firm?
3. How can a service culture of firms across various regions be compared? What impact will it have on the management of people in cross-cultural firms?
4. How can a service culture of excellence be created in a firm?
5. How does teamwork help to improve the service offering?
6. How can training and development contribute to a positive consumer experience?
7. How can the employees in service firms be motivated?
8. How can the employees in service firms be empowered?
9. How can employees in a service firm be made to feel secure?

CHALLENGES OF MANAGING PEOPLE IN A SERVICE FIRM

Services is a dynamic sector, which is growing worldwide. Since the sector is growing and the foreign direct investment is increasing because of the opening of economies, globally there is a demand for professionals in the services sector. Sectors such as software, information technology enabled services (ITES), hospitality, tourism, and health care, are all areas where there is a dearth of professionals. This raises issues on the supply side, which means there are implications for the education side as well as the industry. Some of the challenges are as follows:

- dealing with high rates of attrition
- high level of stress
- high degree of customer interface
- challenges for retaining employees and motivating them
- ensuring adequate supply of professionals into a service stream
- training the people
- managing cultural diversity issues
- performance measurement and rewards.

People Management

The concept of people management is very generic and cannot have a panacea for all the challenges that confront a particular industry. Each industry, which operates in the domain of services, has certain unique challenges before it. The concept of labour markets is extremely vital to understand the dynamics of HR in a particular cultural and industry context. Labour markets are the pool of people available for taking up work assignments. As Riley (1996) points out, at any given point of time, labour markets exist at both the factual and perceptual level. There are people who are looking out for a change and employers who are seeking people for assignments for their firms. According to conventional economic theory, supply and demand is brought into equilibrium by the price of the labour, and it is brought about by the independent and unconnected decisions of thousands of people. The external labour market skills are distributed by the price of labour, yet the internal labour market (within the organization) follows different dynamics. The concept of internal labour markets is based on the idea that sets of rules and conventions within organizations, which act as allocative mechanisms, govern the movement of people and the pricing of jobs. These rules are related to growth opportunities, investments in training, pay differentials, and evaluation of jobs. It is also about openness to external labour markets, which represents the interface between what goes inside the firm and what goes outside.

CHARACTERISTICS OF STRONG AND WEAK LABOUR MARKETS

The characteristics of strong internal labour markets according to Riley (1996) are as follows:
- structural features
- specified hiring standards
- single point of entry
- high skill specificity
- continuous on-the-job training
- fixed criteria for promotion and transfer
- strong workplace customs
- pay differentials remain fixed over time.

Weak labour markets have the following characteristics:
- unspecified hiring standards
- multiple points of entry
- low skill specificity
- no on-the-job training
- no fixed criteria for promotion and transfer
- weak workplace customs
- pay differentials vary over time.

We would expect to find low rates of labour turnover associated with strong internal labour markets. The labour turnover is high with weak internal labour markets. This is, however, a rough indication. Organizations can initiate various measures for improving the internal labour market scenario:
- alter pay and working conditions
- alter training practices
- alter growth opportunities for people in the firm
- use overtime and other forms of increased form of labour supply, which could happen by introducing shifts or may be part-time options as well bringing larger number of people in the work domain
- alter points of entry into the firm
- alter job design and structure of the firm.

Hospitality Sector in India

The Indian hospitality industry is characterized by a weak internal labour market. There is a stream of 10,000 hospitality students graduating every year (Ministry of HRD, Government of India) from various public and private institutions. However, the management trainee positions are merely restricted to about 100–150. Most graduates join as operations trainees and then wait for another few years to become management trainees. The work conditions in most hotels in India, apart from the top luxury brands, leaves a lot to be desired. The attrition rates are high. Long work hours with low compensation motivates employees to look for greener pastures. Many of the multinational brands act as a training ground for interns who later take up more lucrative assignments elsewhere. The reason for shifting jobs are slight increments in salary, the work environment lacks openness, and sharing of concerns by employees is seldom the norm. The employee to room ratio is extremely high.

Hotels deploy more people rather than investing in a multi-skilled task force. These issues can be attributed to the supply side of the labour in this industry. The education system needs to change. Incorporation of management-related modules in the curriculum could be helpful and give insights into management of brands and sensitivity to issues related to strategy, financial management, and people as an important resource.

RELEVANCE OF PEOPLE MANAGEMENT ISSUES

In a service firm, service encounter in many situations involves human interface. At such times, the competence and attitude of an employee determines the outcome of an interaction. There may be instances wherein the features offered by a service are outstanding, yet the employee attitude can completely put off a consumer. There may be a case of an average attribute offering, yet an enthusiastic delivery can be a unique experience for the consumer. There is a need for creating memorable experiences during service encounters, which could result in generating loyal customers for the firm. If the employee is a strong link between the firm and the consumer, then it becomes pertinent that the employee truly represents the philosophy the firm stands for.

How well this philosophy is conveyed in spirit and deed is determined by numerous factors. These are as follows:

Competence level of an employee   It is important that the person performing the job is well informed and knows his responsibilities. In a restaurant, if a waiter is unaware about the menu and is unable to make recommendations when asked, it indicates lack of detailing and customer orientation. For example, in case of an educational institution, the person who counsels students for possible recruitments into the various programmes should be able to guide them into the accreditation process; provide comparative insights with other similar offerings, and details about placement opportunities.

Vision of the firm   The orientation of the employees is a reflection of the vision of the firm in many situations. A firm that wants to be a lead player will care both for its customers and its employees. It will also inform the people about its vision and commitment to various concerns. For instance, Hewlett-Packard has been known for the 'HP way of life'. This is a reflection on care for its employees and customers. It means creating an environment of openness and trust, and making life easier for employees so that they give their best to the job in hand.

Institutionalization of core values of the firm   Firms with outstanding service cultures make sure that values are communicated across the firm and shared with employees. The signages, specific communication training, and artefacts, all reinforce the values of the firm. Internal newsletters and communication are all reflections of institutionalizing of values. The performance measurement and appraisal systems can be used as powerful systems to ensure that all employees work towards fulfilment of the core values. For instance, Xerox ascribes to four values, namely, employee satisfaction, customer satisfaction, return on investment, and return on assets. People's performance was measured on these dimensions in the firm.

Investment in training   Training helps to make people perform at the desired level of expectation. It helps the service firm to provide uniform service across all outlets. The banking experience at Citibank is uniform across all branches. The experience at any Hilton or Marriott will be identical. This emanates on account of similar vision and similar training imparted at various outlets and properties. Walt Disney makes massive investments in training to ensure an unforgettable experience.

Well-defined processes and structure   This helps to minimize confusion in service delivery. To minimize human error, the flow of activities and processes helps to attain standardization and uniformity of delivery. The process of delineating the workflow is called blueprinting.

Empowerment on certain decisions   The employees with a customer interface help to deal with difficult customer situations. If a person handling customers does not have the authority to deviate from prescribed rules, situations sometimes become difficult to handle. A certain amount of responsibility must accompany the job. However, the recruitment strategy needs to be appropriate so that employees who are performing these roles are adequately mature. Let's take the case of a travel firm that organizes tours. Suppose on a tour the bus breaks down and the guide is not empowered to take instantaneous decisions, it will have a negative impact on the overall experience. The domain of empowerment of employees should be clearly defined. More of this is discussed in the section on service recovery.

Rewards and reinforcement of certain kinds of behaviour   There is sufficient evidence in literature that links profitability in a firm to customer satisfaction. Customer satisfaction is not just dependent on the attributes of the service offering; the entire experience and employees contribute distinctly to the whole experience. If, for instance, we take the case of a restaurant, it may offer great food and ambience but if the staff who takes care of the service is rude or unconcerned, it will ruin the whole experience.

The research in human resource management has shown a connection between employee-oriented practices, employee behaviour, and organizational effectiveness. Service employees provide service to customers commensurate with the treatment they receive from their employers (Schneider and Bowen 1985).

The service quality measures in literature are clear pointers towards the importance of people management. The SERVQUAL instrument to measure the service quality clearly delineates the following dimensions, which contribute to the overall experience:
- Assurance: This is defined as the knowledge and courtesy of the employees and their ability to convey trust and confidence.
- Empathy: Caring, individualized attention, which the firm provides to its customers.
- Reliability: The ability to perform the promised service dependably and accurately.

- Responsiveness: The willingness to help customers and provide prompt service.
- Tangibles: The appearance of physical facilities, equipment, personnel, and communication materials.

The above elements clearly indicate that the employees need to be managed effectively, and in order to maintain quality it is pertinent that the employees are trained and treated well.

The Deming's quality paradigm suggests that the following initiatives have a bearing on institutionalizing quality:

- create constancy of purpose for improvement of product and service
- adopt the new philosophy
- cease dependence on mass production
- end the practice of awarding business on price tag alone
- improve constantly and forever the system of production and service
- institute training
- institute leadership
- drive out fear
- break down barriers between staff areas
- eliminate slogans, exhortations, and targets for the workforce
- eliminate numerical quotas
- remove barriers to pride of workmanship
- institute a vigorous programme of education and re-training
- take action to accomplish the transformation.

The aforementioned points clearly indicate the importance of investment in people in the services industry.

FRAMEWORK LINKING EMPLOYEE SATISFACTION, CUSTOMER SATISFACTION, AND PROFITABILITY

The framework as postulated by Heskett et al. (1994) lists the relationship between employee satisfaction, customer satisfaction, and profitability. The framework postulates that in a firm profitability and revenue growth is driven by customer loyalty. Customer loyalty can only emanate if the customers are happy with the firm and the customers will be happy if their experience with the firm has been good. As employees are an integral part of the whole experience in a service firm, their behaviour will contribute to making the entire experience enjoyable. If the employee is happy with the work, and has the right attitude and training, he/she will be productive and will drive the profitability through repeat business. The internal service culture will, therefore, have a huge impact on the employee satisfaction and orientation.

SERVICES INDUSTRY AND CULTURE

All successful organizations have a distinct service culture. It contributes to people's orientation towards customers, treating each other with respect, and upholding the values as cherished by the firm. Service culture has a bearing on employees' attitudes and work ethics. It is, therefore, important to understand the dynamics of service culture. The roots of the service culture lie in the culture itself. It is also interesting to see how different cultures shape the communication and employee dynamics globally. This section gives insights into culture and service culture and suggests how this can be embedded into the day-to-day lives of employees in a firm.

Culture

Culture is an umbrella word that encompasses a whole set of implicit, widely-shared beliefs, traditions, values, and expectations that characterize a particular group of people. It identifies the uniqueness of a social unit, its values, and beliefs (Leavitt and Bahrami 1988). Hofstede (1980) defined culture as 'The collective programming of the mind which distinguishes the members of one human group from another…the interactive aggregate of common characteristics that influence a human group's response to the environment'. Schein (1990) distinguishes between three levels of culture:
1. Behaviour and artefacts (buildings, art, and literature)
2. Beliefs and values
3. Underlying assumptions

Culture exerts a lot of influence on the employees in a firm (Webster 1992). It:
• provides the central theme around which employees' behaviour can converge
• is the critical key strategic managers may use to direct the course of their firm
• provides a pattern of shared values and beliefs, the norms for behaviour, and a form of control of employees
• influences productivity, the manner in which the firm copes with the various aspects of the external environment, and newcomer socialization
• aids in hiring practices, that is, helps in understanding the characteristics of people who would do well in the firm
• establishes the rationale for 'dos and don'ts' of behaviour.

Culture exists at various levels such as country, industry, and corporate (Pizam 1993). It is interesting to see that different nations and firms can be compared on certain parameters, which help to understand cultures. Each country can be categorized on cultural dimensions as in Hofstede's typology. Each industry also has certain unique characteristics. Similarly, local and multinational firms also have their unique cultures, which are influenced by the national and the industry cultures.

Hofstede (1980) identified the following dimensions of culture that can have an impact on work values in an organizational context:
1. Power distance
2. Individualism
3. Masculinity
4. Uncertainty avoidance

Power distance Power distance defines the extent to which societies accept inequality in power and consider it as normal. This dimension does not deal with mere existence of power distance, which is universal, but the magnitude that is tolerated. The extent to which power is distributed among people, equally or unequally, is reflected in superior– subordinate relationship such as parent–child, teacher–pupil, manager–employee, or sovereign–subject. In societies with large power gaps, the superior exerts more power over the junior partner. Austria and Israel have been categorized as low power distance societies, whereas India and Philippines are high power distance societies.

Individualism   This is the degree to which cultures encourage individual concerns as opposed to collectivist concerns. The driving urge in case of individualist cultures is 'me first'. In a collectivist society, the group concerns take precedence over individual concerns; the conformance to group norms is perceived to be important. Japan is an example of a collectivist society, whereas US is seen to be a highly individualistic society. In an individualistic culture, it is important for individuals to have control over their personal and private life, to stand on their own feet, to make decisions that affect their lives, and to look after themselves and their immediate family members. In a collectivist culture, people are more dependent on others in a group, both financially and morally (Tayeb 1997).

Masculinity   This is a characteristic that opposes feminity. In masculine cultures, the social sex roles are clearly differentiated. Men should be assertive while women are clearly caring and nurturing. Japan is high on masculinity (Tayeb 1997). This trait is reflected in the great emphasis that Japanese parents place on competitiveness and excellence at every stage of their children's education, from kindergarten to the firm for which they end up working.

Uncertainty avoidance   This defines the extent to which people within a culture are encouraged to take risks and can tolerate uncertainty. Cultures high on uncertainty avoidance adhere to rules, work hard, and feel compelled to devise means to beat the future. People weak in uncertainty avoidance tend to accept each day as it comes, take risks easily, and do not work too hard. There are fewer rules, and they can be easily broken and changed.

To institutionalize a service culture, especially in a global context, it is important to understand the cultural context both for dealing with customers as well as employees. In a global workplace, there is a need for understanding the values cherished by a local culture.

Tayeb (1995) has tried to establish links between the culture and the competitive advantage of firms in various countries. The local culture influences institutions in a country, which reflects in the national competitiveness of a nation. We, therefore, have instances wherein workforces from different countries are labelled as hardworking, achievement driven, or laid back. This reflects in work dynamics at the workplace as well.

Service Culture and Excellence

Research into service culture has largely been positioned within the latter (variable) perspective. The prescriptions have often been based on case studies focusing on so-called 'excellent' service firms (Berry 1999; Berry and Bendapudi 2003; Muldrow et al. 2002; Schneider and Bowen 1995). Berry (1999) for example, based his study on award-winning organizations such as Bergstrom Hotels, Midwest Express Airlines, and Dana Commercial Credit. He found that the organizations studied were all driven by seven values:

1. Innovation
2. Joy
3. Respect
4. Teamwork
5. Social profit
6. Integrity
7. Excellence

Excellence in a firm can be achieved through employees (Hesselink and Assem 2002). They have the following observations:

- Excellent leadership will be achieved through clear vision and mission statements, and the distinct role model behaviour of managers who are proud of their organization and know what is expected of them.
- Excellent employees will be created through excellent leadership, good recruitment and selection procedures, good education and training facilities, and clear guidelines about what is expected of them.
- Satisfied candidates will be created through excellent employees who see every candidate as a VIP (very individual person), for whom every little detail is covered and for whom the employees carefully assess what the best service is in each specific situation.
- Satisfied customers will be created through satisfied candidates and excellent employees who treat their customers as individuals, for whom every little detail is covered, and for whom the employees carefully assess what the best service will be in each specific situation.
- Satisfied customers will spread the word to others and return again and thus ensure good financial results.

Exhibit 13.1 is a clear example of how a global service culture can be instituted.

Exhibit 13.1 **Global Service Culture at Walt Disney**

Walt Disney is undoubtedly one of the most successful 'children' brands in the world. It has been very successfully running theme parks for children at numerous cities such as Tokyo, Paris, and at locations in US. As a firm, the following values are an integral part of the Disney culture:

- **Innovation** The firm strongly supports innovation.
- **Quality** The firm is committed to achieving excellence in all its products and operations.
- **Community** The firm is committed to including the entire family in its product offering.
- **Storytelling** Every Disney product tells a story and the firm believes that timeless and engaging stories delight and inspire.
- **Optimism** At The Walt Disney Company, entertainment is about hope, aspiration, and positive resolutions.
- **Decency** The firm honours and respects the trust people place in it.

HUMAN RESOURCE STRATEGY AND SERVICE OPERATIONS

It is important to match the human resource strategy with the service operations of a firm. The services offered by a firm range from being customized to being mass-produced. For example, in case of TGIF restaurants the services are customized, whereas, in the case of McDonald's they are standardized. The human resource strategy must fit the product offering. In a customer service situation, the employee works within the controls set by the organization. In these circumstances, control and commitment are variables of equal importance. To consider all these dimensions of standardization, customization, control, and commitment, Lashley postulated a theory to evolve a human resource strategic framework.

According to Lashley (1998) there are four styles of management. The professional style of management is located in the top right quadrant. The offer to the customers is highly customized with a high degree of internal control by employees. Examples of these services are medicine, consulting, accounting, etc. The human resource strategy is likely to be based around employees exercising a high degree of discretion over their tasks with high autonomy over the organization of work. This strategy places a lot of importance on recruitment strategy and selection processes as well.

The command and control style is characterized by a highly standardized service offering such as McDonald's and Pizza Hut. They organize the human resource management through traditional approaches using external control processes to monitor employee performance. The human resource strategy calls for low discretion to employees and emphasis on systems is very strong. Its selection procedures are simplified. Service interactions are trained and in some cases scripted. The standards are well defined. Employee empowerment in these situations is quite limited.

The involvement style is located in the top left quadrant. This service style is such that it is customized in the intangible component of the customer offer but is highly standardized in the tangible element. Employee performance is controlled through external processes as means of ensuring the totality of the customer experience. An experience in the luxury hotel segment may fall in this category. The processes are system driven and through manuals. This approach includes gaining employee involvement and commitment to service objectives, with little power to influence decisions beyond this. Managers place a lot of emphasis on motivating employees but remain in control of employees' actions.

The participative style falls in the bottom right quadrant. It is characterized by highly standardized offers, but banks more on the internal commitment of people. There is a high degree of predictability of the service offering. This can be in the case of banking, which follows both online and real-time banking options. The services are standardized, yet each service experience may be different and unique in terms of experience. The autonomy is well defined and the powers allocated to employees are outlined. The system works on the moral involvement of employees and there is a moderate trust culture.

So, to conclude, there is no one best way of structuring the human resource strategy, but depending on the service offering and uniqueness of experience which one creates, a different human resource strategy can be initiated.

EMPLOYEE ENGAGEMENT IN SERVICE INDUSTRY

Many approaches have been suggested by experts to overcome inefficiencies in the services operations. Some like Levitt (1972) suggest that managers think like technocrats and take a systems approach to the customer problems. However, over a period of time, concepts such as these have been gradually phased out and by the 1990s 'the employee empowerment approach' was actively being considered. Ashkenas et al. (1994) suggested that 'organizations put aside unrealistic searches for a programmatic holy grail and begin to look within—into their untapped capacity and their ability to inspire commitment'. This approach is now being considered as the panacea for poor customer service and inefficient operations. It is a non-bureaucratic, participation-oriented approach to empowering the employees. It is increasingly being felt by the experts that in a rapidly shrinking global workspace, employee empowerment is an effective way to promote organizational competitiveness. This is more so in customer facing organizations, as service organizations are characterized by extensive customer interactions. Therefore, customer satisfaction is closely linked with service performance and various service encounters.

CREATING AN EMPOWERED EMPLOYEE

Hunjra (2011) has defined employee empowerment as giving the power to the employees to make decisions to ensure maximum satisfaction to the customers. Highly motivated employees can push a company to dizzying heights, while employees with low motivation can drag a company down.

In order for an employee to feel empowered, an organization has to rethink its policies, structures, and practices. An organization also has to implement these so that there is an optimum distribution of power, knowledge, information, and rewards. Additionally, companies have to create multiple management systems to ensure a creative environment in which both the employees and the management can think strategically about their job spans so that they are comfortable in assuming the responsibility of the quality of their work. Additionally, by giving flexibility to employees in how they go about their duties, a service organization can ensure 'out of the box' solutions for unforeseen problems that a customer could be facing. This is especially important because a customer is often physically present during these service encounters and therefore, they are directly affected by any gap in service. They are also a witness to the attitude of willingness that the service employee has displayed, therefore empowering the employee would ensure that customer loyalty is retained.

There are studies which suggest that there is direct, measurable relationship between the employee and customer perceptions of the (hotel) brand and customer spending behaviour. This essentially translates that employee behaviour, viewed from the customer perspective, has a direct and positive impact on how much money customers spend.

Various leadership and management issues need to be resolved if the policy of employee engagement can take off. The leaders and managers need to realize that there is a difference between compliance and commitment, and that an engaged work-force is what is needed to help improve organizational performance.

A lot of empowerment programmes fail at the initial stages because of non-distribution of information, inadequate knowledge dissemination, and improper reward systems. This results in the inadequately trained frontline employees who may have the power to act as customer advocates but do not have the wherewithal to act as responsible business people because they are unaware of the business goals and objectives along with full service delivery process. Research over the years shows that management practices that distribute power, information, knowledge, and rewards make an employee empowered. This facilitates a connection between objective management practices (e.g., job restructuring) and business outcomes. An empowered employee is in control of the all the situations that may occur on the job. Additionally, she has the freedom of doing the same job in many different ways and to act in accordance with the customer expectation. He/she is also aware about the context in which the task fits into various activities, whether upstream or downstream, in the service delivery system. He/she therefore has the ability to respond in accordance with the situation. Lastly, an empowered employee is accountable to the work output and is able to recognize the connection between quality and quantity of work. Such procedures followed by employees are difficult for the competitors to replicate.

A study conducted by Aon Hewitt in 2013 defines engagement as the psychological and behavioural outcome that lead to better employee performance. Accordingly, they put forth an employee engagement model that is supported and tested across the world.

Against the backdrop of uneven global growth patterns, the report says that 'engaging the right employees in the right behaviours remains the critical ingredient of how companies manage the diverse economic conditions facing their organizations today'.

As new employee trends begin to highlight the 'employee demands', companies have to fast track the increasing need of the employee for a higher and better positioning of their efforts in the current market conditions, in order to remain competitive and be able to navigate the service pressures.

A research conducted by Gallup Wright Management in 2013 has concurred by previous views that when employees are engaged at work, they are more productive, drive higher level of profitability, are more customer-focused, and are more likely to stay with their current employer. This further supports the idea that 'how employees feel about their work', spills over to customers, influencing their satisfaction with the service they receive. Additionally, evidence from service encounters at companies such as Xerox, Taco Bell restaurants, Ritz Carlton, and Federal Express, suggests that empowerment does produce more satisfied customers and employees.

Companies that link employee engagement strategies to achievement of their corporate goals end up far ahead of their competitors. Caution should however be exercised at this juncture because one size does not fit all, therefore, a contingency approach to employee empowerment has to be carefully implemented. Therefore, in the words of Bowen and Lawler III (1995), service companies need to develop a data-based approach that could answer the following questions—Are our new work designs and structures making employees feel more empowered? Are increased levels of employee empowerment associated with increases in customer satisfaction? Additionally, service companies also have to take into account the fact that efforts at employee empowerment tend to incur higher employee selection and training costs, and therefore, tracking whether there are returns on these investments is also required.

Insights into Some Best HR Practices in the Context of Services Firms

The last few years have seen services organizations shift their focus to retaining and growing their existing customers. They have also realized that service operations play an important role in improving their profitability. Increasingly, service companies have begun to emphasize on the importance of culture, people behaviours, and their relationships with the customer with the service company, by including them in their core philosophy. Decreasing profitability has forced a rethink on such lines as (a) Do they do the best job when it comes to customer service, (b) What are the channels that provide the best service experience to the customer, (c) How does the customer perceive and factor in the service reputation of the company in his/her buying decisions, and lastly (d) How do the service personnel handle issues and how does it impact the loyalty of the customers.

Treating the service teams with respect

Companies in the hospitality and hospitals, information technology, consumer products, and financial services have begun to put their service associates at par with the customers. They not only value their associates, but also ensure that the associates are treated well, feel important, and respected. Management at such companies understands that good treatment of the employees rebounds on to the customers who in turn feel respected.

Hiring for specific skills

A service company that wishes to run optimally has to invest in correct hiring practices and therefore, has to put in place an extensive hiring protocol. Apart from the qualification, it has to identify and be vigilant about the correct attitude and the cultural right fit within the candidates and then trains them for the specific skills, if it wishes to ensure smooth running of the service operations.

Focus on teamwork

Every process in the service industry has equal importance. Therefore, respect of individual, whatever his/her position in the hierarchy is not negotiable at all levels in the organization. A successful service company has the culture of respecting the teams over individuals.

Motivating through rewards and recognition

Recognizing the contribution of the service personnel is extremely important in the service industry. Outstanding service companies often use simple but extremely creative ways to recognize the contribution of the service associate, for example, a hand written note from the head of the company, or mounting a photograph on the wall of excellence, or sharing recognition from external clients, could provide great inspiration.

Good service companies usually acknowledge people for their achievements and guard against trite forms of gratitude. They have a filter; and avoid favouritism. Doing this well requires listening, thinking, creativity, and time, and its upside potential is very vast.

CREATING THE RIGHT SERVICE CULTURE

To create the right culture in a service organization, the following aspects need to be looked into (Redman and Mathews 1998):

- recruitment
- retention
- teamwork
- training and development
- rewarding quality
- job security

Recruitment

Every organization needs to make efforts to recruit the right kind of people into the firm. The service culture is greatly influenced by the kind of people who work in an organization. If one assesses the role theory as practiced by Disney, it assumes that the service firm is like a stage wherein each participant has a role to play. So, the role needs to be played perfectly. But the pursuit of perfection can be achieved only if the people have the right attitude and invest in inducting the right people into the system. As an example, well-known firms such as Southwest Airlines (an airlines firm in USA), Infosys (a software firm in India), and Four Seasons (an international luxury hotel chain) have well-known recruitment processes in place, which follow the basic values. Hiring people with the wrong attitude can be disastrous and impinge negatively on a firm's service culture.

Job descriptions, expectations from the employees, and mapping their career are some essential prerequisites, which are needed to attract the right candidates for the service firms.

Zeithaml and Bitner (2003) have postulated that there are three aspects related to hiring that need to be kept in mind. These are:

- compete for the best people
- hire for service competencies and service inclinations
- be the preferred employer.

Exhibit 13.2 on Infosys, which is one of the leading software development firms in India, has identified numerous methods to attract global talent that can be groomed.

Exhibit 13.2   **The Case of Hiring and Attracting Global Talent at Infosys**

Infosys, a world leader in consulting and information technology services, partners with Global 2,000 companies to provide business consulting, systems integration, application development, and product engineering services. It was started in 1981 by seven people with $250 and is today a global leader in IT and consulting, with revenues of more than $4 billion. Through these services, Infosys enables its clients to fully exploit technology for business transformation.

(Contd)

Exhibit 13.2 (Contd)

Clients leverage Infosys' global delivery model, which is based on the system of taking the work to the location where the best talent is available in order to achieve higher quality, rapid time-to-market, and cost-effective solutions. Infosys has more than 91,000 employees in over 40 offices worldwide.

As economies expand their global presence, developing human capital has become a top priority. Organizations are realizing that companies can go as far as the workforce can take them. The quality of the workforce has a bearing on the performance of the firm. In 2005, over 1.3 million people applied for a job at Infosys. Only 1% them were hired. In comparison, Harvard University took in 9% of candidates. Infosys has always focused on inducting and educating the best and the brightest, and they have global hiring practices coupled with ever-expanding university programmes such as campus connect and development centres. 'Infosys U' trains over 15,000 new recruits every year and is well prepared to win the battle for top-notch talent. This education programme is supported with a fully equipped $120 million facility in Mysore, which is about 90 miles from Bengaluru. In 2005, Computerworld magazine, while ranking Infosys among the 100 best IT places to work in, placed it at the very top of the list of best places for education and training. Fortune magazine, in its March 2006 issue, stepped inside the gates of 'Infosys U' and emerged with the impression that gaining admission to the 'Taj Mahal of training centres' is harder than getting into Harvard.

In 2006, Infosys Technologies Ltd announced its first large-scale plan to recruit 300 college graduates from universities in the United States and 25 graduates from the United Kingdom in 2007. This was a step towards an ongoing commitment to create a diversified, global workforce. Infosys has recruited people of about 25 different nationalities.

Under this global recruitment initiative, US brought more than 100 American college graduates to India in August 2006. These new employees developed their engineering skills at Infosys development centres across India for six months, before returning to Infosys' office in the US. 'This represents a very important landmark in the evolution of Infosys'. Chairman and chief mentor, Mr N.R. Narayana Murthy, Infosys Technologies Ltd says, 'Through the breadth of understanding and cross-cultural adaptability that can only be found in a diverse workforce, Infosys will play an even more strategic role for its clients.'

Ten young Americans came to work in Bengaluru as part of a pilot programme; the success of this programme started the recruitment of young Americans from US campuses. Applications were admitted from all majors, including liberal arts majors, for the software engineering position. In August 2006, more than 100 new employees from American universities began their careers at the Infosys global education centre in Mysore, India, one of the largest corporate education centres of its kind in the world.

'As we expand our global presence, we need to attract bright talent from the local economies. It was with this in mind that we launched university-level recruiting programmes in the US,' said Mr T.V. Mohandas Pai, member of the board, human resources and education & research, Infosys Technologies Ltd. 'We plan to run a pilot programme at top universities in UK this year for 25 positions. We feel college graduates from the US and UK offer unique skills and perspectives that will blend with the skills of our Indian employees, to expand our capabilities in all areas,' he added.

This will be the first instance of Infosys recruiting graduates abroad for permanent positions from schools such as Stanford Graduate School of Business, MIT Sloan School of Management, Harvard Business School, and the Said Business School of Oxford. These institutions have been competing to visit Infosys' Bengaluru campus for InStep, the Infosys internship programme. InStep received over 11,000 applications for 100 positions in 2006. InStep recruits students from 82 universities in 18 countries to come to India for 8–24 weeks to intern at Infosys.

It attracts talent from across the globe, and students from some of the finest universities in the world compete to get an entry into the firm.

Retention

Service firms have a great challenge before them to hire the right kind of employees and retain them as well. In India, ITES is an emerging area in which many call centres operate, handling jobs that are very elementary, to those that are highly complex. The attrition rate at some of the well-known firms is extremely high. This could vary from 30% to 50% in some firms. This is a serious concern as it has financial implications in inducting and re-training new employees. Schlesinger and Heskett (1991) describe a 'cycle of failure' where high employee turnover results in low productivity, poor service, angry customers, and even more discontented workers, and thus continuing high turnover. Organizations with strategies of high customer service such as Walt Disney and British Airways have programmes aimed at high nurturing of a loyal workforce, in order to achieve a stable workforce.

The newspapers in India are almost always full of recruitment advertisements for ITES services. The reasons are manifold—working on night shifts, lack of clarity on future growth, low levels of maturity, and lack of clear career path. Though the work life offers advantages such as good compensation, transport facilities from home to work and back, and bonuses, lack of normal working hours becomes stressful and also hampers their social life.

Hotel firms in India also face a huge challenge of retaining staff at entry level. The industry struggles desperately to retain good people. With the sector expanding rapidly, there are newer opportunities coming in, hence creating opportunities for attrition. Organizations therefore have to make investments in employee development, benchmark compensation, and provide a culture that cares for its employees and presents opportunities for growth. The adverse work conditions such as long hours, low levels of compensation, lack of compensation for extra hours put at work, a bureaucratic work culture, power distance from the top, and lack of culture for voicing and addressing concerns of employees are all triggers which make people look at greener pastures in other industries. The solution is not just at the firm level, the industry as a whole needs to have a different mindset. The education segment also needs a complete revamp and more growth opportunities need to be provided for people, rather than looking at the growth opportunities with an archaic mindset.

Exhibit 13.3 indicates the range of Tata Consultancy Services (TCS) operations globally. It is India's largest software development firm. With its employees posted all over

Exhibit 13.3 **Tata Consultancy Services**

Tata Consultancy Services (TCS) is among the leading global information technology consulting, services, and business process outsourcing organizations. It offers services to clients across 55 countries and is a pioneer of the flexible global delivery model for IT services. TCS has a

(Contd)

Exhibit 13.3 (Contd)

focus to deliver technology-led business solutions to its international customers across varied industries.

TCS offers a comprehensive range of IT services to clients in diverse industries such as banking and financial services, insurance, manufacturing, telecommunications, retail, and transportation. It has offices in 33 countries, with over 35,000 consultants from 30 nationalities, and more than 1,00,000 person years of experience. The fact is that six of the top 10 corporations in the Fortune 500 list of the largest corporations in the United States are among TCS' clients.

Headquartered in Mumbai, India, TCS has operations in more than 45 countries. It has a training centre in Thiruvananthapuram, India, and the Tata Research Development and Design Centre at Pune, India. The company has developed IT solutions for over 800 customers all over the world and has clients such as Boeing, British Airways, British Telecom, Canadian Depository for Securities, Citibank, Compaq, Dell Computer Corporation, Fidelity Investment, Ford, HSBC, General Motors, General Electric, ING America, Lucent Technologies, Microsoft, Nike, Nortel Networks, Prudential Insurance USA, Qwest, SAAB, Swisscom, Singapore Airlines, Texas Instruments, and SIS (SegaInterSettle).

The company has about 3,00,000 members in its diverse and widespread family. The group's many pioneering initiatives to benefit and empower employees have few parallels anywhere in India.

Maitree is a 60,000 friendship and support network for TCS employees who are working at various locations around the world. This constitutes more than 36,000 employees, including some 1500 foreign nationals, working in offices spread across 32 countries on five continents. Binding these people from Asia's largest software company together is Maitree. Maitree means 'friendship' in a host of Indian languages and acts as friend, guide, and counsellor for the families of TCS employees. It started in February 2002, when Mala Ramadorai, an educationist with long years of experience, decided to start an organization to connect and support the spouses of many TCSers who had to adjust to an entirely different culture at short notice. Ms Ramadorai felt that many ladies just wanted to talk to someone and share their experiences and problems.

Maitree started as a forum where the wives of TCSers on foreign postings could get together for social gatherings and share their concerns such as finding good schools for their children, the best place to shop for Indian groceries, and understanding the local language. It has now blossomed into a 60,000-strong network and plays an integral part in the lives of TCSers and their spouses.

The activities of Maitree fulfil needs at different levels and cut across various age groups, involving employees, their spouses, children, and even parents. TCSers, who work long hours and whose hobbies have to take a backseat owing to work demands, love these extra-curricular initiatives. Yoga classes, theatre workshops, flower-arrangement sessions, ballroom dancing classes, computer workshops— Maitree offers something for everyone. TCS helps in providing relocation assistance and foreign language courses, besides conducting classes in Maths and Hindi for employees posted overseas. 'At the India day we conducted at the Amsterdam office, we presented sarees to the wives of our clients. This helped to break the cultural divide and we now have a Yahoo! Group, which links all the overseas TCS community. Recently, we brought the US and Latin American office into the fold,' adds Mala Ramadorai.

It is said that the family that plays together stays together. Maitree is striving to ensure that the unusually large TCS family stays in touch through sharing of experiences, dissemination of information, and most importantly, friendship.

the world, TCS offers opportunities for fostering a sense of belonging in the community through its initiative named Maitree. It also provides an opportunity for the spouses to channelize their talents.

Teamwork

Most service firms require an extraordinary effort and synchronization to deliver a flaw-less service. The inter-departmental coordination requires people to have an under-standing and sympathetic attitude towards the firm's internal customers. For instance, development of software requires inputs by various people. There are people who understand the flow of work and processes such as programmers and systems adminis-trators, and each person has to work as a team to deliver the whole project effectively. The hospitality industry also depends heavily on the effectiveness of teams for the com-plete delivery of a unified experience. To achieve a level of synchronization and to make the experience uniform for all team members, it is essential that all team members are trained in the systems and processes.

Managing teams

The globalization of firms and tendencies towards outsourcing offers new challenges for firms. There is a need to manage multi-cultural teams and also manage the expecta-tions of virtual teams. As the firms are expanding global operations, they have employ-ees from different countries who have to work with each other. The managers should be sensitive to cultural differences. Having more teams in an organization will lead to a flatter organization structure.

Teams can be defined as small groups of people committed to a common purpose, who possess complimentary skills, and who have agreed on specific performance goals for which the teams holds itself mutually accountable (Katznebach and Smith 1994).

Gordon (2002) quotes Birch (2001) on enumerating the factors contributing to the success of the team. These are:

- clear goals
- defined roles for each member
- open and clear communication
- effective decision-making
- balanced participation

- valued diversity
- managed conflict
- atmosphere
- cooperative relationships
- participative leadership.

Benefits of teamworking   West (2004) enumerates on the benefits of working as a team:

- Teams enable organizations to learn more effectively. When one member leaves, the learning of the team is not lost.
- The diverse range of skills and knowledge of team members can be deployed for cre-ating more effective organizations.
- Teamwork can lead to financial benefits. A synchronized team effort contributes to efficiency and quality, which can impact the bottom line of a firm.
- Change can be easier to implement in an organization where teams work efficiently.

Employees who work in effective teams report lower levels of stress. A sense of support is generated within teams, as members share their struggle. Stress is reduced because team members share their struggles and successes. There is greater clarity on roles as team colleagues help in clarifying what those roles are. Team workers have commented on the satisfaction gained by each one learning from the other.

There can be different types of teams such as:

- production and service teams
- project and development teams
- advise and involvement teams
- crews
- action and negotiation teams.

Jassawalla and Sashittal (1999) in their work on cross-functional teams indicate that though some teams have improved new product processes, in many organizations not all work equally well nor are they collaborative. In a study they conducted of 40 managers across areas such as R&D, production, and marketing functions in 10 firms, there were certain challenges, which they faced such as:

- functional–hierarchical designs
- rigid perceptual and spatial boundaries among the functional group
- differences in priorities and agendas resulting in turf protection behaviours
- errors and rework
- chronic cost escalations
- missed deadlines.

Globally, virtual teams (teams located across different geographical locations) are playing an increasingly important role in international business by offering organizations the opportunity for reaching beyond traditional boundaries (Pauleen and Yoong 2001). While information and communication technologies present real and compelling challenges to facilitators, they also present teams with unparalleled opportunities for expanding on new approaches and ideas. There is, however little research on the effects of crossing organizational, cultural, and time and distance boundaries on relationship building in virtual teams.

As outsourcing becomes important, there may be cultural issues and coordination issues involving teamwork. Pauleen and Yoong (2001) have summed up the issues in managing boundary-crossing (crossing barriers of time and space) virtual teams:

To ensure success in team-based designs such as software, hospitality, and other project-based service firms, certain aspects need to be kept in mind. For example, Callanan (2004) has suggested certain recommendations to ensure success in organizations using team-based designs. These are:

1. Adopt an empowerment philosophy in leadership: The organizational leaders must disallow the Machiavellian philosophy that rewards the hoarding of power and information, and instead adopt an empowerment philosophy. This has implications on the recruitment, selection, and development process of the competencies that support the empowerment. To be empowered, employees should have sufficient amount of maturity, experience, and knowledge. For this, the recruitment strategy of the firm should be appropriate. Power in the wrong hands can be disastrous for a service firm.
2. Help leaders overcome the 'fear of irrelevance': Major impediments to empowerment and success of team-based designs are leaders who fear loss of power. Training imparted to leaders helps them to overcome these fears.
3. Build on successes but see failure as a learning opportunity: Establishing an empowerment philosophy does not happen without conscious efforts. Organizations

need to avoid the temptation to view failures as discrediting empowerment in total. Instead, failures should be viewed as paths to future opportunities.

4. Foster initiative and the acceptance of responsibility. Organizations often fail to recognize that empowerment and a team-based structure will work only if members of the organization are willing to be empowered and to participate in teams and workgroups.

Training and Development

Training is a strategic activity in the services industry as it can be deployed as a tool to create relevant skill sets in people and can contribute towards creating a distinct experience for the people. The availability of required quality and quantity of human resource and maintenance of such employment through training would be HR's strategic response to the worldwide changes that are taking place. In today's world, there is a need to follow the principle 'innovation-training-development-action-sustainable-growth' with true concern for the meaningful development of human society as a whole (Jain and Agrawal 2005).

Jain and Agrawal (2005) have quoted the Buckley and Caple (2000) approach to training and development.

In their analysis of training practices in Indian firms, Jain and Agrawal (2005) indicate that though focus is on the analysis and design, the 'evaluation of training' has been largely ignored. The internal evaluation by professionals and practitioners should be predominant over the ritual type evaluation by system administrators from outside. According to ASTD, in 1997, only 52% of organizations used self-directed data and most organizations train their teams, training only 1% of their employees. Only a very small proportion of employees actually get trained. The actual numbers may be large but in percentage terms this number would be a small proportion of the total number of employees.

Experiential learning through internships helps to train the upcoming workforce to better understand the organization and industry. Internships also immensely facilitate students to mature from academic knowledge to applied working knowledge. 'The internship experience provides students with meaningful experiences applying theories and practices discussed and sometimes applied in the classroom. The implications and influences of workplace are far more extensive than the limits and boundaries imposed by the classroom, peers, and instructors. The environmental, social, and cultural conditions of the workplace can help the students identify their own strengths, interests, and abilities' (Tovey 2001). It can also be inferred that an internship experience is meaningful for both the students as well as for the industry, as they can benefit from the skills, strategies, and innovative approaches that students carry from their experience. Training with an organization can add to the hiring process, as the trainee is already aware of the work ethics, culture, and capabilities that exist in the organization.

It is important to ensure that training and development activities initiated in a firm are relevant to a service firm. Training is a resource extensive exercise and if training is not relevant to employees and the firm's needs, then the desired objective of an enhanced service delivery will not be achievable. The training conducted in a firm should be addressed appropriately. Kirkpatrick (1967, 1987, 1994) suggests the following framework for evaluation of training.

1. Reaction (Level 1)
   - What was the trainees' response to the programme?
   - Did the trainees find it useful?
   - Seeking a reaction from trainees is not enough.

2. Learning (Level 2)
   - Did the trainees learn what they should have learnt? This is important and any effective HRD programme should be assessed on this parameter.

3. Job Behaviour (Level 3)
   - Does the trainee use what was learned in training back on the job? Measuring whether training has transferred to the job requires observation of the trainee's on-the-job behaviour.

4. Results
   - Has the training or HRD effort improved the organization's effectiveness?
   - Is the organization more efficient and profitable? This is the most challenging level to assess, given that many things beyond employee performance can affect organizational performance.

Zeithaml and Bitner (2003) have argued that people have to be developed to deliver service quality. There is a need for taking initiatives such as:
- train for technical and interactive skills
- empower employees
- promote teamwork.

These various issues raise the question of how firms should develop an optimal education and training programme. It appears that educational institutions such as universities or professional training institutes are the most appropriate source for providing generic knowledge. This does not mean that the delivery of this training is dependent on these institutions. Firms, for example, could arrange for staff to complete distance based or e-learning programmes.

Exhibit 13.4 gives an idea about the scope of operations of training activities in the world's second largest railway, which is Indian Railways. Over 2,00,000 people are trained every year in their training facilities. Service firms should develop the capabilities to train their employees to ensure a distinct experience.

Exhibit 13.4 Training Initiatives at Indian Railways

The Indian railway system is the second largest railway system in the world under a single management. Indian Railways has 1,08,706 track kms (63,028 route kms), 7,500 locomotives, 2,22,147 units of freight cars, 42,750 passenger cars, 6,853 stations, and 15,45,300 staff. It operates 8,520 passenger trains every day.

Apart from having its own facilities for production of automotives and other rolling stock and a research design and standard wing to carry out research work in railway technology, standardization, and application to self-sufficiency, Indian Railways has the best training facilities, in Asia and Africa, to train people in rail transport.

(Contd)

Exhibit 13.4 (Contd)

Training is considered the most common mechanism in human resource development. It is actually a process that attempts to fill the gap by way of what the employee has to offer. This is done by way of honing the skills, experience, and knowledge that is required on the job. Following are a few institutes to train executives responsible for maintenance, operation, planning, development of infrastructure, and assets at the Indian Railways:

- Railway Staff College, Vadodara
- Indian Railway Institute of Civil Engineering, Pune
- Indian Railway Institute of Signal Engineering and Telecommunications, Secunderabad
- Indian Railway Institute of Mechanical and Electrical Engineering, Jabalpur

Besides these, there are another 200 training schools located over zonal railways to provide training to supervisors and staff engaged in operations and management.

Rewards

The best people need to be retained and rewarded. They should set up pace and also the role models for others to emulate. Employees should also be treated as internal customers and should be incorporated in the vision of the firm. It is essential that an adequate reward system be in place.

To institute the right reward system in an organization, it is essential to have the right measurement systems in place in the organization. If the performance measurement systems are not appropriate, then the rewards will not be fair, and cannot discriminate between performers and non-performers. Also, the system and the top management must handle the appraisal fairly. It is important not only to be fair, but also to be perceived as being fair. It is of great importance that the systems and processes are in place, if the people have to be retained and rewarded appropriately. For instance, in many start-up corporations, multitasking is done and interdepartmental teams are quite common. At the time of attributing rewards it becomes difficult to attribute and recognize individual effort. In certain corporations, team rewards are instituted to encourage team effort and to motivate the employees.

There are numerous instances where organizations have instituted numerous awards for retaining and attracting better talent. However, it is important that individual effort is recognized, as individual identity is important to each person.

Exhibit 13.5 documents the employee benefits that are offered at one of the most innovative airlines in the world, which has been profitable year after year since its inception.

Job Security

Providing a climate of trust is essential for a firm. It is even more important in case of a service firm, as there is a huge amount of interdepartmental coordination, which is required. A feeling of trust can be evoked if the organization has a specific direction and owns up to its commitments. The employees have to be truly treated as stakeholders in the organization. Lack of trust at the workplace, triggers the desire to look for alternative assignments. This leads to poor performance and non-commitment to tasks

Exhibit 13.5 Training Initiatives at Southwest Airlines

An excellent and effective employee training programme is the key to the success of an organization. Examples of such effective training programmes can be witnessed in the case of Southwest Airlines. This airline company is committed to providing its employees a stable work environment, with equal opportunity for learning and personal growth. Employees are encouraged to be creative and innovative and are an important factor in improving the effectiveness of Southwest Airlines. The website states that, 'Above all, employees will be provided the same concern, respect, and caring attitude within the organization that they are expected to share externally with every Southwest customer.'

The employees of Southwest Airlines have access to the following privileges. This also creates a sense of ownership among employees.

Passes/Travel Privileges Employees can travel for free. This privilege is effective from the first day of employment. Employees, their spouses, eligible dependent children, and parents have unlimited space-available travel privileges on Southwest. They also have discounted travel arrangements with other carriers through the Southwest Airlines Pass Bureau, subject to eligibility requirements and other restrictions.

Profit Sharing and 401(k) Plan Participation in the profit sharing plan is offered to all eligible employees. Company contributions to profit sharing accounts, which are made when the company meets profitability goals set each year, funds the plan.

The 401(k) plan is designed to help employees to prepare for the future. Eligible employees may contribute up to 50% of their pay to the plan, on a pre-tax basis. A company match is offered based on employee groups. Rollovers are accepted from the employee's former employer's qualified plan.

Stock Purchase Plan This plan is specially designed to allow employees to share in the success of the company. Through this plan, employees may invest in Southwest Airlines stock through payroll deductions. Employees pay only 90% of the market value for the stock, while the company pays broker commissions on stock purchases.

Medical Insurance Employees may choose from several different medical plan options depending on their lifestyle, needs, and priorities. Most medical plan options are available to employees at no cost, with family coverage available at minimal cost.

Dental Insurance Dental coverage is also offered through several dental plan options and basic dental coverage is available to employees at no cost. Optional additions and family coverage are available at minimal cost.

Vision Vision coverage is offered to provide affordable vision care for employees and their families. Coverage under the vision plan includes complete eye examinations and lenses and frames, or contact lenses. Under some plans, vision coverage is available only to certain workgroups.

Life Insurance Southwest Airlines employees are provided with a basic life insurance at no cost. Coverage is based on annual salary.

Sick Leave, Vacation, and Holidays Depending on employment classifications, employees are able to accrue time off for personal illness and vacation. Employees celebrate several paid holidays throughout the calendar, based on their employment classifications.

Other Benefits Other benefits such as long-term disability insurance, dependant care spending account, health-care spending account, adoption assistance reimbursement benefit, child and elder care resource

(Contd)

Exhibit 13.5 (Contd)

and referral programme, and mental health chemical dependency employee assistance programme are provided to employees.

Stars of the Month   Each month Southwest Airlines selects an outstanding employee to be the star of the month, in Southwest Airlines Spirit Magazine. Their 31,000 employees have a special quality—Southwest Spirit—which has helped Southwest Airlines to earn five consecutive Triple Crowns in 1992, 1993, 1994, 1995, and 1996, for the best baggage handling, fewest customer complaints, and best on-time performance, according to statistics published in the Department of Transportation (DOT) air travel consumer reports.

---

at hand. Hence, it is essential that open systems be created for employees to share their feelings and be able to contribute and take up feedback positively. In the Indian hotel industry, attrition rates are high for certain brands as the management feels that there is no need for sharing the profitability status, and there are no forums for employees to discuss job related stresses and issues with their managers. When discussion is perceived as being judgmental, then employees' perception about the system is that it is closed, and hence, they would not want to be a part of it, if given a choice.

The public explanation as to why Starbucks is so successful, as suggested by Howard Schultz, who with David Olsen acquired Starbucks in 1987 from its founders, is that the company is absolutely dedicated to brewing the best cup of coffee in the world. It acquires its own coffee beans, roasts and grinds them, and has strict controls on temperatures at which each specialty drink is mixed and served. It also enjoys tremendous publicity for the way it treats employees, backing up its idea that happy employees treat customers well. It offers stock options to full-time employees and medical benefits even to part-timers.

SUMMARY

People management is an important part of management in the services industry. It is essential that people are cared for and are treated as internal customers. Managing people component is challenging as, to provide similar level of experiences people have to be trained well in systems, processes, and responses. The success of the firm to a large extent depends on the quality of people the firm has. The availability of labour or external manpower determines the kind of people that get hired by the firm. An overview of the labour market and how it affects availability of manpower is discussed. This chapter also discusses service culture and its impact on customer satisfaction. The factors contributing to service excellence are discussed along with an overview on the relationship between employee satisfaction, customer satisfaction, and the overall profitability of the firm.

The following factors play an important role in creating the right service culture in the organization: recruitment, retention, teamwork, training and development, rewards, and job security.

All these processes have to be managed judiciously to have the right people in the jobs. They have to be trained well so that there is a uniformity of service experience. Caring for employees and investing in their development will lead to higher retention, saving costs for the firm, and hiring for replacement. Fostering teamwork is a prerequisite for a successful service firm. The rewards and recognition keep the employees motivated. Investments will have to be made in recruitment, training, and development, team building, and creating a sense of trust in employees, for lasting success.

KEY TERMS

Customer satisfaction When the service delivery by an organization matches with the customer's expectation, it leads to customer satisfaction.

Job security Providing a climate of trust to the employees, treating employees as true stakeholders in the firm, and owning up to its commitments provides a sense of job security to the employees.

Labour market An informal market where workers find paying work, employers find willing workers, and where wage rates are determined. Labour markets may be local or national (even international) in their scope and are made up of smaller, interacting labour markets for different qualifications, skills, and geographical locations.

Recruitment Process of identifying and hiring the best-qualified candidate (from within or outside an organization) for a job vacancy, in a most timely and cost-effective manner.

Rewards Something that is offered or given in return for some service or attainment.

Teamwork Cooperative or coordinated effort on the part of a group of persons acting together as a team or in the interests of a common cause.

Training and development The field concerned with workplace learning to improve performance. Such training can be generally categorized as on-the-job or off-the-job.

EXERCISES

Concept Review Questions

1. Evaluate the role of employees in service delivery.
2. Discuss critically the relationship between employee satisfaction, customer satisfaction, and profitability of the firm.
3. How can training and development contribute to effective service delivery?
4. How can teamwork be instituted in a service firm?
5. Evaluate the service culture of a firm with examples.
6. How does the labour market have an impact on the people management issues in a service firm?
7. What are the characteristics of weak labour markets?
8. How can rewards be instituted as motivators in a service firm?

Critical Thinking Questions

1. There is a restaurant with 20 tables with as many as 10 staff allocated for these tables. There are just about four tables that are occupied during lunch, which is served as a buffet arrangement. However, during service, there is little eye contact with the staff. The guests have to wait for 10 minutes to have a refill of water. Food is not replenished in the buffet without asking.
   a. Analyse the service culture of the restaurant.
   b. What interventions can be initiated to change the attitude of the staff?
2. A woman boards an aircraft with hand baggage. She tries to stack it on the luggage bin but is unable

to do so independently. Aircraft crew standing close by do not help her. The woman requests the crew. The lady crew responds, 'Stand up on the chair and then keep the baggage.' Bewildered by the response, the guest just stares at her. Then she remarks, 'I will never fly this airline again.'

What is the HR issue in this context? How can the airline avoid such encounters?

3. A tourist takes a boat ride as part of an itinerary and at one of the destinations the boat starts leaking and passengers are advised to get off. The tourist is stranded with no response from the captain or the firm.

Discuss the critical people management issues related to this episode.

4. In an aircraft, the crew is serving the meals and the staff is clumsy. While the meal is being served, the coffee spills over one of the guests. There is little apology on the part of the crew. Will the guest want a future association with the airline?

Internet Exercises

1. Identify any two firms operating in a similar service industry. Browse through their website. Critically compare the HR concerns and compare employee orientation in the two firms.
2. Search for firms that have received global appreciation for service excellence. (Hint: You may look at firms that have international awards such as

Malcolm Baldridge or European Award for Quality Management.)

3. Identify two firms in India and China that have been identified as the 'Best places to work'. What are the similarities and dissimilarities?

4. Evaluate the leadership in two firms in India and Europe in service industries such as banks, hotels, and airlines. Compare and contrast them on HR aspects.

CASE STUDY | **Talent Management and Employee Engagement: Insights from InfoEdge Enterprises Ltd***

The current case study takes the context of InfoEdge Enterprises Ltd (name has been disguised) and looks at aspects that lead to talent management and employee engagement. The company is part of the growing software services industry in India and faces the usual challenges in attracting and retaining talent on account of shortages of the talent pool. Employees are critical successful factors that contribute to competitive advantage and therefore, firms rely on unique competencies of their workforce for business growth. Even for the best employers in the year 2009, voluntary attrition rate was 22% and for the rest it was 35%.

The key driver of engagement for best employer has been identified as career opportunities. It is the number one positive impact driver for employee engagement. The role of their manager and their own responsibility plays a big role in ensuring their future success in the organization.

The best companies invest in equipping managers to provide direction to employees' careers by

- providing clear career planning discussion guidelines
- coaching managers in career conversations

InfoEdge

InfoEdge is headquartered in Hyderabad. It has more than 9,300 associates across 30 global locations. The clients for InfoEdge span across various businesses such as aerospace, consumer, energy, medical, heavy equipment, hi-tech, transportation, telecom, etc. In terms of service offerings, InfoEdge Enterprises Ltd offers leading edge engineering design services, product development and life cycle support, process, network, and content engineering to major organizations. The organization banks upon offering 'global delivery and collaborative engineering' to its clients. The goal of the firm is to cross the billion dollar mark in the next few years.

Snapshot of Business Growth for InfoEdge

InfoEdge has over 20 plus years of experience in the business. 57% of the revenues come in from North America and has many Fortune 500 companies as its customers as well. 98% of its business comes in from repeat customers. The turnover of the company has shown a consistent growth pattern. This is despite the global recession and a tough business environment.

Employee Engagement at InfoEdge

It is interesting to see how InfoEdge has evolved and grown despite market uncertainties. A lot of factors contribute to an organization's growth where employee engagement practices contribute majorly.

Engineering services firms are a lot about people and technology. The IP and learning play an important role in developing deeper insights into business practices. It is interesting to see how growing firms like InfoEdge engages their employees and deploy talent management practices.

InfoEdge strongly believes in employee engagement practices. InfoEdge has deployed a very specific framework for employee engagement. The company strongly feels that employee engagement is a measurable degree of the employees' emotional attachment to their jobs, colleagues, and

*Jauhari, Vinnie, Rajesh Sehgal, and Pooja Sehgal (2013), 'Talnet managment and employee engagement: Insight from Infotech Enterprises Ltd, *Journal of Sevices Research*, April–Sept, vol. 13, no. 1.

organization which profoundly influences their willingness to learn and perform at work.

The core philosophy at InfoEdge around employee engagement involves the following elements:

- Engagement of employees with their manager and the organization
- Leadership by example
- Policies, people, and practices

Employee engagement levels

InfoEdge tracks employee engagement at two levels:

- Manager level
- Company level

To measure employee engagement, a metric called engagement index is measured. This is tracked at a manager level and a company level.

Engagement of employees at a manager level Managers engage with their employees in numerous ways. Managers get a feedback on their management style from their employees on a quarterly basis. The variable pay of managers is dependent on the achievement of engagement index with their teams. The engagement index is measured for every manager at InfoEdge. There are numerous elements which constitute the engagement index of the managers. Some of these elements are mentioned here:

1. Guidance on work
2. Belief that the actions are fair
3. Accountability and credit sharing with the team
4. Role clarity and goal setting
5. Behaviour of the manager—politeness, courteousness, and respectful towards the subordinates
6. Communication and listening skills of the manager
7. Facilitation of growth and development of the team members
8. Decision-making style—is it participative, inclusive, or directive
9. Appreciation and recognition of good work
10. Providing feedback on tasks accomplished
11. Belief in manager—keeping commitments
12. Demonstrating dominant leadership—this measures whether a manager displays emotion, and provides guidance on goals among other factors.

Based on the score of engagement index, a manager comes up with a plan of action reviewed by the reviewing manager and also the subordinates on a quarterly basis. Based on the progress of the action plan, the subordinates award smileys to the manager on a quarterly basis. These are then tracked to see whether the teams are happy and engaged with their managers. Based on the engagement index scores of managers, training interventions are initiated with the managers on coaching and engaging with employees annually.

Engagement at company level There are numerous questions which should be tracked at a company level. InfoEdge deploys a seven dimensional framework to achieve the same. The company level engagement of the employees can be tracked by measuring various aspects such as

1. Relationship with co-workers, customers, and other stakeholders
2. Rewards in the organization—compensation, benefits, and recognition
3. People practices which includes company reputation and people assessment
4. Quality of work life in the organization
5. Growth opportunities for employees
6. Career and learning opportunities created for the employees
7. Resources available to achieve the objectives of the employees

The employee engagement is measured at both the company and the manager level and is reflected in the performance management system as well.

Leadership by Example

InfoEdge being a global organization, looks for a leadership talent that has a global orientation and an engaging and an open mindset. There is a lot of clarity on what constitutes leadership behavior. InfoEdge has developed a leadership quotient which comprises of factors that have an external and internal impact. The external factors are related with some of the following aspects:

Global strategic mindset This is to retain a global mindset and the ability to work across different cultures. The idea is to think about the Big Picture, not compromising on short-term achievements, and then act and take decisions appropriately.

Customer leadership Understanding the customer needs and endorsing them internally, developing customer relationships, and influencing them effectively.

Creating collaborative partnerships This reflects an ability for cross pollination of ideas and builds teams with different competencies. The leadership allows flourishing of different ideas. The leader engages in thought leadership activities and builds partnerships with numerous stakeholders. He/she engages beyond the call of duty.

Adapting to change The leader is willing to adapt to the change. He responds to situations proactively with speed. He is continuously reinventing himself and also rocks the boat so as to avoid complacency.

The aforementioned four factors help InfoEdge to be prepared to leap to the next phase of growth and be actively engaged with the external community.

Employee Engagement Policies, Systems, and Practices at InfoEdge

InfoEdge strongly feels that systems, policies, and practices contribute to employee engagement. InfoEdge's framework of engagement is called Infotouch. Please see Fig. 13.1 which represents different facets of policies which help employees to engage more intensely with InfoEdge. Infotouch is an acronym which represents various ways through which the company engages with its employees. It is about setting an internal culture which helps to foster bonds with employees and their families and external stakeholders to evoke a sense of respect, connectivity, and imbibe a fun element. The culture is institutionalized by way of setting up communication practices and adopting regular and annual rituals which evoke a sense of belonging in stakeholders.

Infotouch is InfoEdge's Associate Engagement Model which believes in the Philosophy of Touching the Mind, Heart and Soul of every stakeholder (associates, families, and friends)

- Mind represents the Rational side of 'Connect' with InfoEdge vision, mission, and business aspirations

I	**Internal Communication & Branding**
N	**New Adventures** (Social Interest Groups)
F	**Fun @ Work**
O	**Outperform** (High Performance Work Culture)
T	**Talent Development** (Learning)
O	**Opportunity** (Career Growth)
U	**Unique Work Practices**
C	**Connect with Managers**
H	**Health & Welbeing**

Fig. 13.1   Infotouch: Framework for employee engagement practices at Infotech

- Heart represents the Emotional side of 'Delight' with InfoEdge values, work practices, and interpersonal relations
- Soul represents the Spiritual side of 'Shared Dreams' with InfoEdge irrespective of directly being associated as employee or not

When an employee is engaged, he/she proactively seeks opportunities to serve the mission of the organization. He /she is willing to travel the extra mile and is willing to be constructively critical for the good of the organization. At a higher level of engagement, an employee becomes an advocate wherein he contributes discretionary effort for executing projects. He sees a mutuality of interest between his values and aspirations of the organization (Mercer Consulting). The level of employee engagement may vary across industry segments as well and several organizational factors may have an impact on employee engagement. Country specific culture may play a big role in employee engagement practices as well.

In India, establishing family linkages helps build up bonds. Activities which help employees to find new talents in themselves or pursue their passion helps them to engage better.

Company Practices

Different processes are aligned to the values of the organization and team activities are structured in a manner which ensure engagement keeping in mind different outcomes. Engagement element percolates various initiatives such as building bonds with the families of employees. Growth opportunities are created in the organization for employees. The company has adopted practices which builds close connectivity with the teams. It is a culture where numerous channels are created to build and connect with employees. A continuous and inspiring communication with internal and stakeholders helps the people stay inspired and motivated.

Internal communication and branding

The people element is seen as a resource and various initiatives are taken to promote communication with people such as
- Internal mailers
- Rewards and recognition programs which have been clearly communicated
- Internal referral programs
- Reflection and newsletter circulation
- Engagement communication workshops
- Rendezvous with senior management
- HR Newsletter 'InTouch'
- Women's Day Celebration

Women are treated as an equally important resource. Women's day is celebrated and there are women related initiatives clubbed under an initiative called 'Spoorti'. This is to celebrate the spirit of womanhood. It involves creating opportunities to unfold their potential, mentorship opportunities, and encourage women to aspire for growth. There are groups of women created with ten members each and projects are rolled off and other activities are created which help them realize their potential and also create great networks and support within the organization. Developmental efforts are also targeted at these groups.

New adventures (social interest groups)

There are social interest groups which have been created which are a voluntary effort by employees. These groups are formed on the basis of common interests outside the work domain. There are groups which would be involved in performing arts or painting or walking clubs. There could be groups interested in poetry. These groups then engage in social activities and provide an opportunity to connect with each other in a social setting. After office hours, these groups may host activities and plan for their creative initiatives.

Fun at work

Fun at work helps people to be happy and helps them to contribute more meaningfully at the workplace. There are various initiatives which are initiated to create a climate of well-being and belongingness. Numerous celebrations are organized which help the employees to connect and celebrate. Some of the key events which are hosted at InfoEdge are listed here:
- Mother's day
- Monthly birthdays
- Festival celebrations
- Team outings
- Online gaming competition
- Kids connect where kids and families get connected
- Gym
- Social events

Outperform (high performance work culture)

InfoEdge makes special efforts to recognize and reward talent. It is not only for big achievements but also for numerous other initiatives for which people can thank and recognize each other. This creates opportunities for bonding and comradeship in the organization. There are numerous forums which are created such as 'Hall of fame', 'Appreciation tree', and overseas holidays for the best teams. There are long service tenure awards which are in place for the employees.

Appreciation tree

An initiative to spread positive vibes throughout the organization by giving the associates an opportunity to thank and appreciate their peers or someone whose help or guidance made a difference to them. Keeping this in mind, InfoEdge initiates a 'Mutual admiration week' in which an appreciation tree is stuck at different places and the leaves are given to all employees to be used to recognize and thank their colleagues.

Talent development (learning)

Talent development is a key priority at InfoEdge. There is a strategy deployed to manage the future talent in the organization. Individual development plans for senior managers are in place. There is a provision for executive coaching and mentoring. Future stars are identified and a high performer's club program is in place. They also have a four tier leadership development program. The levels at which these are initiated are—first time managers, senior managers, strategic managers, and managers in individual contributor roles. At each level, the requirements are unique and tailor-made programs at each level have been implemented. There is a unique work practices program which relooks at all people practices. There are awards for initiating best practices. There are specific training budgets for each of these levels as well as prescribed training man days for various positions.

Opportunities for career growth

InfoEdge strongly believes in investing for employees' growth. There are higher education opportunities that are created for the employees. Their career development plans are discussed. Job rotations are initiated and succession plans are discussed. There is a four tiered approach towards development which is adopted. Employees are encouraged to participate in national and international conferences. InfoEdge follows a layered approach to leadership development. There are four levels identified. It is the first time managers, senior managers, strategic managers, and the individual contributors. Also, efforts are made to spot the talent internally and develop the same for senior positions. All job positions are shared internally

first before opening to the external market. 70% of hiring for senior positions is from internal talent. Star performers are identified and are developed to take on the key positions in the organization. There are also very clear job descriptions in place. There are clear guidelines on how an employee could evolve from being in one role to another and how would the skill set be aligned as one moves from one role to another role. There is a clear emphasis on succession planning in the organization. The same is done at various levels in the organization. Round-tables are held in which future talent is discussed. Both at the top level and horizontal level, the star talent is tracked. In talent management discussions, the chief managing director is also involved. The growth opportunities are not only around the position growth, but knowledge growth is also an important component. While most IT organizations involved in software area would invest in training opportunities specially in technical areas, InfoEdge offers opportunities to work for Fortune 500 clients and also work on cutting edge technologies. Some of the unique technologies on which InfoEdge employees work are: engineering services, next engine aircraft, and mood lighting in the aircraft. The challenge in the work assignment helps engage employees meaningfully along with very clear growth opportunities and employee investments.

Unique work practices

InfoEdge creates unique opportunities for its employees to be connected with the organization. There are numerous forums created for the same throughout the year. The company strongly believes in creating growth opportunities for all its employees. It also provides opportunities for innovation in their roles and encourages and rewards out-of-the-box thinking. It encourages risk taking and also clearly states this in its leadership manual and in identification of future talent as well. It also provides lot of learning opportunities as well as discussed earlier. There are initiatives such as Walk a Mile wherein the senior managers visit the offices of the younger managers and understand the challenges in their roles. They have lunch together and get an opportunity to discuss various facets of their job challenges and opportunities around the same. Rendevouz is another opportunity which has been created for the employees. Senior leaders may come and address 200–300 people and talk to them on various issues which may be related with business opportunities, environment, or technology areas. There is also an initiative wherein the CEO delivers talks and all global employees get connected and get an opportunity to interact with him.

Connect with managers

The senior leaders get involved in creating the right kind of climate in the organization. Spending time with employees at least once in six months, creating right forums for expression, and sharing of ideas is created from time to time. The culture of respect and trust is enshrined in numerous rituals that are practiced by the firm. Know your leaders sessions are well received where success stories and experiences are shared.

The engagement index is measured for all managers as well at an organizational level. This has also been explained in an earlier section. Employee engagement index is an important contributor which reflects in the performance measurement of a manager.

Summing Up

Talent management is one of the key priorities for successful firms. A clear strategy to attract the right people and the ability to leverage their competencies for organizational growth can make a big difference. Firms adopt a variety of measures for managing talent. Talent management starts from attracting and recruiting the right talent for the organization; training and developing them; and engaging them meaningfully which leads to their growth and organizational growth. In order to retain talent, employee engagement is a very important tool. Engagement is not just about delivering on the job. It involves a deeper emotional bond with an organization where a person steps beyond the call of duty to achieve goals for an organization. It is about connecting with the organization emotionally and also demonstrating resilience and going out of the way, accomplishing goals for the organization.

There are different components which contribute to employee engagement. Some of these components are work environment, leadership, management style of a manager/leader, rewards, and recognition among other aspects. Psychological security plays a very big role in employee engagement. The role of a manager assumes a lot of importance in this context. A manager plays a very important role in engaging his teams meaningfully. His behavior and ability to create a challenge in the job roles and fairness in his conduct can go a long way in institutionalizing employee engagement in an organization. The leadership and values espoused by leadership helps engage employees. Leading by example, transparency, and clear directions for the growth of the firm enables a connect and inspiration in the hearts of people. Compensation, rewards, and recognition are all enablers for employee engagement. As discussed earlier, instilling fun elements and creating opportunities beyond the job roles also enables employee engagement. CSR activities, involvement with families, and helping employees bond with each other all help in achieving higher engagement levels in the organization. A powerful communication strategy internally also keeps the employees connected with the firm. Learning and growth opportunities enable employees to be connected and engaged with the firm. Challenge in job roles and ability to see the career trajectories is important for employees. Recognition of performance is an important contributor to employee motivation and engagement. Monetary and non-monetary aspects are both important. Community efforts, social activities, and women empowerment efforts initiated in a firm's context are all ways to create a greater understanding of organization orientation and building a culture where individuals are valued and they get opportunities to contribute and also discover themselves.

Questions

1. 'Some factors impact employee engagement more than the others. A firm should only focus on factors that matter more.' Discuss the statement.
2. Evaluate the employee engagement practices at InfoEdge. Are there elements missing which InfoEdge should look at to manage their talent better?

REFERENCES

Ashkenas, R.N. and R.H. Shaffer (1994), 'Beyond the fads: How leaders drive change with results', *Human Resource Planning*, vol. 17, issue 2, pp. 25–44.

Beich, E. (2001), *The Pfeiffer Book of Successful Team Building*, Jose V-Bass/Pfeiffer, San Francisco.

Berry, L.L. (1999), *Discovering the Soul of Service: The Nine Drivers of Sustainable Business Success*, The Free Press, New York.

Berry, L.L. and N. Bendapudi (2003), 'Glueing-in customers', *Harvard Business Review*, vol. 81, no. 2, pp. 2–7.

Brinkerhoff, R.O. (1987), *Achieving Results from Training*, Jossey-Bass, San Francisco.

Buckley, R. and Jim Caple (2000), A *Systematic Approach to Training: The Theory and Practice of Training*, Kogan, Stylus Publishing Co., 4th edn, pp. 17–26, 269–274.

Bushnell, D.S. (1990), 'Input, process, output: A model for evaluating training', *Training and Development Journal*, vol. 44, no. 3, pp. 41–43.

Callanan, G.A. (2004), 'What would Machiavelli think? An overview of the leadership challenges in team-based structures', *Team Performance Management*, Bradford, vol. 10, no. 3/4, p. 77.

Desimone, R.L., J.M. Werner, and D.M. Harris (2002), *Human Resource Development*, Thomson, Singapore.

Desimone, R.L., J.M. Werner, and D.M. Harris (2002), *Human Resource Development*, Thomson South Western, Bengaluru.

Galvin, J.C. (1983), 'What trainers can learn from educators about evaluating management training', *Training and Development Journal*, vol. 37, no. 8, pp. 52–57.

Gordon, J. (2002), 'A perspective on team-building', *Journal of American Academy of Business*, Cambridge, Hollywood, vol. 2, no. 1.

Heskett, J.L. et al. (1994), 'Putting the service–profit chain to work', *Harvard Business Review*, March–April, p. 166.

Hesselink, M. and F. Van den Assem (2002), 'Building people and organizational excellence: The start service excellence programme', *Managing Service Quality*, vol. 12, no. 3, p. 139.

Hofstede, G. (1980), *Culture Consequences: International Differences in Work-related Values*, Sage, Beverly Hills, California.

Holton, E.F. III (1996), 'The flawed four-level evaluation model', *Human Resource Development Quarterly*, vol. 7, pp. 5–21.

Hoque, K. (1999), 'Human resource management and performance in the UK hotel industry', *British Journal of Industrial Relations*, vol. 37, no. 3, pp. 419–443.

Jain, R.K. and R. Agrawal (2005), 'Indian and international perspectives on employee training practices: A trend report', *South Asian Journal of Management*, New Delhi.

Jassawalla, A.R. and H.C. Sashittal (1999), 'Building collaborative cross-functional new product teams', *The Academy of Management Executive*, vol. 13, no. 3, p. 50.

Jones, G. (1997), 'Conference presentation', Institute of Personnel and Development Conference, Harrogate, October.

Katznebach, J.R. and D.K. Smith (1994), *The Wisdom of Teams: Creating the High Performance Organization*, Harper Business Book, US.

Kaufman, R. and J.M. Keller (1994), 'Levels of evaluation: Beyond Kirkpatrick', *Human Resource Development Quarterly*, vol. 5, pp. 371–380.

Kirkpatrick, D.L. (1967), 'Evaluation' in R.L. Craig and L.R. Bittel (eds), *Training and Development Handbook*, McGraw-Hill, New York, pp. 87–112.

Kirkpatrick, D.L. (1987), 'Evaluation', in R.L. Craig (ed), *Training and Development Handbook*, 3rd edn, McGraw-Hill, New York, pp. 301–319.

Kirkpatrick, D.L. (1994), *Evaluating Training Programmes: The Four Levels*, Berrett-Kochles, Warr, San Francisco.

Kirkpatrick, D.L. (1996), 'Invited reaction: Reaction to Holton article', *Human Resource Development Quarterly*, vol. 7, pp. 23–25.

Kraiger, K., J.K. Ford, and E. Salas (1993), 'Application of cognitive, skill based, and affective theories of learning outcomes to new methods of training evaluation', *Journal of Applied Psychology*, vol. 78, pp. 311–328.

Lashley, C. (1998), 'Matching the management of human resources to service operations', *International Journal of Contemporary Hospitality Management*, vol. 10, no. 1, pp. 24–33.

Leavitt, H.J. and H. Bahrami (1988), *Managerial Psychology*, University of Chicago Press, Chicago.

Leopold, J., L. Harris, and T. Watson (1999), 'Strategic human resourcing principles, perspectives and practices', *Financial Times*, Pitman Publishing, London.

Levitt, T. (1972), 'Production line approach to service', *Harvard Business Review*, Sep–Oct, pp. 41–52.

Lucas, R. (2002), 'Fragments of HRM in hospitality? Evidence from the 1998 workplace employee relations survey', *International Journal of Contemporary Hospitality Management*, vol. 14, no. 5, pp. 207–212.

Miller, B.W. (1992), 'It's a kind of magic', *Managing Service Quality*, vol. 2, no. 4, pp. 191–193.

Muldrow, T.W., T. Buckley, and B.W. Schay (2002), 'Creating high-performance organizations in the public sector', *Human Resource Management*, vol. 41, no. 3, pp. 341–354.

Pauleen, D.J. and P. Yoong (2001), 'Relationship building and the use of ICT in boundary crossing virtual teams: A facilitated perspective', *Journal of Information Technology*, vol. 16, pp. 205–220.

Phillips, J.J. (1996), 'ROI: The search for the best practices', *Training and Development*, vol. 50, no. 2, pp. 43–47.

Pizam, J. (1993), 'Managing cross cultural hospitality enterprises', in Peter Jones and Pizam Abraham (eds), *International Hospitality Industry—Organizational and Operational Issues*, Longman Group, Essex, England.

Probst, G., S. Raub, and K. Romhardt (2000), *Managing Knowledge: Building Blocks for Success*, John Wiley & Sons, Chichester.

Redman, T. and Brian P. Mathews (1998), Service quality and human resource management: A review and research agenda', *Personnel Review*, vol. 27, no. 1, p. 57.

Riley, M. (1996), *Human Resource Management in the Hospitality and Tourism Industry*, Butterworth–Heinemann, Oxford.

Robson, J. (1993), 'Soaring to new heights', *Managing Service Quality*, January, pp. 465–468.

Schein, E. (1990), *Organizational Culture and Leadership*, Jossey Bass, San Francisco, California.

Schlesinger, L.J. and J.L. Heskett (1991), 'Breaking the cycle of failures in services', *Sloan Management Review*, vol. 32, no. 3, pp. 17–28.

Schneider, B. and D.E. Bowen (1985), 'Employee and customer perception of service in banks: Republication and extension', *Journal of Applied Psychology*, vol. 70, pp. 423–433.

Schneider, B. and D.E. Bowen (1995), *Winning the Service Game*, Harvard Business School Press, Boston, Massachusetts.

Seely, Brown J. and P. Duguid (2000), *The Social Life of Information*, Harvard Business School Press, Boston, Massachusetts.

Storey, J. (1989) (ed), *New Perspectives on HRM*, Routledge, London.

Storey, J. (1995), *Human Resource Management: A Critical Text*, Routledge, London.

Tayeb, M.H. (1987), 'Contingency theory and culture: A study of matched English and Indian manufacturing firms', *Organization Studies*, vol. 8, pp. 241–262.

Tayeb, M.H. (1995), 'The competitive advantage of nations: The role of HRM and its socio-cultural context', *International Journal of Human Resource Management*, vol. 6, pp. 588–605.

Tayeb, M.H. (1997), *The Management of Multicultural WorkForce*, John Wiley & Sons, New York.

Tovey, J. (2001), 'Building connections between industry and university: Implementing an internship programme at a regional university', *Technical Communication Quarterly*, Spring 2001, vol. 10, no. 2, ABI/INFORM Global, p. 225.

Towers, T. (1994), *The Handbook of Human Resource Management*, Blackwell, Oxford.

Warr, P., M. Bird, and N. Rackham (1970), *Evaluation of Management Training*, Gower Press, London.

Watson, S. and N. D'Annunzio-Green (1996), 'Implementing cultural change through human resources: The elusive organizational alchemy', *International Journal of Contemporary Hospitality Management*, vol. 8, no. 2, pp. 25–30.

Webster, Cynthia (1992), 'What kind of marketing culture exists in your service firm? An audit ', *The Journal of Services Marketing*, Santa Barbara, Spring, vol. 6, no. 2, p. 54.

West, M. (2004), *The Secrets of Successful Team Management*, Duncan Baird, London.

Worsfold, P. (1999), 'HRM, performance, commitment, and service quality in the hotel industry', *International Journal of Contemporary Hospitality Management*, vol. 11, no. 7, pp. 340–348.

Zeithaml, V.A. and M.J. Bitner (2003), *Services Marketing: Integrating Customer Focus across the Firm*, 3rd edn, McGraw-Hill, New York.

'Best practices of great service companies by Bob Livingston', http://www.businessknowhow.com/manage/greatservice.htm, accessed on 15 January 2015.

Bowen, David E. and Edward, E. Lawler III (1995), 'Empowering service employees', http://sloanreview.mit.edu/article/empowering-service-employees, accessed on 4 November 2014.

George, Michael (2013), '5 steps to creating employee engagement', Cloud Powered Business Blog, Gallup, Wright Management, http://appirio.com/category/business-blog/it/2013/07/5-steps-to-creating-employee-engagement/, accessed on 4 November 2014.

Hewitt, Aon (2013), '2013 trends in global employee engagement' (Report), http://www.aon.com/attachments/human-capital-consulting/2013_Trends_in_Global_Employee_Engagement_Highlights.pdf, accessed on 15 January 2015.

Hunjra, Ahmed Imran (2011), 'Impact of employee empowerment on job satisfaction: An empirical analysis of Pakistani service industry (online), (cited 2 Nov 2014), http://works.bepress.com/cgi/viewcontent.cgi?article=1008&context=ahmed_hunjra, accessed on 15 January 2015.

'Select best practices from the world's best', http://www.greatplacetowork.in/best-companies/worlds-best-multinationals/best-practices#, accessed on 15 January 2015.

http://corporate.disney.go.com/careers/culture.html, accessed on 10 January 2015.

http://www.greatplacetowork.in/best-companies/indias-best-companies-to-work-for/818-2014, accessed on 15 January 2015.

14   Managing Service Processes

OBJECTIVES

After reading this chapter you will be able to understand the

- concept of service processes
- relationship between profitability and service process
- essentials of a service blueprint
- importance of a customer's role in service delivery
- characteristics of a service guarantee
- dimensions of service process matrix

30 Minutes or Free

With the addition of 110 outlets in FY13, Domino's, with over 550 outlets, is the fastest growing pizza outlet in the country today. As of now, Domino's accounts for over 70% of the pizza home delivery market.

Ajay Kaul, CEO, Jubilant Foodworks, the master franchisee for Domino's Pizza and Dunkin' Donuts in India, credits this expansion to the customer insight developed by the company since its advent in 1990. Domino's is credited of converting the parantha eating Indian people into pizza aficionados.

The proposition of delivery in 30 minutes was one such action taken to cash in on paucity of time with the working couples. Another way to cash in on this was to offer the pizza free if the delivery was late. This was a risky undertaking given that traffic in India and maze-like residential areas could derail the profitability of the venture. However, it

was achieved by scouting for most efficient delivery routes months before an outlet opened in any area. Equipped with clipboards, paper, and pencil, employees painstakingly sketched maps of every lane, and landmarks such as fire stations and temples, and marked the address of every building, to prepare for deliveries in the area. Armed with hand-drawn maps, these delivery men test-drove through lanes to familiarize themselves with the topography of the area and also chart out the shortest possible routes to the nearest landmarks.

Once on the job to deliver pizzas, the delivery men are also not allowed to race to their destinations either—their motorbikes are modified to restrict their maximum speed to 45kph. That means riders must know every street, pothole, traffic light, choke point, construction site, and police roadblock in their sectors of fast-changing, densely populated cities, which is where their earlier route familiarization exercises come handy. The delivery men are not penalized by the company for late deliveries. Further, the company also trains its store teams—especially its delivery people—not to feel upset if a pizza is late. Additionally, customers are also reassured that workers do not pay for late pizzas out of their own pocket, with all staff wearing badges on their uniforms declaring 'I am not punished for late deliveries.'

After going through the chapter, you will be able to answer the following questions:

1. Which aspects of a service process contributed to driving Domino's sales in India?
2. Discuss the lessons learnt from Domino's planning process for their efficient delivery.

INTRODUCTION

Managing service processes has a very special significance in the service industry as it offers a process for delivery of the services. Efficient service offering creates unique customer experiences, which would make the consumers use the services. Consumers do believe in a moment-of-truth, which is a point in service delivery where customers interact with service employees or self-serve equipment, and the outcome may affect perceptions of service quality (Lovelock and Wright 1999). So, the service providers must ensure that the front- and back-end processes are aligned in such a manner that they demonstrate a positive moment-of-truth for the customer.

This chapter gives an overview of service processes and explores the relationship between profitability and service blueprinting. It also provides an insight into managing the dynamics of demand and supply. It assesses various waiting line strategies and assesses the role of customers in service delivery. The concept of service guarantees has also been explained.

SERVICE PROCESS

The choice of a service process depends on numerous factors. There is a need to understand the service context and the nature of the service offering. Lovelock and Wright (1999) have provided an insight into the classification process of service, which affects the nature of the operation chosen. The contextual elements that are factored which deciding on a service process are discussed in detail in this section.

Degree of tangibility The degree of tangibility has an impact on the way the service process is structured. A highly intangible service, such as consulting, will need to create tangibility around its offering. This may be in terms of reports or other evidence, which may evoke a feeling of trust in the minds of the consumer.

Direct recipient Depending upon whether the recipient of the service is a person or a thing, or both, the process of service delivery will vary. For example, a hair salon will target its offering on a person; whereas a service centre offering repair services for equipment, may offer pick up and drop services and give guarantees on the quality of

Table 14.1 Direct recipients of service

Nature of service act	People	Possession
Tangible action	Service directed at people's bodies (health-care services)	Service directed at people's possessions (car repair)
Intangible action	Service directed at people's minds (art performance and religion)	Service directed at intangible assets (religion and counselling)

the service offering. Table 14.1 gives an idea of various factors that may be considered while deciding a service process.

Place and time   The place and time of offering of services will also determine how the service processes are structured. For instance, in many developed economies, such as Japan, food is available through vending machines on account of high labour costs and convenience factors. Some hotels, which do not have restaurant facilities and student canteens in universities in Japan, offer food vending machines where different combinations of food are displayed and one can choose from a variety of options.

Customization vs standardization   The service firm also has to make a key decision as to whether it will have a standardized offering for customers or will opt for customization. Many large service firms, especially restaurants and hotels, prefer a standardized offering and offer standardized services across various outlets, globally. On the other hand, some automobile firms offer customization services, such as special designing of interiors and moulding the external body of the cars.

Consumer relationship   The nature of the relationship in terms of a firm looking for spending a large amount of time with the customer versus a scenario wherein the processes are largely automated, also determine the nature of service process. A salon would prefer to offer personalized service, while a banking outlet would prefer to automate its offerings wherever possible.

Demand and supply   In the case of the supply being balanced with demand and there existing a fair amount of competition, service firms are careful of their offering and the way they treat customers, as the switchover threshold may not be very high. Such firms have to be very careful of how they manage their processes.

Service Process and Profitability

Certain services rely heavily on consumers' word-of-mouth for new business generation. Earlier research has established the importance of word-of-mouth with regards to obtaining lawyers, travel agents, hotels, financial planning, tax accountants, insurance agents, banks, automobile mechanics, etc. (File et al. 1992). The research conducted by File et al. points out that the variety of intensity of client participation during the service delivery process is predictive of positive word-of-mouth and referrals. The study conducted on 331 service recipients indicates that four dimensions of client participation are highly predictive of both positive word-of-mouth and new client referrals. The four salient participation factors are tangibility, empathy, attendance, and meaningful interaction. These findings support interactive marketing management for providers of complex services and form the basis of a specific delivery system.

A customer service can be regarded as a process that consists of actual steps to satisfy customer requirements. A customer service process model is required for analysing customer expectations and designing customer service. A better service design provides the key to market success and growth (Shostack 1984). In the service industry, there is still a gap in the rigorous process design standards prior to introducing new services. Before implementing or initiating any changes in the service processes, it is essential to identify bottlenecks and rationalize them. Exhibit 14.1 illustrates how service processes help in precipitating sales. Service blueprinting is one such model.

Service Process and Productivity

Byus and Lomerson (2004) have discussed that the primary strength of a consumer-derived, value-based performance measure is its ability to reconcile many of the differences which exist when considering performance analysis among the business and economics description. They have proposed a consumer value model, which supports

Exhibit 14.1 **Service Process as Facilitation to Product Sales**

Some services help to precipitate product sales. A unique example is wine production, a service experience, which may have an impact on wine sales. O'Neil et al. (2002) have discussed wine tourism and have given an insight on how winery operators invite customers to their wineries and this has a positive impact on future wine sales. Wine tourism involves customers visiting a vineyard where experience of tangible and service production processes are an essential part of the service benefit. The tasting of a tangible product (the wine) is an important element of the benefit from a visit. This latter benefit is one that many vineyard operators focus on, and many see cellar door visits as a means of promoting their product and introducing new customers to it. This research was conducted in Australia.

They suggest that high levels of service can encourage the development of relationship marketing strategies, as currently interpreted, (for example, through the use of mailing lists and targeted incentives) as well as a relationship to a brand in a more traditional sense (Fig. 14.1).

The research identified the importance of service related cues to the sale of the tangible product of wine. The research indicates that service process factors were more closely linked to wine purchase than tangible elements.

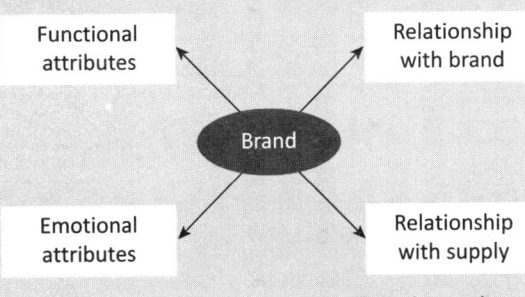

Fig. 14.1   Elements in a successful relationship

the fundamental promises inherent in the marketing concept. Customer focus, integrated organizational effort, and long-term profitability are some of the factors. Improving value as perceived by the customer will enhance long-term profitability of the firm. Consumer value, when used as an integral part of the strategic performance measurement process, is a useful tool for deciding which processes and activities produce the greatest value. Consumer value can provide a substantive proof for allocation of resources of the firm.

SERVICE BLUEPRINTING

The concept of service blueprint and deploying the same in the service industry has been explained in this section.

Building a Service Blueprint

To have an effective service process, it is necessary to document the flow of activities and map them carefully. A service blueprint offers this facility. Zeithaml and Bitner (2000) have elaborated on the service blueprint. Blueprinting is a device that addresses the challenges of designing and specifying intangible service processes (Shostack 1984). According to Zeithaml and Bitner (2000), a service blueprint visually displays the service by simultaneously depicting the process of service delivery, the points of consumer contact, the role of customers and employees, and the visible element of services (Fig. 14.2).

They have outlined the following steps to build a service blueprint.
1. Identify the process to be blueprinted.
2. Identify the customer or segment targeted.
3. Map the process from the customer's point of view.
4. Map contact employee actions, onstage and backstage.
5. Link customer and contact person activities needed to support functions.
6. Ask for evidence of service at each customer action step.

The blueprinting process in case of a fine dining Indian restaurant is illustrated in Table 14.2.

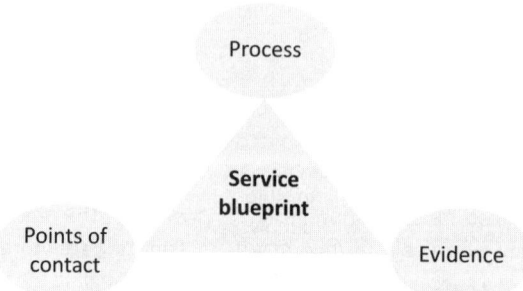

Fig. 14.2 The service blueprint

Table 14.2 Blueprinting for restaurant services

Process name	Start	End	Critical incident
Greeting and seating	Customer arrives and escorted, preference sought	Customer is seated	✓
Menu delivery	Customer is seated	Customer receives the menu	
Order taking for dinner	Customer receives the menu	Customer orders drinks	✓
Drinks are delivered	Drinks are ordered	Drinks are delivered	✓
Order taking for food	Customer receives the dinner menu	Customer orders the meal	✓
Meal delivery	The table is laid	The food is served	✓
Clearing of table	Checks for additional requirement	Clears plates	
Finger bowls	Served	Cleared	
Billing	Customer asks for the bill	Customer receives the bill	
Payment	Customer is handed the bill	Customer pays	✓
Bill settling	Customer makes the payment	Change is brought back	✓
Leave-taking	Customer leaves the table	Customer departs	✓
Problem	Problems are identified	Problems are resolved	

Advantages of blueprinting The blueprinting process offers numerous advantages, such as, it:

- brings clarity to the service delivery process
- enables identification of critical incidents, which contribute or damage the consumer experience
- provides insights on areas where employees need to be trained
- enables further improvement of the process
- helps to put coordination activities in perspective
- can be used to assess and control costs
- facilitates external and internal marketing and can be a source of competitive advantages.

MANAGING DEMAND AND SUPPLY

Managing demand is critical in providing a better service experience. The excess demand may lead to chaos and long queues in a service operation wherein the consumers experience may suffer. Demand and supply mismatch could manifest by (i) demand exceeding supply, (ii) supply exceeding demand, and (iii) matching demand and supply.

Lovelock (2001) provides an insight into understanding the patterns of demand, raising the following issues.

- Do they follow a predictable cycle?
- What are the causes of cyclical variation?

There may be day-to-day strategies for shifting demand to match capacity. If the demand is too high, then some of the following strategies may be initiated.

1. Use signage to communicate busy days for reservations; this could be reflected in advertisements as well.
2. Provide incentives to consumers to use non-peak times. For example, restaurants and hotels offer seasonal discounts.
3. Take care of loyal consumers first. For example, AmEx gives priority to its own credit card users by designating separate queues for them.
4. Charge full price. When the demand is high, service marketers are likely to enhance revenue by deploying premium pricing to contribute to their profitability. For example, hotels in Delhi charge a higher price on account of higher number of tourists visiting India during the peak seasons (winter/spring).

Jaisalmer's desert safari tours offer different rates according to the tourist season

Credit: IndiaPicture/Mahatta Multimedia Pvt. Ltd.

If the demand is too low, then some of the following strategies may be initiated.

1. Use sales and advertising to increase the demand.
2. Modify the service offering and appeal to new marketing segments.
3. Offer discounts.
4. Modify hours of operation.
5. Remove the obstacles for consumption.

Waiting Line Strategies

There are numerous strategies to manage the waiting time. Dickson et al. (2005) have placed them in the three following categories.

1. Manage the reality of the actual wait through use of techniques that help match capacity with the customer.
2. Manage the perception of wait by responding to how customers perceive the wait.

3. Make the wait invisible by developing virtual queues, which allow the customer to participate in other activities. Dickson et al. have highlighted the major limiting factor with a reservation system when there is a fixed and predictable capacity. When the capacity is variable and demand is unpredictable, such as fast food or an attraction in a theme park, the reservation does not yield the required solution.

For example, FASTPASS™ system installed at Walt Disney World helps to manage virtual queues. More than 50 million guests each year use this system. When guests insert their park admission ticket into a specially designated FASTPASS turnstile, it places them in a virtual queue. Based on the number of guests in the virtual queue and the current processing capacity, the computer estimates the time it will take for their position in the virtual queue to get to the front of the line. There are some possible applications of virtual queuing. On cruise lines or at resorts, there are numerous activities, such as shooting, dinner shows, games, excursions, etc.

Some of the waiting line strategies that can be adopted are outlined ahead:
1. Introduce a token system
2. Establish reservation system
3. Segment different waiting customers into loyal customers, premium customers, etc.
4. Make waiting fun for the consumers
5. Bring clarity about the waiting time
6. Offer value to the service
7. Solo waits feel longer than group waits, so a method that takes care of this aspect may be devised.

Queuing Strategies

Capacity management is about maintaining a good balance between the costs of capacity and demand, in relation to the demand. 'The capacity of a facility is the maximum load that can be handled by it during a given period' (Bedi 2007). If there is a discrepancy in demand and supply, and there is no option but to reserve in advance, such as in the services sector, the customers have to wait in a queue. This increases the risk that many customers may switch loyalties. However, the advantage is that the service personnel can be kept busy and facilities can be fully utilized.

In the services sector, as the rate of arrivals approaches the service rate, the average length of the queue increases. Thus, an imbalance of supply and demand will have a different impact on the front and back stages of a service system. Capacity in service operations is generally divided into fixed and variable capacity*.

Fixed capacity   This is determined by physical sources such as facilities, computers, and beds among others. It is generally represented by significant strategy choices and investments, and takes time to acquire and deploy. These largely determine the maximum capacity of the service; for example, hotel rooms, seats on airplanes, telephone lines, etc.

Source: * Based on data from http://courses.ischool.berkeley.edu/i210/f07/lectures/210-20070919.pdf.

Variable capacity   Scheduling of equipment and deliveries is a critical issue in service design. If facilities (trains, buses) and equipment can be easily relocated, rescheduled, or reconfigured for different tasks or functions, they can be viewed as variable capacity. The following rules can be used to manage back-stage service operations:

1. Shortest processing time: Perform the service that will take the least amount of work to complete.
2. Promised completion of date and time: Perform the service that has the first due date.
3. Start date: Perform the service that has the earliest start date.
4. Slack time remaining: Perform the service on the job for which the amount of slack is the lowest (slack is the difference between the due date and the amount of work left).
5. Idle capacity: Manage the amount of idle capacity.

CUSTOMERS' ROLE IN SERVICE DELIVERY

The changing business dynamics has redefined the role of consumers in the service process. Customers can increasingly participate in the service delivery. They can actually control or contribute to their own satisfaction (Schneider and Bowen 1995).

Martin and Pranter (1989) have defined compatibility management as, 'A process of first attracting homogeneous consumers to the service environment; then, actively managing both the physical environment and customer-to-customer encounters so as to enhance satisfying encounters and minimize dissatisfying encounters; for example, health clubs, hospitals, public transportation'. The level of participation may be different across different service areas (Hubbert 1995). It could be low, moderate, or high.

1. Low: Consumer presence required during service delivery; for example, fast food delivery or online payment.
2. Moderate: Consumer inputs required for service creation; for example, haircut or full-service restaurant.
3. High: Customer co-creates the service product; for example, counselling, consulting, gym, or insurance plan.

Customer Role in Service Processes

Customers play different roles in different service segments. Customer role is defined as a set of behaviour patterns learned through experience and communication, performed by an individual in a certain social interaction, in order to attain maximum effectiveness in goal accomplishment (Bateson 1989). There is still a lot of room for research on the customer role in service processes. The customer behaviour in services in usually perceived as volatile and unpredictable. Chervonnaya (2003) has identified 10 major customer roles in services and has tried to relate them to specific service processes.

Depending on the specific requirements of the role, customers can be expected to possess different types of skills. 'The ten roles which a customer can perform can be identified with the help of existing academic studies and can fit into the eight categories listed in this section. The roles "inert" and "idle" can be coupled together with the first item and "decision-maker" and "hunter" can be coupled together in the eighth item' (Chervonnaya 2003). These eight categories are discussed as under.

Passive consumer   A customer could act as a passive consumer of service benefits; for example, a passive patient or an 'inert' patient. They have low motivation or it could be by virtue of their socio-economic or demographic background. It could also depend on the category of service that is being accessed and by the demand–supply situation. In India, for example, given the large number of patients who frequent out-patient departments in government hospitals, or even private hospitals, many patients even if they would want information on line of treatment, do not get satisfactory answers. This is on account of demand–supply mismatch, and long queues, which doctors have to manage.

Learning   A customer can be a source of producer learning. These are referred to as 'instructor customers'. In an educational set-up, the experience with various cohorts of students is an immense source of learning.

Resource   Customers often serve as resource by contributing information input. Such customers are referred to as 'ingredient customers'. The decisions of service employees is linked to their ability to clarify the problem.

Co-producers   These are customers who have to participate in the service process; for example, students taking up full-time courses, patients undergoing medical treatment, or consultancy, wherein the attitude and the nature of process impacts the delivery process.

Auditor customer   Here, the customer evaluates service quality not only on outcomes but also in the process of service delivery itself.

Competitor   He/she is a self-service consumer who is competing with the companies that supply the same service (Zeithaml and Bitner 2000).

Marketing   Here the customer recommends the services to others.

Decision-maker   The customer often engages in the decision-making process. He/she decides whether to produce service on her own or which producer to choose.

Models of Service Process

Mayer et al. (2003) have proposed a model of service process, which consists of an interactive hierarchy with two primary dimensions—the process of service assembly (PSA) and the process of service delivery (PSD). During a service encounter, customers' perceptual filters modify both PSA and PSD. The model is based on the premise that the result of service process assembly and delivery is encounter satisfaction, which is the customers' perception of his discrete experience with a service. Thus, encounter satisfaction is posited to be the outcome of the service process model. Bitner and Hubbert (1995) have concluded that encounter satisfaction is a separate construct from overall satisfaction and service quality, as it relates it to a discrete service experience. Mayer et al. (2003) state that the process of service assembly is composed of steps, tasks, procedures, mechanisms, and activities necessary to the rendering of a service. They have proposed the following eight descriptors (parameters) in the model.

1. Technology
2. Visibility
3. Customization
4. Physical appearance
5. Accessibility
6. Employee costume
7. Amount of interaction
8. Delivery method

Model for process of service delivery   As in the process of service assembly, the process of service delivery is composed of various steps, tasks, and mechanisms. Mayer et al. (2003) outlined eight situational descriptors of service delivery. They are as follows:

1. Duration
2. Work area appearance
3. Employee appearance
4. Empathy
5. Assurance
6. Employee effort
7. Reliability
8. Customer participation

Apart from the service process model, the customer's perceptual filters, such as brand image, mood, and perceived risk also have an impact on encounter satisfaction. See Exhibit 14.2 for how models of service delivery are evolving.

Exhibit 14.2   **Using Collaboration as a Tool to Change Customer Service**

Waiting too long to respond to customer complaints means losing customers to more agile competitors. These competitive threats also highlight that customer demands are always in a continuous flux and that customer services is a continually evolving process. It is for this reason that companies have looked to collaboration tools as a way of changing the face of customer service. In addition to the tried and trusted telephone contact points, customers are now also open to options such as the social media, chat, do-it-yourself, and videos.

Since the advent of the customer contact centres in 1980s, organizations are looking to improve their customer service besides looking for ways to lower business costs and enhance profitability and business processes.

Nearly all the organizations have gone through the first two phases of improving customer service wherein they focused on (i) lowering cost to service by consolidating infrastructure, employing efficient occupancy strategies, and inducting better technologies, and (ii) by improving customer relationship through understanding customer context, deploying customer service agent/resource, and taking the service to the doorstep of the customer.

In the current phase, the companies are focusing on improving customer experiences by using new media such as the video, chat, mobile content, and social media. The companies in turn benefit by enhanced speed and close rate of sales. This brings together various touch points and throws up numerous challenges for the companies, which they overcome by turning to Unified Communications and Colloboration (UCC) platforms. It unites all the collaborative applications such as VoIP, presence, chat, conferencing, video mobility, and social media. Additionally, UCC makes contact centre agents more agile, collaborative, and responsive because technology breaks down time, distance, and media barriers.

SERVICE GUARANTEES

Service guarantees help service firms to infuse greater confidence among consumers for their service offering. Many services require immense human involvement and hence, consumers expect a degree of assurance that these will be delivered to their expectations, or the standards set by the firm.

For instance, IT firms, which sell big servers for banking and airline reservation systems assure extensive service guarantees. The service has to be flawless as the damage caused by failure can result in a completely chaotic situation. Real estate firms, which build apartments/houses, offer guarantees in terms of time of delivery and specification of materials used. If projects get delayed, compensation at a predetermined rate is offered to the consumers. Many mobile firms offer lifetime cards to ensure a lasting relationship with the consumers. Domino's offers a guarantee on time of delivery. If the pizza is delivered late, no charges are made for home delivery. The challenge for the service firms, thus, is to heighten the service reliability and implementation of service guarantee.

Characteristics

Marmorstein et al. (2001) have raised the issues related to service guarantee. They suggest that for a guarantee to be effective, it needs to be credible, simple, and meaningful to the consumer. It must be the centrepiece of an organization's commitment to quality, and not just a marketing campaign. The study conducted by Marmorstein reveals that a service guarantee is more credible among companies, which explains why their services have improved.

The study also points out that the customer's main interest is to receive a reliable service. Being awarded compensation for problems is of only secondary importance. Firms should, therefore, concentrate first on improving their service levels and only subsequently, introduce a compensation policy. Exhibit 14.3 provides an insight into service improvement processes. Service guarantees have been discussed in detail in Chapter 10.

Exhibit 14.3   **Service Process Improvement: Ten Lessons from Japanese Manufacturing**

Service process can make huge contribution to efficiency.

Kannan (2005) has pointed out ten service process lessons that can be drawn from Japanese manufacturing firms. These are as follows.

Lesson 1   Service process quality improvement increases revenues and at the same time reduces costs. Japanese manufacturing techniques have proven that you can increase quality and, at the same time, cut costs.

Lesson 2   Service process improvement is a continuous and never-ending effort.

Lesson 3   Reducing *muda* (wasteful activity).

Lesson 4   Reducing *mura* (inconsistencies).

(Contd)

Exhibit 14.3 **(Contd)**

Lesson 5 Reducing *muri* (physical strain).
Lesson 6 *Genchi gembutsu*—In Japanese, this means going to the actual scene (*genchi*) and confirming the actual happenings or things (*gembutsu*).
Lesson 7 Multi-skill development and job rotation.
Lesson 8 *PokaYoke* methods—In Japanese, it means fool proofing. Mistakes and rework can be avoided by carefully mistake proofing every step of a service process.
Lesson 9 Fixing root causes rather than symptoms.
Lesson 10 Address non-value-adding activities.

Source: Based on Mayer et al. (2003) and Kannan (2005).

SERVICE PROCESS MATRIX

Schmenner (2004) has suggested an evolved service process matrix based on a matrix developed earlier and the gaps therein. He has based his approach on the 'theory of swift, even flow'. He suggests that from an operations standpoint, the 'degree of interaction with and customization for the consumer translates into variation in the provision of a service. The services could be mapped on a two-dimensional scale. The X-axis could be titled the degree of variation, and the Y-axis could be labelled as relative throughput time.

Interaction and customization are common sources of variation and they are unquestioned drags on service productivity. A service may call for much variation in their provision (for example, Subway's sandwich). As illustrated in Fig. 14.3, the critical interval (the throughput time) on the Y-axis is the clock time between—(1) the moment when the service and any facilitating goods are available for use in the 'service encounter', and (2) the moment when that service encounter is completed. The matrix, therefore, examines productivity and not necessarily profitability.

Moving up the diagonal is a move to a greater productivity although not necessarily to greater profitability. Off diagonal location in the matrix can be very profitable.

To deliver flawless service operations, different processes have to be performed. It is not just about the processes visible to the customer, but those invisible to the customer that have an immense impact on the overall delivery of the service. A case in point is fast food chain McDonald's operations in India. In order to standardize its offering and to make a pleasant experience for its customers, the organization makes huge investment in the supply chain management control and the quality of the delivered food products. It has an impressive investment in numerous firms, and immense amount of support and standardization efforts. The case of McDonald's efforts is detailed in Exhibit 14.4. Additionally, as we saw in the opening case, companies like Domino's go an extra mile to tap the markets of tier 1 and tier 2 cities of India such as Chandigarh, Bareilly, and Jabalpur, besides difficult to access and navigate areas like Old Delhi's Daryaganj.

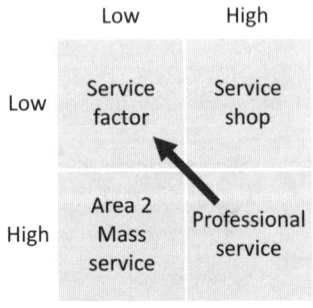

Fig. 14.3 Degree of variation

Credit: Adapted from Schmenner (2004). Used with permission.

Exhibit 14.4 **McDonald's Planning Supply Chain Two Years ahead of Service Delivery**

One would not be wrong in saying that McDonald's is the world's most popular and largest fast food chain. The American company started operations in India in October 1996 and has now expanded to destinations such as Vadodra, Ahmedabad, Ludhiana, Jaipur, Noida, and Doraha, apart from the popular cities and metros.

McDonald's local suppliers in India provide the ingredients of the best quality. There is complete adherence to the government's regulations on food, health, and hygiene, as well as international food standards. Their quick, friendly service is the worldwide mantra and the stringent cleaning standards ensure that all tables, seats, and high chairs are sanitized.

Efficient supply chain management is also a cornerstone of McDonald's success over the years. This means helping poultry farmers and farmers to improve yields on the crop. The suppliers are made to upgrade their systems, minimize waste, and speed up production. Prior to production, McDonald's looked at 250 ingredients that went into making their Indian offerings. The Indian management zeroed in on five products, which account for 80% of McDonald's ingredient costs. These include the patty, iceberg lettuce, buns, potatoes, and cheese. Until 1996, iceberg lettuce was nowhere on its supplier Trikaya's crop menu. Since lettuce is highly vulnerable to weather changes and McDonald's accepts only good quality material, the crop has to be harvested at the right time. To avoid calamities, McDonald's suggested that the lettuce seeds be planted on raised beds or moved to non-flood areas. A lettuce crop has a 3-month cycle. Once the seed is planted, it lies in the nursery for 30 days. For the next 60 days it is in the fields. Once harvested, its shelf life can be 15 days depending on how quickly the temperature is lowered to two degrees centigrade.

McDonald's planning of the supply chain is so intense that it begins the journey two years prior to the product hitting the market. This gives the suppliers enough time to upgrade their technology.

MASS PRODUCTION AND DELIVERY

Service processes can work even in some very unconventional contexts. The case of 'Mumbai *dabbawallas*' (tiffin carriers) is a case in point. This is a mass delivery system run by *dabbawallas* who collect and deliver packages within hours. There are lessons to be learnt from this unique, simple, and highly efficient 120-year old logistics system. The efficiency of the process has earned the *dabbawallas* a six-sigma rating from the *Forbes* magazine. The six-sigma rating means that they have 99.99% efficiency in delivering the lunch boxes to the right people (Exhibit 14.5).

Exhibit 14.5 **Mumbai Dabbawallas: A Lesson in Managing Service**

The Nutan Mumbai Tiffin Box Suppliers Charity Trust, better known as the Mumbai *dabbawallas*, are a supreme example of flawless service operations being managed in the food delivery segment in Mumbai. This case is a mass delivery system run by 3,000 semi-literate *dabbawallas* who collect and deliver 1,75,000 packages within hours. Such is the efficiency of their supply chain management that Forbes gave them a six-sigma performance rating; this indicates 99.999999% correctness, that is, one error in six million transactions.

About 5,000 *dabbawallas* work everyday through a system of multiple relays to deliver tiffin boxes in Mumbai. This exercise begins at nine in the morning and lasts till five in the evening. So, wherever you may

(Contd)

Exhibit 14.5 (Contd)

be in Mumbai, a metropolis with a population of more than 16 million, you never fail to receive home food in time for lunch. The *dabbawallas* have been functioning for about 100 years and are rightly recognized as the best network management system in the world.

The history of *dabbawallas* runs parallel to the history of Mumbai's development. As the population started growing, people started to settle further from the original fort complex. Residential colonies started to move further away and a lot of office goers found it difficult to get home for lunch. Also, carrying lunch boxes from home was not that fashionable. In 1890, a Parsi broker hired a young man to fetch his lunch every afternoon. Business picked up and more and more people had to be hired. A charitable trust called Nutan Mumbai Tiffin Box Suppliers Charity Trust was registered in 1956.

Although most tiffin carriers are illiterate, they are the ultimate practitioners of logistics management. The recruitment usually happens by word-of-mouth and a majority of them hail from neighbouring towns and villages in western Maharashtra. The recruitment policy is such that even before a new recruit leaves his hometown for Mumbai, his area of operation and remuneration are decided. While one set of tiffin carriers collect the tiffins from homes and take them to stations such as Borivili or Kandivili, another set unloads them at Andheri, Dadar, or Churchgate. A third set waiting at the respective stations sorts out and assembles their respective sets of tiffins, and each carrier then sets out for the delivery.

As per the *dabbawallas*, their USPs are:

- They rely on low capital and use cycles, wooden carriages, and local trains to achieve their target.
- There are several groups that work independently and network with each other to achieve one goal.
- They meet once a month where all the groups gather and thrash out issues.
- There is no retirement age.
- They have a simple lifestyle and their job involves a lot of physical exercise; thus, they rarely suffer from illnesses.
- The *dabbawallas* have a credit society, which helps them during credit crunches.
- They are respected as they are considered *annadattas* or food providers.

SERVICES PROFITABILITY AND SERVICE PROCESSES

There is a relationship between service processes and profitability. Efficient service processes help to reduce the time of delivery to the final consumer by expediting the service delivery, with minimal interventions. On the flip side, technological interventions have enhanced the efficiency of many a customer service. A case in point is the induction of hand-held devices to improve in-flight customer service in Delta Airways (Exhibit 14.6).

Exhibit 14.6 Using Hand-held Devices to Improve In-flight Services

Delta Air Lines serves more than 160 million customers each year. Delta was named by *Fortune* magazine as the most admired airline worldwide in its 2013 World's most admired companies airline industry list, topping the list for the second time in three years.

In 2013, Delta launched another initiative in its effort to improve and rationalize customer service. In line with its corporate policy, Delta has continued its investment in technological innovations. It has equipped

(Contd)

Exhibit 14.6 (Contd)

its 19,000 flight professionals with new Windows 8 phone hand-held devices for streamlining on-board purchasing to improve the customer experience.

The Windows 8 device, a Nokia Lumia 820, enables Delta flight attendants to offer:

- Near real-time credit card processing for on-board purchases, including upgrades to Delta's popular economy comfort seating.
- Convenient e-receipts that can be emailed to customers.
- Customers' use of pre-paid credit cards for on-board purchases.
- Quicker transaction processing times.
- In the near future, the ability to read coupons displayed on a customer's mobile device.
- More efficient service recovery.

The new hand-held device is Delta's latest investment in technology for customers and employees, which in the past year has included the Fly Delta app for iPad, the launch of the new delta.com in December 2012, and revamped self-service kiosks in September 2012. Delta also offers its popular Fly Delta app for iPhone, Windows Phone, Android and Blackberry smartphones, and today offers in-flight Wi-Fi on more than 800 aircrafts.

Credit: IndiaPicture/Mahatta Multimedia Pvt. Ltd.

RESEARCH INSIGHT

The Perceived Service Quality Concept—A Mistake?

Grönroos, Christian (2001), 'The perceived service quality concept — A mistake?', *Journal of Managing Service Quality*, vol. 11, issue 3, pp. 150–152.

This study compares traditional marketing models to service marketing models, stating that the most important characteristic of services is the fact that services are processes, not things. A service firm has no products, only interactive processes. While the consumption of physical products can be described as 'outcome consumption', the consumption of services can be characterized as 'process consumption'. In this context, it describes the development of the perceived service quality concept.

SUMMARY

Managing services is a complex task, which requires a lot of planning for front as well as back office operations. Various categories of services are offered, which can be classified in numerous ways. Marketers have to plan their strategies appropriately so that they address issues of demand management. Service experience is a critical element and the service encounters have to be managed well. The role of the customer in a service process has to be assessed carefully. Also, service guarantees have to be looked into. The chapter has discussed the roles that service providers will have to manage. It has also examined the case of a leading multinational fast food chain, which has maintained global standards to provide quality service to consumers. The company manages its supply chain to maintain quality standards. Another case of service operation, which meets the six-sigma rating in spite of a semi-literate workforce, is also cited to emphasize the significance of designing and managing the service process.

KEY TERMS

Blueprinting The detailed modelling of the production process for a new product or service.

Customer roles The redefined role of customers in the service process, indicating the fact that customers can increasingly participate in the service delivery.

Demand–Supply Synchronization of demand–supply is critical to service experience. Excess demand may lead to chaos and long queues and the experience may suffer.

Mass production A type of process in which high volumes of identical, or very similar products are made in a set sequence of operations.

Service delivery The process of offering service, including the place and time. Service delivery determines how service processes are structured.

Service guarantees The process of offering a guarantee on the service delivery in order to make the service credible, simple, and meaningful to the customer.

Service processes The various processes involved in the delivery of services to the customer. Efficient service processes create unique customer experiences, which help customers make use of the services.

Service profitability The fact that efficient service helps to reduce the time of delivery to the final customer and hence makes it profitable.

Waiting line strategies Numerous strategies adopted by companies to manage the waiting time of customers.

EXERCISES

Concept Review Questions

1. Discuss the relationship between profitability and service processes.
2. What is the significance of managing the blueprinting process in a service firm?
3. What are the roles played by the consumers in the service processes?
4. How can the service processes be managed to create profits?
5. Does the workforce always need to be educated in order to provide good quality service?
6. What are the lessons, which can be learnt from McDonald's supply chain interventions? How are they related to service process management?

Critical Thinking Questions

1. An entrepreneur is setting up a new restaurant, which offers multi-cuisine in a modern ambience in Gurgaon, a suburb of Delhi. The area has lot of malls and footfalls (visitors) are high as many of these malls have multiplexes as well. What are the service process issues that the entrepreneur must keep in mind?

2. A multinational bank claims that it provides 24 × 7 services on online banking facilities. A person visits a branch and asks for half-yearly statements. The staff at the counter is rude and tells her to come back later. The consumer files a complaint by calling customer services but she does not get any response from the bank for six months. What kind of service issues would you like to raise here with the bank?

3. Evaluate the service guarantees of five service firms. Which are the common elements in these? Where are the common gaps? What are your recommendations about an ideal service guarantee? What dimensions should be incorporated in a service guarantee?

Internet Exercises

1. Go to the website of Haldiram's. What would be your comments on the service processes adopted by the food chain?

2. Critically analyse the service process adopted by Domino's and Pizza Corner in the Indian market by collecting information from Indian websites.

CASE STUDY | **Flipkart—India's Most Valuable Online Retailer**

Flipkart is a home grown company founded by former IITians—Binny Bansal and Sachin Bansal. It became a part of Singapore-based holding company after its 2012 restructuring. According to a company spokesperson, the Bansals, along with senior management, control about 25% of Flipkart, pegging their net worth at around $375 million (₹2,250 crore) at current valuation.

Flipkart.com was valued at about ₹9,900 crore in November 2013, thus becoming India's most valuable online retailer. It has over 10 million registered users and ships over 130,000 items a day.

Over the past five years nearly $550 million have poured into Flipkart by the investors, thus reposing faith into the winner-takes-it all strategy of the company and rapidly growing retail online market. In other words, investors such as Accel partners, MIH Indialconic Capital Llc,. and Tiger global have turned a blind eye to the environment characterized by poor storage facilities, transportation bottlenecks, and suppliers from the unorganized retail sector.

E-commerce flourished because of limited reach of the brick and mortar retailers, and also because people outside the large cities were jumping on the bandwagon of personal computer and mobile-based access to the Internet.

Hence, what started as a website that would sell books online in 2007, had expanded by 2012 into an online enterprise offering electronics and mobiles, apparel, footwear, toys accessories, sports ebooks, and fitness equipment along with baby products, kitchen, travel gear, and home products thrown in with good measure.

Expansion and growth meant that there was a constant requirement for capital infusion. In October, Flipkart raised $160 million mostly from a new set of investors such as Morgan Stanley Investment management, Sofina SA, Vulcan Capital Management Inc., and Dragoneer Investment Group Llc. In all, Flipkart has raised $360 million in a climate where e-commerce investors have hesitated to fund start-ups or existing sites, having burned their fingers earlier by placing their bets on the sector.

Founders Binny Bansal and Sachin Bansal have, as part of their business strategy, insisted on using the invested money for scaling infrastructure and building capacities, which has delayed the profitability of the business.

With an eye on the future, the e-commerce market is expected to grow from current $1 billion to $56 billion by 2015, of which they hope to be a large part. Flipkart has decided to grow horizontally by focusing on the niche markets such as lingerie and baby products.

The hallmark of such a strategy is low margin of profits and capital-intensive nature of the business. This gives Flipkart a limitless ability to raise money, gain a significant edge over the rivals in the business, besides an opportunity of acquiring smaller firms, such as weRead, a social media-based book recommendation and reviewing site, which it acquired in 2010, and Letsbuy, an electronic portal in 2012. It is also actively considering the acquisition of online fashion portals such as Zovi and Yepme.

Flipkart has reported an annualized gross merchandise sale (or total value of transaction) of about $600 million (over ₹3,680 crore) in the 3rd quarter of 2013. It plans to take the annual gross sales to $1 billion (over ₹6,100 crore) in the next 12 months before starting work on an overseas listing. In FY2013, Flipkart India Pvt. Ltd earned a total income of ₹1,180 crore and reported a loss of ₹281.7 crore before extraordinary items and tax. However, Flipkart faces many challenges as it continues to grow both in size and products.

In order to become a money spinning enterprise in line with the Chinese e-commerce firms, Flipkart needs to address the several challenges, namely change the economics by bringing down the delivery costs like the Chinese firms. At present, most of the online companies in India suffer losses because of high delivery costs.

Binny Bansal says developing the market will be done by pampering customers so that they are unable to find a better service and catering to every demand that comes their way. For sellers, PayZippy acts as a marketplace. PayZippy is Flipkart's payment solution open to other online sites and their customer. This ties very well with the 'philosophy of pampering customers'. Flipkart proposes to develop into an ecosystem and not just remain a seller. The idea is to create technology solutions that can then be used to solve multiple problems. Therefore PayZippy is open to be used by other merchants for payment purposes by overcoming internal challenges ranging from managing a growing company, diminishing stake of the promoter, being continuously motivated, and hiring right kind of talent.

According to Mekin Maheswari, head of the human resources function, 'managing people, about 10,000 of them, will be critical for the company that expects to post sales of $1 billion, that is, about ₹6,200 crore by 2015'. Additionally, he says, 'at present, less than 1% of Indians buy online and this will grow 20–30 times in the next few years. In order to manage this growth, the organization should have a very strong foundation and needs strong people and leadership capabilities'.

Questions

1. Analyse the investment triggers of Flipkart.
2. Discuss 'Flipkart is actually selling convenience'.
3. Identify the growth challenges faced by Flipkart.

REFERENCES

Bateson, John, E.G. (1989), *Managing Services Marketing: Text & Readings*, Dryden Press, Hinsdale, IL.

Bedi, K. (2007), *Production and Operations Management*, 2nd edn, Oxford University Press, New Delhi.

Byus, K. and W.L. Lomerson (2004), 'Consumer or originated value: A framework for performance analysis', *Journal of Intellectual Capital*, vol. 5, no. 3, p. 464.

Chervonnaya, O. (2003), 'Customer role and skill trajectories in services', *International Journal of Service Industry Management*, vol. 14, no. 3/4, p. 347.

Dickson, D., R.C. Ford, and B. Laval (2005), 'Managing real and virtual waits in hospitality and service organizations', *Cornell Hotel and Administration Quarterly*, February, vol. 46, no. 10.

File, K.M., B.B. Judd, and R.A. Prince (1992), 'Interactive marketing: The influence of participation positive word-of-mouth and referrals', *The Journal of Service Marketing*, vol. 6, no. 4, p. 5.

Hubbert, A.R. (1995), 'Customer co-creation of service outcomes: Effects of locus of causality attributions', *Doctoral dissertation*, Arizona State University, Arizona.

India Committee of the Netherlands (1997), 'No roses without a thorn', *India Committee of the Netherlands*, Utrecht, Netherlands.

Lakshman, N. (2003), 'From supply chain to customer value: The McDonalds' way', *Indian Management*, August.

Lovelock, C. (2000), *Services Marketing: People, Technology, Strategy*, 4th edn, Prentice Hall, New Jersey.

Lovelock, C. (2001), *Services Marketing*, Pearson Education, Asia, Delhi.

Lovelock, C. and L. Wright (1999), *Principles of Service Marketing and Management*, Prentice Hall, New Jersey.

Marmorstein, H.O. Sarel, and W.M. Lassor (2001), 'Increasing the persuasiveness of a service guarantee: The role of service process evidence', *The Journal of Service Marketing*, vol. 15, no. 2, p. 147.

Martin, C.I. and C.A. Pranter (1989), 'Compatibility management: Customer-to-customer relationship in service environments', *Journal of Services Marketing*, vol. 3, no. 3, summer, pp. 5–15.

Mayer, K.J., J.T. Bowen, M.R. Moulton (2003), 'A proposed model of the descriptors of service process', *Journal of Services Marketing*, vol. 17, no. 6, pp. 621–639.

O'Neil, M., A. Palmer, and S. Charters (2002), 'Wine production as a service experience: The effects of service quality on wine sales', *The Journal of Service Marketing*, vol. 16, no. 4, p. 342.

Schmenner, R.W. (2004), 'Service businesses and productivity', *Decision Sciences*, vol. 35, no. 3, p. 333.

Schneider, B. and D.E. Bowen (1995), *Winning the Service Game*, Harvard Business School Press, Boston.

Shostack, G.L. (1984), 'Designing services that deliver', *Harvard Business Review*, Jan–Feb, pp. 13–39, 133–139.

Zeithaml, V.A. and M.J. Bitner (2000), *Service Marketing Integrating Customer Focus Across the Firm*, Irwin McGraw-Hill, Boston.

http://articles.economictimes.indiatimes.com/2013-10-15/news/43068438_1_binny-bansal-flipkart-dragoneer, accessed on 26 January 2014.

http://articles.economictimes.indiatimes.com/2014-01-17/news/46301491_1_payzippy-digital-media-and-payments-mekin-maheshwari, accessed on 26 January 2014.

http://courses.ischool.berkeley.edu/i210/f07/lectures/210-20070919.pdf, accessed on 4 December 2008.

http://economictimes.indiatimes.com/news/news-by-industry/services/retail/flipkart-can-acquire-fashion-portals-like-zovi-yepme/articleshow/28489509.cms?intenttarget=no, accessed on 26 January 2014.

http://news.delta.com/index.php?s=43&item=2084\, accessed on 26 January 2014.

http://www.bpic.co.uk/articles/dabawallas.htm, accessed on 23 June 2008.

http://www.business-standard.com/common/story-page_c_online.php?leftnm=10&bKeyFlag=IN&auto no=40629, accessed on 23 June 2008.

http://www.ft.com/intl/cms/s/2/42134ce2-5f24-11e2-8250-00144feab49a.html#axzz2sAYSQQlh accessed on 26 January 2014.

http://www.mcdonaldsindia.com, accessed on 23 June 2008.

http://www.mid-day.com/news/city/2003/october/66240.htm, accessed on 23 June 2008.

http://www.mobilitytechzone.com/topics/4g-wirelessevolution/articles/2013/08/22/350495-delta-flight-attendants-will-use-windows-phone-handheld.htm, accessed on 26 January 2014.

Kannan, N. (2005), 'Service process improvement: Ten lessons from Japanese manufacturing', *BP Trends*, July 2005, http://bptrends.com, accessed on 31 December 2005.

15 Managing Demand and Supply

Fluctuations in Demand

Devya was confused. She had recently hired two more people to cater to the clientele at the Connaught Place outlet where she was retailing her high-end designer clothes. She had done this as the existing staff could not service all the customers resulting in them walking away to competition. She realized that in spite of this, on weekdays from 5 o'clock till the closing time, the customers still had to wait to be shown the right size or design. Weekends were also busy and she had a feeling that she was losing out on business.

She had thought of hiring more staff but she would rather do that at the production end as she wanted to showcase different designs every week. This would keep the customers excited and they would want to come back for more. Also, the two people recently hired were not being optimally

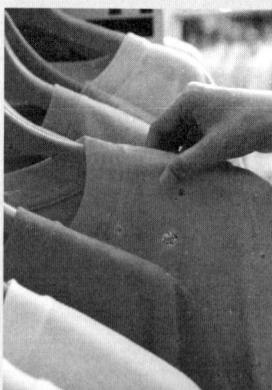

Credit: IndiaPicture/Mahatta Multimedia Pvt. Ltd.

utilized during the off-peak hours. Devya had even toyed with the idea of hiring part-time employees but then, they were not trained to handle the kind of clientele she was dealing with.

After going through the chapter, you will be able to answer the following questions:

1. What is the difficulty that Devya is facing?
2. Why cannot she overcome this difficulty by doing the obvious, that is, hiring more people?

INTRODUCTION

Services industry is distinct from other industries because unlike other industries the product traded is not tangible. Once the moment is gone the product perishes. That is it cannot be stored like a product and then sold at a later date. According to Fitzsimmons (2014), 'a service is a time-perishable, intangible experience performed for a customer acting in the role of a co-producer'. Service firms on the other hand facilitate the production and distribution of goods, and support other firms in meeting their goals, and add value to our personal lives. A case in point being the hospitality industry which creates packages according to customer requirements or the airline industry which develops offers to attract travellers to fly during lean season. All this is done to fill the rooms/airline seats with guests so that there is optimum capacity utilization and an increased profitability. This is done as the airline seats that are not sold in the lean period cannot be inventoried and stored for a period when the demand exceeds the capacity of the flight. A critical aspect of the service industry is managing and balancing the demand and supply sides of the industry. This is a feat that the service manager must be adept at all times, while keeping in mind the perishable nature of the 'product'. This chapter focuses on how service firms can manage sales so that there is no loss to the company because of no demand or more demand than they can cater to.

NEED FOR MANAGING DEMAND AND SUPPLY

Managing demand is critical in providing a better service experience. The excess demand may lead to chaos and long queues in a service operation wherein the consumers experience may suffer. Demand and supply mismatch could manifest by:

Demand exceeding supply   This results in price increase of the product and as in our case, the availability of the services. The price increases because there is fewer products supplied and more people are purchasing the product. A higher demand will increase the price of the product.

Supply exceeding demand   This is known as a surplus. In such a scenario the price of a product will decrease. The price decreases because there are more products supplied than people that are purchasing the product. When the supply of a product/service exceeds the demand of a product/service, the price will decrease.

Matching demand and supply   This a self-regulatory mechanism that is created by economic forces. This in turn determines the cost of goods or services offered at an obtainable optimum price. It is a largely self-regulatory mechanism generally resulting in market equilibrium where products demanded at a price are equalled by products supplied at that price.

Lovelock (2000) provides an insight into understanding the patterns of demand, raising the following issues.

• Does demand follow a predictable cycle?
• What are the causes of cyclical variation in demand?

It is imperative to therefore understand demand patterns and market segments that create demand at various points in time, in a fluctuating service business. An organization therefore has to chart the demand patterns over a relevant time period either formally through predictive systems or informally by observing the consumer trends.

The graphic representation thus created can then be used to predict variations of demand levels. Depending upon the nature of the service industry, these representations can then be used to forecast the demand levels on hourly, weekly, monthly/seasonally, or yearly basis. Additionally, these representations can also deduce—what are the underlying causes for fluctuating demand? This in turn can help the service provider to serve its customers efficiently and profitably.

There could also be a 'hand of' in the demand fluctuations. These random variations are often unpredictable and depend upon (a) seasons which call for medical services, natural disasters that need of medical, telecom, and insurance services and (b) unpredictable acts of terrorisms and political action. These make countries going to war or deploying troops overseas call for movement or creations of niche services within the services sector, for example, AT&T used its ingenuity, capacity, and responsiveness to overcome the communication hurdles of the American army personnel that were deployed in the Gulf war. It installed temporary telephone installations that helped the deployed personnel to place 2.5 million calls to their family and friends.

Detailed records of customer transactions can help in identifying myriad patterns within the market segment. Additionally, a service manager can also analyse a segment for its demand predictability or randomness. A case in point would be scheduling of Monday as the Open day for walk-in patients or the Out Patients' Department in the hospitals and clinics. This is based on the rush that the hospitals observe at the start of the week. Hospitals therefore schedule the specialists and consultants for the middle of the week.

Demand Issues and Capacity Constraints

The need for understanding demand patterns arises because a company plans for serving a set number of customers. Their resources are managed around this. Thus, Devya in the opening case knows that the customers are not being serviced appropriately and were walking away to competition especially from 5 o'clock onwards. This was also happening on weekends and the existing staff was not being able to cope with the clientele flowing in. Hiring more people was the obvious solution but the two salespersons she had recently employed were not being optimally utilized during the off-peak hours. This shows that companies have capacity issues which can be any of the following:

Constraint in the financial resources   Companies have a limit as far as their financial resources are concerned. Their budget is planned and they have to build their infrastructure within these resources. This is done keeping in mind a fixed number of customers that they want to serve. Thus, the number of rooms built in a hotel, number of tables that can be accommodated in the restaurant, and the number of beds in a hospital are all planned. The supplementary facility like car parking is also planned for a fixed number. If over time there is an increase in the number of customers, then the infrastructure will have to be enhanced to accommodate the increased number.

Constraint in the physical facility   Hotels, hospitals, clinics, and classrooms are all designed for a particular capacity. The furnishings, service production (if required, say, in hotels or restaurants), etc. are all planned for this capacity. If the number of customers is more than the capacity planned for, then it will be difficult to accommodate all.

Constraint in operational resources   Airports, warehouses, restaurants, etc. plan to serve a fixed number of people to a maximum limit. Their resources are planned accordingly and include labour, facilities, and equipment. For example, airports can accommodate a fixed number of flights and customers, their check-in facility detecting instruments are all as per these numbers. If more customers come in, it would put a drain on the resources resulting in delays and inconvenience to all.

Constraint in human resource personnel   Companies hire a specific number of employees to serve the customers according to the planned capacity. If the demand exceeds the optimum capacity, then it leads to crowding in the service outlet, employees are overworked, and service quality might deteriorate.

Constraints on time   Service organizations are characterized by simultaneous production and consumption. Hence, in a given time (say lunch hours from 1200 to 1500 hours), they can serve a specific number of people. If more number of people turn up, then within the existing operational facility it might not be possible to effectively serve all the customers while maintaining the promised service quality.

Thus, companies plan their outlets to effectively service a fixed number of customers. The following situations can arise as far as demand for the service is concerned:

Demand exceeds available capacity   When demand is more than the capacity of the organization to serve them, then it results in loss of business as all the customers cannot be accommodated. For example, on weekends in Connaught Place in New Delhi, most of the restaurants are full and there is a lot of waiting for the customers. Many times the customers do not like to wait and so, business is lost for that restaurant.

Demand is more than the optimum capacity   When demand is more than the optimum capacity then all the customers get occupancy. But because of the crowding, employees might be overworked leading to deterioration in the quality of service. Customers would hence not get the quality they would otherwise have got leading to dissatisfaction.

Balance between demand and supply When the demand is as per the optimum capacity planned for the outlet, then the employees are busy but not overworked. Customers get good service quality as planned.

Excess capacity When the demand is low, there would be less number of customers than what have been planned for. This would result in resources not being utilized to the fullest. These resources are wasted and impact profitability. The customers who do come in might feel the absence of other customers disturbing. They might also attribute the low turnout to the quality of service delivered at the outlet (Lovelock, Wirtz, and Chatterjee 2007).

This highlights the fact that the resources of the service organization is fixed to serve an optimum capacity. To accommodate an increased demand, the facility needs to be upgraded which results in incurring further costs. This might be a drain on the financial resources for companies when the demand is fluctuating and might not always be so high.

Companies therefore need to plan their demand and capacity so that there is uniform demand always resulting in optimum utilization of all resources. The following section looks at how organizations can strive to maintain this balance.

Managing Demand and Capacity

Service managers face various issues while managing supply and demand in services, such as (a) having limited ability to alter capacity in terms of the extent of the change and response time to make the change, while having to deal with rapid fluctuations in demand, (b) the need to deliver consistent levels of customer service, and (c) the varying degrees of uncertainty in demand. These issues often affect their ability to maintain quality standards while trying to achieve productivity targets (Lovelock 1984, Rhyme 1988, Heskett, et al. 1990). Additionally, the nature of the process of service delivery restricts the options of the manager to match the supply with demand across the entire delivery system. Therefore, the only options of operational control, that are left open for a service manager is (a) holding (pre-inventory or work storage) in anticipation of demand, (b) altering the capacity, and (c) influencing the demand in other creative ways. However, managers in capacity constrained services such as hotels, airlines and utilities, where profitability is closely linked both to the prices charged and the existent capacity—have to match service production with supply and demand.

It can therefore be said that capacity management is both the ability and the capability to balance customer demand and service delivery by the manager. Additionally, a manager has to be adept (a) in forecasting the nature of the demand and (b) in managing capacity options to meet the expected customer requirement. According to Sasser (1976), there are two basic strategies for managing capacity in services, namely the level strategy and the chase strategy. In the case of the level strategy, the focus is usually to influence demand in line with the capacity, while in the case of the chase strategy, the supply can be changed in line with the demand.

A service manager can allocate demand to the most profitable business segments by identifying which demand to serve and at what price. In service industry allotment, management and overbooking techniques can help in reducing inventory spoilage. Additionally, demand segmentation and price optimization can enable the service manager to differentiate and manage high demand periods, and to better balance supply and demand. Further, companies can generate incremental revenue by recapturing excess demand, that which could not be accommodated during the peak time, during the off-peak time.

There may be day-to-day strategies for shifting demand to match capacity. If the demand is too low then some of the following strategies may be initiated.

Sales and advertising strategies

Direct selling   A customer can buy products online with a credit card on the Internet. This is especially true for supplies and other commodity items that can be grouped by category and offered in a catalogue format by numerous companies. There are literally millions of websites using this approach.

Generate sales lead   Smaller firms have limited budgets, which can be best used for advertising in order to generate quick leads which can be converted into sales. Advertisements of such nature encourage customer response by making a free offer of, for example, a free initial consultation, free estimate, free evaluation of a problem, or some such free information. These leads if funnelled properly to the sales team, can enhance a company's gross sales each year.

Educate your prospects   Advertising can help a customer to differentiate between different brands of a product. In addition, it can also highlight key differences like how a particular product works, what are its benefits, what are its reliability factors, etc. It also conveys information about your services and unique approach, business, and philosophies to the customer. Usually, service firms take a very educational approach to tell the readers of the advertisement/viewer of the TV ad or the listener of the Radio spot about their products. A case in point is the advertisements of insurance and financial companies, which are filled with facts and comparative figures. Readership of these advertisements are high because of the information that they have.

Create awareness   A service company just by placing an advertisement ensures that it has a presence and is ready for business at all times. This creates awareness in the minds of the customers and also gives them alternatives to the existing service providers.

Establish credibility   It is important that the service company uses advertisements to establish its credibility in the market and in the minds of its customers by using authentic and trustworthy sources. By giving useful information to current and potential clients, a service company can assist them in making better buying decisions. This is a nice way to retain and build relationships.

Keep the name of the company in limelight   A service company by regularly advertising in select media can help build familiarity with the company's name and establish its identity. In order to convince a customer to do business with it, a service company must first cross its 'threshold of consciousness.' The first time a prospective customer sees the brand name he/she may not recognize the brand name. The second time, they might think they have seen this name before. But on the third time, most prospective customers will begin to remember the name and what the company stands for.

The bottom line however is that advertising is a costly affair and building awareness through the use of paid advertising is an expensive proposition. The most cost-effective way for top-of-the-mind customer recall is through the combination of advertising and the word-of-mouth publicity that a service company earns through its efficient and timely service.

Modify the service offering and appeal to new marketing segments

The basis of this strategy is to identify groups of customers in different market segments that could benefit from a given service by highlighting the relevance and suitability of that service. This could be done by:

Innovating through disruptions These innovations could be incremental service refinements or radical breakthroughs, in a manner that is valued by major customers in the major markets. Disruptive innovations that are radical in nature more often than not initially result in worse performance compared with established products and services in mainstream markets. However, disruptive innovations are often cheap, simple, small, and more convenient to use. For example, creating an expertise in servicing a domestic water filtering device which is not dependent upon electricity but has high end filter membranes installed, could take away a large chunk of customers from the service agents of the regular water filters.

Create or overtake the existing markets through disruptive actions This is done through identification of a new area of competition outside the existing market. For example, customers who as a rule find themselves at sea with complex technologies, welcome service companies that can help them identify and overcome their technology block. These customers are the worst nightmares of the existing service providers. Moving into this domain may create new avenues of growth for any service company willing to cater to the tech-challenged customer. The new service provider can harness asymmetries of motivation created by low-end disruptions.

Service companies can thus use this new plane to disrupt the strangle hold of bigger corporations. Service companies typically start small in such markets which are usually ill defined. The existing companies do not feel threatened by the new entrant as it does not affect their core business. A case in point would be the stand-alone service centres of vacuum tube television sets, that are often unable to take on new age service centres dedicated to new improved television sets. The older lot therefore can either be pushed out by the creeping march of the new age centres or reinvent themselves according to the times.

Offer discounts This is a common response to low demand. This strategy is all about price differentiation and the price sensitivity of the customer. It is all about supply and demand curves, for example, business travellers are less sensitive to the cost than the families travelling on vacation.

Modify hours of operations   Theatres and banks often operate on different timelines to accommodate their customers. Additionally, schools with large auditoriums and playgrounds rent these facilities during their summer vacations when these facilities are not in use.

Remove obstacles to consumption   Highly sophisticated services are based on a credible commitment of the service provider and the trust of the client and therefore, entry of these services in a market may not be enough for them to take off. There are many barriers such as those of laws, tariffs, and taxes besides 'movement of natural persons' for the provision of services, that could cause hindrance in the establishment of these services.

If the demand is too high, then some of the following strategies may be initiated.

Use signage to communicate busy days for reservations   Additionally, boarding and lodging industry and parking lots often put small sign boards outside their facility to indicate a full capacity. This could be reflected in advertisements as well.

Provide incentives to consumers to use non-peak times   For example, restaurants and hotels offer seasonal discounts. Power companies are currently experimenting with dynamic pricing by using 'time of use' rates in order to lower peak demand of electricity.

Take care of loyal consumers first   For example, AmEx gives priority to its own credit card users by designating separate queues for them. Banks and sports clubs also give preferential treatment to their high value clients in terms of facilities like last minute seasonal passes/privilege cards to a theatrical or sporting event or accessing out-of-stock products.

Charge full price   When the demand is high, service marketers are likely to enhance revenue by deploying premium pricing to contribute to their profitability. For example, hotels in Delhi charge a higher price on account of higher number of tourists visiting India during the peak seasons (winter/spring).

Service inventory and capacity constraints

Companies in the service industry, namely leisure and entertainment, cargo and freight, hospitality, media, and passenger industries serve different segments of customers with diverse products and services. It is therefore important that the service companies have the ability to identify each customer segment and its willingness to pay. The service managers need to optimally match the service demand to their complex capacity constraints, thereby dramatically increasing their revenue and profits. It is therefore imperative that companies in the services sector allocate the right amount of perishable inventory or constrained capacity to the right customer segments to achieve maximum profitability.

Consequently, a service manager needs to identify an appropriate form of service inventory and thereby, offer value through competitive pricing, fast response time, customization, and good quality produced through a set of processes.

There are two types of service inventory namely (a) work storage based on information and (b) facilitating goods.

A work storage based inventory is created when a service company in anticipation of the customer needs, does some amount of work and stores it, even before the customer requests for the service. For example, these could be legal documents as provided by the real estate companies, books and magazines in case of publishing houses, etc. Forms and reports provided by consultancy firms also come under this category.

Facilitating goods on the other hand, are the goods which are given as or along with the core service. They are the materials or items purchased or consumed by the buyer and/or provided to the customer, for example, food and beverages provided by the airlines, repair parts/consumer goods provided by repair and maintenance stores, etc. These could also be goods provided by retailers.

Ideally a service inventory can be built in the following circumstances:

1. When the cost of building the inventory is low and when there is a possibility of it being used by the customer.
2. When customized service can be delivered through application of standard process, for example, online auctions, self-service check-ins at airports, and automated teller machines at banks.
3. When there is the presence of frequent users of the customized services, for example, hotels store data about repeat customers and adapt it to other customers. Web portals build high levels of service inventory because the marginal cost of adding and storing records is miniscule, and there is a greater breadth of coverage which increases the value of the service to customers.
4. When there is a presence of system modularity that allows the service inventory to increase the variety of offerings exponentially.

Application of Theory of Constraints in Service Industry

According to Goldratt's (1990) Theory of Constraints, a service organization cannot achieve optimum performance level until it can identify and manage the constraints that it faces.

The Theory of Constraints helps the service manager to identify the weakest elements of the processes that occur within the service organization. In other words, Theory of Constraints can help a service organization to identify/fine-tune its goals, zero-in on the constraints affecting the performance of the organization, and develop effective solutions to facilitate improvements in the processes, namely, policies and procedures regarding manpower, training, empowerment, can-do attitude, etc. Additionally, uniqueness of each sector of the service economy ensures distinct actions to improve throughput, inventory, and operating expenses.

Throughput This is the rate at which a service system generates revenue for services in a way which is consistent with the organizational goal, for example, throughput in banks is created when banks invest in such markets as real estate, investment firms, customer lending, and institutional lending. Moreover, service firms can generate money by offering a variety of services depending upon its area of operation.

Inventory According to Goldratt (1990), inventory is the money the service organization invests in purchasing, both tangibles and intangibles needed to generate throughput, except for labour and overhead.

Operating expense This includes all the financial resources, both direct and indirect, that a service firm spends converting inventory into throughput, with the objective to increase throughput and/or decrease inventory and operating expenses in such a way as to increase profit, cash flow, and return on investment.

A service firm as mentioned earlier can thus differentiate itself from its competitors on the basis of its supply and demand strategies. These critically separates service firms from good service firms, thereby helping to (a) offset market fluctuations and (b) generate stable and high-margin revenue flow.

WAITING LINE STRATEGIES

Matching capacity and demand entails a number of strategies as discussed earlier. However, it is not always possible to maintain this fine balance. It might not be economically viable to increase the service capacity or demand fluctuations could be so high that the loss in sales during peak periods might not make economic sense to invest further. Companies can then look at managing demand at their sales outlet. For example, a hairdresser might face a lot of demand during a particular period but absolutely no footfalls might occur at other points of time. Hence, investing in increasing the service capacity would lead to very low return on investment. Thus, it would make more sense to manage the customers during high demand periods. This can be done by ensuring that the customers wait for the organization to deliver them their services. However, it is easier said than done. Customers are hard pressed for time and there are a number of service providers in the market waiting eagerly to serve the customers. Thus, waiting for the services might not be something that the customers would be happy about. These waiting lines can be on the phone (when services are provided at an arm's length) or at the physical outlet. In either case, the customer might get impatient and quit leading to a loss in potential business for the service organization. Thus, companies need to take cognizance of the delay and explore the reason for the same.

They can build in operational efficiencies so that the delay is reduced and customers are serviced quicker. For example, automated teller machines (ATMs) has reduced the waiting lines in the banks. Companies can also opt for a reservation system so that customers can book their services in advance and do not have to wait for the same. However, not all customers will reserve their orders in advance and for them, the companies need to have a queuing system and manage the customers' perception of these waiting periods. The queuing system can be managed by following any of the alternative configurations listed here.

Single line and single server There can be only a single line and the customers can queue up there. The service provided can be in single stage or a sequential stage when there are a number of serving operations. For example, if you have to get a visa, then there can be a number of sequential stages such as getting the filled form verified, going through the various identification processes, etc. In these sequential stages, if there is delay at any one stage, then there would be a piling up.

Parallel lines and multiple servers   This occurs when there are a number of servers or service lines and the customer can choose which line they want to wait in. This example is common in toll gates, fast food restaurants, etc. where a number of service providers are sitting at the billing counter and the customer can choose which one to approach. The drawback of this system is that the other line may move faster leading to dissatisfaction among the customers.

Designated line   Here, the service provider can dedicate lines for specific services, for example, if you are travelling first class, business class, etc., then there are different check-in counters at the airports for these travellers.

Single line and multiple servers   This can be done to avoid the problem of some lines in the parallel lines moving slower. The customers here wait in a single line and as soon as any server is free, they go to that server.

Taking a number   Here, the customers are allocated a number and they wait for their turn to come. For example, in a bank, if you want to withdraw money, then a token is allocated and the customer is then served as per the token number. The benefit of this is that customers have a fair idea of the time it is going to take to be served.

The queuing system can be differentiated on the basis of factors like paying price premiums where companies can charge more prices for the same service (for example, airlines can charge different prices from the customers boarding the same flight for the same destination). These customers are then given differential treatment—for example, different lines for faster check-ins, boarding, etc. Another basis is the importance of the customer where loyal customers who frequent the service outlet can be given preferential treatment by providing them special wait areas, serving complementary refreshments, etc. Service outlets can also differentiate the customers on the basis of urgency. For example, patients arriving in emergency health care are given preferential treatment. Also, less complicated requirements of the customer that can be catered to quicker can also be given preference, like in banks and supermarkets.

Companies can also solicit the support of the customers by involving them in the service process. For example, if a customer wants to book a ticket at the PVR Ambience Mall, then they can do this online through Bookmyshow.com, or at www.pvrcinemas.com at the booking window of the PVR, or mobile ticketing through Airtel, Idea, or Vodafone. They can also get tickets home delivered by calling on the PVR telephone numbers for group booking.

Managing waiting time[*]

The waiting time for the customers can be managed to make the waiting tolerable if not pleasurable. The idea is that the waiting time does not lead to dissatisfaction and feelings of displeasure among the customers. The perception of the waiting time by the customers can be managed by the following:

---

*(Based on Lovelock et al. (2007) and Zeithaml et al. 2011)

Keeping customers occupied during the wait time   Customers can be kept occupied while they are waiting for the service to be delivered. For example, Allen Solly showroom in inner circle, Connaught Place, New Delhi offers coffee and muffins to the customers waiting for their family or friend to make a purchase. Physicians and dentists stock magazines in their waiting rooms to keep the customers occupied. This is because the waiting time is then perceived to be shorter and the wait is also bearable.

Keeping the customers informed on the time it would take while they are waiting   The customers can be informed about the time they would have to wait for them to be served. For example, restaurants when fully occupied generally book the tables on a first come basis. They also generally tell the customers how long it would take for their turn to come. This is helpful as customers can then utilize this time to finish any pending work. However, the drawback is that these customers might not come back and end up in another restaurant down the block. To overcome this, the restaurant can start the process of serving the customers. They can, for example, have a waiting area where the customers can be served a welcome drink. They can then be asked to place the order so that the time to serve them when they actually occupy a table can be shortened.

Reducing the anxiety during waiting period   Customers generally get anxious while waiting as they feel that the wait is indefinite. To manage this, companies can keep the customers informed about the balance waiting time at regular intervals.

Explaining the reason for the delay   The customers can be informed about the reason because of which the delay has occurred. If consumers are informed, they feel less irritated. For example, a longer waiting period on a visit to the doctor can be explained by informing about the reason—probably the doctor was attending to a critical patient which took longer, an emergency situation wherein someone was badly hurt, etc. Once explained to the customers, it would lead to acceptance and they would feel less irritated.

Making waits equitable   Customers get irritated when they feel that a person who has arrived after them was served before they got a chance. Hence, the waiting line strategies need to be in place so that customers who came in first are served before the others.

Waiting in groups   Customers accept the waiting time more amicably when they are waiting in groups rather than alone. This is because there are fellow customers to talk to that keeps the customer occupied.

YIELD MANAGEMENT

Yield management acknowledges the fact that the services cannot be inventoried and therefore need to be sold at the best price to get the maximum revenue. This entails the employment of differential pricing for the same product or service. The airline industry was the first to experiment with the idea of yield management when in the early 1970s, it offered discounted fares so that the seats would be occupied. To overcome the possibility of high-fare passengers shifting to the discounted rates, the fares were discounted well in advance (say, 21 days prior to the flight), and the number of seats that could be sold at these discounted prices were limited. 'The systematic process of predicting demand and accurately controlling seat inventory allocation marked the beginning of what came to be called "yield management" as yield was an important airline statistic representing revenue per passenger per mile' (Cross 1995 cited in Cross, Higbie, and Cross 2009). This yield management was adapted by lodging industry 'in the late 1980s and early 1990s' and revenue management 'as an essential way to offer and control differentially priced, time-sensitive products to diverse market segments to increase the hotel revenue' (Hanks, Cross, and Noland 1992 and Cross, Higbie, and Cross 2009).

Exhibit 15.1 **Tracing Yield Management**

The airline industry was the first to introduce differential prices 'for essentially the same seats during early 1970s'. British Overseas Airways Corporation (now British Airways) in 1972 offered 'early bird discounts to stimulate demand for seats that would otherwise fly empty'. The fares for the US scheduled airlines were set by Civil Aeronautics Board which in mid-1970s set up the concept of 'public charters' where charter airlines could 'sell seats on a quasi-scheduled basis for fares far less than the cost-plus fares offered by the scheduled airlines.' Bob Crandall who was then the Senior Vice President, Marketing, American Airlines called a meeting to brainstorm how they could lower their costs to compete. They realized that they had a revenue problem as millions of seats were flown empty per year. They started with the 'Super Saver Fares' in 1977 and in each flight 30% of the seats were allocated to this. They quickly realized that fluctuating demand patterns by route, time of day, and day of week required a different mix of discount seats. Large databases were constructed and computer systems were developed to forecast and monitor passenger demand. Skilled analysts were trained to oversee the system to account for variance and allocate seats with greater precision. Bob Crandall is credited with giving this integrated set of people, process, and systems a name—'yield management'. Other airlines such as Delta Airlines, United Airlines, KLM Royal Dutch Airways, British Airways, and Lufthansa also adopted yield management.

J.W. Bill Marriott Jr heard about yield management directly from Bob Crandall at a chance meeting in the mid-1980s. Marriott International had many of the same issues that airlines did—perishable inventory, customers booking in advance, lower-cost competition, and wide swings with regard to balancing demand and supply. Bill Marriott adopted the practice of yield management at all the Marriott Hotels and called it revenue management. By mid-1990s, Marriott was adding $150–200 million to the annual revenue due to successful implementation of the revenue management. Other hotel chains were quick to adopt this as were restaurants, cruise lines, golf courses, rental car firms, etc. United Parcel Service (UPS) then carried this science to business-to-business (B2B) operations where they applied this to control price discounts offered to clients.

Early 1990s saw revenue management being applied to ad sales on television. Canadian Broadcast Corporation was the first to implement this in 1992. National Broadcasting Company (NBC) and American Broadcasting Company (ABC) adopted this in late 1990s for ad sales. Ford Motor Company was the first to apply this model on 'non-perishable inventory' in mid-1990s. Ford applied this on the marketing programs

(Contd)

Exhibit 15.1 **(Contd)**

to understand what customers wanted—cash rebate, product configuration, vehicle type, etc. This led to an understanding of the customer preference in different geographical markets and across different product lines. This resulted in making more money from the same number of vehicles.

Post the tragic events of 9/11, service providers realized that just controlling inventory and selling at the lowest price available was not sufficient. Intercontinental Hotels Group (IHG) took an initiative to 'understand the price sensitivity of consumer demand.' They realized that customer perception of rates offered changed when the competitor changed its rate. This brought a twist to the revenue management as now they could 'simultaneously optimize price based on forecasted demand, price elasticity, and competitive rates.'

Source: Based on Cross, Higbie, and Cross (2010)

$$\text{Yield/Revenue} = \text{Actual revenue/potential revenue}$$

where

$$\text{Actual revenue} = \text{Actual capacity used} \times \text{Average actual price}$$
$$\text{Potential revenue} = \text{Total capacity} \times \text{Maximum price}$$

Consider a hotel property has 150 rooms with a maximum room rate of ₹2,000. Thus, the potential revenue = $150 \times 2,000 = $ ₹300,000

Now assume that the hotel rents 80 rooms at ₹2,000 at a point of time. In a second instance it rents 120 rooms at ₹1,000 and in a third instance it rents 100 rooms at ₹1,500.

In the first instance the hotel's actual revenue is $(80 \times 2,000) = 160,000$.

In the second instance the hotel's actual revenue is $(120 \times 1,000) = 120,000$.

And in the third instance the hotel's actual revenue is $(100 \times 1,500) = 150,000$.

Then the third case scenario is the one that gets the maximum revenue for the hotel.

Now assume that the hotel rents 50 rooms at ₹2,000; 40 at ₹1,500, and 60 at ₹1,000. In this case the hotel's actual revenue will be $(50 \times 2,000 + 40 \times 1,500 + 60 \times 1,000) = $ ₹220,000 which is the maximum. The yield/revenue management approach is to maximize the yield/revenue to get maximum returns from different customer segments.

Thus, we can say that the yield/revenue management is to efficiently distribute the available services to get the maximum revenue. It allows the managers to forecast business demands and price it dynamically so that demand can be met with maximum revenue to the organization. However, this should be strategically enforced otherwise the following issues might hamper the business.

Focus on profitability rather than customers Customers paying a higher price for the same service might feel dissatisfied once they know about the differential prices charged. This can be overcome by giving preferential/complimentary services to the customers who have paid a higher price for the same service so that they feel that they have got a fair value for their money spent. Also, the loyal customers can be identified and low prices can be offered to them first so that they feel that favourable treatment has been offered to them.

Internal focus   Revenue management's focus is internal, that is 'to predict and optimize the impact of transactions on the hotel.' This can be overcome through 'customer-centric revenue management' (Cross and Dixit 2005) where revenue management can be used 'as an external device to grow and develop customers and customer segments' (Cross et al. 2009).

Lack of proper training   Employees need to have a sound understanding of the science involved in revenue management. This is generally lacking and companies need to have proper training in place to make the employees understand how it works and how decisions are made. This can be overcome through the obvious, that is, provide relevant training to the employees designated for this task.

Lack of access to information   Service providers need to have a central reservation system for yield management to be effective. However, when companies do not have such centralization, they find it difficult to operate yield management effectively.

Overbooking   Yield management works effectively when service providers overbook, that is, book more number of customers than is possible to service. Customers that are a victim of this and whose service experience was not satisfactory as a result would be alienated (Zeithaml et al. 2011). Thus, service providers need to be cautious when overbooking happens and ensure that such customers are adequately compensated by enforcing service recovery and/or recovery paradox.

Yield and revenue management has been developed to provide solutions to business issues. It can be applied to not only services but products as well. The idea is to understand the demand and supply and what motivates the customers to make the purchase.

RESEARCH INSIGHT

Demand and Capacity Management Decisions in Services: How They Impact on One Another
Klassen, Kenneth J. and Thomas R. Rohleder (2002), 'Demand and capacity management decisions in services: How they impact on one another', *International Journal of Operations & Production Management*, vol. 22, issue 5, pp. 527–548.

Service managers are continually challenged with balancing customer demand and service capacity. Recent studies have raised awareness of various demand and capacity management practices available to services, but little numerical work has been done to identify how these decisions work together and how they relate to one another. For instance, reducing prices may attract customers during a slow period, but the extent of impact this should have on cross-training staff is not clear. A simulation based on theoretical and empirical insights explores the impact of various decisions on profitability and operations. The decisions modelled include the impact of automation, customer participation, cross-training employees, informing customers about the operation, and others. It is shown that demand and capacity decisions do indeed impact on each other—sometimes in ways that are not initially obvious. Results provide useful thought-starters for service managers striving to improve their operations.

SUMMARY

Services by their intrinsic nature are perishable and cannot be inventoried. This leads to a situation in which demand and supply needs to be balanced for optimum revenue generation. Excess demand can lead to deterioration in the service quality and ultimately, loss in sales. Excess supply can also lead to loss in revenue as there were no customers to avail the services created. Service providers need to study and understand the demand fluctuations so that the same can be predicted for the future and strategies put in place to gain maximum revenue for the demand available. Thus, companies can use sales and advertising to increase demand and modify the service offering to attract new segments of customers. They can also offer discounts, modify hours of operations, etc. to manage demand and supply.

Companies can adopt waiting line strategies to retain their customers when there is excess demand for the services offered. The waiting period is very cumbersome for customers and service providers need to manage this waiting period so that the customers do not leave without availing the services. A number of waiting line strategies can be used by service providers to manage the customers while they are waiting for the services to be delivered to them.

Yield/revenue management talks about situations when there is low demand and how companies can, through attractive pricing techniques, attract new customers. This strategy is increasingly being used by companies to balance pricing and capacity utilization to increase sales.

KEY TERMS

Demand   Number of consumers willing to purchase the service.
Supply   This includes the total amount of services or goods that a service organization has to offer for all the consumers.
Waiting line strategies   When demand is more than supply, consumers have to wait for their turn to experience the service. These are the strategies that are

employed by service organizations to manage this waiting time so that consumers stay and their overall satisfaction is not diminished.
Yield/Revenue management   Balancing the capacity of the service organization so that the best price is charged for the same service from different segments of consumers to whom service is sold so as to maximize revenue.

EXERCISES

Concept Review Questions

1. Why is there a need to manage demand and supply in service organizations?
2. Discuss the various situations that can arise when demand varies.
3. What can companies do when the demand for the service is low?
4. Discuss various strategies that can be adopted by companies when demand is high.
5. Write a note on service inventory and capacity constraints.
6. Write a note on yield management.

Critical Thinking Questions

1. What are the various constraints that service organizations face while servicing the customers? Which are the three most important ones and why?
2. Differentiate between optimum capacity and maximum capacity. What are the implications of these for a service organization?
3. Discuss the theory of constraints in context of any service organization.
4. What are the waiting line strategies? Discuss the ones that can be adopted by (a) banks, (b) hotels, and (c) airports. Give reasons for your answer.

5. Discuss the relevance of yield management in service organizations.

Internet Exercises

1. Visit the website of two hotels in Shimla or any other hill station. Identify the strategies that they are adopting for managing their demand.
2. Visit the website of an airline. Can you identify any yield management strategies? Discuss the same.

What further strategies can you suggest to the airline so that the regular consumer segment is not alienated?

3. Visit the website of a local restaurant. Can you identify any strategies that they are adopting so that the consumer does not have to wait for the service once they actually visit the restaurant? If not, then what can you suggest to the service provider? Make relevant assumptions.

CASE STUDY | **Driving Sales and Customer Satisfaction***

Introduction

Abhijat had taken over the management of his father's hotel at Khan Market in New Delhi. He could now apply all the decisions he had been itching to take for so long, though his father would be there to guide him. The property was a 12 table restaurant that had been doing fairly well. On weekends there was a waiting time for half an hour and on an average, the business was good compared to the competitors in the vicinity. He had eight waiters serving at any given time. Abhijat knew for sure that customer satisfaction was of paramount importance and the customer would come back only if he/she was satisfied with the service and the food. He was paying a handsome amount to the chef and the kitchen staff and believed that good talent did not come cheap. Profit was good and he had some money kept aside that could be ploughed back into the business.

The problem was that on weekends he was not being able to manage the demand. People had to wait for half an hour and many times they would not come back. He knew for sure that they were walking away to competition. He felt that he was losing out on business. On the other hand, his staff was sitting idle on weekdays—specially on Tuesday and Wednesday when the footfalls were minimum. His father was not willing to make any changes and so his hands were tied. With relief he realized that now was the time when he could break the shackles and implement his decisions.

Though Abhijat wanted to grow his business, he knew that he could not do this by alienating his customers. If the customers wanted to linger after dinner, he would let them be. The waiters would grumble about the waiting customer but Abhijat would not let them bother the customer. He wanted the customer in the restaurant to be happy and satisfied with the experience and not feel rushed. He had to make the waiting customer come back on weekends and attract more customers on weekdays.

Abhijat hired a resource person—Raman, whose duty was to stand outside the hotel on weekends and note the names and mobile numbers of people who were waiting for their turn. This ensured that the first come customers were served first. If people wanted to shop while waiting for their turn, Raman would politely call them once their turn came. Abhijat ensured that these numbers and names were entered into the system. Thus slowly, he started working on creation of his database. He knew his loyal customers by face and now he knew them by name also. Their order was entered along with their phone numbers thus, giving him an idea of their favourite dishes. The people who did not return were also noted and the next day he would personally send an SMS apologizing for the unavailability of a table when the customer had visited. This was followed with a phone number where customers could make a reservation so that they were sure of their place during crowded times. In the end,

*Dr Kirti Dutta

he gave an offer of 5% discount to make-up for not being able to serve them if the customer decides to visit them on the coming Tuesday/Wednesday.

The Result

Within a month Abhijat could see the result. He was able to serve twice the number of customers. His staff could recognize the regular customers by name. They would ask if the customer wanted their favourite dishes and this brought a smile on the customer's face who would gush that how could he remember amid so much rush. Abhijat could feel the customers smiling more while leaving the restaurant. The other benefit was that there was a noticeable rise in footfalls on Tuesdays and Wednesdays which was mostly thanks to the promotional offer he was providing, but Abhijat was happy. At the end of the first six months of taking over, he had doubled the revenue of the restaurant.

Questions

1. What was the problem that Abhijat was facing?
2. What demand and supply management strategy did he implement?
3. What further strategy can you suggest to Abhijat to increase the revenue of his small business?

REFERENCES

Cross, R.G., J.A. Higbie, and D.Q.D. Cross (2009), 'Revenue management's renaissance: A rebirth of the art and science of profitable revenue generation', *Cornell Hospitality Quarterly*, vol. 50, issue 1, pp. 56–81.

Cross, R.G., J.A. Higbie, and Z.N. Cross (2010), 'Milestones in the application of analytical pricing and revenue management', *Journal of Revenue and Pricing Management*, pp. 1–11.

Goldratt, E.M. (1990), *What is This Thing called Theory of Constraints*, North Press Inc, New York.

Fitzsimmons, James A. and Mona J. Fitzsimmons (2014), *Service Management: Operations, Strategy, Information Technology*, Pearson, Singapore.

Hanks, R.D., R.G. Cross, and R.P. Noland (1992), 'Discounting in the hotel industry: A new approach', *Cornell Hotel and Restaurant Administration Quarterly*, vol. 33, issue 1, pp. 73–79.

Heskett, J.L., W.E. Sasser, C.W.L. Hart (1990), *Service Breakthroughs*, Free Press, New York.

Lovelock, C. (2000), *Services Marketing: People, Technology, Strategy*, 4th Edition, Prentice Hall, New Jersey.

Lovelock, C.H. (1984), *Services Marketing*, Prentice Hall Inc., New Jersey.

Lovelock, C., J. Wirtz, and J. Chatterjee (2007), *Services Marketing: People, Technology and Strategy*, 6th Edition, Pearson Prentice Hall, New Delhi.

Rhyme, D. (1988), 'The impact of demand management on service system performance', *Service Industries Journal*, vol. 8, no. 4.

Sasser, W.E. (1976), 'Match Supply and Demand in Service Industry', *Harvard Business Review*, November–December.

Zeithaml, V.A., M.J. Bitner., D.D. Gremler, and A. Pandit (2011), *Services Marketing*, 5th Edition, Tata McGraw-Hill Education Private Limited, New Delhi.

http://hbswk.hbs.edu/item/3374.html, accessed on 25 September 2014.

http://www.ambiencemalls.com/ambiencevk/index.cfm?md=content&sd=entertainment, accessed on 10 October 2014.

http://www.ceps.eu/system/files/Access%20Barriers%20to%20Services%20Markets_0.pdf, accessed on 30 September 2014.

http://www.frontpagepr.com/advertising/ways_advertising_can_increase_sales.asp, accessed on 25 September 2014.

16 Customer Feedback and Service Recovery

OBJECTIVES

After reading this chapter you will be able to understand the

- customer response
- feedback and service management orientation
- service system failure
- concept of service recovery
- importance of service recovery
- strategies for an effective service recovery
- design and implementation process of service guarantees

Bharti Airtel: Listening to Customers

The telecom industry in India is highly competitive and mobile number portability (MNP), which allows users to retain their number while changing operators, is an added challenge that they have to face. Data from telecom regulator shows an increase in the number of MNP requests from 106.9 million (in November 2013) to 111.9 million (in January 2014). The real revenue driver is the 5% of post-paid customer segment, which is very sensitive when it comes to quality of service and customer experience. Thus, Airtel, that serves over 200 million customers, is investing in retail and online presence to enhance customer quality so as to impact customer satisfaction. The company has over 100 company-owned company-operated stores and is looking at

enhancing customer experience at the stores. The company is constantly looking for ways to enhance the service experience at the store as otherwise customers can migrate to other operators some of whose services are at a lower cost. Airtel spoke to customers and realized one of the common problems—they dislike the 24 hour wait to get new connections activated. So the company went back to the drawing board and with a few modifications to the existing process, were able to reduce the activation time drastically.

Another insight was that the customers wasted time while waiting for their turn and so to deal with this problem a position of queue concierge was created. The customers are greeted at the entrance of the store by executives who understand their requirements and then assist them in not only the buying decision but also in filling forms and clicking photographs (Aulakh 2014). The endeavour is to keep the customers happy through their customer service so that they do not migrate to other service providers.

After going through the chapter, you will be able to answer the following questions:
1. Bharti Airtel has achieved the distinction of being 'India's largest mobile operator' and has 200 million customers. Why is it focusing on current users rather than on adding more users?
2. How has Bharti Airtel used customer feedback to its advantage?

INTRODUCTION

In the preceding chapters we have discussed customer expectations, service quality, and customer perceptions about services. We have studied the gap model and have seen that what the customers want and what is delivered to them is often not at par. Providing a 'zero-defect' service should be the objective of all service providers but problems arise when gaps are left in the service delivery (Weun et al. 2004). The importance of customers is highlighted by the fact that it costs a lot more to attract a new client than to retain an old one (Oliver 1999). However, it is estimated that businesses typically lose 50% of their customers every five years (Mack et al. 2000).

CUSTOMER RESPONSE

A physical product once purchased is consumed over a period of time. However, services product needs to be purchased every time they are to be consumed. A customer will re-purchase from the same service provider provided they are satisfied with the service or might turn to another service provider if they are not satisfied with their service for any reason. The customers' behavior will reflect their thoughts and feelings that the service provider has been able to rouse in them during the service delivery. While the preceding chapters have discussed the concept of service quality and how the service provider can create and manage expectations and perceptions, and enhance service delivery, this chapter looks at the post-purchase phase when the customer has consumed the service. The customer will respond to the service delivered according to the quality of services rendered. So customer's perception can be delighted, satisfied, or unsatisfied (see Chapter 7) and response is whether they consume the service again or not. Thus, the consumers can:

- not come back if they are dissatisfied
- not come back and talk negative about the service experience (either to service provider and/or family and friends and/or to third party both offline and online) if they are highly dissatisfied
- come back and re-purchase if they are satisfied
- re-purchase and recommend the brand to family and friends

Customers can choose any combination of the above alternatives depending on their perception of the service provided. The unsatisfied customer is an area of concern for managers as they not only lead to loss of revenue by not coming back, but also lead to further loss as they create negative word of mouth. The spread of Internet can take this to unfathomable heights as word of mouth spreads beyond the immediate sphere of family and friends. Thus, it is important to keep track of customer's satisfaction level through feedback from the customers (see Exhibit 16.1).

Exhibit 16.1 **Making Feedback Count**

Getting customer feedback can be easy when the customer has time but can be difficult at times when they are hard pressed for time and do not want to give a feedback unless the experience was towards the ends of the continuum (too good or too bad). Companies in this case will have to formulate a strategy to solicit their feedback actively, for example, like KFC where the bill advertises a 15% discount for feedback on their website. Not listening to the customers on the other hand is not an option now as it might cause long-term damage. A leading American Airline learnt this after they lost $180 million in market cap over four days when a YouTube video of a song posted by an unhappy customer got half a million views. The airline had refused to pay $3,500 for a broken checked-in guitar.

The next challenge is to educate the employees so that they get the complete picture of the customer's experience that is in line with the brand promise. Organizations need to train their employees for delivering the promised experience and also need to empower them. Top leadership's commitment to a customer-centric culture and aligning incentives to chosen metrics helps build a service environment where everyone is aligned towards the common goal of customer satisfaction. While operational improvements eliminate technical and functional deficiencies, service improvements generate emotional

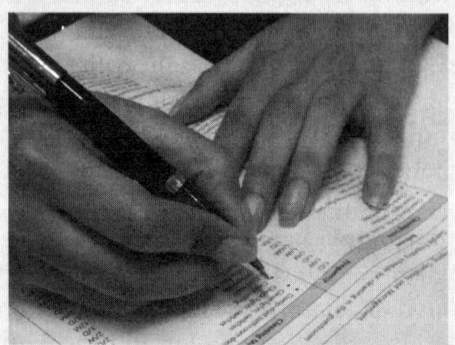

uplift for customers and loyalty (a buyer's deeply held commitment to stick with a product, service, brand, or organization consistently in the future) and advocacy (actively supporting a product or service through positive word of mouth) tend to build from satisfaction (the degree to which a customer's experience exceeds that customer's expectations). Positive advocacy can have a multiplier effect on business while negative word of mouth can destroy years of work (Mall and Rana 2014). Thus, organizations not only need to get the customer feedback but also need to have a strategy in place so that there is customer delight in all the 'moments of truth'.

FEEDBACK AND SERVICE MANAGEMENT ORIENTATION

Feedback is important for services organizations as the purchase of services is on a continuous basis and a satisfied customer is likely to make repeat purchases. Also, it is important to delineate the unsatisfied customer as if these customers are not among the complainers to the company then they will be creating negative word of mouth about their unsatisfactory experience. Service providers need to know who the unhappy customer is so that they can be addressed and their grievances can be handled satisfactorily. The management orientation has a crucial role to play as they can:

a) pay lip service to the customer and completely ignore the reason and continue business as normal leading to repeated dissatisfactory performance
b) look into the reason that caused service dissatisfaction and do something about it for the unsatisfied customer
c) not only address the unsatisfied customer but look into the reason that caused dissatisfaction and take corrective action so that it is not repeated in the future

Management that is customer-oriented, has a strategy in place to keep the customer's happy and is consistently looking at how the service delivery can be improved for a better customer experience. For this they start with getting customer feedback so that they can identify the reasons for dissatisfaction. Companies can collect customer feedback through the following (Lovelock, Wirtz, and Chatterjee 2007).

Feedback forms   Service providers can ask customers to fill a feedback form post the consumption of services. For example, it is very common in airlines to get customers to fill the feedback form towards the end of their journey. Hotels also have feedback forms that they collect from the customers.

Transactional surveys   These surveys are typically done at the end of a particular transaction to gauge the level of customer satisfaction with that particular transaction. For example, if a customer makes a purchase at the Decathlon cash and carry store in Sarjapur, Bengaluru, then at the time of billing as soon as the cashier makes the bill (on the computer screen facing the cashier) three faces appear on the touch screen facing the customer. One is a smiling face titled excellent experience, the other is a satisfied face titled satisfied, and the third is an angry red face saying dissatisfied. The customer is then requested to press any face as per their perception of the service provided. The cashier cannot proceed forward till the customer does the needful. This allows them to get back to every dissatisfied customer to understand the cause of discontent and to set things right (Retail Angle 2010).

Mystery shoppers   Service providers can have mystery shoppers who experience the service (just like a normal shopper but are sponsored by the service provider) to assess the skills of the employees providing the service.

Unsolicited feedbacks   Sometimes the service providers do not specifically ask for feedback but the customers give it anyway—especially when they were highly satisfied/dissatisfied with the service. These feedbacks can be both verbal and written and customers can give these in person or write mails (both online and through post). For example, post terror attack on The Taj Mahal Palace Hotel at Mumbai on 26 November 2008, the hotel received over 500 emails from various guests who narrated the heroic deeds of the staff and thanked them for saving their lives (Rao 2010).

The collection of the feedback in itself is of no value till action has been taken on the same. Management has to ensure that there is a reporting system in place that analyses the feedback and sends the relevant information to the concerned department/ employee so that corrective action can be taken. This error and corrective measure needs to be further documented and circulated to other departments as well so that the same mistake is not repeated there.

SERVICE FAILURE AND RECOVERY

The inability of the services organization to deliver as per customer expectations constitutes service failure. The multidimensional nature of the service encounter creates an environment where failure may often be the norm, not the exception (Mack et al. 2000). According to Palmer et al. (2000), service customers perceive failure when something goes wrong, irrespective of responsibility. We can define service failure as 'during the course of a service experience by the customer, when the customer perceives services quality to fall below the customer expectations and invokes feelings of mistrust in the customer's perception about the service provider, it is called as service failure'.

Failure can occur if the service is unavailable when promised, is delivered late or too slowly, the outcome is not as per expectations, or the employees are indifferent and uncaring (Zeithaml and Bitner 2000). The problem of service failure is further compounded by the fact that there is increased competition in most service industries (Lee et al. 2003). Also, few companies can claim to offer a product so unique that competitors cannot offer it (La and Kandampully 2004). Thus, the customer has many options to choose from. Hence, in an era of increased competition and perceptual differences between customers and the service providers leading to service failures, service recovery becomes an important strategy to reduce dissonance among customers.

A failure to deliver a service as per his expectations creates depredation in the customer's psychology, which if left unattended can ring the death knell for the organization. Grönroos (1988), in his six criteria of good perceived services quality gives due importance to service recovery saying that 'If the customers realize that whenever something goes wrong or something unpredictable happens, the service provider will immediately and actively take action to keep them in control of the situation and find a new, acceptable solution then they are bound to have a better perception of the organization'. Thus, service recovery involves what a service provider does in response to service failures (Weun et al. 2004).

It has also been defined as 'Service recovery is a service employee's performance resulting from a customer's perception of initial service delivery falling below the customer's zone of tolerance' Zeithaml et al. (1993). Keaveney (1995) stated that if organizations do not adopt recovery strategies, it could lead to customers switching over to another service provider. Bitner et al. (1990) and Chung and Hoffman (1998) identified three categories of failure.

Service System Failure

This occurs in a core service, such as hotels, and includes product defects, such as cold food, slow or unavailable service, facility problems; cleanliness issues such as dirty silverware, insect, or rodent problems; unfriendly guest policies such as not accepting cheques or credit cards; and out-of-stock conditions such as inadequate supply of menu items. When a customer experiences a problem in the core service delivery, the employee's response determines the customer's perceived satisfaction or dissatisfaction. For example, if there is a core service failure such as slow service, then an unsatisfactory handling of the situation could be either to give no information, or wrong information and make a one hour delay turn into a five- or six-hour wait. On the other hand, a satisfactory handling of the situation could entail explaining the flight delay, giving the correct reply for the time required, and offering refreshments on the house, or some activities to make the wait bearable. On getting a home delivery of the special Navratra *thali* from Nirula's, a customer found that the food was not cooked properly. On calling Nirula's and lodging a complaint, he found that not only were they apologetic, but also offered to send their special sundaes, which could be consumed during the *Navratra* fast. Thus, the customer who was not happy with the service delivery initially, became a satisfied one due to service recovery by the provider.

Failure in Implicit or Explicit Customer Requests

This occurs chiefly when employees are unable to comply with the customer's individual needs such as food not cooked as per the order, seating problems such as seating smokers in non-smoking section, or lost reservations. Consider this instance. A person travelling with a child who gets airsick will need to take care of the child. If the flight attendant helps that passenger it will create a satisfactory experience for him.

Unprompted and Unsolicited Employee Actions

This includes behaviour of employees that is unacceptable to guests such as rudeness, poor attitude, wrong order delivered, or order misplaced or not fulfilled. It would also include incorrect charges such as charging customers for items not ordered or giving incorrect change. According to Bitner et al. (1990), a truly out-of-the-ordinary employee behaviour was when a family, travelling with their teddy bears, returned to their hotel room and saw that the maid had arranged the bears, holding hands, comfortably together on a chair.

According to a study on restaurant failures by Chung and Hoffman (1998), it was observed that the incident rate for service system failure was 44.4%, delivery failure due to implicit or explicit customer requests was 18.4%, and unprompted and unsolicited employee action was 37.2%. All the failures rated above six on a scale of 1–10, where one was a minor mistake. After an average time period of 294 days it was observed that 69.6% of customers facing service delivery failure were retained, 80.6% of them facing customer request problems were still loyal, and 78.4% facing employee action service problems were loyal. Thus, we see that the core service delivery affects customers the most and is the prime candidate for managerial intervention.

When a customer experiences a service failure, the type of failure, and the magnitude of the failure prompt the customer to take a follow-up action. Even if the customer decides not to complain to the service provider, he may still not be satisfied with the service and may decide to switch over to another service provider, and may also complain to family and friends. Alternatively, he can complain to a third party (Exhibit 16.1). This strategy of the customer is dangerous for the service provider as it does not give him a second chance to rectify the problem. If the consumer complains to the service provider, he gets the opportunity to satisfy the consumer by offering a recovery. The cumulative value of the service provider is the effect of the customer's perception of the recovery strategy along with the initial perception the customer had about the service provider.

AIMS OF SERVICE RECOVERY

The following points must be kept in mind while organizing a service recovery. They are to (1) satisfy customers who have experienced a service failure, (2) retain those customers who have experienced a failure, and (3) improve organization-wide processes as a result of information from failures.

Customers' Response to Service Failures

When customers choose a service organization to purchase a service, they have their own perceptions about it. On experiencing the service they develop their perceptions about the quality of the service at the time of delivery. If this is in accordance with their perceived perceptions, it leads to customer satisfaction. However, if the service rendered is below their expectation it leads to service failure.

If a service failure occurs the customer has two options—either to complain about it to the provider or to nurture the grievance quietly without telling the service provider about it at that point of time. If the customer complains, it gives the service provider a chance to retrieve the situation. It is the customers who do not complain that are a cause of concern for the service providers as they nurture negative feelings and are the ones who are never likely to return for re-purchase of services. Moreover, they can also spread negative word of mouth to relatives, friends, and acquaintances. That is more harmful, as then, the service provider faces the danger of losing all potential customers. The effectiveness of the service recovery influences the customer's perceptions about the service provider, which along with their initial perception, form the overall perception of the value of the service provider in the eyes of the customer. This perception can however, have negative implications if the service recovery was below their expectations. If the service recovery has met the expectations of the customers it can lead to customer satisfaction, and if the service recovery was above expectations it would lead to customer delight, and the recovery paradox would come into play. (The concept is discussed in detail later in the chapter).

Types of Complainers

Broadly, there are two types of customers—those who complain and those who do not. Several authors have uncovered the following four reasons why customers are reluctant to complain (Bamford and Xystouri 2005).

- The customers believe that the organization will not be responsive.
- They do not wish to confront the individual responsible for the failure.
- They are uncertain about their rights and the firm's obligations.
- They are concerned about the high cost in time and effort of complaining.

Zeithaml and Bitner (2000) identified four types of complainers—passive, voicers, irates, and activists.

Passives This group of customers is least likely to take any action. They do not say anything to the service provider, are less likely to spread negative word of mouth, and are unlikely to complain to a third party. This is because they doubt the effectiveness of complaining, thinking that the consequence will not merit the time and effort they are going to spend on it.

Voicers This group of customers actively complains to the service provider but is less likely to spread negative word of mouth, switch patronage, or go to a third party for redressal of their complaints. They are the service providers' true friends, helping them to improve their services by giving them a second chance.

Irates They are most likely to complain to friends and relatives, and switch over to another service provider. They are angry with the service provider, and are about average in their complaint to the service provider. They are less likely to give the service provider a second chance and will switch services, and complain to family and friends.

Activists In comparison to others, they have a higher propensity to complain to the service provider, relatives, friends, and to third parties. This fits in with their personal norms. They are highly optimistic about the positive consequences of all types of complaints.

Table 16.1 provides an insight into the various types of complainers.

We see that when customers complain they believe it is a social obligation to do so—to bring about a change for the better so that others do not face the same problem, and/or to punish the service provider.

Table 16.1 Types of complainers

Types of complainers	Action taken
Passives	No action
Voicers	Complain only to service provider and not to anyone else.
Irates	Complaint to service provider is average and more likely to spread negative word of mouth, and switch service providers. Unlikely to complain to third parties.
Activists	Above-average propensity to complain to all parties and most likely than others to complain to a third party.

CUSTOMER RECOVERY EXPECTATIONS

When customers complain there can be only two outcomes (Berry 1990). They are either satisfied or not satisfied with the company's response. As a service provider, the focus is to create more of the former than the latter outcomes. What customers expect when they voice their grievances is of primary importance. There are three specific types of justice that customers look for following their complaints (Berry 1990).

Outcome fairness Customers expect the compensation or the service recovery strategy to match the level of dissatisfaction. They expect objectivity in that, they want to be compensated no more or less than the mistake the service provider has committed, and equality in getting the same compensation that any other customer would get.

Procedural fairness In addition to compensation, customers expect the policies, rules, and the timeliness of the complaint process to be fair. The complaint process should be easy and hassle free, handled quickly, and by the first person the complainant contacts. The service recovery procedures should be adaptable and should match individual circumstances.

Interactional fairness Along with the outcome and procedural fairness, customers expect the recovery process to be carried out politely, with care and honesty. If customers feel the employees are uncaring and have done little to resolve the problem, it can hamper the recovery process. The skills and demeanour of employees influence the customer's evaluation of service quality. On their part, employees, due to lack of training and empowerment, may feel frustrated and show an indifferent attitude, especially if the customers are irate, it would adversely affect the recovery process.

If the customers feel that the problem faced is not handled properly they can file a complaint under the Consumer Protection Act, 1986. For banking grievances customers can also file a complaint under the Banking Ombudsman Scheme that has been revised by the Reserve Bank of India (RBI) with effect from 2006 (Exhibit 16.2).

Recovery Paradox

A good recovery can turn angry, frustrated customers into loyal ones and may create more goodwill than if things had gone on smoothly in the first place (Hart et al. 1990). For example, if a person orders a meal and finds that what he has received is not as per quality, and the restaurant manager immediately gets him another meal along with drinks at no extra cost, the customer is thrilled. The manager's gesture also affects the customer's purchase decision in the future. Some authors have suggested that companies should plan to disappoint customers so that they can recover and gain a higher level of loyalty from them than they would have gained in the first place. This idea is termed as the *recovery paradox.*

In their study, Weun et al. (2004) have offered mixed views concerning service recovery paradox. They argued that post-recovery satisfaction can be higher than pre-failure satisfaction for minor failures provided they are handled exceptionally well. As these failures become more severe they are unlikely to generate positive feelings towards

Exhibit 16.2   **Thinking Out of the Drop Box**

Imagine a situation where a customer deposits a cheque in the drop box but later finds this payment is not reflected in her account, or that no credit is reflected in the future bills, or the bank denies having received the cheque in the first place. In this case, the unfortunate part is that the customer has no substantiating evidence that she indeed deposited the cheque in the drop box before the due date.

In such a scenario where no foolproof system of accounting exists in the case of deposits through the drop box, the Committee on Procedures and Performance Audit on Public Services recommended that an acknowledgement at collection counters should exist, and that no branch should refuse an acknowledgement to the customer. RBI has even advised the banks to send reminders to all customers around the due date, or if no payment has been received. Any late payment charges levied without sending reminders will amount to deficiency in service.

Another fact is that in cases where a cheque is lost due to the bank's negligence or late pick-up of the cheque from the drop box, the consumer can file a complaint under the Consumer Protection Act, 1986. In case of a belated collection, a photocopy would suffice, whereas in case of a loss of cheque the consumer will have to produce sufficient evidence that the cheque was indeed deposited; the photocopy and pay-in slip would not be helpful as there is no endorsement from the bank on these.

Some ways in which customer litigation can be prevented are:

- Customers who have online viewing and transaction facilities can see whether the amount is reflected in the statements or not. The amount is ideally reflected as soon as the cheque is sent for clearing.
- Most of these collection machines have automatic systems to scan the cheque and issue a pay-in slip. A person deputed at the collection counter can endorse the pay-in slip, which can act as a proof of deposit and provide relief to the customer in case of a lost cheque.

the service provider regardless of how they are handled. Mack et al. (2000) have also researched that the customers who perceived their service failures as minor, rated the recovery efforts as very good (over 78% of the customers felt so), but the customers who had faced a major service failure were more likely to judge the recovery effort as poor (approximately 58%). Thus, if the management has to derive value from the recovery paradox it should not focus on the core services for doing this.

CUSTOMER SWITCHING BEHAVIOUR

Customers are spoilt for choices and the increasing competition in the marketplace provides them with a number of alternatives. Thus, if the service provider does not deliver the promised service during the 'moments of truth' then the customer might not give them a second chance and might defect to other service providers. Hence, it is up to the service providers to solicit the feedback as explained above and then to have a recovery strategy in place as detailed here.

Recovery Strategies

Service recovery strategies describe the actions of service providers in response to defects or failures (Grönroos 1988). A service provider can either do nothing, or do whatever it takes to fix the problem. The commonly used actions are apology and compensation (Bitner et al. 1990, Hoffman et al. 1995, and McDougall and Levesque 1999).

Apology   Service providers apologize for the service failure.

Assistance   This includes the actions taken to rectify the problem. This is the single most effective recovery strategy as it brings the customer back to the original purpose of buying the service. For example, if the customer has to wait for a service even with a reservation, the recovery strategy could include a reduction in the time that he waits for it.

Compensation   This includes monetary payments to the customers for the inconvenience experienced. It is generally resorted to when customers feel that assistance alone cannot offset the trouble 'cost' of the problem. Compensation can be in the form of free food, discounts, or a coupon for a drink or meal at a restaurant.

The effectiveness of recovery strategies is situational and is influenced by the type of service. According to McDougall and Levesque (1999), effectiveness of a recovery strategy depends on the following factors:
- What is done? This includes the recovery action taken by the service provider.
- How it is done? This includes the way in which the service provider has handled the problem, that is, responsiveness, empathy, and understanding. Even if the best of service recovery strategy is offered, but its delivery process is done grudgingly, the customer can see through it and the impact or effectiveness of service recovery stands diluted. Service providers should thus show sincerity in the process of fixing the problem and try to add value beyond the fix.

Types of Service Recovery Strategies

This section elaborates on the various strategies for handling service recovery.

Encourage customers to complain   The service provider should see the process of service recovery as an opportunity and encourage the customers to complain. For example, British Airways analysed its datamine of consumer complaints and transformed it into meaningful information pointing to persistent service problems. They analysed the information and found ways to improve customer satisfaction (Exhibit 16.3). The customers can be encouraged to complain if they find that the service provider has clear procedures for complaint handling, and these are easily accessible and user-friendly. Also, showing the customers that the organization is serious about the complaints received and acts on them, further motivates them to state the service failures that they have encountered.

Timely action   This is the most obvious service strategy and focuses on getting the service recovery right the first time. Service providers should create a culture where the staff is encouraged to acknowledge and deal with service failures, and bring it to the notice of the management. If justice is delayed to customers who are already facing a service failure, it will just add fuel to the fire. The staff should thus be efficient and understand the need of the hour.

Exhibit 16.3   **Service Recovery Strategy of British Airways**

Once dubbed 'awful', British Airways is today one of the most profitable and respected airlines in the world. In the 1980s, the BA management knew something was very wrong. Many customers were complaining about flight delays and food problems. The customers who complained were just one-third of the customers who had actually faced a problem in service delivery. The company estimates that unresolved customer service problems cost it as much as $600 million in lost revenue. The airline's management was determined to 'melt the complainant iceberg'. Its approach was first to change the culture via extensive employee training. The next move was to revise performance measures. Instead of emphasizing on complaint reduction, new steps such as rewarding employees who helped bring hidden problems to the surface, were introduced.

The five-step process

This redesigned process was supported by investments in a database engine and workstations capable of simultaneously displaying a customer's scanned-in letter, and relevant data in other systems such as frequent-flier status. The airline's employees were taught to use their judgement to determine how best to respond to customer problems.

Previously, when customers wrote to complain about flight delays or food, service representatives consulted a two-inch thick manual and followed a 13-step investigation process. It sometimes took them as long as twelve weeks to respond. This long method was condensed into five important steps:

- listen
- apologize
- express concern
- make amends
- record the event.

One manager observed, 'We have nothing to gain by squabbling with customers'. However, BA has everything to gain by turning dissatisfied customers into loyalists.

Staff empowerment and training   It is very essential to empower the frontline staff so that they know the extent to which they can go in solving issues. Doing this also gives the staff the added confidence that they have the power to deal with the service failures to some extent. Moreover, if the staff is empowered to take some decisions, they do not need to contact higher authorities for approval at the time of service failure. This also helps provide the customers timely service recovery, thus enhancing their view of service recovery further. The management should include service recovery aspects in the responsibilities chart of the employees so that they have a clear understanding of what is expected of them. This should also be reiterated to them from time to time during training sessions. The staff should be trained on how to deal with angry customers and how to help them solve problems. For example, American Express customer service representatives handling cardholders' monthly statements are trained and empowered to solve 85% of the problems on the spot (Berry et al. 1990).

Creating the right employee behaviour   Apart from the 'what' aspect, the 'how' aspect of the service recovery should also be highlighted to the employees. The importance of dealing with customers with empathy and compassion should be highlighted so that when they are resolving service failures they can be highly effective, and in the process create a recovery paradox. Employees, by creating 'warmth' in service delivery, are found to positively precipitate the relationship experience (Lemmink and Mattsson 2002). Similarly, we can say that at the time of service recovery this will create a short-term emotional judgment, which will have a long-term effect on the customers' perception.

Empower customers   Some service firms have a recovery strategy that empowers the customers too. This means that they allow the customers to solve their own problems and come up with solutions they seem fit for the service failures.

Follow up with timely personal communication with customers   Companies should undertake a follow up with the customers who have complained about service failures. This would help the service provider in various ways as illustrated here:

- Make sure that the customer is satisfied and is not holding a grudge.
- Communicate to the customer that her satisfaction is important to the organization.
- Create an opportunity for a dialogue—to listen, ask questions, explain, apologize, and seek suggestions from the customer.
- Regain the customer's favour.

Document the service failure   This is an important aspect of service recovery strategy. The purpose is to ensure that the service failures are understood by the staff at all levels so that the same failures are not repeated. It can also be referred to when a similar failure occurs, to understand the recovery strategy used and the impact of the same (that is, did the customer return or not).

Recovery Strategies for Managers

We see that service failures occur as a norm, but it is the way the employee handles the failure that creates a lasting impression on the customers. The knowledge of the service process, service delivery, and its operation, and the system standards enables employees to inform customers about what can and cannot be done to address their problem. In many cases, information alone can create satisfaction. For many encounters, action of some kind is needed to create satisfaction. These responses can be standardized or tailored to the situation. In either case, when information has to be given or some action has to be taken, if the employee is in the know and empowered then he/she can fix situations and respond to requests in effective ways. Thus, managers should undertake the following measures in this direction.

- Identify what information customers consider important and disseminate that information to the employees.
- Identify the range of action alternatives the employees can exercise.
- Train the employees to practice a range of action alternatives, which they can use at the time of service recovery.
- Develop a set of 'Plan B' actions with the employees and incorporate them as 'fail-safes' in the service system.

- Along with this, the employees must be empowered, that is, given discretion to take whatever action they deem necessary to retrieve the given situation (Weun et al. 2004).
- Unprompted and unsolicited employee action is, however, less subject to management control. To overcome this, an organization can, through the recruitment and selection procedures, hire employees with a strong service orientation. According to Chris Dunn, Regional Director of Talent Management, Marriott Hotels International Ltd, most of the employees working at Marriott are Indians who are doing quite well for themselves because the Indian culture of hospitality is quite close to the Marriott culture of serving the associates, the customer, and the community.

Effectiveness of Recovery Strategies

Many studies have been conducted to gauge the effectiveness of the recovery strategies. Researchers have found that a good service recovery is a key factor in building ongoing relationships with customers who were initially unhappy with the service delivery (Bitner 1990; Maxham 2001; and Smith et al. 1999). According to Weun et al. (2004), it is the severity of the service failure or the perceived intensity of the problem that influences the evaluation of a service provider after a service failure. If the service failure is severe, then despite adequate service recovery the customers will still perceive the loss to be greater. This will also affect the customers' trust, their commitment, and word of mouth publicity. A customer who reports satisfaction with the service recovery may not necessarily possess an equally high level of commitment to the service organization. Thus, managers should engage in additional efforts after the service recovery to attempt to build customer commitment. Satisfaction is a major driver of customer commitment and if service managers continue to satisfy customers after a service failure, then customer commitment can still be developed. McDougall and Levesque (1999), in a study on the effectiveness of recovery strategy on customers who had to wait for services even after making reservations, found that irrespective of the recovery strategy taken, the customers showed a negative future intention towards the service provider. Thus, the customer is not willing to forgive and forget. The service provider has to do it right the first time to ensure customer loyalty. Alternatively, we can manage the whole recovery process and create a value enhancement for the organization.

Value Enhancement through Service Recovery

La and Kandampully (2004) proposed a model of value enhancement that is inspired by service failure and recovery. They proposed that service recovery that leads to value enhancement takes the firm through three stages of service orientation—operational, strategic, and service vision.

Operational

This stage of service orientation includes measures that are primarily aimed towards recovering from service failure. These would include the following:
- provide alternatives of recovery so that the customer's needs are met
- acknowledge the understanding of the service failure

- provide immediate rewards for employees involved in successful recovery
- provide further training to employees who contributed to the initial failure.

Strategic

Once the recovery process is in place, the organization graduates to the next level of value enhancement, which entails strategy planning on the basis of learning and realignment as a result of the damage control systems in place. It entails the following measures:

- Align the firm's external orientation with internal orientation to create right customer perception and minimize service failures.
- Conduct a systematic analysis of the entire service delivery system to create a foolproof method and do it 'right the first time'.
- Learn from the service failure and recovery to realign the inner mechanism so that the same mistake is not repeated in the future.
- Create a culture of learning by assimilating and disseminating information.
- Effect improvements that will reflect on the firm's competency and market performance.

Service vision

Once the two stages are achieved, steps can be taken to initiate innovative value enhancement that progresses through the operation, strategy, and vision of the firm for the ultimate benefit of customers, employees, and the firm itself.

Although the service recovery is often regarded as an operational concern, if integrated with strategic and conceptual issues, it can contribute to the firm's business orientation immensely and continually, thus creating a competitive advantage. Moreover, the organization-wide realignment and reorientation will create superior customer value.

SERVICE GUARANTEES

Due to the characteristics of services, the customers cannot be sure of the quality of a service until they experience it themselves. As costs are involved and the process cannot be undone, in order to generate a feeling of trust and commitment, the service providers try to give guarantees in a bid to ensure that the service delivery is going to satisfy the customers. A service guarantee is a commitment the service provider gives to the customer concerning all or part of the service process and may also include a compensation for the customer if the commitment is not honoured (Kashyap 2001). Guarantees are common in manufactured products and have recently been applied to the services sector. According to Wirtz (1996), guarantees can be used as a quality tool, marketing tool, and customer service tool. The different types of service guarantees are illustrated in this section.

Unconditional service guarantee An unconditional service guarantee, guarantees cent per cent customer satisfaction irrespective of any terms and conditions. This applies to the customer's overall satisfaction.

Exhibit 16.4 **Introduction of Loan Back Guarantee by GE Money**

GE Money, India has decided to introduce a 15-day loan back guarantee to bring in transparency while approving mortgages, loans against property, and personal loans.

This guarantee will give its customers, an option of returning a loan within 15 days if they find a gap in delivery in key terms and services versus the promise made to them while applying for the loan. No processing fee or penalty on loan will be levied on the customer. Also, even before the customer has availed the loan, he/she will be provided with a document called the 'most important document', which will contain the paperwork on the important terms of the loan and the simplified tariff card.

This campaign seems to be an attempt by GE Money to provide small-ticket loans to customers with inadequate ability to pay. The size of this business seems to be anywhere around ₹31,440 crore. Some competitors feel that this step only provides a warranty and does not improve product quality.

Conditional service guarantee A conditional guarantee is when the service provider intends to promote a certain element of the service offering. For example, Bharti group is giving guarantees on the Touchtel (fixed line telephone) service in Chennai. In the service level agreement, Touchtel mentions issues such as down time (how long a telephone connection will be out of service in case of a fault), billing errors, and in the case of the DSL service, speed of the Internet connection. The service is provided in key cities, such as Hyderabad, where the business segment is viewed as a potential area that the service provider can tap (Ramakrishna 2004). Exhibit 16.4 elaborates the concept further.

Designing the Service Guarantee

Fabien (2005) gave a model to support the decision of service guarantee development. The proposed model advocated five steps, namely, preliminary analysis, service quality signalling, guarantee design, implementation and communication, and performance analysis.

Preliminary analysis

A preliminary analysis on taking a decision on service guarantee is undertaken at the outset. It can be done by analysing the external and the internal factors.

External factors The following external factors are taken into account while conducting a preliminary analysis.

Industry standards An industry that has few acknowledged standards or where service supply variability is high can be recommended to give guarantees.

Competition Being the first firm to offer guarantees, always provides a competitive advantage to the firm. For example, Standard Chartered Bank became the first bank in Singapore to offer service guarantees (Exhibit 16.5).

Legal aspects The regulations that govern the transactions must be considered in detail. Legally, a commitment constitutes a type of contract, and failure to honour the same can have negative implications.

> **Exhibit 16.5** **Stanchart Innovates with Service Guarantee**
>
> Standard Chartered Bank will offer a new service guarantee, known as the overnight document checking service, to its Singapore customers. As a result of this commitment, trade customers will have a quicker turnaround time, which in turn, will help the company's cash flows and reduce interest costs. This service will help customers to submit export letters of credit documents to the bank till 6.00 pm, along with a commitment that any notice of discrepancy will be delivered by the next working day. In case this deadline is not met, the service guarantee offers customers the ability to claim a credit note of up to SG$100 in commission fees of their next trade transaction. This is a value-added service that will allow the trade customers to speed up their trade capabilities and further strengthen the company's position in the market.

Customer expectations This is of utmost importance as what the customers expect and what they want is vital and the organization providing service guarantees should be aware of this. It will also help them spend the money in the right direction.

Risk perceived by customers Service guarantees assume special significance when customers feel that the risk associated with the purchase of service is high, or they do not feel qualified to assess the service, or where they feel emotionally involved in the service. In such cases if a service guarantee is offered by the service provider it can positively influence the purchase decision of the customer.

Perceived image of the firm A firm with a low perceived image is bound to benefit from providing service guarantees as it will reassure the potential customers about the service quality. On the other hand, for a well-known organization, the strong corporate image is a guarantee in itself. If such firms provide guarantees it will create doubts in the minds of the customers.

Uncontrollable factors These are the factors beyond the firm's control. For example, an airline cannot guarantee flight departure times because of a number of external factors, such as weather condition, air traffic, etc.

Internal factors The following internal factors should be considered during a preliminary analysis on service guarantees.

Process fit This is one of the most important internal factors that should be taken into account because if the process is lacking or not fit enough, then the firms should not provide the guarantees. For instance, if a bank promises a financing proposal within 72 hours of receiving an application, then they must make adequate provisions for the human resources and processes to achieve success in the service guarantees.

Management of contact and support staff The cooperation of the contact and support staff is a must when providing service guarantees. The contact and support staff should be made aware that if they do not perform within the stipulated time, it is going to cost the firm monetarily as well as create negative perceptions about the organization.

Process used to manage customer's comments A firm that clearly informs its customers about the standards they are entitled to expect and compensation they will receive if the same is not met, actually motivates the clients to express service dissatisfaction. Once a firm offers guarantees, there is bound to be a surge in customer complaints. The firm should have a process in place to manage these complaints so that they can recover the customers they would have otherwise lost due to service failures. Service guarantees thus help to retain the customers who would otherwise have been lost and also help the firm to make improvements in their service delivery process.

Employee motivation   It is important for the employees to be motivated so that they can perform and honour the service guarantees. An employee who is aware of, and comfortable with the service guarantees can concentrate on meeting the commitments and improving processes in case of service failures. The guarantees provide a 'framework' for the employees and give 'meaning' to their work. However, if the guarantees are unrealistic they can de-motivate the staff, as they cannot meet the unrealistic promises made by the company.

Pricing strategy   The final, but not the least important point to consider is compatibility of the service guarantee with the pricing strategy. Service guarantees have cost implications in the form of retribution to customers, training to employees, introduction of new systems, and upgradation of existing systems. Firms offering service guarantees are found to charge more than their competitors not following this policy. It has been observed that customers are often willing to pay more to prevent poor service delivery.

Service quality signal

Service guarantees help the organization to send signals of their service quality to potential and existing customers, competitors, and partners (subcontractors, distributors, suppliers, etc.). If customers who have different options to choose from, base their purchase decisions on the quality of the service, they are influenced by the service guarantees, which in turn can motivate them in favour of the service provider.

Guarantee design

The guarantee design is successful if a firm takes into consideration the following aspects:
- It bases the design on customer expectations on a regular basis and adopts a customer-oriented approach when designing its service.
- It defines a service standard, and reviews the efficiency and effectiveness of its service process on a regular basis to ensure that promises are honoured every time.

The service guarantee is not only a 'persuasive focus of communication' to attract new customers, but also helps the employees to understand better their respective roles in the 'service chain'.

Implementation and communication

A service guarantee once designed should first be pretested within a group of customers from the target market. After the necessary amendments are made, the service guarantee needs to be communicated to the customers for its implementation. This communication should be done in a phased manner, spread over six months to two years, to allow the firm to perfect the applications of the guarantees. While launching service guarantees, a media offensive strategy helps maximize the effect.

Performance analysis

It is important for a firm to know the effectiveness of a service guarantee for a given period and in a given commercial environment for it to continue to provide the same effectively and profitably. The costs involved in service guarantees should be evaluated. The costs include the money and resources spent on (1) market research required for the preliminary analysis, (2) pretesting the guarantee, (3) measurement of performance indicators, (4) time spent on designing guarantees, (5) communication campaign, (6) compensation for dissatisfied customers, (7) cost of process triggered by request for compensation, (8) legal options required in case of failure to fulfil a guarantee, and (9) costs involved if the service guarantee is withdrawn prematurely.

It is not easy to isolate the impact of a given marketing strategy. A number of factors, such as price wars, counter-attack by competitors, or changes in economic environment, all add to the complexities. Another way to ensure the effectiveness of a service guarantee is to study certain performance indicators before and (six months) after its launch even though the marketing communication is spread over a period of many months. Some of the relevant indicators that can be studied are (1) customer retention rate, (2) net margins, (3) net profit, (4) number of new customers, (5) gross revenue generated before and during the service guarantee period, (6) number of applications for compensation, (7) value of compensation offered, and (8) value of transaction entered into by a customer after compensation.

A study of these indicators provides information about the immediate or short-term benefits of guarantees. It is also important to consider the medium- and long-term benefits of the guarantees. A higher customer retention rate points towards customer loyalty which will prove beneficial in the medium and long-run, when the loyalists turn advocates for the service organization, providing them service satisfaction through guarantees. The senior management's determination and commitment to provide customer satisfaction creates a positive culture where all the employees learn about the importance of a happy customer. This results in lower employee turnover, and higher employee loyalty and commitment towards the organization. Subsequently, this gets reflected in their service quality, and ultimately in customer satisfaction.

An ideal service guarantee should be (1) transparent, (2) offered unconditionally, (3) credible and realistic, (4) focused on the key service features, (5) supported by significant compensation to the customers, (6) easy to understand and communicate, (7) easy to invoke, and (8) easy to implement.

An unconditional guarantee offers to provide full customer satisfaction. However, it is found that unconditional guarantees are viewed as 'blank cheques' where the customers do not have to give reasons for their dissatisfaction. Thus, organizations can balance an unconditional guarantee with promises concerning the performance of certain elements of the service.

Disadvantages of Service Guarantees

Service guarantees pressurize employees to meet the guarantees, which can be difficult if systems are not in place. This causes disillusionment and frustration among them when they cannot meet the customer expectations, and results in confrontations (quarrels, foul language, etc.) with them. The result is not only a high rate of customer loss, but higher employee turnover too. So, for a service guarantee to be successful it is not only important to keep the customer expectations in mind but also to have an internal focus, and get the processes in order, and ensure that the workforce is also in tune with the guarantees.

RESEARCH INSIGHT

Establishment and Applications of the Integrated Model of Service Quality Measurement

Yang, Ching Chow (2003), 'Establishment and applications of the integrated model of service quality measurement', *Managing Service Quality: An International Journal*, vol. 13, issue 4, pp. 310–324.

The improvement of service quality has become a major strategy for improving competitiveness. The identification of customers' requirements and the measurement of satisfaction levels are therefore two crucial activities for enterprises. However, firms frequently fail to understand customer requirements, and the usual methods for measuring customer satisfaction are incomplete. The present research establishes an integrated model for achieving multiple targets in measuring service quality, that is, to identify the important quality attributes that are identified by customers, to understand customer satisfaction levels with respect to these quality attributes, to discover the difference between employees' perceptions and the customers' perceptions of these quality attributes, and to use the analytic results to improve service quality. This integrated model is valuable for practical implementation in industries, and as an important reference for academic research on service quality.

SUMMARY

Service failures are not an exception in an organization that focuses on services delivery. Failures are bound to happen in service organizations. It is thus imperative that an organization be aware of the different service failures and how the customers respond to the same. It is interesting to note the importance of service recovery on the value of the service. It is, therefore, important for an organization to salvage the situation by providing recovery strategies. If good recovery strategies are adopted and if the initial failure is not severe, it is possible to create a higher satisfaction in the customers. This can only happen if the customers bring the service failures to the notice of the organization. Recovery strategies not only provide satisfaction to customers encountering a service failure (recovery paradox), but also help in retaining the customers, and when tied strategically with the business orientation can lead to creating a competitive advantage. Service guarantees are used as a tool to help the organization to coax the customers to bring the failure points to the notice of the organization. This then gives the organization a chance to recover the customer's trust. The various service guarantees that can be used by an organization and the guidelines to help an organization design its own service guarantees have been discussed.

KEY TERMS

Complaint handling   The process of dealing with customer grievances.

Complaints   An after-effect of service failure, when the customer nurtures negative perceptions about the same. A complaint gives the service provider a second chance to retrieve the situation.

Customer dissatisfaction   This arises when the service rendered to the customer does not meet his expectation. This can lead to a customer complaint or a silent customer who does not complain about the service problem.

Feedback   Customers are an important source of feedback; they can provide information or opinions about the performance of a product, system, intervention, or employee.

Service failure   When the service rendered to the customer is below his expectation, it leads to service failure.

Service guarantee   A promise made by a third party who is not party to a contract between two others, to accept liability if one of the parties fails to fulfil the contractual obligations.

Service recovery   A strategy devised to reverse the decline in profitability of a firm or subsidiary, enabling it to achieve a viable and sustainable future.

Value enhancement   The logical flow of service failure leading to service recovery and finally, enhancement of value of service.

EXERCISES

Concept Review Questions

1. Critically discuss the importance of the concept of service recovery.
2. What is 'recovery paradox'? Do you agree with the concept? In what situations will the recovery paradox fail? Give examples to support your answer.
3. Discuss any two recovery strategies that you think are best suited for a fast food restaurant. Give reasons to support your chosen strategies.
4. What are service guarantees? Discuss the circumstances under which an organization should adopt or stay away from offering service guarantees.
5. Critically discuss the importance of service guarantees in the process of service recovery.

Critical Thinking Questions

1. Describe the last service failure you experienced. Discuss your response to the service failure. Give reasons for the same. In retrospect do you think it was the right action to take? Why?

2. Discuss an incident in which you faced a service failure and complained to the service provider. What was the response of the service provider? What recovery strategy did he/she choose and what was the effect of the same on your overall perception of the service provider value?
3. Identify a service organization you patronize regularly. Design a service guarantee for the same.

Internet Exercises

1. Visit the website of any two hospitality chains that provide service guarantees. Compare the guarantees provided. As a customer what would your response be to both the organizations and why?
2. Visit the website of your insurance agent. Is there any provision for customer complaint? If yes, try and file a complaint and wait for the response. How would you have handled the same situation if given a chance?

CASE STUDY   Customer Feedback for Online Shopping*

Online shopping

Welcome to the connected world! It is a world that provides a number of alternatives and saves you from the hustle and bustle of going to the market. A world where you can get a bouquet delivered to your girlfriend at her doorstep on Friendship or Valentines Day, while sitting on your sofa in 2–3 minutes flat. It saves you from slogging out in the sun, going from store to store searching for the perfect product. Now, you can savour the comfort of your house and between sips of your tea can complete your shopping chores. There are a number of websites you can log on to or you can download their apps on your mobile phone and shop on the go. India's online fashion retailer Myntra is planning to launch an artificial intelligence powered chat-based personal shopping assistant that will guide the consumer through the browsing session. The first quarter of 2014 Myntra experienced 80% growth in sales coming from the mobile platform and it is expecting to clock a sales of over ₹6,000 crore in early 2016 (Nair 2014).

Online shopping offers a number of benefits right from time saving to making shopping easier. Therefore, if you have to purchase a shirt, you just need to open the website and go to the clothing section. There you proceed to the catalogue of shirts and can choose from various brands in just a few clicks. The variety is huge and that too from the cheapest to the most expensive so that customers can choose as per their budget and choice. The product is delivered in a promised period of time and the order can also be tracked online.

The Myntra Experience

In a similar experience, suppose a dress was ordered from Myntra and the customer gets an alert that his order for a given amount has been placed successfully. This is followed with an SMS about the placed order along with tentative delivery period. On the day of delivery, an SMS is also sent to the customer that the order has left the warehouse and will be delivered by end of the same day. The delivery is not accompanied with a return option as in the case

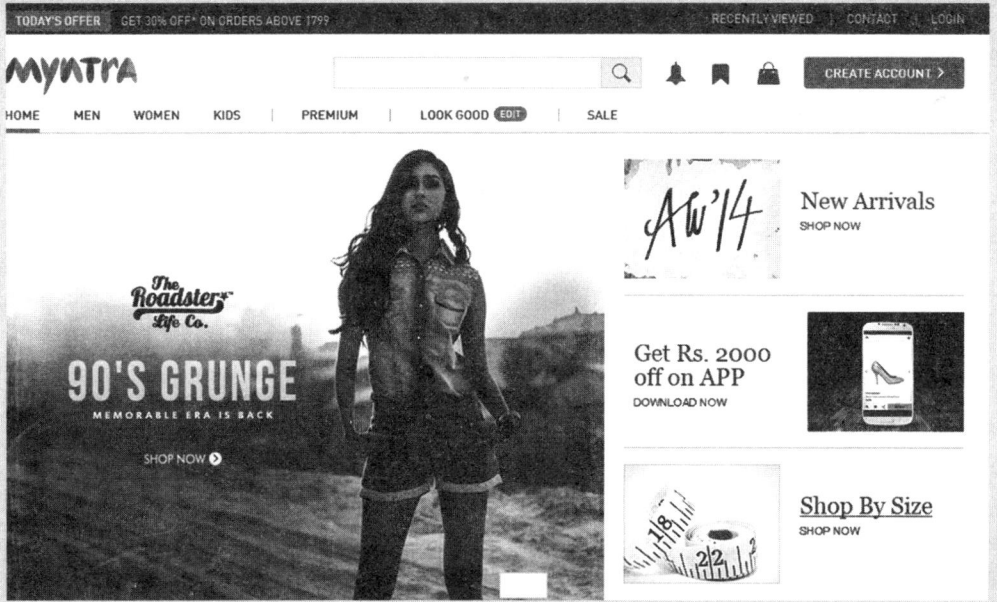

*Jaya Rishi Kinger and Mohita Sethi

of Jabong. However, if you want to return the product for any reason—say wrong size, colour, etc.— you can do so within a period of thirty days by calling the customer care executive and give the reason for return. Myntra then arranges for the re-pickup of the delivered product. The customer is informed about the promised date by which the courier guy will come to re-pickup the product. At this time of pick-up, the customer also has to fill a return form stating the reason for return. The money can then be either refunded to the customers' bank account or the money can be converted to Myntra cash in the customer's account. This can then be used to make a purchase within a period of one year. After the delivery a feedback form is mailed to the customer's email id to solicit a feedback about the service.

Myntra has a referral policy also and customers can refer their friends to Myntra's website and if the referral makes a purchase then the referee gets points' proportional to the amount of purchase. This is a one-time policy and the referee gets 25% on minimum order value of ₹999 and the maximum bonus points for the referee is up to ₹500. Myntra has a formal system of getting the feedback. After the product has been delivered they send a mail to the customer asking for the feedback for every purchase made.

Retaining the Customer

In case the customer wants to return the product the same is facilitated by Myntra but even if the customer is satisfied with the refund the company loses that sale. Here we need to identify the root of the problem to identify where the deal went wrong— was the information appropriate, did the product live up to the promise, etc. The same is documented as the reason for the return. The idea is that even if the sale is lost the customer is retained and confidence is inculcated that the customer can return the product to the company. There are online blogs like mouthshut.com that has 511 online reviews for Myntra (as on 16 August 2014). Of these out of the top 5 most read ones, 4 are about the negative experiences of the customers. The fifth one goes on to say how the customer was apprehensive about placing the order after reading the earlier reviews but was then very happy with the experience.

Word of mouth has long been used to influence the service purchase among family and friends. The Internet has added to this by connecting us with others globally so that we can learn from their experience before making a purchase. According to a study by BCG, 9% of urban Indian consumers use the Internet during the purchase process. This number will grow to 29% by 2016 with their main activities being searching for information and social networking (Mall and Rana 2014).

Conclusion

Online shopping is highly competitive with a number of well entrenched players and international players also developing India-specific strategies. Companies need to pay attention to the services they are offering and keep their customer satisfied as a bulk of the online activities is concentrated in the pre-purchase activity and an unfavourable review is enough for a potential customer to turn their back on you. Also, online recommendations and feedback are public, permanent, and non-controllable (Mall and Rana 2014). Thus, companies need to have an effective feedback system where they should actively seek feedback and not just mail it to the customers as like the authors there might be other people who do not have time to respond. This can be followed with a call from the executive to know about the customers' satisfaction level. Customers can be actively involved regarding how to improve the service delivery experience. The fruitful results of an effective feedback system can only be had if a system is developed where the reasons for service failures are consistently updated and corrective action taken. This should be a never ending process to maintain the clientele and to expand the business.

Questions

1. Discuss the service delivery process of Myntra and comment on the feedback method employed.
2. What kind of complainers can you identify in the reading?
3. Do you think the policy of refunding the money or making it available as Myntra cash is a good enough recovery strategy? Why or why not?

REFERENCES

Aulakh, G. (2014), 'Bharti Does a "Quality" check to beat competition blues', *The Economic Times*, New Delhi, dated 8 April, p. 8.

Bamford, David and Tatiana Xystouri (2005), 'A case study of service failure and recovery within an international airline', *Managing Service Quality*, vol. 15, no. 3, pp. 306–315.

Bendapudi, N. and L.L. Berry (1997), 'Customers' motivations for maintaining relationships with service providers', *Journal of Retailing*, vol. 73, no. 1, pp. 15–37.

Berry, L.L. (1995), 'Relationship marketing of services: Growing interest, emerging perspectives', *Journal of the Academy of Marketing Science*, vol. 23, no. 4, pp. 236–245.

Berry, L.L., Valarie A. Zeithaml, and A. Parasuraman (1990), 'Five imperatives for improving service quality', *Sloan Management Review*, vol. 31, no. 4, pp. 29–38.

Bitner, M.J., B.H. Booms, and Tetreault M. Stanfield (1990), 'The service encounter: Diagnosing favourable and unfavourable incidents', *Journal of Marketing*, vol. 54, no. 1, pp. 71–84.

Cash Jr, James I. (1995), 'British Air gets on course: Airline uses information technology to support service recovery strategy', *Information Week*, 1 May.

Chung, Beth and Douglas K. Hoffman (1998), 'Critical incidents', *Cornell Hotel and Restaurant Administration Quarterly*, vol. 39, no. 3, pp. 66–71.

Doney, P.M. and J.P. Cannon (1997), 'An examination of the nature of trust in buyer-seller relationships', *Journal of Marketing*, vol. 51, no. 2, pp. 11–27.

Dutta, Kirti, Umashankar Venkatesh, and H.G. Parsa (2007), 'Service failure and recovery strategies in the restaurant sector: An Indo-US comparative study', *International Journal of Contemporary Hospitality Management*, vol. 19, no. 5, pp. 351–363.

Fabien, Louis (2005), 'Design and implementation of a service guarantee', *The Journal of Services Marketing*, vol. 19, no. 1, pp. 33–38.

Goel, Sumit (2006), 'Thinking out of the drop box', *The Economic Times*, 13 October, p. 9.

Grönroos, C. (1988), 'Service quality: The six criteria of good perceived service quality', *Review of Business*, vol. 9, no. 3, pp. 10–13.

Gwinner, K.P., D.G. Dwayne, and M.J. Bitner (1998), 'Relational benefits in service industries: The customers' perspective', *Journal of the Academy of Marketing Science*, vol. 26, no. 2, pp. 101–114.

Hart, C.W.L., W.E. Sasser Jr, and J.L. Heskett (1990), 'The profitable art of service recovery', *Harvard Business Review*, July–August, pp. 148–156.

Hoffman, K.D., S.W. Kelly, and H.M. Rotasky (1995), 'Tracking service failures and employee recovery efforts', *Journal of Marketing*, vol. 9, no. 2, pp. 49–61.

Juttner, U. and H.P. Wehrli (1994), 'Relationship marketing from a value system perspective', *International Journal of Service Industry Management*, vol. 5, no. 5, pp. 54–73.

Kashyap, R. (2001), 'The effects of service guarantees on external and internal markets', *Journal of Academy of Marketing Science*, vol. 1, no. 10.

Keaveney, S.M. (1995), 'Customer switching behaviour in service industries: An exploratory study', *Journal of Marketing*, vol. 59, April, pp. 71–81.

La, Kahn V. and J. Kandampully (2004), 'Market oriented learning and customer value enhancement through service recovery management', *Managing Service Quality*, vol. 14, no. 5, pp. 390–401.

Lee, S.C., S. Barker, and J. Kandampully (2003), 'Technology, service quality and customer loyalty in hotels: Australian managerial perspective', *Managing Service Quality*, vol. 13, no. 5, pp. 423–432.

Lemmink, Jos and Jan Mattsson (2002), 'Employee behaviour, feelings of warmth, and customers' perceptions in service encounters', *International Journal of Retail and Distribution Management*, vol. 30, no. 1, pp. 18–33.

Lovelock (1993), *Product Plus*, McGraw-Hill, New York.

Mack, R., R. Mueller, J. Crotts, and A. Broderick (2000), 'Perceptions, corrections, and defections: Implications for service recovery in the restaurant industry', *Managing Service Quality*, vol. 10, no. 6, pp. 339–346.

Mack, Rhonda, Rene Mueller, John Crotts, and Amanda Broderick (2000), 'Perceptions, corrections, and defections: Implications for service recovery in the restaurant industry', *Managing Service Quality*, Bedford, vol. 10, no. 6, pp. 339–346.

Mall, A. and K. Rana (2014), 'Listening to your customers is not easy', *Brand Equity*, *The Economic Times*, New Delhi, 09–15 July, pp. 2–3.

Maxham, J.G. (2001), 'Service recovery's influence on consumer satisfaction, positive word-of-mouth, and purchase intentions', *Journal of Business Research*, vol. 54, pp. 11–24.

McDougall, Gordon H.G. and T.J. Levesque (1999), 'Waiting for service: The effectiveness of recovery strategies', *International Journal of Contemporary Hospitality Management*, vol. 11, no. 1, pp. 6–16.

Nair, R.P. (2014), 'Myntra plans to offer chat-based shopping assistant', *The Economic Times*, New Delhi, p. 6.

Oliver, R. (1999), 'Whence consumer loyalty', *Journal of Marketing*, vol. 68, pp. 33–44.

Palmer, A., R. Beggs, and C. Keown-McMullan (2000), 'Equity and repurchase intention following service failure', *Journal of Services Marketing*, vol. 14, no. 6, pp. 512–528.

Ramakrishna, N. (2004), 'Touchtel to guarantee service levels to users', *Businessline*, 20 March, p. 1.

Rao, T.V. (2010), Book extract 'Managers who make a difference—Sharpening your management skills' cited in 'Nurturing Organizational Values', *The Strategist*, *Business Standard*, New Delhi, 22 November, p. 2.

Smith, A.K., R.N. Bolton, and J. Wagner (1999), 'A model of customer satisfaction with service encounters involving failure and recovery', *Journal of Marketing Research*, vol. 36, no. 3, pp. 356–372.

Trade Finance, London, September 2006, p. 1.

Venkatesh, U. and A. Kulkarni (2002), 'Employee motivation and empowerment in hospitality, rhetoric or reality: Some observations from India', *Journal of Services Research*, vol. 2, no. 1, pp. 31–53.

Weun, Seungoog, Sharon E. Beatty, and Michael Jones (2004), 'The impact of service failure severity on service recovery evaluations and post-recovery relationships', *The Journal of Services Marketing*, vol. 18, no. 2/3, pp. 133–146.

Wirtz, J. (1996), 'Development of a model on the impacts of service guarantees', Paper presented at the fourth International Research Seminar on Services Management.

Zeithaml, V.A., L.L. Berry, and A. Parasuraman (1993), 'The nature and determinants of customer expectations of service', *Journal of the Academy of Marketing Science*, vol. 21, no. 1, pp. 1–12.

Zeithaml, V.A. and M.J. Bitner (2000), *Services Marketing*, 2nd edn, Tata McGraw-Hill Publishing Company Limited, New Delhi.

Zhu, Zhen, K. Sivakumar, and A. Parasuraman (2004), 'A mathematical model of service failure and recovery strategies', *Decision Sciences*, vol. 35, no. 3, pp. 493–525.

Banerjee, G. (2007), 'GE Money introduces loan-back guarantee', http://www.livemint.com/2007/11/07221434/GE-Money-introduces-loanback.html, accessed on 7 November 2007.

http://airtelbroadband.in/experience6.htm, accessed on 19 October 2006.

http://www.retailangle.com/Newsdetail.asp?Newsid=3305&Newstitle=Simran_Says:_An_interesting_new_retail_store, accessed on 9 August 2014.

Impact of Technology on Marketing of Services

OBJECTIVES

After reading this chapter you will be able to understand the:

- various technology issues pertaining to firms
- impact of technology on service firms
- various challenges for managing the use of online technology

PVR Cinemas—Magic of Innovation

The Internet has helped services firms to provide better customer satisfaction and experience. Priya Village Roadshow (PVR) multiplexes have added a special punch to the cinema experience in India. The technology experience of movie goers starts much before they leave their homes. Besides offering e-tickets and m-tickets, the multiplexes have adopted the latest sound and projection technologies to ensure ultimate viewer satisfaction. Automation technology has reduced the transaction time and the long queues may soon become a thing of the past. The introduction of mobile ticketing at PVR has been a success and the interactive voice response (IVR) mechanism and ticketing kiosks have introduced easier ways of interacting with the customers. The movie schedules are available on the mobile and the user just has to send an SMS. The Intranet boosts the security set-up of PVR Cinemas with a network of close circuit cameras constantly updating the central control rooms.

PVR has a presence in about 97 locations in India. They have edge-to-edge screens and are equipped with modern projection and sound systems. Fourteen PVR screens have moved to the electronic format and plan to roll out digital cinema screens soon. The theatres will soon work on the principle of digitized content being distributed through satellite or fibre networks, uploaded to digital cinema servers that will then serve it to a digital projector for screening.

After going through the chapter, you will be able to answer the following questions:

1. How can technology impact the quality of consumer experience?
2. Why must a service firm deploy technology?

INTRODUCTION

This chapter discusses the technology issues that need to be addressed across various service segments. It also discusses the impact of technology on services firms. Businesses are confronted with enormous challenges to perform. Product life cycles are shortening, development in material science and technology is accelerating, customer sophistication is growing, and concern with the environment and its resources is emerging as a key issue (Zairi 1995). The convergence of technologies is giving rise to new businesses. Mobile commerce and broadband technologies are redefining the domain of entertainment and media businesses. Technology when assessed as an issue, not only impacts the R&D dimension and hence, the development of new products/services, but there are also so many more manifestations of technology at the workplace. These issues are discussed in the following section.

There are numerous aspects that need to be understood in the context of management of technology. Some of these aspects are discussed in this chapter.

Choosing Alternate Technology

This means deciding a particular technology for manufacturing or for providing services. For instance, when telecom firms offer mobile services they have to address complex technology issues.

- Do they need to adhere to the standards set up in the country?
- Do the countries allow alternative technologies to be used in a particular domain? What will be the impact on the customer?
- Will he/she be able to afford the new technology?
- What will be the impact on profitability of the firm?
- Is this technology sustainable over a long period?

Carlson (2004) has discussed the issues of using technology foresight to create business value. He suggests that developing an R&D strategy and identifying new technology-based opportunities is a critical activity today. From incremental maintenance of core technologies to long-term threats and opportunities, such as nanotechnology, a business needs to understand and manage more technology options today than ever before. He suggests that technology foresight is a perspective and a process that can sort the options, identify new technology opportunities, and develop coherence between short- and long-term R&D. He has pointed out some major aspects, which indicate the criticality of technology foresight:

- commoditization of markets, products, and most technologies
- more perfect global markets
- capital availability in second- and third-world countries
- global technology equilibrium (catalyzed by the Internet)
- increasing pace of scientific discovery
- large coherent technology initiatives such as nanotechnology and biotechnology
- relentless productivity increase from information technology.

Exhibit 17.1 gives an insight into how small theatres are using digital technologies, which result in cost savings for them.

Exhibit 17.1 Digital Experience at Cinemas

Digital technology has entered cinemas in small cities such as Cuttack (Orissa) and Pedapally (Andhra Pradesh). With the distributors' permission, a film that does not run well can be changed. The owner of a cinema hall in Cuttack says that though there is a choice to change the film, the publicity required for a film makes this difficult. Different owners have different takes on this. Also, distributors responsible for distributing the movies to particular locations feel that switching movies entails a huge cost, although some lenient ones do allow the cinema owners to discontinue a movie in case there is no crowd. Further, the regional database for digital films is yet to pick up because of the fact that converting print to digital is costly.

Assessment of the Lifespan of Technology

A very important issue, which needs to be addressed, is related to assessment of the lifespan of the technology. The lifespan of the technology needs to be assessed and also some forecasts are essential. It is a very complex task and needs expert insight into the domain. Many technologies, when developed, become the standard for the industry to follow. For instance, the Pentium configuration developed by Intel and the operating system developed by Microsoft have become accepted global standards. Similarly, the UNIX platform too is an accepted global standard. Worldwide, many software professionals have got together to develop an open software system named Linux. So, when such technology becomes an acceptable standard by the industry, it opens doors for new challenges which need to be addressed. For how long can the competitive advantage be maintained? According to Chesbrough (2003), the concept of 'open innovation' is the key to thriving in today's competitive environment. He further adds that open innovation is all about making greater use of external ideas and technologies in their own businesses, while also allowing their unused ideas to be used by other companies.

SERVICE INNOVATION

Increasingly, firms do not consider themselves to be strictly in the services or manufacturing domain. Instead, they view themselves as offering solutions which deploy both products and services. On one hand, manufacturing firms offer hardware/product and after-sales service. On the other hand, service firms that offer service may need to offer hardware in order to facilitate the delivery of the service. For example, the telecommunication service provider may provide the necessary hardware to access Internet and telephone services at the customer location.

Firms need to continuously change and evolve. Innovation is the successful exploitation of new ideas; this definition applies to all firms in the economy and is equally relevant to services innovation as well.

Innovation, if explained using Schumpeter's approach (1934), can emanate from any of the following areas:

1. New product offering: If applied to the services domain, it would mean offering new services or adding new features.

2. Targeting new markets for the services: As an example, a service firm may target new geographies and align its offering to the local needs.

3. New sources of supply: This particular innovation involves using new modes of supply.

4. New methods of production: This applies in terms of deployment of new methods of production. In the services domain, it means the processes for delivery such as ATMs in banks.

5. Use of new technology: The use of IT has led to the emergence of new product offerings. For example, airline or hotel reservations have witnessed a boom in online reservations.

There can be numerous approaches to understanding the concept of service innovation. Soete and Miozzo (1989) provide a more differentiated picture of the services industry, distinguishing between supplier-dominated, scale-intensive physical networks and information networks, and specialized science-based services. The research literature points outs that services deliver a substantial contribution to the innovation processes. Other than technological elements, non-technological elements, such as people and processes, play an important role in the innovation process.

Hertog and Bilderbeek (1999) have put forward the following framework for understanding the process of service innovation. This is referred to as the Dialogic's four-dimensional model of innovation in services. This particular model helps to understand the process of service innovation. There are four important dimensions that help in describing and analysing service innovation. These are:

1. Dimension 1 (new service concept)
2. Dimension 2 (client interface)
3. Dimension 3 (service delivery system)
4. Dimension 4 (technological options)

New service concept This deals with a new service offering or deployment of new technology for offering the service. For example, call centres offering various kinds of support for back office operation. Another example is, using Internet-based technologies for offering online services. New service development has been dealt with in sufficient detail in Chapter 2.

Client interface A second element of service innovation is the client interface. In services delivery, a client is an essential part of the service delivery in many cases. (For example, a student in case of face-to-face teaching in a classroom.) A student's participation as an active learner makes a lot of difference to the overall classroom experience. The calibre of the learner and teacher also impacts the overall learning experience. The deployment of technology facilitates the service delivery more effectively and can be a source of innovation. For example, in airlines, self-operated kiosks, which enable self check-in, make processes less cumbersome and also reduce the waiting time for passengers to check-in. This is particularly helpful when there are long queues due to stringent security measures deployed by the airlines.

Service delivery system This refers to internal delivery mechanisms that have to be managed in order to allow service workers to perform their tasks more effectively. It is closely related to employee empowerment. This theme has been dealt with in detail in Chapter 15.

Technological options   Technology also facilitates service innovation. The offering of value-added services by telecommunication firms is an example. The SMS service and broadband access are some additional features which are offered on the mobile phone.

MAPPING PATTERNS OF SERVICE INNOVATIONS

There are different patterns of service innovation. As innovations can emanate from different sources, the patterns of service innovation can be quite varied. Hertog and Bilderbeek (1999) have postulated the following patterns, which explain service innovation.

Supplier-dominated innovation   In this particular case, the service innovation emanates from the hardware industry. These innovations come in from an external supplier, and are disseminated and implemented by service industry users who, in turn, can satisfy the need of their clients. For example, the use of the microwave has greatly extended food preparation possibilities in cafés and restaurants. Cash registers and mobile phones have been assimilated in many small firms that use little new technology otherwise. In transport and logistics operations, the deployment of on-board computers is a case in point. In financial services, these innovations may pertain to new distribution channels based on technical platforms such as SMS alerts, mobile devices, etc.

Innovation within services   Here the innovation may arise from both technological and non-technological sources, for example, the use of technology for more effective delivery of content in classroom. The relay of lectures online and simultaneous interaction with speakers from a remote location is one example, and franchising in the retailing industry is another.

Client-led innovation   In this case, the service firm responds to the needs expressed by the clients. For example, online banking helps save paper and is a more sustainable way for transactions. Organic products delivered at the doorstep is another example of client-led innovation.

Innovation through services   This pattern is more complicated. The service firm influences the actual innovation in the client firm by providing R&D services or offering IT solutions for making processes more effective. Shippers offering clients tracking and tracing facilities contribute to the reduction of stocks.

Paradigmatic innovation   This pattern affects everyone across the value chain. It is a complex and pervasive innovation, which will affect the usage and consumption patterns of the users. For example, shifting to Dish TV or using set-top boxes for viewing a large number of channels is a case in point. There is a fundamental shift from free viewing of the aired content to paying for viewing different channels. E-commerce also offers a shift in buying and consumption patterns. Online access to research databases, which can be bought online and viewed online, is an illustration of this pattern.

Innovation in a firm's internalized service function Internal services to employees (internal consumers) can also be a source of innovation, impacting their productivity and effectiveness. For example, the deployment of various services such as HR and payroll, travel-related reservations, and IT support through online methods within the organization help to eliminate bureaucracy and to streamline operations, especially where the size of the organization is large.

Innovation in an outsourced service function Many large firms outsource IT solutions or deploy separate departments, which offer solutions to employees within the firm. Security and cleaning services are also often outsourced.

INNOVATION POLICY FRAMEWORK

The innovation policy framework of a country helps to foster innovation in firms. This may vary across various industry segments. For example, in India after de-regulation of the insurance and banking segment, firms have deployed innovative practices to provide better services to consumers. Technology deployment has enabled easy access and online transactions. Stiff competition between the service firms helps consumers and they compete on a better service offering to the consumer.

Government policies play a key role in influencing innovation across various firms. It affects firms as enumerated in this section (DTI 2007).

Creating opportunities The regulatory framework developed by the government helps to create opportunities. Post-liberalization in India, in 2001, services sectors such as telecommunication, finance, and airlines have seen a lot of improvement in service offerings as firms compete with each other for a higher market share.

Enabling framework The government provides a conducive intellectual framework to protect the investments in innovation by the firms. There is also a measurement system for innovation and standards are created to control the processes and protect consumer interests.

Advice and support framework Here, the government offers support for various programmes, access to technology, finance availability, R&D tax benefits, and infrastructure benefits. For example, in India, the creation of science parks has facilitated entrepreneurial growth and exports through software firms operating out of these parks.

Supportive climate for innovation The government provides and works for macroeconomic stability, which ensures investors trust and a climate ripe for investment. A policy of fair competition encourages firms to invest. Sound investments in education policy ensure availability of manpower. The physical and IT infrastructure also become facilitating factors. An effective science policy and trade policy also influences the investments in a particular industry segment.

Deployment of Technology in Service Firm

The choice of technology has a bearing on the functional relationships between employees, consumers, and markets. The choice of technology determines the nature of relationships. However, there is a lot of debate on whether technology should determine relationships, or relationships should determine the choice of technology. The issue is a complex one and does not deserve a simple answer.

The customer expectations should ideally be determinant of the service processes. In order to bring efficiency in the service procedures, some or all of the areas can be automated. Information flow within the organization changes the dynamics of interaction and also shifts the power base in the organization.

The use of ERP, for instance, has had a very positive effect on some organizations whereas some other organizations did not benefit to the extent that they had expected to. In a study conducted by Davenport (1998) and reported in *Harvard Business Review*, a lot of insight is given as to how some organizations had to make massive changes in their organizational structures to integrate the new technologies, which in some cases did not gel well with the customers. So, it is important to assess the use of technology in light of the impact it will have on customers.

Another issue that needs to be addressed here is the category of product/service, which is being discussed. For instance, in high-tech areas, the consumer may not even be aware of the consequences and features of the technology and the service. He/ She sees the offering and buys it. Very soon technological innovation takes place and the product is rendered obsolete. The case of IT products and the services offered by telecom companies are a demonstration of this issue. So, here the customer is not in a position to dictate the choice of technology. After the service providers have learnt from market experience, they can make educated decisions on the shifts in technology that they would like to make.

Trade-off between Cost of Technology versus Returns from Technology

Firms that make investments in technology tend to benefit, especially in the high-tech segment. They make a lot of money through patents, royalty, and licensing revenues. They have the first mover advantage and hence they tend to look for global markets. The emerging economies, however, have a technology lag and often find a contemporary technology out of reach. The issue is certainly one of costs involved and the consequent returns thereof. It is important for service firms to understand these issues. Setting up firms with obsolete technologies will surely have issues with long-term sustenance of the firm.

The issues of energy crisis are imminent in the decades to come. Environmental issues will also have to be addressed. The effects of global warming are quite evident. Firms will have to look at sources of technologies and the conduct of business in such a way that resource consumption and ill effects on the environment are minimized. The issue of technologies is so vast that at any given point even a small organization

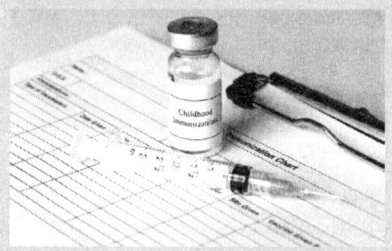
would be using a range of technologies in different domains such as serving markets, communication, and offering services. So, one needs to be clear about whether we are using technology as a supporting device to make a transaction, offer final service to the consumer, or open a door for communication. Understanding the intent is important.

Exhibit 17.2 indicates the change in business format in the health-care segment.

Market Preparedness for Technology

For many service firms, the markets need to be prepared for launch of such services. For instance, in the banking segment in India, there were aspects that needed to be considered when the banks were being automated. What essentially happened was that the nationalized banks such as the State Bank of India (SBI) were not computerized in the 1970s and 1980s and customer transactions were manual. When the move to computerize the bank was initiated, there was at first, a lot of resistance from employees. Massive efforts were made to train the employees. Also, efforts were made to put in ATM machines so that many transactions could be automated. In India, Hindi is a dominant language and when ATM machines were installed, the language concerns of the local population was an important consideration. However, the shift to move to the usage of ATM machines is quite evident, especially in urban areas in India. Service firms have to take these aspects into consideration.

Exhibit 17.3 gives an overview of Apple Corporation and its revolutionary products that have changed the world in a number of ways.

Exhibit 17.3 **Apple—One of the Most Innovative Companies in the World**

Apple Corporation has recently often been named America's most respected company based on a poll of US business people. The iPod, iPad, and iPhone are attributed as the main drivers in Apple's success. The company has been one of the world's most innovative companies and its unique visual identity, store design, and product designs are truly inspiring. This is a major reason why the products of Apple have become an experience in themselves. Apple's 'Think Different' campaign saluted innovators who were dismissed as crazy. The latest iPhone offering by Apple is the 5SiPhone, which has been recently launched in India. Apple has projected worldwide sales of 1051 million by the end of 2013. Before this, the iPod had created a revolution that changed the world of music. This revolutionary MP3 player has sold about 119 million pieces and has helped increase the company's market capitalization from $6 billion to $155 billion.

IMPACT OF TECHNOLOGY ON SERVICE FIRMS

Technology has numerous consequences on the working of service firms. Some of these impacts are detailed as follows:

Productivity

The effective use of technology, especially information technology, has helped to improve the productivity of service firms. A case in point is the banking segment wherein the time for inter-bank transfers from across countries has reduced significantly. Electronic transfers have become an acceptable norm for financial transactions. Similarly, the concept of ATM machines has helped to reduce manpower costs and hence, made processes more efficient for the consumer. Similarly, in the airline and hotel industry, online reservations and tele check-ins have made life much more comfortable for the consumer, with the benefits of saving time and money. Government online portals have really helped, for instance, to systematize the processes for various kinds of licenses such as driving, passport, election I-cards, etc.

Offering New Services

The advent of new technologies has enabled service firms to offer new services. Telemedicine is a case in point. Similarly, software can be downloaded after making a payment. Digital libraries are being created. People can go in for online subscriptions for databases and can access literature online. Gaming and entertainment has been completely redefined. Microsoft, Nintendo, and Sony are some of the key operators offering services in these areas. Biotechnology and prescriptive medicine on account of developments in the genome project are all the consequences of application of technology to conventional fields of science.

The implications for service firms, however, is that they need to have a clear understanding of training of manpower and present standardized offerings. They need to define the processes for management of these services. There is also a need for understanding the critical success factors.

Control Mechanisms

Service firms have devised new ways of imbibing control mechanisms in the organizations. For example, FedEx has a unique tracking system, which it uses for tracking the goods in transit and offers distinct value to its customers. Firms, which have their websites, sometimes install cookies to help to track the usage patterns of the visitors on their websites. This helps them to make suitable modifications in their offering so that customers derive better value from such websites.

The IT systems installed in organizations also enable them to track the time spent by their employees on the IT systems or the usage patterns of the same. Mobile technology has helped to foster increased connectivity but has an impact in terms of invasion of privacy as it makes a person accessible all the time. This impinges on the work–life balance in some cases.

Widening the Reach of Distribution Channels for Service Firms

Service firms can use technology to widen the horizons of reach for the firm. The website and IT can be used effectively to tap alternate segments of the market. The institution of the online reservation system for hotels or airlines has had a big impact on the distribution strategy adopted by the service firms. The commissions of the intermediaries have greatly decreased as firms are trying to tap the customers directly, doing away with the distribution channels.

Internet protocol (IP) has enabled data transmission from different devices and applications over the same network. Apart from simplifying processes, technology also helps reduce costs. IP traffic is carried across a wide area network (WAN) providing connectivity for geographically distributed hosts, or local area network (LAN). To provide IP-based networking services that meet the customers' growing needs is both an opportunity and a challenge for service providers. Internet protocol is the underlying communication technology that enables many new applications such as online reservation systems; it has brought out a radical change to air travel ever since SITA developed the first Internet booking engine 20 years ago. It also drives the self-service business model, which is both convenient for passengers and helps airlines keep ticket prices lower. SITA is the world's leading service provider of IT business solutions and communications services to the air transport industry. It manages complex communication solutions for its air transport, government, and global distribution system (GDS) customers over the world's most extensive communication network, complemented by consultancy in design, deployment, and integration of communication services.

Interlocked Relationships

The use of certain technologies leads to long-term relationships between the service firms. For instance, computer firms tie-up with software vendors and sign long-term contracts. Thus, Hewlett–Packard (HP) may sell Microsoft's operating system, or UNIX servers, as a part of such agreements. Similarly, there are relationships between the telecom companies and mobile phone manufacturers. Software manufacturers also have relationships with companies such as Cisco Systems and Oracle for meeting various needs as required by the customers.

Any changes in such relationships can have an impact on the supplier relationships and hence, on the profitability of the firm.

The implication for this is that firms need to make investments in IT very carefully. There is a need to assess the long-term consequences of such partnerships. There is a need to closely monitor such partnerships and ways to explore changes as and when required.

Managing Customer Relationships

The use of information technology has completely redefined the dynamics of managing customer relationships. Information technology enables creation of databases of consumers, and depending on the categorization of the same service firms can think of appropriate technologies to reach out to these consumers. There is evidence that building of customer relationships can generate business for a lifetime and technology can facilitate this process. However, the use of technology has to be assessed carefully; for example, mobile phone users in India feel abused by the number of telemarketing calls, which they receive for bank loans, credit cards, and promotional SMS messages from a wide variety of suppliers. Firms have been using data mining techniques to foster linkages with customers. Service firms use data mining and data warehousing to know and understand the consumers well in order to customize the strategies. The concepts of data mining and data warehousing have been discussed later in the chapter.

Fostering Linkages with Various Stakeholders

Technology can play a wonderful role in fostering new relationships with various stakeholders in a service firm. These linkages can be created by the use of a website and digital content. Channels of communication can be opened up with academic institutions, which are suppliers of manpower and business ideas, and users of the services namely, society, suppliers, consumers, government, NGOs, and other trade organizations. The links on the website can open doors for potential relationships with various stakeholders in the society.

Global Information Technology Sourcing

The global information technology sourcing (GITS) represents a change that has the potential to transform the manner in which companies do business. Globally, many companies have committed the development and maintenance of internationally sourcing portions of their systems to offshore entities. The globalization of talent, trade liberalization in developing countries, quantum improvements in worldwide telecommunication infrastructure, and cost-cutting pressures on organizations have led to the emergence and acceptance of offshoring as a business model (Legard 2004). Rao et al. (2006) have enumerated eight primary drivers of outsourcing by some of the companies, namely (i) lower cost, (ii) quick access to expertise not available in-house, (iii) flexibility to meet capacity needs while maintaining steady domestic head count, (iv) accessing a global skills-base, (v) access to new markets, (vi) improved quality of product, (vii) developing experience with external collaborations, and (viii) assisting domestic IT staff to improve processes.

India is a widely recognized destination for information technology enabled services (ITES) outsourcing. Bengaluru, Gurgaon, Hyderabad, Pune, and Mumbai are emerging hubs for ITES outsourcing activities.

ISSUES IN MANAGING ONLINE TECHNOLOGIES

Online technologies have a deep impact on service firms. There is a need to assess the issues related to online technologies, which service firms need to keep in mind. Some of these issues are detailed in this section.

Service mix   Service firms have to decide whether they need to open options for online services as well. The service firms that use online technologies manage the demand better. For example, in India every year there are lakhs of applicants for a US visa. In view of such a huge rush of applications, the US consulate in India has now tried to use online technologies to manage the process. The application forms and appointments are made online and real-time information on the status of application is available. This is very different from the cumbersome manual procedures, which used to result in huge delays. Similarly, the airlines industry, as has been explained earlier, is the first fully web-enabled industry.

Costs involved   The dynamics of setting up online businesses involves making fixed-cost investments. The business model is such that fixed-cost investments are higher than operational/variable expenses. So, the service operators should realize this and the profit margins in subsequent years could be very high.

Integration issues   The service firm, when it uses online technologies for conducting business, needs to put a fool proof process in place. It all depends upon the stakeholders it is targeting and the processes that it wants to automate. There are firms that have used online technologies to address the needs of customers, suppliers, potential and current employees, obtain information about philanthropic activities, and open doors for building communication channels with various stakeholders.

If, for example, a particular retail outlet also offers opportunities for online selling, then there is a massive coordination effort required, both for procurement and delivery of the products. Also, secure payment channels need to be created.

Building relationships with consumers   Service firms can exploit online technologies to open doors of communication, both with internal and external customers. This can provide opportunities for improvement of the business. It also reduces the efforts to be made to reach out to the customers.

Website   The website, which the service firms use, can be very dynamic and address the needs of various stakeholders.

 The service industry uses data mining and data warehousing services to improve its operations. Please visit the Online Resource Centre to know more about this.

RESEARCH INSIGHT

Impact of Information Technology on Customer and Supplier Relationships in Financial Services

Mulligan, Paul and Steven R. Gordon (2002), 'The impact of information technology on customer and supplier relationships in the financial services', *International Journal of Service Industry Management*, vol. 13, issue 1, pp. 29–46.

This study examines the role that information technology plays in supporting relationships between customers and suppliers in the financial service industry. It traces the interrelationships among the different sectors of this industry—brokerage houses, retail banks, institutional banks, mutual funds, insurance underwriters, and others—and identifies roles that information technology and electronic service delivery can play in creating and supporting inter-organizational integration across sector boundaries. It further identifies the opportunities for and threats to these relationships caused, in large part, by the continuing evolution of information technology. This study will help managers in the financial services to analyse the opportunities and assess the risks of building tighter relationships with their customers and suppliers through electronic commerce.

SUMMARY

The use of technologies by service firms is a complex issue and needs to be addressed with a lot of care. There are a range of issues that service firms need to address relating to the forecasting of technology, assessment of technology choices, impact on future returns to technology investments, consequences to the society, and organizational issues. Technologies should be used to offer better experience to consumers and not merely imbibe technology for the sake of using it. Technology solutions are usually resource and capital intensive. Any firm has to trade-off between investments and returns. The technology infusion leads to emergence of new services and a better experience for consumers. In certain cases such as multiplexes and Internet, information is available at the fingertips, whereas automated responses for customer complaints is a nightmare in some cases. The firms need to assure consumers that technology solutions will work when operations are scaled up. Deployment of technology may automate transactions but the human effort cannot be completely eliminated. There is really a need to strike an adequate balance between human interface and automation.

The Internet has also affected and transformed the way consumers access services. Ipod is a case in point; it has transformed the way in which music and video is accessed and bought. The access device has changed the face of the music industry.

KEY TERMS

Customer relationship management systems Computer applications that integrate a company's information about its customers with the knowledge of how best to use this information.

Technological change An increase in the level of output resulting from automation and computerized methods of production. Apart from increasing output, technological change can affect the ratio of capital to labour used in a factory. If it involves reducing the labour force it can lead to technological unemployment in an area or industry.

─────────────────── **EXERCISES** ───────────────────

Concept Review Questions

1. How are the changes in technology influencing the service firms?
2. Evaluate the technology issues that service firms should consider.
3. Examine the issues, which service firms have to consider when making choices about which technologies to deploy.
4. New technology deployment has led to emergence of new service firms. Please elaborate using some examples and the challenges faced by them (Hint: You could discuss about Internet-based businesses).
5. How can service firms channelize technology to build relationships with customers?

Critical Thinking Questions

1. A small firm offering real estate consultancy is deploying an agency for reaching out to the consumers in Delhi. It tries to reach them through telecalling to initiate the first contact with the consumer. Please assess the choice of technology medium used by the firm. Also suggest other media that can be chosen, which deploy technology intensively. You may also give an insight into the costs involved in implementing the same. You may make assumptions about the turnover of the firm.
2. Evaluate the use of technology by consumer banks in India.
3. How has the Internet changed the travel choices of Indian consumers? Please carry out a small survey and share the findings in the classroom.

Project Assignments

1. Explore the alternate technologies available for mobile telephony? What are the issues involved for a particular country when choosing a particular technology?
2. Assess the online reservation systems for two international airlines. Which one is better and why?
3. Assess the customer relationship programmes of two service firms in any domain. How has technology been used to implement the programme? Which programme is better and why?

CASE STUDY The Online Advertising Food Chain*

Online advertising is growing by leaps and bounds, but are there opportunities for smaller players?

It is said that during any economic downturn, the first sector to get impacted is advertising as it is the first place where companies like to cut back. However, thanks in part to a small base, the Indian online advertising and marketing sector is growing at a fast pace offering many opportunities for different classes of people.

From around ₹150–200 crore in the financial year 2007, online ad spends targeting Indians are expected to have jumped to around ₹500 crore in FY 2008, according to industry estimates. 'In 2008–09, we expect it to hit ₹900 crore', says Mahesh Murthy, whose firm Pinstorm alone would have bought ₹115 crore worth of ads by the end of this year (Fig. 17.1).

In other words, Pinstorm, which claims a market share of around 15 per cent in India, will alone oversee ad sales almost 50% higher than the total industry turnover of ₹80 crore during 2006.

While still accounting for just around 5% of the estimated ₹15,000 crore spent on advertising in India, online promotions account for between 15 to 20% in places like the US and parts of Europe (Fig. 17.2). Recently, a new media specialist research firm eMarketer, revised down its estimate for online promotion expenditure by US companies due to the economic recession. Yet, the new estimate for 2008 for US companies alone stood at

* Eluvangal, S. (2008), 'The online advertising food chain', *The Online Advertising Food Chain*, DARE, 31 August 2008. Reprinted with the permission of Mr Krishna Kumar, Group Editor, DARE, www.dare.co.in.

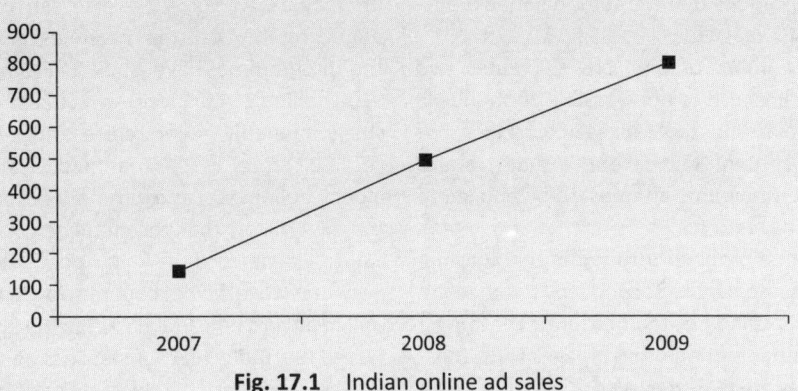

Fig. 17.1   Indian online ad sales

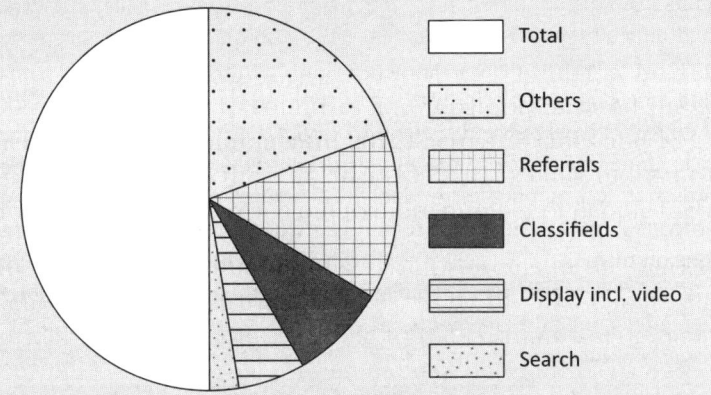

Fig. 17.2   US online ad market (2007)

$25.9 billion (₹111,000 crore), up 23% from its estimate for 2007.

To understand the opportunities thrown up by the new medium, it is important to understand the 'food chain' of the online ad market.

As in traditional mass media advertising, online marketing has also started throwing up different strata of service providers. Between the advertiser on one end and the website owner or publisher on the other, there are many layers of service providers.

The Network or the Media Agency

The most important intermediary is the ad or affiliate network. This is in effect, what brings the advertiser and the publisher together and is the closest equivalent to the media agency of traditional advertising. The simplest model of the online advertising chain can be formed with just these three participants, with the ad network helping the advertiser and the publisher discover each other. In this respect, an ad network is like the traditional media buying agency, helping big companies to buy ad space on TV and newspapers.

However, the analogy cannot be taken very far due to the fact that unlike in the traditional media world, there are no big networks or websites that attract most of the online eyeballs. Each of the billions of pages of web content is a potential vehicle for advertisement and the number of website owners would be in millions, rather than the tens of TV and print publications that a traditional media buying agent has to deal with.

The huge number of 'publishers' creates two problems. One, that it is not possible to manually manage the placement of ads across billions of pages of web content. The second is that it is also difficult to determine the 'ad rates' to be applied to each of these pages.

While the first problem resulted in the automation of ad placements, the second led to the evolution of alternate standards for measuring the impact and reach of a publication or web page. Thus, most of the ads today are placed by algorithms that 'read' the content of a web page and gauge the potential interests of its readers from the content itself.

As for the second difficulty, as it is not possible to keep track of how many visitors each page of a website has, unlike tracking popularity of the 9 o'clock news, ad networks have evolved the concept of pay-per-click. Under this system, the publisher is paid according to the number of relevant visitors to his or her page as measured by the number of people clicking on the ads.

The shift to a pay-per-click model also simplifies the first problem of intelligent ad placements, as the publisher now has the incentive to make sure that the most relevant ads from the network are displayed on his pages. Many older networks, especially those that pay on the basis of sales or leads instead of clicks, still rely on the publisher to choose the best ads on their networks.

However, their success has been eclipsed by the emergence of Google's automated ad placement mechanism called Adsense Adwords. While preventing the network from being overwhelmed by the sheer scale of manually choosing the right ads for the right page, the automated system has the additional advantage of being able to periodically refresh the ads displayed on pages frequented by the same group of viewers, further increasing the chances of clicks.

The automated, and therefore low cost, ad selection system has brought in even relatively low-traffic websites within the reach of ad networks, and therefore, extra ad revenue. The success

of Google's Adwords Adsense can be seen in the huge growth that the revenues generated from the programme have shown. From just around $100 million (₹430 crore) in 2002, the programme single-handedly generated revenues of $5.8 billion (₹24,500 crore) in 2007, around 17.5% of the total global online ads and promotions business. With the $2.4 billion that the number two ad network, Yahoo, generated for its publishers, the two networks together accounted for a quarter of all online advertising and marketing revenues for 2007. Please see Table 17.1 for statistics on Google.

The business of ad networks, therefore, is restricted in its scope for new entrants. However, there are some smaller networks that still rely on the publisher or the website owner choosing the links he/she wants to display. Such networks have survived by specializing in verticals and having a different business model. Unlike the two big networks, which calculate the impact of the ads based on the number of people clicking on them, the specialized networks such as Commission Junction offer much higher commissions to the publisher, but only for getting their readers to fill out forms or purchase online. While each click on the big networks may get you as little as five cents (₹2.30), in these networks, typically called referral networks or cost per action (CPA) or cost per sale (CPS) networks, publishers can expect to make between $10 to $30 (₹430 to ₹1,290) per lead.

Unlike the automated click-based networks such as those of Google and Yahoo, CPS or affiliate or referral networks are areas that are yet to see much

Table 17.1   Google statistics (2007)

Total revenues	$16.59 bn
From Adv and Mkg	99%
From the US	52%
% given to publishers*	79%
Y-on-Y growth	56.50%

* Not applicable to revenues from Google's own pages
Source: Based on data from Google investors relations (2009).

traction in India. Typical 'actions' on the basis of which publishers get paid include filling up a loan request form or a car enquiry form.

A big plus for referral networks is the ability of the publisher or the site owner to fine-tune the displayed ads. For example, a website on the latest cars can host referral ads for cars, spare parts, car insurance, etc. Many publishers prefer such non-automated networks due to the control that it gives them over the links as well as the chances of higher revenues in case of niche websites. For example, if you have one lakh unique visitors per month and around 300,000 visits or impressions, then a referral network may work better for you. If targeted properly, around 9,000 to 10,000 out of the 100,000 can be converted. 'Each hot lead can fetch $25 to $30,' says Suresh Reddy, Chairman and Managing Director of Ybrant Digital, a Hyderabad-based digital marketing company.

The two big challenges in this space are the recent entry of Google's own referral network, as well as the little headway the business has made in India. Traditional affiliate marketing is expected to generate commissions of $2.27 billion this year in the US alone or about 8.75% of the total online ad spend there, according to eMarketer. In India, however, they 'accounted for less than ₹10 crore out of the total ₹600 crore online ad spend last year—around 1.67%,' according to Mahesh Murthy of Pinstorm.

With the recent announcement of the Google Affiliate Network, there are fears that Google may also 'algorithmize' the online affiliate marketing industry, just as it did the CPC industry. Shawn Collins, a long time affiliate-marketing industry observer based in the US, however feels that the higher level of involvement between the brand, the affiliate network, and the publisher will make it unsuitable for automation. Automatic networks are notoriously susceptible to fraud and unscrupulous marketing practices, such as repeatedly clicking on the ads placed on one's own website. 'Affiliate marketing is ultimately about relationships,' he says, 'and companies will not want to expose themselves to liabilities for their brand, can-spam, etc., by automating everything.'

The Optimizers or the Creatives

Most of the smaller companies no longer entertain hopes of growing into big enough ad networks to challenge the hegemony of Google and Yahoo. Many, however, have carved out a niche for themselves, in a role similar to that of a creative agency that makes the ad in the traditional world.

These firms offer their services to advertisers, promising to make their advertising strategy more effective, like a creative agency would. Like a traditional creative agency that is tasked with designing the most effective message within a given TV time slot or newspaper print space, the optimizers set themselves the job of getting the advertisers, value for their money.

Such optimizers owe their emergence and existence to the preponderance of algorithms in determining visibility in the world of online advertising.

Display advertising, whether algorithmized or not, and whether in the form of text links, pictures or video, is usually targeted at static content. However, it suffers from the disadvantage that, like in the traditional media, the viewer or reader is usually trying to focus on something else and the ads turn up as intrusions or distractions. Yet, there is one publisher whose readers are usually receptive to suggestions and advertisements—the search engine.

Thus, notwithstanding the fact that Google and Yahoo operate the largest ad-networks online, they generate more revenues from their roles as publishers of search results than as ad network operators. For example, while Google generated $5.8 billion in 2007 by placing ads on the millions of pages included in its ad network, it generated almost double that, $10.62 billion, by placing ads on its own website—its search result pages (Fig. 17.3). Similarly, Yahoo generated $3.67 billion worth of advertisements on its own pages in 2007, compared to $2.4 billion on those of its partners.

According to eMarketer, search pages accounted for ads worth $8.62 billion of adspent in the US last year, comprising 40 per cent of the total US online adspent. Besides this, even display ads including

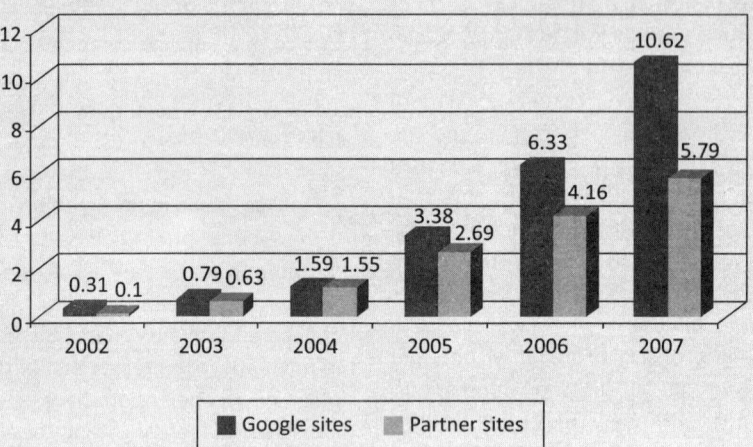

Fig. 17.3 Ad revenues through Google

picture and video ads are increasingly being delivered on the basis of search algorithms applied to the target publisher's page. A new crop of companies have made themselves a business by figuring out the most low cost way to put the advertiser's message in front of the surfer.

'In search, the better you are, the more margins you can deliver,' points out Vivek Bhargava, CEO of a contextual marketing company, Communicate2. 'It's about expertise. If I can get him the same amount of display or traffic for ₹150 for which he is spending ₹200 now, he saves ₹50 and we get a share of the savings,' he adds.

Pinstorm too works on similar principles. 'We will deliver the most bang for the advertisers buck,' says Mahesh. 'In our case, we don't even involve the client in details such as how we are going to use paid listing on search engines, etc. All we say is, let us measure the impact of our campaign, in terms of increased traffic, higher visibility, etc., and pay us for it. Whether we use paid search, or displays, or optimize your website, or write reviews is immaterial.'

Next is What?

The next step, most people realize, is in selecting the ads not just on the basis of the search term or the content of a website, but on the past behaviour of the viewer. This, however, may create further stumbling blocks for the independent 'creative' experts, as most of the user data is with companies like Google and Yahoo who offer 'logged in' and therefore, traceable, experiences to Internet users. While it is easier for Google or a social networking website like Facebook to keep a tab on what their users do online while logged in, it will be trickier for third parties. 'We believe that this information will also be made available to third parties, at least by some providers,' says Mahesh.

Questions

1. What is online advertising and how is it different from traditional mass media advertising?
2. Discuss the various forms of online advertising highlighted in the case study.
3. Discuss the difference between automated click-based network and affiliate or referral networks.

REFERENCES

Al Bawaba (2006), 'SITA survey finds world's airlines on way to become the first totally web-enabled global industry', *Al Bawaba*, London, 13 November, p. 1.

Business Outlook (2006), 20 November, India, pp. 36–40.

Business Standard (2006), 'Digital wave hits small theaters too', 17 October 2006.

Business Standard (2006), 'Catching up on camera', 22 November, New Delhi.

Business Standard, 'Dial E for emergency', 22 November 2006.

Business Standard (2006), 'Wikipedia founder plans rival', 19 October, New Delhi.

Carlson, L.W. (2004), 'Using technology foresight to create business value', *Research Technology Management*, September/October, vol. 47, no. 5, p. 51.

Davenport, T.H. (1998) 'Putting the enterprise into the Enterprise System', *Harvard Business Review*, July–August, vol. 76, no. 4.

DTI (2007), 'Innovation in services', Occassional Paper, 9 June 2007.

Hertog, Pim den and R. Bilderbeek (1999), 'Conceptualising service innovation and service innovation patterns', Research Programme Strategic Information Provision on Innovation and Services (SIID), for the Ministry of Economic Affairs, Directorate for General Technology Policy.

Hindustan Times (2006), 'Robots as waiters at Hong Kong malls', 24 October, p. 25.

Mitsch, R.A. (1992), 'R&D at 3M: Continuing to play a big role', *Research & Technology Management*, September–October.

Rao, M.T., W. Poole, P.V. Raven, and D.L. Lockwood (2006), 'Trends, implications, and responses to global IT sourcing: A field study', *Journal of Global Information Technology Management*, vol. 9, no. 3.

Schumpeter, J.A. (1934), *Theory of Economic Development*, Harvard University Press, Cambridge, Massachusetts.

Soete, L. and M. Miozzo (1989), 'Trade and development in services: A technological perspective', MERIT 89-031, Maastricht.

Zairi, M. (1995), 'Benchmarking in R&D', *Productivity*, vol. 36, no. 3, October–December.

http://investor.google.com/fin_data.html, accessed on 22 January 2009.

http://www.cis.drexel.edu/faculty/thu/DMIR-07/DMIR07.htm, http://www.cyberbee.com/content.pdf, accessed on 25 August 2008.

Livemint (2008), http://www.livemint.com/2008/01/14171331/Apple-will-shine-but-not-as-b.html, accessed on 25 August 2008.

18 Managing Quality and Excellence

OBJECTIVES

After reading this chapter you will be able to understand the

- essentials of service quality
- different models for service excellence
- criteria for choosing TQM framework
- blueprint for service excellence

Schwarz Alpine Growing with Excellence

Growth can be achieved through excellence in quality of service provided is a fact known since ages. Schwrz Alpine Spa and Resort, a family run (Pirktl family), five star property in Tyrol Austria has been doing exactly this since 2003 when they first started working in line with the European Foundation for Quality Management (EFQM). The property has a 27 hole golf course, 4,000 square meter spa, and state-of-the-art health and fitness suite with year round sporting activities in luxury accommodation and Water Worlds with 9 pools. Working for excellence is evident in the awards won by the property not only of EFQM but others also like Tripadvisor Traveller's Choice 2014, Sterne Award 2014, and European Health and Spa Award 2014 to name a few. Their revenue per available room has been increasing over the years and has been more than the target. Also, the customer satisfaction with the available services is above the level targeted (Quality

Austria, Recognition book 2013). The benefits of implementing the EFQM model has been as follows:

- The key results such as employee satisfaction, recommendation, leadership, overall satisfaction with colleagues, and training show positive stable trends for more than 4 years exceeding the set targets.
- Operating profit and cash flow performance has improved year-on-year over the past ten years, in line with the target and comparing favourably with local and national competitors.
- Development, despite the challenging economic conditions, reflected particularly in the positive ongoing company results has made the organisation more flexible and efficient (EFQM 2013).

After going through the chapter, you will be able to answer the following questions:

1. What is Schwrz Alpine Spa and Resort trying to do?
2. What has been the result of their perseverance?

INTRODUCTION

The need to provide excellent services is important keeping in mind the growing competition in the market and the cost involved in attracting and retaining customers. Grönroos (1998) first described products as outcome consumption and services as process consumption. Products are manufactured and thus can be described as an outcome of a series of activities involved in the planning and production of the products. Services involve simultaneous production and consumption and hence, are more of a process consumption rather than an outcome consumption. Since the customers are present at the time of production, the quality of managing the production holds more importance in the case of services. If satisfied with the quality of services, the customers are bound to return and repeated customer satisfaction leads to customer loyalty. Thus, the development of customer loyalty is affected by the quality of service delivered, which in turn, profoundly impacts the organization's profits (Mohsin 2005).

REGULATORY AND COMPLIANCE ISSUES

The major services industries in India are run partially or entirely by the government. However, both foreign and domestic private firms play a large role in advertising, accounting, consulting services, etc. (USTR 2001). The growing awareness of India's potential in the services sector has resulted in an influx of major players into the Indian market. Industries such as insurance, banking, and foreign securities saw a number of foreign players joining the fray. The Securities and Exchange Board of India (SEBI) was established on 12 April 1992 'To protect the interests of investors in securities, and to promote the development of, and to regulate the securities market' (SEBI 2008). The Insurance Regulatory and Development Authority (IRDA) Bill was passed in 1999 and opened India's insurance market to private participation up to 26% of paid-up capital. Reserve Bank of India (RBI) issued new guidelines in 1993 under which new private sector banks could be established (USTR 2001).

The World Bank (2007) report on 'Regulatory trends in service convergence' discusses the regulatory issues that arise with technological convergence and challenge the traditional framework.

Authorization and licensing Conventionally, authorization and licensing were based on the type of service. However, converging technologies and service providers dealing in multiple domains have made it difficult for regulators to clearly classify them. For example, the licensing of Internet protocol television (IPTV) services offered by MTNL, a telecom service provider.

Competition policy Interconnection, ownership, market access, and access to content and services are important determinants of competition policy.

Interconnection Formerly, interconnection models worked within the same facilities. The complexity created by the overlapping of services and networks have made the conventional approaches to interconnection charging unsuitable. For instance, interconnection required between broadcasters and telecom providers for IPTV services.

Ownership Traditional regulations include concentration limits and cross-ownership limits to restrict monopoly of one owner on different media and across different media, respectively. Complications arise as these restrictions are dependent on defining the services in the context of multiple play. For example, should Voice over Internet Protocol (VoIP) be regulated under broadcasting or as a substitute for analogue voice services?

Market access Market access has been heavily regulated in the past and governments have been charging heavy licensing fees to traditional service providers. With new entrants in the market due to convergence, available capacity may increase, making the competition more severe.

Access to content and services Different technologies have a fair chance of catering to varied customer choices and hence should be provided through interconnections with their default carriers.

Managing scarce resources Spectrum management and numbering plans and probability are used to manage scarce resources.

Spectrum management As a conceptual model, it focuses on mitigating three types of conflicts—uses, users, and technologies.

Numbering plans and probability Such regulations were introduced to address voice telephony services. The numbering plans established different ranges for voice services and within fixed telephony it was divided into geographical areas.

Service regulation It constitutes the quality of service, privacy and law enforcement, content regulation, and universal service goals and funding.

Quality of service This is vital as the telecom network has a point-to-point nature, where networks allocate and distribute limited resources across multiple subscribers.

Privacy and law enforcement Voice over Internet protocol (VoIP) calls may travel over public Internet, making it possible that their privacy is compromised, which is actually a legal guarantee in most countries. Voice over Internet protocol may even become a security threat in case government or law enforcement agencies want to survey voice conversations.

Content regulation Via converged content delivery mechanism, content that was formerly dedicated to specific networks can be conveyed on different infrastructures and delivery platforms.

Universal service goals and funding Convergence challenges traditional, universal service policies and the means by which universal service objectives are currently met.

Legal frameworks   As services converge into the same medium, it might become difficult for traditionally separate regulators dealing with different services to assert their jurisdictions in the converged environment.

Traditionally, different services were regulated differently (Table 18.1). However, as convergence has blurred the lines of demarcation among multiple services, media, and networks, very specific and complex regulatory challenges have emerged.

Technological advancement has been the key driver of convergence. This includes digitization, increase in computing power, and consequently data compression, implying that the carrying capacity of channels increases even when the bandwidth is kept constant. Further, the availability of significant broadband penetration; consolidation in the development and provision of content and services; development and online advertising; and the ability to offer new and possibly bundled services and deliver them over one access network to the consumer, are some of the key market factors encouraging convergence. Table 18.2 takes the example of the information and communications industry to draw attention to the need for regulatory frameworks that are sensitive to convergence.

Table 18.1   Regulatory asymmetry across the communications industry

Services/ regulatory features	Data networks	Wireless telephony	Wireline telephony	Cable television	Broadcast radio	Broadcast television
Market entry	Usually open entry is the norm	Difficult due to spectrum constraints	Differs from country to country	Depends on jurisdiction	Difficult due to spectrum constraints	Difficult due to spectrum constraints
Focus of carriage	Quality of service	Spectrum and quality of service	Quality of service	Quality of service	Spectrum	Spectrum
Content regulation	Typically absent	Typically absent	Typically absent	Variable: from mild to strict	Strict	Very strict
Level of competition	Typically competitive	Oligopolies	Monopolies or oligopolies	Monopolies or oligopolies	Monopolies or oligopolies	Monopolies or oligopolies
Numbering issues	IP addresses	Phone numbers, portability	Phone numbers, portability	Channel numbering	—	Channel numbering
Spectrum licensing	Only in case of licensed broadband wireless, market-oriented	Yes, with entry fees and annual charges, often through markets	None	None	Typically administered	Typically administered
Interconnection management	Market-driven	Regulated	Regulated	May be regulated	—	—
Universal service goals	Typically absent	Yes	Yes	Free-to-air channels	Public service broadcasting	Public service broadcasting

Source: Based on the data from The World Bank (2007).

Table 18.2 The genesis of the regulatory challenge

Traditional	Convergent
Each type of content had one dedicated network infrastructure. For example, television carried unidirectional video and audio; and print transmitted text-based content.	Possible to use one network for multiple services with digitization, packet switching, and growth of IP-based networking. For example, data communication over the telephone network.
Regulatory approaches depended on the clear division between the different services and a one-to-one mapping of service to network.	Specific regulations for specific content used over dedicated networks are becoming redundant. Regulators need to respond to the challenges posed by accelerated diffusion of services. For example, VoIP and IPTV.
Essential to ensure that policy and regulation enable free and fair competition and supports the full play of market forces.	Even more essential to ensure that policy and regulation enables free and fair competition and supports the full play of market forces.
Services were clearly classified.	For example, VoIP can allow non-telephony operators to offer voice services. European Union is regulating VoIP as an Internet service. Canada is temporarily regulating VoIP as per existing rules for telephones.

Source: Based on the data from The World Bank (2007).

The breaking down of barriers on corporate activities and strengthening of the market, 'Is supposed to induce or force boards to monitor and work with management in creating more dynamic, efficient, and responsible business structures, which will provide competitively priced, and high-quality goods and services, and produce profits for shareholders. According to this logic, those companies that are well governed will survive and possibly thrive, while those which are not will be taken over or perish' (Reed and Mukherjee 2004). The concept of corporate governance thus came into being and is defined by Nobel Laureate Milton Friedman as, 'The conduct of business in accordance with shareholders' desires, which generally is to make as much money as possible while conforming to the basic rules of the society embodied in law and local customs' (The Institute of Company Secretaries of India 2003). Thus, if companies are practising corporate governance, people feel they will perform better over time. Some feel that corporate governance acts as a 'Means for limiting or reducing the risk to which a company is exposed'. Still others feel that it is a fad and go along with it as so many investors increasingly think it matters (Wallace and Zinkin 2006). Thus, there are various compliance and regulatory issues that guide a firm. However, the best judge of any organization is its customer, and since this book focuses on the services industry it tries to look at service quality and discusses some of the various models of excellence being practised. We thus start with a discussion on service quality.

SERVICE QUALITY

Quality has been defined by a number of people. Some of the definitions are as follows.

According to the British Standard 4778 (1987), quality is 'The totality of features and characteristics of a product or service that bear on its ability to satisfy a stated or implied need', and the stated need here is that of a customer (Lockwood et al. 1996).

According to the German standard DIN 55350, quality is defined as 'The totality of characteristics and features of a product or process, which facilitate realization of given requirements' (Mohanty and Lakhe 2002). Garvin (1984) presented five different approaches to defining quality. These are listed as follows:

Transcendent view   According to this view, quality cannot be analysed or defined precisely. It can only be recognized through experience.

Product-based view   According to this view, quality is a precise and measurable variable, and service can be quantified as a set of tangible attributes.

User-based view   As the title suggests, quality depends upon the user. Thus, it focuses on the ability of the organization to deliver what the customer requires. This takes an external view of the organization and tries to identify the different needs and expectations of the customers.

Manufacturing-based view   This view focuses on the engineering and manufacturing practices, and emphasizes the management and control of the supply side of quality. It takes an internal perspective of the organization and helps them to deliver a standard service to the customers.

Value-based view   This view describes quality in relation to cost and price, that is, cost to the service provider and price to the customer. According to this view, a quality product or service is one that is available to the customers at an acceptable price or cost.

Kasper et al. (1999) defined quality as, 'The extent to which the service, service process, and the service organization can satisfy the expectations of the user'. Kandampully (2000) concluded that service quality is crucial for the success of any service organization, and Grönroos (1988) linked service quality with customer perception of service quality. This concept has already been elaborated in Chapter 7.

MODEL OF SERVICE QUALITY

The most eminent instrument in attempting to systematize the service quality is the SERVQUAL model that was developed by Parasuraman et al. (1985). This model is discussed in detail in Chapter 7.

MODELS OF EXCELLENCE

The earliest approach to looking for quality was the quality inspection approach, which simply introduces the inspection stage to identify the defects in the product or service before it reaches the customer. However, this approach focused on identifying the occurrence of non-conformance rather than identifying the source of the problem and setting things right. Thus, this method gave way to quality control which focused on the fact that quality checks are important throughout the production process rather than at the end. The drawback of this method was that it focused on mistakes and so the quality assurance approach was practised to entrench quality into the process so that mistakes did not occur and if they did, they were identified and corrected. All the concepts discussed till now focused internally, that is, within the organization and attempted to rectify the service product before it reached the customer. The main focus in total quality management (TQM) was on the customers and on the satisfaction of their needs by the continuous improvement of the processes (Lockwood et al. 1996). This is an organizational concept and tries to involve all the people for the successful achievement of customer satisfaction, and the ultimate aim is to achieve organizational excellence. Different frameworks for TQM, namely BS En ISO 9000, Malcolm Baldrige National Quality Award, EQA, and CII awards have been discussed here.

BS EN ISO 9000

The British Standards Institute first published their guidelines in 1979 as BS 5750, based on a series of Ministry of Defence supplier standards. After achieving international success, this, with modifications, became the model for international standards published as ISO 9000 and EN 29000. In 1994, it was adopted as ISO 9000 (Lockwood et al. 1996). According to Asher (1996), 'ISO 9000 is a method for guaranteeing consistency of approach through the use of written procedures, systems audit, and review'. ISO 9000 should not be confused with the quality of the product or service, as it only relates to a documented quality management system operated by the supplier. The main aspects of the ISO 9000 system are the following*:
- Its aim is to produce a product/service 'right first time'.
- It has a 'plan-do-check-act' (PDCA) cycle.
- All documentation is in written form.
- A system of independent audits is put into place to check that the procedures in the quality system are fully implemented.
- The company can have ISO certificate in parts.
- It is used to derive continuous improvement.

  The main strengths of this model are:
- It is more prescriptive in the way the company must work with its suppliers.
- It ensures that company subcontractors have process capability and control over their processes.
- Training is an important aspect.
- There are regular audits and continuous improvement.
- It enables employees at all levels to suggest improved methods of operation.

  The main drawbacks of this system:
- Interpretation of ISO 9000 for a particular industry can often be subjective and auditors form a view based on their experience.
- Achieving certification gives no explicit guarantee of product/service quality.
- The standard only addresses the capability and control of the manufacturing, installation, or servicing process.

Source: * Based on Porter and Tanner (2002).

- Very often, quality audits are not seen as opportunities for improvement, but as policing activities.

  The improvement opportunities in this model:
- Scope of the approach should be broadened to also include customers.
- ISO training should be imparted to the temporary staff as well, especially where they have direct contact with customers.
- The audits must form the basis of improvement action and should encourage the results to be taken in a positive way.

Malcolm Baldrige National Quality Award

The Malcolm Baldrige National Quality Award is one of the best-known quality awards and was used to recognize US companies for business excellence and quality achievement. It was named in remembrance of Malcolm Baldrige who served as the US Secretary of Commerce from 1981 until his tragic death in a rodeo accident in 1987. It was created by public law and was signed by President Reagan on 20 August 1987. This led to a new public–private partnership to promote business excellence. Since then, many countries, such as Australia, Singapore, and Dubai, have adopted the framework and run their own award programmes. The main features of this award are as follows:
- Helps improve quality performance practices and capabilities.
- Facilitates communication and sharing of best practices information among and within organizations of all types.
- Serves as a working tool for managing performance, planning, training, and assessment.
- Results in improvement of overall company operational performance and capabilities, thus resulting in marketplace success.

  The main strengths of this award are:
- customer focus and satisfaction
- translation of customer requirement into design through use of cross-functional teams
- address quality requirements early in the process and provide for a process control plan
- risk assessment is conducted biannually at each production facility and outcomes used as input to the planning process
- focus on corporate responsibility and citizenship.

  The main areas for improvement are*:
- Planned benchmarking approach is utilized but how the benchmarking needs and priorities are determined is not clearly detailed.
- A systematic process does not exist for aggregating customer-related data with other key data to set priorities.
- Trend data regarding the effectiveness of quality-related training and key indicators of effectiveness are not presented.
- How customer satisfaction is evaluated and improved and how gains and losses of customers and customer dissatisfaction indicators are considered, are not clear.

Source: * Based on Porter and Tanner (2002).

European Quality Award

This award is the European equivalent of the Malcolm Baldrige Award*. With the aim of enhancing the competitive position of European companies in the world market, 14 chief executives of leading European companies formed the European Foundation for Quality Management (EFQM) on 15 September 1988. The membership has grown to over 400 members since then. The main aims of EFQM were to (1) support the European organization in making quality an important aspect in achieving global competitive advantage and (2) enhance the quality culture in Europe by deploying quality improvement activities.

So far, four awards, namely Thesis award, Media award, Leadership award, and Award for companies and public services have been developed by EFQM.

The company award will now be referred to as EQA and the main features of this award are that it:

- is based on Malcolm Baldrige Award and Deming Prize model
- focuses attention on TQM as a strategic imperative
- focuses on high level of customer satisfaction, people/employee satisfaction, and sense of social duty
- actively promotes total quality outside the organization also, by presenting papers at quality conference, writing articles, working with local schools and colleges, etc.

The EFQM Excellence Model is a practical tool that can be used in a number of different ways:

- as a tool for *self-assessment*
- as a way to *benchmark* with other organizations
- as a guide to identify areas for *improvement*
- as the basis for a common *vocabulary* and a way of thinking
- as a *structure* for the organization's management system.

The EFQM Excellence Model is a non-prescriptive framework based on nine criteria. Five of these are 'enablers' and four are 'results'. The enabler criteria cover what an organization does. The results criteria cover what an organization achieves. Enablers lead to results, and are improved using feedback from results (EFQM 2006).

The main strengths of this award are:

- focus on TQM both within and outside the organization
- timely recognition and appreciation of the efforts and success of individuals, and teams
- focus on top-down, bottom-up, and lateral communication.

Areas for improvement are as follows:

- Started in 1991, so insufficient history at this time to show that it is a rigorous model for business effectiveness.
- It is very exhaustive. *Source*. * Adapted from Porter and Tanner (2002).

Source: * Based on Porter and Tanner (2002).

CII Awards

The journey of CII began in 1895 when five engineering firms, all members of Bengal Chamber of Commerce and Industry, joined hands to form the Engineering and Iron Trades Association (EITA), with the aim of pressurizing the colonial government to place government orders for iron and steel with companies based in India, instead of in the UK. The name changed to Indian Engineering Association (IEA) when the association decided to forge a commitment for manufacturing and exclude traders from the membership. Till 1942, IEA was the only All-India Association of Engineering Industries and represented big engineering companies, particularly British firms. Thus, the interests of medium- and small-scale Indian firms were not sufficiently represented. The Engineering Association of India (EAI) was formed in 1942, as an affiliate of the Indian Chamber of Commerce. In 1974, IEA and EAI merged to form to the Association of Indian Engineering Industry (AIEI), which was a 'Stronger association capable of harnessing larger resources and providing a wider range of services'. Foreseeing the upcoming challenges of competition due to globalization, AIEI changed to Confederation of Engineering Industry (CEI) in 1974, reflecting greater consolidation and solidarity to put the industry on a stronger footing. On 1 January 1992, in keeping with the government's decision to opt for liberalization of the Indian economy, it was natural that there would be inter-sectoral integration through the process of diversification and expansion, where engineering units could diversify into non-engineering units and vice versa. The name was changed to CII. In 1994, CII adopted the European Quality Award Model and introduced the CII–EXIM Bank Award for business excellence jointly with the Export–Import Bank of India to enhance the competitiveness of India Inc. (Fig. 18.1).

The main features of this award are:

- The CII–EXIM Bank Award for business excellence is the most prestigious award in India that an Indian company can receive.

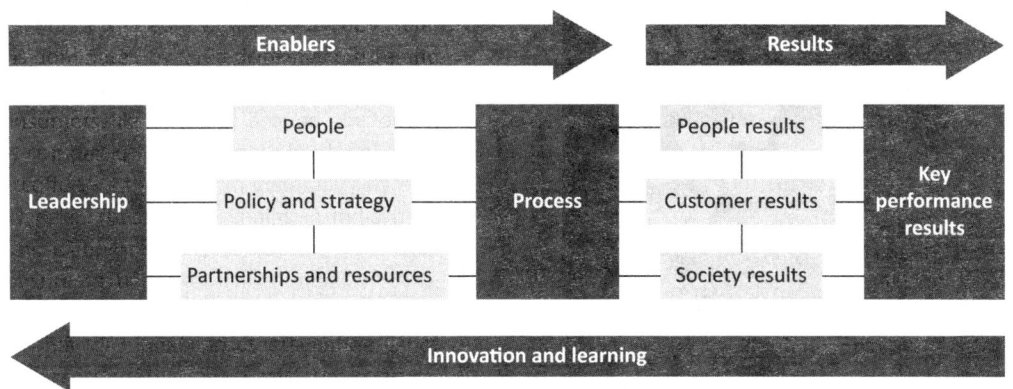

Fig. 18.1 The CII–EXIM bank award model

Source: The CII–EXIM Bank Award for Business Excellence.

Source: * Based on Porter and Tanner (2002) and CII (2006).

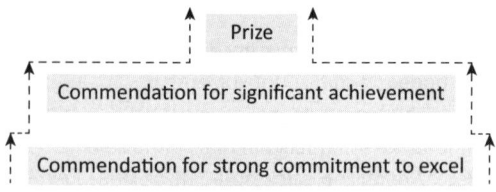

Fig. 18.2 The CII–EXIM Bank Award levels of recognition

Source: Based on CII–EXIM Bank Awards.

- It demonstrates excellence in results with respect to its various stakeholders through excellence in processes and people.
- The award is administered by CII with technical support from EFQM.

The CII Excellence Award is one of the most respected and sought-after awards for business excellence, as it recognizes the best company among Indian industries. It incorporates stringent criteria and rigour in the assessment process, as it is based on the European model for business excellence—the US MB NQA, Japan Quality Award, and Australian Quality Award. The companies that receive this award are comparable to the best globally. 'Excellent results with respect to performance, customers, people, and society, are achieved through leadership driving policy and strategy, people, partnerships, and resources and processes. The arrows emphasize the dynamic nature of the model and show that innovation and learning help to improve enablers, which in turn leads to improved results'. Five Indian companies have received this award till now (CII 2006).

The CII–EXIM Bank Award has four levels of recognition starting from the commendation certificate for strong commitment and going up to the award. Thus, organizations at different levels of competitiveness can benefit from participating in the award process (Fig. 18.2).

CRITERIA FOR CHOOSING TQM FRAMEWORK

After discussing the different models for service excellence, how do we decide which model to choose for an organization? According to Porter and Tanner (2002), the different models can be chosen depending upon—(1) basic philosophy; (2) operational logistics; and (3) experience.

The *basic philosophy* can be used to guide the choice of the TQM. The different philosophies can be listed as follows:
- If an organization's ultimate goal is excellence in business, then it should choose the EQA model.
- If the basic aim is to provide ever improving value to customers, then the organization should choose the Baldrige award.

On the basis of *operational logistics,* an organization can choose either of the frameworks. Thus, if an organization has European operations it is likely to choose the EQA framework. In the same way, companies based in US and Asia-Pacific are likely to choose the Baldrige framework.

An organization's *experience* is also an important factor in the choice of TQM. An organization relatively new to self-assessment will use EQA or Baldrige depending upon its location, but if its business planning process is integrated with well-established self-assessment systems it will have a system based on the Baldrige model (Porter and Tanner 2002).

BLUEPRINT FOR SERVICE EXCELLENCE

The different frameworks talk about excellence in services, but how organizations work strategically to achieve this excellence is a fundamental question. In early 1992, Robert Kaplan and David Norton developed a new approach to strategic management, which acts not only as a measurement system but also as a management system enabling organizations to clarify their vision and strategy and translate them into action. The *balanced scorecard* (BSC) can 'Motivate the management to make breakthrough improvement in critical areas such as product, process, customer, and market development' (Kaplan and Norton 1993). The main features of this approach are listed as follows:

- It is a set of measures that gives top managers a fast and comprehensive view of the business by putting together, on a single management report, many of the dissimilar elements of the company's agenda.
- It includes financial measures that give the results of actions already taken and complements the financial measures with operational measures on customer satisfaction, internal processes, and organization's innovation and improvement activities, that is, the operational measures.
- It puts strategy, not control, at the centre.

The four perspectives of the BSC model are:
1. The customer perspective, or how do the customers see us?
2. Internal perspective, or what must we excel at?
3. Innovation and learning perspective, or how can we continue to improve and create value?
4. Financial perspective, or how do we look to our shareholders?

The companies following TQM lack a sense of integration. The BSC acts as the focal point for the organization's efforts, defining and communicating priorities to the different stakeholders. 'The BSC is not a template that can be applied to businesses in general or even industry-wide. Different market situations, product strategies, and competitive environments require different scorecards. Business units devise customized scorecards to fit their mission, strategy, technology, and culture' (Kaplan and Norton 1993).

Thus, the BSC approach helps companies to become the kind of organization they want to be. It puts vision and strategy, and not control, at the centre assuming that people will adopt necessary behaviours and actions to achieve these goals.

RESEARCH INSIGHT

Management of Service Quality—Differences in Values, Practices, and Outcomes

Lagrosen, Stefan and Yvonne Lagrosen (2003), 'Management of service quality—Differences in values, practices and outcomes', *Managing Service Quality: An International Journal*, vol. 13, issue 5, pp. 370–381.

This article concerns a study with the purpose of identifying differences in the management of quality between manufacturing, private service, and public service organizations. A questionnaire was sent to members of the Swedish Association for Quality. Some interesting differences were identified. Customer orientation is highest in the private service sector and lowest in the public service sector. The manufacturing companies' usage of ISO 9000 is extremely high and their usage of the Swedish Quality Award is fairly low whereas the public service organizations use both these two models equally. This corresponds with the finding that ISO 9000 produces better results in the manufacturing sector whereas The Swedish Quality Award produces better results in the service sector. Generally, the indication is that quality management is most successful in the manufacturing sector and least successful in the public service sector. There is also a difference in that improvements in the manufacturing sector are more often about the processes whereas the organizations within the public service sector more often report improvements regarding personnel.

SUMMARY

Customers are the ultimate deciders of an organization's success. However, the service-providing organizations can also script their own success by providing excellent services and meeting the customer needs and requirements, which in turn, make the customers return repeatedly for the services being provided. The prevalence of various regulatory and compliance issues further necessitates this. This chapter highlights the need for an organization to maintain excellence in the production and delivery of services. It starts by discussing the various regulatory and compliance issues and their relevance in the market. The chapter goes on to focus on the need to manage excellence as a strategic tool, the relevance of service quality maintenance by an organization offering services and its importance to the customers.

Different models based on service quality have been proposed for attaining excellence in services.

This chapter specifically highlights the BS En ISO 9000 model, Malcolm Baldrige National Quality Award, The European Quality Award, and the CII Awards. The main features of these awards along with their strengths and drawbacks and the improvement opportunity have been discussed in detail. The availability of these different models of excellence can be confusing for a service provider. The next section thus highlights the criteria to help the service-providing organizations to decide which framework to choose from the aforementioned models. Finally, the blueprint for services excellence is also discussed in the form of the BSC approach.

KEY TERMS

Balance scorecard (BSC) An approach to management that integrates both financial and non-financial performance measurement in a framework proposed by Kaplan and Norton. The concept was first reported in the *Harvard Business Review* in 1992 and has since been adopted by various organizations.

Convergence The general trend in which computers, telecommunications, and the broadcast media have become increasingly interdependent and have assumed similar functions for many business and other purposes.

SERVQUAL The provision of high-quality products together with a high quality of customer service. It can be identified by a number of factors such as tangibles, reliability, responsiveness, assurance, and empathy.

Total quality management (TQM) An approach to management that seeks to integrate all the elements of an organization in order to meet the needs and expectations of its customers.

EXERCISES

Concept Review Questions

1. Critically evaluate the importance of service quality.

2. Enumerate the different models for service excellence and discuss any one model in detail.

3. Discuss the European Quality Award and Malcolm Baldrige National Quality Award. Highlight the similarities between the two models.

4. Briefly discuss the BSC approach and its relevance in an organization.

Critical Thinking Questions

1. How will you choose an excellence model for an organization operating in China for the past three years? Give reasons for your answer.

2. You are the service provider in the hospitality sector. Try designing the BSC model for your organization. Make realistic assumptions.

Internet Exercises

1. Visit the website of Malcolm Baldrige Quality Award and identify the different organizations that have received the award in the services sector.

2. Visit the website of European Quality Award and compare it with the MBNQA website. Which according to you is more informative, and why?

CASE STUDY **Balanced Scorecards in Managing Higher Education Institutions: An Indian Perspective***

Introduction

Organizational failure can usually be traced to deficient strategic planning, poor organization structure, recruitment and retention of staff, ineffective or non-existent internal control, and a lack of communication and feedback. On a more operational level, poor budgeting and inattention to cash flows are also often the cause of organizational failure. Educational institutions of higher learning are no different; it is just that in the Indian context, traditionally, the government has controlled these institutions and, at times, strategic management and its derivative tenets are not so visible in the initiation and operation of such institutions.

Heimerdinger (2002) indicates a need for training perceived by non-profit managers that manifests the traditional concerns of human services professionals who find themselves promoted into managerial positions without the benefit of traditional formal training in management—referring to those tasks usually defined by activities such as planning, organizing, motivating and controlling, and feedback. Sub-tending all of these is the need for leadership. If we juxtapose the above mentioned comment with the fact that educational institutions of higher learning in India have traditionally been 'administered' (managed) in a way in which academic staff have been given apex positions in the administrative hierarchy, it highlights this need for developing managerial capacity.

Universities worldwide are facing the challenge of being centres of excellence for teaching as well as research. On one hand, universities are increasingly being required to teach ever increasing number of students in multiplying varieties of specializations and disciplines, and on the other, they are being asked to pay more attention to quality of teaching and educational programmes (Smeby 2003). This again indicates the requirement to re-look at the ways institutions of higher learning are to be managed.

This article looks at focusing attention on one of the contemporary tools of management, namely, the BSC, and tries to discuss how it may be beneficial in the strategic management of higher education institutions in India.

Tertiary Education in India

In India, the university system, as we see today, originated about a century and half ago with the establishment of universities at Kolkata, Chennai,

---

* Umashankar, Venkatesh and Kirti Dutta (2007), 'Balanced scorecards in managing higher education institutions: An Indian perspective', *International Journal of Education Management*, vol. 21, no. 1, Bradford. Reprinted with the permission of Emerald Group Publishing Limited.

Mumbai, Allahabad, and Lahore between 1857 and 1902. These were modelled after the British universities of that period. The Central Advisory Board of Education's (CABE) Committee on Autonomy of Higher Education Institutions (2005) in its report states that currently the Indian higher education system consists of 343 university level institutions and about 16,885 colleges, and that there are many nagging concerns about its role and performance. Many of our reputed universities and colleges have lost their pre-eminent positions. Only a few manage to maintain their status and dignity in an environment of complex socio-economic pressures and worldwide changes in approaches to the educational processes. Under the rapidly expanding situation with multiplicity of expectations from the higher education system it has become necessary to identify those attributes, which distinguish a first-rate institution from a mediocre one. The complex array of associated issues deserves a total re-thinking of our approach to higher education. Serious efforts are now underway to develop the policy perspectives in education involving deeper national introspection and fundamental changes in the structure, content, and delivery mechanisms of our university system.

The report further indicates that the enrolment in the Indian higher education system has increased from 7.42 million in 1999–2000 to about 9.7 million at present, indicating nearly 10% annual growth. The colleges account for about 80% of the enrolment with the rest in the university departments. Thus, the programmes available in the college system largely determine the quality of our higher education. In the past decade, there has been a sharp increase in the number of private colleges as well as universities with the status of either deemed to be universities or state universities. The proportion of the eligible age group wishing to enter higher educational institutions will most likely increase significantly from the present level of about 7%. The regulatory mechanisms will perhaps be liberalized. Higher education is continuing to expand, mostly in an unplanned manner, without even minimum levels of checks and balances. Many universities are burdened with an unmanageable number of affiliated colleges; some have more than 300 colleges affiliated to them. New universities are being carved out of existing ones to reduce the number of affiliated colleges. Under these circumstances, our dependence on autonomy as the means to improve the quality of such a huge higher education system poses serious challenges.

Venkatesha (2003) compares and finds a lot of differences in the work culture between the teachers of post-graduate departments of universities with those of colleges. In degree colleges, teaching is the only mandate and pertaining to this, teachers have to improve their knowledge in teaching by undergoing orientation and refresher courses, summer camps, workshops, and participating in seminars/symposia from time to time. On the basis of these activities, teachers are considered for promotion to the next cadre. Some college teachers who are interested in research may conduct research and publish papers. The research activity of college teachers is invariably out of their natural interest rather than a yardstick for their promotion, unlike in universities. Once a university teacher acquires a Ph.D. degree, many university teachers lapse into routine teaching assignments. Because of this type of dual role of teaching and research without defined guidelines, university teachers can neglect either teaching or research, or sometimes both. In Indian universities, teachers are promoted based on their research publications, books written, papers presented in seminars/symposia, membership of various academic societies, etc., but not much importance has been given to the teachers' contributions towards teaching.

This type of situation in our universities tempts many teachers to neglect teaching and take up some sort of research mostly uneconomical, unproductive, outdated, and repetitive, and venture into the business of publishing substandard research articles. The system normally recognizes quantity, like the number of Ph.D. students guided, number of papers published, etc., rather than quality of the research and publications. Unfortunately, no concrete method has been developed so far to judge the teaching and research aptitude of university teachers. Some academicians argue that both teaching and research cannot be done at the same time. However, it is generally thought that education (even from the undergraduate level) and research should coexist to complement each other. Special emphasis on assessment-oriented teaching and research will impart a new dimension to the role of a teacher.

Commenting upon the inherent contradictions in higher education and research in sciences, Chidambaram (1999) indicates a peculiar situation existing in the country. Wherein on one hand, a large number of people are being given postgraduate degrees in science disciplines without an appreciation of their possible future careers; on the other hand, there is a considerable reduction in the number of such talented and motivated students seeking admissions to science courses. The dilution of resources that this irrelevant training represents has the consequence of deteriorating the quality of the training for the really talented people.

Staying on with science education, Narlikar (1999) identifies poor methodology of science teaching that encourages rote learning, ill-equipped teachers and labs, lack of inspirational and committed teachers, poorly written textbooks, and peer pressure to join lucrative courses, as some of the causes of the current sickness that has afflicted the science scenario. Our institutions or universities are just not projecting the romance of science and a proper and correct image. In his opinion, this unfortunate trend can be reversed if society displays a will and creates an environment to cure the causes of the deeply entrenched malady.

Altbach (2005) provides an overview of the ailments afflicting the higher education machinery in India when he says that India's colleges and universities, with just a few exceptions, have become 'large, under-funded, ungovernable institutions'. Many of them are infested with politics that has intruded into campus life, influencing academic appointments and decisions across levels. Under-investment in libraries, information technology, laboratories, and classrooms makes it very difficult to provide top-quality

instruction or engage in cutting-edge research. A rising number of part-time and ad hoc teachers and the limitation on new full-time appointments in many places have affected morale in the academic profession. The lack of accountability means that teaching and research performance is seldom measured with the system, providing few incentives to perform. He goes on to say that India has survived with an increasingly mediocre higher education system for decades. Now, as India strives to compete in a global economy, in areas that require highly trained professionals, the quality of higher education becomes increasingly important. So far, India's large educated population base and its reservoir of at least moderately well trained university graduates have permitted the country to move ahead. He concludes that the panacea to the ailments of Indian universities is an academic culture based on merit-based norms and competition for advancement and research funds, along with a judicious mix of autonomy to do creative research, and accountability to ensure productivity. He rightly says that 'world-class universities require world-class professors and students—and a culture to sustain and stimulate them'.

He recommends a combination of specific conditions and resources to create outstanding universities in India including:

- sustained financial support, with an appropriate mix of accountability and autonomy
- the development of a clearly differentiated academic system—including private institutions—in which academic institutions have different missions, resources, and purposes
- managerial reforms and the introduction of effective administration
- truly merit-based hiring and promotion policies for the academic profession, and similarly, rigorous and honest recruitment, selection, and instruction of students.

Misra (2002) identifies 'management without objectives' as one of the key reasons for the downfall of the Indian university system. He highlights the need for adopting a functional approach in our universities; periodic academic audits; greater autonomy and accountability in all spheres of operations; open door policy welcoming ideas and people from all over; administrative restructuring, decentralizing university departments and schools; and making education relevant to our people and times; as the basic steps towards improving the Indian universities.

The earlier discussion establishes the need for accountability-based autonomy and being consistently relevant to the context in which the Indian universities (or any other universities anywhere for that matter) may exist. This creates the backdrop for adopting the basic tenets of strategic management in the paradigms of operating our universities. The BSC is one such basic tool that can certainly be of assistance in this rationalization process.

The Balanced Scorecard

Kaplan and Norton (1992) first introduced the concept of the BSC in their *Harvard Business Review* article, 'The Balance Scorecard—Measures that Drive Performance'. Focusing on the fact that managers needed a balanced presentation of both financial and operational measures, they propounded four perspectives as the drivers of future financial performance:

1. Customer perspective: How do customers see us?
2. Internal perspective: What must we excel at?
3. Innovation and learning perspective: Can we continue to improve and create value?
4. Financial perspective: How do we look to our stakeholders?

The scorecard provides executives with a comprehensive framework that translates a company's strategic objectives into a coherent set of performance measures. It represents a fundamental change in the underlying assumptions about performance measurement and helps focus the strategic vision.

According to Kaplan and Norton (1993), local improvement programmes such as process reengineering, total quality, and employee empowerment lack a sense of integration. The BSC can serve as the focal point for the organization's efforts. ISO model for excellence introduced in 1987 aims to produce a product/service 'right first time' by standardizing the functions in different departments and performing regular audits; continuous improvement is

observed but it does not take the customers into account. However, the scorecard takes customers as one of the perspectives. It puts strategy and vision, not control, at the centre. It allows people to adopt whatever behaviour and whatever actions are necessary to arrive at these goals (Kaplan and Norton 1992). Thus, the whole arena is open for innovative ideas and action plans.

The BSC is not just a measurement system; it is a management system to motivate breakthrough competitive performance and is most successful when used to drive the process of change (Kaplan and Norton 1993).

According to Kaplan and Norton (1996b), the management shifts from reviewing the past to learning about the future in the BSC application. It retains the measures of financial performance—the lagging outcome indicators—but supplements these with measures and the drivers—the lead indicators—of future financial performance (Kaplan and Norton 2001). This also triggers a double-loop learning process.

The BSC's widespread adoption and use is well documented, for example, Kaplan and Norton (2001) reported that by 2001 about 50% of the Fortune 1000 companies in North America and 40–45% of the companies in Europe were using the BSC (cited in Karathanos and Karathanos, 2005). Kaplan and Norton (2001) formulated a new framework, namely, the 'Strategy Map', a comprehensive architecture for describing strategy. It provides a visual representation of the strategy and is a single-page view of how objectives in the four perspectives integrate and combine to describe the strategy (Kaplan and Norton 2004).

Application of BSC in Education

It is evident that the BSC has been widely adopted in the business sector, but the education sector has not embraced the BSC concept widely as indicated by the dearth of published research on this topic (Karathanos and Karathanos 2005). Cullen et al. (2003) proposed that BSC be used in educational institutions for reinforcement of the importance of managing rather than just monitoring performance. Sutherland (2000) (cited in Karathanos and

Karathanos 2005) reported that the Rossier School of Education at University of Southern California adopted the BSC to assess its academic programme and planning process. Also Chang and Chow (1999) reported in a survey of 69 accounting departments heads that they were generally supportive of the BSC applicability and benefits to accounting education programmes. Ivy (2001) studied how universities in both UK and South Africa use marketing to differentiate their images in the higher education market. At a time when higher educational institutions around the globe face declining student numbers and decreasing funding grants, it becomes imperative for them to determine their images in the eyes of their various publics. Karathanos and Karathanos (2005) describe how the Baldrige education criteria for performance excellence has adapted the concept of the BSC to education, and discuss significant differences as well as similarities between the BSC for business and the BSC for education.

In higher education, as in business, there are acceptable conventions of measuring excellence. Rather than emphasizing financial performance, higher education has emphasized academic measures. As in the case of business, the demands of external accountability and comparability, and measurement in higher education, have generally emphasized those academic variables that are most easily quantifiable (Ruben 1999). These measures usually are built on and around such aspects as faculty/student numbers (ratios), demographics, student pass percentages and dispersion of scores, class rank, percentile scores, graduation rates, percentage of graduates employed on graduation, faculty teaching load, faculty research/publications, statistics on physical resources, such as library and computer laboratories. Ruben (1999) indicates that one area deserving greater attention in this process of measurement is the student, faculty, and staff expectations and satisfaction levels. He opines that in most higher education centres very little attention is paid to systematically measuring students', faculty, and staff satisfaction, despite sharing the widely accepted viewpoint that attracting and retaining the best talent/people is the primary goal and critical success factor for institutions of higher learning.

In a study conducted by Ewell (1994) (cited in Ruben 1999), the measures used in 10 states in the US in performance reports of higher education institutions, were:

- enrolment/graduation rates by gender, ethnicity, and programme
- degree completion and time to degree
- persistence and retention rates by gender, ethnicity, and programme
- remediation activities and indicators of their effectiveness
- transfer rates to and from two- and four-year institutions
- pass rates on professional exams
- job placement data on graduates and graduates' satisfaction with their jobs
- faculty workload and productivity in the form of student/faculty ratios and instructional contact hours.

Karanthanos and Karanthanos (2005) have compared the Baldrige Award and BSC criteria in the context of education and have come out with measures closely aligned among both the instruments (see Table 18.3).

Applicability and Design of the BSC in the Indian Environment

Review of extant literature indicates that business organizations, as well as academic institutions, are fundamentally rethinking their strategies and operations because of the changing environment demanding more accountability. The BSC is described as a novel approach to face these challenges (Dorweiler and Yakhou 2005). The strategies for creating value in education need to be based on managing knowledge that creates and deploys an organization's intangible assets. The scorecard defines the theory of the business on which the strategy is based; hence, performance monitoring can take the form of hypothesis testing and double-loop learning. A good BSC should have a mix of outcome measures and performance drivers (Kaplan and Norton 1996b).

Marketing and communication strategies vis-à-vis institutions of higher education assume greater import as the image portrayed by these institutions plays a critical role in shaping the attitudes and

Table 18.3   Expected measures in BSC and Baldrige criteria for education and business

	Education	Business
1.	Student learning results: Results should be based on a variety of assessment methods, should reflect overall mission and improvement objectives. Should reflect holistic appraisals of student learning.	Customer-focused results: Customer satisfaction measurements about specific product and service features, delivery, relationships, and transactions that bear upon the customers' future actions.
2.	Student and stakeholder focused result: Student and stakeholder satisfaction measurements about specific educational programme and service features. Delivery, interactions and transactions that bear upon student development and learning and the students' and stakeholders' future actions.	Product and service results: Key measures or indicators of product and service performance important to the customers.
3.	Budgetary financial and market results: Instructional and general administration expenditure per student, tuition and fee levels, cost per academic credit, resources redirected to education from other areas, scholarship growth.	Financial and market results: Return on investment, asset use, operating margins, profitability, liquidity, and value added per employee.
4.	Faculty and staff results: Innovation and suggestion rates; courses or educational programmes completed; learning; on-the-job performance improvements; cross-training rates; collaboration and teamwork; knowledge and skill sharing across work functions, units and locations; employee well-being, satisfaction and dissatisfaction.	Human resource results: Innovation and suggestion rates; courses completed; learning; on-the-job performance improvements; cross-training rates; measures and indicators of work system performance and effectiveness; collaboration and teamwork; knowledge and skill sharing across work functions, units, and locations; employee well-being, satisfaction and dissatisfaction.
5.	Organizational effectiveness results (including key internal operations performance measures): Capacity to improve student performance, student development, education climate, indicators of responsiveness to student or stakeholder needs, supplier and partner performance, key measures or indicators of accomplishment of organizational strategy and action plan.	Organizational effectiveness results (including key internal operations performance measures): Productivity, cycle time, supplier and partner performance, key measures or indicators of accomplishment of organizational strategy and action plan.
6.	Governance and social responsibility results: Fiscal accountability, both internal and external; measures or indicators of ethical behaviour and stakeholder trust in the governance of the organization; regulatory and legal compliance; organizational citizenship.	Governance and social responsibility results: Fiscal accountability, both internal and external; measures or indicators of ethical behaviour and of stakeholder trust in the governance of the organization; regulatory and legal compliance; organizational citizenship.

Source: Based on Karanthanos and Karanthanos (2005).

perceptions of the institution's public towards that institution (Yavas and Shemwell 1996). In India, for instance, institutions of higher education are becoming increasingly aggressive in their marketing activities. In this increasingly competitive environment, the marketers of higher education should be concerned about their institution's positioning and image.

The marketing of educational programmes has attracted the attention of researchers who have identified research-based planning and programme development, relationship marketing, and non-traditional methods for education delivery as key areas for future focus (Hayes 1996). Some of the reasons that marketing of higher education has gained importance in the management of higher education programmes and institutions are the founding missions being found increasingly ill-suited for the demands of the marketplace; budgets becoming excruciatingly tight while departments and programmes clamour for more support; the recruiting and fund-raising arenas having become extremely competitive as well as hostile; higher education being more and more dominated by many largely undifferentiated colleges and universities offering similar programmes; demographic shifts in the operating environment marked by diminishing numbers of traditional full-time students, fewer full-pay students, and fewer residential students; escalating demand for adult higher education, and continuing and special focus programmes; and last but not the least, the sharp rise in the cost of higher education (Kanis 2000). In India too, recently, as liberalization has progressed, although in fits and starts, governmental support to institutions of higher learning in the form of grants and subsidies is drying up. The movement of self-sustenance is gaining force. This also adds up and forces managers of educational institutions, especially in the public domain, to re-think their mission and strategies (Venkatesh 2001).

Ruben (2004) says that students are affected not only by the teaching environment, but also by the learning environment, which includes facilities, accommodation, physical environment, policies, and procedures, and more importantly, interpersonal

relations and communication, and from every encounter and experience. Hence, the faculty, staff, and administrators have to set good examples by their deeds and recognize that everyone in an institution is a teacher. Keeping in mind that the continual self-examination by institutions should focus on the institution's contribution to students' intellectual and personal development, we can propose the following model (Table 18.4–18.7) for the BSC approach in the Indian higher education scenario, largely based on the analysis of the findings presented variously by Chang and Chow (1999), Stewart and Hubin (2000), Ivy (2001), Cribb and Hogan (2003), and Karanthanos and Karanthanos (2005):

As listed in Tables 18.4–18.7, a wide range of stakeholders and their diverse claims/interests and objectives have to be addressed in the context of the institution of higher education in India. The first component, customer perspective, is supposed to aim at the immediate needs and desires of the students, parents, faculty and staff, alumni, the corporate sector, and the society at large. It is relevant here to state that looking at students solely as customers becomes a sort of a misnomer, as they are also (if not only) the 'throughput' that eventually gets processed in the institution and ends up accepted (or rejected) at the verge of graduation. Hence, the corporation and society at large should be considered as the real customers. The second component involves the internal business or operations perspective. This inherently focuses on the implementation and delivery of the academic, research, and other programmes by the institution and the degree of excellence achieved in the same. The third component, innovation and learning perspective of the organization, looks at the development of faculty and staff as a precursor and foundation to excellence in programme design and delivery. Finally, the fourth component constitutes the financial performance and its measure. It is clear in the Indian context especially, that although the government eschews the 'profit' word for educational institutions, it emphasizes more and more on self-sustaining programmes and institutions as

Table 18.4   Component one: Customer perspective—including students, faculty, staff, alumni, parents, and corporations

Objective	Measures
Students/Parents	
• Highly-valued programme • Quality academic advising • Flexible course scheduling • Quality instruction • Effective student placement	• External rankings in press, percentage of enrolment out of applications • Student evaluation of advising • Student satisfaction survey • Alumni evaluation, graduating student survey • Accreditation, recruiter evaluation, professional exam passing rate • Percentage of students with job offers at graduation, number of companies recruiting on campus, average starting salaries
Faculty/Staff	
• Growth opportunities • Learning opportunities	• Salary growth over period of time • Courses or educational programs completed • Knowledge and skill sharing across work functions, units, and locations • Employee well-being
Alumni	
• Knowledge updation with passage of time • Knowledge reinforcement	• Alumni feedback • Alumni satisfaction survey
Corporate	
• Hiring quality students • Knowledge extension, i.e., research, consultancy, training, continuing education-related linkages	• Number of students hired • Number of job offers per student • Average salaries offered • Number of people benefiting from training programmes conducted by institution • Grants/endowments garnered from industry
Society	
Good citizenship	• Number of alumni in public service, community service, NGOs. • Philanthropic record of alumni, faculty, staff • Legally clean record of alumni, faculty, staff

a desirable outcome of the strategies and models envisaged and pursued by universities and colleges. Surpluses are important, as only then can institutions look for achieving greater autonomy in designing and delivering ever new courses and programmes that are relevant to the population in context, but expensive to implement.

Kaplan and Norton (1996a) say that companies are using the balanced scorecard to:
• clarify and update vision and strategic direction
• communicate strategic objectives and measures throughout the organization
• align department and individual goals with the organization's vision and strategy

Table 18.5   Component two: Internal business perspective student/stakeholder focus

Objective	Measures
• To achieve continuous improvement of services, facilities, and resources	Meeting service standards, response time to customer, service facilities to staff
• To improve new product and service development	Number of new products and services introduced, i.e., new courses, syllabi, programmes, and curriculum changes
• Quality assurance	Distribution of grades awarded, exit exam, or student competency evaluation
• Internship programme	Number of internships available, number of companies available, student evaluation
• Cost-efficiency	Faculty-to-student ratio, educational expenses per student
• Unique or specialized curriculum	Number of faculty in specialized area, number of schools offering the same programme

Table 18.6   Component three: Innovation and learning perspective faculty and staff, organizational effectiveness, social responsibility

Objective	Measures
• Faculty professional growth	Number of faculty presentations at conferences; number of faculty presentations; number of seminars attended, travel budget for conference attendance
• Staff motivation and development	Percentage of budget spent on staff development; staff satisfaction index in staff survey; number of cross-trained or multi-skilled staff
• Incorporating technology into teaching	Number of courses incorporating new technology
• Innovation in teaching	Number of teaching workshops attended by faculty, number of teaching innovation projects
• Curriculum innovation	Number of curriculum revisions in last five years; number of new courses offered in last five years
• Partnering with corporations for campus recruitment	Number of firms involved; number of joint activities
• Organizational citizenship	Academic excellence; and increased research productivity; increased outreach to community
• Resource management	Number of campus partnerships, entrepreneurial initiatives, trends in energy use

- link strategic objectives to long-term targets and annual budgets
- identify and align strategic initiatives
- conduct periodic performance reviews to learn about and improve strategy

- obtain feedback to learn about and improve strategy.

All the aforementioned benefits are relevant in the context of the institutions higher learning in India. As Pandey (2005), indicates, 'A good aspect

Table 18.7 Component four: Financial perspective

Objective	Measures
• Prosper	Annual grants; amount of permanent endowment
• Succeed	Enrolment trend
• Grow	Enhancement in student intake
• Survive	Level of student enrolment; funding per student
• Maximize asset utilization	More efficient and effective use of facilities, space, services, systems, and resources as measured by various usage studies and statistics

of the BSC is that it is a simple, systematic, easy-to-understand approach for performance measurement, review, and evaluation. It is also a convenient mechanism to communicate strategy and strategic objectives to all levels of management'. According to Kaplan and Norton (2001), the most important potential benefit is that the BSC approach aligns with strategy leading to better communication and motivation, which causes better performance. Considering the linkages in service management profit chain (Kaplan and Norton 2001), we can list the potential benefits as follows:

- Investments in faculty and staff training lead to improvements in service quality.
- Better service quality leads to higher customer (stakeholder) satisfaction.
- Higher customer satisfaction leads to increased customer loyalty.
- Increased customer loyalty generates positive word-of-mouth, increased grants/revenues, and surpluses that can be ploughed into the system for further growth and development.

With growing popularity for Indian engineers and graduates in job employment abroad (*The Times of India* 2006) India has to build world-class quality into higher education. In fact, a critical test of a scorecard's success is its transparency: from the 15–20 scorecard measures, an observer is able to see through the organizations corporate strategy (Kaplan and Norton 1993). Thus, if higher education institutions apply the BSC approach to their organization they will be able to position their students and programmes positively in the minds of the international audience.

Conclusion

Universities need to consciously and explicitly manage the processes associated with the creation of their knowledge assets and recognize the value of their intellectual capital to their continuing role in society in a wider global marketplace for higher education (Rowley 2000).

Translating the BSC approach to the complex world of academia is a challenge (Ruben 1999). There are some critical success factors highlighted for higher education institutions in India. These factors are critical because if they are executed properly, the institution will achieve excellence in its chosen field(s). It serves as a driving force to move institutions towards their goals. In the process of reaching these goals, institutions are confronted with many barriers that are difficult to overcome; however, many barriers originate from the institutions organizational members themselves by way of resistance to change, fear of accountability, and its derivative pressure, lack of commitment, and fear of failure. If quality can be nurtured into the senses of all the functionaries in the institutions, then organizational members will engage in the co-operation and commitment required of them (Kanji et al. 1999). The BSC approach offers an institution the opportunity to formulate a cascade of measures to translate the mission of knowledge creation, sharing, and utilization into a comprehensive, coherent, communicable, and mobilizing framework—for external stakeholders, and for one another.

The current state of Indian universities and other institutions of higher learning can benefit through the application of BSCs to cull out areas that they need to urgently focus upon and design appropriate strategies.

Questions

1. Discuss the scenario of tertiary education in India.

2. What is the balanced scorecard and how can it be applied to business?
3. Critically evaluate the application of balanced scorecard in education.

REFERENCES

Altbach, Philip G. (2005), 'Higher education in India', *The Hindu*, 12 April.

Asher, Mike (1996), *Managing Quality in Service Sector*, Kogan Page Limited, London, Chapter 2.

CABE (2005), 'Autonomy of higher education institutions', New Delhi, Ministry of Human Resource Development, Department of Secondary and Higher Education, Government of India.

Chang, O.H. and C.W. Chow (1999), 'The balanced scorecard: A potential tool for supporting change and continuous improvement in accounting education', *Issues in Accounting Education*, vol. 14, no. 3, pp. 395–412.

Chhaparia, Parul (2006), 'Bahamas come head-hunting to India', *Times of India*, 12 February, p. 7.

Chidambaram, R. (1999), 'Patterns and Priorities in Indian research and development', *Current Science*, vol. 77, no. 7, pp. 859–868.

Cullen, J., J. Joyce, T. Hassall, and M. Broadbent (2003), 'Quality in higher education: From monitoring to management', *Quality Assurance in Higher Education*, vol. 11, no. 1, pp. 30–34.

Dorweiler, V.P. and M. Yakhou (2005), 'Scorecard for academic administration performance on the campus', *Managerial Auditing Journal*, vol. 20, no. 2, pp. 138–144.

Garvin (1984), 'What does "product quality" really mean?' *Sloan Management Review*, 26(1), pp. 25–45.

Grönroos, Christian (1988), 'Service quality: The six criteria of good perceived service quality', *Review of Business*, vol. 9, no. 3, pp. 10–13.

Grönroos, Christian (1998), 'Marketing services: The case of the missing product', *The Journal of Business and Industrial Marketing*, vol. 13, no. 4/5, pp. 322–336.

Hayes, Tom (1996), 'Higher education marketing symposium wins top grades', *Marketing News*, vol. 30, no. 3, pp. 10–11.

Heimerdinger, John F. (2002), 'Commentary', *Nonprofit Management and Leadership*, vol. 13, no. 2, p. 205.

Ivy, Jonathan (2001), 'Higher education institution image: A correspondence analysis approach', *The International Journal of Educational Management*, vol. 15, no. 6/7, pp. 276–282.

Kandampully, J. (2000), 'The impact of demand fluctuation on the quality of service: A tourism industry example', *Managing Service Quality*, vol. 10, no. 1, pp. 10–18.

Kanis, Ed (2000), 'Marketing in higher education is a must today', *Business First*, Louisville, vol. 16, no. 25, p. 55.

Kanji, Gopal K., Abdul M. Bin, A. Tambi, and W. Wallace (1999), 'A comparative study of quality practices in higher education institutions in the US and Malaysia', *Total Quality Management*, vol. 10, no. 3, pp. 357–371.

Kaplan, Robert S. and David P. Norton (1992), 'The balanced scorecard: Measures that drive performance', *Harvard Business Review*, January–February, pp. 71–79.

Kaplan, Robert S. and David P. Norton (1993), 'Putting the balanced scorecard to work', *Harvard Business Review*, September–October, pp. 134–142.

Kaplan, R.S. and D.P. Norton (1996a), 'Using the balanced scorecard as a strategic management system', *Harvard Business Review*, Jan–Feb, pp. 75–85.

Kaplan, R.S. and D.P. Norton (1996b), 'Strategic learning and the balanced scorecard', *Strategy and Leadership*, Sept–Oct, pp. 18–24.

Kaplan, R.S. and D.P. Norton (2001), 'Transforming the balanced scorecard from performance measurement to strategic management: Part I', *Accounting Horizons*, vol. 15, no. 1, pp. 87–104.

Kaplan, R.S. and D.P. Norton (2004), 'How strategy maps frame an organization's objectives', *Financial Executive*, March–April, pp. 40–45.

Karathanos, D. and P. Karathanos (2005), 'Applying the balanced scorecard to education', *Journal of Education for Business*, vol. 80, no. 4, pp. 222–230.

Kasper, Hans, P.V. Helsdingen, and W. de Vries Jr (1999), *Services Marketing Management: An International Perspective*, John Wiley and Sons, England, Chapter 5.

Lockwood, Andrew, Michael Baker, and Andrew Ghillyer (1996), *Quality Management in Hospitality*, Cassel, New York, Chapters 1 and 2.

Misra, R.P. (2002), 'Globalization and Indian universities: Challenges and prospects', unpublished speech at the Third Dr Amarnath Jha Memorial Lecture, delivered at Lalit Narayan Mithila University, Darbhanga, Bihar on 2 September 2002.

Mohanty, R.P. and R.R. Lakhe (2002), *TQM in Service Sector*, Jaico Publishing House, Mumbai, Chapter 1.

Mohsin, Asad (2005), 'Service quality perceptions: An assessment of restaurant and café visitors in Hamilton, New Zealand', *The Business Review*, Cambridge, vol. 3, no. 2, pp. 51–57.

Narlikar, J.V. (1999), 'No fizz and spark—decline in science education', *The Times of India*, 6 May, p. 10.

Pandey, I.M. (2005), 'Balanced scorecard: Myth and reality', *The Vikalpa*, vol. 30, no. 1, pp. 51–66.

Parasuraman A., V.A. Zeithaml, and L.L. Berry (1985), 'A conceptual model of service quality and its implications for future research', *Journal of Marketing*, vol. 49, no. 4, p. 47.

Porter L. and S. Tanner (2002), *Assessing Business Excellence*, Butterworth–Heinemann Publications, Oxford, Chapters 2, 4, and 6.

Reed, Darryl and Sanjoy Mukherjee (2004), *Corporate Governance, Economic Reforms, and Development: The Indian Experience*, Oxford University Press, New Delhi.

Rowley, Jennifer (2000), 'Higher education ready for knowledge management', *The International Journal of Educational Management*, vol. 14, no. 7, p. 325.

Ruben, Brent D. (2004), *Pursuing Excellence in Higher Education: Eight Fundamental Challenges*, Jossey Bass, San Francisco.

Smeby, Jens Christian (2003), 'The impact of massification of university research', *Tertiary Education and Management*, vol. 9, no. 2, pp. 131–144.

Stewart, A.C. and J. Carpenter-Hubin (2000), 'The balanced scorecard: Beyond reports and rankings', *Planning for Higher Education*, Winter 2000–01, pp. 37–42.

The Institute of Company Secretaries of India (2003), *Corporate Governance (Modules of Best Practices)*, 5th edn, The Institute of Company Secretaries of India, New Delhi.

The World Bank (2007), 'Regulatory trends in service convergence', Policy Division, Global Information and Communication Technologies Department, Washington, D.C., United States.

Venkatesh, Umashankar (2001), 'The importance of managing point-of-marketing in marketing higher education programmes: Some conclusions', *Journal of Services Research*, vol. 1, no. 1, pp. 125–140.

Venkatesha, M.G. (2003), 'Teaching versus research in Indian universities', *Current Science*, vol. 84, no. 11, pp. 1384–1385.

Wallace, Peter and John Zinkin (2006), *Mastering Business in Asia Corporate Governance*, John Wiley & Sons (Asia) Pte Ltd, New Delhi.

Yavas, U. and D.J. Shemwell, (1996), 'Graphical representation of university image: A correspondence analysis', *Journal for Marketing for Higher Education*, vol. 7, no. 2, pp. 75–84.

Cribb, G. and C. Hogan (2003), 'Balanced scorecard: Linking strategic planning to measurement and communication', 24th Annual Conference of the International Association of Technological University Libraries, http://www.iatul.org/conference/proceedings/vol13/papers/CRI BB_fulltext.pdf, accessed on 22 January 2009.

http://www.balancedscorecard.org/images/BSC.jpg, accessed on 19 December 2006.

http://www.ciionline.org/Common/201/images/Business%20Excellence%20Model.pdf, accessed on 19 December 2007.

http://www.cii-iq.in/pdfs/excellence.pdf, accessed on 25 January 2009.

http://www.efqm.org, accessed on 19 December 2007.

http://www.efqm.org/Default.aspx?tabid=35, accessed on 5 September 2008.

http://www.efqm.org/success-stories/customer-and-people-oriented, accessed on 17 September 2014.

http://www.quality.nist.gov/Ambassador/Slides/Criteria%20for%20Performance%20Excellence.ppt#6, accessed on 19 December 2007.

http://www.quality.nist.gov/PDF_files/2008_Business_Nonprofit_Criteria.pdf, accessed on 5 September 2008.

http://www.qualityaustria.com/uploads/media/recognition_book_2013.pdf, accessed on 17 September 2014.

http://www.schwarz.at/de/alpenresort-schwarz/aktuelles/alpenresort-schwarz-erhaelt-das-praedikat-exzellent-vom-deutschen-wellness-verband-wp427-33.html#comments, accessed on 17 September 2014.

http://www.schwarz.at/de/alpenresort-schwarz/
auszeichnungen/, accessed on 17 September 2014.

http://www.sebi.gov.in/Index.jsp?contentDisp=
AboutSEBI, accessed on 5 September 2008.

http://www.thehindubusinessline.com/2006/09/01/
stories/2006090102460300.htm, accessed on 6
September 2008.

http://www.ustr.gov/assets/Document_Library/
Reports_Publications/2001/2001_NTE_Report/
asset_upload_file786_6575.pdf, accessed on
5 September 2008.

Ruben, Brent D. (1999), 'Towards a balanced scorecard of higher education: Rethinking the college
and universities excellence framework', Higher
Education Forum, QCI Centre for Organizational
Development and Leadership, Rutgers
University, http://www.qci.rutgers.edu, accessed
on 2 January 2006.

19 Ethics in Service Firms

OBJECTIVES

After reading this chapter you will be able to understand the

- concept of ethics and values
- importance of ethics in an organization
- guiding principles of ethics
- describe ethics in an organizational context
- myths around organizational ethics
- issues relating to ethics in service firms

Business Ethics: Why are They Assuming Importance?

Good ethics and corporate governance are considered important behavioural traits that can help an organization build brand equity and ensure stable growth for the company. As companies globalize, marketing, manufacturing, and distribution networks are being set up abroad. But as this happens, ethics and governance are topics that should gain more importance. It represents the responsibility of the company towards all its stakeholders, employees, and the government. Making ethics part of the organizational culture has to be an ongoing process. Training programmes can help employees to consider their value systems when they are faced with ethical dilemmas. Global companies have customers who demand to see and expect ethical behaviour and governance. This refers to documentation, systems, and processes such as ISO 9001 and CMM.

This essentially helps establish credibility and governance policies and processes, to help the company be the next 'wave' globally. Thus, it becomes the company's responsibility to put in place some strong governance policies and help them lead by example. These policies go a long way in helping them to establish best practices in the industry.

The trend in India is very positive as it has been seen that the corporate sector in India is moving towards zero tolerance towards instances of misconduct or erratic behaviour of employees. For example, in companies such as Coca-Cola, TCS, and KPMG, a recruit whose ethics are suspect, are refused. Companies like Motorola expect their employees to under commit and over-deliver, while Infosys puts in value systems on the wall to ensure that everybody follows them.

After going through the chapter, you will be able to answer the following question:

How important are business ethics in a country like India?

INTRODUCTION

The words 'ethics' and 'values' have been in use since ages. However, the aspect and meaning ascribed to these words has been different. This chapter attempts to reconcile some of the views on the subject and analyses them for managerial implications. The Oxford dictionary defines *values* as moral or professional standards of behaviour, principle, artistic, legal, and scientific values, and *ethics* as a science that deals with morals. Chakraborty (1991) elaborates that values serve the process of 'becoming' in the sense of transformation of the level of consciousness, purer higher levels. They help us distinguish between the 'desired' and the 'desirable', between the 'delectable' and the 'electable', and between the 'short-term' and the 'long-term'. While education is more germane to values, training relates more closely to skills.

ETHICS

Miller (1960) states that ethics is a part of reality. It is the recognition of and responsibility for the realities involved in any relationship. He believes that God's will is done when man relates himself to the task of bringing creation to its fullest expression. Human relationships are of three orders:
1. *With things:* which are below human beings in creation. It signifies dominance.
2. *With persons:* who are alongside. It signifies mutuality.
3. *With God:* who is above human beings. It signifies dependence.

Any attempt to treat a relationship other than as in reality, denies the basic reality of the relationship. Ethics, as elaborated by Miller, is respecting other individuals' dignity and entity. It also gives a direction for formulation of ethics with respect to various entities.

Ethics is about honouring one's word. It is to stand by your commitment and carry conviction in your action. There are no overtones of being right or wrong, for these are subjective words. This can have negative implications also, because if someone stands for something outrageous and stands up with conviction, it can have serious repercussions. The guiding spirit for the conviction must come from a well thought out process of self analysis and analysis of the context. It is here that one's sense of judgement becomes important.

Ethics cannot be talked of in an absolute sense since there are a number of elements attached to them, so there are bound to be differences. However, the important thing is that ethics becomes meaningful when supported by analysing the context and applying judgemental power. 'A person will be committed to values only when he sees them to be precious to him. People make such choices that make them feel good' (Shah 1995).

Sources of Values

Steiner (1975) remarks that there are five principal repositories of values that influence a businessperson—religious, philosophical, cultural, legal, and professional. A common bond threaded through these systems binds together the great majority of individuals in a society.

Classification

It is desirable to classify ethics into two categories—(1) professional ethics; and (2) personal ethics.

Professional ethics   These reflect the ethics or commitment of word in the worklife. It relates to one's commitment to professionally laid out principles and objectives.

Personal ethics   These reflect one's value system and feelings about a number of issues.

Both professional and personal ethics have a common core. There has to be an overlap between the two. Ethics are like habits; they reflect in all circumstances. A person who is committed will maintain commitment in all relationships. A person in the habit of lying will lie even without the circumstances demanding it.

Ethics in Business

Although philosophical debates about ethics can be traced back to antiquity (Small 1993), it is only relatively recently that there appears to have been a marked surge in interest in the area of business ethics as a discipline.

Smith and Johnson (1996) point out that, for instance, one orientation is to identify business ethics with application of normative ethical theory to business (for example, Ozar 1979; Davis 1982; Goodpaster and Matthews 1982; and Velasquez 1988).

Velasquez (1988) argues that business ethics is applied ethics. It is the application of our understanding of what is good and right to the assortment of institutions, technologies, transactions, activities, and pursuits which we call 'business'.

This implies that even with the systematic attempt to integrate models of moral problem-solving with practical moral dilemmas in business, there may be no one correct solution to a given problem. There may be different explanations for alternate solutions. This situation raises two issues. Firstly, that of praxis—business ethics is an applied, practical area of investigation. It is not simply the study of ethical thought divorced from the social context of business activities. Its test bed must be business environments with all their complexity, confusion, and uncertainty. Secondly, there is no one set of universally agreed cannon. Instead, any business practitioner is confronted by an array of competing views, derived from moral philosophies, each articulating different prescriptions about what is good or bad for the conduct of business behaviour.

Raphael (1981) puts the issue quite succinctly when he observes that in philosophy, far more than in science, one is left in the end with a number of possible theories, none of them proved, none of them definitely disproved. The individual must then decide for himself which, if any, to accept. So, do not expect moral philosophy to solve the practical problems of life or to be a crutch on which you can lean. A study of philosophy makes it more necessary, not less, to stand on your own feet, to be self critical, and to be obliged to choose for yourself.

As Raphael implies, perhaps the main value of moral philosophy to the businessperson is its ability to facilitate critical self-reflection rather than the provision of clear guidelines that enable the construction of optimal solutions. Of the problem, some commentators avoid defining business ethics purely in terms of the application of ethical theory to business affairs. For instance, De George (1986) argues that business ethics is an interdisciplinary field in which the methodologies of the various areas of business education are as applicable as those of ethical and philosophical analysis. McHugh (1988) provides a good induction of this variety of academic influence when he indicates that there are a dozen or so disciplines which can be said to have a claim to providing an input to business ethics. These include philosophy, sociology, psychology, history, law, politics, and economics.

The subject matter of business ethics is more than an individual responsibility and the application of moral beliefs to business practice.

There will be different answers to ethical issues depending on the assumptions or 'mode of engagement', of whoever is proposing the answers. Many commentators (e.g., Buchholz 1989; Stace 1988; and Sumner 1988) have differentiated what may be called 'prescriptive', 'cognitive', or 'absolutist' moral statements from what are termed, 'descriptive', 'non-cognitive', and 'relativist' moral statements. How a person is oriented with regard to this dichotomy determines the extent to which he or she believes it is possible to specify what is good or bad, right or wrong, for people in general, and for members of business organizations.

Typically, Hoffman and Moore (1990) observe that 'It is…the study of what is good and right for the human being. It asks what goals people ought to pursue and what actions they ought to perform. Business ethics is a branch of applied ethics; it studies the relationship of what is good and what is right to business.'

CODE OF ETHICS IN THE ORGANIZATIONAL CONTEXT

Code of ethics is a formal statement of the company's values concerning social issues. The purpose of a code of ethics is to communicate to employees in plain language what the company stands for. Codes of ethics are valuable when they explicitly state those behaviours that are expected and those that will not be tolerated, and are backed by management's actions. Without top management support, there is no assurance that the code will be followed. Codes serve to remind employees of existing values and guidelines and to tell the public at large what the company stands for.

Why must Business Pursue Ethical Practice?

Steiner (1975) writes, 'Businessmen think that practising good ethics will help their business because customers repeat sales, employees like to work for an ethical manager, a good reputation will attract business, a reputation for sharp business practice is not an asset, and consistent behaviour is valued by customers'.

In the organizational context, ethics can have the following implications:

Motivation   A leader's staunch belief in certain values, which can improve productivity, can be transcended to his subordinates. The motivating power should be the benefits attached to adopting a particular set of values.

Interpersonal ethics   In an organization, if the commitments between various departments are kept, deadlines are adopted, and work gets done, then surely we can have more efficient organizations.

Customers   A word of commitment made by the organization with customers, if kept, can win loyal customers, for example, companies proclaiming service time of 4 hours in case of breakdown must stand up to it. In the long-run, these are the factors which shape the organizational futures.

The value management may, therefore, be precisely said to be the development of an individual's self-management in a community. It involves the development of personal commitment to the company as well as to a set of necessary rules and to psycho-social responsibilities.

Thus, every profession has certain professional ethics, which must be adhered to. A person deviates when his/her perception of reality varies and the ends become more important than the means themselves. The pursuit of ethics by employees can only be possible when the top management approves it and leads by example. Everyone wants to identify with a dependable person, a person who carries conviction and stands by his/her word. It is a commitment which makes all the difference.

ETHICS AND SERVICE FIRMS

This section offers insights to managers on issues around ethics. Different management sectors are chosen and problems are highlighted.

The pursuit and understanding of ethical issues is critical for service and product firms. The boundaries between traditional manufacturing and service firms are diminishing because the manufacturing firms also look at the service dimension of the products that are being offered. Any cost-intensive product such as automobiles, computer, electricity, and generators, when purchased, also has an after-sales service dimension to it. So, the services attached to the product have a huge revenue generation capacity.

Ethics play an important role in being the foundation for conduct of business and fostering relationships with the consumers. The perception of quality of service relies on factors such as reliability and integrity, which are based on both personal and professional ethics. Every industry has certain professional ethics, which must be adhered to in order to foster lasting relationships with consumers and the society at large. The driving force for long-term sustenance of the businesses will not come from mere marketing gimmicks and promises but from value delivered to the stakeholders, and most importantly, relationships fostered with the communities.

To gain a deeper insight into the range of issues involved in ethics, a few examples will provide issues which could be raised in the domain of service firms.

Management Education

India is a flourishing market for higher education. There are both private and public players. There are nearly about 1,000 management institutes and university departments. Foreign direct investment and liberalization measures have opened up immense opportunities for management jobs. The demand–supply gap has led to an increasing level of entrepreneurship in the service industry. There is still no foreign direct investment in the education segment and there are ambiguities in the regulatory mechanism. The accreditation of private technical institutions is under the purview of All India Council of Technical Education. There have been a lot of cases involving student anxiety over the validity of their degrees. The University Grants Commission (UGC) and All India Council for Technical Education (AICTE), which are responsible for ensuring proper planning and coordinated development of technical education system throughout the country, have identified a lot of institutions that are providing engineering and management education without their approval. Apart from these, there are universities which have closed down indefinitely and created havoc among students and parents alike. There have been cases of severe depression among students. This makes it all the more important for AICTE to keep a check on these unapproved institutions and the so-called 'deemed' universities without UGC's approval. The ethical factor to understand here is whether it is fair on these institutions to play with student's useful years for the sake of their business and profits.

The last few years have witnessed the mushrooming of numerous private institutions. Management institutes face severe dearth of faculty, lack of systematized mechanism for quality control, lack of research orientation, inadequate research infrastructure, poor delivery mechanism, and hence, poor output. These problems are a major challenge for Tier II and Tier III management schools. The Tier I schools include the IIMs, IITs, and other premium management institutions in India. The signalling effect of education is lost and firms have to make massive investments in de-learning and re-training the graduates emanating from some of these institutions.

The Private University Bill has been passed in some of the states in India. There are a few private universities which have been set up in India. However, in Chhattisgarh there were over hundred universities created in a span of less than one year. This resulted in small time institutes registering themselves as universities and admitting students in various programmes.

There was then a Supreme Court ruling which took away the status of private university from many of these institutions. This created a lot of confusion in the market and many of the students who had already taken admission in the so-called universities had to confront a lot of problems later, as the existence of that university was no long valid.

This raises further, the ethical issues of motive of existence for such service firms. There are issues of charging hefty fees without offering corresponding student experience. There have also been issues on offering placement for such students.

Admissions to Schools

Admissions of students to primary schools in Delhi have been a very contentious issue. Most of the private schools in Delhi had cumbersome admission procedures. There are long queues for filling up forms, questionnaires to be filled, with complex questions assessing one's view on the philosophy of life. Parents as well as children are interviewed. The court intervened and has now mandated certain criteria for regulating admissions to the primary schools. The question is: Should a three and a half year-old child and his parents be interviewed for admission to the primary school? What ethical issues are involved here?

Health Care

This is another sector wherein lots of ethical debates have arisen. Some of the questions which have been raised are:

1. Should tests on animals be banned?
2. What should the firms disseminate to people who are willing to go in for clinical trials for new drug development?
3. Should patients be advised of the consequent side effects of drugs administered to them?
4. What are the consequences of carelessness on the part of hospital staff when a patient is undergoing treatment in the hospital?

Also, another issue dominating the Indian health-care scenario is the rampant illegal trade of organs. China and India are the leading nations in terms of illegal organ trade. The ethical issues arising in this case are kidneys being removed without informing the patients and refusal to pay as promised for the donation.

Telecom

This is an emerging area in services and hence then are a lot of issues, which may lie in the domain of ethics, and which could be discussed. Some of these issues are:

- Should firms be offering lifetime connections for mobile phones? The tenure of licensing to operate in a region is fixed. So, is it ethical to make offers which may not hold valid when external circumstances change?
- Mobile phone users in India get numerous promotional SMS messages and automated calls for product promotions. Is it not an invasion of privacy for a consumer? Is it ethical for mobile phone companies to share the mobile number database for commercial purposes?
- Mobile service operators offer free phones at lower prices clubbed with services, which may already be obsolete in terms of technology. Is it ethical to offer that stock at subsidized prices to the consumers?

RESEARCH INSIGHT

Establishing Ethical Boundaries for Service Providers: A Narrative Approach
Bush, Victoria, Sharon Harris, and Alan Bush (1997), 'Establishing ethical boundaries for service providers: A narrative approach', *Journal of Services Marketing*, vol. 11, no. 4, pp. 265–277.

The arena of services marketing provides numerous opportunities for ethical violations. As competition intensifies, service providers strive harder to please the customer which can increase the temptation to make ethical compromises. The paper presents the narrative paradigm as a normative model for ethical decision-making in the services marketing environment. The narrative paradigm is learned through socialization and can be applied to the performances of service providers. By viewing services rendered from the narrative perspective, service marketers may be able to discern hidden moral issues or potential controversial activities. It goes on to introduce the concept of services as a performance and the current status of ethics in marketing with implications for the service industry. The paper introduces the narrative paradigm and gives examples of how it can be applied to the service marketing environment.

SUMMARY

This chapter introduces the concept of ethics and values and provides an overview of the same. The sources of ethics have been explained and its importance in an organization is discussed. While explaining the concept of ethics in an organizational context, the guiding principles around ethics are also provided. The chapter also provides an insight on issues of ethics in service firms.

There could be a range of ethical issues which could arise related with a service offering. These could be related with keeping up the promises made to the consumer, or the delivery mechanism of the same, or other aspects related to the conduct of the business. The service firms need to be extremely cautious of the perception that they are creating in the mind of the consumer.

This chapter also addresses some of the myths associated with ethics. The code of ethics in an organizational context has also been discussed. The benefits of managing ethics at the workplace have also been discussed.

KEY TERMS

Code of conduct   A set of conventional principles and expectations that are considered binding on any person who is a member of a particular group.
Corporate governance   The manner in which organizations, particularly limited companies, are managed, and the nature of accountability of the managers to the owners.

Ethics   A science that deals with morals.
Myths   A fiction or half-truth, especially one that forms part of an ideology.
Values   They are moral or professional standards of behaviour—principle, artistic, legal, or scientific.

EXERCISES

Concept Review Questions

1. What interventions should firms initiate to create the perception of being an ethical organization?
2. What are the common elements of ethical issues raised in select services sectors as enumerated?
3. Evaluate the principles which govern ethics in an organization.

Critical Thinking Questions

1. SMS (short messaging services) in India are an acceptable way of communicating. Consumers are constantly bombarded with SMS messages by various firms. Consumers can choose the 'do not disturb' facility offered by mobile service operators, but even then the customer has no respite.

Please analyse the situation from an ethical perspective.

2. Is it right to overbook an aircraft and then offload passengers at the last minute in a budget airline? Please evaluate from an ethical perspective.

3. In India, the demand for higher education is greater than the supply. Higher education institutions use various techniques for eliminating applications for various courses. Please analyse the situation from the ethics viewpoint.

Internet Exercises

1. Browse through the website of Infosys and Tata Consultancy Services. Compare and contrast the ethical principles followed by the two firms.

2. Identify issues of ethics for the hotel industry by choosing a particular country's context.

CASE STUDY — **Information Technology, Corporate Business Firms, and Sustainable Development: Lessons from Cases of Success in India***

This paper critically analyses some cases of success of interventions initiated either by corporate firms or supported by the corporate firms which lead to community development. These cases highlight practices, which can be adapted in any part of the world. These interventions are a win-win situation both for the firms and the communities involved. A multiple case study approach has been adopted. The range of interventions vary from being very specific to being very wide in their approach, and help the grass-roots level communities to emerge out of the poverty trap. The analysis culminates in development of a framework, which attempts to link the nature of the intervention with the stage of development. The study concludes that the interventions have to be linked with the stage of development and resource strength in a particular geographical location. The resource may be a raw material or manpower, which can lead to the turnaround of that region. Where the stage of development is low and where people do not even have access to basic amenities, the nature of interventions have to be wide so as to simultaneously have positive impacts on food, shelter, water, education, employment, and women empowerment (as in SWRC Barefoot College initiative). In such cases, sophisticated technologies may not generate the desired effect.

For areas which have some basic resources, IT and other related technologies can be channelized as in the case of HP and TARAhaat for evolving new commercial products and services. The ITC case study is an outstanding example of self-sustaining intervention which leads to identification of a new business channel, and which also empowers rural communities and brings in efficiency in the business processes. The policy implications are suggested and pointers towards aspects that need to be taken care of to make these interventions successful have also been delved upon.

Each country has a unique historical background and a culture which needs to be preserved. Blind aping of western models for initiating development is not healthy as that replicates the same culture diluting the individualistic characteristics. This research which reflects the participative approach directed to alleviate poverty and empower people at the grass-roots levels. These are interventions which have been initiated and targeted at various stages of development. The nature and extent of intervention varies as it moves from a lower stage of development to a higher stage. The development in a country can be sustainable if strategies are aligned to the resources available in abundance. The study proposes models for development and links the nature

---

* Jauhari, V. (2005), 'Information technology, corporate business firms and sustainable development: Lessons from cases of success from India', *Journal of Services Research*, vol. 5, no. 2, October 2005–March 2006. Reprinted with the permission of *Journal of Services Research*.

of intervention with the stage of development of that geographical area.

The ITC E-choupal Initiative

This is an experiment which demonstrates the identification of strengths that exist at village level, identification of a methodology which results in higher incomes, use of information technology which creates empowerment, and redefines the roles of individuals. It also demonstrates a unique innovation on the part of the corporate firms to redefine the supply chain management practices, which contributes to added value.

ITC is an Indian diversified firm which operates in the area of tobacco, hotels, consumer products, and agri-based products. The corporate aim was to:

- become India's largest agri-produce processor, servicing 1,00,000 villages covering 10 million farmers by 2007
- create an information superhighway to the rural economy
- establish a single point of contact between farmers and a range of suppliers of agri inputs and consumer goods—Monsanto, Eicher, and Nagarjuna Fertilizers.

The Indian Backdrop

One of the interventions suggested to alleviate poverty is to increase the productivity of small farmers. Seventy per cent of the world's poorest farmers live in rural areas and depend on agriculture (Human Development Report 2003). A typical village in India does not have basic amenities such as electricity and water. Illiteracy levels are high. However, the same group became adept at using e-commerce, which changed their lives. At the same time it is also interesting to see how the rural market in India behaves with regard to the demand for consumer goods (Table 19.1).

In agricultural products, there are *mandi*s, which are agricultural markets set up by the state governments to procure agricultural produce directly from the farmers. Table 19.2 lists the number of villages and *haat*s in India. Located in high production centres of different crops, these markets can be

Table 19.1 Distribution of villages in India

Population	Number of villages	% of Total villages
Less than 200	1,14,267	17.9
200–499	1,55,123	24.3
500–999	1,59,400	25.0
1000–1999	1,25,758	19.7
2000–4999	69,135	10.8
5000–9999	11,618	1.8
10,000 and above	3,064	0.5
Total number of villages	6,38,365	

Table 19.2 Villages and haats in India

State/UT	Number of villages (number of haats)
Jammu & Kashmir	6,652 (NA)
Himachal Pradesh	19,831 (10)
Punjab	12,729 (16)
Chandigarh	24 (0)
Uttarakhand	16,805 (NA)
Haryana	6,955 (0)
Delhi (rural)	165 (28)
Rajasthan	41,353 (261)
Uttar Pradesh	1,07,440 (14,121)
Bihar	45,113 (10,681)
Sikkim	452 (19)
Arunachal Pradesh	4,065 (NA)
Nagaland	1,315 (46)
Manipur	2,391 (7)
Mizoram	817 (49)
Tripura	870 (736)
Meghalaya	6,023 (319)
Assam	26,247 (4,044)
West Bengal	40,783 (456)

(Contd)

Table 19.2 (Contd)	
State/UT	Number of villages (number of haats)
Jharkhand	32,615 (NA)
Orissa	51,352 (3,887)
Chhattisgarh	20,308 (NA)
Madhya Pradesh	5,392 (NA)
Gujarat	18,544 (NA)
Daman & Diu	23 (0)
Dadar & Nagar Haveli	0 (6)
Maharashtra	43,722 (3,578)
Karnataka	29,483 (1241)
Andhra Pradesh	8,183 (NA)
Goa	359 (8)
Lakshadweep	24 (0)
Kerala	1,364 (670)
Tamil Nadu	16,317 (1169)
Puducherry	92 (0)
Andaman & Nicobar	547 (0)

Table 19.3   Regulated agri-produce markets (*mandis*) in India

State	Number of *mandis*
Andhra Pradesh	23
Assam	35
Bihar	828
Goa	5
Gujarat	30
Haryana	75
Himachal Pradesh	29
Karnataka	44
Kerala	5
Madhya Pradesh	84
Maharashtra	827
Orissa	123
Punjab	667
Rajasthan	384
Tamil Nadu	270
Tripura	21
Uttar Pradesh	645
West Bengal	456
Chandigarh	3
Delhi	17
Pondicherry	5

categorized as grain *mandis*, cotton *mandis*, soya *mandis*, etc. There are about 6,800 *mandis* in India (Table 19.3). The average population catered to by each *mandi* is 1.36 lakh. Most agricultural areas with population more than 10,000 have *mandis*.

Annamalai and Rao (2003) have criticized the *mandi* system, stating that it does not serve the farmer well and is burdened by inefficiency. Depending on the geographic proximity, the farmer takes his goods to the nearest *mandi*. The system is viewed as based on exploitation. There are multiple points before the supplies are bought that contribute to wastage.

The Business Model (ITC)

The model is centred on a network of *e-choupals*, or information centres equipped with a computer connected to the Internet, located in rural villages. ITC appointed *sanchalak*s (coordinators) and *samyojak*s (collaborators) into the system as the provider of logistics support. Each *e-choupal* serves about 10 villages within a five-kilometre radius. There are a million farmers being served in nearly 11,000 villages through 2000 *e-choupals* in four states (Madhya Pradesh, Karnataka, Andhra Pradesh, and Uttar Pradesh).

Traditionally, the soya or wheat crop would be traded at *mandis*. Farmers were exploited by traders, who often bought the wheat at low prices claiming it to be of poor variety. Storage, transport, and handling facilities were limited. So, intermediaries like traders were needed.

Intermediary margins were high, accurate market signals were non-existent, wastage was rampant, and processing yields were low. Conventionally, a typical farmer would sell to a small trader called the *kaccha adat*. This man in turn, sold it to a larger trader called the *pakka adat*. From here the produce found its way to the local *mandi* where a large trader came into the picture. Going through a loop like this meant procurement costs were as high as ₹700 per tonne of soya. In addition, there were losses in transit and a tax burden as well. This is reflected in Fig. 19.1.

Brokers compare these statistics with the American mid-west market. Its farmers produce 36 bushels of wheat per acre, one of the highest yields per acre and its millers achieve flour extraction levels of 75%. Average waste levels are 2%, which are the lowest in the world and well ahead of the 8–11% in India. Wheat farmers in the US now get 92% of the delivered mill price as opposed to less than 70% that Indian farmers now take home. ITC started the process of disintermediation. So, by providing the information access to the farmer rather than the intermediary, the value is added directly.

The ITC Model for Soya Procurement

So, ITC identified coordinators at the village level who were called *sanchalaks*, who used the net to provide spot quotes after examining the produce sample. If the price was right, the farmers would take the produce to the ITC collection centre. The *samyojaks* were the collaborators who would coordinate the group of villagers. They would perform the documentation work and supply farm inputs from ITC and partner companies to *sanchalaks*. They would also build relationships with the *sanchalaks* and farmers.

When ITC started the experiment it was the middle of 1990s. ITC first leased few centres and started scouting for villages around these centres. The computer was placed at the *sanchalak*'s house who would head each *choupal*. He was trained to use the computer. He was carefully chosen so that farmers could trust him—neither too big, which would distance him, nor so small that he may not be respected. ITC started to pump information on *mandi* prices through the Internet to the *sanchalak*'s home. Information on best farming practices and weather forecasts were also made. The *sanchalaks* were paid 0.5% for each tonne of soya that originated from their *choupal*. There were commission agents in *mandis* whose role was redefined by ITC. They were called *samyojaks* or coordinators. They would use their ties to nominate *sanchalaks* but also do the relevant *mandi* documentation. For villages situated far off, the *samyojaks* would aggregate the grain and bring it to ITC. For this he was paid a commission of 1%. As a result, ITC reduced the cost of procurement from ₹700 a tonne to ₹200 per tonne. This is reflected in Fig. 19.2.

Financial Feasibility

On an average it cost ₹40,000 to set up a basic *choupal*. In places where connectivity was poor ITC had to invest in VSATs. These investments escalated

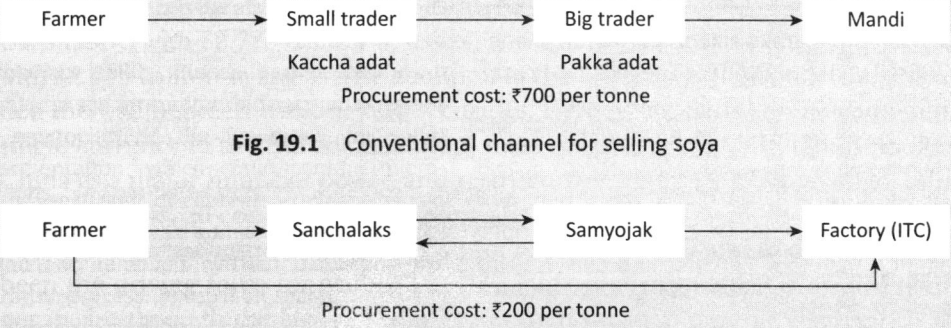

Fig. 19.1 Conventional channel for selling soya

Fig. 19.2 E-choupals

the costs to ₹1 lakh. In Madhya Pradesh alone, when the experiment started ITC had 1,045 *e-choupals* spread over 6,000 villages serving over six lakh farmers. This was for soya crop which was a five million tonne crop in Madhya Pradesh. For it wheat was 14 times bigger.

ITC's Game Plan

There would be 1.5 million outlets in the country. There would be an army of mobile traders and cycle distributors. There would be a huge earning on transaction fees for every deal that took place. The market for agricultural products is valued at ₹1,75,000 crore. The tobacco market is just ₹15,000 crore. So, it makes a lot of business sense to diversify the risks and add new business areas, which also contribute not only to the bottom lines but to the profitability as well. The investment made by ITC would be recovered in five years for wheat procurement. The infrastructure created can be used for other purposes as well. It also sets up a relationship at the grassroots level. In years to come, this can open doors for more revenues to come in as it will also expose the community to new products.

ITC had tied up with Monsanto for seed selling. The FMCG products and consumer durables could be delivered through the same network.

The investments in the e-commerce initiatives are different as compared to the normal manufacturing operations. The cost curves for e-based businesses also behave differently. Choi et al. (1997) and Choi and Whinston (2000), discuss investments in the e-businesses. The total cost curves of many physical products and services are U-shaped. First, as the quantity increases the cost declines; but later, the cost increases due to the growth of both the fixed and the variable costs (especially administrative and marketing costs). In contrast with digital products, the variable costs per unit are low and almost fixed, regardless of the quantity. Therefore, cost per unit declines as quantity increases due to pro-ration of the fixed component of the cost over more units. This results in increasing returns with increasing sales (Turban et al. 2002).

Most FMCGs currently operate where they are viable while servicing populations above 1,00,000. There are enormous pockets of widely dispersed markets where population sizes are below 2,000. ITC with 1.5 million outlets across the country, an army of mobile traders, and cycle based distributors, claim to understand the nuances of catering to these populations. By collaborating with ITC, a potential seller does not have to invest in infrastructure. ITC simply takes a small transaction fee for every transaction, for every deal taking place on its network. The market for agricultural produce is ₹1,75,000 crore, out of which ITC only accounts for ₹15,000 crore.

Comparison with Traditional Models

The agribusiness initiatives taken by some of the other farmers have not been successful. Initiatives by some of the well-known companies such as Mahindra and Mahindra, Tata Chemicals, EID Parry, Rallis, and Nagarjuna Fertilizers took up agribusiness ventures by setting their own models. Most of them faced problems for growth. The 'Shubh Labh' venture started by Mahindras had set up 36 centres in 10 states by the end of 2002. Even ikisan.com (Nagarjuna Fertilizers), Indiagriline.com, and Parry's corner (EID Parry), which tried to create an e-marketplace could not scale up.

Problems

Firstly, there was a lack of trust from the farmers as these models depended on the intermediaries who were not trusted by the farmers. Secondly, these models had high fixed costs. The fixed cost of a Rallis Kendra was ₹0.5 million to 0.6 million, whereas the variable cost came up to ₹1 million (this included the cost of a PC, telephone, furniture, 2–3 motorcycles for field staff, rentals, and salaries). Rallis covered 20,000 acres but could not scale up. Every centre had 6–8 employees. For 10 centres, 60 people were to be employed. Taking an average salary of ₹0.15 million would mean an outflow of ₹100 million per month in salaries itself. Unless volumes went up, operating costs would be high.

Thirdly, there were issues of channel conflict. Also, many companies did not have enough knowledge in procurement. Corporations need the organizational knowledge of handling samples. The market does not reward you for scaling, but for taking positions.

From the organization's perspective, profits do not come easy in the agribusiness unless the organization has sufficient control over the supply chain of the agricultural produce. In Madhya Pradesh, the farmers were located in remote villages scattered throughout the state. The next issue before the organization was that of the middlemen for obtaining good quality products. The middlemen exerted influence on the farmers by concealing the prevailing market prices and other related information. They made large profits for themselves by blocking access to such information.

On the farmers' side, there were issues such as they were trapped in a vicious circle of low investment, low productivity, weak market orientation, low value addition, low margin, and low risk-taking ability. So the paradoxical condition was that despite abundant natural resources, Indian farmers remained globally uncompetitive. This was evident in Indian performance on the global scale. The immediate aim for the *e-choupal* initiative was to integrate ITC's association with rural suppliers as well as to develop new markets for its own and third-party goods.

The rural symphony started in Madhya Pradesh, which was dominated with firms such as Ruchi Industries. ITC soya *choupals* are located all over Madhya Pradesh and cater to more than 6,000 villages. The vision is to get farmers a better price for their crops.

 You can visit the Online Resource Centre for more on such cases.

Conclusion

There is no unique solution for development efforts. Different geographical areas are at different stages of development and therefore, one solution cannot be an answer. A mix of interventions is required. The solution may have technology ITC Initiative:

- The initiative such as the one taken by ITC in India is an interesting case. There is a resource base available.
- The effort is directed at system inefficiencies and then linked with improving procurement from the villages. It results in cost savings for the farmer.
- It opens new doors of opportunity for the firm for additional revenues. It gives impetus for expanding into more areas for procurement. ITC started with soya procurement and then moved over to wheat procurement.
- Here, initiatives such as those by HP and the barefoot college can bring in a holistic development and empowerment of communities.

The interventions that are initiated have to be sustainable and self-propagating. So, an important dimension is the financial feasibility to create a spiral effect that leads to that region's growth. ITC's model is an indication that being commercially savvy and also having community orientation is possible. There is a huge potential to convert the latent demand into an active demand and bring in new numbers in the list of potential consumers.

The involvement of the local community and their role makes a huge difference. There is a need to redefine the roles and also make them understand the outcome of such interventions. When there is a realization that such interventions will lead to a larger good of the community, then their motivation levels are higher. Corporates will have to look for such unique value drivers, which may not just come through artificial means such as expenditure on advertising. After all, many products that actually sell in the market do so because of the superficial differentiation. So, efforts which are directed at doing things differently, which lead to a positive impact on the resource usage and recycling the existing resources, will be desirable.

ITC management of the bureaucracy is also unique. When *e-choupals* were conceived, they faced a fundamental regulatory obstacle. The Agricultural Produce Marketing Act, under whose aegis *mandis* were established, prohibits procurements outside the *mandi*. ITC did not use the *mandi* infrastructure and invested on building the electronic infrastructure. Since ITC paid the tax on the produce sourced, it did not risk the relationship with the government and *mandis*.

Question

What are the lessons on ethics that you have learnt from the discussion of ITC in this case study?

REFERENCES

Al Gini (1998), 'Moral leadership and business ethics', in *Ethics the Heart of Leadership*, Joanne B. Ciulla (ed.), Praeger, London.

Annamalai, K. and Sachin Rao (2003), *What Works: ITC's E-Choupal and Profitable Rural Transformation*, World Resources Institute.

Assisi, C. and I. Gupta (2003), 'ITC's rural symphony', *Business World*, 10 January.

Buchholz, R.A. (1989), *Fundamental Concepts and Problems in Business Ethics*, Prentice Hall, Englewood Cliffs, New Jersey.

Chakraborty, S.K. (1991), *Management by Values towards Cultural Congruence*, Oxford University Press, New Delhi.

Choi, S.Y. and A.B. Whinston (2000), *The Internet Economy: Technology and Practice*, Smartcon.com, Austin, Texas.

Choi, S.Y. et al. (1997), *The Electronics of Electronic Commerce*, Macmillan, Indianapolis, Indiana.

Cooke, R.A. (1986), 'Business ethics at the crossroads', *Journal of Business Ethics,* vol. 5, pp. 259–263.

Davis, M. (1982), 'Conflict of interest 2', *Business and Professional Ethics Journal*, vol. 1, no. 4, pp. 17–29.

De George, R.T. (1986), 'Replies and reflections on theology and business ethics', *Journal of Business Ethics,* vol. 5, pp. 521–524.

Doft, Richard L. (1985), *Management*, Dryden Press, Chicago.

Donaldson, T. (1989b), *The Ethics of International Business*, Oxford University Press, New York.

Dunn, D. and K. Yamashita (2003), 'Micro capitalism and the mega corporation', *Harvard Business Review*, August.

Epstein, E.M. (1989), 'Business ethics—Corporate good citizenship and the corporate social policy process: A view from the United States', *Journal of Business Ethics*, vol. 8, pp. 583–595.

Goodpaster, K.E. and J.B. Matthews (1982), 'Can a corporation have a conscience?', *Harvard Business Review*, vol. 60, no. 1, pp. 132–140.

Grenier, Louise (1998), 'Working with indigenous knowledge', *A Guide for Researchers*, IRDC.

Hofstede, G. (1991), *Culture and Organization: Software of the Mind*, McGraw-Hill, London.

Holliday, C. (2001) 'Sustainable growth, the DuPont way', *Harvard Business Review*, pp. 129–134.

Hornsby, A.S. (1993), *Oxford Advanced Learners Dictionary,* Oxford University Press, Calcutta.

Hoffman, M. and J.M. Moore (1990), *Business Ethics: Reading and Cases in Corporate Morality*, 2nd edn, McGraw-Hill, New York.

Human Development Report (2003), Oxford University Press, New Delhi.

Joanne B. Ciulla (1998), 'Leadership ethics: Mapping the territory', in B. Ciulla (ed.), *Ethics: The Heart of Leadership*, Joanne Praeger, London.

MacIntyre, A. (1989), *A Short History of Ethics*, Macmillan Press, London.

Mahoney, J. (1990), 'An international look at business ethics', *Journal of Business Ethics,* vol. 9, pp. 545–550.

McHugh, F.P. (1988), *Keyguide to Information Source in Business Ethics*, Nichols, New York.

Miller, Samuel H. (1960), 'The tangle of ethics', *Harvard Business Review*, Jan–Feb.

Ozar, D.T. (1979), *The Moral Responsibility of Corporations in Ethical Issues in Business*, in T. Donaldson and P. Werhane (eds), Prentice Hall, Englewood Cliffs, New Jersey.

Payne, S.L. and R.A. Giacalone (1990), 'Social psychological approaches to the perception of ethical dilemmas', *Human Relations*, vol. 43, no. 7, pp. 649–665.

Peterson, C., V. Sandell, and A. Lawlor (2001), *What Works: Tarahaat's Portal for Rural India,* World Resources Institute, July.

Pope Pius XI (1985), 'Quadragesimo Anno (On reconstructing the social order)', in David M. Byers (ed.), *Justice in the Marketplace: A Collection of the Vatican and U.S. Catholic Bishops on Economic Policy, 1891–1984*, United States Catholic Conference 61, Washington DC.

Primeaux, P. (1942), 'Experiential ethics: A blueprint for personal and corporate ethics', *Journal of Business Ethics,* vol. 11, pp. 779–788.

Raphael, D.D. (1981), *Moral Philosophy*, Oxford University Press, Oxford.

Reinhardt, F. (2003), 'Tests for sustainability', *The Global Competitiveness Report 2002–03*, Oxford University Press, New York.

Shah, N.B. (1995), 'Value/ethics in management: Relevance and application', in S.K. Chakraborty (ed.), *Human Values for Manager*, Wheeler Publishing, New Delhi.

Small, M.W. (1993), 'Ethics in business and administration: An International and historical perspective', *Journal of Business Ethics*, pp. 293–300.

Smith, Ken and Phil Johnson (1996), *Business Ethics and Business Behaviour*, Thomson, London.

Srinivas, M.N. (1996), *Indian Society through Personal Writings*, Oxford University Press, New Delhi.

Stace, W.T. (1988), *Ethical Relativity and Ethical Absolution in Ethical Issues in Business: A Philosophical Approach*, 3rd edn, in T. Donaldson and P.H. Werhane (eds), Prentice Hall, Englewood Cliffs, New Jersey.

Steiner, G.A. (1975), *Business and Society*, Random House, New York.

Sumner, W.G. (1988), 'A defence of cultural relativism', in T. Donaldson and P.H. Werhane (eds), *Ethical Issues in Business: A Philosophical Approach*, 3rd edn, Prentice Hall, Englewood Cliff, New Jersey.

Transparency International (1996), 'Sharpening the response against global corruption', *Transparency International Global Report 1996*, Berlin.

Turban, E., D. King, J. Lee Warkentin, and M.H. Chung (2002), *Electronic Commerce*, Prentice Hall, New Jersey.

Velasquez, M.G. (1988), *Business Ethics: Concepts and Cases*, 2nd edn, Prentice Hall, Englewood Cliffs, New Jersey.

World Bank (2003), 'World development indicators', The World Bank, Washington.

Sarvani, V. (2003), 'ITC's e-choupal: Taking e-business to farmers', *Case Folio*, July. Also available on www.icfaipress.org.

Sharma, M. (2000), 'Information technology for poverty reduction', www.ouhk.edu.hk/cridal/wrapup/discuss/messages/22.html, accessed on 5 July 2014.

www.ndtv.com (2001), 'Pro poor policies let down by the lack of reform', accessed on 1 March 2001.

20 Strategies for Business Growth

OBJECTIVES

After reading this chapter you will be able to understand the

- strategic management framework for the service industry
- options available for growth of a service firm
- concepts related to green field ventures
- meaning of joint ventures
- concepts related to mergers and acquisitions (M&A), strategic alliances, franchising, and licensing
- relevance of management contracts in emerging forms of entrepreneurship

INTRODUCTION

This chapter elaborates on the strategic management framework for the service industry. It traces the evolution of the strategic management framework. This chapter discusses the various strategic options for growth of a service firm. These options could be green field ventures, joint ventures, mergers and acquisitions (M&A), strategic alliances, franchising, licensing, and management contracts. The factors affecting the choice of entrepreneurship have also been elaborated upon.

STRATEGIC MANAGEMENT FRAMEWORK

Strategy, as has been treated in the conventional management literature, is associated with the growth of the business—keeping in mind the vision and matching external environmental dynamics with the internal resource base in the organization. Andrews (1971) defined the strategy as a match between what a company *can do* (organizational strengths and weaknesses) within a framework of what it *might do* (environmental opportunities and threats). Strategic management literature has postulated several frameworks to further the understanding of the concept of strategy. External business environment influences the strategic behaviour of a firm. For example, a mature industry has a relatively stable business environment, which then elicits behaviour that focuses more on cost-saving and process-related improvements in business. A high-tech industry, however, is characterized by a lot of changes. In such an industry, the product life cycles are short, customer aspirations change very fast, the competition is aggressive, and customers have to be educated about new products—their features and advantages. Examples of these product categories are electronics products, telecommunications, wireless-based products, aeronautics, chemicals, pharmaceuticals, etc.

Since the beginning of strategic management discipline, the four major corporate strategy frameworks that have emerged are strengths, weaknesses, opportunities, and threats (SWOT) in the 1960s, strategic planning matrix in the 1970s, competitiveness in the 1980s, and core competencies in the 1990s. There is also abundant literature available on style of leadership, which has an impact on the behaviour and orientation of a firm. The leadership may vary from being bureaucratic to entrepreneurial. The organization structure and the business environmental behaviour have also been explored in strategic management literature.

Resource-based View of Firm

It combines the internal analysis of the phenomenon within companies with external analysis of the industry. The resources may be tangible, intangible, and in a form such as supply chain management or managerial capacity. Based on the resource-based framework, the firm can assess its portfolio of products or services on the BCG framework or Ansoff grid parameters. Also, all these resources can be assessed on the following dimensions (Collis and Montgomery 1995):

- Test of inimitability
- Test of substitutability
- Test of durability
- Test of competitive superiority
- Test of appropriability

In all these tests the focus is on this resource base, keeping in mind the market conditions and competitive factors.

Porter's (1980) view on competitive advantage discussed the competitive dynamics of the firm. He has postulated various frameworks which facilitate a better understanding of the firms in light of the competitive dynamics. For instance, the five-force framework or the value chain analysis helps firms to understand the sources of competitive advantage for the firm.

Collis and Montgomery (1998) have even discussed the context in which the resource-based view of the firm could be further analysed. They have pointed out that the resource continuum can be extended across numerous factors such as:

- nature of resources which can vary from general to specialized
- scope of resources which can vary from wide to narrow
- coordination mechanisms which vary from transferring to sharing
- control systems which can range from financial to operating systems
- corporate office size which can vary from small to large.

McKinsey's 7-S framework also prescribes a model for managing organizations, which considers the following factors:

- strategy
- shared values
- systems
- skills
- styles
- structure.
- staff

The strategic view of the firm suggests that there should be a source of competitive advantage. This source should be sustainable in the long run.

Sustainable Competitive Advantage

The main reason for analysing competitors is to enable the organization to develop competitive advantages against them, especially advantages that can be sustained over time. The real advantages come from advantages that competitors cannot easily imitate, not those that give only temporary relief from the competitive battle. To be sustainable, competitive advantage needs to be more deeply embedded in the organization—its resources, skills, culture, and investment over time. Sources of sustainable competitive advantage can take many forms, for example:

- differentiation
- superior quality
- low costs
- superior service
- niche marketing
- vertical integration.
- high performance or technology

OPTIONS FOR GROWTH OF SERVICE FIRM

Strategic management takes a long-term perspective of the firm. It helps to chart out long-term plans for growth of the firm. Some of the different options for growth for national and international expansion of the firm are as follows:

- green field ventures
- franchising
- joint ventures
- licensing
- mergers and acquisitions
- management contract.
- strategic alliances

GREEN FIELD VENTURES

A *green field venture* is a firm, which has been started from scratch. It is a new venture created by bringing in capital, land, and labour, and is often a painstaking exercise. The risk in creating a new venture is substantially high. It also varies from industry to industry.

Many firms have grown only by internal or organic development. This means starting the firm's operations from scratch. The advantages of organic growth may be summarized as follows:

- The cost of development is spread over time.
- The firm experiences minimal disruption.
- The firm can build up its own internal team (it does not need to inherit resources, as in an acquisition or merger).

However, there are also obvious disadvantages:

- It can be a slow process and the final cost may be high.
- The means of development is perceived by some to be conservative and cautious.
- There may be operational and bureaucratic delays.
- It may take many years to build up a brand.
- It may be entirely dependent on the promoter's initial vision and his experience may be a limiting factor.

External growth on the other hand is perhaps more visible and can be more risky. Mergers and acquisitions also offer speed in development. They also provide immediate access to necessary resources, knowledge, and competitive positions, which are the other benefits.

JOINT VENTURES

A *joint venture* is an entity that is formed by a legal agreement between two or more parties. The various parties have a financial stake and the profit-sharing arrangement is agreed in advance.

It is also a manifestation of an organization's entrepreneurial orientation. India took the initiative to start joint ventures in the late 1950s. The first Indian joint venture was sanctioned as early as 1959. This paved the way and opened new vistas for closer economic and trade ties between India and other developing countries.

Joint ventures benefit the investing firm, the investing country, and the host country. Some Indian firms had earlier invested abroad due to severe cuts imposed on the expansion of large houses under the Industries Development and Regulation Act and the MRTP Act prior to liberalization, but most of them are lured by the attractive incentives offered by many developing countries in the form of tax holidays, export incentives, freedom to remit profits and repatriate capital, and in many cases, protective tariffs. The Indian entrepreneur gets first-hand market information, widens his contacts, and thus gets an opportunity to increase his exports. For example, Indian joint ventures can be established in Mauritius to take advantage of the benefits offered by the government.

Joint ventures may have the following advantages:

- Lead to increased export of capital goods, spare parts, and components from India.
- Exports of technical know-how and consultancy services also increase.
- It helps in projecting India's image as a supplier of capital goods and technology.
- They can help in the utilization of idle capacity in the capital goods sector and thus, in reducing costs in general.
- They may lead to greater employment.
- The country also gains by greater inflow of foreign exchange in the form of dividends, royalties, and technical know-how fees.
- These also help to achieve India's aim of achieving collective self-reliance and annual cooperation among the developing countries.

Developing countries generally welcome India's joint venture because intermediate labour-intensive technology developed by India is more suited to their requirements, and they can adopt it directly without any or slight modifications. Moreover, most developing countries, because of their limited home market, may not be able to afford large-scale capital intensive technology provided by developed countries and thus prefer the medium-scale technology developed by India. Finally, host countries perceive little threat to their political or economic independence from Indian joint ventures.

Joint ventures in India

Indian companies convince their partners of their clout and influence. The business is secondary; the priority is having a tie-up. However, after the initial enthusiasm, the ardour begins to wane. The transnational—almost invariably, a company with superior financial, managerial, and technological muscle—begins to ask the basic question, 'What can my Indian partner contribute that will endure?' In most cases, the answer is straightforward—nothing. The foreign investor then wants control, whereas the Indian company, with its access to the media and politicians cries foul. This is the first set of problems that are visible. Not enough time is spent by either party to identify their complementary core competencies. The Indian companies keep looking for alternative collaborations. A clash of managerial cultures and styles is inevitable. The problem can be overcome over time if there is investment in training and the development of skills. But this is not something Indian companies are comfortable with. A third set of problems arises when foreign companies want management control since they are bringing in the technology. So, in technology-driven businesses, Indian companies might have to play second fiddle initially. However, there is nothing wrong in this. If Indian managements believe in sustaining their presence in a particular industry, they will see the value of investing in research, technology, and networking, and earn the right to be equal partners.

Joint ventures obviously bring together contrasting management styles. Generalizations are tricky, but it would not be an exaggeration to say that the managerial ethos in Indian companies reflects that of our society—in-egalitarian, stratified, secretive, and top-down. In the final analysis, it is this that creates strain and tension. Transparency is unwelcome not only to Indian politicians, but also to Indian industrialists, as they are used to a feudal system of management. Nationalist slogans are used to garner public support, but the root of the problem lies in the fear of exposure and the loss of control. A joint venture is bound to have its ups and downs, but given a measure of trust, communication, and sensitivity of both sides, things can be managed smoothly.

MERGERS AND ACQUISITIONS

Some definitions regarding takeover and merger are provided in this section.

Takeover of a company means assumption of management control of that company by getting substantial powers of management (Thakur 1995). This is normally done through an acquisition of a sufficient number of shares carrying voting rights and then taking charge of the management of the company by getting appointed to the Board. The purpose of takeover is generally unilateral and the offer company decides the maximum price (Verma 1995).

The draft regulation of SEBI on takeovers does mention takeover and an informal definition of a takeover bid is also given. A *takeover bid* is generally understood to mean an offer made to the holders of securities carrying voting rights in a company or convertible into securities carrying such rights, to acquire their securities for a consideration, the purpose of the offer usually being to acquire control of the company, or consolidate control by the existing management.

The omission of a formal definition seems to be conscious. It seems that the legislature does not want to enter into disputes on whether the acquisition of shares is for a takeover or is a genuine investment. The provisions of the law are triggered as soon as shares exceeding the specified limits are acquired. However, the flip side of this is that when a person purchases shares for a genuine investment, he has to adopt the same procedure as required for a takeover.

Merger or *amalgamation* on the other hand, refers to the physical joining of two companies. This takes place either by dissolving both the companies or forming a new one to take over their businesses, or by one company dissolving and transferring its existence to the other. In a sense, takeover may precede a merger, though a takeover is not necessary for a merger to take place.

Verma (1995) defines merger as the combination of two or more companies into a single company, where one survives and another loses its corporate existence. The survivor acquires the assets as well as liabilities of the merged companies or company. The company which survives is the buyer and retains its identity, while the seller company is extinguished. Merger is also defined as amalgamation. It is the fusion of two or more existing companies. All assets, liabilities, and stock of one company stand transferred to the transferee company in consideration of payment in the form of equity shares of the transferee company, or debentures, or cash, or a mix of two or three modes.

Amalgamation is used interchangeably with merger. The common literal linkage between these two terms is through the word combination. The Oxford dictionary defines both these words as combinations, carrying a sense of mixing or uniting two or more things together, or in the corporate sense, uniting or combining two undertakings together. The essence of amalgamation is blending of two or more existing undertakings into one undertaking, which may take one of the following forms:

- Absorption: This occurs when one or more undertakings blend with another.
- Merger: Two or more undertakings blend to form a new one. This is precisely known as merger, since the blending companies merge their respective separate identities to form a new undertaking.

MERGERS AND ACQUISITIONS IN INDIA

The Indian economy has seen a rise in the mergers and acquisitions (M&A) activity since the liberalization process gathered momentum from 1991 onwards. The number of M&As has increased and each industry is witnessing change. The privatization of industries such as power, steel, and telecom has opened new opportunities. The Monopolistic and Restrictive Trade Practices (MRTP) Act, 1969 that was implemented to check concentration of economic power and control the growth of monopolistic and restrictive trade practices has been weakened. The industrial policy, announced on 24 June 1991 by the government, assured the dismantling of the shackles of the regulatory system. Amendments were made in the MRTP Act, omitting all restrictive sections discouraging the growth of the industrial sector. To attract foreign investment in the industry, relaxations were made for foreign direct investment (FDI) up to 51% foreign equity in high priority industries that has further been enhanced in many sectors. The spate of M&A activity in the industry has increased, led by changes in economic policy.

Further trends in M&A activities in the first quarter of 2014 across the globe indicated that the M&A environment created in 2013 increased acquisition opportunities for those firms which had access to capital.

Additionally, not only did the global deal value increase in 2014, it was of a much higher value due to large mega deals, than due to the deal volume. A KPMG (2014) M&A report quotes several experts, who say that that acquirers have learned the lessons from the previous years and are therefore paying more attention to finding the right strategic fit. It further quotes a technology investment advisor, who stated that clients are more selective with their targets. Therefore, though the deal volume has not increased as anticipated, clients are willing to pay a premium for targets that meet their selection criteria/growth plans. The M&A has also swept the industrial manufacturing sector where the companies are seeking quality of deals; because investors have become more critical and request for more robust growth strategies from the company.

Significance

A study by Jauhari (2001) foresees the impact of liberalization of economy on the M&A activity in the country. This is because of the excess capacities in the Indian industry, over-fragmentation, lack of requisite size of the firm, the firm's viability, lack of financial resources, and commercial orientation. All these factors characterize Indian industry, as the environment was such that a long period of licensing regime ensured that industry could not expand beyond a particular size and political influence helped getting licences for setting up firms. In many sectors, this led to monopolies as a result of which there was little competition. The industry did not really invest in R&D and innovation as it was able to sell whatever was being produced. So, there was no incentive for making any improvements, which led to stagnation in the Indian industry. Suddenly, in 1991, the liberalization process initiated by the government changed the rules of the game. Profitability coupled with productivity and customer orientation became important terms, which Indian industry had been evading for long years. Since the shakeout in the Indian industry is inevitable on account of increased competition, M&A activity is bound to take place. So, it becomes necessary to understand what needs to be kept in mind to manage these better.

According to Thomson Reuters analysis (2014), the global M&A trend has been replicated in India. In FY14, the Indian M&A market registered an aggregate disclosed deal value of US$22.6 billion, representing an increase of 12% against the US$20.1 billion seen in FY2013. Although, the number of M&A transactions involving Indian companies was relatively low in FY14, and stood at 674, which was down by 20% against 843 deals in FY13. It summarized the trend as follows:

- Transactions value increase, replicating global M&A environment trends, with big-ticket announcements driving deal value
- FY14 records deals worth US$22.6 billion, up by 12% compared to FY13
- Cross-border deals dominate, accounting for three-fourths share of all mergers and acquisitions.

Some significant overseas acquisitions by Indian firms since 2007

1. Corus Group (UK)—Acquired by TATA Steel—US$12.11 billion on January, 2007
2. Novelis US—Acquired by Hindalco Industries—US$6 billion February, 2007
3. Algoma Steel Canada—Essar Steel Global—Canadian $1.85 billion on April, 2007
4. Minnesota Steel US—Essar Steel Global—US$1.65 billion on April, 2007
5. Jaguar Cars and Land Rover UK—Acquired by Tata Motors—US$2.3 billion on March, 2008
6. Imperial Energy(UK)—Acquired by ONGC—GB1.3 billion on August, 2008
7. Zain Africa—Acquired by Bharati Airtel—US$10.7 billion on February, 2010
8. Honiton Energy Holdings China—Acquired by Tanti Group—US$2 billion on April, 2010
9. Marcellus Shale US—Reliance Industries–US$1.7 billion on April, 2010
10. Abbot Point Coal Terminal Australia—Adani Enterprises–US$2 billion on May, 2011

Findings

The following are the findings of the study.

M&A activity in India (2012–13)

India's GDP growth rate has continued to stay ahead of other emerging markets because of the resilience of domestic consumption demand, despite depreciating rupee, inflation, and high fiscal deficit. The M&A activity has continued despite slowdown and the total deal activity stood at US$32bn across 738 deals in CY2013. Another reason for the slowdown has been an uncertain political and economic climate.

According to the International Mergers & Acquisitions Review 2014, India faced key challenges in 2013 such as:

- A sluggish growth despite the services sector doing well
- High deficits in both fiscal and current account
- A high inflation of approximately 10% resulting in high inflationary pressure on the economy
- Volatile exchange rate wherein the Indian Rupee (₹) depreciated against the US$.
- Uncertain political scenario.

The year 2013 saw some important overseas acquisitions, for example, Apollo Tyres' acquisition of Cooper Tire for around USD 2.5 billion in the United States, while Oil India's and ONGC Videsh acquired a stake for about USD 2.5 billion in the Rovuma-I gas field in Mozambique.

While the year 2012 saw outbound investments, there was some stability and improvement over 2011 with deal values of about USD 14 billion. These values indicate that the deal activity was broadly tracking the general market sentiment during this period.

Strategically speaking, there were several factors that have motivated Indian corporates to actively focus on the global markets and on cross-border acquisitions. Easy availability of financing has made it easy for companies to make acquisitions and to grow organically across geographies.

Given here is the list of 11 most talked about M&A deals across India:
1. Flipkart–Myntra—$300million (estimated)
2. Asian Paints–ESS Bathroom Products—Amount undisclosed
3. RIL–Network18 Media and Investment—4,000 Crore
4. Merck–Sigma Deal—$17 billion in cash
5. Ranbaxy–Sun Pharmaceuticals—$4 billion
6. TCS–CMC—Amount not disclosed
7. TATA Power–PT Arutmin Indonesia—₹47 billion
8. Tirumala Milk–Lactalis—₹1750($275 million)
9. Aditya Birla Minacs–CSP CX—$260 million
10. Sterling India Resorts–Thomas Cook India—₹870 Crore
11. Yahoo–Bookpad—$15million

The total number of M&As has been increasing every year, though there is a change in the composition of the same. An analysis of M&A activity reveals that the number of acquisitions as a percentage of total M&A activity declined vis-à-vis the number of mergers. This is probably because many more Indian firms are restructuring themselves and are merging different group entities, which explains the increased number of mergers in the second phase.

Following are the reasons why Indian companies have become active in cross-border acquisitions:
- Search for new markets
- Need for new technologies
- Access to natural resources
- Product and market diversification
- Rise of global finance
- Vertical Integration
- Regulatory evolution
- Bureaucracy and lack of single window clearance

Overview of M&A activity of the Indian firms 2013–14

M&A in India totalled US$5.7bn in Q3 2013, 28.6% off the value of the preceding quarter (US$8bn). India's M&A through Q1–Q3 2013 was valued at US$17bn. Unilever's US$3.5bn acquisition of an additional 14.8% stake in Hindustan Unilever was the largest deal in India so far this year and accounted for 20.9% of aggregate M&A value in the country. Its size propelled the value of deals in the consumer sector from 306.1% to US$4bn, making it the most active sector for M&A in India. The Pharma, Medical & Biotech sector was the only sector to witness a second successive growth in M&A value. An aggregate US$1.8bn worth of deals occurred in the sector during Q1—Q3 2013, which were accounted for by Abbott's landmark acquisition of Piramal Healthcare. On the other hand, the Q1–Q3 2013 figure (US$8.7bn) exceeded

Q1–Q2 2013 by 124%. This arose from two acquisitions worth US$5.1bn by state-run ONGC and Oil India off the coast of Mozambique.

International M&A activity

- Q1 2014 global M&A increased 5.7% over Q4 2013 (US5$566.6bn)
- Eight mega deals in Q1 (worth US$166.3bn) were announced
- The mega deals accounted for a 27.8% share of global M&A
- TMT M&A (US$176.1bn) had the highest share of global M&A at 29.4%, the highest valued Q1 since 2006 (US$188.9bn)
- Technology M&A (US$54.3bn) saw the highest value for an opening quarter on Mergermarket record, up 55.1% compared.
- Pharma, Medical & Biotech M&A (US$63.2bn) was over four times the Q1 2013 value of US$14.2bn

Reasons for M&A Activity in India

This section illustrates the reasons for M&A activity since the liberalization of the Indian economy.

In 1991 there was a shift in the industrial policy that paved the way for M&A in India. These reforms removed the restrictive provisions of the Monopolies and Restrictive Trade Practices (MRTP) Act, and restrictions of the Foreign exchange regulations, besides establishing anti-competitive provisions, through the establishment of Competition Commission of India (CCI) in 2002. This commission was aimed at checking activities such as collusive biddings, formation of cartels, and consolidation via M&A in order to reduce the hegemony of large companies.

The 1989–90 reforms have been instrumental in reducing market and firm level rigidities, ensuring corporate restructuring, and policy modifications in order to meet the emerging competitive challenges. This in turn ensured that firms retain their competitiveness and also increase their market worth. This aspect has since reflected in the aggressive growth of domestic investment activities leading to an increase in the M&A activities in the last decade. The outcome of this policy shift has been two fold—(a) domestic enterprises have consolidated their position to face increasing competitive pressures, and (b) multinational enterprises (MNEs) from India have aggressively pursued their desire, substantially establishing their presence and control in the international markets.

Another peculiar aspect of the M&A activity in India is the initiative taken by the services sector, which has used the M&A route to expand both domestically and globally. This was then followed by the manufacturing and the pharmaceutical sector along with the IT, automotive chemicals, and the steel sector.

M&A activity has increased because of the growing need for investment especially in infrastructure and industry. This has resulted in a more investor-friendly climate in the country. Additionally, with opening up nearly all the sectors to FDI in a varying degree, it has permitted FDI investors to acquire shares on the stock exchange to boost and consolidate shareholdings of FDI investors in India. Additionally, simplification

Table 20.1   Sectoral trends of the inbound
M&A 2012–13

Sector	CY2012	CY2013
Consumer, non-cyclical	20%	21%
Communications	13%	20%
Technology	9%	14%
Industrials	16%	12%
Consumer, cyclical	13%	10%

Source: Based on the data from International Mergers &
Acquisitions Review 2014

of regulations on foreign portfolio inves-tors has facilitated investment routes into the country resulting in increased foreign investments. Simultaneously, Indian busi-ness is increasingly engaged in both hori-zontal and vertical integration, this in turn helps in enhancing synergies that are inte-gral in M&A transactions.

M&A laws in India are still evolving, creating a peculiar situation in which the regulators are constantly trying to catch up the global M&A waves that are striking the shores of the country. This creates substantial confusion wherein the regulators variously interpret a stated law. An example of such an interpretation is the definition of 'control'. Though this definition is consistent across various laws, it is still subject to interpretations of various regulators. This has resulted in increased confusion of foreign investors.

The basic tenets of the Indian law involving M&A transactions are undergoing a sea change. Numerous bills pertaining to M&As, namely Goods and Service tax, Direct Tax Code, reforms on pension funds, and banking and insurance are waiting approval from the parliament. It is therefore hoped that the once these legislations are implemented, they will smoothen the process of M&A deals in India. Additionally, a conducive legal environ-ment would become the mainstay of global corporate climate for the Indian companies.

The SEBI Takeover Regulations 2011 has helped in simplifying the open offer and disclosure regimes in India. This was followed by the new Companies Act 2013, which proposes to modernize and simplify corporate laws in India. An important feature of M&A activity in India is its sectoral composition of the inbound M&A in 2012–13 (Table 20.1).

Conclusion

It can be concluded that corporates have enthusiastically embraced M&A after years of recession, especially when there is a healthy availability of cash reserves, and improving employment numbers. Additionally, there are several factors such as easy availability of finance, opening up of rigid regulatory frameworks, etc. that have motivated the corporates to focus on achieving the next level of growth. Despite the enthusiasm, deal makers recognize that successful deals require superior strategies, comprehensive due diligence, and well-developed integration plans, and it is only when these very complex processes have occurred, should the deal makers go ahead for increasing shareholder and investor returns through acquisitions.

Managing cultures

The managing of cultures between different merging entities is also extremely impor-tant. There are a number of issues which need to be addressed.

Sharing of power at the top   When two companies merge, decisions need to be taken regarding who will be at the helm of affairs at the top. This transition has to be smooth and in the interest of the organization. Also, several sensitive decisions need to be taken regarding which employees will stay and who will leave. An acquisition/merger is accompanied by a sense of fear in the employees about their survival in the organization. This leads to the management of another important aspect—the communication process.

Communication channels   These need to be set up right in the beginning. Asea Brown Boveri had handled the acquisition of ABL in India very well. Letters from the CEO had been sent to employees at ABL giving them information about the proposed change. Such communications instil a lot of confidence in employees. In contrast, the merger of Compaq with Digital was fraught with uncertainty and suspicion, and many employees from Digital left. Such a scenario can be devastating, as losing good employees is a far bigger loss.

Setting up a code of conduct   There can be differences in work cultures. These are more striking if a cross-border merger is involved. For instance, in the merger between Daimler and Chrysler, there was clearly a difference between the work styles. Chrysler liked to pride itself on a buccaneering approach, where speed and ingenuity is prized. The engineers, designers, and marketing people all worked together on each model. On the other hand, Daimler has a more traditional chimney structure in which designers and marketing people mix less, and engineers are in charge.

Mergers should not be a strategy in their own right. Many mergers are undertaken in the name of cost cutting. The merged banks had generally cut performance more slowly than their non-deal making peers. Many companies went in for a merger as it was difficult to survive. McDonnell merged with Boeing as its biggest customer was cutting its spending to half. Chrysler merged with Benz as it was finding it hard to survive.

There are industry sectors where size matters. According to some estimates, an automobile maker has to produce a minimum number of cars to survive. There has been substantial restructuring in recent years as a result of weak demand, over-capacity, and environmental pressures. In 2014, five automobile manufacturers in the world produced 72.23 million units in 2014 constituting a large portion of the world's production and the 10 largest manufacturers constituted nearly 80% of the world's total production.

In the banking sector, the biggest bank in the world today is Industrial and Commercial Bank of China with $3.062 trillion in assets, according to SNL Financial, followed by UK's HSBC with $2.723 trillion in assets, and the third bank is France's Crédit Agricole with $2.615 trillion in assets. The abolition of the Glass Stegall Act in US in 1999 dismantled the wall between banking and securities. Deregulation and the introduction of the single currency in the European Union, financial liberalization in Japan, emergence of China as a major financial power, and restructuring of banking in countries affected by financial crisis, all contributed to large scale M&As.

In the pharmaceutical industry, costs for expensive R&D and to derive synergies have been the driving force for acquisitions. All large pharmaceutical firms have grown bigger in size through the M&A activity rather than through organic growth.

However, despite the talk of a lot of activity taking place in the domain of M&A, one needs to look at its total contribution in the world economy. In developing countries, the advantage of M&As is rarely access to proprietary technology or skills. The advantage lies more in rapid market entry, local market knowledge, established distribution systems, and contacts with the government, suppliers, or customers (*World Investment Report* 2000). In cross-border mergers/acquisitions, the acquisition offers saving of time as compared to setting up a green field venture along with other reasons advocated earlier. However, from a developing country's perspective, foreign acquisitions do not add to productive capacity but simply transfer ownership and control from domestic to foreign hands accompanied by laying-off employees, or closing production or functional activities. However, any country where M&As are being looked at, should also take into account the development priorities of the country. Not only the financial implications, but other social and cultural implications must also be weighed when evaluating a merger/acquisition.

STRATEGIC ALLIANCES

Global networking, partnership alliances, and information sharing are utilized by world-class organizations. Alliances enable companies to focus on their core skills and competencies. Globalization and technology are changing the nature of business like never before. Both technology and globalization are intimately linked. By reducing the costs of communication, IT has helped to globalize production and financial markets. In turn, globalization spurs technology by intensifying competition and by speeding up the diffusion of technology through FDI. Together, globalization and IT crush time and space. During the past two decades the global network of computers, telephones, and televisions has increased its information carrying capacity a million times over. Today, a $2,000 laptop is more powerful compared to a $10 million mainframe computer in the mid-1970s. A fibre optic cable can carry 1.5 million conversations, whereas a transatlantic telephone cable could carry only 138 conversations simultaneously. No communication medium has grown as fast as the Internet. Anybody with a computer, a modem, and a telephone can teleshop, telebank, and telelearn, 24 hours a day.

Traditionally, the concept of the firm came in because different functions had to be coordinated. Ronald Coase, a Nobel prize-winning economist in 1937, asked why workers were organized in firms instead of acting as independent buyers and sellers of goods and services at each stage of production. He concluded that firms were needed because of the lack of information and the need to minimize transaction costs. A world without firms, in which production was organized entirely through markets, would require full information and no transaction costs; but in the real world it takes time and money to find out about the product being bought and sold. A firm resolves these problems. The size of firms is determined by the relative costs of buying in services from outside and the overhead cost of providing them in-house. For instance, a car firm can either make the tyres itself or buy them from a supplier. The tyres will probably cost less if bought in the competitive marketplace, but some of this saving may be offset by higher transaction and coordination costs. The higher these costs are, the greater the likelihood that firms will find it more profitable to provide services internally, which will increase their size. However, IT—in the form of e-mail, Internet, fax machine, and computerized billing—reduces these costs, and so increases the attraction of buying goods and services from outside. As these costs fall, the traditional logic of the firm becomes less persuasive. All kinds of goods and services can be outsourced and many employees can be replaced by outsiders, linked by electronic networks. In this way, IT encourages vertically integrated corporate giants like AT&T to break themselves up into smaller more efficient firms loosely connected by networks. Two opposing forces are therefore at work. In industries such as software and entertainment, where network externalities are powerful, IT will favour a greater concentration of business to exploit larger economies of scale, so the firm will tend to increase in size. Elsewhere, falling communications costs will favour decentralization and one would see the emergence of a lot of strategic alliances.

Another factor driving the concept of strategic alliances is customer focus. Organizations are now focusing on providing complete solutions rather than offering isolated products. For instance, Intel and Canon have little in common except digital technology, but they can all come together to provide a complete solution to the customer. Canon can click pictures, Intel can process pictures using the microprocessor, and Canon can make multiple copies using its photocopiers. There are also some other reasons which lead to strategic alliances. For instance, Bowersox (1990) points out the forces for impetus of strategic alliances.

- The political legal terrain of the 1980s stimulated the development of integrated-services practices. Deregulation of transportation and communications, coupled with relaxed anti-trust enforcement—intended to give productivity a change—generated an atmosphere conducive to innovation.
- The explosion in IT has made computerization cheap and computers hold logistic alliances together.
- Today's emphasis on lean organizations (cost conscious and focusing on areas of expertise) makes managers more likely to turn to external specialists to solve problems or perform tasks outside the organization's sphere of expertise. The objective of competing more effectively—through greater asset utilization, higher leverage, and faster responsiveness—is a prime stimulant towards logistic collaboration.
- An escalating competitive environment forces the players to do all they can to become lowest cost competitors. Efficiency in logistics is particularly important for companies that are doing business abroad.

Strategic alliances—The concept

Different researchers have delved upon various aspects of strategic alliances. Some of them have propounded a specific definition while others have deliberated upon the form of manifestation of strategic alliances. The different perceptions are outlined in Table 20.2.

Table 20.2 provides an insight into the concept and views of the various researchers on strategic alliances. It is observed that strategic alliances are seen as distinctly separately from the M&A activity. It could be seen as a step towards strengthening of competitiveness, sharing of risks and resources, gaining knowledge, obtaining an access to new markets and technology, and carrying out a new project. It has also been seen as a partnership in which each partner retains his own individual identity. Joint ventures are seen to be a manifestation of strategic alliances. Thompson, however, in contrast to the others does consider mergers to be a manifestation of strategic alliance.

Table 20.2 Perceptions of strategic alliances

Author	Year	Definition/Manifestation
Forest and Martin	1988	Strategic alliances could take a form of operational joint venture, equity investment, client sponsored research contract, marketing distribution agreement, research institute agreement, collaborative R&D, R&D limited partnership, and technology licensing.
Thomson	1990	Strengthening of competitiveness in terms of technology, cost, or marketing with an aim to increasing competitive advantage without either merger or acquisition, primarily because of inherent problems. Thompson has cited six categories of strategic alliances—mergers, new business, development of business jointly, special agreement between marketers and their suppliers, making strategic investment in another firm, and international trading partnerships.
Bowersox	1990	Has delved upon logistic alliances: • extended organization • concentration of relationship continuum instead of series of single transactions • combine resources of service providers • vertical alignment between two or more proprietary markets • horizontal alignment of product marketers.
Mohr and Spekman	1994	Firms comprising the alliance share costs, risks, and benefits of exploring and undertaking new business opportunities.
Orsino	1994	Alliances with supplier, horizontal integration, new product or market access, and mutual marketing relationship.
Raphael et al.	1995	Classifies the types of alliances as machine, entrepreneurial, complementary, and customer partnerships.
Luffman	1996	Type of business partnerships in which the firms concerned, each of which retains its own corporate identity, provides its partners with particular skills, competencies, and resources for their mutual benefit. It can also involve equity investments.
Wright et al.	1996	Define strategic alliances as partnerships in which two or more firms carry out a specific project or cooperate in selected areas of business. According to them, the strategic alliances can take one of the following forms—joint ventures, franchising, licensing, joint operations, joint long-term supplier agreement, joint marketing agreement, and consortium.
Rangan and Yoshino	1996	An arrangement that links specific facets of the business of two or more firms. The basis of the link is a trading partnership that enhances the effectiveness of the participating firms' competitive strategies by providing for mutually beneficial exchange of technologies, products, skills, or other types of resources. They suggest that strategic alliances simultaneously possess the three following characteristics: (1) Two or more firms that unite to pursue a set of agreed upon goals, yet remain independent subsequent to the formation of the alliance. (2) The partners share control over the performance of assigned tasks associated with the alliance and in the benefits derived from it. (3) The partners contribute on a continuing basis to the alliance.
Dacin and Levitas	1997	Strategies for firms from multiple countries to share risks and resources, to gain knowledge, and to obtain access to new markets.

(Contd)

Table 20.2 (*Contd*)

Author	Year	Definition/Manifestation
Das and Teng	1997	Inter-firm cooperative arrangements aimed at pursuing mutual strategic goals, e.g., joint ventures, joint R&D, product swap, equity investment, sharing, licensing, and others. They do not consider internalization, including M&As, as strategic alliance.
Harrigan	1998	Diversification by strategic alliance refers to arrangements in which corporations join forces to form a cooperative partnership. Typically, neither company owns the other, though often they create a third commercial entity usually referred to as a joint venture, that they co-own.
www.Business Dictionary. com, Web Finance, Inc.	2008	Agreement for cooperation among two or more independent firms to work together towards common objectives. Unlike in a joint venture, firms in a strategic alliance do not form a new entity to further their aims, but collaborate while remaining apart and distinct.

Yoshino and Rangan (1995) base their premise for analysis of alliances on the argument that an alliance-seeking firm acts in two dimensions—cooperation and competition—that generally play out as cooperation and conflict. They examine the strategic alliances on four dimensions:

1. Flexibility
2. Protection of core competencies
3. Learning
4. Value addition

Burton (1995) delves into two paradigms of business strategy—competition and collaboration. In the competitive paradigm, he credits Porter (1980) who in the conduct of business strategy equated it with execution of competitive strategy and achievement of sustainable advantage for the business. The alternative paradigm emphasizes the positive role of cooperative arrangements between industry and participants, and the consequent importance of what Kanter (1995) termed collaborative advantage, as a foundation of superior business performance. Burton has propounded that an all or nothing choice between a single-minded striving for either competitive or collaborative advantage would be a false one. The real strategic choice problem that all businesses face is where (and how much) to collaborate and where (and how intensely) to act competitively. He has provided a framework of analysis to explore issues concerning the coherence of the firm's composite strategy. It seeks to overcome the one-sided application of the competitive strategy model, which can lead the firm down strategic routes that do not optimize its overall advantage.

A study carried out by McKinsey examined the partnerships of 150 top companies—50 each from the US, Europe, and Japan. Of these, 49 cross-border strategic alliances were studied in detail. This study was published in HBR in 1991, and was reprinted in the 1993 book, *Collaborating to Compete*, edited by McKinsey consultant Joel Bleeke. The major findings are as follows:

• Alliances between strong and weak companies usually do not work because they do not provide the skills needed for growth. This leads to mediocre performance.
• The hallmark of lasting alliances is their ability to grow beyond the initial goals. For this, ventures need autonomy and flexibility.

- Alliances with equal financial partnerships are more likely to succeed than those in which one partner has a majority interest.
- Clear management control is what matters more than financial ownership.
- More than 75% of the alliances that terminated ended with an acquisition by one of the partners.
- The hallmark of successful alliances is their ability to evolve beyond initial expectations and objectives.
- Corporate partnerships with an even or nearly even financial stake are more likely to succeed than those in which one partner holds a majority interest. Nearly 65% of the joint ventures that had partners with different geographic strengths, succeeded. The story is different in cross-border acquisitions where the success rate was just 9%, when the acquiree and the target company did not have significant overlapping in the same geographic markets.

Forms of Alliances in India

Alliances in India take one of the following forms:

- marketing tie-ups
- operations handling
- joint ventures
- technology licensing
- manufacturing

- MoUs
- services
- supply
- setting up a new business.

There is, however, no data to support that a particular form of alliance will be more successful than others. The alliance may or may not involve an equity stake. In joint ventures there is certainly an equity stake, which makes each of the partners more responsible and hence, there is a greater sense of commitment. However, in India there is a lot of problem with joint ventures. One of the reasons is the level of liberalization, which has removed restrictions from a lot of industrial segments as a result of which many foreign companies that were earlier going in for joint ventures prefer to set up a 100% subsidiary.

Breaking a Strategic Alliance

The number of newly forged alliances has been growing at more than 25% annually in recent years (Bleeke and Ernst 1995). The failure rate of these alliances has been consistently very high (Parkhe 1991). Inter-firm trust, managerial coordination, and opportunistic behaviour of the partners, are just a few issues that complicate the management of these alliances.

A lot of reasons emerge as being a case for breaking these alliances. Some of these are:

- consolidation of business
- increase in stake by the foreign partner
- cash crunch
- difference in business priorities
- change of business focus

- lack of trust
- lack of ability to stick to the deadlines
- government policy
- mismatch of corporate cultures.

Levitas et al. (1997) remark that approximately 50–60% of alliances formed are unsuccessful in accomplishing the partners' objectives. Besides the inherent risk, one of the most often cited reasons for alliance failure is the incompatibility of partners. The choice of the right partner can yield important competitive benefits, whereas the failure to establish compatible objectives can lead to insurmountable problems. Corning Glass Works, which has developed numerous successful strategic alliances, has undertaken a long courtship with potential partners to assess their motives and the quality of their management as one of its guiding principles in selecting partners (Slocum and Lei 1993).

Levitas et al. (1997) identify the following reasons for incomplete agreement on alliance objectives:
- cultural heritage
- level of economic development.

On one hand, partners from developed countries look to partners from developing countries to provide access to local knowledge, including customs and business practices, political connections, as well as the ability to satisfy the host government's foreign investment requirements. On the other hand, partners from lesser developed or developing countries seek access to technology, export opportunities, and an opportunity to gain international alliance experience. Thus, partners differ by level of economic development, motives for setting up alliances, and expected benefits (Beamish 1988, 1994). Differences in government support and foreign policies can influence the alliance process.

The difference in value systems too has an impact on the nature of an alliance. For instance, the US has a cultural heritage based on rugged individualism and belief in free market, whereas Korean culture is strongly influenced by Confucian ideology. It has been suggested that Koreans are less egocentric than the Americans; Koreans' standards of success and failure are more closely associated with the approval or disapproval of others than with inner personal standards or goals, more common among Americans (Brandt 1987). Korean managers have a stronger long-term orientation than US managers (Kim et al. 1990). Korean culture is more concerned with the interests of the community. In Korea, state run capitalism operates with a vast network of institutionally defined relationships between business and government. Korean managers have had to develop the requisite partnering skills needed to be effective in collaborative ventures. In sharp contrast, there is a clear separation between private business and public government in the US. There have been few attempts by the US government to foster industry. Relations between government, business, and labour are often adversarial (Lodge and Crum 1985).

Way to Go ahead with Alliances

The following are the recommendations which seem to emerge:
- There is a greater need to have an objective before going in for an alliance.
- There is also a need for assessing the strengths and contributions by both the partners.
- There is a need for ensuring a cultural match between the different partners involved in the alliance.
- There needs to be a commitment from all the partners involved in the alliance, and the roles of the partners must be clearly identified.

- A level of trust needs to be built up between the partners. This can only be done if the business processes are documented, the procedures for decision-making are fair, and financial transactions are transparent. Financial irregularities can be disastrous for the partnership.
- Indian companies also need to put their value systems in place. Unless that happens, no amount of technical excellence can really lead to an improvement in the working of any enterprise. As Ghosal (1999) points out, arrogance, lack of respect for individual dignity—one's own and that of others—an opportunistic relationship with employees within the organization, and with customers and suppliers can be detrimental in the long run. These companies must commit to a process of shaping and embedding a new set of values within their organizations.
- If equity stakes are involved, then the level of commitment becomes higher and there is a greater degree of seriousness in the venture.
- Both the partners must ensure a greater degree of value addition.
- There should also be a clear identification of critical success factors in the alliance.
- When forming alliances between international partners, the differences in culture, infrastructure, and economic development and government policies should be incorporated (Dacin et al. 1997).
- Certain variables should be avoided when choosing a partner for strategic alliance. Alliances should not be formed to correct a weakness because the weaker party ends up at the mercy of the stronger, for example, GM's alliance with Toyota. GM entered the alliance with an inability to manufacture high quality cars. Ten years later, GM was still not able to strengthen the weakness.
- Proprietary technology should not be licensed. Sony acquired transistor technology from Bell Labs for a small price of $25,000 and there are literally no radio manufacturers in US.

Some of the aforementioned aspects will help to sustain the alliance for a longer time. Alliances will be formed as there is a trend towards subcontracting activities in which the organization does not have core competencies. The duration of the alliance, however, depends on the degree of trust and adjustments, which both the partners are willing to make.

FRANCHISING

Franchising is one of the many ways in which a business can grow. It is being adopted by a number of businesses and has led to an emergence of international brand names such as Kentucky Fried Chicken, Coca Cola, Pepsi, and retail chains such as Pierre Cardin, Benetton, Van Heusen, and Bata.

The following sections attempt to explain the concept of franchising, the advantages it offers to the franchiser (one who owns the brand), and the franchisee (one who buys the business concept and the brand name from the franchiser). It also elaborates upon the relationship of franchising with entrepreneurship and the franchising trends in India.

Organizations have to find new mechanisms for growth from time to time. Different organizations have gone in for different strategies for growth. Franchising has emerged as one such strategy for growth among other prevalent activities. It is a way of expansion of one's business after establishment of a brand name, by lending it for a royalty on sales. On a macro level, franchising can serve to widen the entrepreneurial base of the country. It is a concept, by virtue of which one invests one's own money for buying an established brand name for selling a particular product or service, to become a part of a retail chain or an established business, but retain the ownership of the business. It, therefore, gives an entrepreneur access to an established business format, thereby reducing the chances for failure.

Bidlake (1990) remarks that franchising is gaining an increasingly respectable image as more large professional companies use it as a route to rapid expansion with low capital outlay. Jarillo (1993), for instance, traces the emergence of the Kentucky Fried Chicken chain, which was started in 1956, when an old native of Kentucky, Colonel Sanders started selling to some of his friends the right to open restaurants to cook and sell a chicken dish after a Southern recipe, which he had perfected in the previous 20 years. Just eight years later, he presided over the entrance of 700 Kentucky Fried Chicken restaurants throughout the world, selling the same menu to the same standards. This is what is called franchising. Orsino (1994) writes that franchises are built on the premise of superseding regional differences—no matter where you travel across the country, when you go to a franchise operation you know exactly what to expect in terms of quality, pricing, and service. Uniformity and predictability are paramount.

Franchising is one of the most creative of the various marketing techniques. The key to a successful franchise operation is a strong system. It is a system that provides the appearance that all outlets belong to a chain, the know-how to franchisees to keep one step ahead of the competition, and abundant opportunities to all who want to fulfil the dream of owning one's own business.

Definition

Franchising is a system or method of marketing a product or service, wherein the franchiser who has developed a special product service or system that has gained national recognition grants a right or licence to small independent businessmen throughout the country to merchandise this service or product under the national trademark and in accordance with a proven successful format. This increases the franchiser's exposure to more national business and gives the franchise a greater chance for success in a given field with a smaller amount of capital investment.

The franchise system of distribution is a significant part of the US economy and is viewed as a dynamic, growing, business activity, increasingly accepted and respected by the public, all levels of the government, and by the business community. It has become a powerful force because of the following reasons (Ayling 1988):
- overcomes shortage of capital
- overcomes high interest rates
- attracts highly motivated operators

- fast growth of operating units
- greater market penetration.

Franchising also offers advantages to the person who buys an existing franchise, that is, the franchisee. Pecenko (1993) elaborates it as follows:

Data from the US illustrate that after one year in business, 97% of franchisees are successful business operators, as compared to a 62% rate in the case of fully independent entrepreneurs. After five years of franchise operation, 92% of the participants observed are still successful, compared to only 23% of the independents. Entrepreneurs, when going in for a franchise operation as a franchisee, find it less risky to enter the market due to the following circumstances:

- The enterprise concerned starts an already established business.
- Consumers are accustomed to franchiser-sold products.
- The entrepreneur concerned is assisted by his franchiser throughout the creation of the new company and later on in its operation.
- The entrepreneur gets access to fields of activity too expensive to venture into on his own (due to R&D and/or promotional costs).
- The entrepreneur may also get access to foreign funds when needed, since he has become part of an already established business organization.

The word franchising is derived from a French verb '*franchir*', which means 'to free' (used in the context to express freedom from servitude or restraint) (Hall and Dixon 1989). The definition of franchising as given by the International Franchising Association is: 'A franchise operation is a contractual relationship between the franchiser and the franchisee in such areas as know-how and training, wherein the franchisee operates under a common trade name, format, and procedures, owned or controlled by the franchiser, and in which the franchisee has or will make a substantial capital investment in his business from his own resources.' Ayling (1988) mentions that the definitions for franchising given by International Franchise Association and British Franchise Association have a number of things in common:

- There must be a legal contract outlining the terms and obligations agreed between franchiser and franchisee.
- The franchiser must initiate and train the franchisee in all aspects of his business prior to its opening.
- After the franchisee's business has opened, the franchiser will continue to provide him with support in all aspects of the operation.
- The franchisee is permitted, under the control of the franchiser, to operate under a particular brand name, business format, and procedure, and with the benefit of the goodwill generated by the franchiser.
- The franchisee will be required to make a substantial capital investment from his own resources.
- The franchisee will own his business.
- The franchisee will pay the franchiser for the rights he acquires, through the front-end 'licence fee' and ongoing management services fees for continuing support.

- The franchiser will generally grant the franchisee a geographical territory and/or a vertical market sector in which to operate.

Hall and Dixon (1989) have delved upon some of the prerequisites to expand through franchising:
- The business must be capable of standardization.
- It must have a unique selling point.
- There should be a relatively high profit margin.
- It should be simple for the franchisees to operate.

For franchising effectively, the following are some of the essential points to observe. To set up the franchise, the franchiser will have to:
- market the franchise
- set up at least one pilot operation
- have sufficient capital and skills to support the network
- draw up a comprehensive operating manual
- draw up a detailed contract
- select suitable franchisees
- train them and give continuing assistance.

The franchise operation accompanied by complete business management assistance is called *business format franchising*.

Scope of franchising

Looking at the present trends in the US, it seems that franchising can be attempted with nearly any type of business. Perhaps, more than any other method of marketing, franchising has reflected the demographic changes in society as well as the prosperous economic climate of recent years.

However, the Indian scenario is very different. In India, it all started in the soft drink industry with Coca Cola, in 1954. The soft drink industry is one area where franchising has really worked well; the other being bakery, as illustrated later. For example, Parle had 60 franchisees in India and 14 abroad. It was the leading soft drink industry in India.

In the soft drink industry Pure Drinks, UB group, and the Pepsi Company have all taken up franchising. Britannia, Spencer's, and Bakeman's had also undertaken franchising, though Bakeman's moved out of the bread industry and restricted itself to biscuits and other confectionery items.

Franchising has been adopted as a route to growth by many firms operating in India such as Archies, McDonald's, Domino's Pizza, NEXT Stores, Ferns N Petals, NIIT, schools such as Delhi Public School, hotel brands such as Radisson, Country Inns and Suites, and Park Plazas.

LICENSING

Licensing is also one of the corporate entrepreneurial activities undertaken by organizations for growth. There are organizations, which do not have the resources to develop

their own technology. Ramu (1997) remarks that many MNCs use licensing for entry into foreign markets. There may be factors such as:
- prohibition of FDI
- absence of a large market
- scale not being attainable
- general lack of interest in international operations
- limited availability of resources.

He has talked about four forms of licensing:
- basic licensing
- management contract
- franchising
- contract manufacturing.

Basic licensing

Here, an organization allows another firm to use its technology, patents, and or trademarks for a fee.

Management contract

This entails the responsibility for the operation of one enterprise by another. The latter takes over the responsibility of management and training of personnel. This is primarily a non-market relationship.

Kotabe et al. (1996) identify technology licensing as a step toward or an alternative to wholly-owned subsidiaries. They remark that the recent trends in technology licensing indicate that it is used increasingly as a conscious, proactive, component of a technology-based firm's global product strategy. Barney (1991) mentions that the resource-based view of the firm implies that technology is a combination of physical, capital, and organizational capital resources. The firm uses such resources to gain sustained competitive advantage. Anecdotal evidence such as Philips, Matsushita's Digital Compact (Kotabe 1992), and Motorola's licensing of proprietary microprocessor technology to Toshiba (Hamel et al. 1989), implies that technology licensing is being used as an explicit, proactive element of the firms' global market strategy. This includes the use of technology licensing as a tactic to achieve rapid market penetration (Lei and Slocum 1991), a means of established standards (Hagedoorn 1993), and a method of amortizing R&D costs (Ohmae 1990).

In India, there are a lot of licensing agreements under various kinds of technology transfer agreements. Dubey (1996) examines the use of Sierra Industrial Enterprises, which have snapped up a licence in 1996 for representing the $5.6 billion Beaverton (US)-based Nike in India. Nike has adopted the licensing route, which only involves lending its brand name designs and marketing experience in return for a fee amounting to 5% of sales, net of tax.

Sierra has further entered into a sourcing arrangement with Moja Shoes, a company floated by US-based non-resident Indians Dilip Mathur, Mahesh Nathani, and Ravi Akhori. Sierra has also forged alliances with 20 small units in and around Delhi, Bengaluru, and Ludhiana for sourcing apparel and sports accessories.

Management contracts in hotel industry

The management contract is a business format which separates ownership from operation. In the hotel industry, it has provided the opportunity for much-needed capital to fund the demand for new construction in world markets, while creating the vehicle for hotel management companies to expand their networks and market shares with reduced exposure to investment and political risks. The growth in contacts has also been driven by hotel owners; the need for experienced and established operators for their own peace of mind, and to satisfy investors' demands.

There is no standard definition of a hotel management contract; however, it is usually defined as a formal arrangement under which the owner of a hotel employs the services of an operator to act as his or her agent to provide professional management of the hotel, in return for a fee. The operator assumes full responsibility for the management of the business, while the ultimate legal and financial responsibilities, and rights of ownership of the property, its furniture, and equipment, its working capital, and the benefits of its profits (or burden of its losses) remain those of the owner. The owner may be a private individual, a financial institution, a real estate company, or a government. The operator is most likely to be an established hotel chain offering marketing strength, brand names, bargaining power, systems and procedures, project design and management, technical services, training, and management development. However, the rate of growth in the number of independent hotel management companies is increasing; these include groups that do not have their own international brand and reservations system, and who operate hotels for a variety of owners.

The owner usually seeks an effective return; the contractor an effective earnings stream. Typically, the fee structure is in two parts: a base fee of around 3% of hotel turnover and an achievement fee of around 10% of gross operating profit or earnings before debt, interest, and tax (EBDIT).

Economic changes impacting upon the hotel industry, accelerated competition among operators worldwide, and greater performance demands by owners and lenders, are leading to adjustments in contract provisions and increased owner bargaining strength.

Management contracts in food service industry

A management contracting arrangement, relevant to this industry sector, is defined by Sharma (1984) as 'An arrangement under which operational control of an enterprise, which would otherwise be exercised by the directors and managers appointed or elected by its owners, is vested by contract in a separate enterprise that performs the necessary management functions for a fee'. This fee may be made up in several ways. These include a straight fee; one linked to the turnover of the business; one in which purchasing discounts are returned to the client organization to offset against the fee; or a combination of the above. It is not uncommon for contractors to gain as much income from purchase discounts obtained, but not passed on to the clients, as it earns from the fees charged. This will result in local management following a strict policy of using authorized suppliers in order to maximize such discount earnings to the contracting organization. Contracts are usually of the following types, or may be a combination, dependent upon the nature of the client's business:

- management fee (sometimes called 'cost plus')
- fixed costs
- full cost recovery (nil cost)
- commercial return
- guaranteed performance

An increasing trend is for contractors to offer a range of services in addition to catering, such as office cleaning, and accommodation and grounds maintenance, which will save the client having to deal with several different organizations for different services. Therefore, the term 'food service' may be too narrow.

Most of these business formats have implications for the organizational and operational tie between the hospitality firm and the unit or subsidiary, particularly related to the degree of control. The formats chosen depend upon whether the business is based on assets or cash flow.

All these forms of growth put a strain on the head office organization in terms of the extent and range of support services offered. All methods stretch the managerial and operational capabilities of the firm. However, they do make contractors and franchisers quite different types of competitors.

CHOICE OF EMERGING FORMS OF ENTREPRENEURSHIP

As discussed in the previous section, a firm can choose between a range of options. The choice of these strategies may depend on numerous factors. These may depend, for instance, on the resources of the firm. A resource-intensive firm will like to expand through green field ventures. It may also license its brand name. Franchising offers opportunities to the firm wherein the resource constraints are taken care of by franchisees making their own incentives. Mergers and acquisitions help to give access to established businesses, which help to enhance market share or quick access to complementary services. However, the culture match offers a huge challenge to the success of the merger. Outsourcing helps to manage costs better. Information technology enabled services are being increasingly outsourced. India is emerging as a very strong destination for outsourcing of ITES. Outsourcing helps firms to focus on core competencies and to outsource certain functions. The outsourced businesses range from very simple tasks such as call center management, data entry, and customer processes, to high-end research-based functions.

Technology helps to go in for outsourcing solutions, especially in the case of managed services through the use of IT. Firms that offer outsourcing services also adopt specific strategies wherein they work for one major firm as an in-house outsourced services firm or another firm which deals with multiple vendors.

There is no unique recommended strategy. The strategy depends on the context, market, resource access, and long-term situational advantage. The success of a strategy lies in implementation and control. Great strategies will not turn into a success in reality, if the implementation is flawed.

SUMMARY

This chapter analyses the strategic options available to a firm for expansion of their operations. There are numerous strategies which a firm can adopt—green field ventures, joint ventures, franchising, strategic alliances, and M&As, among others. There are advantages and disadvantages in each case. A green field venture option is time consuming and tedious but has advantages of a fresh start and does not come along with cultural baggage. However, the time taken to start the operation varies from state to state and also across various countries. Mergers and acquisitions may be a faster route for growth. However, in this case there may be challenges with regard to the culture of the two firms, and also the actual financial situation and competencies of firms in question. The time for an acquisition/merger may depend on the legal environment in a country. However, in this decade, Indian firms have been very aggressive about identifying firms abroad, and steel plants, automobile manufacturing, IT firms, research-based firms, pharmaceutical operations, etc., have been acquired by Indian

entrepreneurs. This has been facilitated by a changing legal environment, which governs the M&A activity. The airlines sector has also seen M&A activity on account of a better coverage of geography and economies of scale.

Franchising in India has also seen tremendous growth across various segments such as hotels, restaurants, schools, and retailing. It is a quick way of getting access to a brand and standardizing one's operations. However, a pilot operation is essential before embarking upon franchising as a strategy for growth.

Strategic alliances also have been witnessing lot of growth and there are several manifestations of these alliances—manufacturing, marketing, R&D, supply chain, etc. There are challenges like agreement on terms by the partners and also, levels of trust play an important role.

To conclude, there is no best strategy that can be suggested. The choice of a strategy depends on the context, types of firms involved, investment, and timeframe in consideration.

KEY TERMS

Acquisitions   The act of contracting, assuming, or acquiring possession of something.

Entrepreneurship   The assumption of risk and responsibility in designing and implementing a business strategy or starting a business.

Franchising   A system, in which a licence is given to a manufacturer, distributor, trader, etc. to enable them to manufacture or sell a named product or service, in a particular area, for a stated period.

Green field ventures   A green field venture is a firm which has been started from scratch. It is a new venture creation by bringing in capital, land, and labour.

Management contracts   The practice in which a domestic firm supplies the management know-how to a foreign company that provides the capital in order to create a joint venture.

Mergers   A combination of two or more businesses on a relatively equal footing that results in the creation of a new reporting entity.

Strategic alliances   Agreements between two or more firms to engage in an activity on a shared basis. The outside activities of each partner are not affected by the alliance, which is designed to build on the expertise of each.

Strategic management   The process of managing, in a way that is consistent with the corporate strategy or in such a way as to capitalize on the opportunities that present themselves.

Strategy   Growth of the business considering the vision, and matching the external environmental dynamics with the internal resource base of the organization.

EXERCISES

Concept Review Questions

1. What are the alternate strategies for growth, which service firms can adopt?

2. In a financially constrained situation, which is a better strategy to adopt—franchising or acquisition?

3. Critically analyse strategic alliances as a strategy for growth of a service firm.
4. Evaluate the advantages and disadvantages of setting up green field ventures.

Critical Thinking Questions

1. A small entrepreneur is making an investment of ₹50 crore in setting up a restaurant. What alternatives should he evaluate before venturing from a strategic perspective?
2. Franchising a brand has its advantages and disadvantages. Take the case of a successful and an unsuccessful enterprise, which opted for franchising. Identify reasons for the success and failure of franchising as a strategy for each enterprise.
3. A small restaurant owner offering Indian cuisine is running his business in an upbeat mall in South Delhi. He wants to expand his brand nationally. Suggest a strategy for expansion given the context that he has financial constraints.
4. A fast food chain with a similar brand offers different experiences to consumers at its outlets in Delhi and Mumbai. These are franchised outlets. Identify the underlying issues.

Internet Exercises

1. Access the website of McDonald's and Domino's. Compare and contrast the franchising information available on these chains.
2. Carlson Hospitality owns a number of brands such as Radisson Country Inns and Suites. Evaluate the strategies adopted by the Radisson chain for growth, globally.

CASE STUDY   Biocon: A Strategic Insight

Biocon

Biocon is India's leading biotechnology enterprise. The company has evolved from an enzyme manufacturing company to a fully integrated biopharmaceutical enterprise, focused on health care. Biocon applies proprietary fermentation technologies to develop innovative and effective biomolecules in diabetology, oncology, cardiology, and other therapeutic segments. Biocon's success lies in its ability to develop innovative technologies and products and to rapidly leverage them to adjacent domains. This unique 'integrated innovation' approach has yielded a host of patented products and technologies that have enabled multi-level relationships with their global clientele.

Biocon Limited has three subsidiary companies:

1. Syngene International Private Limited provides chemistry and molecular-based custom research services in early stage drug discovery and development. Kiran Mazumdar Shaw formed Syngene in 1994 when she learnt that there were opportunities in the field of contract research. She floated Syngene as a separate business and did not expect Biocon to put in funds frequently. Kiran usually pauses before entering another space, testing the waters first, and expanding only when she is sure of its potential. Hence, for four years Syngene progressed at a slow pace and took off only in 1998.
2. Clinigene International Private Limited conducts longitudinal research in diabetes and offers a wide range of comprehensive services in drug development and clinical trials. In the late 1990s Gordon Ringold, a former business associate who had formed Surromed in the US, told Kiran about the exciting possibilities of clinical research, and Clinigene was formed in the year 2000 (Biocon Annual Report 2006 , Hari 2002).
3. Biocon Biopharmaceuticals Private Limited (BBPL) was set up on 17 April 2006 in collaboration with CI MAB, representing the Centre of Molecular Immunology, Cuba. The state-of-the-art cGMP compliant facility is designed to manufacture a broad range of novel and bio-similar therapeutic products through large-scale cell culture fermentation for the treatment of cancer, autoimmune, and metabolic diseases (Capitaline database).

In 1978, Biocon started with extracting two enzymes—papain and singlass, from papaya and catfish. It produced low-cost enzymes for the food and beverage industry to increase the translucence of fruit juices, for example, or to lighten the structure of bread. It then moved into pharmaceuticals, supplying generic ingredients used in the manufacture of cholesterol-lowering statins to companies such as Myland in the US and Sandoz in Germany (Elliott 2005). In the 1980s, Biocon started R&D to manufacture enzymes through fermentation. Biocon also decided to focus on solid-state fermentation at a time when only the Japanese could handle it with ease. The R&D team knew nothing about designing a manufacturing plant, let alone about solid-state fermentation. The first blueprint for a fermenter was ready in 1989 and Biocon commissioned its first commercial plant in 1991 (Hari 2002). Initially, Kiran had promoted the company as a joint venture with an Ireland-based MNC, Biocon Biochemicals. However, in 1989 Unilever Plc acquired Biocon Biochemicals Ltd in Ireland and merged it with its subsidiary Quest International (Biocon Annual Report 2006). In 1998, Unilever inked a deal with ICI to sell its speciality chemicals division of which Quest International was a part. This year was crucial for Kiran as it was the year she married John Shaw (then the Managing Director of Madura Coats). Shaw with his wide experience and large savings helped Kiran to buy Unilever's share in the company. Unilever had let Kiran float other companies but did not allow her to veer it away from its original business of making and selling enzymes. Thus, Biocon became an independent entity.

By the late 1990s, Biocon had become well entrenched in the fermentation space. It designed a new reactor called the PlaFractor for solid-state fermentation, which could contain micro-organisms well, and its contents could be mixed while fermentation was going on. Things could be added and removed without disturbing the fermentation process. To top it all, it consumed less energy than the Japanese model. In 2001, Biocon became the first Indian company to be approved by US FDA for the manufacture of lovastatin, a cholesterol-lowering molecule. In the same year, it also received the US 2001 worldwide patent for its PlaFractorTM.

In 2004, Biocon announced a strategic partnership with Vaccinex Inc to discover and co-develop at least four therapeutic antibody products. In the same year, Biocon created a buzz in the stock market with its hugely successful IPO. Biocon closed day one of the listing with a market value of $1.11 billion. It became the second Indian company to cross the $1 billion mark on the day of listing. After this success, Biocon announced research collaboration with North Carolina's Nobex Corporation to jointly develop oral insulin for the treatment of diabetes on a global scale. It then launched Insugen TM, the new generation bio-insulin, manufactured in Asia's largest human insulin plant. Currently, 75% of insulin sales come from overseas markets such as Latin America, the Middle East, and Southeast Asia. In April 2006, Biocon invested ₹1 billion in a new facility at Bengaluru to make monoclonal antibodies for cancer and autoimmune diseases (*The Financial Express* 2006). Table 20.3 shows Biocon's drug discovery pipeline. In June 2006, Kiran set up the Biocon Park, which is India's largest biotech hub comprising an integrated cluster of research labs and manufacturing facilities on a 90-acre expanse in Karnataka Area Industrial Board in Bommasandra Industrial Estate Phase IV, on the outskirts of Bengaluru. The park was built with an investment of ₹600 crore and is the single largest capital investment made by Biocon in 27 years of its history. The multi-product facilities cater to cardiovascular cholesterol reduction, immunosuppressant in organ transplants, diabetes, and cancer (*Pharmabiz* 2006).

The People

Biocon has a flat management structure. Kiran realized that for such a structure to work she had to adopt a 'networking management' style wherein there is high level of networking and communication, thus helping people to make their own decisions. This has inspired her employees, as is evident from their long tenures at Biocon and the less than 1% attrition rate (Elliott 2005, Biocon Annual

Table 20.3 Biocon's drug discovery pipeline

Drug	Preclinical	Phase I	Phase II	Phase III	Launch
IN 105		Diabetes			
BVX 10	Inflammation				
BVX 20	Oncology				
BIOMAb EGFR™				Oncology	
TI hT		Oncology Inflammation			
Oral BNP	Cardiovascular				
Streptokinase				Cardiovascular	
GCSF				Oncology	
Insulin					Diabetes

Source: Based on the data from Biocon Financial Report (2006).

Report 2006). Most of the top executives at Biocon have been there since the beginning. Kiran started the R&D division with Shrikumar Suryanarayan from IIT-Madras whom she had met in the early 1980s when he was a student and wanted enzymes for his project. When Suryanaranyan completed M. Tech., he had a number of offers for Ph.D. programmes and wanted Kiran to help him choose. Instead, she offered him an opportunity to start an R&D division for her and today he heads this division. Murali Krishnan is another example. He was helping Biocon in 1981 while studying to become a chartered accountant. He joined the company soon after, without completing his CA, and is the president of Biocon Group Finance. Biocon, Syngene, and Clinigene together employ approximately 2,000 qualified personnel—from biologists, chemists, IT specialists, medical practitioners, pharmacologists, engineers, and finance/legal/ marketing analysts, to general administrators. 10% of the employees hold a Ph.D. degree, 30% have a Masters degree in science, and the remaining are graduates with a Bachelors degree in science, commerce, or arts. 30% of Biocon employees are women. The employee attrition rate is less than 1% and the average age of employees in the company is 28. The employees say they enjoy working at Biocon because of the leadership style Kiran has adopted. Her husband, who has worked in several countries as a senior manager with Coats Viyella, marvels at the open culture at Biocon. According to ICICI Ventures who have closely studied Biocon, all the senior managers of the company have a say in the business.

Competition

As per Ibef (2015), the Indian biotechnology sector is expected to grow from the current US$5–7 billion to US$100 billion by 2025 according to Association of Biotechnology Led Enterprises (ABLE). The Indian biotech industry holds about 2% of share of the global biotech industry.

The Associate Chamber of Commerce and Industry of India estimated that over $4 billion was likely to be invested in the Indian biotech industry by 2010, primarily in the areas of health care, agriculture, environment, and food processing. It further stated that India would become a global player through export of bioproducts, particularly to neighbouring countries, West Asia, Southeast Asia, and certain developed countries.

Biocon is a biopharmaceutical company with strong capabilities in statins, immunosuppressants, recombinant insulin, and a wide product range across key therapeutic segments including diabetology, cardiology, and oncology. Biocon extended its R&D to new domains of knowledge, spanning bioprocess development, gene expression technologies, secondary metabolites, bioconversions, and proteomics. Today, it leverages its multiple expertise to leading-edge recombinant biopharmaceuticals and human therapeutics. The invention of the PlaFractor and through it, the ability to pioneer novel production processes for therapeutic molecules, is testimony to Biocon's path-breaking R&D capabilities and exceptional engineering skills.

Biocon launched BIOMAb-EGFR, a therapeutic monoclonal antibody-based drug for treating solid tumours of epithelial origin, such as head and neck cancers. The drug is the first of its kind to be clinically developed in India and is the first anti-EGFR humanized monoclonal antibody for cancer to be made available commercially anywhere in the world. The product has shown consistent positive outcome in clinical trials initiated both in India and globally, and is being studied in global clinical trials for colorectal, lung cancer, glioma, and pancreatic cancers. Over the years, Biocon has invested in cutting edge research with the objective of reducing therapy costs for chronic conditions. The company has taken a range of novel biologics, biosimilars, differentiated small molecules, and affordable recombinant human insulin and insulin analogs from 'Lab to Market.' It has made a big contribution INSUGEN®, an indigenous recombinant human insulin. It has developed world's first antibody for treatment of plaque psoriasis. Biocon spent ₹3,287 million on R&D in the year 2014–2015 generating a revenue of ₹31,429 million with 7,500 employees (Biocon Annual Report 2015).

Biocon launched a comprehensive portfolio of renal therapy products, which are priced 35% lower than those available in the market. Biocon's nephrology division is committed to finding solutions to kidney disorders using the highest standards of biotherapeutics and will simultaneously strive towards reducing the risks of the disease in the future through progressive research and innovative therapies. The new immunosuppressant drugs for renal therapy include Ranodapt, Tacrograf, Cyclophil ME, Rapacan, and Erypro. *Immunosuppressants* are medicines that inhibit or prevent the activity of the body's immune system. The company's newly carved nephrology division expects to release more drugs in the market. To achieve this, Biocon will continue to increase investments in the R&D division.

Many Firsts

Biocon is the first Indian company to manufacture and export enzymes to USA and Europe, which it started in 1979. In 1989, it became the first Indian biotech company to receive US funding for proprietary technologies. It is the first company to have solid substrate fermentation technology from pilot to plant level. The commercial success of Biocon's proprietary fermentation plant has led to a three-fold expansion. In 1993, its R&D and manufacturing facilities received ISO 9001 certificate from RWTUV, Germany. In 2002, Clinigene's laboratory became the first in India to receive CAP accreditation. In 2003, Biocon became the first company worldwide to develop human insulin on a Pichia expression system.

Biocon's Business Model

Biocon is India's largest biotech company with a presence in biopharmaceuticals, enzymes, customs research, and clinical research. It is difficult to say whether it is an enzyme company, a biotech company, or a pharmaceutical company. Biocon has a multi-business revenue share model with pharmaceutical products, research services, and enzymes (Fig. 20.1). Thus, we can say that Biocon is a biotech-turned-pharmaceutical company (Hari 2002). However, Chairman Kiran Mazumdar Shaw says that Biocon is rapidly transforming into an innovation-led organization where they have developed a balance between all-round revenue growth and risk mitigation in order to build a strong and sustainable business for the long term.

The integrated business approach has enabled Biocon to establish a significant presence in the global biopharmaceutical market. From early stage drug discovery to clinical development and commercialization, Biocon leverages its collective expertise and resources to provide an innovative range of products and services. This integrated business model allows it to offer its strategic global partners

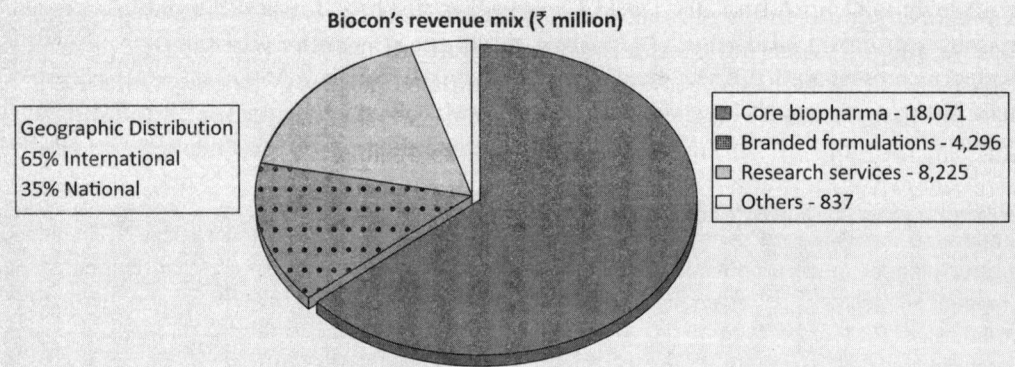

Fig. 20.1 Biocon's multi-business revenue share

Source: Based on the data from Biocon Annual Report (2015, p. 10).

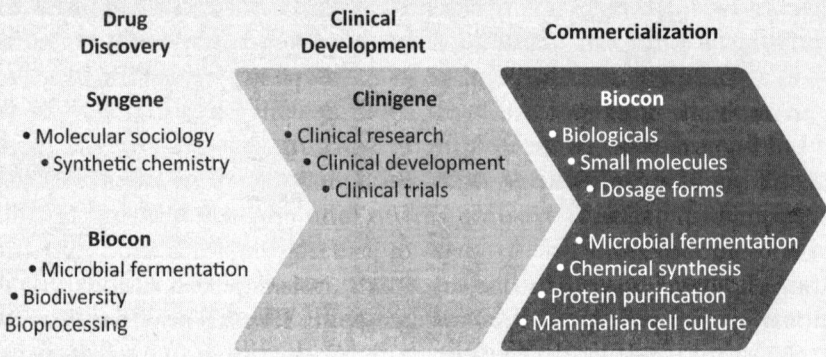

Fig. 20.2 Biocon's business model

Source: Based on the data from http://www.biocon.com.

customized, high-value solutions at any stage in the life cycle of a drug—right from discovery to market. The three stages are as follows (Fig. 20.2).

Step 1: Early stage drug discovery At Syngene, a Biocon subsidiary, Biocon offers outsourced, high-value R&D—from target identification and validation to small molecule and library synthesis. With its reputation for meticulous intellectual property right protection, it provides pharmaceutical and biotechnology majors customized solutions in the areas of synthetic chemistry and molecular biology.

Step 2: Clinical development At Clinigene, another Biocon subsidiary, Biocon specializes in Phase I–IV clinical trials and studies, using well-characterized

clinical databases in diabetes, oncology, lipidemia, and cardiovascular diseases. It offers its services at its College of American Pathologists (CAP) accredited (CAP is widely recognized as the 'gold standard') and National Accreditation Board for Testing and Calibration Laboratories (NABL) accredited central reference laboratory and the state-of-the-art bioavailability and bioequivalence centre (BA/ BE centre).

Step 3: Commercialization Biocon's track record of commercialization has been outstanding. Biocon's biopharmaceutical foray began with statins and immunosuppressants. Their commercial success is evident in the rapid market share they have gained in the US and Europe. In fact, Biocon continues to be the only Indian company to have US

FDA qualification for Lovastatin. FDA has inspected and accepted Biocon's facilities for Simvastatin, Pravastatin, Pioglitazone HCl, and Lovastatin (submerged fermentation). Biocon has also commercialized human insulin (rDNA) based on the Pichia expression system and submitted a drug master file for the same to the US FDA (www.biocon.com).

Biopharmaceuticals have been and will continue to be the mainstay of the company, promising exciting growth opportunities. This segment is involved primarily in the manufacture and marketing of active pharmaceutical ingredients (APIs) that require advanced fermentation and other skills and that offer significant market potential in the regulated markets once the product goes off patent. Within this segment, statins constitute major products. Biocon has received US FDA acceptance for its Pravastatin, Simvastatin, Lovastatin, and Pioglitazone manufacturing facilities. Biocon has already established itself as a leading exporter of Lovastatin to the US and Simvastatin to Europe. Apart from statins, other major biopharma's APIs are for immunosuppressants and anti-diabetic drugs.

The focus on statins augurs well, as statins are cholesterol-lowering agents used to treat/prevent coronary diseases, and are amongst the largest selling drugs worldwide. Patent at expiration of Pravastatin in Europe will augment statin growth in the year ahead followed by a quantum jump in the US markets in 2006 when both Pravastatin and Simvastatin go off patent. Biocon perceives the recent announcement of Simvastatin going OTC as an additional opportunity.

Biocon has also successfully developed recombinant human insulin at a commercial scale.

Reason for Success

Ever since Biocon became the buzzword in the market for the emerging field of biotechnology, Kiran has been a much-quoted personality. According to her, her belief in the field, a magnificent team of people who shared her passion for the subject, determination, and urge to succeed have all contributed to Biocon's reputation as the leader in the field. Another reason is that Biocon extends its friendliness to its customers. It not only gives customers a product, but also provides information on the market, a strategy, and a future. According to the managing director of Delhi-based Harvest Gold Foods, 'only Biocon works with the customer to reduce costs' (Hari 2002). Biocon has been driven by its strategy to provide affordable access to advanced biopharmaceuticals for global patient populations. Through their approach of 'exclusively inclusive' they have developed a portfolio of products that can benefit millions of patients world over. In 2015, Biocon probably has one of the largest portfolios of generic insulins and biosimilar protein therapeutics in advanced stages of development with six molecules in phase III clinical trials, namely rh-Insulin, Glargine, Pegfilgrastim, Adalimumab, Bevacizumab, and Trustuzumab. Biocon is the largest producer of insulin in Asia. Biocon has brought affordable oncology therapeutics to Indian market.

The primary reasons for the success of the firm are explored as follows:

- The firm had a distinct strategy and focus area. It focused on a gap in the market and was able to expand its market around the area. It focused on enzymes and steadily extended its operations in the field. Initially, it sourced technology and even acquired the stake from Hindustan Lever in order to retain its competitive edge.
- Biocon has built global scale and cost competitive complex manufacturing capabilities to address needs of patients worldwide.
- The business model of the firm is very sound. It offers and maps the entire value chain in the drug development and delivery process. It covers the entire spectrum from discovery and development to commercialization. The focus on diseases such as diabetes and cancer is appropriate as there is a lot of room for development. Over the years, it has evolved from a firm focused on enzyme manufacturing to a fully integrated biopharmaceutical enterprise. It followed an integrated innovation approach to yield patented products and technologies, which enabled multi-level partnerships. It also tapped the global market and was not restricted to the Indian market. The export orientation of the firm enabled it to prepare itself for a global strategy rather than have a micro perspective. The firm prepared itself for discovery, clinical development, and commercialization.

- There was a creation of a high performing team. The team dynamics and the complementary roles played by team members are critical to the success of any venture. The firm clearly demonstrates that it has used the networks of the founding entrepreneur as well as its employees to have a committed team at the top, who have stayed with the firm for an extended period, thereby lending stability, and building and nurturing the R&D culture and a penchant for innovation.
- There was a system of capitalizing on the university linkages. The firm has strong linkages with the academic community and thereby works closely with the educational system as well.
- The firm spends 10% of biopharma revenues in R&D every year. ₹3.29bn in R&D was spent in FY15 (Biocon Annual Report 2015, p. 17).

Questions

1. What are the key strengths and challenges for Biocon?
2. Critically evaluate the growth strategy adopted by Biocon.

REFERENCES

'After the deal', *The Economist*, 9 January 1999.

Andrews, Kenneth, R. (1971), *The Concept of Corporate Strategy*, Dow Jones Irwin, Homewood.

Ayling, D. (1998), 'The universe of franchising', *Management Today*, April.

Banker (2000), 'Top 1000', July.

'Barista brewing aggressive expansion plans', *Express Hotelier and Caterer*, 6 December 2004.

'Barista Coffee sets up new company in Sri Lanka', *Express Hotelier and Caterer*, 22 December 2004.

Barney, Jay (1991), 'Firm resources and sustained competitive advantage', Journal of Management, vol. 17, no. 1, pp. 99–120.

Basant, R. (2000), 'Corporate response to economic reforms', in Nagesh Kumar (ed.), *Indian Economy Under Reforms*, Bookwell, New Delhi.

Beamish, P.W. (1988), *Multinational Joint Ventures in Developing Countries*, Routledge, London.

Beamish, P.W. (1994), 'Joint ventures in LDC's: Partner selection and performance', *Management International Review*, vol. 34, pp. 60–74.

Bhandari, A. (1996), 'Survival of the fittest', International Times, *The Economic Times*, 13 August.

Bhargava, V. (1997), 'TCS, Microsoft, and NIIT to jointly launch EX-NGN', *The Economic Times*, 19 December.

Bidlake, S. (1990), 'Franchisers fix a firm line', *Marketing*, 12 July.

'B.K. Modi sells entire telecom equipment JV stake to Alcatel', *The Economic Times*, 23 March 1999.

Bleeke, J. and D. Ernst (1995), 'Is your strategic alliance really a sale?', *Harvard Business Review*, vol. 73, no. 1, pp. 97–105.

Brandt, V.S.R. (1987), 'Korea', in G. C. Lodge and E. F. Vogel (eds), *Ideology and National Competitiveness: An Analysis of Nine Countries*, Harvard Business School Press, Boston, Massachusetts, pp. 207–239.

Bowersox, D.J. (1990), 'The strategic benefits of logistics alliances', *Harvard Business Review*, July–August, vol. 68, no. 4, pp. 36–45.

Brown, M. (1997), 'Outsourcery', *Management Today*, January.

Burton, J. (1995), 'Composite strategy: The combination of collaboration and competition', *Journal of General Management*, vol. 21, no. 1, Autumn.

Capitaline (2005), '300 More Café Coffee Day outlets by 2007', *Capitaline.*

Chandrashekharan, A. (1998), 'A twist in the noodle battle', The Strategist, *Business Standard*, 15 September.

Collis, D.J. and C.A. Montgomery (1995), 'Competing on Resources: Strategy in the 1990s', *Harvard Business Review*, vol. 73, no. 4, July–August, pp. 118–128.

Collis, D.J. and C.A. Montgomery (1998), 'Creating corporate advantage', *Harvard Business Review*, vol. 76, no. 3, May–June 1998, pp. 70–83.

Das, T. (1996), 'MNCs: India's strategy needs rethink', *Economic Growth and Social Change*, March.

Financial Times, 6 April 1997.

Forrest, J.E. (1990), 'Strategic alliances and the small technology based firm', *Journal of Small Business Management*, July, pp. 37–45.

Ghosal, S. (1999), 'The value of values', Corporate Dossier, *The Economic Times*, 5–11 March.

'Global IT giants in pact supply equipment to ISP's', *Business Standard*, 30 November 1998.

Goyal, M. (1999), 'Public bond, private life', *The Economic Times*, 26 February–4 March.

Gupta, N.S. (1995), 'Alliances emerge as the 90s weapon', *The Economic Times*, 10 September.

Hagedoorn, J. (1993), 'Understanding the rationale of strategic technology partnering: Interorganisational modes of cooperation and sectoral differences', *Strategic Management Journal*, vol. 14, no. 5, pp. 371–85.

Hakusho, Toshi (2000), *Japan External Trade Organization*, JETRO, Tokyo.

Hamel, G., Y.L. Doz, and C.K. Prahalad (1989), 'Collaborate with your competitors and win', *Harvard Business Review*, vol. 67 (Jan/Feb), pp. 133–39.

Haldipur, R. (1998), 'Management and strategy lessons from Microsoft and Bill Gates', *Indian Management*, October.

Hall, Peter and R. Dixon (1989), *Franchising*, Pitman, UK.

Hari, P. (2002), 'The world of Biocon', *Business World*, 2 December.

Hodgetts, R.M., F. Luthans, and S.M. Lee (1994), 'New paradigm organizations: From total quality to learning to world-class', *Organizational Dynamics*, Winter.

'How mergers go wrong', *The Economist*, 22 July 1999.

Jauhari, Vinnie (2001), 'Managing mergers and acquisitions', 6th *International Conference on Global Business and Economic Development*, Bratislava, Slovekia, 7–10 Nov.

Jauhari, V. and K. Misra (2001), *Business Strategy*, Excel, New Delhi.

Jarillo, J.C. (1993), *Strategic Networks—Creating the Borderless Organisation*, London.

Kanter, R. M. (1994), 'Collaborative advantage: The art of alliances', *Harvard Business Review*, July–August, pp. 96–108.

Kim, K.J., H.J. Park, and N. Suzuki (1990), 'Reward allocations in the United States, Japan, Korea: A comparison of individualistic and collective cultures', *Academy of Management Journal*, vol. 33, pp. 188–198.

Kotabe, M., A. Sahay and Preet S. Aulakh (1996), 'Emerging role of technology licensing in the development of global product strategy: Conceptual framework and propostions', *Journal of Marketing*, vol. 60, January, pp. 73–88.

Kotabe, M. (1992), *Global Sourcing Strategy: R&D Manufacturing and Marketing Interfaces*, Quorum Books, New York.

Lei, D. and J.W. Slocum Jr (1991), 'Global strategic pay offs and pit falls, *Organizational Dynamics*, vol. 19, Winter, pp. 44–62.

Levitas, E. (1997), 'Selecting partners for successful international alliances: Examination of US and Korean firms', *Journal of World Business*, vol. 32, no. 1.

Levitas, E., M.A. Hitt, and M. Tina Dacin (1997), 'Competitive intelligence and knowledge development in strategic alliances', *Competitive Intelligence Review*, vol. 8, no. 2, pp. 20–27.

Lodge, G.C. and W.C. Crum (1985), 'The pursuit of remedies', in B.R. Scott and G.C. Lodge (eds), *US Competitiveness in the World Economy*, Harvard Business School Press, Boston, Massachusetts, pp. 479–502.

Mathai, P.G. and T. Surendar (1999), 'Pharma drama', *Business World*, 7–21 April.

Mitra, A. (1999), 'Zee may tie with French firm for DTH network', *Business Standard*, 26 March.

Mohr, J. and R. Spekman (1994), 'Characteristics of partnership success: Partnership attributes communication behaviour and conflict resolution techniques', *Strategic Management Journal*, vol. 15, pp. 143–152.

Mukherjee, S. (1999), 'Posing a challenge to BHEL', *Business Standard*, 24 March.

Ohmae, K. (1989), 'The global logic of strategic alliances', *Harvard Business Review*, March–April.

Ohmae, K. (1990), *The Borderless World*, Harper Collins, Glasgow, England.

Orsino, P.S. (1994), *Successful Business Expansion*, John Wiley, New York.

Parkhe, A. (1991), 'Inter firm diversity, organizational learning, and longevity in global strategic alliances', *Journal of International Business Studies*, vol. 22, pp. 579–601.

Peters, T. (1993), *Liberation Management*, Pan, London.

Pecenko, B. (1993), 'Franchising effects on small business entrepreneurship', *Public Enterprise*, vol. 13, no. 1–2, pp. 9–16.

'Pharmaceuticals: On tonic of mergers', Data India, *Business Standard*, March 1998.

Porter, M.E. (1980), *Competitive Strategy: Techniques for Analyzing Industries and Competitors*, Free Press, New York.

Rajadhyaksha, N. (1994), 'Are Indian brands worth so much', *Business World*, 5–18 October.

Ramu, Shiva, S. (1997), *International Licensing—Managing Intangible Resources*, Response Books, New Delhi.

Roy, R. (1999), 'Philip Morris set to acquire Godfrey Phillips', *Business Standard*, 2 April.

Sharma, D.D. (1984), 'Management contracts and international marketing industrial goods', in E. Mayhack (ed.) *International Marketing Management*, Praeger, New York.

Thakur, J.M. (1995), *Takeover of Companies: Law, Practice, and Procedure*, Snow-white, Bombay.

Venkiteswaran, N. (1997), 'Restructuring of corporate India: The emerging scenario', *Vikalpa*, vol. 22, no. 3, July–September.

Verma (1995), *Corporate Mergers, Amalgamations and Takeovers*, Bharat, New Delhi.

Verma, Vinnie (1999), 'Indian pharmaceutical industry: Some perspectives and issues in the coming decade', *Chemical Industry Digest*, January.

World Investment Report (2000), 'Cross Border Mergers & Acquisitions and Development', United Nations, Geneva.

Wright, P., M.J. Kroll, and J. Parnell (1996), *Strategic Management Concepts*, Prentice Hall, Englewood Cliffs, New Jersey.

Yoshino, M.Y. and S. Rangan (1995), *Strategic Alliances: An Entrepreneurial Approach to Globalization*, Harvard Business School Press, Boston MA.

Asia Times (2004), 'Fresh entries stir up Indian coffee market', http://www.atimes.com/ind-pak/DD30Df03.html., accessed on 8 December 2008.

'Award for Biocon CMD', *Business Line*, 11 October 2005, http://www.thehindubusinessline.com, accessed on 15 October 2005.

Biocon Annual Report (2006), Capitaline Database. http://www.biospectrumindia.com, accessed on 2 July 2007.

'Biocon chief tops poll of biotech personalities outside US, Europe', *Business Line*, 10 March 2006. http://www.thehindubusinessline.com/2006/03/10/stories/2006031003290800.htm, accessed on 12 May 2006.

'Biocon to sell insulin in US, Europe; up R&D', *The Financial Express*, 14 September 2006, press releases on www.biocon.com, accessed on 5 December 2006.

Biocon (2015), *Annual Report 2015*, www.biocon.com/drs/Biocon. Annual Report, accessed on 20 July 2015.

Business Standard (2004), http:indiacoffee.org/news letter/2004/jn/news_eyes.html, accessed on 25 June 2006.

Elliot, John (2005), 'Biotech Queen', *Fortune*, 14 November 2005, press releases on www.biocon.com, accessed on 5 December 2006.

http://thefirm.moneycontrol.com/story_page.php?autono=1053242, accessed on 5 December 2006.

http://trak.in/tags/business/2008/07/15/indian-mergersacquisitions-full-private-equity-funding-growth/, accessed on 22 September 2008.

http://trak.in/tags/business/2014/10/21/top-10-indian-mergers-acquisitions-2014/, accessed on 5 December 2006.

http://www.biocon.com, accessed on 28 September 2006.

http://www.euromoney-yearbooks-international-mergers-acquisitions-review-2014.pdf, accessed on 5 December 2014.

http://www.ey.com/IN/en/Newsroom/News-releases/EY-indian-m-and-a-transactions-on-rise-reflect-global-trends, accessed on 5 December 2006.

http://www.ey.com/Publication/vwLUAssets/EY-Firepower-Growth-Gap-Report-2014/$FILE/EY-Firepower-Growth-Gap-Report-2014.pdf, accessed on 5 December 2006.

http://www.forbes.com/sites/halahtouryalai/2014/02/12/worlds-100-biggest-banks-chinas-icbc-1-no-u-s-banks-in-top-5/, accessed on 5 December 2006.

http://www.investmentbank.kotak.com/downloads/euromoney-yearbooks-international-mergers-acquisitions-review-2014.pdf, accessed on 5 December 2006.

http://www.mergermarket.com/pdf/Mergermarket TrendReport.Q12014.Global-FinancialAdvisor LeagueTables.pdf, accessed on 5 December 2006.

http://www.nishithdesai.com/fileadmin/user_upload/pdfs/Research%20Papers/Outbound_Acquisitions_by_India_Inc.pdf, accessed on 5 December 2006.

http://www.virtualbangalore.com/Ppl/PplKiranM.php> http://nrcw.nic.in/shared/sublinkimages/166.htm, accessed on 25 September 2006.

Ibef (2015), 'Biotechnology industry in India', India Brand Equity Foundation (Ibef), www.ibef.org, accessed on 29 July 2015.

Indiacoffee.org (2004), 'Coffee consumption in India: Perspectives and prospects', http://indiacoffee.org/newsletter/2004/april/cover_story.html, accessed on 5 December 2006.

'Kiran Mazumdar is Eminent Businessperson', *The New Indian Express*, 25 February 2006, press releases on www.biocon.com, accessed on 5 December 2006.

Pharmabiz (2006), 'President Kalam dedicates BioMAb EGFR to the nation', 7 June, www.pharmabiz.com. accessed on 18 June 2006.

Shaw, Kiran Mazumdar (2006), 'We aim to make healthcare affordable to masses', *The Financial Express*, 29 January, press releases in www.biocon.com, accessed on 5 December 2006.

'Tata Coffee sells stake in Barista', http://in.news.yahoo.com, accessed on 5 March 2005.

The Economic Times (2005), 'Biotech turnover could touch $5bn by '10: Shaw', *The Economic Times*, 23 April 2005, press releases on www.biocon.com, accessed on 5 December 2006.

Thomson Reuters (2014), Mergers and Acquisitions, Review, www.dmi.thomsonreuters.com, accessed on 5 December 2014.

Emerging Service Sectors in India

Medanta—The Medicity

It is one of the largest multi-super specialty medical institutes in India. The hospital was founded in 2009 by renowned cardiovascular and cardiothoracic surgeon, Dr Naresh Trehan, and is located in Gurgaon, which is a part of the National Capital Region of Delhi, India. It is primarily known as an institute specializing in cardiology. Adhering to NABH standards, the hospital was accredited in 2013 by ISQua (International Society for Quality in Healthcare).

It is spread across 43 acres in Gurgaon NCR. It has 1,250 beds and over 350 critical care beds, besides 45 operation theatres. Medanta currently has 32 institutions, departments, and divisions that cater to over 20 specialties. In a nutshell, Medanta is an institution that matches the highest standards of healthcare delivery across the world. It offers not only the best technical facilities, but also clinical research, education, and training.

As a private sector multi-specialty hospital, Medanta has caused a flutter in the ₹1,50,000 crore Indian healthcare market. 'Our healthcare costs are already 15–20% lower than the current market rate,' Trehan says, adding, 'Medanta will make the highest-end healthcare affordable to the masses, including the weakest sections. Already, the hospital offers 5% free and another 20% as subsidized treatments'.

According to sector analysts, Medanta has followed a distinctive pricing strategy to take on its rival hospitals such as Fortis, Apollo, and Max Healthcare among others. It targets a large patient pool and therefore is able to keep its prices down.

According to Muralidharan Nair, Partner, Life sciences practice, Ernst & Young, 'Indian healthcare market is increasingly becoming price-driven and if Medanta is able to sustain its price advantage, other big hospitals in the National Capital Region would be forced to lower their healthcare costs as well'.

At a primary level, Medanta is a composite of multi-super specialty institutes that are led by renowned medical practitioners who spearhead their respective fields. As an equity partner, Punj Lloyd developed the infrastructure for the sprawling healthcare facility.

Nair further goes on to say that it is 'without any doubt, that Trehan has adopted a multi-pronged strategy in the creation of Medanta'. He further adds that 'Trehan is very well respected and has successfully leveraged his reputation in the medical fraternity and managed to attract the best talent available'. And given its proximity to Delhi international airport, Medanta is able to attract medical tourists from around the world for cheaper medical care.

After going through the chapter, you will be able to answer the following question:

1. What should Medanta do further to create a services brand that is attractive to both foreign and Indian patients?

Source: Based on Choudhary (2010) and Mathew (2010).

INTRODUCTION

According to Organisation for Economic Co-operation and Development (OECD) forecasts for the year 2050, India will be the world's third largest economy after China and USA. The Indian economy is set to grow at the rate of 10–11%. In 2007–08, the size of the Indian economy is set to cross $2 trillion (India Economic Survey 20014–15), while its GDP size would cross another milestone of $3 trillion after five years in 2019, according to IMF's latest world economic outlook. While the share of agriculture and allied sectors in GDP declined to 15.2% during eleventh plan and further to 13.9% in 2013–14 according to provisional estimates. The industry on the other hand grew by a meagre 1% in 2012–13 and slowed down further in 2013–14 posting a modest increase of 0.4%. The services sector accounts for 54% of GDP and has been growing at the rate of 9% since the mid-1990s (Eleventh Five Year Plan 2007–12). The services sector in India continues to be broad-based. India's services sector has remained resilient during the world economic crisis and is exhibiting visible signs of fresh growth during 2014–15, despite showing a subnormal growth during the down-turn. As the world GDP growth and trade show signs of improvement, key service sectors such as IT, transport, logistics aviation, and retail trading, have also begun to rebound. The growth of financial services comprising banking, insurance, and business services in the year 2012–13 was 12.9% (KPMG, Economic Survey Highlights 2013–14). Services exports have shown an average growth rate of 28% since the last decade. India has about 65% share of the global offshore market and a 46% share of the global business offshoring industry (BPOs). Exports of software services account for 46% of India's total service exports. Travel on the other hand accounted for nearly 12% share. However moving in tandem with global exports of financial services, India's exports of financial services registered a high growth of 34.4% in 2013–14 (KPMG, Economic Survey Highlights 2013–14). However, the Economic survey 2013–14 has identified potential high ticket items such as tourism and hospitality sector, port services, shipping, ship building and ship repairs and railways that have both manufacturing, and employment linkages.

The following topics cover four major sectors in India, such as biotechnology, healthcare, retailing, and banking.

Healthcare is an important emerging sector with many large corporate hospitals being created. India's big pharmaceutical firms such as Ranbaxy have also forayed into speciality hospitals. India has earned a name for itself in heart care and other specialized streams such as ophthalmology. Medical tourism is also booming.

The section on retailing gives an insight into the dynamics of the retail segment. In India, the segment has been dominated by the unorganized sector for centuries. With the emergence of specialty malls it displays a huge potential for growth.

The section on banking gives a perspective on the nature of services offered by this segment. It compares the role of the public and the private sectors. It also delineates the role of technology in this segment. An insight into the service mix elements—product, price, place, promotion, people, physical evidence, and process has also been delved upon.

HEALTHCARE SECTOR IN INDIA

The healthcare segment has an immense bearing on the growth of an economy. It is an extremely competitive global industry. Patients are prepared to travel to remote parts of the world in order to receive the service quality they hope for, and prefer to go to private hospitals for better service. There is little research comparing service opportunities in the private and public sector segments. Health service quality is a multidimensional variable and one can use SERVQUAL to measure the service quality. SERVQUAL represents six dimensions of service quality: tangibles, reliability, assurance, responsiveness, empathy, and accessibility.

Different research studies indicate that the analysis of healthcare can be broken into various segments such as patient confidence, business competence, treatment quality, supportive services, physical appearance, waiting time, and empathy (Jabnoun and Chaker 2003).

The experience of patients in the public and private healthcare segment may be very different. The most significant and widespread global trend in healthcare over the past decade has been the increasing share of for-profit healthcare and its commercialization across societies (Table 21.1). This has paralleled the process of economic globalization and is intrinsically linked to it. The process of the private sector entering into the healthcare segment began in the late 1970s, and early 1980s and 1990s. The factors which influence private participation in the healthcare segment are as follows (Baru 1998):

- Global actors including bilateral and multilateral agencies, pharmaceutical, medical equipment industries, insurance companies, and research institutions have played a critical role in shaping health policies across the world.
- The role of the state in each country, especially in terms of investments in public health services, pharmaceuticals, medical equipment, and insurance sectors in each of these countries.
- The growth of the middle-class and their influence on both the demand and supply of private health services.

Table 21.1   Growth of the healthcare industry in India

Year	Revenue
2008	$45 billion
2009	$52 billion
2010	$70 billion
2017 (Forecast)	$160 billion
2020 (Forecast)	$280 billion

Source: Based on the data from India Brand Equity Foundation report on Healthcare Industry in India (2014).

The trends in public investments have been similar to those in Pakistan and Bangladesh. While the Bhore Committee had recommended that 12% of total outlay must be earmarked for health, the figure never crossed 3%. Over the years it has witnessed a decline and is clearly inadequate for expansion of facilities. This gets reflected in the stagnation of public services from the 1980s through the 1990s. There is a shortage of paramedical staff in rural areas and this has negative consequences for the quality of services in the public sector.

Healthcare in India

The late 1980s saw the mushrooming of a number of corporate hospitals. Many of the corporate hospitals failed because they emerged in isolation and were not part of a larger picture. However, with liberalized health insurance and increasing awareness, and the spread of corporate hospitals, things are looking up.

Most Indian metros have hospitals with world-class infrastructure, processes, and outcomes. However, 70% of the healthcare infrastructure is confined to the top 20 cities of India. In order to reach the remaining population, innovations both in healthcare products and delivery are required.

The growth drivers of healthcare sector in India include (i) affordable treatment costs, (ii) rising population of the country and awareness among people about healthcare disorders, (iii) increase in focus on models like public private partnership (PPP), (iv) constantly rising interest of people in medical tourism, (v) rising disposable income, (vi) quicker diagnosis, leading to timely treatments, (vii) initiatives such as wellness check-ups and medical insurance taken by corporate houses, and (viii) rising penetration of health insurance.

Indian healthcare industry is all set for expansion because of several reasons (see Exhibit 21.1). One of the important reasons is the increase in medical tourism in India. The medical tourism industry in India is growing at a CAGR of 15% and is expected to touch $250 billion by 2020 (Brand Equity Foundation Report, 2014).

Indian healthcare has evolved over the years from being a government-led charitable care system to that led by the private sector. Healthcare in India today provides existing and new players with a unique opportunity to achieve innovation, differentiation, and profits. This leaves a lot of scope for private and international players to enter the sector.

Health Tourism

According to a KPMG–FICCI report (2014) medical tourists are defined as people from various countries who travel across international borders to receive some form of medical aide or treatment. In 2012, the global medical tourism industry was estimated at

Exhibit 21. 1   Reasons for the Growth of India's Healthcare Sector

- To standardize the quality of service delivery, control cost, and enhance patient engagement, healthcare providers are focusing on the technological aspect of healthcare delivery.
- The mobile health industry in India is expected to reach $0.6 billion by 2017. Strong mobile technology infrastructure and launch of 4G is expected to drive mobile health initiatives in the country. Digital health knowledge resources, electronic medical record, mobile healthcare, and hospital information system are some of the technologies gaining acceptance in the sector.
- Telemedicine is a fast emerging sector in India. In 2012, the telemedicine market in India was valued at $7.5 million and is expected to rise at a CAGR of 20% to $18.7 million.
- With increased private participation, the healthcare sector has also witnessed rise in FDI inflows. As per law, 100% FDI is permitted for all health-related services under the automatic route. Demand growth, cost advantages, and policy support were instrumental in attracting FDI inflows into the healthcare sector. During April 2000–March 2013, FDI inflows for drugs and pharmaceuticals stood at $10.3 billion, while inflows into hospitals and diagnostic centres, and medical appliances stood at $1.6 billion and $0.6 billion, respectively.
- India's competitive advantage also lies in increased success rate of Indian companies in getting abbreviated new drug application (ANDA) approvals. India also offers vast opportunities in R&D as well as medical tourism.

around $10.5 billion. It is expected to grow at a CAGR of 17.9% from 2013–19 to reach $32.5 billion in 2019. Additionally, due to the highly fragmented nature of the industry there are various estimates of the market size.

There are two segments of people who travel to other countries—people who are looking at rejuvenation therapies and those who travel for medical treatment. The latter category is classified as the economy segment as medical care costs in their own country are considerably higher. This segment is price sensitive, which in turn is the exact reason for them to travel to any particular destination.

Indian medical value travel industry has emerged as the fastest growing segment despite the global downturn. However, it is fragmented in its approach because it is usually an individual hospital initiative in the country, unlike countries such as the USA, Japan, Jordon, and Malaysia, which are more organized in promoting themselves. On the other hand, India as a country has not leveraged its competitive and comparative advantage appropriately in the healthcare sector.

The USP of Indian medical tourism industry is the combination of high quality facilities, competent, English-speaking medical professionals, cost effectiveness, and various tourist attractions. Various estimates peg the cost of treatments in India between $3,000 and $10,000, while dental, eye, and cosmetic surgeries cost 3–4 times less in India as compared to western countries. Additionally, medical tourists usually get a package deal that includes flights, hotels, treatment, and, often, a post-operative vacation from travel agents.

Healthcare has emerged as one of the largest service sectors with estimated revenue of around $30 billion constituting 5% of GDP and offering employment to around

Rejuvenation therapy is popular with tourists arriving in India

Credit: IndiaPicture/Mahatta Multimedia Pvt. Ltd.

4 million people. It is estimated that by 2025, Indian population will reach 1.4 billion with about 45% constituting urban adult (15 years +). To cater to this demographic change, the healthcare sector will have to be about $100 billion in size contributing nearly 8–10% of the GDP of that year. By then, it is estimated that the 10 large national healthcare networks would be able to absorb 30% of the market share. The leaders in the Indian healthcare sector are already being benchmarked to international quality and efficiency standards. According to an industry report, the growth of this sector has begun to contribute to 6–7% of GDP (CII).

The key advantage of Indian healthcare sector are (i) cost advantage, (ii) no waiting time, as compared to advanced nations such as the US and UK, (iii) diagnostics and pathology services, which are outsourced by foreign hospital chains due to the high cost differential in India, and (iv) clinical trials, which can be easily carried out because of the availability of a huge patient pool along with the cost advantage with testing of drugs possible at 60% of the price.

Within the country the healthcare system is expanding and developing rapidly both in terms of services and spending in the public as well as private sectors. The share of the private sector in healthcare delivery is expected to increase from 66% in 2005 to an estimated 81% by 2015. Growing awareness about quality healthcare across the country has also contributed to a substantial demand for high-quality and specialty healthcare services in tier-II and tier-III cities. Many healthcare players such as Fortis and Manipal Group have entered management contracts to provide an additional revenue stream to hospitals.

Additionally, there is a huge potential for health insurance, because only 10% of people have some sort of health coverage in the country and therefore the potential market for health insurance is very large. McKinsey–CII estimates the number of potential insurable lives at 315 million with a potential of $7,700 million in health insurance premium by 2015.

Government Policy

In the mid-1980s, the healthcare sector was recognized as an industry. Hence, it was possible for the players to get long-term funding from financial institutions. The government also reduced the import duty on medical equipment and technology, paving way for technological upgradation in the industry.

Since the national health policy, with its main objective of 'health for all' by the year 2000, was approved in 1983, little has been done to update or amend the policy even as the epidemiological profile of the country changed and new health problems arose from ecological degradation. The focus so far has been on medical care and not on comprehensive healthcare.

The hospitals are also handicapped with government regulations, which do not allow them to advertise. As hospitals spend millions of rupees in technology and infrastructure, it becomes necessary for them to attract patients and generate funds.

In India, approximately 60% of the total health expenditure comes from the self-paid category as against government's contribution of 25–30%; the contribution from insurance companies is negligible.

The majority of private hospitals are expensive for a normal middle-class family. The opening up of the insurance sector to private players has helped improve the access to healthcare establishments. Health insurance will make healthcare affordable to a large number of people.

The health insurance segment is increasingly penetrating the health sector in the country. Total premium has seen a growth of 17% in 2012–13 when compared with the previous fiscal. So far the total premium collected by the health insurance companies in the fiscal year 2012–13 stands at ₹15,701 crore as compared to the last fiscal. According to Insurance Regulatory and Development Authority (IRDA), 'Health insurance continues to be one of the rapidly growing sectors. This segment of non-life insurance business has continued to grow at double digit figure for the past five years, although the growth rate has receded considerably from the high level witnessed during the period from 2006–07 to 2010–11'. The combined share of the four public sector insurers in the total health insurance premium was 61%. Private insurers accounted for 28% and the rest was made up of the stand-alone health private insurers in the total premium. Health insurance segment has grown at a CAGR (compounded annual growth rate) of 30.05% during the past seven years and that is substantially higher than the CAGR (17.5%) of gross domestic premium growth for the same period. According to IRDA the high CAGR of health segment has led to a noticeable rise in its share in non-life premium. Health segment's share stood at 22.19% in 2012–13 up from 10.91% in 2005–06.

Despite this, if the world figures are considered, only 2 million people (0.2% of a total population of 1 billion) are covered under Mediclaim, whereas in developed nations like the US, about 75% of the total population are covered under such insurance schemes. One reason could be that the agencies that offer the scheme have never marketed health insurance aggressively. Moreover, agencies like GIC take up to six months to process claims and to reimburse customers after they have paid for treatment out of their own pockets.

Issues Related to Private Health Insurance in India

Mahal (2002) in his outstanding work on private health insurance in India suggests that the introduction of private health insurance can contribute to increasing the aggregate costs of healthcare in several different ways. In their interactions between the healthcare providers and customers' such as doctors and patients, it is given that the former have much better information about their patient's health status and future course of treatment than the latter. The patient is fairly dependent on the course of treatment recommended by a physician. One consequence is that in a regime of pure indemnity insurance, providers have an incentive to provide more care than may be medically appropriate. The problem will arise when the patient can choose his/her doctor and treatment freely and then present the bill to the insurer for reimbursement. There is another dimension to the whole process. Once insured, an individual faces a reduced incentive to take health precautions. Also, a sick person may feel less compelled to control her consumption of healthcare and expensive diagnostic examinations if medical care costs are covered by insurance.

Key Success Factors

Location of the hospital is a key success factor. The major factors in deciding the location of a hospital are:
- a central place having easy accessibility
- space around the hospital for future expansion
- space to make provision for residential quarters for the staff
- hostel facility, if there is to be a college on campus.

It is also beneficial if the hospital is located in a place where there is no other hospital in the vicinity. For example, when Apollo opened in Delhi, there was no other hospital for 200 km, which proved to be a boon for them.

Also, diseases which are characteristic of a certain region, can affect the location. For example, studies conducted by Fortis show that north Indians are more prone to cardiac diseases and so it has set up a 200-bed cardiac hospital and 12 smaller cardiac centres in and around Mohali (Chandigarh).

In case of Mumbai, where space is a problem and there are already a lot of hospitals, super-speciality hospitals make more business sense. Technology plays an immense role in delivering better quality healthcare through application of telecommunications technology or rather tele-medicine. This will help transfer of electronic medical data, including high-resolution images, sounds, live video, and patient records from one location to another through telephone lines, ISDN, modem, Internet, satellites, video-conferencing, etc.

Mathur (2003) has evaluated the impact of IT on healthcare management in India. The role of IT in healthcare and its impact through services trade depends on three related aspects:

1. Power and reach of telematic connectivity, which determines who will be included.
2. Legitimacy of service providers seeking return on investments.
3. Structure of responsibilities for healthcare, which are a part of the government frame in local and national jurisdictions.

The stakeholders' goals by performance criteria as postulated by Mathur (2003) are indicated in Table 21.2.

Hospitals need to have long-term understanding with Preferred Provider Organizations (PPOs), which further have an understanding with corporates. In case an employee in any of these corporates has an illness, it is referred to the PPOs, which sends them to the hospital for check-up and treatment.

The success rate of crucial operations and surgeries reflect the technological and knowledge-based edge of a hospital over its competitors. Such successes are discussed in health magazines and newspapers, which becomes a natural advantage for the hospital.

Some hospitals by means of their past track record have created a niche market for themselves. For example, the Hinduja Hospital in India is known for its high-quality healthcare at reasonable rates, whereas Lilavati Hospital is known for its five-star services. Hospitals can also promote medical colleges. This helps them to generate extra resources in the form of fees, using the same infrastructure.

Sources of revenue

The general perception that large hospitals with high bed-occupancy rate are profitable is misleading. Experience from around the world shows that hospitals with more than 250 beds do not do well. Many Indian hospitals are following the US healthcare industry practice by decreasing the average length of stay of patients and increasing patient turnover. Research conducted in the US shows that 80% of the revenues from a

Table 21.2   Stakeholder goals by performance criteria

Healthcare stakeholders	Criteria		
	Choice	Efficiency	Cost
Consumers	Does choice of healthcare commodities, services, and facilities expand?	Countervailing institutions? Quality standards? Competition?	Pricing? Safety? Data privacy?
Service providers	Which cross border networks?	Synergy effects in innovation of production and distribution?	Reduced costs on development and delivery?
Insurers (Firms, employers)	Data-based calculus for financing? Consolidation?	Scale effects? Cross border delivery?	Reduced costs? Health maintenance organizations? Moral hazards? Leakages?
Governments	Designing health systems with national/global scope?	Side effects/spillovers? Equitable norms?	Burden on public finances? Trade balance? Investment flows? Human capital?

patient comes within the first 72 hours of admission. Hospitals generate a lot of revenue from general inspection if the patient turnover is very high.

A large percentage of revenue comes from specialized services like operations and surgeries. For these reasons, many corporates are planning for small, 100-bed specialized hospitals, which cater to specific diseases such as cardiac, cosmetic surgery, and neurology.

Research has also shown that there is a lot of scope for super-speciality hospitals with 100–50 beds, which generate revenues equivalent to a large 500-bed general hospital. Typically, large hospitals with approximately 500-bed capacity take about 9–10 years to break even, whereas super-specialty hospitals with about 100 beds only take about 6–7 years to break even.

General room charges do not contribute significantly to the hospital revenues, unlike intensive care units (ICU). The general room to ICU/ICCU room ratio depends upon the type of the hospital. In case of general hospitals, the ratio is about 8:2, whereas in case of a specialized hospital, it is about 6:4. Hospitals have in-house doctors and visiting consultants. The visiting doctors contribute a certain percentage (approximately 15%) of their billings to the hospital revenues. Hospitals can also generate revenue from medicines if they are supplying them in-house. Some hospitals make it mandatory for their patients to buy medicines from the hospital's chemist shop. A margin of 15–20% can be charged for such medicinal supplies.

Though many hospitals run by trusts do not earn this way, new entrants or corporates, for whom the private healthcare sector is a direct extension of their line of business (for example, pharma companies), can generate good returns from the supply of medicines. Hospitals promoting medical studies generate extra resources in the form of fees, using the same infrastructure. For example, Manipal Hospital charges more fees from foreign students.

More and more overseas Indians fly home to visit their doctors here because they have complete confidence in them. They get world-class treatment at a fraction of the cost they would have to pay abroad, as liberalization has speeded up the entry of the latest state-of-the-art equipment.

Medical charges in India are between one-tenth and one-thirtieth of that in the US. For example, a bypass surgery, which costs $3000 in the US, costs only ₹35,000– 40,000 in India, with the same technologies and facilities.

This is also because Indian doctors are amongst the best in the world. They prefer to consult these doctors for their chronic diseases such as high blood pressure, diabetes, neurological problems, and even dentistry.

Modern Healthcare Management

Third-party administrator (TPA) can play a major role by managing the healthcare needs of groups of individuals. A TPA will negotiate better deals for their customers and sort out the medical claims for a fee. On the other hand, a PPO can manage almost all the healthcare needs of their customers. However, PPOs cannot provide insurance cover, as they do not assume the risk of their clients. But now, with private insurance operators coming into the picture, most PPOs and TPAs will turn into health maintenance organizations (HMO), by linking their products with insurance companies, or even hospitals. (As of today, HMOs are not allowed in India).

A key aspect of HMOs is that they carry the risk of their customers, and hence they will want to know the bio-informatics and the epidemiological data of clients. Understanding the disease trends of their clients helps them to know which risk to carry, how much, and at what price.

Experience, mostly in the US, has shown that HMOs have lowered the cost of treatment (it is in their interest to make sure payouts to hospitals are reduced), ensured preventive care, and made the healthcare industry, by and large, more professional.

For the healthcare boom to succeed, it is imperative that hospitals do not fail. Overseas, where the HMOs have a say in the way hospitals are run, they keep a tight control of costs and revenues. HMOs have still not made their entry in to the country, but PPOs, thanks to the sheer quantum of business they bring, are already influencing the way hospitals are managed, in the same way that mutual funds keep the companies they invested in on their toes.

Hospitals can become integrated healthcare systems, that is, when medicines, food services, laundry, and linen, will become 'purchased' services. These third-party operations will increase the profit margins.

The corporate hospitals will play a positive role in the healthcare sector by taking the load off government hospitals, whose performance has not been up to the mark.

Over the years many mergers and acquisitions have occurred in hospitals in the US. A major advantage of these mergers is the move towards more integrated healthcare systems, which can achieve economies of scale by rationalizing capacity and amalgamating functions such as information technology, consultants, emergency transport, database, and research and development.

But healthcare is primarily a local market business and it is very important to consider the following factors before going in for mergers:
- relative sizes of the hospitals
- their geographical proximity
- the relationship between individual hospitals and physicians
- degree of unity in leadership structures of separate institutions.

Again, research in the US has shown that merged hospitals in narrowly defined geographic areas, with few or no competitors, have succeeded in exerting a favourable influence on the services.

The key to success appears to be a strong orientation to performance, as well as standardizing and integrating work processes, functions, suppliers, and investments, but not necessarily on a centralized basis. For example, Apollo in Chennai, Hyderabad, and Delhi will be separate hospitals postmerger, but functions will be centralized.

Some type of mergers can be for synergy of skills. For example, to help the merged organizations benefit from one another's individual strengths by applying them across the board. It also helps them to make joint investments in branding or information technology and also to react effectively to the changed market forces.

Alternatively, hospitals can go in for group purchases, as in America. The buying power of large PPOs in USA such as Premier, VHA/UHC and AmeriNet gives them the clout to exert price pressure on suppliers, particularly for products in lower demand. As PPOs have become consolidated, manufacturers have to offer bigger discounts in order to hold on to their contracts. So, there exists a lot of supply management opportunity, which will affect spending productivity.

Outlook

Demographic data available from the National Centre for Applied Economic Research (NCAER) states that the national average of the proportion of households in the low income group (annual income < ₹25,000) has declined from 58.84% in 1990 to 49% in 1996. On the other hand, the middle and higher middle income group (annual income > ₹50,000) has increased from 14% to 20%.

With the opening up of the insurance sector, a lot of private players will come out with innovative insurance products, which will further drive the healthcare revenues.

Considering the middle and higher middle income groups, we get a conservative estimate of 35–38 million households or 200 million insurable lives. They provide a ready market for corporate hospitals. The Indian healthcare industry can replicate the success of the IT industry if the resources are utilized well and the demand–supply gap is reduced. The fact that patients from about 55 countries are treated in Indian hospitals and thousands of international patients visit Apollo Hospitals and Fortis healthcare annually, indicate that the potential of this industry is huge. It is important that the healthcare facilities are made accessible to more and more people. The future step towards this should be expansion, that is, to set up private hospitals and healthcare facilities in Tier II and Tier III cities and towns of India. For this to become a reality, creation of better infrastructure for increased access to these locations is extremely important.

BIOTECHNOLOGY INDUSTRY IN INDIA

Biotechnology holds a lot of promise for India. As a stream of science, it has the ability to deliver the next wave of technological change. The growth of the sector can usher in employment generation, intellectual wealth creation, enhance industrial growth, and generate entrepreneurial opportunities.

Comparisons can be drawn between the growth of the IT sector and the biotechnology sectors in India:
- In the biotech area, the assets are more capital intensive.
- The return on investment takes a longer time to materialize.
- Intellectual property assets are important.
- A high level of skill and education are required.
- There are strong roots in the education system. In a lot of incubation projects, academics have taken a lead in setting up new ventures.
- There are gaps in the competencies available and the skill set required by the industry.

There are three main segments in the biotechnology segment:

1. Biopharmaceuticals (i.e., vaccines, therapeutics, diagnostics, and animal healthcare products)
2. Bioindustry (i.e., enzymes, organo-amino acids, and yeast-based products)
3. Bioservices (i.e., clinical research, contract research, contract manufacturing, and bioinformatics)

Insight into the Biotech Industry in India

The biotech industry is growing at an average rate of about 20% and according to a study it may reach $7 billion mark by the end of FY15. India's biotech industry is made up of bio-pharmaceuticals, bio-services, bio-agriculture, bio-industry, and bioinformatics.

According to a study conducted by The Associated Chambers of Commerce and Industry (Assocham), 'The biotechnology industry in India, comprising of about 400 companies has grown three-fold in the last five years to reach $4 billion in FY13'.

From the perspective of revenue generation of ₹1,600 crore, the bio-pharma sectors lead the growth of the biotech industry. Additionally, India has emerged as a leading destination for clinical trials, contract research and manufacturing activities, which accounts for revenue generation worth about ₹3,800 crore.

Increasing investments, outsourcing activities, and exports are the key drivers for growth in India's biotech sector.

Government Interventions

The government of India has over the years been spending higher amounts of money on the department of biotechnology. The government has decided to initiate the following strategic actions for the promotion of the biotechnology sector in India in order to:

- create a national task force on education and training
- formulate a human resource development strategy
- deploy initiatives towards curriculum development
- take measures to strengthen the teaching and R&D in life sciences and biotechnology in universities
- create science and technology leaders for the industry.

Table 21.3   Biotech industry market break-up

Segment	2012–13 (as percentage of the total market)
Biopharma	64%
Bioservices	18%
Bioagri	14%
Bioindustrial	3%
Bioinformatics	1%

Source: Based on the data from India Brand Equity Foundation (IBEF) (2014).

Table 21.3 illustrates the biotech industry market break up in India.

Table 21.4 lists the top 10 biotech companies by turnover.

India's Strengths in the Sector

India's strengths in the biotech segment are as follows:

- Availability of skilled and educated manpower.
- Indian companies are committed to global standards.

Table 21.4   Top 10 biotech companies by turnover

Rank	Company	Revenue (in $ million)
1	Serum Institute of India	437.1
2	Biocon	344.5
3	Nuziveedu Seeds	143.2
4	Novo Nordisk	131.1
5	Reliance Life Sciences	144.4
6	Rasi Seeds	42.1
7	Panacea Biotec	32.1
8	Bharat Biotech	71.6
9	Ankur Seeds	62.7
10	Mahyco	45.3

Source: Based on the data from ABLE–Biospectrum Industry Survey, June 2013, Aranca Research.

Allocation of budget to the department of biotechnology between 8th to 12th five year plans (₹ crore)

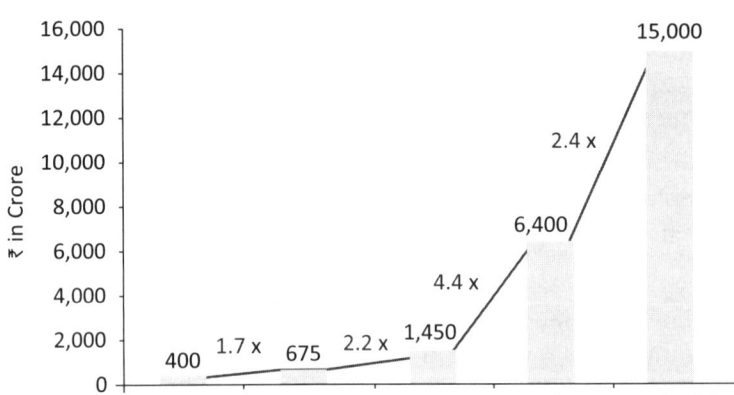

Fig. 21.1   Budgetary allocations to the Department of Biotechnology
Availability of venture capital and a growing economy

Source: Based on a presentation by Dr M.K. Bhan, Department of Biotechnology
Association of Biotechnology Led Enterprise (ABLE).

- There are a large number of companies operating in various areas.
- There is a strong MNC presence, which helps firms to compete.
- Have competencies in specific areas such as vaccines.
- There are enormous strengths in areas of bioinformatics.
- Have capabilities to manage clinical trials. There is a high incidence of infectious/lifestyle diseases and an excellent pool of doctors and physicians.
- There is a huge network of research laboratories.
- Rich biodiversity is available in India.

The Department of Biotechnology intends to support the creation of incubators in biotech parks promoted by private industry or through public–private partnerships. Concessions will be provided to firms located in biotech parks.

According to the Technology Information Forecasting and Assessment Council of India (TIFAC) there were 2378 biotechnology patent applications which were filed bet ween 1995 and 2003 (TIFAC 2004).

There is evidence of a large number of alliances being fostered between academia and industry.

The outsourcing of clinical trials is on the rise. Also, there are a large number of alliances being forged with foreign firms in different areas such as agriculture, health-care, environment, and industrial biotechnology. There are clusters of biotech firms in Hyderabad, Bangalore, Mumbai, Delhi, and Chennai.

Challenges

The biotechnology sector faces the following challenges:
- It is a highly competitive sector with a large number of small firms.
- There is a need for a large number of science graduates and also for research capabilities.
- This segment requires intensive research investments both by firms and educational institutions. The educational institutions will also need to make higher investments in research programmes which are also aligned well with reality.
- The intellectual property issues also have to be dealt with, specially in the context of international collaborations.
- Venture capital support is required for the incubation of new biotechnology firms.

Conclusion

There is a need to prioritize research areas and make focused investments. Coordination between agencies is also required. In addition, there is a need for making investments in innovation and nurturing local research talent, and India needs more Ph.D.s in these areas. Technology entrepreneurship should be sustained in the universities. The regulatory framework needs to be strengthened. Entrepreneurship in this sector should be encouraged and firms should be more open to collaborations and networks.

THE RETAILING SECTOR IN INDIA

Modern retail globalization is accelerating. Since 2001, more than 89 new markets have been entered by more than 49 new retailers. India is an attractive destination as far as retail is concerned. According to the Global Economic Outlook 2014, India contributed towards 4% of the global GDP, which increased to 6% in 2012 and is expected to reach 8% by 2025.

'India remains an appealing long-term retail destination for several reasons, starting with its demographics—a population of 1.2 billion people, half of whom are younger than 30 years and roughly one-third of whom live in cities. Indians' disposable incomes are increasing, allowing them to spend more and try new products, brands, and categories while spending a lower proportion on food'. (AT Kearney 2014).

The retail sector in India can be broadly divided into two segments—value retailing, which is typically a low margin-high volume business (primarily food and groceries), and lifestyle retailing, a high margin-low volume business (apparel, footwear, etc.). The sector is further divided into various categories, depending on the types of products offered. Food dominates market consumption with 60% share followed by fashion. The relatively low contribution of other categories indicates opportunity for organized retail growth in these segments, especially with India being one of the world's youngest markets (Equity Master 2014).

Transition from traditional retail to organized retail is taking place due to changing consumer expectations, growing middle class, higher disposable income, preference for luxury goods, change in the demographic mix, etc. The convenience of shopping with multiplicity of choice under one roof (shop-in-shop), and the increase of mall culture etc. are factors appreciated by the new generation. These factors are expected to drive organized retail growth in India over the long run (Equity Master 2014).

Concerns for the industry include an opaque real estate market with high prices and low availability, high borrowing costs, personnel shortages, expensive supply chains, and unpredictable politics both locally and regionally. More retailers today are focusing on 'improving operations and back-end processes to increase profitability'. Lean models—in terms of size, capital spending, and operating costs—are gaining hold, and even incumbent retailers are reducing store sizes and opening new stores only in carefully selected locations (AT Kearney 2014).

AT Kearney (2006) studied that successful retailers:
* enter a high potential market early
* take their time to develop
* are willing to experiment with a variety of store formats
* assemble a team comprised mainly of local nationals who know the market and the culture, and then
* give these local managers substantial authority to find the formula that works.

But speed to market alone doesn't equal success and global retailers like Carrefour and Auchan do not find the Indian market attractive due to FDI rules (Agarwal 2014).

INDIAN RETAIL INDUSTRY

The Indian retail industry, traditionally dominated by the family-run *kirana* stores, has faced a tremendous metamorphosis both in format and structure. Indian retailing has the highest retail density in the world (Vishvas and Murugaiah 2006) and the past few years have witnessed the evolution of organized retailing with numerous players, both national and international, joining the fray. The total retailing market in India in 2014 stood at $490 billion. The organized sector accounted for $39.2 billion, that is, 8% of the total (Ministry of External Affairs, GOI 2014). This organized retailing is expected to cross ₹47 lakh crore by 2016–17 (Capital Market 2014). Today, the organized retail sector has 300 malls, 1500 supermarkets, and 325 departmental stores (Vishvas and Murugaiah 2006).

Retailing is India's largest industry and accounts for 22% of GDP and contributes to 8% of the total employment in India (Reuters 2011). According to AT Kearney's 2006 Global Retail Development Index (GRDI), India occupied the first ranking, which had been taken over by Vietnam. It was studied that India consistently ranked in the top ten in GRDI from 2001–2012 (AT Kearney 2011a, 2011b, 2012). However in 2013 it stood at 14th and in 2014 it stood at 20th position (AT Kearney 2013, 2014). India remains an appealing long-term retail destination for several reasons. Indians' disposable incomes are increasing, allowing them to spend more and try new products, brands, and categories while spending a lower proportion on food (AT Kearney 2014).

The rise of the double income family (resulting in increased purchasing power), higher mobility, availability of credit cards, changed lifestyle, and scarcity of time, necessitate the need for convenience shopping. Organized retailing in India is predominantly an urban phenomenon and players are now moving to tier II and III cities as tier I cities have been explored enough and have reached a saturation level (Equity aster 2014). Many players are trying to recreate the ambience and experience of foreign shopping malls and are providing wide product range, quality, and value for money to create a memorable shopping experience (Kaushesh 2002).

Retail Defined

Gilbert (1999), defines *retail* as, 'Any business that directs its marketing efforts towards satisfying the final consumer based upon the organization of selling goods and services as a means of distribution', and *international retail* as, 'the process of a retailer transferring its retail operations, concept, management expertise, technology, and/or buying function across national borders'.

'Any retail outlet chain (and not a one-stop outlet) which is professionally managed (even if it is family run), has accounting transparency (with proper usage of MIS and accounting standards), and organized supply chain management with centralized quality control and sourcing (certain part of sourcing can be locally made), can be termed as organized retailing in India' (Vishvas and Murugaiah 2006).

Indian Retail Structure

The Indian retail industry is divided into organized and unorganized sectors. *Organized retailing* refers to 'trading activities undertaken by licensed retailers, that is, those registered for sales tax, income tax, etc'. This includes retail chains, hypermarkets, large retail business, etc. The *unorganized retailing* sector refers to local *kirana* stores, mom-pop stores, *paan/beedi* shops, convenience stores, hand-cart and pavement vendors, etc. There are more than 12 million mom-pop stores in India (*Retail Merchandiser* 2006). According to KSA Technopak, organized retail constituted just 2% of retail sales in India in 2002, and went on to 7% in 2011–12 wil become 10.2% by 2016–17 (Table 21.5).

The initial growth in organized retailing was slow and concentrated in the metros. Due to the high investment required for real estate, the real estate developers have been

Table 21.5 Retail industry in India

	2011–12	2016–17
Estimated size of retail in India	₹23 lakh crore	₹47 lakh crore
Share of organized retail in India (%)	7	10.2
Size of organized retail in India	₹1.61 lakh crore	₹4.79 lakh crore

Source: Based on Assocham statistics cited in Capital Market 2014.

the major players in organized retailing in India such as DLF, Rajan Raheja, K. Raheja, and DS group (Fitch Report 2003).

The study of development of retailing in India brings forth some interesting facts.

Region-specific retail   Retailing is region-specific with players making their presence felt in a particular region, for example, Apna Bazar has 75 stores in Mumbai only, and Foodworld has 75 outlets in South India, and Wills Sport has 29 stores in Delhi (*The Economic Times* 2003).

Emergence of discount formats   As Indians are more price conscious and look for value for-money, large discount format stores, that is, hypermarkets have emerged as major competition to both organized and unorganized retail.

Large number of international players   With the government announcing that international brands can now set up their retail chain with majority stake, a large number of international players are eyeing India. Some of the international players already in the market are Landmark Group, Dubai; Metro, Germany, Mango, Spain; McDonald's, USA; Dominos, USA, etc. (Fitch 2003).

Mall development   Malls started developing in India in the late 1990s with Crossroads in Mumbai and Ansal Plaza in Delhi taking the lead. The total organized retail supply in 2013 stood at approximately 4.7 million sq ft, witnessing a strong year-on-year growth of about 78% over the total mall supply of 2.5 million sq ft in 2012 (Ministry of External Affairs, GOI 2014).

Business Models for Retailing

Every product/process has a life cycle. If we analyse the global retail trends we see that in the past 11 years (i.e., 1995–2006) the market attractiveness follows the same consistent pattern, that is, opening, peaking, declining, and closing. This usually happens over a period of 5–10 years.

Marketers can plan the business models when they are entering a country based on which life cycle stage the country is in at that point of time. The business model or retail format is the type of mix the retailers adopt regarding the nature of merchandise and services offered, pricing policy, advertising and promotion, store design, store size, and location (Lamba 2003). However, AT Kearney (2006) says that the business model chosen should match with the market stage of the country you are entering. Some of the different business models for retailing are as follows:

Convenience stores   These are the modern version of the friendly neighbourhood stores, easily accessible and having the essential items; for example, 7-Eleven chain of convenience stores, Spencer's (220 stores in 2013), etc. (IBEF 2013).

Department stores   These are usually multi-tiered large stores that stock a vast range of products in a variety of departments. Their number in India has grown by 24% per annum over the past five years and their sales have grown even more rapidly by about 34% annually over the period 1999–2003. The upper-middle and high income classes predominantly frequent these stores. Most department stores stock a range of branded goods to cater to the customer's demands. Examples are Shoppers Stop and Lifestyle, and Trent. Reliance Retail has launched Reliance Trends in this format (IBEF 2013; Jhamb and Bhardwaj 2006).

Specialty stores   As the name suggests these stores offer a particular line of merchandise and cater to a niche market. They offer lower prices than other types of retailers selling similar items, for example Bata, Tanishq, Titan, etc.

Supermarkets   These are departmentalized self-service stores offering a wide variety of food and household goods. They offer products at lower prices by reducing the margins. In India, there are no major national supermarket chains and most of the organized retailers prefer to operate in particular regions, for example, Foodworld. In 2007, Reliance Fresh was also launched by Reliance Industries in the supermarket format (INR News 2007).

Superstores   These are also called combination stores and are larger versions of supermarkets. They are usually situated on the outskirts of the city and occupy a large area. Popular examples are Wal-Mart, K-Mart, and Target.

Discount stores   As the name suggests, in this format the consumer gets the items at a discounted price. Indian customers have already experienced these discount stores like Giant by the RPG group and Big Bazaar from Pantaloon. Big Bazaar's promoters did not have the product expertise in all the products offered at their stores. So they came up with 'consolidator' concept where different national players were given a space in the stores with the understanding that they would provide the best deal in town (Shah 2002).

Hypermarkets   These are larger retail stores which combine superstores and discount stores. Hypermarkets result in a colossal retail facility carrying an enormous range of products. They have the potential to satisfy all the routine weekly shopping needs of the customers in a single trip. Big Bazaar and Giant are the main players in India. Reliance announced its entry in the retailing sector with an investment of ₹25,000 crore (*The Economic Times* 2006). This retail rollout was launched on August 14, 2007 as India's largest hypermarket under the name 'Reliance Mart' in Ahmedabad. At the time of the launch, it carried a range of over 95,000 products catering to the entire family (INR News 2007). The other hypermarkets in India are HyperCITY, Spencer Hyper, etc.

Warehouse stores   Just like the low-cost airlines, warehouse stores project a low price image by offering their merchandise in a no-frills environment. They carry limited merchandise, displayed in simple cut boxes and price them low by cutting on the profits.

Shopping malls   These are a common mall where a variety of retailers are located and are not retail stores in the true sense. Recent times have seen the emergence of many malls in India. One of the reasons for this can be the convergence of retail and entertainment sectors (*The Economic Times* 2003). The first malls to develop in India were Spencer Plaza in Chennai (1998), Crossroads in Mumbai (1999), and Ansal Plaza in Delhi (2000). 'A mall without walls is the latest innovation in mall formats to hit India in the form of Bangalore Central launched by Pantaloon Retail (India) Ltd in May 2004 in Bangalore. Unlike the regular malls which are consortiums of clearly demarcated shops, the seamless mall is akin to an enormous trail outlet housing hundreds of well- known brands, sharing space with each other. The brands are showcased category-wise and once the customer focuses his attention on a desired category, competing brands vie with each other for a share of his mind space and pocket. Common facilities such as centralized billing, marketing, and loyalty programmes benefit both, the customers and participating brands. Besides this, it also houses a coffee shop, a food court, a supermarket, a pub, a fine-dining restaurant, a discotheque, and even India's first in-house radio station Radio Central' (Bharwani and Bhushan 2005).

Cash and carry   This is generally targeted towards small wholesale customers who buy in bulk and pay in cash. Whereas the other models concentrate on business to customer, this model targets business to business customers. Hotels, restaurants, caterers, and exporters generally prefer this model as they get products at a price lower than the market price. The basic concept is a retailer selling to another retailer and not competing with it. German giant Metro AG has entered India as a cash and carry store and has five stores across Mumbai, Kolkata, Hyderabad, and Bangalore (IBEE 2013).

Direct catalogue retailing   This is a successful business proposition as entrepreneurs can set up the business without going into the heavy investment of owning/renting an elaborate showroom. They can successfully run the venture of mail order retailing even from their warehouse. However, this is not a good idea in India where customers like to feel the product and satisfy themselves before going for the final purchase, and where there is scepticism about getting the product after having made the payment in advance to an unseen company.

Web stores   With the widening and ever-increasing use of the Internet non-store retailing is also spreading at a fast rate. India's online retail industry has grown at a swift pace in the last five years from around ₹15 billion ($249.64 million) revenue in 2007–08 to ₹139 billion ($ 2.31 billion) in 2012–13, translating into a CAGR of over 56%. The nine-fold growth came on the back of increasing internet penetration and changing lifestyles, and was primarily driven by books, electronics, apparel, beauty, and personal care.

According to Crisil Research, the online retail business in India is expected to grow at a whopping 50–55% annually to become a ₹50,000 crore ($8.32 billion) business in the next three years. During the same period, ecommerce companies could capture around 18% of the country's organized retail market, up from their current share of about 8%. India's urban population has contributed immensely to the growth of the online market in the country. Mumbai has left behind all other cities in India in shopping online; Delhi ranks second and Kolkata ranks third in the preference for online shopping in 2013. In the next 7–10 years, around 30–40% of the total retail in India's top 75 cities is expected to be carried out online, as per Arvind Singhal, Chairman and Founder, Technopak Advisors.

In India, Flipkart and Snapdeal dominate the online marketplaces. Snapdeal brands itself as the biggest online marketplace in India and allows more than 20,000 businesses to sell on its platform. The growing online retail market has become a very lucrative business for international majors as well (Ministry of External Affairs, GOI 2014)

Future of Retailing

Foreign direct investment (FDI) in retail as of 2014 stood at 100% for single-brand retail and 51% for multi-brand retail. 100% FDI is also allowed in cash and carry format. Foreign chains investing more than 51% have to source 30% of their products locally and 50% of an 'initial' mandatory investment of $100 million has to be spent in setting up cold storages and warehouses (Prusty and Bose 2013). However it is up to the state governments to allow the retailers to set shop in their state—a step that has made it hard for new retailers to form unified strategies for the Indian market as a whole. Still, foreign retailers are allowed 100% of single-brand stores, and many opened outlets in 2013, including US brands—Stuart Weitzman, Michael Kors, and Columbia Sportswear and German multinational Bosch (which sells appliances, power tools, and security systems at its first branded store in India) to name a few. Other retailers have indicated interest in opening single-branded stores, including IKEA, Burger King, Gap, Skeyndor, H&M, Richemont, AEON, and Swiss Military' (AT Kearney 2014).

The other concerns for the industry include an opaque real estate market with high prices and low availability, high borrowing costs, personnel shortages, expensive supply chains, and unpredictable politics both locally and regionally. More retailers today are focusing on improving operations and back-end processes to increase profitability. Lean models—in terms of size, capital spending, and operating costs—are gaining hold, and even incumbent retailers are reducing store sizes and opening new stores only in carefully selected locations.

India's e-commerce market is expected to grow more than 50% in the next five years, as its young population increases Internet access and speed. Cash-on-delivery options have been an important step to growth. Inventory management, logistics planning, and resource availability are important hurdles for online retail in India' (AT Kearney 2014).

THE BANKING SECTOR IN INDIA

The banking sector is the backbone of any financial system and economy. Commercial banks play an important role in the development of underdeveloped/developing economies by mobilization of resources and their better allocation. The Indian banking system has changed a lot over the last five decades, especially in the last 20 years, with India taking to the path of free market economy and globalization. From private ownership and control of commercial banks to public ownership and government control by way of nationalization, the system changed further in the wake of liberalization and introduction of new players in the shape of private sector banks and foreign banks. This brought the element of stiff competition in the environment with the introduction of new technologies and ideas, new perceptions of quality, along with a high degree of professional management and marketing concepts, in to the Indian banking system.

The public sector banks, which still account for the major part of the Indian banking industry in terms of size and reach (Table 21.6), are facing stiff competition from private and foreign banks as also from the non-banking financial institutions.

The foreign banks which form only 0.37% of the total number of branches (as on March, 2013) in India still manage to gather 4% of the total deposits (as on March, 2013). (See Table 21.7 for more details on the financial figures of public, private, and foreign banks).

Banking Trends in India

The banking system in India has undergone major changes in the last century. The Indian banking system is regulated by the central bank of the country, that is, Reserve Bank of India (RBI), which was nationalized in 1949. RBI is the primary regulator for the banking sector and the government exercises direct and indirect control over banks through RBI to protect the depositors and to stabilize the banking system. Extensive powers have been conferred on RBI under the RBI Act and Banking Regulations Act.

RBI, as banker to the government, transacts government business and manages public debt besides giving temporary (ways and means) advances. It is the sole agency in India to issue currency notes. As the controller of banks, RBI grants licenses to conduct banking business and issues directions to carry on banking business. It carries out inspection

Table 21.6   Banking sector in India

	Public sector banks	Private sector banks	Foreign banks
Number of banks	26	20	43
Number of branches (as % of total)	82.05	17.58	0.37
Number of ATMs (as % of total)	61	38	1
Total deposits (%)	77	19	4

All figures for the period 2012–13.
Source: Based on the data from RBI (2013a) and Indian Banks' Association (2014).

Table 21.7   Financial figures of banks in India (₹ in crores)

	Public sector banks		Private sector banks		Foreign banks	
	31.03.12	31.03.13	31.03.12	31.03.13	31.03.12	31.03.13
Deposits	50,02,013	57,45,697	11,74,587	13,95,836	2,76,948	2,88,000
Investments	15,07,270	17,59,056	5,25,982	6,25,931	2,00,651	2,28,063
Advances	38,77,307	44,72,845	9,66,403	11,43,249	2,29,849	2,36,680
Total assets	60,39,620	69,61,988	16,93,128	19,89,797	5,88,179	6,21,562
Gross NPA	1,17,262	1,64,462	18,768	21,070	6,297	7,977
Net NPA	59,162	89,950	4,401	5,994	1,411	2,661
Interest income	4,84,740	5,54,872	1,34,555	1,66,486	35,997	42,248
Other income	50,347	56,785	25,048	29,793	10,896	11,213
Total income	5,35,087	6,11,656	1,59,603	1,96,279	46,893	53,461
Interest expenses	3,28,597	3,87,929	86,784	1,07,133	14,982	18,741
Operating expenses	90,155	1,01,890	34,030	40,490	13,254	14,206
Total expenses	4,18,752	4,89,819	1,20,814	1,47,623	28,237	32,947
Operating profit	1,16,335	1,21,838	38,790	48,656,	18,573	20,432
Provisions & contingencies	66,823	71,256	16,071	19,660	9,147	8,846
Net profit	49,514	50,583	22,718	28,995	9,426	11,586

Source: Based on the data from RBI (2013a) and Indian Bank' Association (2014).

of banks for financial supervision and exercises management control. Being a bankers' bank, RBI keeps deposits of the commercial banks and provides financial assistance to them as lender of last resort and also by refinancing their outstanding export credit. Till the onset of banking reforms initiated in early 1990s where as controller of credit, RBI fully regulated and fixed bank rates and interest rates, and also exercised selective credit control and other methods for monetary control through tools of maintenance of statutory reserves, as banks have to maintain credit reserve ratio (CRR) and statutory liquidity ratio (SLR), that is, a certain percentage of their assets with RBI in the form of cash/eligible securities (for more see next section marketing mix for the banking sector). However, reforms ushered in gradual deregulation in the interest rate regime, which enabled banks to price the banking products.

In 1947 there were 558 commercial banks in India, which were reduced to 91 in 1967 due to liquidations and mergers. State Bank of India, the biggest Indian commercial bank was formed in July 1955 to break the ownership and control of few leaders of commerce and industry over the economic power and banking system. These consisted of mainly private banks under the ownership of big industrial houses, catering primarily to the needs of a few big leaders in commerce and industry. Also, in order to have balanced geographical growth of banks, especially in rural areas and small towns that accounted for the majority of the population, 14 major banks were nationalized by the government in 1969.

The government as the owner of the banks decided the agenda for the banks and directed the flow of credit. The focus changed from class banking to social banking. The thrust of the banking system was on extensive branch network in unbanked areas, promotion of savings and tapping more deposits, providing credit to priority sector of the economy, which while contributing a lot to the economy was not getting adequate credit, and for rural development.

This social transformation process resulted in unprecedented expansion of the banking and financial system. However, the regulated business environment, poor quality of credit portfolio due to social lending without adequate safeguards against defaults, thin margins on social lending, disruptive tactics of trade unions, increasing number of loss- making branches due to unmindful branch expansion in rural areas, and other factors, resulted in sacrifice of service quality, operational productivity, and profitability of these organizations, which still survived due to the regulated business environment. The regulated environment killed the scope for competition among banks.

However, the acute financial crisis at the beginning of the 1990s, which brought India on the verge of default in its foreign exchange repayment commitments for the first time since independence, necessitated liberalization. The Narasimham Committee set up to suggest ways and means to reform the financial sector to avoid recurrence of the above situation, recommended the adoption of transparent accounting procedures (prudential norms) by banks in line with international norms and entry of private players into the market. The later recommendations dealing with restructuring of the financial sector to make it more robust included interest deregulation as one of the important measures. In the wake of liberalization, the decision to take the path of free market economy and globalization, necessitated reforms in the financial sector to become internally viable and internationally competitive.

To strengthen the banking system, a lot of measures have been taken to restructure banking in India with the introduction of prudential norms on capital adequacy, asset liability management, asset classification, income recognition and provisioning, accounting standards and transparency in disclosures, corporate governance, risk management, etc. The entry of foreign/private banks, deregulation of interest rates, disintermediation, and other policy measures initiated competition in the banking industry. The government support in the shape of recapitalization has been provided to a very few weak banks only. To meet the capital adequacy requirements the public sector banks are resorting to raising capital from the public, leading to reduction in the government shareholding. Public sector banks were forced to focus on improved quality, greater efficiency, and higher productivity. Profitability has taken the centre stage. Globalization has rendered it necessary to be cost-effective, customer-oriented, and technology-based.

The reforms after 1991 have resulted in widening and deepening of the financial system. The growing competition and highly stressed profits have not only introduced new marketing concepts in the Indian banking sector but has also brought customer satisfaction to the centre of the focus. It has become very important for banks to retain their existing customer base as well as to enlarge it.

Marketing Mix for the Banking Sector

The key marketing mix elements for the banking sector are as follows:

Product   Banks offer different types of products. In addition to the traditional products like plain vanilla deposit accounts and loans banks have now added a wide portfolio of products, a large number of which are technology enabled. Some of these are (i) car loans, (ii) housing loans, (iii) education loans, (iv) services of saving/current accounts, (v) discounting/underwriting of bills, (vi) corporate banking products specifically designed for each key account, (vii) credit and debit card instruments, (viii) fund transfer mechanisms, (ix) issuance of drafts and banker cheques, (x) investment advisory services, (xi) cash management services, (xii) investment products, and (xiii) consumer loans.

This form of retail banking is a fairly new concept in India. It is at a level which is still far below the other Asian markets and thus, the scope for growth continues to be immense (Goyal et al. 2004). Within the retail portfolio there is not much difference in the products being offered by most of the players in the Indian banking sector.

Pricing   Pricing management is significant in India because other non-banking financial institutions charge least possible fees for services rendered. The onset of reforms in 1990s brought in an era of gradual deregulation of interest rates. This brought in picture the concept of 'benchmark prime lending rate (BPLR), taking into account actual cost of funds, operating expenses and a minimum margin to cover regulatory requirement of provisioning/capital charge and profit margin'. This reform gave banks leverage in regulating interest rates above or below BPLR based on 'activity/sector of borrower, risk/premium applicable for particular industry, recovery position of the sector, rates prescribed by other banks, government/RBI policy etc.' (RBI, 2013b). The concept of Base rate provided further leverage to banks in determining the interest rates.

Promotion   Despite interest deregulation to some extent, banks still do not have much leverage in price discrimination and as the products also are very similar, the banks have to actively promote/market themselves in order to gain business. Also, the introduction of different international players in the market and the increasing variations of products being introduced, promotion now occupies an important place. Online banking is also an effective medium of promotion for the various bank schemes and acts as a marketing tool (IIBF 2005). They are promoted actively through the print media, radio, television, outdoor hoardings, and banners. Banks also organize customer meets, which is a forum to mobilize business and provide promotional materials such as pens, calendars, and diaries.

Place   Banks are easily accessible from the different branches present in an area. Changing technology has also brought about changes in the channels of distribution of banking services. Services are being increasingly distributed via the following means:

ATMs   The automated teller machines (ATMs) have come up as an alternative to new branches and reduce the operating costs. They are located at convenient locations in cities, provide easy access to consumers, and have helped banks in market penetration. Banks have also been gaining synergies through ATM sharing arrangements.

Tele-banking Telephone banking or tele-banking is another delivery medium for banking services, which is accessible 24 hours. A customer can call the bank any time and inquire about balances or transaction history, or can even transfer funds between accounts. Telephone banking has led to growth of call centres, and many banks such as ICICI, HDFC, Standard Chartered, and American Express have deployed call centres for better customer support and care. Public sector banks have also following suit with SBI and PNB taking the lead.

Cards These are also called plastic money. A number of options are now available like:

Credit card These are a source of revolving credit. They allow the user to make payment on purchases by using this card (at a fixed rate of interest) without having to go through the hassles of managing hard cash.

Debit card This also allows the user to make purchases or obtain cash by debiting the payments to the cardholder's bank account where credit balance exists.

Platinum card This is a credit card aimed at more affluent customers.

Smart card These cards have integrated chips (IC) installed and have a memory and a processor. They have to be paid for in advance and can be reloaded with funds and used for a range of purposes.

Online banking or e-banking This is also referred to as anywhere banking. The customer can transact business from any corner of the world via the Internet. Thus, any computer having an internet connection can provide banking facility to the customer. This allows faster, more efficient, and more personalized service to the customer. At the retail end, banks offer internet banking through a large number of branches, for example, account enquiry, money transfer requests, etc. Corporate customers are also being offered internet banking services, for example, online funds transfer facility, trade finance management, funds management, upload features, MIS/reconciliation, multi-level authorization, etc.

Mobile banking The guidelines issued by RBI in October 2008, permitted banks to facilitate funds transfer from one bank account to another bank account, both for personal remittances and purchase of goods and services. Banks were directed on the regulatory/supervisory issues, registration of customers for mobile banking, to ensure technology standards, interoperability, interbank clearing, and settlement arrangements for fund transfers, customer grievance and redressal mechanism, and transaction limits in an attempt to ensure safe, secure transfer of funds. In line with these guidelines, banks have been offering mobile banking services to their customers through various channels such as SMS, USSD channel, mobile banking application, etc. However, real time inter-bank mobile banking payments has been facilitated through the setting up of the Interbank Mobile Payment Services (IMPS), now termed as Immediate

Payment Service, and operated by the NPCI with the approval of the Reserve Bank of India. The IMPS has enhanced the efficiency of mobile banking by enabling real time transfer of funds between bank accounts and providing a centralized interbank settlement service for mobile banking transactions. The IMPS has also been enhanced to support merchant payments using mobile phones to promote less cash society. The committee considered options of using mobile for the merchant payments whereby the merchants on initiating the payment request completes the transaction by accepting an OTP generated by customer on his mobile. The committee also considered a standard and simple process to generate OTP across all banks. Mobile telephony in India has a huge potential with 873.4 million mobile connections as on 30 June 2013 in the country, of which about 350 million are in rural areas. The number of subscribers who access Internet by wireless phones has grown to about 143 million. With sizeable proportion of households (41.3%) not having a bank account, and large unbanked sections of population residing in the villages (as per Census 2011, only 54.4% of rural households had access to banking services), mobile banking offers a huge opportunity for banking industry to leverage upon the mobile density in the country (RBI 2014).

Process   With the basic product offered by different banks being the same, the differentiation comes in the form of mode of delivery. The foreign/private banks score in this area by having a better organized delivery. However, banks as a whole are making an effort to be more consumer responsive by providing a time-bound delivery (Goyal et al. 2004). Installation of a number of electronic mediums such as ATMs and tele-banking, has caused less crowding in the counters at the banks, helping the bank employees to deliver a more personalized and quicker service to the customers. They are hence able to deliver customer value.

People   When banks upgraded their technology they realized that they did not need the number of staff they had. By announcing attractive schemes to the employees so that they could take voluntary retirement, different banks were able to retain the quality staff that was open to adapting to the new technologies being introduced. Still, the public sector banks are saddled with a de-motivated, ageing workforce, lacking in attitude towards productivity, and service to customers. These act as a major deterrent for the customers who increasingly prefer to deal with the private sector banks that have young, high-performing, tech-savvy, and motivated personnel who are open to mould with the changing scenario effectively. Since people are an important component in the service delivery, public sector banking needs to have an effective human resource management.

Physical evidence   In keeping up with the change in technology the ambience of the banks was also paid attention to. The growing competition from foreign banks, which had a well-appointed and standardized office (Goyal et al. 2004) forced the public sector banks to sit up and take note of their ambience. Keeping in mind that the surroundings in which customers make transactions has a lasting impression on them, banks concentrated on proper maintenance of premises, cleanliness, basic amenities, decor, sitting arrangements, placement of vouchers at convenient locations, and all counters had signboards prominently displaying the nature of transactions being handled at those counters for the convenience of the customers (PNB Monthly Review 2005).

Critical Factors for Success

Consumers find banks to be preferred places for monetary transactions. Safety, better interest rates, and ease of management attract customers for money deposits and on the other hand, attractive interest rates and flexibility of payment along with pleasing and friendly services make them a good borrowing option also. Customers seeking other services, say, like locker services are interested in friendly service and operational facility for longer hours. Some of the critical factors for overall banking success are:

- The ability of the services product is one of the most important factors. The needs of the customers are varied and banks providing a whole portfolio of services are required to satisfy these needs.
- The availability of the services at an arms length is what the customers are looking for. These include the branch networks, ATMs, computerized and IT enabled services, etc.
- Incidence of affable services.
- Using the Internet as a service channel rather than a pure sales tool (KPMG 2006).
- Recognition of and relationship with the customer.
- Mature, enthusiastic, knowledgeable, friendly, and cooperative staff providing prompt and reliable service.
- Reward for the customers in the form of interest rates.
- Management of customer perceptions about the bank.
- Trust and confidence in the bank.
- Ambience.
- Complaint redressal mechanism and availability of help desks for customer convenience.

CONCLUSION

Public sector banks have the advantage of having reach and a long history, which brings credibility, but at the same time the quality of services provided is questionable in the mind of the customers. They are further disadvantaged by being bureaucratic, having social obligations, lending to priority sectors at low rate of interest, having an ageing workforce with a low level of motivation, and low per employee business. They further lack expertise and are faced with delayed decision-making. Attitudinal differences affect the productivity and performance of employees and thus affect the overall profitability of the banks.

The private/foreign banks on the other hand, are at an advantage as they have started afresh, are thin and lean, have a tech savvy, young, and highly motivated workforce. However, the disadvantage is that they have fewer traditional channels of distribution, thus causing lower reach and are unable to tap the big rural market/agriculture sector. They are also facing a quicker turnover of their employees.

Product and pricing are somewhat differentiated but not substantially among different banks it is only the quality of services mainly, which makes considerable difference in the Indian banking sector at a time when the expectations of the customers are on the rise. The public sector banks are changing but there is still a gap between the level of services expected by the customers and the services being provided to them.

SUMMARY

This chapter gives an insight into the four sunrise services sectors—healthcare, biotechnology, retailing, and banking. For each section, the overview of the industry and the government policies affecting these sectors along with the major players have been highlighted.

There are certain similarities across all the sectors. All these sectors other than banking have large number of small players. In healthcare and biotechnology there is a need for investment in research and development (R&D) as that would lead to competitive advantage. There is also a need for a very strong university–industry relationship. There is a need for trained manpower and more research oriented output from academic institutions in these segments. The large players in these two segments have focused on issues such as international expansion, fostering strategic alliances, investing in R&D, and undertaking global operations. Technology entrepreneurship should be sustained in the universities; regulatory framework needs to be strengthened; entrepreneurship in these sectors should be encouraged; and firms should be working towards opening collaborations and networks. All these have been dealt in detail in this chapter.

The retailing sector also promises huge opportunity for growth in India. Characterized largely by unorganized sector, the country finally sees emergence of malls and organized retailing is slowly gaining firm ground. There are different models which retailers deploy for operations. India has seen a large number of domestic brands that have created a foothold in the domestic market. The entry of foreign players will make the Indian market even more competitive. However, addressing people's issues is a key challenge in this segment. As the business grows, finding the right talent and utilizing technology to enhance productivity would be important factors that need to be addressed.

The banking section shows that the product and pricing are still very much regulated. It is mainly the quality of services and not the services themselves, which makes a lot of difference in the Indian banking sector at a time when the expectations of the customers are on the rise. The public sector banks are changing but still there is a gap between the level of services expected by the customers and the services being provided to them. There is a lot that needs to be attended to in providing better experiences to customers in banks. All other aspects, such as technology deployment, can be replicated but the element of a distinct service culture and customer focus creates a unique advantage for the banks along with their portfolio of offerings.

KEY TERMS

Critical success factors The strengths and weaknesses that most affect an organization's success. These are measured relative to those of its competitors.

Intellectual property (IP) An intangible asset such as copyright, patent, trademark, or design right. Intellectual property is an asset, and as such it can be bought, sold, licensed, or exchanged.

Marketing mix The factors controlled by a company that can influence consumers' buying of its products.

Reserve Bank of India (RBI) This is the central bank of India and the preamble to the RBI describes the basic functions of the bank with regard to regulating the issue of bank notes and keeping of reserves with a view to securing monetary stability in India, and generally operating the currency and credit system of the country to its advantage. It is also the sole agency in India for issue of currency notes.

Retail   Any business that directs its marketing efforts towards satisfying the final consumer based upon the organization of selling goods and services as a means of distribution.

SERVQUAL   A service quality measurement model that is used to compare customers' expectations before a service encounter and their perceptions of the actual service delivered. It represents six dimensions of service quality, namely, tangibles, reliability, assurance, responsiveness, empathy, accessibility, and affordability.

EXERCISES

Concept Review Questions

1. Discuss the major challenges in the healthcare sector in India.
2. Critically discuss the success factors in a healthcare sector using conceptual and practical aspects.
3. Analyse the role of paying capacity of a consumer and issues of the insurance sector in enabling the wider consumption of healthcare services.
4. Profile the major challenges across the service mix elements in the healthcare segment in India.
5. What are the key factors that have contributed to the growth of the biotech industry in India?
6. Critically assess the strengths and challenges for the biotech industry in India?
7. Compare and contrast the similarities and dissimilarities between the IT and biotech industry and state the factors that biotech firms should consider when setting up operations in India.
8. What is retailing? Critically evaluate the concept of retailing, globally.

9. What are the different models of retailing and how do they vary over the product life cycle?
10. If a consumer durable firm is entering the Indian market which model of retailing should it adopt and why?
11. 'Retailing is here to stay'. Critically discuss in context to the Indian scenario.
12. Critically discuss the best segment to enter for retailing, the part of the country, and the format it should adopt.
13. What are the reasons for the nationalization of banks?
14. Discuss the impact of the nationalization of the banks on the Indian economy.
15. What further changes can you suggest to improve the functioning of the banking sector?
16. Critically evaluate the impact of information technology on the functioning of banks.
17. How has the paradigm shift occurred in 'place' of the marketing mix for the banking sector?

REFERENCES

Baru, Rama V. (1998), *Private Healthcare in India: Social Characteristics and Trends*, Sage Publications, New Delhi.

Bharwani, Sonia and Sudhanshu Bhushan (2005), 'The emergence of malls as a retail format in India—Some perspectives, trends, and paradigms', Paper presented at the International Conference on Services Management, 11–12 March 2005, New Delhi.

Brand Equity Foundation Report (2014), *Healthcare Industry in India*, Brand Equity Foundation, India.

Capitaline Plus Report (2006) on 'Healthcare in India'.

'Changing gears: Retailing in India', *The Economic Times*, 2003.

Dobhal, Shailesh (2006), 'Net's cast wider than you thought', *The Economic Times*, 5 July, p. 1.

'E-shopping to get festive boost in metros: Assocham', *The Economic Times*, 6 October 2008, p. 4.

Gilbert, David (1999), *Retail Marketing Management*, Pearson Education, pp. 6–7, Harlow, England.

Goyal, Parul, Kirti Sharma, and Vinnie Jauhari (2004), 'The State Bank of India: A progressive study of transformation of a socialistic welfare organization into a market entity', *Journal of Services Research*, vol. 4, no. 2.

Indian Institute of Banking and Finance (2005), *Principles of Banking*, Indian Institute of Banking and Finance, Mumbai.

Jabnoun, N. and M. Chaker (2003), 'Comparing the quality of private and public hospitals', *Managing Service Quality*, vol. 13, no. 4, pp. 290–299.

Jha, S.M. (2000), *Bank Marketing*, Himalaya Publishing House, Mumbai.

Jhamb, Sujata and Astha Bhardwaj (2006), 'The case for FDI in the retail sector—India', presented at Fourth International Conference on Globalization and Sectoral Development, 17–19 February 2006, IILM, New Delhi.

Lamba, A.J. (2003), *The Art of Retailing*, Tata McGraw-Hill, New Delhi.

Mahal, Ajay (2002), 'Assessing private health insurance in India: Potential impacts and regulatory issues', *Economic and Political Weekly*, 9 February.

Mathur, A. (2003), 'The role of information technology in designs of healthcare trade', Indian Council for Research on International Economic Relations, New Delhi.

Padhy, Kishore C. and Manoranjan Padhy (2002), *Banking Future: The Coming Shape of Money and Finance*, Dominant Publishers and Distributors, New Delhi.

Punjab National Bank, *Monthly Review*, June 2005, New Delhi.

'Reliance now sells retail tale to India', *The Economic Times*, 28 June 2006.

Shah, Kinjal (2002), 'Discount stores: Is it the answer?', *Marketing Series, Retailing the Sunrise Sector*, Institute for Chartered Financial Analysts of India.

Sobti, Renu (2003), *Banking and Financial Services in India*, New Century Publications, Delhi.

The Marketing Whitebook 2005, *Business World*, New Delhi.

Toor, N.S. (2006), *Handbook of Banking Information*, Skylark Publications, New Delhi.

Vishvas, Radhika and V. Murugaiah (2006), 'FDI in retailing—Challenges and opportunities,' *Marketing Mastermind*, July.

Agarwal, S. (2014), http://www.livemint.com/Industry/lNu6op68qAiuR6ml2yuJtl/Auchan-Max-Hypermarket-part-ways-over-FDI-compliance-issues.html.

AT Kearney (2011a), available from http://www.atkearney.com/documents/10192/481787/GRDI-A_10-Year_Retrospective.pdf/3c6eb3b2-dfe6-4cd0-9d7b-8ce37e9482fe, last accessed on 17 August 2014.

AT Kearney (2011b), http://www.atkearney.com/documents/10192/372586/Retail_Global_Expansion-GRDI_2011+%281%29.pdf/3903b4b7-265c-484e-932c-50169e5aa2f3, last accessed on 8 December 2014.

AT Kearney (2012), available from http://www.atkearney.com/documents/10192/302703/Global+Retail+Expansion+Keeps+On+Moving.pdf/4799f4e6-b20b-4605-9aa8-3ef451098f8a, last accessed on 8 December 2014.

ATKearney(2014),http://www.atkearney.com/consumer-products-retail/global-retail-development-index/full-report.

Bhushan, Ratna (2003), 'Food for retail thought', *The Hindu Businessline*, http://www.thehindubusinessline.com, accessed on 1 July 2006.

Capital Market (2014), 'India's overall retail market to reach ₹47 lakh crore by 2016-17: Assocham', dated 12 February 2014, *Business Standard*, http://www.business-standard.com/article/news-cm/india-s-overall-retail-market-to-reach-rs-47-lakh-.crore-by-2016-17-assocham-114021200773_1.htm.

Equity Master (2014), http://www.equitymaster.com/research-it/sector-info/retail/Retailing-Sector-Analysis-Report.asp.

Global economic outlook (2014), available from https://www.conference-board.org/data/globaloutlook/.

http://articles.economictimes.indiatimes.com/2013-12-02/news/44657410_1_healthcare-sector-healthcare-delivery-fortis.

http://economictimes.indiatimes.com/News/News_By_Industry/Services/Retailing/Organised_unorganised_retailers_can_co-exist_in_India/articleshow/3564943.cms.

http://en.wikipedia.org/wiki/Store, accessed on 10 October 2008.

http://icmr.icfai.org/casestudies/catalogue/Marketing/MKTG114.htm, accessed on 14 July 2006.

http://www.aima-ind.org/AIMA_Yellojobs_Online_survey_16May2008.pdf, accessed on 10 October 2008.

http://www.assocham.org/prels/shownews.php?id=1865, accessed on 22 January 2009.

http://www.atkearney.com, accessed on 17 July 2006.

http://www.atkearney.com/documents/10192/1315829/Global+Retailers-+Cautiously+Aggressive+or+Aggressively+Cautious.pdf/b8f528f4-cb6f-411d-8ae6-7afb7fbc7b7e, last accessed on 8 December 2014.

http://www.atkearney.com/documents/10192/1315829/Global+Retailers-+Cautiously+Aggressive+or+Aggressively+Cautious.pdf/b8f528f4-cb6f-411d-8ae6-7afb7fbc7b7e, last accessed on 8 December 2014.

http://www.biospectrum.com, accessed on 14 June 2006.

http://www.business-standard.com/article/companies/biotech-industry-to-touch-7-bn-mark-by-fy15-end-study-114050601009_1.html.

http://www.cii.in/sectors.aspx?enc=prvePUj2bdMtgTmvPwvisYH+5EnGjyGXO9hLECvTuNu2yMtqEr4D408mSsgilyM/.

http://www.cii.in/sectors.aspx?enc=prvePUj2bdMtgTmvPwvisYH+5EnGjyGXO9hLECvTuNu2yMtqEr4D408mSsgilyM/, last accessed on 30 October 2014.

http://www.domain-b.com/organisation/Nasscom/20080211_indian_it.html, accessed on 10 October 2008.

http://www.domain-b.com/organisation/Nasscom/20080709_NASSCOM.html accessed on 21 January 2009.

http://www.expresshealthcare.in/200809/market28.shtml, accessed on 12 October 2008.

http://www.financialexpress.com/news/magic-of-medanta/648319/0.

http://www.fitchindia.com, last accessed on 14 December 2006.

http://www.iba.org.in, accessed on 13 July 2006.

http://www.ibef.org/industry/healthcare-india.aspx.

http://www.icmr.ucfau.org, last accessed on 14 July 2006.

http://www.imagesretail.com/india_retail_report.htm, last accessed on 10 July 2006.

http://www.inrnews.com/realestateproperty/india/ahmedabad/relianceretail_launches_hyper.html, last accessed on 12 November 2008.

http://www.kpmg.com/IN/en/IssuesAndInsights/ArticlesPublications/Documents/KPMG-FICCI-Heal-Sep2014.pdf.

http://www.kpmg.com/IN/en/services/Tax/FlashNews/India-Economic-Survey-2013-14%E2%80%93Key-Highlights.pdf, last accessed on 8 December 2014.

http://www.kpmg.no/?aid=9166399, last accessed on 21 December 2006.

http://www.livemint.com/2008/03/24002940/328-new-malls-by-2010-retail.html, last accessed on 12 October 2008.

http://www.oifc.in/healthcare.

http://www.pwc.in/industries/healthcare.jhtml.

http://www.rbi.org.in, last accessed on 15 July 2006.

http://www.rediff.com/money/2002/oct/26heal.htm.

http://www.rediff.com/money/2002/oct/26heal.htm.

http://www.rediff.com/money/2002/oct/26heal.htm, last accessed on 12 October 2008.

http://www.retail-merchandiser.com, last accessed on 11 July 2006.

http://www.reuters.com/article/pressRelease/idUS123461+02-Jun-2008+PRN20080602, last accessed on 15 October 2008.

http://www.sify.com/finance/medanta-has-no-effect-on-competitors-news-news-kdlcbbjadec.html.

http://www.thehindu.com/business/Economy/health-insurance-segment-clocks-double-digit-growth/article5545858.ece.

Indian Banks' Association (2014), available from http://www.iba.org.in/, last accessed on 19 August 2014.

Kanwar, Onkar S. (2005), 'Retailing in India: FDI and policy options for growth', http://www.ficci.com/media-room/speeches-presentations/2005/feb/feb23-retailing-onkar-htm.htm, last accessed on 8 August 2006.

Prusty, N. and N. Bose (2013), 'India eases investment rules for retail', available from http://in.reuters.com/article/2013/08/01/india-retail-fdi-idINDEE9700CJ20130801, last accessed on 17 August 2014.

Reuters (2011), last available from http://www.reuters.com/article/2011/05/11/idUS29963+11-May-2011+BW20110511.

RBI (2013a), available from http://rbidocs.rbi.org.in/rdocs/Publications/PDFs/ORTP21112013_F.pdf, last accessed on 19 August 2014.

RBI (2013b), available from http://rbi.org.in/scripts/NotificationUser.aspx?Id=8008&Mode=0, last accessed on 10 October 2014.

RBI (2014), available from http://rbi.org.in/scripts/PublicationReportDetails.aspx?UrlPage=&ID=760#4, last accessed on 15 October 2014.

Technology Information Forecasting and Assessment Council (2004), *Intellectual Property Rights*, vol. 10, nos 6–7, June–July, http://www.pfc.org.in/fac/june04.pdf, last accessed on 18 July 2006.

Index

About the Authors

 **Vinnie Jauhari** is Director, Education Advocacy, Microsoft Corporation India Pvt. Ltd, Gurugram. She was earlier Director, Institute for International Management and Technology (IIMT), Gurgaon. With a PhD from Indian Institute of Technology (IIT) Delhi and a postdoctoral degree from UN University Tokyo, Dr Jauhari has published over 100 papers in national and international journals and has authored 12 books. Recipient of several international awards for her work in education, she brings in a blend of corporate and academic experience of over 20 years in the domain of services and innovation. She is the co-author of *Innovation Management* (OUP).

 **Kirti Dutta** is Professor (Marketing), Ansal University, Gurugram. She has over two decades of work experience including 11 years of industry experience. With a PhD in branding, communications, and consumer behaviour, Dr Dutta is an avid researcher and has over 75 national and international research papers and publications to her credit. She is also on the review panel of a number of international journals. Dr Dutta has also authored a textbook on *Brand Management* (OUP).

Related Titles

Consumer Behaviour [9780198062929]

Rajneesh Krishna, *Dean, FLAME School of Communication*

Consumer Behaviour is a comprehensive textbook designed for students of postgraduate management programmes specializing in marketing. It aims to help readers understand and analyse the behaviour of Indian consumers and develop winning marketing strategies.

Key Features
- Discusses in detail the sociological and psychological aspects to explain core concepts of consumer behaviour
- Provides Indian perspective to help readers relate to the choices and actions of consumers
- Explains psychosomatic concepts that impact consumer behaviour such as need, motivation, emotion, perception, memory, attitude, and personality
- Includes chapters on consumer research and consumer decision-making processes and models.

Retail Management, 2e [9780198061151]

Chetan Bajaj, *fellow of the Indian Institute of Management (IIM) Bangalore;* **Nidhi Varma Srivastava**, *Marketing Science Director at Millward Brown, India;* **Rajnish Tuli**, *Marketing Science Director at Millward Brown, South East Asia, Singapore*

The second edition of *Retail Management* is a comprehensive textbook, which has been extensively updated with new chapters and case studies. Specially designed to meet the requirements of management students specializing in marketing, it presents the key concepts of retail management through examples and cases.

Key Features
- Includes chapters on financial planning for retail, organizational structure and HR strategies, supply chain management and information systems, store operations, managing retail chains and franchising, and international retailing
- Contains classroom-tested cases from international as also Indian chains and stores
- Includes useful appendices containing the relevant provisions and formats of the Shops and Establishments Act, Central Sales Tax Act, Consumer Protection Act, The Prevention of Food Adulteration Act, The Standard Weights and Measures Act, Sale of Goods Act, The Essential Commodities Act, and Service Tax rules

Managing Retailing, 2e [9780198075943]

P.K. Sinha, *Indian Institute of Management (IIM) Ahmedabad;* **Dwarika Prasad Uniyal**, *Lal Bahadur Shastri National Academy of Administration, Mussoorie*

The second edition of *Managing Retailing* is a comprehensive textbook designed to meet the needs of postgraduate management students. Based on original research, it provides an in-depth coverage of retailing theory and explains the key concepts of retailing through numerous illustrations, examples, exhibits, tables, figures, and case studies.

Key Features
- Explores the issues faced by retailers in India and other Asian countries
- Includes chapters on category management, store loyalty, and retail technology
- Looks at the store as a social unit with its own code of conduct, language, and norms

Brand Management: Principles and Practices [9780198069867]

Kirti Dutta, *Dean and Professor (Marketing), G.L. Bajaj Institute of Management and Research, Greater Noida*

Brand Management is a comprehensive textbook designed for students of postgraduate management programmes specializing in marketing. It explores the core concepts of branding and illustrates them through numerous examples, exhibits, figures, images, case studies, and videos.

Key Features
- Provides rich learning from brand practices of Indian brands like Kingfisher, Maggi, Airtel, Aircel, Micromax, ITC, and LIC
- Discusses practices of global and Indian companies such as Singapore Airlines, Lux, Amul, and Tata Group, and includes exhibits with marketing insights from industry
- Includes exclusive chapters on creating a brand, understanding organizational culture, consumer behaviour, e-branding, and managing brand architecture

Other Related Titles